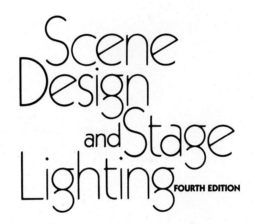

Scene Design and Stage Lighting

FOURTH EDITION

Scene Design and Stage Lighting

FOURTH EDITION

W. Oren Parker
Carnegie-Mellon University

Harvey K. Smith

HOLT, RINEHART AND WINSTON

New York   Chicago   San Francisco   Atlanta
Dallas   Montreal   Toronto   London   Sydney

Dedication

To Donald Oenslager, Frank Bevan, and Stanley McCandless, whose influence has been felt by many of our contemporary scene, costume, and lighting designers, including this author.

Cover: Stage setting designed by Robert Edmond Jones

The two drawings by Robert Edmond Jones, *The Ancient Mariner* and *Love for Love* (pp. 73 and 375), are used by permission of the publishers, Theatre Arts Books, New York. Copyright 1925 by Theatre Arts, Inc.; copyright © 1970 by Theatre Arts Books.

Library of Congress Cataloging in Publication Data
Parker, Wilford Oren.
    Scene design and stage lighting.

    Bibliography: p.
    Includes index.
        1. Theaters—Stage-setting and scenery.
2. Stage lighting.   I. Smith, Harvey Kennedy,
joint author.   II. Title.
PN2091.S8P3   1979   792'.025   78-23608
ISBN 0-03-020761-4

Printed in the United States of America

9012 039 98765432

Textbook manual by author W. Oren Parker
Sceno-Graphic Techniques, revised and enlarged 1964.
Carnegie-Mellon University Bookstore, Pittsburgh, 15213
or
1974 Scenographic Media, Box 2122, Norwalk, Conn. 06851

Preface

The original aim of *Scene Design and Stage Lighting* was to bring to the study of scene design the background and training requisite to designing in the modern theatre. It brought the conception, technical execution, and lighting of scenery into a united design approach. Over the years there has been pressure to divide and expand each area separately. The temptation has been resisted in the belief that the major purpose of the book — to bring lighting and scene design together — is more important than ever.

Since the original edition the theatre has experienced many changes. Forms and techniques that were then ideas are now actualities. Led by the innovative thinking of international designers such as Josef Svoboda and Ladislav Vychodil, lighting has become a forceful design statement. The dramatic presence of light as scenery has not, however, separated lighting design from scene design but has served to bring the two closer together.

Although the innovative designs of European scenographers have a continuing influence on costume and scene design in this country, there is a growing tendency to look with new insight toward our own stage design heritage. The past designs of Robert Edmond Jones, Donald Oenslager, and Jo Mielziner, for example, are worthy of study by the beginning designer along with those of many contemporary designers. In the same manner, the pioneer work in lighting design by Stanley McCandless cannot go unmentioned; he was one of the first to put lighting into the hands of the artist.

In the last five years we have seen little physical change in the theatre. It has been a period of general refinement of our philosophical attitude toward the designing of scenery and lighting. The ever-expanding scope of stage lighting has affected the foundation of design principles. No longer can lighting be thought of as something to be studied later, it must be included in the very beginning of the study of design in the theatre. Hence, this edition has provided extensive reorganization of basic design principles to include light as an element of design.

The treatment of the execution of scenery has been altered in this edition to make room for new construction techniques and tools as well as the addition of scenery-painting procedures not mentioned in preceding editions.

To create a more concise working textbook, one chapter has been eliminated and others have been condensed. The color section has been revised to include new examples of the use of color in the theatre.

The introduction to lighting design has been changed to fit the new concept of design elements, thereby bringing to the lighting designer the same principles of design used by the visual artist. The latest in instrument design and lighting consoles has also been included.

This edition would not have been possible without the aid of numerous friends and former students. I wish to thank the very busy Gilbert Hemsley, Jr., John Ezell, and Steve Ross for their assistance and many photographs; Cletus Anderson for his advice and contributions to the color section; James Bakkom for generous and informative pictures; William Nelson and Michael Gare for the photographs from the Carnegie-Mellon University Department of Drama files.

I also wish gratefully to acknowledge the aid of Howard Bay, Don Beamen, June DeCamp, Robert Dopel, Charles Elson, Ed Kook, Charles Levy, William Matthews, Robert Melloncamp, Michael Price, Patricia Simmons, and Fredrick Youens.

A special thanks for the most helpful and cooperative staffs of the Library and Museum of the Performing Arts, Lincoln Center; Beinecke Rare Book and Manuscript Library, Yale; the Harvard Theatre Collection; the Yale Theatre Collection; and the United Scenic Artists of America, Local No. 829. I also appreciate the valuable assistance of Mrs. Frank Bevan, Mrs. Donald Oenslager; my understanding editor, Ruth Chapman, and my patient wife, Teschie.

W.O.P.

Pittsburgh
August 1978

Contents

PART 1

The
Design
Concept

Introduction

1

INTRODUCTION

The paths leading to designing in the theatre are numerous and varied. They may come from within the theatre itself or from the outside world. The talents of an actor or director gifted with a sense of theatre and visual ideas can lead him to design just as surely as can the more practiced talents of the visual artist equipped with a natural ability to draw and paint and a strong desire to be in the theatre. A student from the latter background standing at the threshold of training for a career in design for the theatre may puzzle over what the future holds. The flush of excitement and sense of involvement of first experiences in the theatre should not obscure the need for an artistic commitment toward a goal which can lead to creative achievements and personal fulfillment in the distant future. But, to reach this goal he must first thoroughly understand the complex form of the theatre as an art.

The theatre of today, along with all arts, is experiencing a time of rapid change. In a short interval its literary form, its physical form,

4

and, in some cases even in the basic idea of theatre itself, its theatrical form have undergone changes. Some are natural developments or extensions of the theatrical form; some are self-conscious changes for change's sake; while others, by their obscurity to present-day theatregoers, await the new audience of the future. All these evolvements in some measure affect the designer and his position in the theatre.

The student designer is perhaps confused by the action of numerous groups, whose activities vary from do-it-yourself happenings to psychedelic sing-alongs, as to their current claims to the title of *theatre*. To set the performing arts aside from self-entertainment and group therapy, it may be wise to clarify in the beginning what is meant by *theatre,* or the theatrical form.

THE THEATRICAL FORM

The theatrical form in its simplest description is the communication of ideas between two groups: performers and audience. The assembly of audience and performers, or *performance,* is the presentation of ideas by the performers to the audience. These ideas may range from the very ancient to the most topical, from the profound to the absurd, and at the same time be either sentimentally obvious or intellectually obscure. As a further modification, the performance itself can exist in a number of styles and descriptions and in a variety of physical forms. As theatrical styles are discussed in detail later, it is more important in an introduction to elaborate on the description of the types of theatrical forms and the variety of physical forms, or theatre struc-

FIGURE 1–1a. GRAND OPERA. In the proscenium stage form, the Metropolitan Opera House, Lincoln Center, New York, is a dazzling example of the overwhelming scale and grandeur that is associated with grand opera and the musical theatre. Architect—Wallace K. Harrison. (Photo—Joseph W. Molitor)

FIGURE 1–1b: LIGHT OPERA.   Uilheim Hall, Milwaukee's Performing Arts
Center.   Architect—Harry Weese.   Theatre Consultant—George C. Izenour.
(Photo—B. Korab)

6 tures, that go to make up our sometimes controversial, frequently exciting but always interesting, contemporary theatre.

The three types of theatrical forms that involve the designer most are: the *literary form,* or drama; the *musical form,* including opera and book musicals; and, for want of a better name, the *audio-visual form,* which places the emphasis on sound and sight and not on the spoken word, as in ballet, modern dance, and the recent experiments in visual sound. It stands to reason, of course, that all three types can be united into a *total theatre* or joined unilaterally in such combinations as dance-drama or choral readings.

Of the three forms, the literary form, or drama, has so dominated the theatre scene that the word *drama* has become synonymous with *theatre.* The significance of drama to the designer is evidenced by the fact that the major portion of a designer's training for the theatre is spent in learning to interpret and expand the ideas of the playwright.

In recent years the dominance of the literary form has been challenged in this country by the musical theatre. Characterized for so long by its two extremes of either lighthearted musical comedies for the tired businessman or the heavy fare of Grand Opera for the cultural elite, the new musical theatre has approached total theatre in many of its productions. The strong book musical such as *West Side Story* becomes near-opera in its musical dimension while its "book," or libretto, drawing a strong contemporary parallel to the classic *Romeo and Juliet* theme, retains a popular appeal.

At the same time opera has been undergoing a resurgence that in part reflects an influence of the book musical. An operatic performance, historically dominated by the composer and his music, is more often than not a contest of virtuosos. Although most operas are inspiring to hear and delightful to see, their librettos often leave much to be desired. The present movement toward such new opera forms as Gunther Schuller's *The Visitation* brings more meaning and reality to the words of the singer and a greater unity and strength to an already powerful theatrical form.

The need for the presence of the designer in the literary and musical theatre is obvious, for both place great demand on the visual background to set style and often to make an integral comment. The audio-visual theatre, however, is almost entirely a visual show. What the performer wears (or does not wear) and his visual surroundings become extremely important. Technical advances in the handling of lights and the electronic production of sound have opened new vistas in this type of theatrical experience. One of the most novel concepts in the audio-visual theatre is revealed in the performances of *Laterna Magika* in the Czechoslovakian theatre, where the mediums of dance and pantomime are combined with moving picture projections to create a new and imaginative theatrical form. The recent visual-music experiments of Iannis Xenakis in the French Pavilion at the 1967 Canadian World Exposition and the proposed theatre of sound and sight by Jacques Polieri in Paris are audio-visual theatre forms of the future. They promise either to eliminate the performer altogether or to lift him to unexperienced dimensions by the use of light projections. Innovations of this type have the potential of developing into an exciting, abstract, though largely sensational, theatrical form of the future with many opportunities for stage designers and theatre technicians.

THE PHYSICAL FORM

The various types of theatrical form in a general way determine their own physical form. The size of a theatre for a musical produc-

FIGURE 1–2. PROSCENIUM THEATRE.   The new playhouse at Pennsylvania State University includes many of the recent improvements of the proscenium form such as an elevator system to provide a flexible apron arrangement, side stages, and a steeply graded auditorium for optimum vertical sightlines. Architect—Harry Kale of Eschbach, Pullinger, Stevens, and Bruder.   Theatre Consultants—Walter H. Walters and William H. Allison.   (Photo—Pennsylvania State University Photography Studio)

FIGURES 1–3a and b. COMBINATION THEATRE.   Renderings of the two seating arrangements of the small 350-seat theatre at the Janet Wallace Art Center of Macalester College, Saint Paul, Minnesota. The Macalester Theatre is one variation of the ever-increasing number of convertible theatres being built: proscenium position, p. 8; thrust position, p. 9.   Architects—Perry, Shaw, Hepbern, and Dean.   Theatre Design and Engineering Consultant— George C. Izenour.

tion, with its presentational style and spectacular scale, for example, is the opposite of the needs of a theatre for drama, which is more intimate in nature. Both have clung in the past to the traditional proscenium arrangement of audience and stage. The physical shape of new theatres, however, has undergone a variety of changes which are discussed in detail in Chapter 2. Like the innovations in theatrical form, many new theatres contain either modernized improvements on the conventional proscenium shape or are completely different in form and production concept, while a few try to combine both by converting at will from a conventional to an unconventional seating arrangement.

NEW THEATRES

The fallout from the so-called cultural explosion has sprinkled new theatres of all forms over the entire country. It has, in turn, stimulated a revival of professional resident companies from coast to coast, bringing live theatre to an ever expanding audience.

Designed primarily for drama and possibly intimate musicals, many recent theatres have taken on the new-old form of the thrust and arena stage. Prompted by the desire to bring the audience closer to the actor, these variations either partially or completely surround the acting area with seats. Although these shapes inadvertently reduce the theatricality present in the conventional proscenium theatre, they in a sense give the theatre back to the actor and playwright by minimizing the scale of a production.

Perhaps some of the more unique concepts of new theatre shapes are those advanced for audio-visual theatres. While none have been built, their projected schemes foresee a radically different audience-performer relationship. The audience, for example, may be separated into groups with widely different views of a constantly changing performance area. Aside from these audio-visual theatres of the future, dance and ballet have their own special requirements in this type of

FIGURE 1–4a. THRUST STAGE.   A view from the side of the extreme thrust stage of the Tyrone Guthrie Theatre in Minneapolis, Minnesota. This 1400-seat theatre was designed solely for thrust-stage productions.   Architect—Ralph Rapson. Theatre and Lighting Consultants—Tanya Moiseiwitsch and Jean Rosenthal.

FIGURE 1–4b. THRUST STAGE. A more intimate thrust-stage theatre in Milwaukee's Performing Arts Center. Architect—Harry Weese. Theatre Consultant—George C. Izenour. (Photo—B. Korab)

FIGURE 1–5. MODIFIED THRUST STAGE. A view of the thrust stage arrangement of the Vivian Beaumont Theatre in Lincoln Center, New York. The 1140-seat auditorium also has a modified proscenium arrangement. Architects— Eero Saarinen and Associates. Theatre Consultant—Jo Mielziner. (Photo—Ezra Stoller. Copyright © 1965 Lincoln Center for the Performing Arts.)

theatrical form. While dance can give shape to its performance area by the pattern of its choreography, it is more fully enjoyed if viewed from a slightly steeper angle than is provided in the normal theatre seating arrangement.

The trend toward minimum-production theatres, such as the thrust and arena stages, may be disturbing to the beginning designer because of the extreme limits of the staging. Although minimized, however, the need for design is still present. The emphasis merely has changed from the background to what the actor wears and to what he sits or stands upon. Costumes, properties, and lighting rather than elaborate scenic backgrounds become the major areas of design concentration.

In spite of the popularity of these current forms there are signs which indicate that the proscenium theatre has far from passed from the scene. Arena stage directors, feeling the strain of continually try-

FIGURE 1–6. SEMI-THRUST STAGE.   With only a slight thrust, the stage at the Dallas Theatre Center can vary from extended apron or open staging to proscenium staging. The flare of its sightlines, however, makes open staging the best arrangement by removing any feeling of a proscenium opening. A built-in turntable is provided as the basic aid for the shifting problems of this type of stage. Scene is from Shakespeare's *Taming of the Shrew.*   Architect —Frank Lloyd Wright.

ing to top themselves on a bare stage, are beginning to use more and more production devices to vary the staging. Similarly, after three or four years of staging plays on a thrust stage, the audience and director are now quietly admitting that not all plays lend themselves to thrust staging and perhaps a proscenium type theatre could *also* be used.

In an effort to find a form midway between thrust and proscenium staging there are a few examples of the unique uses of the proscenium theatre form. The picture-frame feeling is reduced by extending the apron of the stage and doing away with the traditional act curtain. The result gives the illusion of a thrust into the audience and at the same time provides a stage far more flexible for the limited use of scenic elements than the true thrust stage.

NONTHEATRE FORM

Partly as a reaction to the theatre building boom there has been a move toward creating theatre in nontheatre structures. The conventional audience-performer arrangement is altered to fit into an old garage; a deserted warehouse; a gymnasium or ballroom. The unusual relationship of the seating arrangement and performance area is a part of the theatrical experience and is sometimes more exciting than the show itself. It does, however, free the audience and the performer from any preconceived notion of what will be seen or can be done in this unconventional atmosphere.

No matter what direction the physical form of the modern theatre may take from year to year, it is evident that the designer must be trained to work in all types of theatre and, of course, with all theatrical forms.

FIGURE 1–7. AUDIO-VISUAL THEATRE. A sketch after Jacques Polieri's projected scheme for a "Théâtre du Mouvement Total," a theatre in which the audience, while being carried on slowly moving platforms, is totally surrounded by an experience of sound and visual effects. Architects—Pierre and Etienne Vago.

FIGURE 1–8. ARENA THEATRE. A scene from the production of *Project Immortality* at the Arena Stage in Washington, D.C., a successful example of the theatre-in-the-round form. Architect—Harry Weese. (Photo—Capitol Photo Service, Inc.)

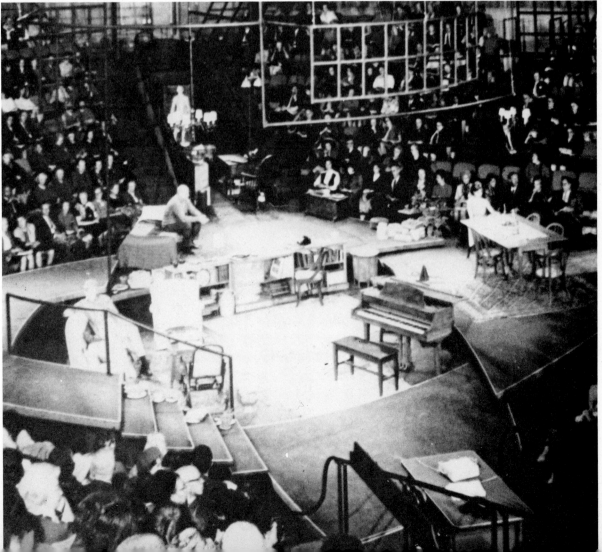

14   SCENE DESIGN

The theatrical form, of which scene design is a vital part, combines many related arts into the very intricate, sometimes frustrating but always fascinating, art of the theatre. In the drama, or literary theatre, the written words of the playwright are transformed by the director and his fellow artists into an audible and visible expression of the author's ideas for an audience. In the presentation of a play, scene design exists solely to bring, through the stage setting, visual substance to the dreams of the playwright.

In simplest terms, scene design is the designing, executing, and lighting of a stage setting. It is a very limited and specialized area of design based on a wide background of semirelated knowledge as well as specific training in modern theatre practice.

THE TOTAL VISUAL EFFECT

Scene design in the modern theatre is concerned with the total visual effect of a dramatic production. In any production the total visual effect is the sum of all the elements that depend upon being seen to make their impression on the audience. The scenic background

FIGURES 1–9a and b. TOTAL ENVIRONMENT THEATRE.   The Theatre Mobile, one of the three theatres at La Maison de la Culture, Grenoble, surrounds the viewer with the action and environment of the production by moving both the audience and the scene. *(a)* A view of the revolving seat-bank and encircling ring. The enclosing wall can be pierced at frequent intervals or remain a surface for light projections. *(b)* A cutaway model of the theatre showing its egg shape. The small end of the oval functions as a conventional stage when the seat-bank is focused in that direction.   Architect—André Wogenscky.   (Photo—Ifert and Meyer, *Cimaise* Magazine, June– September 1968)

FIGURE 1–10. DANCE THEATRE.   An audio-visual theatre that involves the performer. This projected theatre designed especially for the dance incorporates a flexible stage and steeply banked semicircular seating to bring the pattern of the dance into the full view of everyone.   Architect—Elizbabeth Harris.   (Photo—J. Alex Langley. Copyright © 1962, reprinted by permission of the American Federation of Arts.)

is the largest and most obvious visual element that supports the spoken word of the dramatic form. The designing of a setting, however, is not confined to creating the color and shape of framed pieces of scenery alone. It also includes the planning of the quality and intensity of the lights that reveal the scene; the selection and styling of the furniture and set-dressings; the careful consideration of the actors' costumes to blend or contrast with the background; and, because a dramatic production is not a static form, scene design must also provide for the easy movement of actors. The combination of all these visual elements represents the total visual effect.

The visual requirements of a script may be as simple as those of *Our Town,* which all but eliminates physical elements of scenery, or as complicated as those of *Aida,* which requires vast quantities of spectacular background. In either case the visual elements, simple or complicated, have to be designed, prepared, and lighted by someone.

16 THE SCENE DESIGNER

The esthetic responsibility of the total visual effect is normally in the hands of the scene designer, although his importance and influence may vary with the extent of his talent, experience, and personality in comparison to those of his fellow artists. A beginning designer is frequently dominated by a more experienced director until he develops enough ability and confidence to warrant full membership on the production team.

The Qualities of a Designer. There are so many things a beginning designer is expected to know almost at once that he may be puzzled as to where to begin. He will soon find that if he wishes to design for the stage, he must have or quickly develop three qualities that are directly related to or influenced by the specific demands of the modern theatre. He needs the vision and imagination of the creative artist; the ingenuity and the skills of the stage artisan; and above all the knowledge and sense of theatre of the actor, director, and playwright.

To be a creative artist in the theatre, he must be talented and articulate in line, color, and form. Through the visual arts he must be able to bring meaning and visual significance to the stage picture. He achieves this through his imaginative or creative quality backed by training in design, drawing and painting techniques, and the study of period decoration.

As a stage artisan or craftsman he must be able, through the use of unique materials and theatrical techniques, to bring substance to his own ideas with skill and dispatch within the structural limitations of his medium. This is his practical or technical quality. To create a design that can be wholly realized, he must know the structure of scenery, the limitations of materials, the methods of moving scenery, and lighting techniques.

As a collaborating artist the scene designer should make an important visual contribution to the dramatic form. Through his study of dramatic structure and perception of the playwright's goals he is better able to find the author's image and bring a visual interpretation of the theme onto the stage. Awareness of the necessary movements of the actors and directing techniques helps him to create a proper environment to support the action of the play. This is his theatrical quality. He must have a strong sense of theatre to bring a theatrical flare to his designs while still keeping them in proportion to the dramatic import of the play and movement of the actors.

DESIGN COLLABORATION

Within the realm of the total visual effect are several areas of design concentration. In this age of specialization, not all productions are designed by one designer. Frequently, the design of a large production is divided between a scene designer, a costume designer, and a lighting designer. In this case the work of the three is a collaborative effort dominated by the basic ideas of the scene designer. The design of the scenery either directly controls or indirectly influences the total visual effect of any dramatic production. The scene designer, however, cannot design a setting without considering costumes and lighting even though their design and supervision may be in the hands of someone else.

A designer also cannot design a scene without thinking of the movement of the actors, although the final action and positioning of the actors is the prerogative of the director. The floor plan of a setting influences the ease or effectiveness of the actors' movements whether the director is aware of this influence or not. He is, perhaps, more aware of the restrictions of a poor floor plan than of a successful one. Nevertheless a good floor plan is a highly important part of the total visual effect.

In theatre forms such as the thrust stage and arena theatre the visual effect often centers around the costume design rather than the scene design. Conventional scenery is either minimized or eliminated entirely, placing greater emphasis on the design of properties and small fragments of scenery to help establish locale.

Costume design is an essential part of the total visual effect and, although it directly concerns the actor, it complements or highlights the scene design. But, while deeply engrossed in his own contribution, the scene designer must always remember that to see and hear the actor interpret his role is the main reason the audience comes to the theatre. The costume gives meaning to the individual character, and

FIGURE 1–11.
HISTORICAL THEATRE.
The Goodspeed Opera House, East Haddam, Connecticut, a nineteenth-century opera house, faithfully reconstructed into a modern producing theatre. (Courtesy Michael P. Price, Producer)

18

at the same time places each character in proper relationship to the total visual effect. The major role of the scene design and of the lighting design is to supplement and emphasize the costume or actor in the ever moving stage composition.

Whether the attributes of the artist and artisan are found in one person or separate individuals, the ultimate goal of scene design is the same. Designing for the stage means working within the limitations of the physical stage (or the limitations of an individual stage) and with the techniques and materials common to the theatre, while satisfying the visual requirements of the script.

FUNCTION OF SCENE DESIGN

Scene design, like other kinds of creative design, is the creating of a form to fulfill a purpose or function. The function of scene design is obviously linked with the dramatic form which it serves. Scene design, in providing a visual support to the dramatic form, is an integral part of the modern theatre. Its function, as a result, is woven into the philosophy of modern theatre practice. The basic concept of present-day theatre, as a playwriting and play-production unity, has brought scenery out of the pretty background class into full partnership in the production of a play. The scene designer brings to the production a visual expression of the author's aim. It is a fusing of the visual effect and the basic intent of the play into a single dramatic impression.

The function of scene design can be more clearly revealed by looking at the dramatic form of the play itself, thereby illustrating

FIGURE 1–12. EXTENDED APRON.   The greatly altered and highly mechanized new forestage of the Stratford-on-Avon Shakespeare Theatre. One-half of the acting area is downstage of the old proscenium line.   (Photo—Joe Cocks)

the relationship of scenery to the action of the play—and in turn to its visual contribution toward placing the action, establishing the dominant mood, reinforcing the theme, and staging the story.

FIGURE 1–13. OPEN STAGING. Two-thirds of the acting area in the new Chatham College Theatre is in front of the proscenium opening and combines large forestage and side stages.   Architects— Johnson and McMillin, Associates.   Theatre Consultants—Oren Parker and William Nelson.   (Photo— D. Meisle)

ACTION

If scene design is to bring to the play a visual expression of the author's intent, the designer must first examine the action of the play and the kind of people involved in the action. Unless it is completely abstract, every play (or any other theatrical form such as ballet or pantomime) presents a conflict. Out of the conflict, whether of heroic proportions, or of a simple domestic problem, comes the action of the play. The action of the play is the force that moves it forward and makes it a living, breathing form. Dramatic action is a combination of physical or bodily action, visual movement, dialogue, and character- ization. Characterization creates sympathy or repulsion for the figures caught in the action. The characters either create the conflict, or are shaped by the conflict in the ensuing action.

The Scene of Action.   By incorporating all the elements of the total visual effect, scene design creates in visual terms the scene of the action. At the same time, it is more than just a place; it is an en- vironment for the action. Sometimes the scene or elements of the scene may become a part of the action which can be seen in the frankly theatrical use of scenery in a farce or musical comedy. The scene, on the other hand, may recede into the background and become a wit- ness to the action, to be more felt than seen.

20

CHARACTERIZATION

Character development or characterization, also, bears a relationship to the environments of the scene. The people in the action react in accordance with, or in opposition to, their surroundings. The influence of the characters on scene design, sometimes subtle, sometimes symbolic, is, on occasion, more obvious. When the place is an interior, a study of the people living in the house gives the designer many important clues for details. For example, the family of Grandpa Vanderhof and his bizarre friends in *You Can't Take It with You* certainly contribute a wealth of detail as to the kind of house and collection of curios that make up the environment of the play.

The basic function of scene design, then, is to create the appropriate surroundings and environment for the action of the play. The first function of scene design toward creating an appropriate environment is to fix the action of the play in time and place.

FIGURE 1-14. NONTHEATRE FORM. *(a)* Theatre in an old railroad round house. *The Round House* —outskirts of London. *(b)* Theatre in the park. *The Park Players* —Pittsburgh. *(c)* Theatre in a garage. *The Performance Group* —New York.

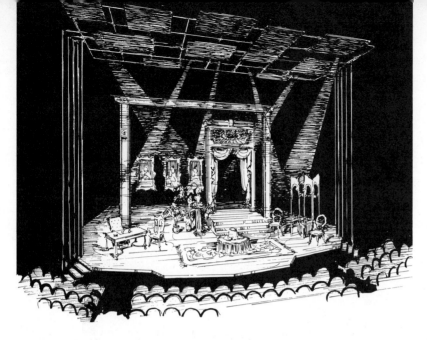

FIGURE 1–15. ALTERED PROSCENIUM THEATRE. A unique use of the proscenium theatre by the American Conservatory Theatre in San Francisco. With a firm conviction in the proscenium as an important visual frame of reference, the director and designer covered or minimized the gaudy proscenium decor of a conventional theatre, extended the stage floor forward over the orchestra pit (less than six feet), and then created a second temporary frame in keeping with the style of the production at a point well below the middle of the original stage. The new stage floor was ramped slightly to improve the sightlines and the traditional act curtain was ignored. The result is an illusion of tremendous thrust into the audience and at the same time provides a stage that is far more flexible for the use of limited scenery than the thrust stage. Designer—Stuart Wurtzel.

TIME AND PLACE

The action of the play must take place somewhere. It is usually in a place calculated, by the author, to establish the proper atmospheric surroundings for the action. This place, even though it be in limbo, makes a visual impression on the audience. The author many times visually establishes a mood by where he places the action in time as well as locale. A specific time in the historical past can prepare a state of mind in the audience as much as the absence of either time or place.

Although time and place are linked with the over-all mood, the connection is sometimes rather loose and may merely suggest a place that carries connotations of the atmosphere inherent in the play. The first act of Anouilh's *Legend of Lovers,* for example, is set in a French provincial railroad station in the early twentieth century. A closer examination of the play shows that it is not a literal station but a point where travelers pause as they come and go between this life and the life hereafter. Time is of very little importance except that it is not contemporary.

ESTABLISHING THE MOOD

The second function of scene design is to establish in the visual elements of the surroundings an expression of the dominant atmosphere, or mood. Scene design aims to create in this first impression an expression of the mood and its relationship to the action and characters. Mood can be described as the quality of a play that, when properly transmitted, effects a state of mind and emotional response in the audience. It can be expressed in such words as sparkling, warm, gloomy, violent, earthy, mystic, and so forth. Some more general expressions of mood are tragedy, comedy, farce, and the like, that are also used to define a type of play.

Figure 1–16. MOOD COMEDY. *Born Yesterday.* Designer—Donald Oenslager. Director—Garson Kanin. Producer Max Gordon, 1946. (Photo—Vandamm, Theatre Collection, New York Public Library)

A play, it can be argued, is the dramatization of a mood, a theme, and a story. All three elements are always present in a play but one may be emphasized over the other two. Hence, a play may be primarily a dramatization of mood with theme and story in a secondary position; the plays with mood dominating seem to be at the extreme ends of the emotional scale. A tragedy is usually a mood-dominated play as is low comedy or farce. The tragedy *Legend of Lovers,* just mentioned, is an example of dramatization of mood. *Born Yesterday* is another example, although it is in the opposite mood.

Scene design, besides placing the action of the play, creates a visual expression of the mood. It is the ball, sometimes the bouncing ball, the designer must always keep in sight as he moves through the mass of technical decisions and mundane problems that occur during the execution of his design.

FIGURE 1–17. *HEARTBREAK HOUSE.* Designer—James Russell. (Photo—Morris Shapiro)

The relationship of mood to action is stressed, for on occasion a visual atmosphere is established in contrast to the apparent mood of a play. Comedy scenes are sometimes played in the ghostly surroundings of a haunted house, or tragedy against the gay background of a street carnival. The contrasting moods combine into a single dramatic impression. Hence, fun in the haunted house might turn into farce, and murder at the Mardi Gras may become irony.

Tragedy, of course, frequently begins in a lighter mood which may or may not be expressed in the surroundings. A gay scene may have an air of foreboding which anticipates the approaching tragedy.

REINFORCING THE THEME

If scene design is a visual expression of the author's intent, the theme of the play is the next area of study. The theme of some plays is clearly apparent, especially if the author is using the dramatic form as a pulpit or soapbox to lampoon society or government.

Theme is, of course, closely linked with mood as well as with the storytelling part of the dramatic form. Comedy often carries a message to an unsuspecting audience as effectively as does the more direct approach of the serious play with a strong story line.

An example of an expression of theme in scenery is found in Shaw's *Heartbreak House.* The living room of Captain Shotover's house is designed like the fantail of an ancient sailing ship. The incongruity

FIGURE 1–18. *LEGEND OF LOVERS.* Designer—Eldon Elder, 1951–1952.

24

of this misplaced bit of architecture is a constant visual symbol of the lack of purpose and aimlessness of the cultured, frank, charming, unconventional people that live in it.

The expression of theme in scenery cannot always be done so pointedly. More often the theme is treated with subtlety and in symbols known only to the designer and his muse. The most obvious example of a theme-oriented play is found in the documentary theatre. Removed from the fictional format of literary theatre, the documentary theatre is free to move to its objective with dramatic and theatrical directness. The most familiar documentary theatre, stemming from Germany in the 1930s, is that of Bertolt Brecht and Erwin Piscator. Their theatre of alienation was sociopolitically oriented and frankly aimed at the elimination of capitalism as a social and political way of life.

Although impact of the message has lessened as audiences have become more sophisticated and tolerant to shock, the documentary theatre remains as a vital theatrical form exerting a strong influence on modern theatre practice and design. Light projections using mixed-media of film and live actors to express theme have become the hallmark of documentary theatre. There is also the conscious effort to bring real-life objects and true materials to the stage in an attempt to remove scenery (and all of theatre for that matter) from the world of make-believe and playacting. The effect on the young designer is evident in the freedom of present-day stage design from the taboos of illusion and sentimentality that dominated the romantic world of make-believe.

FIGURE 1–19. THEME, DOCUMENTARY THEATRE. *The Clown* by Bertolt Brecht. Designer—Stanford Thomas. (Photo—Nelson)

STAGING THE STORY

Story is the connecting thread that holds together the other elements in a complete dramatic form. It is the train of related incidents that brings continuity to the many events in a play. Story is probably more important to the theatre than to other art forms. The expression of an idea in the theatre is dependent upon having and holding the audience's attention every moment. The theatre audience, if confused, cannot turn back the pages, like a novel reader, and reread a passage for clarification. An engrossing story can hold an audience spellbound as the playwright leads them where he wills. A good storyteller, of course, uses mood to create the atmosphere for his story. He can also use the story to make a point, which is apparent in plays with strong themes. Any good play usually has a good story, but a play that is dominated by the dramatization of story is primarily dedicated to telling an interesting tale, whether it be of love, adventure, intrigue— the list is long and varied. This type of play is fundamentally entertainment which may on occasions have a profound theme, but more often is based on a very simple premise.

As the environment of a story-dominated play is usually real, the designing problem becomes a selection of realistic details and forms that place the action and establish the mood. This, more often than not, has been accomplished by the author in his choice of realistic location for the scene of the action. A more important contribution of design than the re-creation of a specific locale is the staging of the action. Staging, or fitting the action on the stage, provides the areas, levels, and properties in such a way as to allow the continuous flow of action so necessary to telling a good story.

The staging can sometimes become complicated, as is demonstrated in the three-room apartment of *Voice of the Turtle* or the cross-section of the house in *Desperate Hours,* both examples of story-dominated plays. The designer, as a contribution toward staging in *Voice of the Turtle,* is called upon to divide the stage into the various areas of an apartment, all of which must lend themselves to an easy flow of action and good sightlines and still seem architecturally logical. Many English and French so-called bedroom farces are story-dominated plays that depend heavily on staging. The juxtaposition of hallways, doors, closets and the ever-present bedroom, all visible to the audience, is necessary to the fast pace and split-second timing of the nonsensical action of the story. Staging problems are a part of the scene designer's knowledge of the theatre as a medium and are discussed more fully in the next chapter.

FIGURE 1–20a. STAGING. An example involving exterior areas as well as the interior of one of the houses. *At the Seventh Hour.* Designer—John Kurten. (Photo—Morris Shapiro)

OTHER THEATRICAL FORMS

The question may be raised whether or not the functions of scenery for a play or any other literary form in the theatre can be applied to other theatrical forms such as mime, ballet, audio-visual, and unstructured theatre. Unless the production is totally abstract or completely unstructured the guide lines are the same. The absence of a predetermined story line may limit the planning of staging but, eventually, staging is involved even if the action is accidental or improvised.

Theme and mood are both present in any theatrical form. The psychedelic extreme imparts an essence of theme through the atmospheric senses of sight and sound. Although classical ballet usually has a story line, its modern counterpart frequently does not. Hence the decorative background of ballet that sets the locale and mood of the dance has given way to the limited use of scenery in the form of stylized properties more expressive of theme than anything else. Mime, both group and solo, is the most absolute of the theatrical forms. Imagination supplies the scenic background and hand props. Although the same thinking is involved, the skill of the performer, rather than the designer, creates the mood of the locale in the minds of the audience. Mime is sometimes incorporated into literary theatre. The pantomimed props and scenery in *Our Town* is an example, as well as the imagined costume in *The Emperor's New Clothes*.

In ballet the miming of dialogue by the dancers is a conscious control or theatrical convention that has little to do with the scenic background except that it establishes a performing *style*. The importance of style to a designer is discussed later in Chapter 4.

Whether the play or production is story-dominated, mooddominated, or out-and-out propaganda, it is the function of scene design to place visually the action of the play in an environment that will bring significance to the dramaturgical elements. Theatrical form is a complicated medium and a strict taskmaster. It requires of the designer, as well as his fellow artists, a complete understanding of theatrical organization and working methods before he can create freely and imaginatively.

FIGURE 1–20b. STAGING. *The Desperate Hours* at the Ethel Barrymore Theatre, New York. Setting and lighting— Howard Bay, 1955. (Photo— Courtesy the Library and Museum of the Performing Arts, Lincoln Center)

Scene Design and the Theatre

2

THE THEATRICAL MEDIUM

Materials and techniques which are the bases of scene design must have a direct influence on the final design form. These materials and techniques evolve a medium through which the design is transmitted. Each medium requires a specific handling which gives it an individual effect. A painting, for example, may be done in an oil, watercolor, or fresco medium. Scene design, however, does not stand alone; it is a part of the over-all dramatic form. As a result the scene designer is not only concerned with the media of canvas, paint, and wood, but also with theatrical materials and theatrical techniques. A scene designer may draw sketches or make models, but his designs do not reach a full state of expression until they are on stage in a theatre. If the materials and techniques of the theatre are to be used intelligently, the designer must have an awareness of the theatre as a medium of expression.

The basic communicative qualities of scene design are the same as in any other visual art—color, line, and form create the same emo-

28

tional response on the stage as they do in a poster or display design. Any structural difference traceable to materials and techniques lies in the function of scene design in the theatre. In order to understand, at least in general terms, the extent and limitations of the materials and techniques of his medium, the beginning designer must develop an awareness of the theatre as an organization, a show, a machine.

THEATRE AS AN ORGANIZATION

The preparing of any production requires the close cooperation of many specialists. The theatrical medium brings together the writer, actor, director, designer, and audience. The ultimate success of a play often rests on the efficiency of the producing organization in: (1) selecting a play; (2) procuring financial backing and establishing a budget; (3) securing a theatre; (4) selecting and rehearsing the actors; (5) designing the scenery and costumes; (6) building, painting, and lighting the sets; and (7) promoting an audience. Lack of cooperation or understanding, complicated by faulty planning in any phase of the organization, can weaken the production as a whole.

Like any other well-functioning organization, there must be a guiding force. The director or producer is the dean of the production group and the chief interpretive artist for the playwright. His basic over-all concept of the production brings a unifying control to the visual elements, acting style, and literary interpretation.

The designer's contribution towards the production is, of course, a vital part of the visual concept. He is, nevertheless, a part of the organization and its collaborative effort, which may mean subjugating personal triumph many times for the good of the whole. Great moments of unified achievement in the theatre are usually experienced when the goal of the production is placed above individual gain.

The designer, besides being aware of his general relationship to the over-all production plans, needs to know the specific organization of his own area of theatre—design, technical production, and lighting. A thorough knowledge of backstage and scenery-shop organization often leads to a more efficient production as well as resulting in a more faithful reproduction of design ideas. Because of its specialized nature, the personnel organization of designing and technical production is **discussed in detail in Chapter 10.**

THEATRE AS A SHOW

The designer's awareness of the theatre as a show emphasizes the temporal quality of scenery, the dramatic qualities of the visual elements, and above all the sense of joining with an audience to give a performance.

As a performing art the theatre has a feeling of immediacy and audience relationship that does not exist as completely in other art forms. It is true that a painting has an audience, or viewers, too, but the painting remains a painting without the viewers. A theatrical performance without an audience, however, is little more than a rehearsal. The audience and its participation are a vital part of the theatrical medium. Consequently, the theatre's almost total dependence upon an audience gives it a temporal quality that becomes an intrinsic part of the medium.

The direct influence of this temporal quality brings about a specific attitude towards scene design and the structure of scenery, for although scenery may look solid for the most part, it must be lightweight and portable to move easily from scene to scene or from audience to audience. And, finally, when the production reaches its last curtain, the usefulness of the scenery ends. It is doomed to storage, rebuilding, or destruction.

The dramatic qualities of scenery are, of course, mainly achieved through the versatility of the designer's use of the visual art form. A dramatic quality more specifically related to the theatre is the use of proportion or scale. The theatre, more than other art forms, is an overstatement of life. Even a realistic play is drawn a little sharper and greater than real life. Any idea, no matter how significant, will make little impression on an audience if it is merely stated.

The size and distance of the audience in relation to the performance has an influence on the scale of any overstatement in scenery. If, for example, the theatre is large and the audience is at a great distance from the performance, the scenery has to take on an increased scale just to be in proportion to the size of the auditorium and stage. But whether it is a musical spectacle at Jones Beach or a drama of intimate proportions in a vest-pocket theatre off Broadway, the electrifying qualities of the theatrical medium are always present.

THEATRE AS A MACHINE

The modern stage is a complex machine which promises to become even more complicated in the very near future. A practical understanding of this machine is of prime importance to anyone expecting to design in the theatre. The designer's use of the physical stage and its equipment means working with theatrical techniques. The influence of these techniques on final design form predicates a scene-designing philosophy. Hence, the scene designer, like the architect, painter, sculptor, must know and use his medium, the theatre, with all the imagination and ingenuity he can bring to bear. To superimpose a design form without regard for theatrical techniques and the limitations of the physical stage is as ill conceived as architecture that forces interior planning into a predetermined exterior shape.

THE PHYSICAL STAGE AND ITS AUDITORIUM

To a beginning designer, the most important step toward learning his new medium is to become acquainted with the physical stage. He needs to know the actual shape and physical make-up of the performance area, for they define the space in which he must work.

THE PROSCENIUM THEATRE

In the contemporary theatre the stage has various forms based upon the relationship of the audience to the stage area. The most common form is the proscenium type of theatre, where the audience is arranged on one side of a raised stage area. The enclosed stage is open to the audience through the proscenium opening. The early concept of this proscenium opening was of a decorative frame to separate the audience from the play in an artificial and often unrelated manner. Modern theatre structure tries to blend the proscenium opening with the auditorium so that the stage and audience are not separated but flow one into the other. The proscenium wall of the modern stage is merely a masking wall to hide the stage machinery, lights, and scenery storage from view.

THE TEASER AND TORMENTORS

Because the proscenium opening is a part of the architecture of the theatre, it has fixed proportions. There are frequent needs to change the size of the opening to fit the scale of an individual production or setting. For this reason the teaser and tormentors, which are adjustable framing members, are located immediately upstage of the proscenium opening. The tormentors are the right and left vertical frames which move laterally onstage to reduce the width of the opening. The teaser is the top horizontal frame which is lowered to reduce the height of the opening. While both help shape the proportion of the frame, they also mask, or hide from view, the backstage area of the setting.

The framing of a stage opening is usually accomplished in one of three diffcrent ways. The teaser may be a neutral-colored cloth border hung in fullness or pleats accompanied by a corresponding cloth tormentor which can be pulled open or closed on a horizontal traverse track. A second variation is to frame the cloth teaser, thereby forming a continuous flat plane hanging overhead. The matching framed tormentor which sits on the floor can be easily moved on stage or off to narrow or widen the opening.

32

The most complicated masking arrangement furnishes the framed teaser and tormentor with a "reveal," or thickness, on the onstage edges. This gives the framing members a heavy look and at the same time provides better masking of the spotlights directly upstage of the opening. The reveal may be attached perpendicularly or beveled at about a 45-degree angle (Figure 2–1).

The downstage edge of the setting usually does not attach directly to the reveal of a framed tormentor. It is held free to allow space for lighting instruments. The free edge of the set is supported by a "return," which turns the set offstage parallel to the tormentor.

Sightlines.   After he knows the size and shape of the stage area, the designer is interested in the sightlines of the auditorium, to determine how much of the stage is in view. The proscenium theatre has a characteristic sightline problem that varies only slightly with the different patterns of seating arrangement. If the flare of the seating arrangement is very wide, for example, people sitting on the extreme right side of the auditorium see very little of the left side of the stage and vice versa. Similarly, persons sitting in a very steep second balcony see very little of the back wall of the setting. If the auditorium floor is flat without a gradient, or if the stage floor is unusually high, the audience does not see the stage floor and sees very little even of the actor's legs as he walks upstage.

The designer must know these extreme sightline conditions in order to plan his setting to bring important areas into the view of all the audience. It is not necessary to find the sightline of every seat in the house but only of the extreme or critical locations.

The extreme horizontal sightlines are drawn from the points farthest to the right and left of where a member of the audience can be seated.

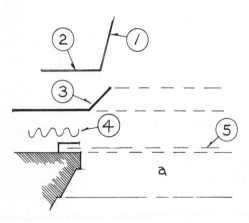

FIGURE 2–1. THE TORMENTOR AND TEASER.   The proportion of the frame for a stage setting is established by the tormentor and teaser which may assume one of several forms. Shown are three of the more conventional types. Left *(a)* Plan shows (1) right wall of setting, (2) right return, (3) stage-right tormentor, (4) house curtain, (5) asbestos curtain. Opposite page *(b)* drapery border with legs on short traveler racks, *(c)* framed border and wings without reveals, and *(d)* framed with beveled reveals, showing (1) detachable plug to change the height of the reveal. Section *(e)* shows (1) position of light bridge or first pipe, (2) framed teaser with beveled reveal, (3) framed tormentor and beveled reveal, (4) house curtain, (5) smoke pocket.

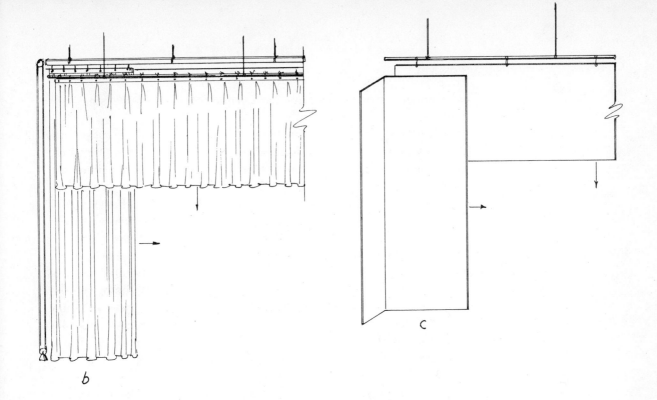

b

c

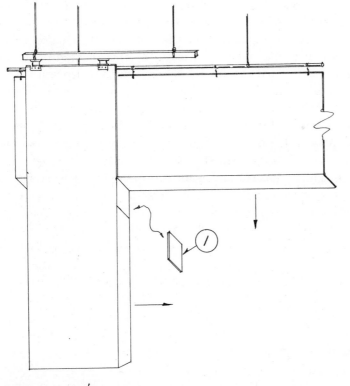

1

d

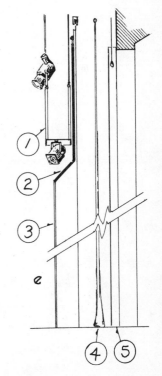

1

2

3

4   5

e

34 The horizontal sightlines are located on the plan of the stage and auditorium (Figure 2–2b).

The extreme vertical sightlines are harder to locate, for they are found on a sectional view of the auditorium and stage which frequently isn't available to the designer. The vertical extreme sightlines are drawn from the front row upward and from the last row in the balcony downward. On occasion, when a large balcony overhangs a considerable portion of the orchestra, it is necessary to consider a vertical sightline from the last row of orchestra seats (Figure 2–2a).

From the pattern of extreme sightlines, the designer can see how much of the stage is in view to each member of the audience. In Figure 2–2b, for example, the horizontal sightline (4) shows the designer how far onstage a person sitting in this seat can see and how much of the stage-right wall he can't see. In this manner, the designer consults the sightlines of an auditorium in order to plan efficiently the use of stage areas for staging the action of the play.

Staging. The designer uses the sightlines of a theatre in two different ways: first, when he is studying the staging of the play, to develop the design form, and then later, for more technical reasons, to check the masking of the nearly completed setting.

When he is planning the staging, in collaboration with the director, the designer maps out the arrangement of properties, levels, and general floor plan to facilitate the easy flow of the play's action. Because the designer is thinking like a director at this point, the staging is more than a traffic pattern for the actors. Its chief concern is to help bring into focus each scene or moment in the play with the proper degree of relative importance to the other moments.

The designer, through composition of the visual elements, can alter the basic value of any stage area. Due to their position on the bare stage, certain areas are stronger than others. The very nature of the proscenium theatre makes an actor standing downstage nearer the audience more important than an actor in an upstage position. The relative importance of the various positions on a bare stage is shown in the diagram (Figure 2–3a) by first dividing the stage into six equal parts and then numbering the areas in the order of their importance.

Such devices as raking or angling the side walls of a set to force the action in the weak upstage left and right areas toward the center, placing furniture to bring important scenes into good sightlines, and using levels in the upstage areas to increase their importance are just a few examples of staging techniques in scene design.

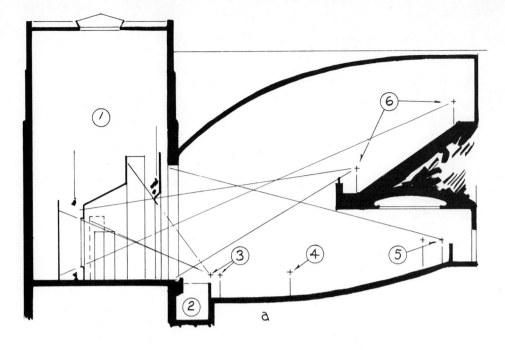

FIGURE 2–2. SIGHTLINES. *(a)* Sectional view. *(b)* Plan of auditorium and stage: (1) stage area, (2) orchestra pit, (3) front row end seats, (4) widest part of the auditorium which determines the splay of the seating arrangement, (5) back row of the orchestra, (6) balcony seats.

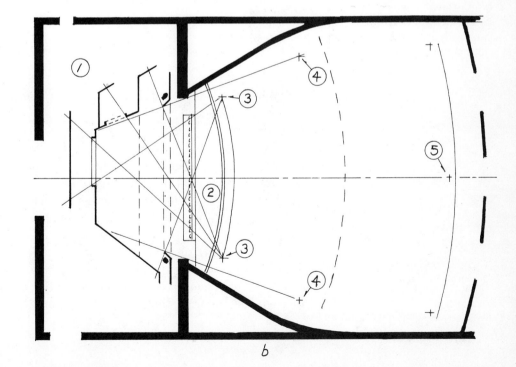

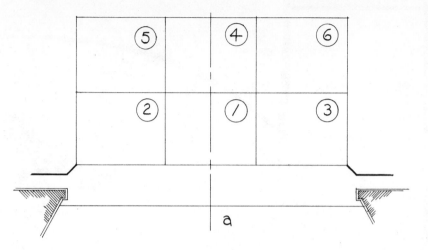

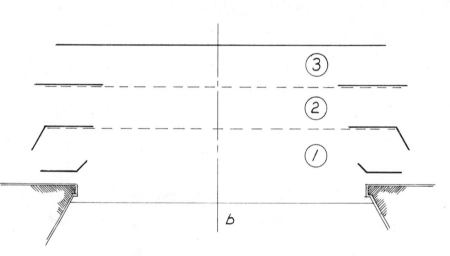

FIGURE 2–3. STAGE AREA.
(a) The stage divided into basic areas for easy identification. They are numbered in order of their relative importance: (1) downstage center, (2) downstage right, (3) downstage left, (4) upstage center, (5) upstage right, and (6) upstage left. *(b)* A second method of dividing the stage by a series of horizontal planes determined by the location of portals or wings. They are numbered from downstage to upstage.

When the stage is cut, left to right, by a series of portals made up of vertical wings and horizontal borders, as in the wing and backdrop type of plan, the staging becomes more two-dimensional. It falls into a series of horizontal planes related to the portals, each traditionally referred to by numbers. Beginning at the apron the downstage strip is number one, the next number two, and so on upstage. The staging can be directed by indicating whether an actor or piece of scenery is to be in "one," "two," or "three," as desired (Figure 2–3b).

STAGING IN FRONT OF THE PROSCENIUM

Two variations of the proscenium theatre are the *extended apron* and the *thrust stage*. Both are outgrowths of the desire to break through the frame of the proscenium in an effort to reduce the distance between the audience and the actor. Each is a part of the contemporary trend or revolt from the romantic theatricality of the past which depended upon a certain esthetic distance to complete its illusion. Although the extended apron and thrust stage are not new forms in the history of the theatre, they are very much a part of present-day staging and represent a space in which today's stage designer must be prepared to work.

THE EXTENDED APRON

While somewhat alike in shape the apron and thrust stages differ in the arrangement of their respective audiences. The extended apron plays to a seating arrangement similar to that of the proscenium theatre with only slight differences in sightlines. The greatest change occurs in the vertical sightlines caused by the increased gradient. The necessity to keep an actor in full view and in a position well ahead of the proscenium results in a steeper rate of rise in each successive row of seats.

The extended apron is usually equipped with access openings or doors within each flanking wall ahead of the proscenium opening. The forestage area may be used in conjunction with proscenium staging, allowing elements of the scene to spill out onto the side stages, or in a more formalized manner, with all action originating on the apron.

The most flexible form of apron stage is illustrated in Figure 2–4, which shows how the area ahead of the proscenium opening can be modified by the use of elevators or removable platforms and seats to one of three variations: (a) full extended apron; (b) side stages with orchestra pit; (c) regular proscenium staging with additional seats.

THE THRUST STAGE

The thrust stage or open stage, as it is sometimes called, is as the name suggests a stage thrust out into the audience area. With seats arranged on three sides of the peninsula-shaped acting space the bulk of the audience is closer to the actor than would be in conventional seating. Semipermanent elements of scenery or an architectural background make up the fourth side of the theatre (Figure 2–5).

Though in appearance the thrust stage is structurally related to the proscenium theatre, its chronological development stems from the arena theatre. The long-felt need in the theatre-in-the-round for greater variety of staging and a stronger axis of visual composition led to a semicircular grouping of seats around the thrust stage. At the same

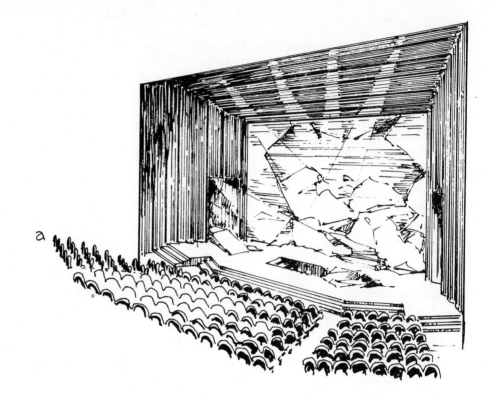

a

FIGURE 2-4. THE FLEXIBLE APRON.   A proscenium-form theatre equipped with a flexible apron which when raised or lowered can assume a number of shapes. *(a)* The apron raised to stage level providing an extended apron ahead of the proscenium opening with entrances from the sides and through the apron floor. *(b)* The apron lowered to orchestra-pit level for a musical production. *(c)* The apron at auditorium level. This arrangement with the extra seats is for a proscenium production.

time, the widely diversified sightlines are an obvious improvement over the limited angle of view of the proscenium theatre. Since the upstage portion of the stage is anchored to the structural part of the theatre, a rather important axis is established in the opposite direction.

The strong visual axis, however, has its shortcomings. The people sitting in the end seats of the right and left sides have a radically different compositional view. This is even more in evidence if the seating arc is greater than a semicircle where the audience in the extreme side seats may find themselves enjoying a vista that approaches a rear view. The ideal configuration seems to be slightly less than semicircular, thereby providing a more equitable distribution of seats without losing the sense of close contact with the actor which is so much a part of both the thrust stage and arena theatre concept.

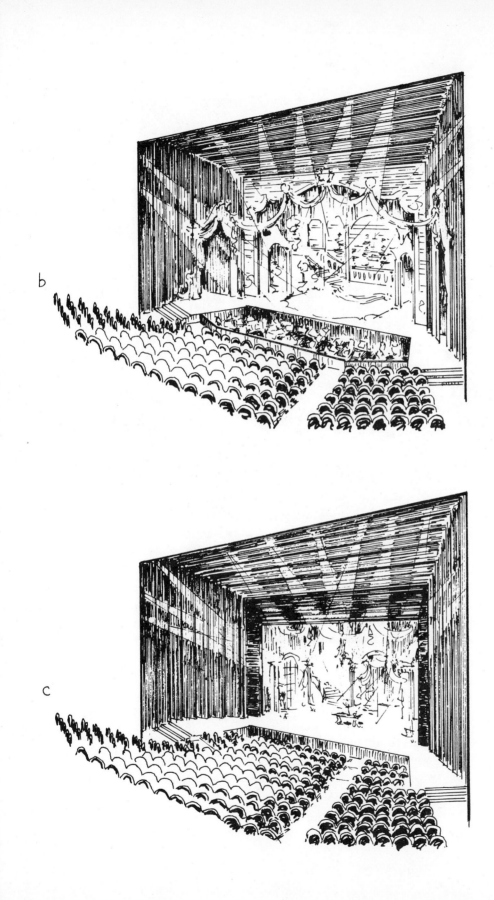

FIGURE 2–5. THE THRUST-STAGE THEATRE. With seats on three sides of the stage area, the thrust stage and its background can assume a great variety of forms other than the conventional living-room interior in the illustration. Entrances can be made from the audience tunnels, the sides, through the stage floor, and from the back.

The features of an ideal thrust stage that influence design are the extreme conditions of both the horizontal and vertical sightlines as well as the basic aim of this theatre type to simplify the amount of scenery needed to establish the locale. The abnormally wide horizontal sightlines force the use of conventional scenery to the back wall with properties and levels utilized on the stage to set the scene. The sharp vertical sightlines, owing to the steeper gradient, make the floor treatment an important part of the design.

Both the apron and thrust stages, because of their exposed positions, work best with one fixed setting or modified act changes. Any speedy change of locale is somewhat awkward and depends upon the ingenuity of the director to stage it visually, or resort to the uncertainty of a "blackout" change.

The design limitations of both the apron and thrust stages are offset by the improved flexibility of the staging. The three-quarters facing of the thrust stage plus the presence of actor's entrances from the audience area as well as the unconventionality of the theatre itself continuously encourage a greater use of style and design detail than is called for in the proscenium theatre. Costumes and properties become the center of the visual composition with most of the environment only suggested.

ARENA THEATRE

Another familiar stage form is the arena type of staging where the audience encircles the stage area. The scale of arena staging can vary from an intimate theatre-in-the-round to an arena the size of Madison Square Garden, with many sizes and variations in between (Figure 2–6).

Although the sightlines of arena staging are greatly improved over the proscenium type of theatre the stage form is very limiting to the designer in terms of conventional scenery and techniques. The visual elements have to be confined to small low units or open pieces that can be seen through. Design detail becomes more important because of the intimacy of the theatre and the lack of larger elements of scenery in the composition. This type of staging is intentionally simple, depending upon a suggestion of scenery to set the scene and stimulate the audience's imagination to fill in the rest.

FIGURE 2–6. THE ARENA THEATRE. The audience surrounds the stage area which may or may not be raised. Any use of scenic elements is limited to properties or an occasional open set piece.

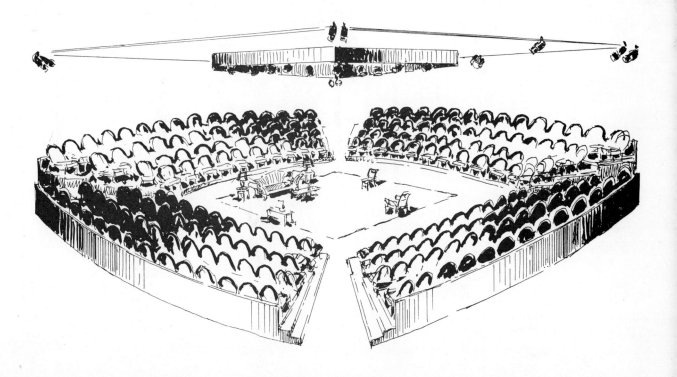

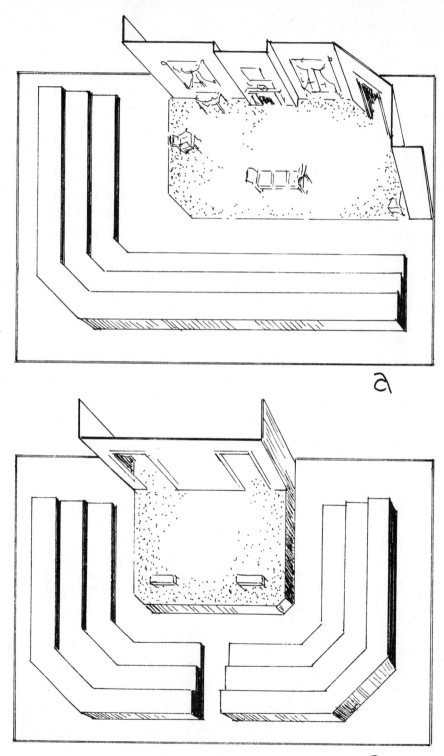

a

c

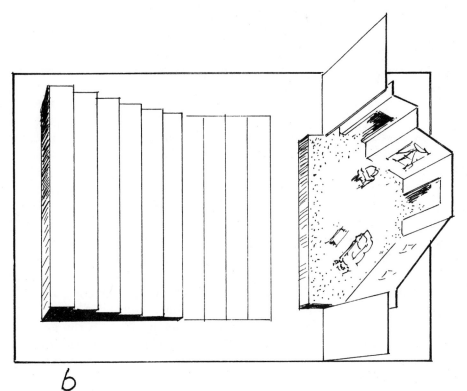

_b_

FIGURE 2–7. FLEXIBLE STAGING. The seat- platforms and stage are movable and thereby able to assume a variety of arrangements. The audience partially surrounds the stage area which may have a limited amount of scenic background. (_a_) L-shaped arrangement, (_b_) proscenium type. On page 42; (_c_) U-shaped with the audience seated on three sides of the stage, and (_d_) the audience split to produce a number of acting areas.

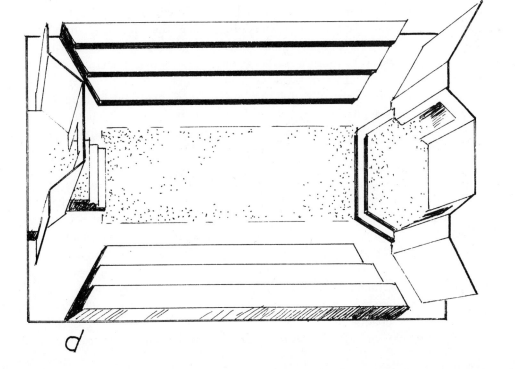

_d_

FLEXIBLE STAGING

Flexible staging is an outgrowth or expansion of arena staging. It is obvious that arena staging has some advantages over proscenium staging, but on the other hand there are many plays that do not lend themselves to arena presentation.

Flexible staging provides an area for the easy changing of the stage-audience arrangement. Within this flexible space the staging can be altered from arena staging to three-quarters-round, or to proscenium-type staging (Figure 2–7). Ballroom or cabaret staging is a further variation with the audience on two sides and a small stage or bit of scenery at one end, or both. The sightlines vary, of course, depending on the type of staging. When the seats are arranged for proscenium-type staging there is a decided improvement in the sightlines over the conventional proscenium theatre. The seating is usually arranged with a negligible flare, thereby creating good sightlines for the entire house (Figure 2–7b).

Flexible staging offers many exciting designing and directing possibilities. Its main drawback is the relatively small audience capacity, which limits its commercial use. A more serious handicap is the loss of time and energy which occurs during the changing of the theatre from one arrangement to another. It is, however, an excellent staging medium for experimentation in new dramatic forms.

STAGE LIGHTING

Of all the techniques within the theatrical medium affecting scene design and the structure of scenery, lighting is the most influential. Because lighting technique will be covered in great detail later it will not be necessary to more than point out its general influence on the materials and structure of scenery.

The use and control of lighting is strictly a theatrical technique, born and developed in the theatre. It is an additional element of design that gives the scene designer a greater flexibility in composition than occurs in any other visual art form.

Aside from its design possibilities, the presence of light on the stage has an unavoidable effect on the structure and materials of scenery. The scene designer must consider in advance the relative changes in the intensity of light and the position of the light source which may determine whether an area of scenery is to be opaque, translucent, or transparent. In the making of transparent or translucent pieces of scenery, the pattern of the framing and the location of the seams have to be carefully considered. Frequently the design is altered slightly to conceal or modify a seam or structural element. Conversely, opaque areas should not be neglected, for a strong backing light may reveal an interesting but unwanted pattern of framing.

Often the design of the lighting comes too late in the planning of a setting, almost as an afterthought. This sometimes reflects an indifference or unawareness of the theatricality and compositional value of light itself. An alarming number of young designers either cannot or do not want to be bothered with lighting their own sets. The continuation of an unfortunate disinterest of this kind can only lead to the surrender of a portion of scene design to specialists who are willing to give the thought, time, and skill necessary to design and supervise the lighting of a stage setting. Lighting is too important a part of the theatrical medium not to be considered in the beginning along with the other theatrical techniques which condition the design and structure of scenery.

OTHER THEATRICAL MEDIA

Although television and motion pictures stem from traditional theatre as a variation of the dramatic form, their individual techniques make them separate theatrical media.

MOTION PICTURES

The advent of the wide screen, curved screen, stereophonic sound, multiprojectors and the like are now leading to new production techniques and new theatre shapes. The scene designer's approach and the use of scenery is nevertheless basically the same as in the conventional theatre. There are the same signposts within the script and the same demands for visual expression. The difference in the finished form of the scenery is a result of the difference in theatrical techniques.

Motion pictures, for example, do not have the sightline problems that plague a scene designer on the stage. The camera is the eye of the audience. What it sees the audience sees. Through the camera the audience can move in, around, and through the scenery. As a result, a movie audience doesn't have as much of a sense of the whole design as does a theatre audience. For this reason, details in design become much more important in the movie. Details that are hardly seen on the stage are enlarged tenfold on the screen.

There is also, of course, a different audience relationship. Movies, although capable of raising an emotional response in an audience, lack the personal contact of living theatre. A moment in the theatre is a moment that will never occur again in exactly the same way. The next night's performance will vary as the audience varies.

TELEVISION

Present-day taped television is virtually the same theatrical technique used in motion pictures. Live television drama has given way to the more dependable and flexible process of shooting an entire

46

show ahead of telecast time on electronic tape. Although a different technical process, the end result is similar to motion pictures. The comparative smallness of the reception screen and the absence of the combined reaction of a theatre audience are the two major differences. The latter deficiency is often compensated for by taping the show before a live audience or by dubbing-in "canned" audience reaction later.

The television scene designer's problems correspond to those of the motion picture designer. The immediate background of a close-up or medium shot becomes comparatively important because of the small size of the reception screen. Many of the familiar movie tricks are also possible in television. The designer can use "supers" (superinposed images) and "process shots" (rear projection screen behind the actor with a moving projection) although the former is accomplished electronically rather than by photography as in the movies.

Scene Design as a Visual Art 3

THE FUNDAMENTALS OF DESIGN

The exciting interplay of line, color, and form in a vibrant stage setting or the subtle refinements of an inconspicuous scenic background do not happen by chance. The proper integration of color and style of costumes and the dramatic presence of light in the stage scene is dependent upon an understanding between the designers of the principles of design. To create a setting the scene designer uses, either consciously or intuitively, well-established rules and fundamentals of design common to all the visual arts. A knowledge of these fundamentals is of value to the beginning designer as an analytical and constructive aid to the development of the final design form.

DESIGN

The abstract use of the word *design* immediately suggests the existence of *man* the artist. Design is *order* and order is the work of man. Yet *design* exists all around us in *nature*, for nature has a certain order and harmony. The artist is able to see design in nature and

48 make conscious rules and definitions of the presence and scope of design in nature for use in a creative work.

Nature, however, is inanimate and therefore not conscious of its design. The artist can bring two things to design that do not exist in nature: emotion, or feeling, and intellect, or thought. The emotional aspect of design is very individual and is a part of the creative dream sometimes called talent. It is difficult to gauge and impossible to teach. On the other hand, the intellectual part of design can be measured and defined in terms of composition. Although the desire to create may begin with emotion or feeling, the artist cannot rely on feeling alone or he will produce nothing. The merging of emotion and intellect is the beginning of the creative process that gives birth to design form.

Designing a visual form to fit a specific function within the structural limitations of the theatre is a creative process. The first step in the creative process of designing scenery or costumes, as in the other visual arts, is a study of the interrelationship of the elements of design and the principles of composition.

COMPOSITION AND THE ELEMENTS OF DESIGN

Composition, in general terms, is the composing or organizing of the elements of design in space into a unified *form*. The result may be a single *form* or the interaction of several *forms* acting as a whole. The elements of design are the elemental factors that make up the visual form whether it be a two-dimensional shape or a three-dimensional sculptural object.

The elements of design can also be thought of as forces that, by manipulation, can singly dominate a composition and help give the form *meaning*. The reason or meaning of any visual form brings a unity of purpose to a composition that is particularly important when designing in the theatre. The meaning attached to the designing of a visual form may be dictated from the outside, or come from within the artist, often formulated by the simple desire for personal expression.

The objective or subjective reason for creating might be used to define the difference between a *designer* and an *artist*. The former is more frequently asked to create a visual form to fit predetermined requirements while the artist is prompted by a personal cause or inner drive that has to be expressed in some mode of creativity. Although the artist's and designer's work pattern and creative process are often the same there still remains this basic distinction.

It is obvious that the designer in the theatre is working, for the most part, objectively to a set of well-defined functions with an occasional opportunity for a self-expressive "ego trip."

The elemental factors that make up a visual form can be listed in the order of their importance to the creative process. They are: line, dimension, movement, light, color, and texture. Of these elements, *line* and *color* are the most forceful while *light* and *movement* are more unique to the theatre.

LINE

Line, as an element of design, defines *form*. It is a most important force in a composition because it is present in many different ways. Line can enclose a space as *outline* and create shape (two-dimensional form), or as *contour-lines* suggest three-dimensional form. Line in a composition can appear as *real line* in many different modes (straight, curved, spiral, and so on) or as *suggested line* simulated by the eye as it follows a sequence of related shapes.

Line is a path of action and therefore cannot help but take on a sense of *direction* and become a part of *movement*. This is particularly true when the form is *linear* in shape. It soon becomes apparent that an arrangement of several linear shapes does not only assume a direction but

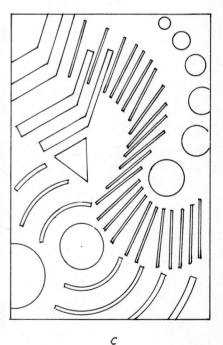

a   b   c

FIGURE 3-1. REAL LINE AND LINEAR SHAPES.   *(a)* Examples of real line. Straight, curved, subtle and strong reverse curves, serpentine and spiral. *(b)* Real line can enclose space and create shape. Some shapes are linear, thereby taking on line characteristics by assuming direction and attitude. *(c)* Suggested line. The eye will follow a line suggested by: repetition of shapes; parallel lines; concentric circles; gradation of size or color; or a shape that points.

FIGURE 3–2. LINE AND COMPOSITION. *(a)* The composition is dominated by the use of curved lines. Some lines are projected, others are three-dimensional step forms, and some are bent pipe and rope. *The Atlantide* by V. Nezual. Designer—Ladislav Vychodil—Bratislava. *(b)* A composition dominated by angular lines. The unique use of a gauzelike drop made of cord embedded in flexible, transparent plastic forming a light-catching background that appears, then disappears when the exterior is more important. *A View from the Bridge* by Arthur Miller. Designer—Ladislav Vychodil.

also takes on an *attitude* toward each other, be it one of harmony or opposition.

The use of line and shapes with line characteristics becomes a vital force in any *form* or arrangement of forms. A composition may use *line* as a dynamic force with a sense of violent action or as a static force with a feeling of strength and stability.

FIGURE 3-3. LINEAR FORM IN COMPOSITION. Stage compositions dominated by the use of linear forms. *(a) Iphigenia auf Tauris*. Designer—Ruddi Barch. (Photo — German Information Center) *(b) Pelléas et Mélisande.* Designer—Robert Edmond Jones. (Courtesy Yale Theatre Collection)

FIGURE 3-4. SUGGESTED LINE IN COMPOSITION. The eye is led by the repetition of form to the center of interest. *Lohengrin*, Metropolitan Opera, New York. (Photo—Sedge Leblang) Designer—Charles Elson.

DIMENSION

Dimension is the size or mass of *form*. There are forms so small they are invisible to the eye without the aid of magnification and forms so large the mind cannot comprehend them. Dimension, as an element of design, is not only concerned with the size of a shape or mass of a three-dimensional form, but also with the relationship of the size of one shape to another—large to small, large to large, etc. *Real dimension* is always present in a two-dimensional shape, but, of course, becomes *suggested dimension* when a three-dimensional form is represented on a two-dimensional surface.

Dimension, in addition, includes the amount of space between forms in a composition. The size of the interval has a definite effect on the apparent size or mass of the form and its proportional relationship. The prominence or recession of the interval or size of mass is, of course, influenced further by the use of color, light, and texture. The proportional

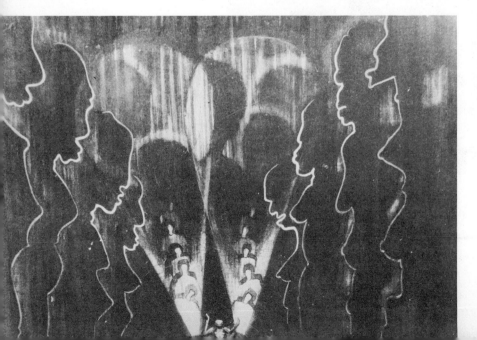

FIGURE 3-5. DIMENSIONAL RELATIONSHIPS. The scale of the forms dominates the composition. *The Emperor Jones*, the slaveship scene. Designer—Donald Oenslager.

relationship between interval and mass also begins to establish a rhythm or sense of *movement.*

MOVEMENT

Movement is the action of *form.* It is the kinetic energy of composition. Motion in design is always present even in a static composition. The pattern of optical signals that touch the retina and then the brain is a continuous flow and hence mobile in character.

The *real movement* of form within a composition is very much a part of stage design. The movement of light, of the actors, and on occasion animated elements of scenery are unique to the theatre.

FIGURE 3-6. MOVEMENT IN COMPOSITION.   *(a)* The kinetic energy of optical motion dominates the composition. *The Love for Three Oranges,* cabalistic scene. Designer— Donald Oenslager. *(b)* Transferred motion. An airplane in flight. The real movement of lights, clouds, and wind gives the fixed airplane the appearance of movement. *Flying High.* Designer—Edward Haynes.

The movement of the eye or *optical motion,* however, is a type of movement that is present in any fixed arrangement of forms. The use of *suggested line* (one characteristic of *line*) stimulates optical motion as the eye is led from one shape to the next.

Optical motion begins with an intuitive sense of *orientation* that everyone has or has experienced. It provides the basis for an interpretive feeling of movement frequently so subtle the viewer does not distinguish the effect as a product of optical motion. The tendency of the viewer, for example, to interpret a diagonal line extending from the lower left to upper right corner of a composition as an upward motion is a product of orientation. It is a part of the *left to rightness* common to us all as well as the fixed association of a *top and bottom* to all compositions.

Movement also involves the fourth dimension—*time.* The interval and size of form relationship (mentioned earlier) cause a kind of movement or rhythm. The interval spacing or *tempo* may be staccato, pulsating, or ponderous in its timing. The vibration of repeated shapes, complementary colors, rapid changes of direction, and high contrasting areas are all visible examples of *optical motion* which can be recognized as the trade mark of op art.

Although orientation brings an instinctive sense of movement to a composition, the designer has many means of controlling optical motion. Strong direction can be countered, reversed or subtly changed by altering the *position* or *attitude* of the forms in relation to each other. The outline of the form itself can establish a direction as well as the use of other elements of design such as color and light.

Another interesting phenomenon of movement is its *transferability.* Both real motion and optical motion can be transferred to a static object. A simple figure or shape placed against a busy or pulsating background will appear to dance or vibrate itself. This unwanted optical motion can happen to pictures in a setting if they are hung on a background of vibrant wallpaper. Real motion can also be transferred from a moving background to a fixed object in the foreground. Most everyone, for example, has experienced the sense of motion while sitting in a stationary railway car when the adjacent train begins to move. The technique of moving the background behind the actor or fixed scene to create the illusion of movement in the scene is frequently used on the stage.

LIGHT

Light reveals *form.* It is the first definition of form. Although not traditionally viewed as an element of design, its dominant presence in all areas of stage design make it imperative that *light* be considered as a basic influence in the beginning of the creative process and not something to be studied later.

Light, as an element of design, must be thought of in three different ways. First as *real light* capable of revealing form. Second, as light having its own design-form. And lastly, as *simulated light* as it might appear in a two-dimensional representation of a three-dimensional form.

The design potential of light is inherent in the physical characteristics of light itself. The three variants of light are *intensity, color,* and *distribution.* By controlling its brightness, color, and direction, light becomes a strong factor in creating a design-form.

Intensity is the brightness of light. It can be the *actual* or *comparative* brightness of light itself. The actual brightness of the sun, for example, can be contrasted with the comparative brightness of automobile headlights at night. Spotlights in a darkened theatre offer the designer the same comparative brightness under more controlled conditions.

FIGURE 3-7. LIGHT IN COMPOSITION. The use of the distribution, color, and movement of light in this production of *Prometheus Bound*, designed by Donald Oenslager, was unique for its time. Produced at Yale in 1939 (conceived much earlier), it represents the kind of innovative use of light we accept as modern practice. Within the simple "gray gauze box" sitting in space, through which light could penetrate, wash with color, project on its surfaces, or make it disappear before our eyes, we watched the anguishes of Prometheus unfold. Lighting — Stanley McCandless. Costumes — Frank Bevans.

The ability of light to transmit and reveal *color* is one of its most dramatic qualities. Setting aside the physics of color and its origin in the light spectrum (see Chapters 8 and 12) and turning to the design aspect of color in light, we find that its chief contribution is the transmitting of color or *colored light*. The modifications of local color of form by colored light is a design technique unique to the theatre. *Color modification* and the additive mixing of colored light are two rather basic concepts of color as a quality of light that have to be understood by all designers in the theatre.

Distribution is the energy path of light. The control of the distribution of light gives it *direction* and *texture* as a design feature. The various kinds of distribution begin with the general radiation of direct emanation through the more specific reshaping of the light rays by reflection and optics, to the parallel rays of the laser beam. The sharp or soft-edged quality of the light beam coupled with its degree of brightness give *texture* to light.

It is easy to see how a knowledge of the distribution of light can affect the design form by the introduction of *highlight, shade,* and *shadows* into composition. Beside the atmospheric quality that light can add to a composition there is the obvious design character of an exposed light source such as candelabras, chandeliers, or visible lighting instruments.

The final use of *real light* is as its own design form. Patterns of light can be projected over a form as a part of the composition, or the projected image can be the entire composition. Although the use of light as projected scenery can be thought of as a medium in itself, it is, however, still a visual art and therefore draws upon the same fundamentals of design for its realization.

The use of *simulated light* is most often present in the designer's sketch, where it represents the effect of light in the composition. Although *line* is used first to represent three dimensions, the added use of simulated light and its shades and shadows is the designer's most effective way to represent three-dimensional form in a sketch or backdrop. However, the most successful use of *simulated light* in a sketch or painting is based upon a first-hand knowledge of what *real light* can and does do.

COLOR

Color modifies *form*. As an element of design it is a powerful stimulus that can: change the dimension of form; reverse the direction of line; alter the interval between forms; and generate optical motion. Color in the theatre comes from two basic sources: pigment or dye present on the surface of the form or color transmitted by light which colors or modifies the color of the form.

Color in either light or pigment has three characteristics or variants: *hue, value,* and *chroma.* A specific color can be thought of in terms of its *hue,* which is the color's wavelength or position in the spectrum; its *value,* signifying the color's black-to-white relationship; and its *chroma,* indicating the color's degree of purity (saturation) or freedom of neutrality. Until it is time to go into all the aspects of color in detail (Chapter 8) only the black, white, and gray steps of value will be used to demonstrate the effects of color in design.

TEXTURE

Texture is the *tactile* aspect of *form.* It is the treatment of surfaces *Real texture* gives the surfaces of a form an additional quality of design. A surface can be highly polished, rough-hewn, rusticated, or squeezably soft. Real texture is best revealed by directional light (distribution) to heighten its effectiveness. Certain textures can be *represented* or painted, such as marble and wood grain. Represented texture appears best under general light and if it is carefully painted and lighted can achieve the same tactile sense as a real texture.

FIGURE 3-8. TEXTURE IN COMPOSITION.   This small but expressive scene design illustrates the dominance of texture in a composition. Designer—Vladimir Suchanek, Bratislava.

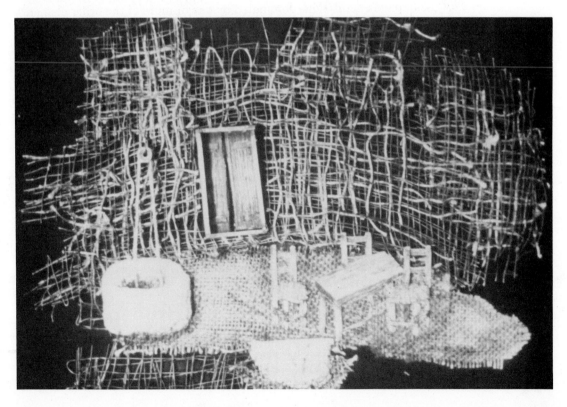

58 THE PRINCIPLES OF COMPOSITION

The elements of design are the raw materials ready to be brought together into some order or purpose. Composition is the organization of these elements into a unified form. The principles of composition are the various ways the designer can control and use the design elements to bring unity, interest, and meaning to a stage composition. Unity brings into play two controls, *harmony* and *contrast.* The interest or appeal in a stage setting is the direct result of the manipulation of these controls.

HARMONY

The simplest act of bringing order to disorder is to sort unrelated objects into groups which have some sequential relationship or continuity. The objects may have in common a similarity of shape, color, or texture. Repetition, then, is a basic control. The repetition of one or more of the elements of design shows the presence of outside control. The repeated use of line or linear forms, for example, can dominate a composition although the other elements of design are present. In both designs shown in Figure 3-2 two different modes of *real line* dominate each composition in a dramatic way. The repetition of line also affects the over-all mood of the design as well as establishing strong optical motion. Examples of set designs dominated by one or more of the other elements of design are illustrated on the following pages.

Although repetition is one of the easiest and quickest ways to bring harmonious control to a composition, there is the danger of becoming monotonous or gauche. The possible monotony of repetition can be relieved with a little contrast or variation.

CONTRAST

The designer depends upon contrast to create form. Form cannot be revealed without contrast as is evident in the examples of the absence of contrast occasionally seen in nature. The protective coloration of an animal or bird reduces contrast to the point of making it invisible against the background. This is nature's way of providing protection, but ask an actress in a red dress how she feels when she sits on a matching red sofa. Complete harmony or lack of contrast is as unfortunate as so much contrast as to lose the sense of control. Between the two extremes lie infinite variations.

VARIATION

When the repetition of one element produces monotony a variation of one or more of the other elements can add interest to the composition. The frenzied *motion,* for example, that dominates Donald Oenslager's design for the cabalistic scene in *The Love for Three Oranges* is relieved by the variation of *dimension* and direction, and is enhanced, if we could see it, by the contrast of *color* (Figure 3-6a). It is also interesting to note in Mr. Oenslager's designs for *Prometheus Bound* (Figure 3-7) that, although the design is dominated by the use of *light,* the manipulation of the direction, distribution, and intensity of light is the major variation brought to a rather simple form. *Color* of the scenic form in this production was held under strict control. The over-all tonality was gray or neutral with moments of color achieved through the use of colored light.

PATTERN COMPOSITIONS

The injection of variation into composition to relieve repetition establishes a rhythm as the variation itself begins to repeat. This is the basis of most pattern compositions which exist in two forms: border and over-all patterns. Although more obvious, the manipulation of the elements of design are the same as any composition except for *light.* The openness or closedness of a pattern involves light, particularly if the structure is a grill or lattice designed to let light pass through. The rhythm of the variation repeat, or motif, as it is called, is known by the terms of its relative positions. That is to say, the motif may be placed in relative positions of alternation, opposition, or inversion.

The motifs may be placed in alternation by alternating their position in relation to a central axis without changing the original direction of the pattern. To place motifs in opposition tends to break the rhythm into a series of static arrangements, creating a feeling of stability. To place the motifs in inversion takes the direction out of the movement, especially if used in an over-all pattern. Inversion is frequently used in textile patterns permitting the material to hang either up or down without the motif appearing to be upside down.

These arrangements can be combined and compounded into numerous variations of each element of design, thereby adding interest to the border or pattern composition (Figure 3-9).

An analysis of border designs may seem unrelated to scene design. However, a border or pattern is a type of composition. It has an obvious control that is easy to see and study. The same control appears with a subtler and less restricted handling in the composition of a setting. Besides, pattern composition as found in wallpaper, paneling, and cornice decorations still occupies a large part of the scene designer's time.

GRADATION

The variation of motifs within a border composition can, as has been shown, establish a rhythm or feeling of movement. The feeling

FIGURE 3-9. PATTERN COMPOSITION. *(a)* Border motifs in repetition, *(b)* motifs in opposition, *(c)* motifs in inversion, and *(d)* motifs in alternation. Overall patterns. The same motif is shown in four variations of the many methods of creating an overall pattern such as wallpaper. The inserts indicate the geometry of the control. *(e)* Diaper. *(f)* Scale. *(g)* Ogee. *(h)* Vertical stripes.

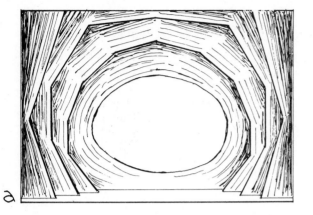

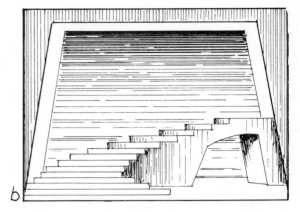

of movement or change is frequently desired in composition of a stage setting where the controls will be less obvious. The sequential controls of a border composition are sometimes too obvious or abrupt. Sharp contrasts can be reduced by the use of the sequence of gradation, which by transitional steps softens contrasting elements and at the same time brings a feeling of movement into the stage picture. The graded wash of a skydrop as the dark blue at the top gradually becomes lighter near the bottom, is an example of gradation of the value of a color. The use of gradation may occur in line, shape, or in any one or more of the elements of design. The resulting feeling of movement in the composition is free of the repetitive rhythm of the pattern composition (Figure 3-10).

FIGURE 3-10. THE SEQUENCE OF GRADATION. *(a)* Gradation of shape from a rectangle to an oval opening, *(b)* gradation of value in the sky and of direction in the steps.

COMPOSITION AND SPACE

Space is to the scene designer what a block of wood or stone is to the sculptor. The space in and around the stage becomes an area to enclose or leave open, to light or leave dark, to flatten out or to create the illusion of even greater depth.

For the scene designer the perception of space begins in two-dimensional forms with the relationship of *figure* and *ground*. Ground, often background, is a two-dimensional plane. In the simplest example, it can be likened to a sheet of drawing paper. The figure or shape outline has to be in contrast to the ground to be visible. An example of figure is the enclosure of a portion of the ground by an outline. For greater contrast the figure may be filled with a flat tone or color.

The space feeling of a composition made up of a single figure and ground is flat. As figures or large shapes are overlapped, one figure becomes the ground for the other and composition begins to take on depth.

The ground may be simple with a textured or patterned figure, or in reverse, with a complicated ground and simple figures (Figure 3-11).

The composition of a wing and backdrop type of setting is an example of the use of figure and ground in scene design. The flat plane of each wing when contrasted against the adjacent wing gives an illusion of space that belies their two-dimensionality, especially when other signs of space are used.

Up until now the figure has been thought of as an outline, or outline and flat tone. The figure can also represent a solid with not only height and width, but also a depth or thickness. The representation of volume in outline or in solid areas is also an indication of space. The outline itself may be varied in thickness and the ground modeled to accentuate the three-dimensional or plastic qualities (Figure 3–12a).

The figure can be given further plasticity by chiaroscuro modeling, which is to model in light and dark tones without regard for a light source. Chiaroscuro modeling combined with the sequence of gradation emphasizes the structure of solids and gives stronger indication of space (Figure 3–12b).

The next step to heighten the three-dimensional quality of the form is to model it in light and shade as if coming from a definite light source. The direction of the light and the cast shadows help to describe the form and place it in space (Figure 3-12c).

The final exploit of space perception is the illusion of literally breaking through the plane of the drawing paper with the use of per-

FIGURE 3-11. FIGURE AND GROUND. *(a)* Ground, undefined space, *(b)* single figure defining a portion of the ground, *(c)* several figures, *(d)* the upstage figures become the ground for the downstage figures helping to establish the planes in space, *(e)* an example of complicated figures against a plain ground with the reverse in the center.

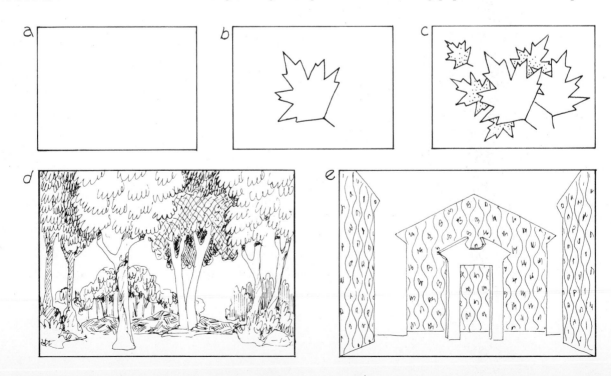

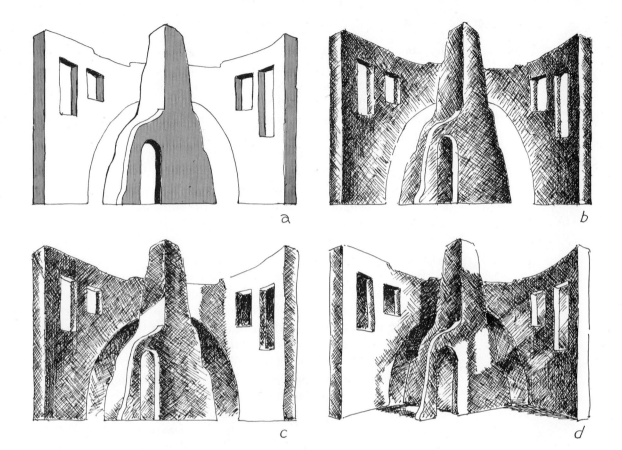

FIGURE 3-12. COMPOSITION AND SPACE. Composition with the definition of form in space. *(a)* Simple outline and outline and flat tone. *(b)* Chiaroscuro or shading to bring out the form within the outline. *(c)* Cast shadows which establish a light source and increase the feeling of space. *(d)* Total effect combines perspective with directional lighting to create the illusion of three dimensions.

spective. Perspective and the shadows of directional lighting are combined to achieve a total effect, a feeling of space in two-dimensional form (Figure 3–12d).

COMPOSITION AND UNITY

The composition of a stage setting is expected to bring a unity to the over-all arrangements of the visual forms. Besides the unifying effect of harmony expressed in the sequence of repetition and gradation, scene design needs a greater sense of unity to bring strength to stage composition. The compositional unity of a scene design is dependent in part upon first, balance and movement, and second, proportion and rhythm. At first glance, balance and movement may seem the same as proportion and rhythm; however, a closer analysis will show that they are related but not the same. Balance and movement are the outward, more obvious expressions of the subtler, more sensitive effects of proportion and rhythm.

Unity suggests balance, a balance of the forces within the composition. These forces are the forces of tension, attraction, attention, and movement that exist between the forms of a stage design. All scenery forms have mass and size (dimension), which means that their proportion must be considered. And lastly, the proportional relationship between forms cannot help but bring rhythm into the composition whether it be static or dynamic in feeling.

BALANCE AND MOVEMENT

Balance is described as being the balance of forces within a composition. But what is the visual expression of a force? The strong visual pull of attraction and attention are forces. The intense colors of a poster attract the eye. The attention value of the poster contains the interest and meaning that stimulate a response in the viewer.

These two forces, attraction and attention, are of significance to scene design. Many times a setting has to make a telling effect in the opening moments of a play and then have sufficient attention value to sustain interest through the two hours of performance.

A visual expression of tension also exists between forms. The degree of tension is dependent upon the interval or space between forms. The space between the finger of God and Adam as He is giving life to man in Michelangelo's Sistine Chapel ceiling mural is an example of tension. The spark of life can almost be seen. If the fingers were touching, or moved further apart, the tension would be absent. Tension as a force is found in the composition of a setting in the spacing of scenery masses, the grouping of furniture, or in the relationship of the actor to the scenery and furniture.

Another example of a force in composition is the force of gravity, and man's unconscious reaction to it. It has probably the greatest effect on balance. Man reacts to visual signs with an organic sense of balance schooled by a lifetime of living with the pull of gravity. Because of this, an unsupported heavy object may seem to be falling, as does a leaning object, unless its center of gravity holds it in balance. Also, a recognizable shape in an unnatural position may cause a feeling of imbalance. The reverse is also true. To abstract a recognizable shape, the designer sometimes consciously uses unnatural position as pure design in an effort to deny reality.

As well as a sense of balance from left to right and up and down, man has a perception of depth. This allows him to judge whether objects are in the same plane or are receding in proper order. However, it is the same sense of depth on the part of the theatre audience that is fooled, by altering the signs of space perception with perspective foreshortening, into seeing more distance than is actually on the stage.

Movement as a contributor to unity is concerned with *change* and *time*. The harmonious and progressive change of the sequence of gradation is an example of movement as the eye is led, step by step, through the change of color, form, dimension, or direction.

Movement as a contributor to unity is concerned with *change* and *time*. The harmonious and progressive change of the sequence of gradation is an example of movement as the eye is led, step by step, through the change of color, shape, size, or direction.

A well-organized form has a firmly established movement plan. Some arrangements of form stimulate a greater sense of movement than others. Some cause a different kind of movement such as a precarious balance of tension. The plan of movement within a composition, in any event, is a closed plan, always staying or returning to the over-all form.

In the theatre, as has been noted, the inclusion of time in actual movement is quite apparent. The actors move from area to area; the lights dim and brighten; scenery, on occasion, moves in view of the audience. All these are part of the composition of the dramatic form and involve the element of time. The element of time, however, exists in a fixed composition too.

There is an interval of time as the eye follows the pattern of movement through a composition. The interval is minute, of course, when compared to the broader movements on stage. The visual change can lead the eye, abruptly or gradually in terms of time, over the movement plan of a composition. (See *Optical motion*.)

PROPORTION AND RHYTHM

The second portion of obtaining unity in a composition is the use of proportion and rhythm. Proportional judgment is probably the beginning or indication of talent. A certain amount can be acquired by training and sharpened by analysis, but the greater portion is intuitive or sensed by the artist.

Proportion is the ratio of something to something else. It is natural to relate proportion to the human figure, especially on the stage where the actor is a part of the total composition. If human scale is half of the ratio, the size of a form in relation to the human is a matter of proportion. In the theatre this is referred to as *scale*. The designer is constantly checking the size of a form in ratio to human scale (Figure 3–13). Some productions demand a greater scale or an increased ratio of the size of surrounding forms to the actor.

Proportion can also be linked to the reason or function of a visual form. The proportion of a chair as a visual form, for example, depends upon how it is to be used. A simple dining-room side chair is small when compared to the scale and grandeur of a canopied throne chair. Stage settings and even entire productions can differ in scale

FIGURE 3-13. SCALE.   The feeling of scale in a stage setting is linked to the size of the human figure. In these two examples, the design forms are identical in size. Their scale changes in relation to the size of the figure in the composition.

for similar reasons. The proportions of the ballroom scene in *Romeo and Juliet,* for example, are of more significance than the scale of Friar Laurence's cell; similarly, the pageantry of *Henry the Eighth* demands greater scale as a production than *The Merchant of Venice,* which is of more intimate proportions.

Many forms and arrangements of forms, however, are not associated with human scale. Besides the concept of proportion as scale there exists a proportional relationship of one form to another, as well as the space between forms. Perhaps more important is -the proportional relationship of forms to the surrounding space. The rhythm and proportions of a sculptural arrangement of forms set in an unbound space, for example, may seem different from a similar arrangement of shapes framed or confined within a rectangular shape such as a proscenium opening.

Although scene designing, at least in its formative stages, composes within a rectangular or near-rectangular shape, it is also concerned with the freer compositions of the nonproscenium stage. Designing for nonproscenium theatre approaches the use of sculptural techniques to create a desirable proportional relationship between

FIGURE 3–14. CHANGE OF SCALE.   An example of increased human scale.
The larger-than-life actors are in the Guthrie Theatre production of *The
House of Atreus,* an adaptation from Aeschylus' *Oresteia* by John Lewin.
Designer—Tanya Moiseiwitsch.

scenic forms in a more or less undefined space. Whereas the composition within a proscenium frame is viewed basically from a frontal direction, nonproscenium scenic forms have to be composed satisfactorily for viewers from all directions.

As balance is linked to movement, so proportion is joined with rhythm. The space between forms and the attitude of one shape toward another creates a rhythm in the composition. Rhythm is a type of movement that repeats or recurs at intervals, or completes a cycle. The proportional relationship between forms establishes a rhythm, as does the subdivision of a single form.

The conscious inner relation and rhythm is present in a stage composition in many ways. It may appear in the quiet dignity of a formal arrangement or in the vigorous movement of a dynamic composition. It may be expressed in the rhythmic flow of harmonious forms or in a nervous, staccatolike organization of shapes.

Rhythm, as a unifying factor, is usually expressed in the lines or the linear qualities of a stage composition. The use of actual lines or the feeling of a line caused by the position and direction of one shape to another results in a rhythmic movement that may be as strong or as subdued as the designer desires. Diagonal lines and lines parallel to the diagonals give a greater sense of movement than the use of strong horizontal and vertical lines which tend to stop movement (Figure 3–15).

Although the rhythm of straight lines is more bold and forceful than curved lines, curved lines have infinitely greater variety. The rhythm of a curved line may have the grace of flowing lines, the turbulence of reverse curves, the whirl of a spiral, as well as the repetition and order of interlaced geometric curves, such as circles and ovals.

Whether the rhythm of a stage composition is dominated by straight or curved lines, it eventually becomes a part of the basic movement plan. Likewise, the proportional relationship of forms, which determines the rhythm, seeks a balance, resulting in a greater feeling of unity.

COMPOSITION AND INTEREST

Besides maintaining unity in his stage composition, the designer tries to bring interest and meaning to his setting. Any meaning attached to the scenic forms of the composition is, of course, a part of the designer's interpretation of the scenic requirements of the play as he brings visual substance to the playwright's ideas (Chapter 1).

FIGURE 3–15. RHYTHM AND MOVEMENT IN
COMPOSITION.   *(a)* A composition based upon
diagonal lines has a definite sense of movement. *(b)* A
composition based upon strong horizontals and
verticals has a static feeling.

A stage setting, however, can fulfill all the scenic requirements of the play and still not be interesting. Just what makes one setting for the same play more interesting than another?

A setting is interesting many times because of a unique and daring design interpretation which stimulates an intellectual response in the audience. This is possible when the play is a classic or familiar to the audience. Continental scene designers consistently produce exciting and quite different design approaches to well-established classics. Likewise, in university and community theatres, where people are going to see a production or interpretation of a well-known play more often than a new play, the emphasis is frequently on the design idea, or an exciting production scheme.

The designer, unfortunately, cannot take such great liberties with a new play. Here the audience is seeing the play for the first time and will not appreciate too intellectual an approach unless it is a part of the production scheme. It is more important that he first stimulate the proper emotional response to the play.

The second thing that makes one setting more interesting than another is what the designer does to the balance of his composition. A mechanical balance of the design forms may bring unity to a composition but still be monotonous and uninteresting. Any interesting composition varies or stretches the balance into a more exciting arrangement of forms without losing unity.

TYPES OF PROPORTIONAL BALANCE

There are several arrangements of forms that are organized in a manner to bring a sense of balance or equilibrium to a specific area. The arrangements are classified as axial, radial, and occult balance.

Axial balance is a symmetrical arrangement of forms of equal weight on either side of an axis. The axis may be an actual line or a central-division line. A composition based on such a symmetrical balance may seem dignified and classical in feeling, though rather static and severe in effect (Figure 3–16a).

The formality of the symmetry can be eased a little by using an asymmetric arrangement wherein the basic forms remain in symmetry with a variation of color or detail taking place within the over-all forms.

A stage setting of a formal or architectural nature frequently employs symmetrical balance, both within the composition (individual wall treatment) and as a whole. Sometimes a near-symmetrical arrangement is used to give the effect of symmetrical balance in a softer, freer manner (Figure 3–16b).

Radial balance is a symmetrical balance around a center and the movement is always circular. It is most useful in a decorative pattern or ornamental detail, although it may occasionally be seen in the floor plan of a setting (Figure 3–16c).

Occult balance differs from axial balance in the absence of any axis or focal center. It is the balance of unlike elements, the felt balance of mass against space. There are no rules except the judgment of the designer. The result is a feeling of greater movement and excitement which lends itself readily to dramatic uses (Figure 3–16d).

As occult balance is dependent upon the interrelationship of elements within the composition, the use of proportion and rhythm aid the designer to arrive at the delicate balance present in an occult arrangement.

CENTER OF INTEREST

Unless the composition is an over-all pattern, it is organized about a center of interest, or focal point. This is a point in the composition (not necessarily in the center) to which the eye of the viewer is led by either obvious or subtle means. The leadlines which are present in the movement plan of the composition lead the eye to the center of interest. Besides the focal center there may also be secondary areas of interest as well as intriguing bits of detail within the composition which hold attention yet do not detract from the main point of focus.

A stage setting is usually designed around a strong center of interest with important secondary areas. Although the concept of the setting as a background has its own center of interest, the true center of interest in the total visual effect is on the actor. As was mentioned earlier, a stage composition is a fluid, ever-changing thing with a different center of interest for each scene.

Fortunately, stage lighting, costume colors, and the movement of actors all help to make any change of emphasis rather simple. By dimming most of the lights and brightening one area, stage lighting can easily bring focus to a specific point on the stage as can the color of a costume in relation to the setting and to other costumes in the scene. The movement of the actor can also be used to change the center of focus, as is so effectively demonstrated in a ballet or group-dance composition. The mobility of the actor allows the director to compose with actor groups or picturization so as to direct the interest of the audience to any portion of the stage setting. The contributions of stage lighting, costumes, and actor picturizations toward the complete stage composition all serve to emphasize the importance of the visual side of the theatre as well as underlining the function of scene design as a visual art.

a

FIGURE 3-16. BALANCE IN COMPOSITION. *(a)* Symmetrical
balance. *Fidelio*. Designer — Donald Oenslager. (Photo — Grimes) *(b)*
Asymmetrical balance. *Up in Central Park*. Designer — Howard Bay.
(Photo — Graphic) *(c)* Radial balance. *Les Troyens*. Designer — Peter
Wexler, Metropolitan Opera. (Photo — Copyright © Beth Bergman) *(d)*
Occult balance. *The Ancient Mariner*. Designer — Robert Edmond
Jones.

b

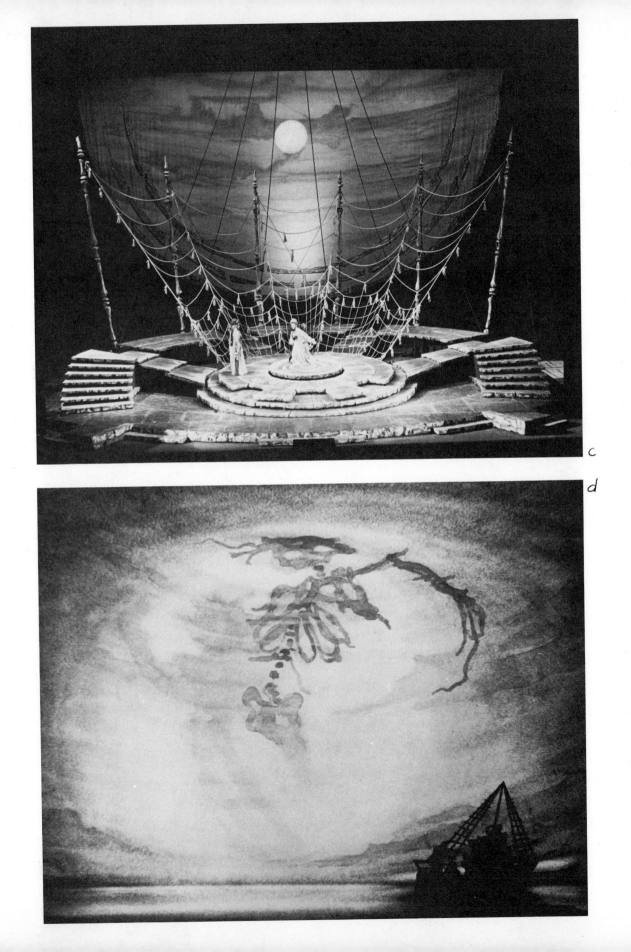

c

d

The
4 Design Idea

At this point, the beginning designer is conscious of the responsibilities of scene design to the play. He is aware of the influences of the theatrical medium and is familiar with the intricacies of the creative process. But, he may ask, how does one get an idea for a design?

It is impossible to set down universal rules for developing a design idea; there are as many methods as designers. And an individual method is often so subjective and intuitive that it is of little value to another designer as a way of working; each must and usually does develop his own method of reaching his inner reservoir of creative ideas.

Still, it is possible to make recommendations and to point to examples of good design, but the actual conquest of an idea is the designer's individual struggle.

The design idea, of course, doesn't exist until the play becomes a production and the written word becomes dialogue and visible action. It is the individual expression of the artistic imagination, theatrical sense, and technical ingenuity of the designer through the visual control of line, color, and form. The design concept is often evident as a visual theme with variations that weave through a complicated setting or series of settings, bringing unity of thought to the whole. Many times the theme is so subtle that only the trained eye of another designer can see and appreciate its presence.

The design idea is aimed at stimulating an intellectual or emotional response in the audience. The control of the design elements may be broad and sensational to arouse primitive emotions, or they may be subtle and refined to stimulate an intellectual response. Good design is the result of logical yet imaginative thinking and intuitive feeling expressed through an idea or central theme.

The ideas for many an inspirational setting have been worked out on the back of an envelope during a coffee break, or have been virtually completed before the author has finished the third act. Although this is frequently the pace at which a scene designer is expected to work, it is hardly a practical procedure for an inexperienced designer.

ANALYSIS OF THE PLAY

The developing of a concept for a setting begins with the study of the play. Ideally, the play is analyzed from three separate readings, assuming that the designer will have the script longer than overnight, or for more than two hours on a train. The three separate readings represent the logical steps towards accumulating information that shapes and inspires the design idea.

The designer's first reading of the play is for its content. He allows himself to react as a member of the audience, avoiding any preconceived image of the background other than the author's description. In this way his first impression is an over-all response that helps him answer these questions: What kind of a play is it? What is the action and where is it taking place? What is the dominant mood? Is the play a comedy? Or is it a tongue-in-cheek satire with political overtones? Is it a tragedy of classical proportions or a domestic misunderstanding? And so on.

The scene of the action often suggests or sets the atmosphere of a play. A deserted house on a stormy night for a mystery or a love scene by candle light are typical examples. The action, however, is not always in harmony with its surroundings but may be in opposition or contrast to its environment.

The mood of a play or scene often suggests *color* to the designer. Out of the mood of the environment comes the over-all tonality of the play, which often can be expressed most forcefully in color or the absence of color.

The second reading is for the play's intent. What is the author saying? It is a more careful reading—between the lines and within parentheses. What is the theme? What is the style? Has the author expressed a point of view through allegorical symbols or in daily-life realism? Has he soared into the realm of epic poetry, or has he dropped into the lusty imagery of sidewalk prose? In the style of the play the designer finds a clue to the degree of reality or unreality of the scenic environment.

From the theme of the play the designer can usually find a visual image that can lead to a design concept. And from the style of the play the designer gets an indication of the *form* of his design. Style and form interact, for style influences form. A realistic style implies realistic forms; a fantasy or dream suggests unreal forms. And so on.

THEATRICAL STYLES

The theatre combines many styles. It brings together the literary style of the script, the acting style, the over-all production style of a director, and the visual style of the setting, costumes, and lighting.

Style, among other meanings attached to the word, is a mode of expression or presentation in creative form. The creative forms or elements of scenery, levels, and lightings which make up the stage setting can take on many modes or styles in keeping with the degree of reality or ideality of the play.

Scenery Styles. As a visual art, scenery styles can be defined first in terms of the degree of representation of nature. To deal with the extremes, a strictly representational style is imitation. Its main object is to produce a lifelike copy of nature. The design form is represented as near to its natural form as the technical skills of the artist will permit.

The nonrepresentational style, the opposite extreme, is ornamental. Its main object is sensation. The interplay of sheer form and color becomes important. There is no attempt to create a form that bears any resemblance to nature or man-made objects.

In between the two extremes of the representational and nonrepresentational styles lie as many degrees of realism, abstraction, or complete nonobjectivity as the designer dares to define.

Most styles, except for complete nonobjectivity, stem from realism. That is to say, the natural source of the abstracted design form is recognizable although it may have been distorted or abstracted in a decorative or stylized manner (Figure 4–1).

Secondly, scene design, more than other visual arts, is often subject to period and national style. A scene designer, for example, may be called upon to produce a Rococo room in French, German, or Venetian tastes. He may, however, vary the degree of realism and simplify authentic detail within the style line and still retain the flavor of the period and country.

REALISM—INTERIOR. *First in Heart.*
Designer—William Eckart (Photo—
Shapiro).

FIGURE 4-1. SCENERY STYLES. The
thirteen photographs on pages 77 through
83 illustrate realism, stylization, and both
fragmentary and suggested scenery
types.

REALISM—EXTERIOR. *The Three Sisters.*
Designer—Alvin Schechter (Photo—Baker).

STYLIZATION—PAINTED. *Happy as Larry*.
Designer—William Bohnert (Photo—Shapiro).

STYLIZATION—CARICATURE. *Tango* by S.
Mrozek. Designer—Travers Mercer (Photo—
Nelson).

STYLIZATION—PAINTED. *The Beaux' Stratagem* by George Farquhar. Designer—Charles Dox (Photo—Nelson).

ANTI-ILLUSIONARY SCENERY. *Puntila* by Bertolt Brecht. An example of Brecht's aversion to illusionary or "make-believe" scenery. Real, unconventional textures such as the straw-covered portals, unpainted old boards, and a brass sun are used. The result is of course not realism but stylization which, though denying illusion, is still theatrical. (Photo—Nelson)

SURREALISM. *A Dream Play* by August
Strindberg. Designer—Beeb Salzer (Photo—
Rabin).

SURREALISM. *Right You Are If You Think You Are*
by Luigi Pirandello. Designer—William Matthews
(Photo—Feinstein).

FRAGMENTARY SCENERY.   *(a) Beethoven.*   Designer—Ariel Balif (Photo—Shapiro).
(b) A view from the wings of a setting for the operatic version of Eugene O'Neill's
Mourning Becomes Electra at the Metropolitan Opera, New York. The highly stylized
interpretation of the stately Classic Revival style is achieved by the imaginative use of
textured surfaces and exposed structural members.   Designer—Boris Aronson
(Photo—Gary Renaud)

SUGGESTED SCENERY. *Children of the Ladybug.*
Designer—George Corrin (Photo—Shapiro).

SUGGESTED SCENERY. *The Merchant of Venice.*
Designer—Robert Joyner (Photo—Nelson).

PERIOD THEATRICAL STYLE.   Not a revival but a concept in the
manner of a specific period theatrical style. *The Merchants* by Plautus
becomes a Roman vaudeville with an ''ad-drop'' oleo for a background.
Designer—Donald Oenslager. Costumes: Frank Bevans. (Courtesy
Yale School of Drama Library).

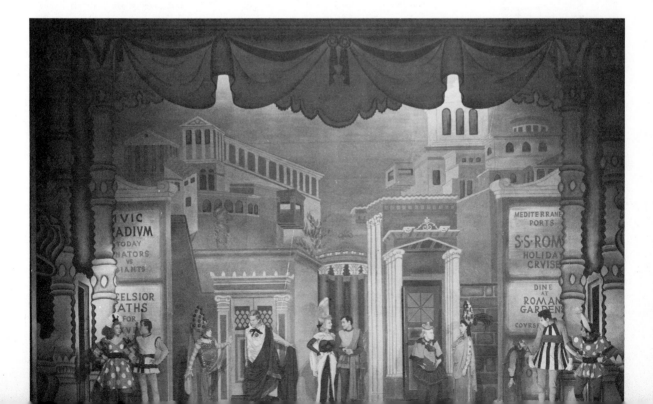

Theatre history also has period styles that frequently affect the style of scenery. The painted realism and staging conventions of the nineteenth century and earlier take on a theatrical feeling when compared with the ultrarealism of the box set and removed-fourth-wall style of the early twentieth century. The melodrama revival is a familiar example of the use of a theatrical-period style in scenery.

Modern theatre forms such as the arena, thrust, and open stage definitely establish a scenery or production style. The audience is asked to accept a convention of staging which is not dependent on realism and relies on the nature and arrangement of properties and the imaginations of the audience to create the environment of the scene. The novelty of the style in comparison to conventional proscenium staging is a part of its appeal.

The third influence on scenery style is that of the individual. The scene designer, as he develops, usually acquires a personal or individual style that creeps into everything he designs. This may change slowly or have phases, but it still exists as a personal stamp on everything he does.

Although style, especially individual style, is a part of each designer's creative ability and therefore is more closely related to the fundamentals of design (Chapter 3), it must at the same time be correlated with the other theatrical styles, acting, and writing.

Acting and Literary Styles. With the scenery style, the dramatic form combines the literary and acting styles. They all have an effect on each other and must have some degree of unity or the dramatic form is weakened.

The literary style reveals through dialogue the degree of ideality represented in the play. The style of a play may capture a cross section of life, such as Elmer Rice's *Street Scene,* or it may be as expressionistic as the treatment of Mr. Zero's problems in Mr. Rice's *The Adding Machine.*

The epic style of Brecht and his attempts to denude the stage of illusion or any visual make-believe obviously has its influence on scenery style. By appealing to the intellectual side of the members of his audience, and denying them any escape into sentimentality, he forces them to listen, and perhaps more important, to react. The belief that any reaction, even the shock of unconventionality, was better than having a passive, hypnotized audience is reflected in elements of scenery. Thus, a barren stage, the presence of *real* materials and textures, exposed lighting instruments, and clear unatmospheric lighting create the essence of his scenes.

Paradoxically, the opposition to the fakery of illusionary scenery in the effort to free the theatre of conventionality actually imposes

a new system of theatrical hocus-pocus. The result is a scenic stylization in tune with present-day junk sculpture and pop art which the
audience responds to in vicarious recognition of its unconventional
cleverness.

The acting style of today, for the most part, is believably real
when compared to the highly mannered period examples of the seven-
teenth, eighteenth, and nineteenth centuries. Acting style, however,
may vary from naturalism to conform with the style of a specific
drama. It takes its cue, as does scenery, from the literary style of the
play.

There are many examples of conflicting styles: one illustration is
the nineteenth-century conception of opera. A stilted literary style
was combined with a presentational acting style of singing dialogue—
both set against a conflicting background of painted realism. Today,
the style of the scenery has been brought closer to the less realistic
acting and writing styles to form a more unified and convincing art
form.

Scene design, as a visual art, can reinforce and heighten literary
and acting styles. Strangely enough, it can on occasion be a contrast
to the acting style without breaking the unity of the production. The
designer has always felt that stylized scenery does not necessarily
call for stylized acting, as was demonstrated so expertly in Jo Mielziner's setting for *Death of a Salesman*. The reverse, however, is not
true. If the acting is stylized, the scenery must be, too. The important
thing is that the audience will accept any degree of departure from
the real in scenery as long as it is consistent and in good taste.

WORKING WITH THE DIRECTOR

During this formative stage there is only so much a designer can do
alone. From the beginning there is a need of close communication with
the director, especially if there is a strong directorial concept to be
considered in the design. Directorial influence on design can vary from a
complete hands-off-solve-it-yourself attitude to a this-is-what-I-want
directive. A more equally balanced collaboration is, naturally, ideal. One-
sided experience can dominate the results of the union and personality
clashes can turn off the creative process. The most successful and unified
productions are usually the result of the mutual respect and open-
mindedness of both the designer and the director.

The collaboration, of course, begins with talking. Preliminary discus-
sions can lead to agreement of: what the play is about; the dramatic
image; general atmosphere, colors, style, staging, and directorial concept.
Talk, however, has its limits. Words have a way of triggering a different
image in each individual. Right or wrong, the designer must very soon put

some visual impressions on paper. Only then can the designer and director begin to communicate.

An understanding and agreement of *style* is probably the most important part of the designer-director collaboration, especially if other designers are involved in the production (costume and lighting). Although the impact of a style confusion appears later in the execution of the design it is significant enough to be mentioned now at the formative stage.

The theatre, as we have seen, brings together many styles. During production, the director is the only one with an over-all view and therefore must be responsible for coordinating the various styles as the show is being put together. The lack of immediate communication to the designer or designers of directorial changes or style adjustments in other areas of design can lead to conflicts at a time in the production schedule when it is too late to make changes. The best-laid plans can go astray without constant supervision and communication on the part of the director. An experienced designer soon learns to not take anything for granted and makes frequent checks with the director and other areas of design.

FINAL READING

After a discussion with the director to reach a mutual understanding of the theme, style, and general interpretation of the play, the designer returns to the script for the third reading.

This reading of the play is for its technique. Close attention is paid to the physical requirements of the plot structure and the changes of locale if there are many scenes. The action and staging requirements are examined to determine such things as: the number of people in a scene, the types of entrances and exits, references in the dialogue to the scene, bits of action hidden from one actor but visible to the audience, and so on, all leading to the development of a basic idea and scheme of production.

SCHEME OF PRODUCTION

The design solution of a multiscene play, which is known as a scheme of production, brings scenery-handling techniques into the design concept. The design idea is developed around a method of handling the numerous changes of scene. The kinds of changes and the methods of handling scenery, such as wagons and turntables, are discussed fully in Chapter 10 and indicate the necessity of designing a large production around at least a basic scheme for moving the scenery.

Although discussed separately, a scheme of production is, of course, closely related to *style*. Many times the designer, through his scheme of production, establishes certain conventions he expects the audience to accept which, consequently, create a scenery style. Conversely, a scenery style may dictate how the scenery is to be handled, thereby becoming a scheme of production.

The Unit Setting.   Scenery moving is reduced by the various uses of a unit setting. This form of setting is based upon the retention or reusing of elements of scenery to simulate a change of scene. This is usually accomplished by repeating either the plan, design shape, or color in the various settings. The design shapes and colors, for example, may be varied in each setting although they are placed in identical floor plans, or the same shape can be moved to a variety of positions.

A unit setting can be used in two different ways, either as a cleverly camouflaged method of reusing scenery unbeknown to the audience, or as an obvious device that becomes a unifying force for the production, as well as simplifying scene changes (Figure 4–2).

FIGURE 4–2. THE UNIT SETTING.   The production scheme for Anouilh's *Colombe* as it was produced by the Yale Dramatic Association. The repetition of the theatre proscenium form brings a visual and thematic unity to the production.

UNIT SETTING. Continuation of the production scheme for Anouilh's *Colombe* at Yale.

Simultaneous-Scene Setting. Sometimes a production scheme can eliminate any actual movement of scenery by placing two or more locales on the stage at the same time. The action moves from one area to the other without a break. The only movement is in the changing of lights. The areas retain their initial identity throughout the show. They may be different rooms in a house, different houses in the same town, or remotely located scenes (Figure 4–3).

Although the simultaneous-scene setting is mentioned here as one of the many schemes of production, it was, of course, discussed earlier as a kind of production that emphasizes the important design function; *staging the story* (Chapter 1). Even though the scenic elements and furniture in the simultaneous-scene setting may appear as extreme realism, the style of the setting is, in the final analysis, unrealistic. The audience is asked to accept theatrical conventions such as *cut-away walls* and *strange locale juxtapositions* to facilitate the staging of the story.

FIGURE 4–3. A design by Peter Larkin for *Inherit the Wind*. Ink and wash, 1955. From *The Arts of the United States: A Survey in Color,* conducted by the University of Georgia. Reproduced by courtesy of Mr. Larkin.

Formal Setting. A freer example of the simultaneous-scene setting is the use of an arrangement of abstract or architectural forms in such a way as to allow a flow of action over the set, relying on lights to change the composition. Three or four basic areas may be established, but they do not take on the connotation of a specific locale. A formal setting locates the action only in a very general way. It is dependent upon the actor, properties, and dialogue to establish the specific locale of the scene. Occasionally a formal setting is dressed with a minimum of moving set pieces to add variety (Figure 4–4).

FIGURE 4–4. FORMAL SETTING. Example of a setting based on an interesting arrangement of steps and levels, providing several acting areas for the fluid action of the play. Changes were achieved by the clever use of lighting to reveal portions of the basic setting in a variety of interesting compositions. *Divine Comedy.* Designer—Peggy Clark (Photo—Shapiro).

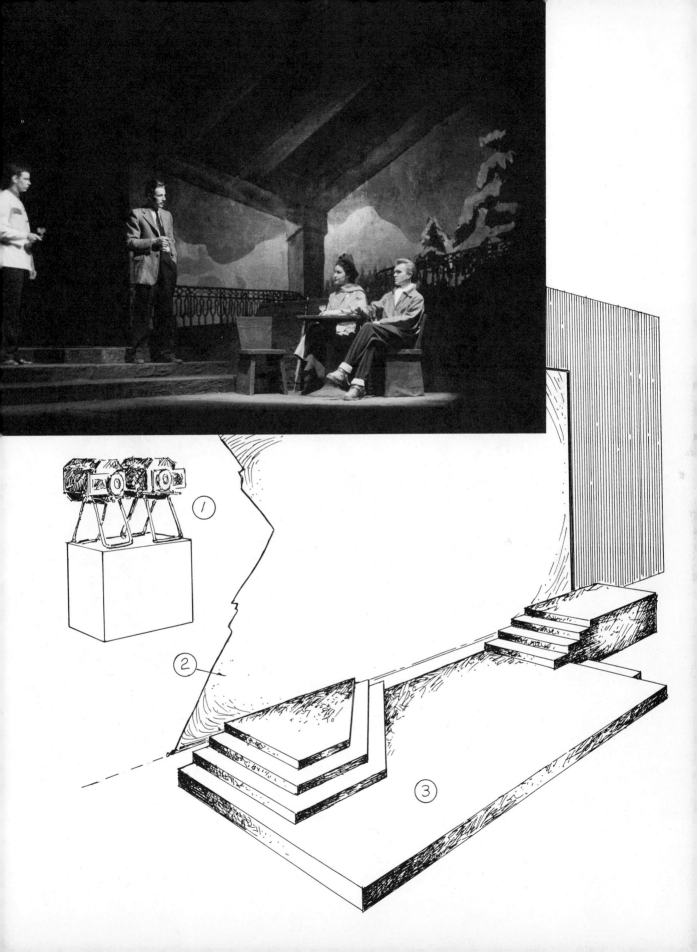

92 FIGURE 4–5. PROJECTED SCENERY. *(a)* One slide of a multiscope production of *Snows of Kilimanjaro*. The diagram shows the screen, projection equipment, and setting relationships. (1) A pair of 5000-watt projection machines. (2) Translucent rear-projection screen. (3) Formal arrangement of platforms. Designer—Robert Thayer (Photo—Shapiro). *(b)* A scene from *The Measures Taken* by Bertolt Brecht, illustrating the documentary use of projections. The screen is used as a visual support to the theme of the play rather than in the more conventional way to establish environment or locale. Designer—Frederic Youens (Photo—Nelson).

Projected Scenery.   Included with many production schemes for handling multiscene shows is the use of light projections as scenery. The rear projection of a design onto a translucent screen makes the shifting of a scene as simple as the changing of a slide (see Chapter 18).

Because projected scenery is *light* and not *paint* it has a strong dramatic quality which tends to dominate the scene. It becomes in a sense an actor rather than scenery. Projected scenery when used correctly as an integral part of the play functions best for a non-realistic or abstract production where the scenery is acting and not just background.

Brecht, for example, used the screen as an actor. He frequently projected poignant messages or illustrative images on the screen more as an instrument of propaganda or idea than as a visual background to set the scene. It is a classroom or documentary technique which when used in dramatic surroundings serves to heighten his epic theatre.

In spite of its limitations and dominating characteristics, projected scenery can be used as a highly dramatic and exciting production scheme. Many production designs have been based on projected scenery with successful results (Figure 4–5).

PRELIMINARY STUDIES

The designer's first impression of a design concept may have been formed as early as the first reading of the play only to be substantially revised or rejected after a closer study of the script in the second and third readings. Often a first impression is right, but sometimes it is wrong and the designer finds it hard to get it out of his mind. For this reason the beginning designer may be wise during the first reading of a new play to keep his mind open and free of preconceptions until all the facts are accumulated. At that time everything usually falls into place with little or no effort.

An idea may first appear to the designer in the form of an interesting floor plan to be developed later into a related elevational drawing, or the reverse—as a decorative shape or historical form that must be adjusted to a workable floor plan.

Preliminary studies usually consist of small, free-hand thumbnail sketches and rough floor plans. After consultation with the director, the tentative ideas of the designer are ready to be expanded into a more complete form of presentation.

THE PRESENTATION OF THE DESIGN IDEA

A designer may present his ideas in two forms: as a two-dimensional sketch, or, as a three-dimensional model. Sometimes both the sketch and model are used. The sketch is used to sell the idea and the model is made later to more clearly indicate the space relationships and acting areas to the director and builder.

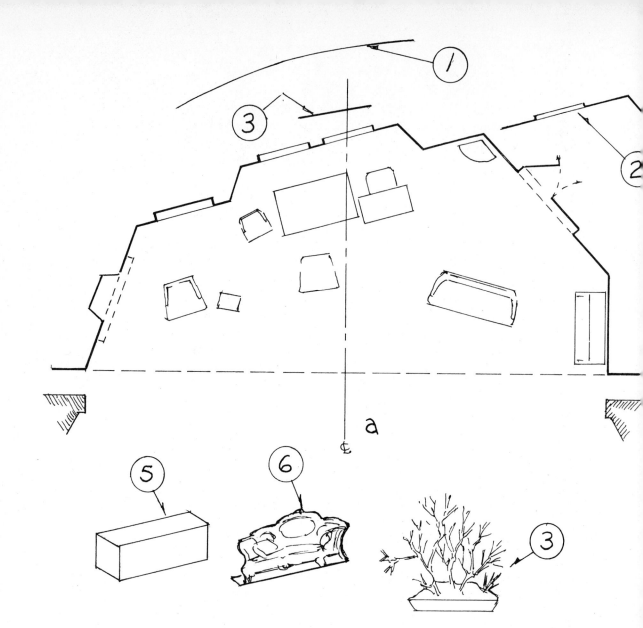

FIGURE 4–7. THE MODEL. (a) Plan for model is the same as floor plan for the stage setting at a smaller scale, usually ¼″ = 1′0″. (b) Perspective view of assembled model. (c) Layout of set before corners have been scored or tabs cut prior to folding for assembly. (1) Sky backing. (2) Hall backing. (3) Treetop set piece. (4) Portal or tormentor-teaser proportion. (5) Block furniture to approximate space it will occupy onstage. (6) Cutout furniture. (7) Double doors.

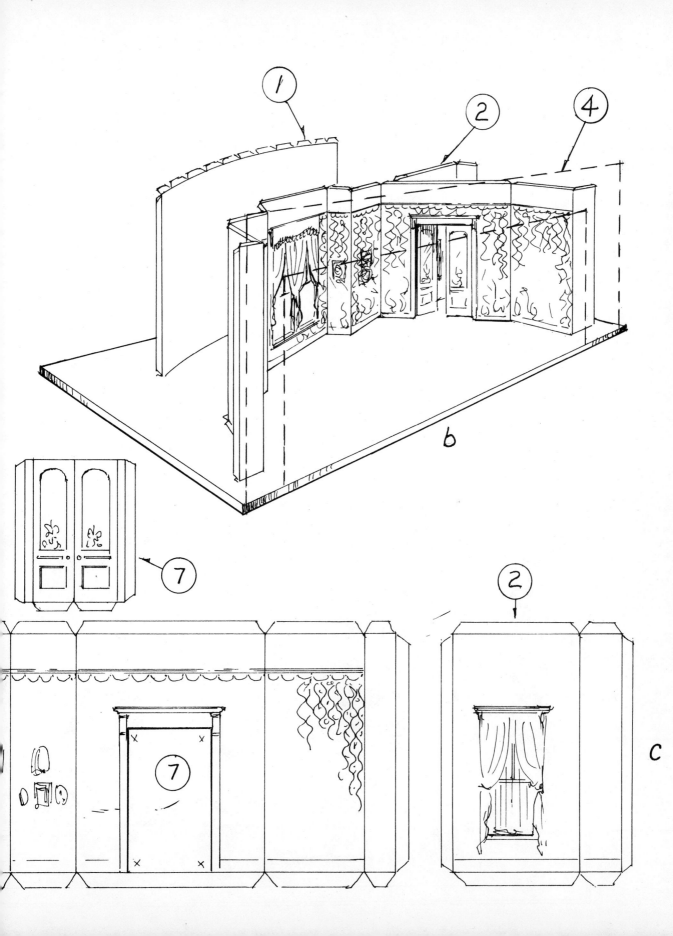

THE SKETCH

Although scene design is essentially a three-dimensional art form, the sketch medium is used to present the design idea. The sketch can be rendered in color and perspective to show atmosphere that would be difficult to accomplish in a model. Many sketches can be made to show changes in lighting, scenery, and composition of the actors. The sketch is lightweight, easy to carry around, and therefore adaptable to the selling of an idea.

What is represented in the sketch depends a little on the working arrangement of the designer. For example, it may be an established designer working with a new producer, an established producer working with a new designer, or a producing team, experienced in working together for some time.

The producer views the sketches of an established designer more with a knowledge of what the designer has done in past settings than for what is actually shown in the sketch. He knows that after an agreement on the general concept the experienced designer will fill in the details and create a setting to a high standard of excellence in keeping with his reputation.

Because a new designer doesn't have past examples of his work, his ideas are bought or rejected on the strength of his sketch. In addition, of course, he must be able to back up his ideas with faithful execution.

Under either condition, the sketch tries to catch a moment in the play. The designer usually picks a moment that will best show the setting and still express the dominant mood of the play. The sketch is an idealized drawing of the total visual effect which serves as a goal for the execution and guide for the lighting. Supplementary sketches are sometimes needed to show what would happen at another dramatic moment with different lighting and actor grouping.

In the purest sense, however, the sketch is only a means of presenting an idea. It is not the final design and therefore should not be displayed or judged as a complete art form. A stage setting is not complete until it is on the stage, lighted and viewed in the context of the action of the play and the actors' movements. The judgment of the success or failure of a design in the final analysis is based on how it functions under finished performance conditions rather than as a beautiful sketch.

FIGURE 4–6.　THE DESIGNER'S SKETCH.

The sketch is not meant to be a working drawing. Although it maintains a consistent proportion to show the actor-scenery relationship, it is not necessarily drawn to an accurate scale. It is possible, however, to execute from a carefully proportioned sketch if large portions of the set are parallel to the footlights as in a wing and backdrop setting. The colors in the sketch are not intended to be the scenery colors, but represent the color as it would appear under the stage lights in the total visual effect.

If the designer is a member of an established producing group such as summer stock or television, his sketch may take on a different character. The designer, director, builder, and painter are so used to working with each other that much is understood without being set down on paper. The designer's sketch becomes schematic with marginal notes. They are carried just as far as is necessary to convey the idea. They are not drawn for the layman but for the designer's professional colleagues. He will resort to a full sketch or model only if he is trying something experimental which needs careful explanation.

The sketch is always accompanied by a floor plan. If the floor plan is drawn to scale and the sketch is in good proportion, the director and others concerned with the production can form an accurate opinion as to how the actual setting will look (Figure 4–6).

THE MODEL

Although the sketch has been pictured as the prime means of presenting an idea, it is frequently backed up by a model. Because of the three-dimensionality of scenery, some designers prefer to work directly in the model form of presentation. The model gives a true indication of the space relationships of scenery and actors and is, therefore, of interest to the director when he is planning the staging.

Within the model, each piece of scenery is constructed to an accurate scale, thus giving the designer a miniature preview of how the setting is going to look. Because the model is three-dimensional, composition and sightlines can be checked from all the extreme angles of view.

Besides being a means of presentation, the model also can be used to check construction and effects before making a sketch. In this way the new designer is assured that his sketches can be reproduced in full-scale scenery without technical difficulties.

Figure 4–7 illustrates the steps in making a simple paper model. The paper used is white three-ply bristol upon which is drawn a continuous elevation of each wall in the setting with pictures, draperies, and some furniture in place. All corners of the room are left joined

FIGURE 4-8A. DESIGNER'S SKETCH for *He Who Must Die*, a translation and adaptation of Nikos Kazantazakis' *The Greek Passion*. Designer — Rolf Beyer .

FIGURE 4–8B. DESIGNER'S MODEL for *He Who Must Die.*

so they can be scored and folded to fit the floor plan. Tabs are left on the top and bottom to stiffen the walls as well as to provide a glueing surface with which to attach the model to the floor plan and ceiling piece.

The scale of the model varies with the designer. Some like to work at the scale of one inch equals one foot while others prefer a smaller scale. The ¼-inch scale model is a convenient size for fast execution, which sometimes is important. Also in the smaller scale it is easier to make changes and experiment than in a larger scale.

The sketch and model are the designer's means of presenting or selling a design concept. Once the director and designer have reached an area of agreement and the idea has been bought, the designer has to prepare another type of presentation; this time to the artisan and craftsmen who will build, paint, and light his design.

FIGURE 4–8C. COMPLETED SETTING for *He Who Must Die* (Photo—Street).

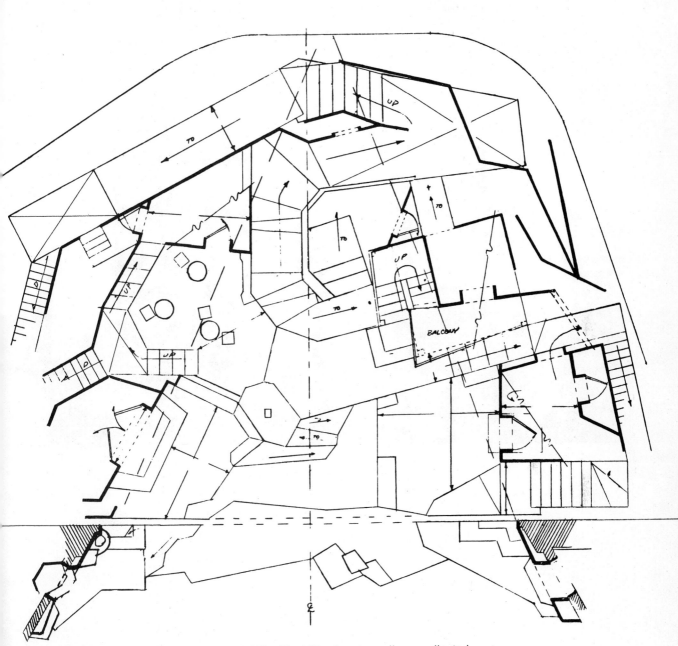

FIGURE 4–8D. FLOOR PLAN for *He Who Must Die.* An unusually complicated floor plan showing many different levels. The double-weight lines indicate scenic elements. The single-weight lines define the shapes of the various levels. Note how top levels have been cut away in some places to show the shape of walls underneath.

This particular drawing was prepared to aid the director in planning the action of the play. It is therefore stripped of dimensions to clean up the drawing. Normally each change in level is dimensioned by noting its height off the stage floor.

FIGURE 4-9A. THE PRELIMINARY SKETCH.   A designer's first
thoughts. Sometimes in color, more often in black and white. Shown in ink
and wash is a preliminary sketch for *Grand Hotel*. Designer—Anon Adar,
Tel Aviv. More designers' sketches and other means of presentation can
be found on pages 93–99.

FIGURE 4-9B. DESIGNER'S SKETCH.   *Can Can*, Dance Hall Scene.
Designer: Jo Mielziner. This sketch by Jo Mielziner, a master of the
watercolor medium, is a delightful example of the technique. He uses the
vibrant and transparent qualities of watercolor to catch the theatricality of
the period and locale. (Courtesy Jo Mielziner estate)

5 Drafting the Design

Although scene design is three-dimensional in final form, most of the presentation of the design idea in preparation for construction is two-dimensional in character. The graphics of presentation is the visual language, or fundamental means of communication between the designer, stage technicians, and director. The planning of a show throughout all its phases relies upon a common knowledge of simple drafting techniques to communicate technical and artistic information. If the designer wants his ideas carried out efficiently and accurately he must give simple, clear, and accurate information.

DRAFTING EQUIPMENT

A student designer who is about to turn into a draftsman for the first time will need to become acquainted with his new tools and materials. Although drafting for the theatre is similar to architectural drafting and engineering drawing it is not necessary for the scene designer to outfit himself quite so elaborately. For the beginner, a list of basic drafting equipment should include:

(*a*) A drawing board or drafting table
(*b*) Drawing board padding
(*c*) T-square or traveling straight edge
(*d*) Set of triangles or Set-square
(*e*) Small set of drafting instruments
  1. Compass
  2. Lengthening bar
  3. Inking attachments
  4. Dividers
  5. Bow compass
  6. Ruling pen

(*f*) Scale rule
(*g*) Pencils or leads
(*h*) Tracing paper
(*i*) Accessories
  1. Erasers
  2. Erasing shield
  3. Drafting tape
  4. Sandpaper pad or lead pointer
  5. Drawing cleaning powder

A good *drawing board* is made of clear white pine, cleated to prevent warping, and for most purposes about 24 inches by 30 inches in size. A *drafting table,* the top of which is a drawing board, should be a little larger. A top of about 30 inches by 42 inches gives additional work space around the drawing.

Drawing boards need to be padded to keep the pencil from following the grain of the wood. *Laminene,* a tinted paper made just for this purpose, is an excellent drafting surface.

The *T-square* guides off one side of the drawing board to establish the horizontal lines in the drawing. Its accuracy depends upon the straightness of the working edge and the squareness of the head and blade. A 30-inch T-square made of hardwood with a transparent-edge blade and fixed head is best for all around service. A traveling parallel straight edge which serves the same function as a T-square is attached permanently to the top of a drafting table. Its length, of course, is determined by the longest dimension of the top.

Two transparent celluloid *triangles* give the customary set of angles as well as perpendicular lines when they are guided off of the T-square. A 6-inch 45-degree and an 8- or 10-inch 30–60-degree triangle are the most convenient sizes.

An instrument that lends itself to drawing the many odd angles so frequently found in a stage setting is the *set-square*. It is a com-

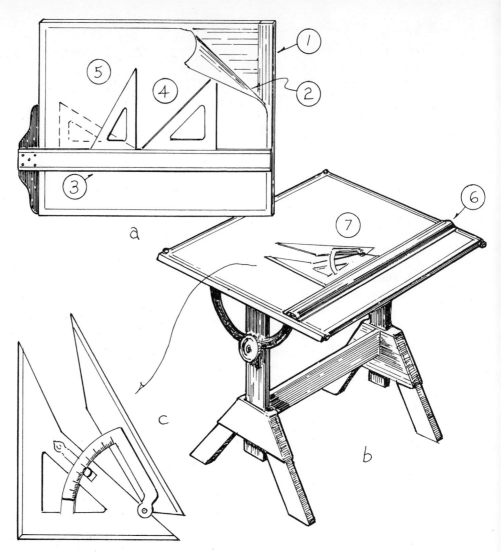

FIGURE 5–1. DRAFTING EQUIPMENT. *(a)* Drawing board and tools. (1) Cleated white-pine drawing board. (2) Tinted Laminene padding for drawing-board surface. (3) T-square. (4) 45-degree triangle. (5) 30–60-degree triangle. *(b)* Drafting table with adjustable tilt and height. (6) Parallel straight edge attached to the top of the drawing table by a cable system that allows it to travel from top to bottom and remain parallel. (7) Set-triangle that is able to adjust to many different angles. (c) Detail of set-triangle.

bination triangle and protractor with an adjustable edge that allows the selection of any angle between 45 degrees and perpendicular.

When assembling drawing instruments for the first time, it is wise to invest in a good set. The accuracy and clarity of the work depends on the quality of the instruments. Buying a cheap, low-grade set is a nuisance from the beginning and worthless in a short while. It is better to economize in the number or size of the set and buy good instruments.

The basic drafting instrument is the *compass.* It is necessary to draw a circle or swing an arc. Many small drafting sets are comprised of just a compass with lengthening bar and inking attachments. Extra points are also provided to turn the compass into dividers.

The *lengthening bar* is an attachment that increases the length of one arm of the compass making it possible to swing a larger radius to make an arc or circle. An *inking attachment* can be fitted to the same arm of the compass or to the end of the lengthening bar. The

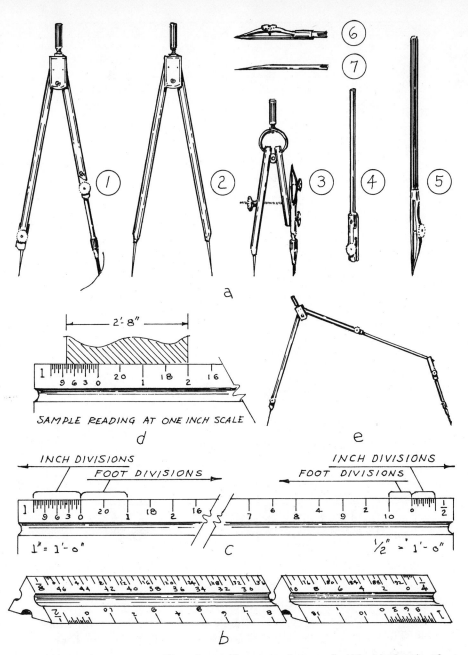

a

d

SAMPLE READING AT ONE INCH SCALE

e

INCH DIVISIONS

FOOT DIVISIONS

1" = 1'-0"

INCH DIVISIONS

FOOT DIVISIONS

½" = 1'-0"

c

b

FIGURE 5–2. DRAFTING INSTRUMENTS. *(a)* The minimum set of drafting instruments. (1) Compass. (2) Dividers. (3) Combination bow compass and bow dividers with inking tip and divider points to replace pencil lead. (4) Extension arm for compass. (5) Ruling pen. (6) Inking tip for compass. (7) Divider point. *(b)* Architect's scale rule, triangular form, three edges, six faces, and twelve scales. *(c)* Drawing of one face to demonstrate the method of reading a scale rule. The face shown contains two scales: 1" = 1'0" to the left and ½" = 1'0" to the right. To read the 1-inch scale, for example, inches are read to the left of zero while foot divisions are read to the right. *(d)* Drawing showing a sample reading of a surface 2'8" in dimension at the scale of 1" = 1'0".

inking attachment, like the *ruling pen,* has a double-blade tip that holds ink and is adjustable to a thick or thin line.

Dividers are used to hold or transfer a dimension. The compass can perform the same operation, but with less accuracy. Bow instruments such as the *bow compass* and *bow dividers* are better for small circles and measurements, and for retaining a recurring dimension or arc.

A set of drafting instruments containing a four-inch compass and dividers with lengthening bar and inking attachments plus a bow compass and bow dividers would fulfill the average drafting requirements.

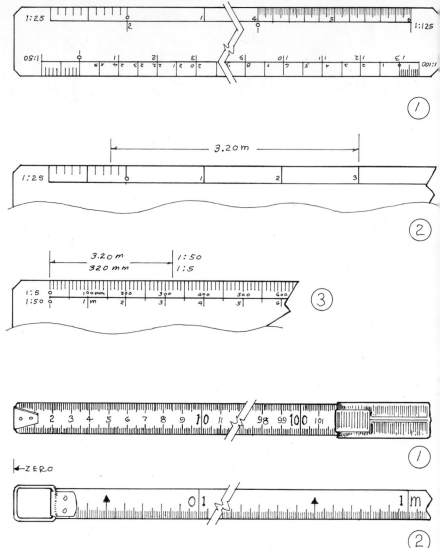

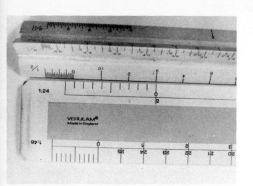

FIGURE 5–3. METRIC-SCALE RULES AND MEASURING TAPES. *(a) Metric conversion scale rule.* The metric scale 1:24 is shown in direct comparison to the scale of one-half inch equals one foot. *(b) Metric-scale rules.* (1) The open divided-scale rule. This example has two scales on each edge. Centimeter divisions are shown outside the zero mark while meter divisions are indicated toward the center of the rule. Draftsmen in the theatre will find this the easiest rule to use. (2) Use of the open divided rule for dimensioning. (3) The fully divided scale rule shows centimeter and millimeter divisions the full length of the rule. *(c) Metric measuring tapes.* (1) The three-meter tape. Numbers note centimeters; the smallest divisions are millimeters. (2) The thirty-meter tape. The major divisions are at ten-centimeter intervals with the millimeter the smallest division.

Most scenery is too large to be represented in a drawing at actual size, so it is necessary to reduce the size in regular proportions. The *scale rule* is devised to make the change in proportion as painless as possible. The most useful scale rule is the triangular form, which provides twelve different graduations (Figure 5-2). To the beginner, a confusing factor is the discovery that there are two types of scale rules: the Architect's scale, which divides the proportional foot into twelfths or inches, and the Engineer's scale, which divides the inch into decimals or tenths, with divisions from ten to sixty. The names are trade names, not an indication of the profession using them. Engineers have as much use for the Architect's scale as do architects. Inasmuch as stage sets, like houses, are built in feet and inches, the planning of scenery is done with the Architect's scale rule.

The Metric Scale. There are firm indications that in the not too distant future the United States will join the majority of nations and convert to the metric system of measurement. Leading up to that event and briefly after the change-over there will be a period of constant cross-reference until feet and inches have been wiped out of the mind as a scale reference. Until that moment the theatre drafts- man may be required to know and use both systems. Plans and con- struction drawings for European and British imports are usually in the metric system and have to be transposed or executed according to metric rules without converting to feet and inches.

To convert into the metric system or to redimension a drawing in meters the draftsman can use a specially prepared conversion scale rule (Figure 5–3a). To make the conversion accurate the scales that are provided are in an unusual ratio for direct drafting in the metric system. The ratio 1:24 shown in the illustration is equal to the scale of one-half inch equals one foot ($\frac{1}{2}'' = 1'0''$). This is an odd ratio for the metric system and can lead to mistakes in the shop.

The metric drafting-scale rule (Figure 5–3b) uses two basic divi- sions: the millimeter (mm) and the meter (m), which is 1000mm. Although not indicated on the rule the centimeter (cm) can be deter- mined by noting every 100mm or by moving the decimal point of the reading. Small measurements are dimensioned in millimeters (450- mm), whereas greater distances are indicated in meters and centi- meters (20.52m). As a present-day point of reference it will be noted that 25mm is approximately equal to one inch, which is an easy number to remember if it is necessary to convert or refer to feet and inches. Hence the ratios; 1:12.5m is approximately one-inch scale; 1:25m = one-half-inch scale; 1:50m = one-quarter-inch scale, and so on.

Although the centimeter does not appear on the drafting scale it is used on the measuring tape (Figure 5–3c). The tape is numbered in centimeters (cm), each being divided into tenths (mm) with, of course, 100cm equaling one meter.

Drawing pencils and leads for lead-holders have varying degrees of hardness and softness. Soft lead produces a blacker line than hard lead. The leads are graded by letters from 6B, which is very soft, through HB and H, which are medium soft to firm, to 6H, the hardest lead. The combination of H, 2H, and 4H leads gives the variety in line quality necessary for a good blueprint.

The choice of drafting paper depends, of course, on what type of drafting is planned. An ink drawing, a pencil drawing, or a preliminary study each require different *tracing papers*. There are many kinds of paper and no standardization of the numbering system, so the be- ginner is wise to seek the advice of a competent dealer. He can rec- ommend the proper density of tracing paper to insure a clear, good- contrast print.

The accessories that complete the draftsman's list of equipment is made up of such items as a *sandpaper pad* to keep a proper point on the pencil, or compass lead, and a *lead-pointer* for pointing the leads of the draftsman's mechanical pencils; a *ruby eraser* and *erasing shield* for erasing pencil-line mistakes and an art gum eraser or *drawing cleaning powder* to help keep the drawing paper clean; and *drafting tape,* which is used to fasten the tracing paper to the drawing board.

DRAFTING TECHNIQUES

In the theatre, drafting practices are so numerous and loosely defined that it is difficult to unify them. There are as many ways to draft a show as there are designers. A close inspection, however, reveals that each designer differs only in the amount of information he gives and in the way he organizes his material. All have in common a background of engineering drawing and its basic principle—orthographic projection.

THE ORTHOGRAPHIC PROJECTION

In spite of its academic sound, the orthographic projection is a simple drawing. Orthographic means straight line. A straight-line projection is a method of representing the exact shape of an object in a line drawing on a plane perpendicular to the lines of projection from the object. It is easier to understand when it is compared to the converging line projection inherent in the foreshortening of a perspective drawing or photograph. A perspective of a three-dimensional object is very descriptive and easy to visualize. The object, however, is not represented in true dimension due to the foreshortening of some surfaces.

For example, it is easy to recognize the familiar three-step unit from a perspective drawing (Figure 5–4a). The carpenter, however, needs more information than a pretty sketch. He wants to know its height, its width, and its depth. An orthographic projection is a draftsman's way of drawing the three steps to give this information. It reveals the object one view at a time and from all angles. The observer is free to move around the object to view it from front to rear and from top to bottom. Each view is seen in true dimension by straight-line projection.

VIEW ALIGNMENT

Obviously, a series of unrelated views of an object are of little value unless they are organized in a connective manner to show the position of the object in space. Hence, there is a conventional arrangement of views that is the basis of all drafting techniques.

To understand the method of transposing the views of the object in space onto the drawing board requires some visual imagination. Using the three-step unit as an example, it is imagined in the center of a transparent cube. Projected on each side of the cube is a line drawing of the object as it appears in each view. With the side con-

FIGURE 5–4. THE
ORTHOGRAPHIC
PROJECTION.

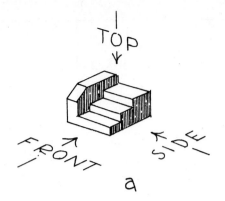

a

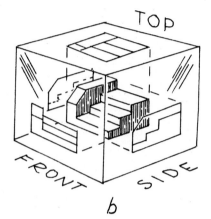

b

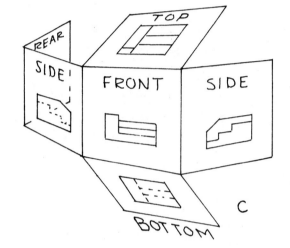

c

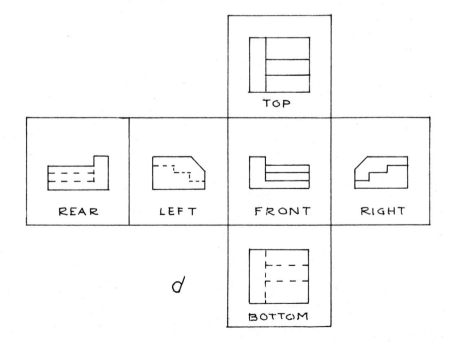

d

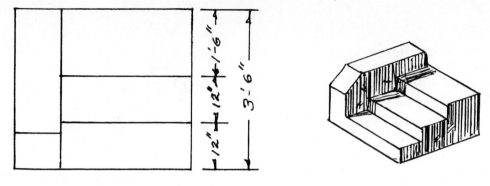

TOP

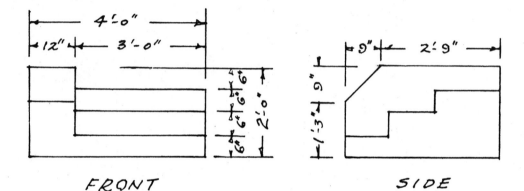

FRONT

SIDE

FIGURE 5–5. SCALED AND DIMENSIONED DRAWINGS. Designers' working drawings generally show three views of the object, drawn to scale and dimensioned. Occasionally one view may be omitted or an additional view (such as a section) included, depending upon the complexity of the subject.

taining the front view as the center, the other faces of the cube are unfolded to either side, to the top, and to the bottom (Figure 5–4b).

The front view is always the most recognizable one, showing the main characteristics of the object. It is the key view that gives the carpenter his bearings for visualizing the three-step unit in three dimensions. The top and side views are shown above and to the side of the front view providing the three principal views of the object.

Borrowing from architecture, some views are referred to as elevations, a term that is applied to all views seen in a horizontal direction. The horizontal views include the front elevations, side elevations, and rear elevations.

An academic and less frequently used expression is to refer to the views as projections. The front, top, and side views become respectively the vertical, horizontal, and profile projections. It is just another way of describing the three principal planes of projection.

Of course the carpenter does not refer to the drawings as orthographic projections. To him they are working drawings, for with the simple addition of a few dimensions and material specifications to the orthographic projection of the three-step unit, the carpenter is ready to start building (Figure 5–5).

DESIGNER'S WORKING DRAWINGS

As the designer begins his working drawings, which are flat and less descriptive than his sketch, he soon discovers that the draftsman has a way of making the lines speak for themselves. In the draftsman's language, symbols and conventions are words. His vocabulary has lines of all types. There are thick lines, thin lines, dotted lines, dashed lines, straight lines, and curved lines. Each has a different meaning and function. The draftsman's language, like any language, depends on a mutual knowledge of the symbols to read correctly a set of working drawings.

DRAFTING CONVENTIONS AND LINE SYMBOLS

The first and simplest convention is the drawing of lines in different weights or thicknesses. The various types of line symbols are grouped into three weight classes: light, medium, and heavy. A line is made heavy or light depending on its eye-catching importance on the blueprint. Obviously, heavy lines are going to be seen first, medium-weight lines second, and lightweight lines last. The use of different weight lines gives the blueprint a feeling of depth. It is a very slight third dimension, but it is enough to make the print easier to read. Beyond the slight descriptive quality of the weight of a line there is the meaning or symbol of the function implied in the use of certain lines that needs to be explained.

MEDIUM-WEIGHT LINES

It is easiest to begin with the medium-weight lines for they are used the most and have already been seen in the orthographic projection of the three step unit (Figure 5-5). They are the *outline lines* that represent the shape of the object, showing the edges and surfaces as they appear at the angle of the view. The visible outline is a solid line indicating the visible surfaces. The *hidden* or *invisible outline* is a dotted line indicating the hidden surfaces not visible in the view (Figure 5-6).

Next is the *adjacent-parts* or *alternate-position line.* It is similar to the hidden outline in looks, for it is a dashed line. The hidden outline, however, is used to show something that is there but hidden from view. The alternate-position line, on the other hand, is like a ghost. It is used to indicate something that was there but has been removed from view. The dashed-line symbol can be used to note an adjacent piece of scenery or the alternate position of a moving part. The use of the adjacent-parts line appears in the designer's elevations of Figure 5-9.

The final medium-weight line is the *center line,* symbolized by an alternating dash and dot. The center line is used to establish the

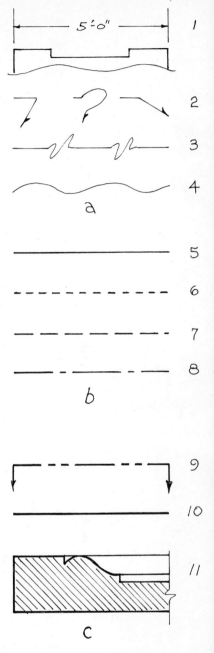

FIGURE 5-6. LINE SYMBOLS. *(a) Lightweight lines.* (1) Dimension and extension lines. (2) Leaders. (3) Long break line. (4) Short break line. *(b) Medium-weight lines.* (5) Visible outline. (6) Hidden outline. (7) Adjacent parts or alternate position line. (8) Center line. *(c) Heavyweight lines.* (9) Cutting plane line. (10) Section outline. (11) Section lines and section outline.

center of circles and the dividing line of symmetrical parts. The center line is a familiar symbol in the floor plan of a stage setting where it marks the center of the proscenium opening. It is an important reference line for the location of a set onstage.

LIGHTWEIGHT LINES

The lightweight lines are many and have a variety of uses. Their function is to give additional information about the object and still not detract from the over-all picture created by the outlines. That is why they are light in weight.

Dimension lines, with arrowheads at the ends, mark the extent of the surface that is being dimensioned. Figures, set into the line, show the exact distance. If dimension lines are set too close to the drawing, or within the drawing, they may become confused with outlines. To keep the dimension line away from the object, the *extension line* is used. These lines are solid, and are drawn perpendicular to the surface of the object. As the name implies, they extend the surface to the dimension line. Although the arrowheads of the dimension line touch the extension line, the extension line itself is held clear of the object, about one-sixteenth of an inch, wherever possible (Figure 5–6).

Leaders, relatives of dimension lines, are made with one-sided arrowheads that touch the surface where a note or dimension applies. If the leader is always drawn slanted or curved, there is less chance for anyone to confuse it with the dimension line.

Break lines are space savers that denote a shortening of length or height. Occasionally, the draftsman wants to draw a unit of scenery which is too long to fit on the paper. He can reduce the length by taking a piece out of the center and using a break line to show that the piece is not represented in full length. The break line can also be used to indicate that the outer surface of an object has been cut away to show inner structure. The *long break line* is a straight line with spasmodic eruptions occurring at intervals while the *short break line* is a more subtle curve with less regularity.

HEAVY-WEIGHT LINES

Heavy-weight lines are used solely to indicate the cross section of an object, or the cutting away and removing of a portion to reveal the inside. The *cutting-plane line,* drawn over an adjoining view to locate the position of the cut, consists of a repeating dash and a double dot. The arrowheads point the direction seen in the sectional view (Figure 5–7c).

The other heavy-weight line is the *section outline* which appears in the sectional view. It is a heavy solid line that outlines the cut surface to emphasize it over the uncut surfaces. The cut surface is further set apart by the use of *section lines* which are light-weight crosshatched lines drawn within the cut-surface outline.

SCALED DRAWINGS

The most important part of a set of working drawings is the dimensions. Although the carpenter may understand the drawings, he can't begin to build until he has some indication of size. He relies on a scaled drawing or a dimensioned drawing for such information. Most misunderstandings that occur between the drawing board and the finished setting are over dimensions such as the wall that is too small for the side board or the door that is too large for the door opening.

Many errors can be avoided if the designer uses a scaled drawing. If it is carefully drawn, it not only provides the carpenter a way to figure sizes, but also gives the designer a fairly accurate basis for studying the proportional relationship of various elements of the set.

The usual scale of a working drawing is half inch equals one foot ($\frac{1}{2}'' = 1' - 0''$) which means that every half inch on the drawing is equal to one foot at full-scale or actual size. Decorative details which might not be clear at the small scale are frequently increased to the scale of $1'' = 1' - 0''$ or larger. Any important bits of detail that the designer wants accurately reproduced, such as wallpaper patterns, scrolls, brackets, railings, and the like, are presented at full scale.

DIMENSIONS

An unscaled drawing needs some indication of size before the carpenter can begin building. The placing of dimensions opposite a surface is done in a manner to show its exact limit and measure. Dimensions, however, are not reserved strictly for unscaled drawings. It is common practice to place dimensions on a scaled drawing to save time in the shop. A properly given dimension includes the dimension line, figure, and extension lines.

SECTIONS

On many occasions the designer feels the need of supplementing the working drawings with another view that will add information to the normal top, front, and side views. The additional view most frequently used is the section. A designer often finds it easier to explain a three-dimensional piece of scenery by cutting it open to show the inner structure or exact contour. Because it is a more descriptive view, the section is sometimes used in place of a side or top view.

There are many types of sectional views and a variety of uses (Figure 5–7), but the two sectional views used consistently in the theatre are the floor plan and the hanging section. Of the two drawings the floor plan is most important to the designer, although he may use the hanging section to check technical details and vertical sightlines.

FLOOR PLAN

Long before starting the working drawings of a set, the importance of the floor plan is realized. A designer continually thinks of the plan while the idea of the setting is being developed. The plan grew with the design, pushed one way for esthetic reasons, altered another way for practical reasons, modified for staging reasons and, finally, solidified into the key working drawing and information center, the floor plan.

All phases of production seek information from the floor plan. To explain the design of his set adequately, the designer finds it necessary to refer often to this plan. The carpenter consults it to lay out the construction. The director and stage manager are unable to map out the staging without understanding and studying it. The setup, rigging, and lighting depend on information in the floor plan to complete the final assembly of the set on the stage.

The floor plan is a horizontal section with the cutting plane passed at a level that shows (when the upper portion of the set is removed) the most characteristic view of the shape of the set. Because a stage set is made up of many small units of scenery, the floor plan is also an assembled view. The floor plan, then, reveals the horizontal shape of the set, locates it on the stage, shows the scenery assembled, and identifies with labels the units and pieces that make up the complete setting.

SYMBOLS

The floor plan is usually drawn at the scale of ½″ = 1′ − 0′ or smaller. At this scale, it is necessary to use symbols and conventions

FIGURE 5–7. SECTIONAL VIEWS. *(a)* Revolved section, drawn directly on the elevation to indicate contour. *(b)* Removed section, a revolved section that has been removed and set to one side of the elevation. *(c)* Cross section B–B is a vertical section and A–A is a horizontal section, frequently called a *plan*. *(d)* Half section, used on a symmetrical object combining the cross-section and elevational views.

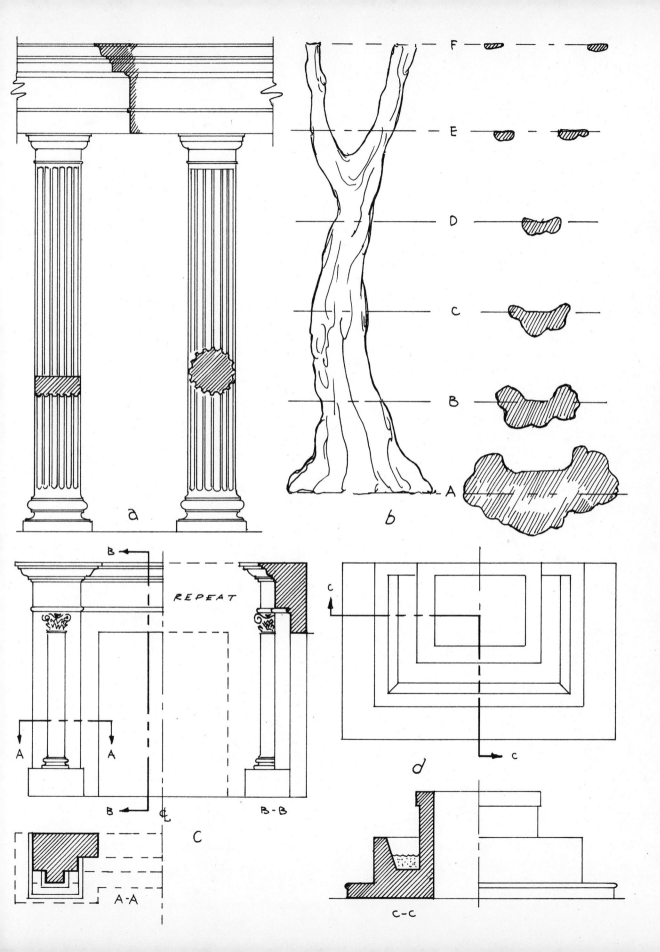

a

b

REPEAT

B

A   A

B

C

A-A

B-B

c

d

C-C

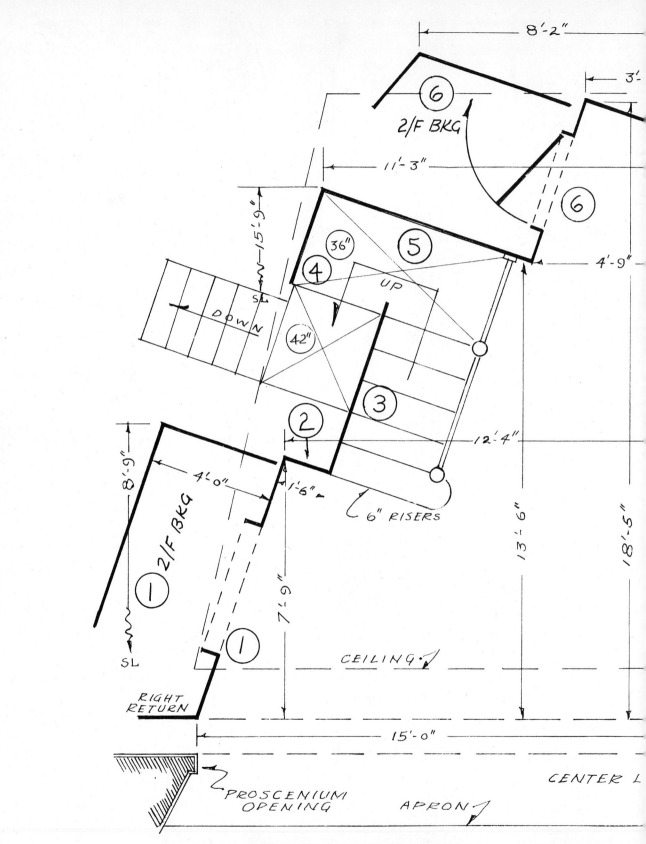

FIGURE 5–8. THE DESIGNER'S FLOOR PLAN.   A horizontal section taken through all wall openings and above all steps and levels wherever it is feasible. The dark solid lines represent a cross section of

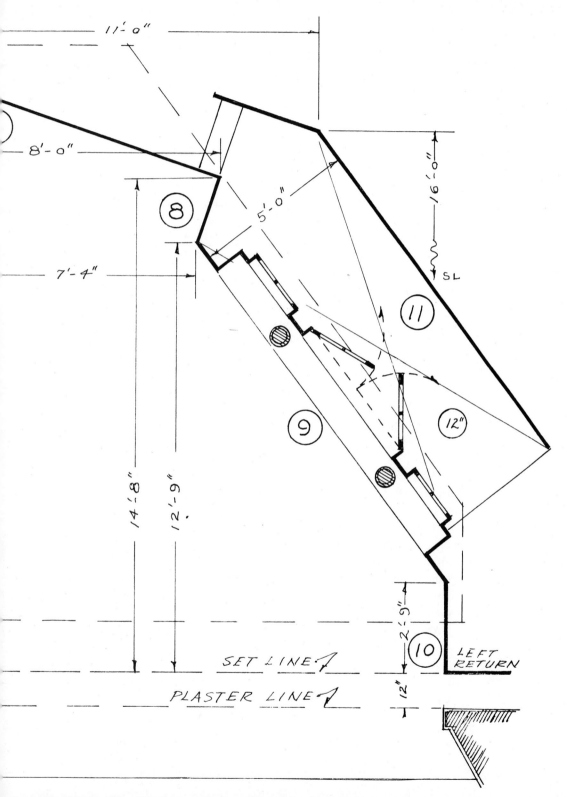

11'-0"

8'-0"

5'-0"

6'-0"

SL

7'-4"

⑧

⑪

⑫"

⑨

14'-8"

12'-9"

2'-9"

⑩ LEFT RETURN

SET LINE

PLASTER LINE

12"

the walls of the setting. The lightweight solid lines outline the steps and
levels seen in a top view. The dotted lines within the wall openings
indicate a "header" or presence of wall above the opening.

to help explain the set with a limited amount of detailed drafting. Most of the symbols shown in Figure 5–8 are familiar ones; their use and meanings are logical enough if it is kept in mind that a plan is a sectional view.

DIMENSIONING THE FLOOR PLAN

The floor plan is dimensioned from two reference lines, the center line of the proscenium opening and the set line—a dashed line drawn from the right return to the left return of the set to mark the downstage extremity of the set. It is not necessary to dimension the plan in great detail because all the scenery will appear in separate elevational views with complete dimensions. If it is kept in mind that the floor plan is also an assembled view, it will help to determine what dimension the stage carpenter needs to know to locate and assemble the set on the stage.

How wide are tormentors? How deep is the back corner of the set? Distances to the left and right use the center line as a base line while all depth measurements are taken directly or indirectly from the set line. Any point on the stage is located by its distance right or left of the center line and its measurement upstage from the set line. After all important corners and backings are located, a few additional dimensions may be needed, such as over-all dimensions of a wall or unit of scenery, and radius dimensions of circles or arcs that may be in the floor plan.

LABELING

Part of the function of an assembled view is to identify and label the parts that make up the whole. The floor plan gives this information in varying degrees of completeness depending upon the working conditions and the nature of the show. In designing for summer stock or university and community theatres, where the bulk of the structural planning falls on the designer's shoulders, he may want to be more specific in his labeling of each piece of scenery in the show. The label becomes an easy, accurate means of identification for a single piece of scenery or assembled units of a setting.

As in the theatre, the floor plan of a television show contains a careful notation of each piece of scenery. Television scenery is almost entirely of stock units and standard sizes. The designer's labels and notes on the plan are a catalog, or index guide, for assembling the set in the studio.

DESIGNER'S ELEVATIONS

Of almost equal importance to the floor plan, as a working drawing, are the designer's elevations. Compared to the floor plan, which is an assembled section showing the relationship of many parts, the elevational drawings are, in a sense, a disassembled or dismantled view of the individual parts. Because the elevation of an assembled set as it would appear in a normal front view has little value as a working drawing, the scene designer uses another technique. The set is taken apart, flattened out, and each piece of scenery is shown in front view at a scale of $\frac{1}{2}'' = 1' - 0''$. Starting with the right return, the setting is drafted to show all pieces of scenery laid out in order, piece by piece, to the left return. All pieces are represented at $\frac{1}{2}$-inch scale in true size and shape.

Each flat wall surface or unit of scenery is outlined. A solid line or space between units marks an open joint. For special reasons, it may be necessary to indicate a covered joint on the line where two or more wings are hinged together to make up a flat wall surface. The covered joint is indicated with a dotted line and a note to hinge and to dutchman, or cover, the joint. Normally, this isn't necessary as the carpenter decides just how an oversized surface will be subdivided. His decision as to how it is to be made is guided by such technical considerations as the size of the stage, the method of handling the sets, and, if the scenery has to be transported, the nature of the transportation. The standard maximum wing width of 5 feet 9 inches is based on the height of a baggage-car door through which all the scenery of a road show must be able to pass if it is traveling by train. If the scenery is moving by truck, or not traveling at all, the maximum standard width can vary accordingly. The designer will do well, however, to keep in mind these technical considerations as he plans his scenery, for they are the limiting features that control the size and shape of his design.

APPLIED DETAIL

Designers vary in the amount of detail they show at $\frac{1}{2}$-inch scale. Although the decorative trim and other details are better shown at a larger scale, it is sometimes wise to at least sketch a portion of the detail on the $\frac{1}{2}$-inch elevations. It not only shows the trim in assembled view but also gives the carpenter some idea of any special construction that may be needed. Because of the light wood frame and canvas construction of scenery, pictures, valance boxes, or lighting fixtures can't be placed in the middle of a wall without providing extra structural support from behind. If the applied details are partially sketched in the elevation, or indicated with the dashed-line symbol of an adjacent part, the carpenter will know where to supply the additional construction (Figure 5–9).

Obviously, the labels of the elevation must agree with the labels

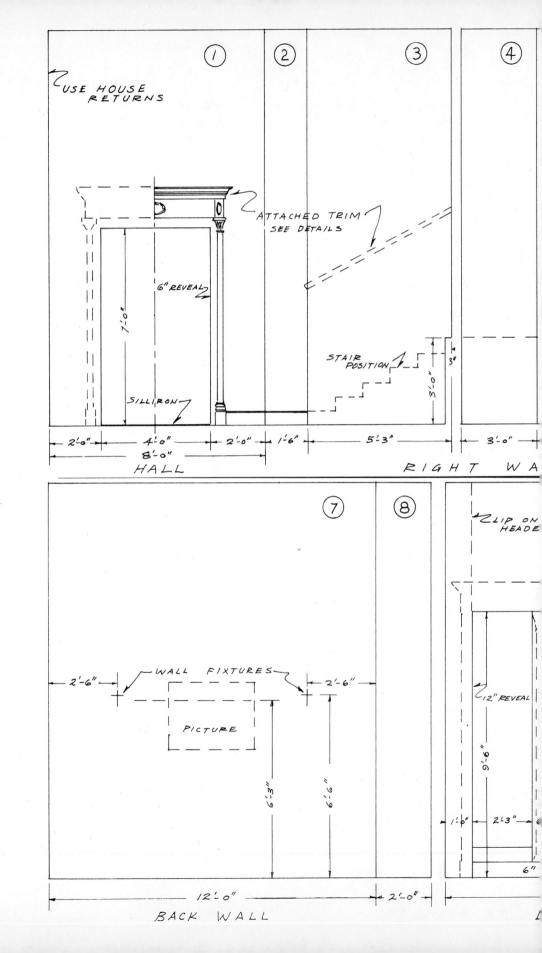

USE HOUSE RETURNS

(1) (2) (3) (4)

ATTACHED TRIM
SEE DETAILS

6" REVEAL

7'-0"

STAIR POSITION

3'-0"

3"

SILL IRON

2'-0" | 4'-0" | 2'-0" | 1'-6" | 5'-3" | 3'-0"

8'-0"

HALL

RIGHT WA

(7) (8)

CLIP ON HEADE

WALL FIXTURES

2'-6" | 2'-6"

PICTURE

6'-3"

6'-6"

12" REVEAL

9'-6"

1'-0" | 2'-3"

6"

12'-0" | 2'-0"

BACK WALL

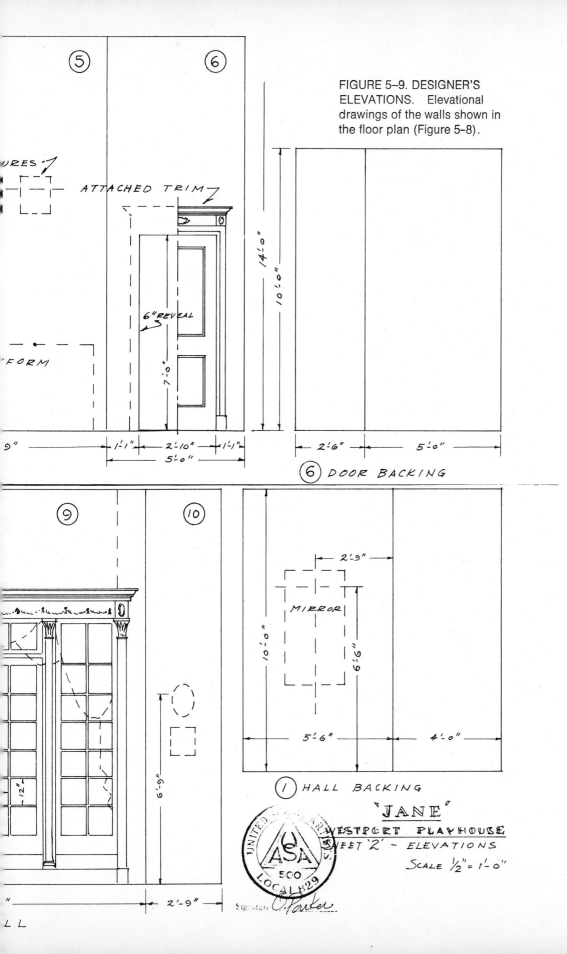

⑤   ⑥

FIGURE 5–9. DESIGNER'S
ELEVATIONS. Elevational
drawings of the walls shown in
the floor plan (Figure 5–8).

URES

ATTACHED TRIM

6" REVEAL

FORM

14'-0"

10'-0"

7'-0"

9"   1'-1"   2'-10"   1'-1"
5'-0"

2'-6"   5'-0"

⑥ DOOR BACKING

⑨   ⑩

2'-9"

MIRROR

10'-0"

6'-6"

5'-6"   4'-0"

① HALL BACKING

12"

6'-9"

6'-9"

2'-9"

'JANE'
WESTPORT PLAYHOUSE
SHEET '2' – ELEVATIONS
SCALE ½" = 1'-0"

Signature O. Parker

L L

of the corresponding units in the floor plan. The accuracy of cross-labeling in especially important when stock scenery is being used, for unless the set is extremely simple, it is the carpenter's only guide as to how the pieces assemble. On occasion, for clarification, a portion of a floor plan may be repeated near the elevation drawings of a complicated unit of scenery. If there is still a possibility of misunderstanding, a pictorial drawing can be included.

COMPOSITIONAL ELEVATIONS

Borrowing a trick from the interior decorator, the scene designer sometimes uses a compositional elevation. It is most useful on an interior setting, for it is an assembled view of each wall with all the set dressings related to that wall in place. Jogs or breaks in the wall are not flattened out but are shown in position. In this manner, the scene designer can study the composition of the furniture, pictures, and window draperies at small scale.

A compositional elevation is usually drawn at ¼-inch scale, or smaller. If it is drawn on graph paper, the necessity of using dimensions is eliminated as sizes and proportions can be calculated by counting the squares (Figure 5–10b).

It can be seen that the compositional elevations are in no way a working drawing for the carpenter. They are of value to the designer himself as an aid in making decisions on furniture and picture sizes during the hectic stages of collecting properties.

PICTORIAL DRAWINGS

The designer's sketch is a type of pictorial drawing, but because of the foreshortening it cannot be used as a working drawing. By imagining a pictorial drawing with the edges of the receding surfaces not converging and sides not foreshortened, a type of drawing is represented that can be drawn to scale and used as a supplementary view to the working drawings. The lack of perspective makes it possible to draw to scale, although the view may have a distorted mechanical appearance.

The two basic kinds of pictorials are the isometric and the oblique drawings. Their difference is dependent upon the angle of the view. The isometric drawing represents an object seen from one corner and slightly above (Figure 5–11a). An oblique drawing shows the object as seen opposite one face with the side angled off to the right or left (Figure 5–11c).

The term "isometric," meaning equal measure as compared to the foreshortened distances or unequal measure of perspective, accurately describes its appearance. An isometric drawing has three axes to rep-

FIGURE 5–10.
ADDITIONAL FLOOR PLANS AND ELEVATIONS.
(a) Furniture plot. An undimensioned although scaled floor plan showing the furniture in place. The grid of two-foot squares helps to indicate the sizes of the furniture pieces and distances between units.
(b) Compositional elevations. A perpendicular view of each important wall as it looks assembled with dress properties and related set properties in position.

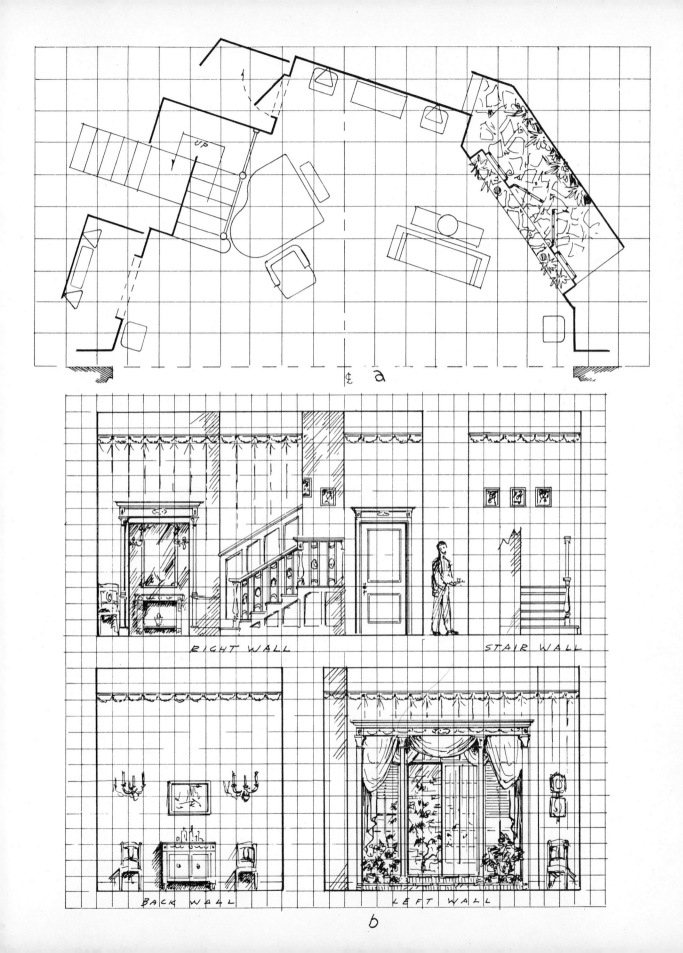

a

RIGHT WALL

STAIR WALL

BACK WALL

LEFT WALL

b

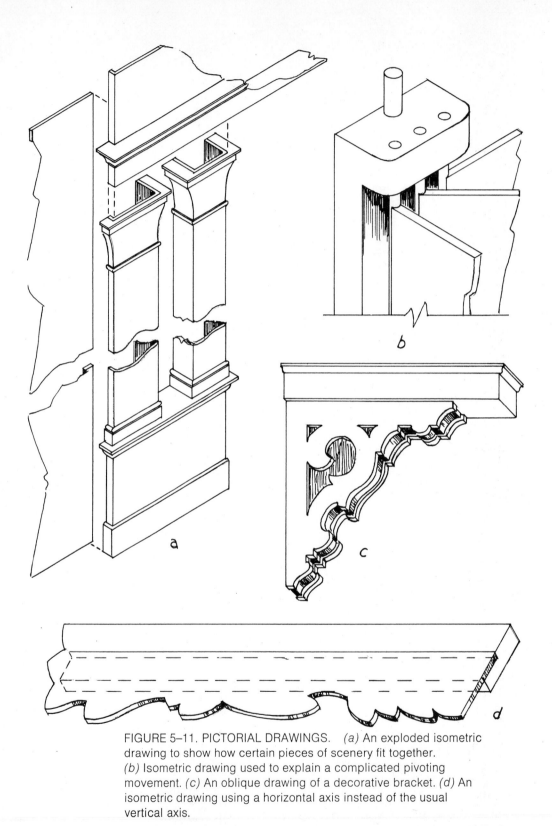

FIGURE 5–11. PICTORIAL DRAWINGS. *(a)* An exploded isometric drawing to show how certain pieces of scenery fit together. *(b)* Isometric drawing used to explain a complicated pivoting movement. *(c)* An oblique drawing of a decorative bracket. *(d)* An isometric drawing using a horizontal axis instead of the usual vertical axis.

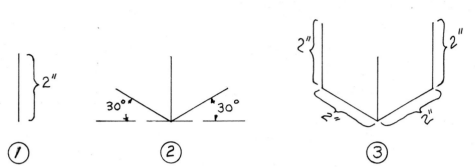
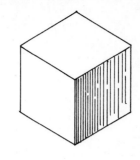

FIGURE 5–12. CONSTRUCTION OF THE ISOMETRIC DRAWING.
The object is a two-inch cube. (1) Vertical axis, the nearest corner
of the cube. (2) Slanted axes, right and left. (3) Slanted lines and
uprights drawn to scale. (4) The completed isometric drawing of the
cube.

resent the principal planes of the object. The first is a vertical line to
indicate all the upright edges; second, a slanted line to the right, 30
degrees to the horizontal, for the horizontal edges of the right plane,
and third, a 30-degree line slanted to the left to represent the horizontal edges of the planes to the left. These lines, and all lines parallel
to them, are known as isometric lines. Conversely, lines that are not
parallel to any of the three axes are nonisometric lines. Heights and
distances can be measured on isometric lines but a nonisometric line
cannot be drawn to scale (Figure 5–12).

Because irregular edges, curves, and angles are distorted in an isometric view, it may be desirable to change the direction of the view to
show them at a better advantage. By moving around the object until
the complicated surface is parallel to the plane of the paper, or frontal
position, it is possible to see the irregular edge or curve without distortion. A view from this direction is an oblique drawing.

The same general pictorial characteristics are present in the oblique
drawing as in the isometric with the exception of a more pronounced
distortion in appearance. Because of the frontal position of one of the
principal planes, two of the oblique axes are at right angles to each other.

The angle of the third axis, representing the plane of the sides,
may vary from 30 to 45 degrees to the horizontal. It can be drawn
either to the right or left, and slanted either up or down (Figure 5–13).
By placing the side that contains the irregular outlines, angles, or curves
in the frontal position drafting time can be saved and the appearance
of the view made more attractive.

To reduce the distortion and improve the looks of the oblique
drawing, the draftsman sometimes uses a cabinet drawing. It is constructed with the complicated face parallel to the picture plane—like
the oblique—but distances measured parallel to the angled axis are

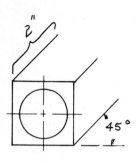

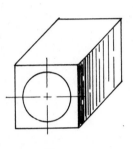

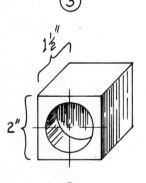

FIGURE 5–13. CONSTRUCTION OF THE OBLIQUE DRAWING.
(1) The principal face with slant line drawn to right, or left. All the lines are drawn to a scale. (2) The completed oblique drawing. (3) An oblique drawing of a circular disk. The center of the circle of the thickness is set to the right on an oblique line. (4) A cabinet drawing. All slanted lines are drawn at a reduced scale to minimize the distorted look of a regular oblique drawing.

reduced in scale. A ratio of two to three or three to four between the frontal planes and the angled axis produces a pleasing proportion. By always labeling the cabinet drawing and giving the ratio of the measurements on the angled axis, the possibility of it being mistaken for an oblique drawing is avoided (Figure 5–13[4]).

Pictorial drawings may be dimensioned like a working drawing. The technique, however, is slightly different. Instead of being perpendicular to the surface, the extension lines are drawn as extensions of one of the isometric planes, and the dimension line is parallel to the object rather than perpendicular to the extension line. To help give the feeling that the dimension is in one of the isometric planes, the figures are slanted with the extension lines. If the object is not too complicated a dimensioned pictorial drawing can be used as a working drawing.

Besides their use as a working drawing, pictorials are frequently used as a supplementary view to explain a bit of complicated assembly, or mechanical detail.

THE PERSPECTIVE DRAWING

A perspective drawing, as has been mentioned, is not a working drawing because of the converging of horizontal lines in the sides of the object. It is, however, a more representational view and in its two-dimensional concept it is more closely related to the designer's sketch than to a working drawing.

The laws of perspective become part of the designer's drawing skill either by observation of normal foreshortening in nature or by knowing the mechanics or graphics of perspective drawing. Figure 5–14 illustrates the basic perspective views of an object in space and orientation to the horizon line (HL). Shown are a combination of views of a cube in simple perspective drawing. "A" represents the cube in a frontal position parallel to the picture plane or plane of the paper. The cube in this position has only one vanishing point (VP-C) on the horizon line. "A-1" represents the cube above HL, "A-2" on HL, and "A-3" below HL.

In "B" the position of the cube is angled to the picture plane and therefore has two vanishing points, VP-R to the right and VP-L to the left. The side walls of the cube converge to their respective vanishing points on the horizon line.

The Graphics of Perspective. The initial concept of the graphics of perspective is *foreshortening*. To understand foreshortening is the first step toward being able to visualize the graphics of perspective. Foreshortening is present, for example, in the converging lines of a fence or railroad where parallel lines appear to meet in the distance. To transpose the visual foreshortening of nature into *graphic* foreshortening on the drawing board, two assumptions have to be made.

Because the eye through peripheral vision is able to see more than is practical to draw, the first assumption is that all verticals are perpendicular to the ground. This is true in the center of the eye's vision but not true of the extreme right or left areas. The vertical lines seem to converge or diverge depending upon whether the observer is on the ground or high above the ground. The second assumption is that the horizon line is straight and parallel to the ground. This is not true of visual foreshortening in which the horizon seems to curve around the observer in a gentle arc.

FIGURE 5–14. GRAPHIC PERSPECTIVE. The front face of box A is parallel to the picture plane. In this position the sides, top, and bottom of the box have a single vanishing point (VP-C). A-1 represents the box above the horizon line (HL), A-2 at HL, and A-3 below HL. The corner of box B is facing the picture plane. In this position the sides have corresponding right (VP-R) and left (VP-L) vanishing points. B-1 represents the box above HL, B-2 at HL, and B-3 below HL.

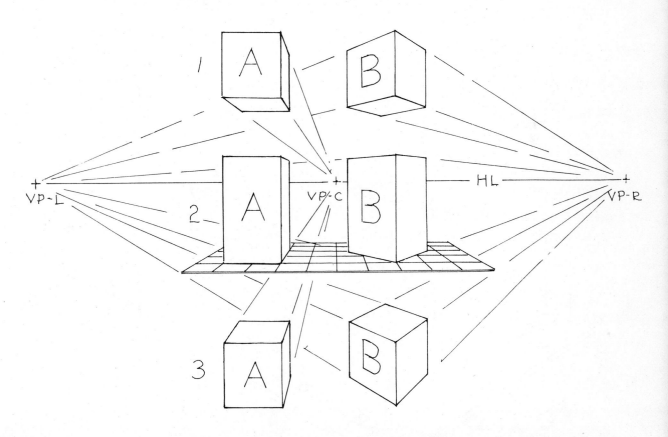

130   Added to these basic assumptions is the positioning of the observer at the *observation point*, which is the most desirable or ideal location. To capture an approximation or illusion of the visual foreshortening on paper the best location of the observation point (OP) would be a distance from the stage or major portion of the stage that provides a cone of vision of not greater than 30 degrees. In other words, the angle between lines drawn from the extreme right and left sides of the object to OP should approximate 30 degrees. It is possible, of course, to set up a graphic perspective system with an OP closer to the stage or with a greater cone of vision than 30 degrees, but the resulting graphic foreshortening is distorted and unnatural. The designer, however, can on occasion use this distorted foreshortening to exaggerate the perspective for design reasons.

FIGURE 5–15. A PERSPECTIVE SYSTEM.   A pictorial arrangement of the components that make up a perspective system. The picture plane (PP) intersects the ground plane forming the ground line (GL). The height (h) of the observation point (OP) determines the distance the horizon line (HL) is above GL. The object is projected into the picture plane by the use of sightlines (SL) from OP. The sides of the cube in PP converge to right and left vanishing points (VP-R and VP-L).

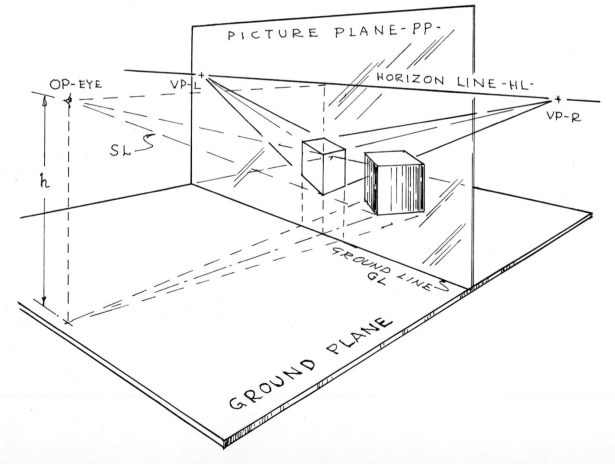

Figure 5–15 is a pictorial representation of the components that make up a perspective system. Besides the components already mentioned, HL and OP, there are also shown the picture plane (PP) and the ground plane (G), which is usually the stage floor. The picture plane is an imaginary transparent plane placed between OP and the object. It is usually perpendicular to the ground and its line of intersection with the ground plane forms the *ground line* (GL). The ability to visualize the picture plane is an important step toward understanding the process of developing the perspective drawing on this plane, after it is folded into the plane of the drawing board. In the theatre, PP is normally considered to be at the proscenium opening or slightly upstage at the front edge of the setting.

Our description of the perspective system is almost complete except for designating the location of the horizon line (HL). The height of OP off the ground determines the height of HL which is drawn parallel to GL on the picture plane. The location of OP is arbitrary. It can be placed in a position to reveal the object either in a favorable or a distorted view, whichever is desired. The normal position for a perspective sketch is a little above ground and on the center line.

It will be noted that all vanishing points fall on the horizon line. This is true of all planes parallel or perpendicular to the ground plane. The shape and vanishing points of an askew (slanted) plane can be plotted by using the floor and perpendicular walls as reference planes.

THE PERSPECTIVE SKETCHING TECHNIQUE

The particular perspective method a designer may choose in preparing his sketch is influenced by his sketching technique and personal method of working. Individual sketching techniques vary primarily with the angle at which the setting is viewed. Whereas most designers prefer to show, for example, a little of the stage floor in their sketch, there are some who like to show no floor at all, while others take an elevated viewpoint showing more floor than is necessary.

There are occasions, however, when a designer may choose an extreme viewpoint for his sketch in order to fit the form of the theatre in which he is working. A high ballroom stage, for instance, with the audience seated on a flat, ungraded ballroom floor creates a situation in which no one is able to see the stage floor. The opposite might occur in an amphitheatre with a rather steep seating arrangement in which the majority of the audience sees a great expanse of the stage floor.

132

The three basic angles of view are illustrated in Figure 5–16. Using the conventional vanishing-point method, the perspective sketch of a simple unit of scenery is shown under three different conditions. First is shown the minimum floor view (a), followed by the extreme no-floor view (b), and, finally, a sketch from a high vantage point (c). In the first condition (Figure 5–16a), OP is at a proper distance from the object, determined by keeping an angle of 30 degrees or less between sightlines (SH) drawn from the outside edges of the object to OP. The horizon line is established at a height of about five or six feet above ground or stage floor. As a result the perspective drawing shows a little stage floor and appears normal.

The vanishing point for each wall is located by drawing a line from OP parallel to the angle of the specific wall until it intersects the picture plane (PP). It is then projected downward until it crosses HL. The point of intersection with HL is the vanishing point (VP) for that wall. The vanishing point for each wall was found in this manner (some of which fall out of view in Figure 5–16b).

FIGURE 5–16. PERSPECTIVE VIEWPOINTS. The three basic angles of view that may appear in a perspective sketch for the theatre. (a) Minimum floor view. HL at about six feet above GL. (b) No floor view. HL is on the floor (GL). (c) Maximum floor view. HL is abnormally high, giving the set the look of being viewed from a high vantage point.

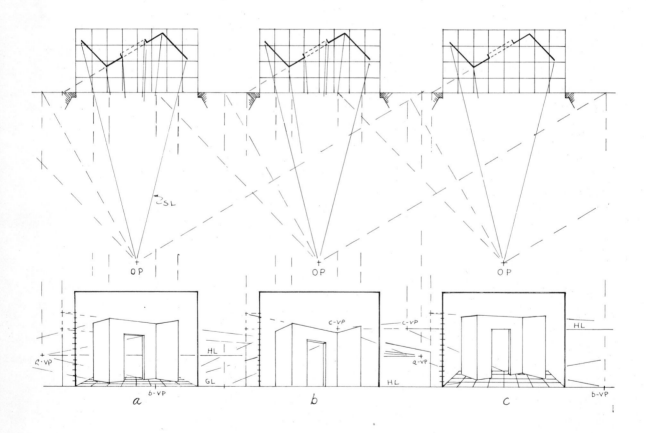

The conditions in Figure 5–16b and Figure 5–16c are the same except for the position of HL. The second view has located the horizon line in the floor or on GL while the third view has raised HL above the normal view to show more of the floor.

The application of normal perspective techniques to the sketch of a stage setting does have one disadvantage. Because the walls of a setting, especially an interior, are frequently raked to bring them into better sightlines, they tend to appear more exaggerated than right angles. To a certain extent this is happening in the real set, for the raked side walls of a box set do tend to make the setting look deeper than it really is. This is not so apparent until it is placed within the two-dimensional form of a sketch. This sometimes requires adjustments either in the sketch or floor plan to bring the elements of the composition into a desirable proportional arrangement. It is important to remember that if the sketch is being developed with the observation point at the conventional distance so as to form a cone of vision of 30 degrees or less, the result does give the designer some clue as to how his set is going to look prior to making a scaled model.

The Perspective-Grid Method. Because of the many angled walls that may occur in a setting the designer seeks to avoid the space-consuming method of a full graphic perspective system involving the location of vanishing points from a sprawling observation point and the precisely aligned floor plan. He looks for an easier way or shortcut to produce an approximation of the perspective drawing. The perspective grid is an aid in simplifying the graphics of perspective of the designer's sketch.

The use of a perspective grid of the stage floor as a guide under the sketch is helpful to the beginning designer as he develops a perspective view of his setting from the floor plan. Like most shortcuts, the grid method is an approximation and therefore less than accurate. The inaccuracies, however, are not alarming and are offset by the time and space saved.

As a technique the perspective-grid method does not employ either the use of an observation point other than the initial setup or the cross-reference of sightline points from an aligned floor plan. It does use, however, the traditional horizon line and vanishing points in addition to measuring points.

The grid which can be prepared in advance and reused indefinitely is developed in one of two ways (Figure 5–17). Both begin with a scaled grid of the stage floor. The upstage and downstage lines of the grid appear in true dimension along the picture plane, or downstage,

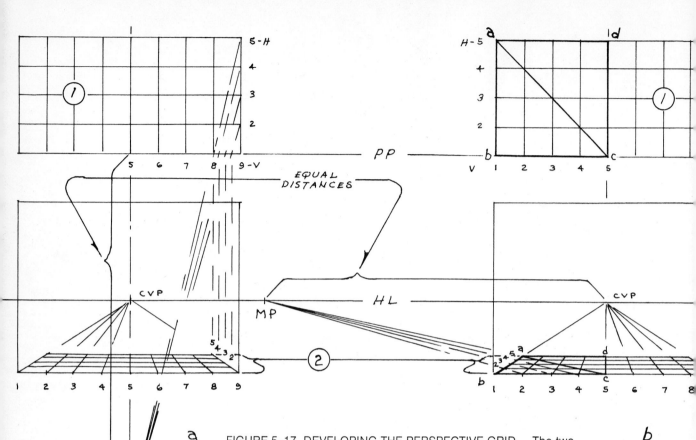

FIGURE 5–17. DEVELOPING THE PERSPECTIVE GRID.   The two
methods of developing a perspective of the stage floor are shown.
(a) The observation-point method: (1) The stage floor is marked in
a grid of equally spaced horizontal and vertical lines. The vertical
lines are numbered from 1 to 9 and the horizontal lines are
numbered on the right from 1 to 5. Because all the vertical lines are
perpendicular to the picture plane (PP) they all vanish or converge
to a single vanishing point in the center (cvp). The location of the
depth in perspective of each horizontal line is accomplished by
sighting a line from OP to the intersection point of a horizontal line
and one of the vertical lines (for example, 5-H on line 9-V). The
point where the sightline crosses PP (at 8-V) is projected downward
until it intersects perspective line 9-V as it is converging toward cvp.
As the horizontal lines are parallel to PP, it can be drawn through this
point to the left, terminating at line 1-V. (2) Each of the horizontal
lines is located in this manner to complete the perspective grid.
(b) The measuring-point method: (1) The gridded stage floor as in
(a). The measuring point (MP) is measured on HL the same distance
from the center line (cvp) as OP was from PP in (a). The perspective
position of each horizontal grid line is located on 1-V by sighting a
line from MP to a series of points on PP representing the true
distances each horizontal line is apart. As the true grid is made up of
squares, vertical lines 1, 2, 3, 4, and 5 are the same distances. The
points where the sightlines from MP cross line 1-V. (2) Locates the
perspective spacing of the horizontal lines. The perspective grid is
then completed in the same manner as in (a).

edge of the plan. All vertical lines converge to a common vanishing point at the center (VPC) because they are perpendicular to PP.

The spacing of the horizontal line parallel to PP can be located by conventional perspective methods shown to the left of the center in Figure 5–17a. Sightlines are projected from the observation point (OP) to each position on the outside edge of the grid. The corresponding positions in perspective are located by projecting downward the point of intersection of the respective sightlines and the picture plane. Once the grid has been developed in perspective the observation point is no longer needed.

Measuring-Point Method. The measuring-point method which is demonstrated in Figure 5–17b dates back to the theatre of the Renaissance. Originally known as the *distance-point method*, it was first evolved in 1435 by Leone Battista Alberti. The system's basic difference is that it does not use an observation point, needing only to know the distance OP would be from the picture plane.

The formula for the method is based upon the reality that in a perspective plan the diagonal of a square if extended will fall upon the horizon line at a point the same distance from the center line as OP is from PP. Figure 5-17b shows how the measuring point is used to locate the position of the horizontal lines of the grid in perspective. True dimension intervals on PP are projected back to MP and where they cross the outside edge of the grid locates the respective spacing of each line. If accurately drawn the right side should match the spacing to the left of the center line.

It is important to remember that to be accurate the measuring-point method is based upon the square or subdivision of the square and its diagonal. If the stage is deeper than the side of the square, the grid should be expanded offstage to make the proper double-square proportion. Although only the floor grid will be used in the perspective method of sketching, the measuring-point system can be used as a measured-perspective technique by establishing an MP to the right and left.

THE PERSPECTIVE FLOOR PLAN

Figure 5–18 illustrates with a simplified example of scenery the steps taken to use the perspective grid as a guide for a sketching technique. Figure 5–18a is a scaled floor plan of the set drawn over a grid of squares. For the sake of clarity in a small drawing the squares shown are 3 feet in dimension. As their size is optional it might be desirable in a larger drawing to use two-foot squares for more dependable accuracy. If the sketch is developed on tracing paper over the perspective grid as is suggested in Figure 5–18b it can be saved for future use.

The first step toward the sketch is the transference of the floor plan onto the perspective grid by locating each in its corresponding square (Figure 5–18c). Vertical lines representing corners and edges are extended upward, for the moment, to undetermined heights. Before individual heights can be found the vanishing points of key walls must be located. The VP of the right and left walls are the easiest to locate because of their sharp angle to PP. As their faces are parallel to each other the same VP will serve both. To locate this important vanishing point the base line of each outside wall is carefully produced from its position on the perspective grid until it intersects HL. This is the approximate VP for the base of both walls and for any line parallel to the respective base lines.

The final step to complete the drawing is to find the height of the doorway and scenic unit. One method is to use the center vanishing point (VP-C) which is the VP for the grid. Figure 5–18d shows how h–1 and h–2 are taken in true dimension from PP back along a perspective line on the grid to VP-C passing through a corner to the critical point of measurement. The point of intersection of the vertical raised from the corner in plan and perspective line h–1, for example, VP-C, determines the height. The height of the doorway and other verticals can be found by the same method.

Furniture, platforms, and set dressing can be located by using the perspective grid and approximate VP in the same manner. The ceiling or overhead area may also be gridded and constructed in perspective to the same HL and OP system to provide a more inclusive guide for the designer's sketch.

On pages 130 to 131 are represented three different uses of the perspective grid as a sketch technique. The first is the conventional interior setting, showing the steps that were taken to develop the final sketch: (a) the scaled floor plan with a grid overlay; (b) the grid in perspective with the walls blocked in and the vanishing points located; (c) the addition of set dressings and furniture; (d) the final sketch with the grid removed.

The second example brings together some unusual conditions. The setting not only thrusts ahead or through the picture plane but also has a ramped floor and slanted ceiling. The floor plan (a) is gridded and shows the location of PP. In the split view (b) the stage left center portion shows the perspective grid and the method of determining the ramp of the floor. It will be noted that a reflected perspective grid was used overhead to plot the slant of the ceiling piece. The final sketch (c) is completed with the grid and construction lines removed.

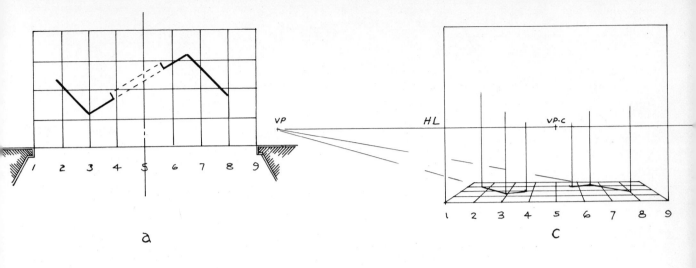

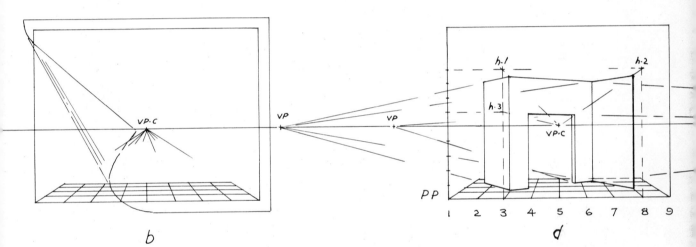

FIGURE 5–18. USING THE PERSPECTIVE GRID. (a) The floor plan of a simple element of scenery drawn on a gridded stage floor. (b) A perspective grid predeveloped by either the observation-point or measuring-point method is covered with tracing paper to preserve the grid for future uses. (c) By referring to the floor plan on the true grid (a), it is reconstructed, point by point, onto the perspective grid. The corners, edges, and vertical sides of openings are extended upward but not terminated. The vanishing point of the two parallel walls is located by projecting the base line in the perspective plan until it intersects HL (vp). (d) The height of the scenery is found by extending one of the corners to PP. The downstage corner resting on V-3 is projected to PP along line V-3. The height is then measured directly above and projected back to VP-C. Where it intersects the vertical of the corner from the plan (c) is the height in perspective. Other heights are located the same way: h-2 is off line V-8; h-3 is the height of the door opening. With the heights all located, the sketch is completed by drawing the tops and all lines parallel to them to their related vanishing points.

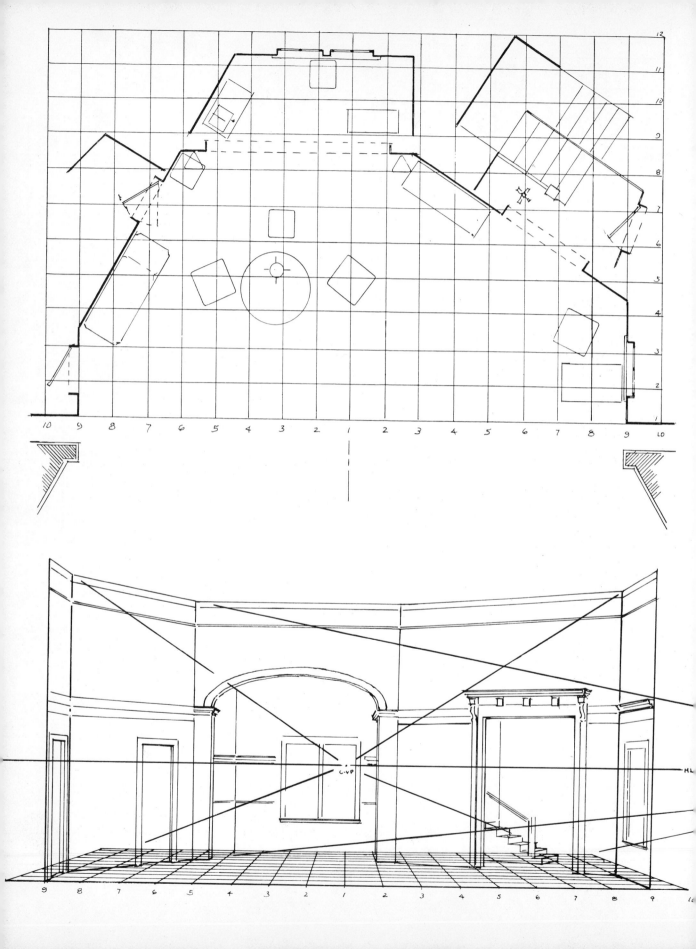

"You Can't Take It With You"

The most difficult form to represent in perspective sketch is the thrust stage. The third illustration presents an adaptation of the perspective grid technique for a thrust stage setting. The perspective grid is developed from an off-center view rather than on the center-line: (a) the floor plan with grid; (b) the perspective grid which, if drawn on tracing paper, can be reversed to present a view from the opposite side; (c) the final sketch.

Any perspective technique in the final analysis should *guide* but not control the drawing. It should *free* rather than restrict the creative style of the designer. The mechanics of the technique should not be used as a means to the end but more as a check when, to the eye of the designer, "something doesn't look just right."

FIGURE 5–19. PERSPECTIVE SKETCH TECHNIQUE—CONVENTIONAL INTERIOR. *(a)* The scaled floorplan with a grid overlay. *(b)* The grid in perspective with wall blocked in and the vanishing points located. *(c)* The addition of set dressings and furniture. *(d)* The final sketch, with grid and construction lines removed.

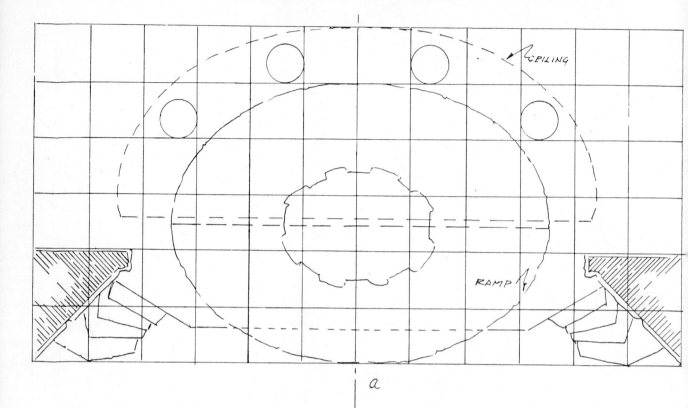

CEILING

RAMP

a

FIGURE 5–20. PERSPECTIVE SKETCH TECHNIQUE—ANGLED FLOOR
AND CEILING.   *(a)* The scaled floor plan with grid overlay. Note the
location of PP. *(b)* A split view showing on the stage-left side the
perspective grid and the method of determining the ramp of the floor in
perspective. The height of the ramp is measured on the PP at a point, h-1,
on the grid. The true height of h-1 is projected upstage along a sightline to
the center vanishing point (c-vp) to intersect a second vertical line on the
upstage edge of the ramp. A rectangle of the ramp is blocked in, within
which the elliptical shape of the ramped floor can be drawn. Because the
stage floor projects past PP, the height of the apron is in perspective. By
extending a sightline through h-2, a vertical projected downward the
height of the stage to the perpendicular at the downstage edge of the
apron determines the height of the apron in perspective. The slope of
ceiling is found by the same method. (1) The perspective grid. (2) A
second perspective grid overhead to locate the slope of the ceiling.
(3) The position of PP on the ramped floor and sloped ceiling. (4) Center
line. *(c)* The finished sketch.

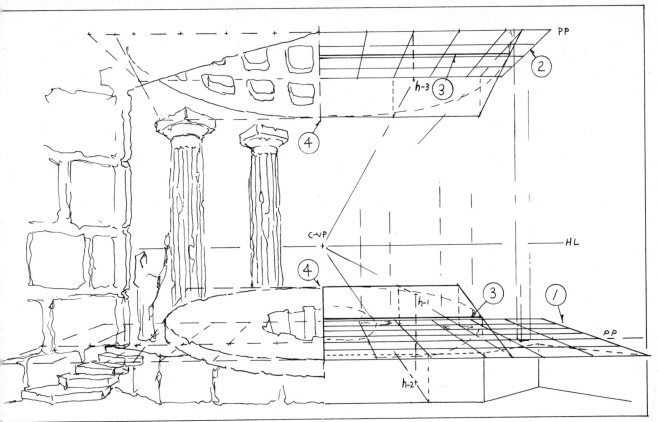

b

c

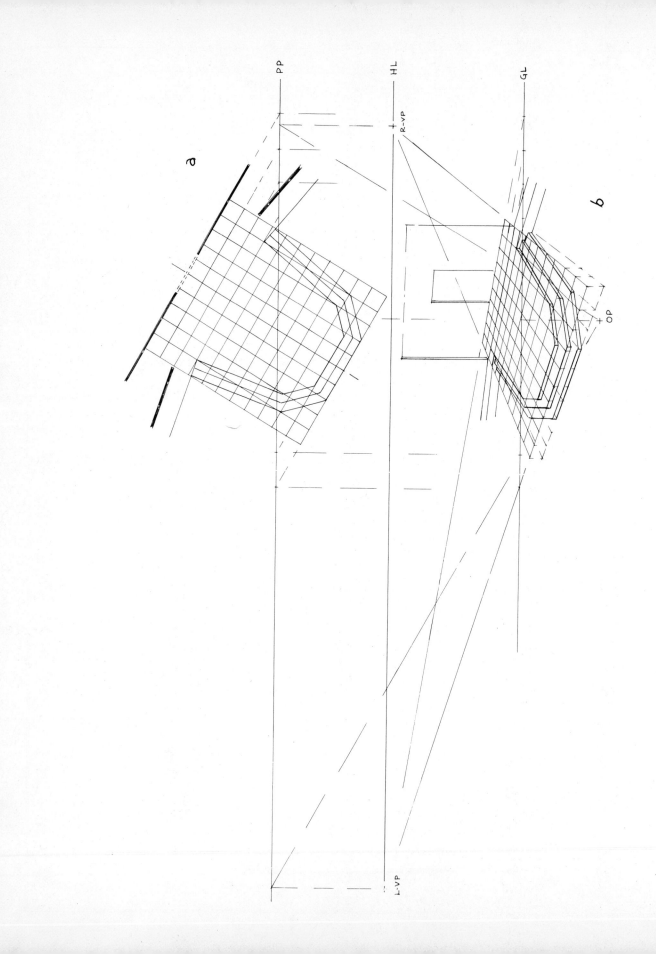

THREE-DIMENSIONAL PERSPECTIVE

The use of three-dimensional forms on the stage, both architectural and abstract, is the sculptural use of space. It is the use of actual space and not the illusion of space. This is best dealt with in three dimensions with the use of models or real forms.

Sometimes, however, the scene designer has to produce the illusion of more space with three-dimensional forms, or combine two-dimensional with three-dimensional forms to create an illusion of space on a shallow stage. With careful study, the same techniques of space perception applicable to two-dimensional forms can be adapted to three-dimensional forms. Figure 5–22 illustrates a method of foreshortening a three-dimensional form. In this example a structure representing a garden shelter has been foreshortened in perspective into a much smaller space than it actually appears to occupy.

The technique of foreshortening a three-dimensional object is dependent upon two views, the plan and side elevation. View (1) in Figure 5–22 is the plan or view looking down on the structure. The dotted lines designated a, b, c, d represent the actual size of the plan

FIGURE 5–21. PERSPECTIVE SKETCH TECHNIQUE—THE THRUST STAGE.   An adaptation of the perspective grid technique to a thrust-stage setting. The perspective grid is developed from an off-center view rather than on the center line. Opposite page: *(a)* The floor plan with grid. *(b)* The perspective grid. Above: *(c)* The final sketch.

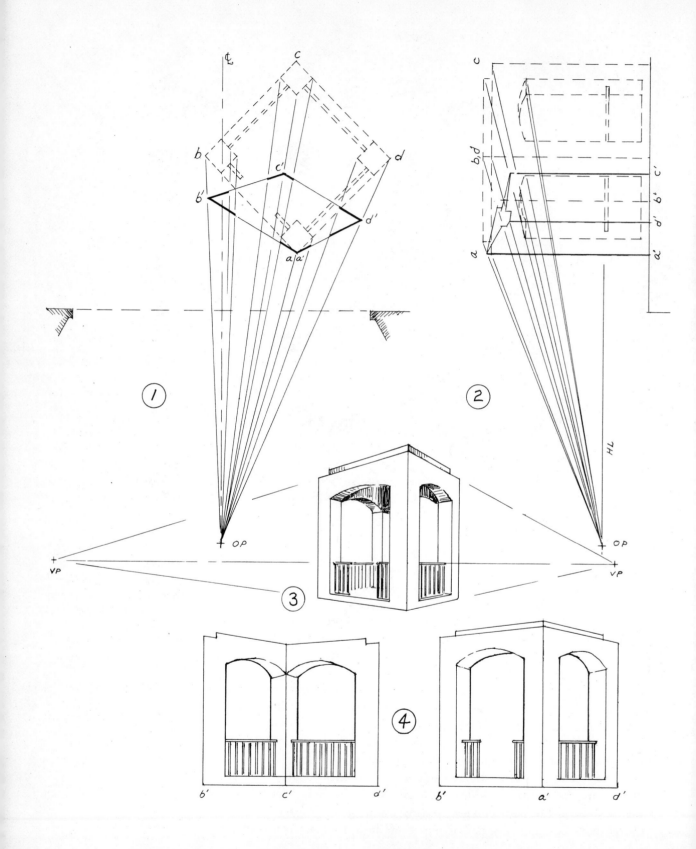

① ② ③ ④

FIGURE 5–22. THREE-DIMENSIONAL PERSPECTIVE.   Illustrated are the steps necessary to foreshorten a scenic element (a gazebo or garden shelter) that in reality occupies in plan the space a, b, c, d to half the depth indicated a′, b′, c′, d′ in the drawing. (1) Using, jointly, the plan (1) and the side elevation (2) to work out the foreshortened heights of each corner, the four walls are redrawn into their new shapes (4). (3) A normal two-dimensional perspective drawing of the gazebo, which is the way it will appear if the foreshortened walls are carefully assembled on the foreshortened plan.

while a′, b′, c′, d′ represent its foreshortened size. Each foreshortened point is located on a sightline drawn from the observation point (OP) to its original position on the actual plan. The position of the foreshortened points a′, b′, c′, d′ is arbitrary depending upon how large or small a foreshortened plan is desired.

    View (2) is a side view of the structure drawn next to and in alignment with view (1). The points a, b, c, d are shown in side view as well as a dotted line drawing of the rest of the elevation. The side view also shows the height of OP through which is drawn the horizon line (HL).

    By projecting each point (a′, b′, c′, d′) of the foreshortened plan into the side view, being careful to relate each to its proper sightline, a foreshortened side view of the structure can be drawn. Because of the height of HL and the theatrical convention of stopping the perspective at the railing, most of the perspective appears at the top of the structure.

    View (4) is a development of the four walls of the garden shelter based upon dimensions found in the two foreshortened views, plan and side elevation.

    View (3) is a normal two-dimensional perspective drawing with OP and HL in the same positions as in (1) and (2). To a certain extent (3) represents how the foreshortened walls of view (4) will look when they are assembled.

    A second method of solving foreshortening is to work directly from the three-dimensional sketch and related floor plan. Figure 5-23 presents the two views of a perspective street scene. The plan has been located in the sketch by the perspective grid technique (Figure 5-18). The base of each house has been produced to find its vanishing point on the horizon line. (HL) house (1), for example, has a base line vanishing point on HL at the point labeled B-VP(1). All horizontal lines above HL, however, vanish to a second temporary vanishing point T-VP(1), closer to the house to force the perspective and thereby foreshorten the house. To layout house (1) in elevation for a model or designer's elevations T-VP(1) must be located in the plane of the element of scenery. This is accomplished by projecting T-VP(1) on HL directly upward until it intersects the produced base line of house (1) in plan.

    The elevation of house (1) (Figure 5-24) can be drawn using T-VP(1) as a VP for all horizontal lines *above* HL. Note that the true distance of T-

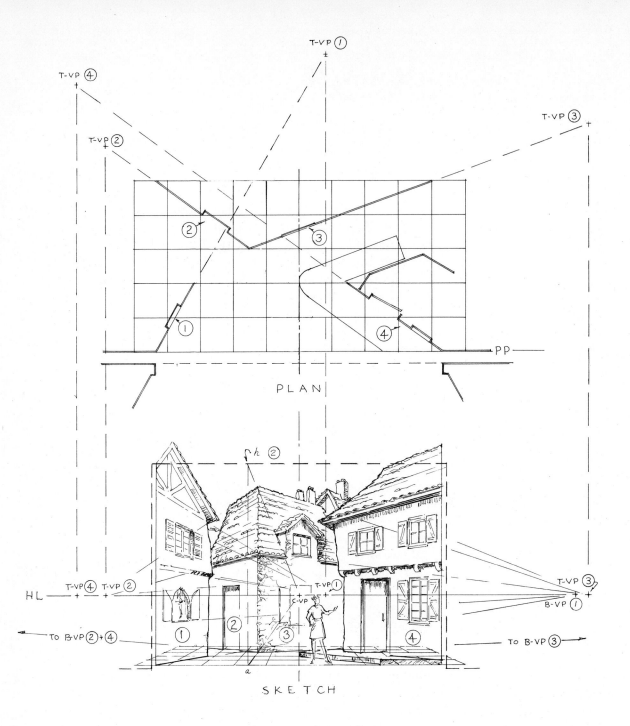

FIGURE 5–23. FORESHORTENED SCENERY. A floor plan and sketch which has been drawn on a perspective grid. All horizontal lines *above* HL converge to a temporary vanishing point (T-VP) to heighten the normal perspective. House (1), for example, has a base line vanishing point on HL at point B-VP (1). All horizontal lines above HL, however, vanish to a second temporary vanishing point T-VP (1) to foreshorten the house.

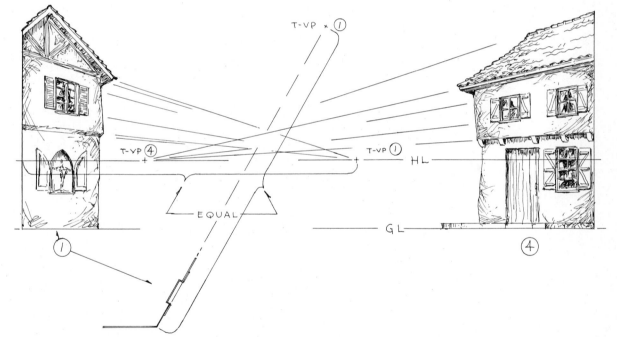

FIGURE 5-24. FORESHORTENING IN ELEVATION.
To resolve the elevation of the foreshortened house
(1) the distance of T-VP (1) from (1) is an important
dimension. The true distance of T-VP (1) in elevation
is found in the plan directly above T-VP (1) on HL. The
degree of foreshortening in any of the houses is the
decision of the designer.

VP(1) in elevation is located in the plan view. The same procedure can be used to develop the elevation of all the foreshortened houses. Because the method is an approximation it is subject to adjustment as the designer develops his sketch.

TECHNICAL PLANNING

The designer is normally not concerned with the details of technical planning. If the scenery, however, is going to be built with unskilled hands, as is the case in most community and university theatres, the designer finds himself the chief guardian of construction. Unless he wants to be tied up with shop supervision at the time when he is busy selecting properties, designing the lighting, and taking care of countless details, it pays for him to make a set of construction drawings.

The simplest way to lay out the framed construction of scenery is to use rear elevations. A view from this direction looks at the scenery as it appears under construction in the shop. A rear elevation shows the framing and profiling, explains the assembly, locates the hinges, and indicates bracing and stiffening. The detail and completeness of the rear elevations can be gauged by the aptitude of the shop help. An experienced carpenter might need a construction drawing for the occasional unusual piece of scenery while inexperienced help would need every piece of scenery detailed (Figure 5–26).

The construction of three-dimensional pieces, such as fireplaces, doors, steps, and rocks, are not clearly explained in a rear elevation. How they are built can be shown by combining sectional views with designer's front and side elevations. The sectional view not only shows the internal structure but helps to explain the contour of the object. Irregular forms, of course, may require many sections. Very special shapes or profiles are often drawn at full scale to serve as a pattern.

THE HANGING SECTION AND PLAN

The hanging section, mentioned earlier, is another important part of the technical planning. It becomes a very necessary drawing to the designer in planning a multiscene production or a heavy hanging show. The designer soon discovers that the flying space is filled very quickly with lighting equipment, traveler tracks, masking curtains, and the like. To avoid a hopeless tangle in the flies, the hanging plot of a heavy show is carefully studied first in plan and section.

The hanging section, which is a sectional view taken vertically through the stage on the center line, is not a working drawing in itself. It provides information that can be used in the floor plan and elevations as working drawings. Besides taking the guesswork out of vertical masking by checking the extreme vertical sightlines, the hanging section gives an accurate picture of floor space problems. It shows the

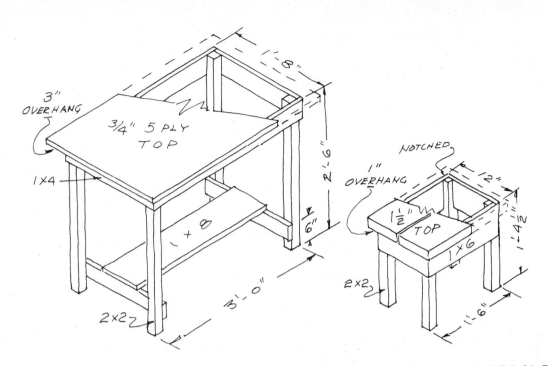

up- and downstage space requirements more clearly than the floor plan which becomes the working drawing.

If the show is extremely heavy it may require a separate hanging plan to indicate the disposition of all the scenery that is to be flown. To keep the plan from becoming confusing, most of the scenery on the floor is not shown. The hanging plan may be very general and schematic, or quite detailed, depending on the proportion of the rigging, the theatre, and the type of show. For a wing and backdrop type of production, for example, it is little more than a listing of drops in the order they will hang and the numbering of the act and scene in which they will work. A more complicated hanging plan would indicate the exact positions of spot lines and extra rigging.

Recent engineering developments in a more flexible flying system and gridiron design than the existing pin-and-rail and counterweight methods indicate a time in the future when the hanging plan will be a required drawing for every show.

PLANNING OF PROPERTIES

The designer is responsible for the selection of properties, for the design of specially built pieces of furniture, and for the furniture plot or general arrangement of properties in the setting.

In planning the properties, the designer's chief concern is to correlate the needs of the director with his own ideas. A meeting of minds can be achieved easily if the designer can show by sketches, clippings, or photographs what he plans and indicate in a scale furniture plot the size and position of set properties as they appear in the setting plan.

FIGURE 5–25. FREE-HAND PICTORIAL DRAWINGS. Dimensioned free-hand isometric drawings of simple furniture. If an object is simple in form, a pictorial drawing with dimensions can serve as a working drawing. There is enough information provided in this type of drawing to allow the carpenter to begin building immediately. A more complicated object would need additional views.

The furniture plot is a schematic plan locating the position of the set properties in each scene. It is generally drawn at ¼-inch scale with all furniture in position. The furniture plot is not dimensioned unless there is need to call attention to a certain measurement. It is drawn on a grid of 1-foot or 2-foot squares, so anyone can figure distances by counting squares. Such a plan is useful to the director and stage manager for laying out rehearsal space and studying the staging. It is valuable to the property man as a visual reference list of his set props. And the designer will find he can use it in planning the lighting of the production (Figure 5–10a).

The floor plan of a television show is handled in essentially the same way. It is drawn at ¼-inch scale over a grid of 1-foot squares shows the set props in place, notes and numbers each piece of scenery.

The construction of a special prop, like any three-dimensional piece of scenery, would require some sort of working drawing. The usual plan, front and side views, can be used or, if the piece is not too complicated, a dimensioned pictorial drawing will serve as a working drawing (Figure 5–24). Again, the designer will find it wise to study out all the important details at full scale.

THE PLANNING OF LIGHTING

The planning of the lighting is set down in the form of a lighting plot and instrument schedule. They are mentioned here chiefly as a portion of the graphics of presentation expected of a scene designer to further explain the design of a setting. The mechanics of developing a lighting plot with regard to instrument performance and dimming control are fully discussed in Chapter 20.

The basic design of the lighting, or ideal, is established in the designer's sketch (Chapter 4). The action of the play is frozen momentarily to illustrate the atmosphere and composition of a dramatic moment. Any change of composition by a movement of lights is often shown in a series of sketches. It is, of course, impossible to make an atmospheric sketch without considering the light sources. The beginning of the lighting plot, then, is in the designer's sketch. But, like the carpenter, the electrician needs more than a pretty sketch before he can start to hang lighting instruments.

The lighting plot is comparable to the working drawing which expresses the design of the set in terms of feet and inches, materials,

FIGURE 5–26. REAR ELEVATIONS.   Detailed construction drawings show the framing of each piece of scenery and indicate how each is assembled. Note the use of vertical and horizontal sections as assembled views.

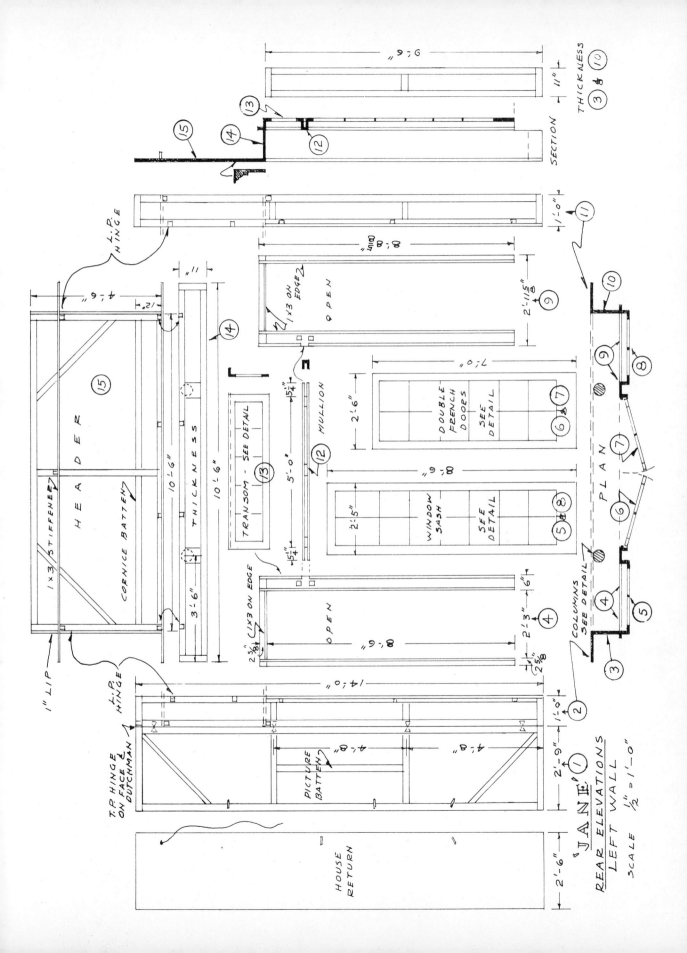

"JANE"
REAR ELEVATIONS
LEFT WALL
SCALE ½" = 1'-0"

152 and shows how it works. The plot translates the designer's ideas of atmosphere, composition, and color into lighting areas, types of instruments; designates their position, use, and color medium.

The lighting plot is drawn on a ¼-inch or ½-inch scale floor plan showing the set props in position, as in the furniture plot. The plan is divided into acting areas, and symbols of instruments are drawn in their approximate hanging position. They are assigned to light a certain area. The division and number of areas may be arbitrary to cover the entire acting area systematically or may be motivated by the action and mood of the play.

Because the lighting plot is so schematic, most of the specific information is presented on an accompanying instrument schedule. The combined lighting plot and instrument schedule tell the electrician the number and type of instrument, the wattage, color, use and hanging position.

PART 2

Executing
the
Design

Scene Design and Technical Production 6

Before the ideas of the designer can reach the stage, his designs, in the form of working drawings, have to go through a preparation or construction period. The scaled model is transformed into full-scale elements of scenery, the graded wash in the sketch becomes a carefully painted backdrop, the insignificant spot on the elevation is fashioned into a pointed bit of detail, and so on, moving towards the moment when all the scenery is fitted together on the stage under lights and in final form.

Although the study of technical production is placed here in the logical order of the development of a stage setting, it also, paradoxically, represents knowledge a scene designer should possess before beginning to design in the theatre. For this reason a study of technical production is a necessary part of a scene designer's training and background. As the architect is familiar with building techniques and materials, so should the scene designer be acquainted with methods of constructing and handling scenery as well as the uses of theatrical materials and techniques. A logical place to begin is with a survey of the tools and

155

materials that are used to make scenery and an examination of the working procedures of a scenery shop.

THE SCENERY SHOP

Scenery is frequently built and painted under the adverse condition of an inadequate shop. The designer soon learns that an ill-equipped shop with sparse working space places a limit on the kind and amount of scenery that can be built and painted. Occasionally he finds himself in the enviable position of being able to plan his own shop, or at least asked to specify the space requirements of the ideal scenery shop. In preparation for such an occasion, the designer should have some knowledge of the space requirements and layout of a good scenery shop.

SPACE REQUIREMENTS

The over-all area of a scenery shop depends upon four things: the size of the stage the shop is to serve, the location of the shop in relation to the stage and storage areas, the number and kinds of productions to be produced in an average season, and the nature of the shop's working procedure and personnel.

The size of the stage, or, in some cases, several stages, which the shop is to serve has a direct bearing on the size of the shop itself. A large stage requires large elements of scenery. A shop serving a large stage, of course, needs the space to execute the expansive proportions of such scenery. In a similar manner, the large amounts of scenery necessary to supply more than one stage would influence the size of the shop. Although the scale of the scenery might be smaller, a shop serving several stages would have to be arranged to handle quantities of scenery.

The location of the scenery shop also affects its size. For example, a shop near the stage could utilize stage space for the construction of scenery and thereby supplement the shop area. On the other hand, a shop in a remote location needs additional space for the storage of scenery and properties as well as the necessary construction and painting areas. Although a distant shop has the disadvantage of causing the additional handling of scenery from the shop to the stage and back again, it does have the decided advantage of being able to operate free of preperformance uses of the stage. A shop adjacent to the stage is doomed to conflict with rehearsals and performances, which will render it inoperative a major portion of the time.

Besides the size of the stage and location of the shop, it is apparent that the number and kinds of productions also help to determine the space requirements of a scenery shop. A repertory company, for example, would require enormous storage space to retain the scenery of numerous productions intact, while perhaps only building one or two new productions a year. An opera or musical comedy production group would have a greater demand for scenery than a season of more intimately scaled productions, and so on.

The final consideration that has some influence on the over-all size of the shop is the shop procedure and personnel. The nature of the shop's personnel and working hours may vary from a staff of full-time professionals to scattered groups of part-time student apprentices or volunteers. A small highly skilled staff working steadily can use building space more efficiently than large sporadic groups requiring sufficient area to do many separate jobs at once to fully utilize the workers' time. A further evaluation of the space requirements resulting from shop procedure includes an analysis of the areas of work, tools and equipment, and materials of the average scenery shop.

AREAS OF WORK

The shop is divided into areas related to the various steps in the process of building and painting. These areas are organized for: (1) storage of materials and tools; (2) the cutting and working of lumber (boring, planing, and so on); (3) the framing and covering of basic units of scenery; (4) the trial assembly of basic units into portions or all of the complete setting; (5) the painting of scenery and properties; and (6) the building of properties which although listed last would be in process along with scenery construction.

(1) The first necessary space in a scenery shop is for the storage of materials and tools. This means lumber racks, paint bins, and hardware cabinets located near their area of use yet convenient to the loading door. Provisions must also be made for the storage of brushes near the painting area and for small tools adjacent to the woodworking area.

(2) The second area, related to the next step in building scenery, is the woodworking area. Here the lumber is cut and worked (bored, planed, jig-sawed, and so on). Convenient to this area is the lumber supply, hardware storage, and the hand tools. Within the area there should be space for the large power tools such as table saws, band saws, drill presses, and the necessary work benches for working wood.

Careful consideration should be given to the lighting of the woodworking area and the other work areas, as well as to the placement of power outlets convenient to the working position of the power tools associated with each area.

(3) and (4) The third space is the assembly area, which ideally should be as large as the playing area of the stage to allow a trial assembly of the setting. The space can also be used for the framing and canvassing of basic units of scenery. Regular-shaped flats are framed and canvassed on a template bench (Figure 6–2), while irregular-shaped units are laid out or "lofted" and then assembled on the floor. The assembly area can also serve as a temporary storage space for completed scenery waiting to be "loaded out."

FIGURE 6–1. SCENERY SHOP LAYOUT.   A bird's-eye view of a scenery shop for a community or university theatre. Although housed in a separate wing to isolate operational noises, it is, at the same time, attached to the left side of the stage it serves *(S)* Stage—left side. *(A)* Assembly area—serves three functions: *(a)* Provides an area equal to the playing area of the stage for trial assembly of part or all of the setting. *(b)* Becomes space to store the offstage wagon of a transverse-wagon scheme for moving scenery. *(c)* Also serves as a painting area; the last stage of scenery construction before moving it onto the stage. The split paint frame (top) often can be used as two separately operated small frames or be locked together as a single large frame. The available floor space can be used for horizontal painting and full-scale lofting. Although the assembly is closed off from the stage by a pair of sound-deadening doors, the work in this area still has to be essentially quiet work, such as painting and lofting, when the stage is in use.
(C) Construction area—where the cutting and working of materials as well as small-unit assembly takes place. This area is further isolated from the stage by sound-deadening doors. *(T)* Technician's or shopman's office. *(B)* Balcony over a portion of the shop—provides extra storage space for materials and supplies. Could also have long cutting table and sewing machine for making stage draperies. *(M)* Metal-working area—removes welding and metal-working tools from main shop area. *(P)* Property shop—area for building, rebuilding, upholstering, and finishing furniture and special properties. *(D)* Drafting room above metal and property shop on the same level as the balcony. (1) Space between shop building and stage house to reduce the amount of structure-borne sound. (2) Vertical painting area with movable palette table. (3) Paint supplies, sink, and burners. (4) Storage bins for scenery waiting to be painted or to be assembled after painting. (5) Drop storage racks on this wall above doors. (6) Lift—serves basement scenery and property storage rooms and balcony storage above. (7) Movable template tables which can be used together or separately. Space beneath top can serve as storage space for plywood and upson board. (8) Lumber storage racks and pullover saw tables. (9) Small tool and hardware storage.
(10) Power tools in woodworking area under the balcony. (11) Canvas and muslin storage.

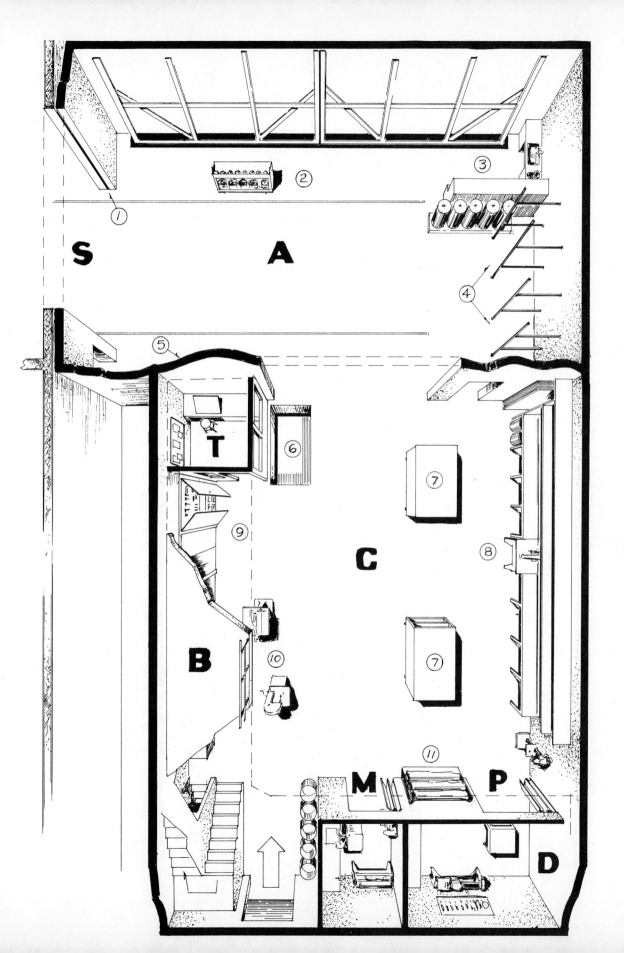

(5) The painting area is another important space in the shop. It should be convenient to a sink, gas or electric burners, and the paint bins. Vertical painting, which occupies the least amount of floor space, requires overhead clearance, or sufficient height to stand the scenery upright. The simplest vertical painting method is to mount the scenery on a fixed frame against a wall and paint from a rolling platform or "boomerang." The most convenient method is the use of a counter-weighted vertical paint frame which lowers into a well, or raises off the floor. The painting is done from different levels or "decks" (see **Methods of Painting, Chapter 9**).

A more precarious method is to raise and lower a painting scaffolding in front of a fixed frame. Besides being laborious and dangerous, the scaffolding has the added inconvenience of usually being some distance from a sink, burner, and paint supplies.

With even the best equipment for vertical painting, it is some-times necessary to paint horizontally on the floor. Certain painting

FIGURE 6–2. TEMPLATE BENCH.   The type shown is adaptable to a shop with limited working space where the same area may be needed for other operations. The template is a waist-high work bench with movable planks in the center (1) to provide support for framing the various widths of regular-shaped flats. The casters on one side (2) enable it to be tipped onto that side and pushed out of the way for storage. The casters on the base (3) provide easy movement when the bench is in working position. Although not equipped with built-in square corners and clinch plates, the template can also be used for such tasks as sabre-saw cutting and small assembly work.

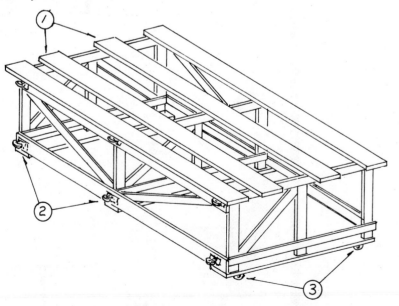

techniques require horizontal painting. The floor of the assembly area, or stage floor, often serves this purpose if it can be worked into the production schedule.

(6) The most frequently neglected area in shop planning is a space to build properties. The altering, repairing, upholstering, and finishing of furniture is a specialized operation which requires different tools, materials, and paints from those found in the scenery shop. A property shop does not need a lot of space. It should, however, be an area near but separated from the dust and confusion of the scenery shop and the splatter of flying paint from the painting area.

TOOLS AND EQUIPMENT

The tools of a scenery shop are primarily for woodworking, with limited provisions for the working of metal. To build scenery it is necessary to cut, pare or shape, bore, and join the wood. The tools to work the wood are either hand tools for limited and special work, or power tools for mass production and precision work. The working and joining of wood, however, is always preceded by careful measuring and marking.

MEASURING AND MARKING TOOLS

(Figure 6–3) Tools for measuring and marking are not only used with each technique of working wood but also in every step in the construction and assembly of the completed setting. Almost all mistakes in building are directly traceable to wrong measurements or a misinterpreted mark. The importance of accurate measurements cannot be overstressed.

A list of the essential measuring and marking tools for a scenery shop should include (Figure 6–3a–h, right, i–o page 162).

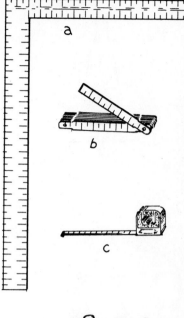
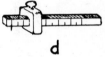
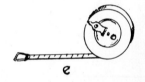

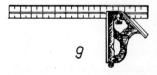
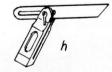

Measuring		*Marking*	
(a)	Framing square	(h)	Bevel gauge
(b)	6-foot folding rule	(i)	Scribe
(c)	6-foot, 8-foot, and	(j)	Tri-square
	12-foot steel tape	(k)	Spline or spring curve
(d)	Marking gauge	(l)	Trammel points and bar
(e)	50-foot steel tape	(m)	Chalk line
(f)	Protractor square	(n)	Centering square
(g)	Combination square	(o)	Spirit level

Some of the tools are obviously for measuring only (6-foot rule and 50-foot tape) and others are made specifically for marking (tri-square,

FIGURE 6–3.

i

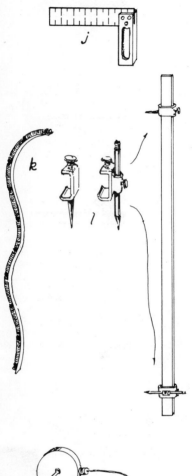

j

k

l

bevel gauge, scribe, spirit level, spline, and center square). There are, however, a few tools designed for both measuring and marking.

The *protractor square* is able to measure an angle in degrees and provide a marking guide.

The *combination square,* with its adjustable sliding bar, is calibrated for measuring as well as establishing a marking guide for the 90-degree and 45-degree angles.

The *framing square* with calibrated edges is a useful tool in marking the angle cut of a stair carriage, and for establishing a right angle for framing.

The *marking gauge* is calibrated to mark for a rip cut, an operation that can be duplicated by the combination square.

Within the group of marking tools, the *tri-square* is calibrated for limited measuring although its chief function is as a marking guide for a 90-degree angle cut. The *bar* or *beam* holding the trammel points is sometimes calibrated to measure the radius of the circle or arc it is to swing. The other tools in this group serve as marking guides only.

The *bevel gauge* is designed for transferring or saving a predetermined angle or bevel.

The *scribe* can follow an irregular surface with one point and scratch or mark the outline of the surface at a fixed distance with the other point.

The *spline and spring curve* are used to mark an irregular curve, or to plot a curved edge in full-scale lofting.

The *spirit level* establishes a true vertical or horizontal, and the *center square* locates the unmarked center of a circle or round stock.

The *chalk line* is for snapping an extremely long straight line that may be used as a framing guide, as a reference line for full-scale lofting, or as a guide line for painting.

CUTTING TOOLS

(Figure 6–4*a–m,* page 163),The chief cutting tool is the saw. A list of saws for a scenery shop is as follows:

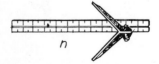

m

Hand Saws	Power Saws
(*a*) Ripsaw	(*g*) Saber saw
(*b*) Crosscut saw	(*h*) Pullover saw
(*c*) Keyhole saw	(*i*) Cut-awl
(*d*) Scroll saw	(*j*) Jigsaw
(*e*) Miter box and backsaw	(*k*) Skilsaw
(*f*) Hack saw	(*l*) Table saw
	(*m*) Band saw

n

o

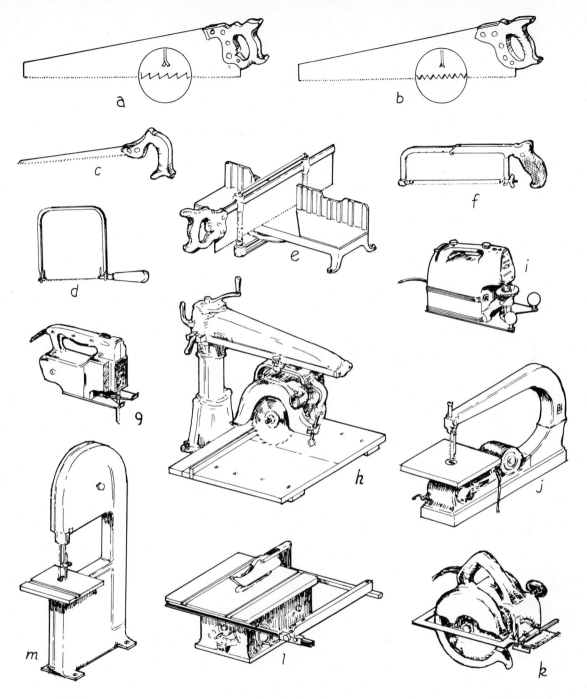

a b c d e f i g h j m l k

FIGURE 6–4.

The specific work a saw can do depends upon the shape of the tooth (pointed or chisel), the set of the tooth (flare of every other tooth in the opposite direction), and the tooth count (number of teeth per inch). Because wood has a grain, which is the alternating density of the fibers within its structure, it requires a different kind of saw to cut across the grain than to cut with the grain. The teeth of a cross-cut saw are sharp and straight to cut through the wood fibers while

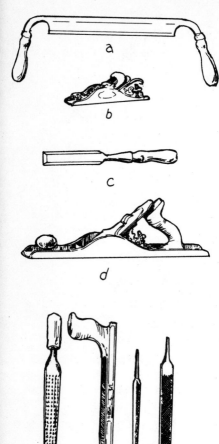

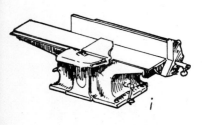

the teeth of the ripsaw are angled and flat edged like a chisel to chip the wood with the grain. The ripsaw has the widest set and the lowest tooth count (6 to 8 teeth per inch). The crosscut saw has a tooth count of 8, 10, to 12 teeth per inch.

The ripsaw and crosscut saw are for straight-line cutting as is the hack saw, which is used to cut metal. A hack saw, with a tempered-steel blade of 18 tooth count, will cut strap iron, bolts, and pipe that are frequently used in scenery construction.

An angled cut or miter can be cut freehand with a crosscut saw, or it can be accurately cut in a miter box with a backsaw. The backsaw, with a high tooth count (10 to 12 teeth per inch) is a stiff-bladed saw with a straight back which serves as a guide in the miter box (Figure 6–4e). It is extremely useful in mitering moldings for a cornice, picture frame, or panel.

Power Saw.   Power tools made for straight-line cutting are the table saw, pullover saw, and Skilsaw. Each may be fitted with a rip or crosscut, or combination blade for specific work.

A 10-inch, tilting-arbor, 1-horsepower table saw, with miter gauge and rip fence is a basic piece of equipment. It is a heavy enough tool to do precision work in quantity. It miters and rips with ease and accuracy.

A 10- to 12-inch one-horsepower pullover saw provides the necessary power for cutting heavy lumber. Its pullover action above the wood and long table make it an accurate crosscut and limited mitering tool. Because the guide fence becomes inaccurate from repeated crosscutting, it is not a very accurate ripping tool.

The Skilsaw, which is a portable circular saw, is designed to be brought to the work rather than for bringing the work to the saw. It can be used to an advantage as a rip or crosscut saw on partially completed units of scenery. Because of its light weight and small blade it is limited as to depth of cut and accuracy. It is, however, a useful tool to have in a busy shop.

Irregular Cutting.   Not all cutting in the making of scenery is straight-line cutting. As a matter of fact a high percentage of the cutting is irregular or scroll work. Cutouts and profile edges require the greatest amount of scroll work.

A hand saw to cut on an irregular line must necessarily have a small blade to be able to turn and follow the irregular line. The scroll saw has a high tooth count of 12 per inch to produce a smoothly cut edge. It has a removable blade for inside cuts. The deep throat of the

FIGURE 6–5.

frame that holds the blade allows the saw to reach well into the work.

The keyhole saw with a tooth count of 8 to 10 is made for heavy, coarse, and fast work. The small blade, although not as small as the scroll saw, allows irregular cutting beyond the limits a scroll saw can reach.

Power Tools for Irregular Cutting. Power tools that speed up the production of scroll work are the band saw, jigsaw, saber saw, and cut-awl. The *band saw* with its continuous blade is limited to outside cutting and to work as large as the depth of its throat. A band saw with a 20-inch throat will serve the average need of a scenery shop if it is supplemented with other equipment to do inside cutting.

The *jigsaw* with its removable straight blade and deep throat is made for both inside and outside scroll cutting. The *saber saw*, which is a portable jigsaw, does not limit the size of the work. It is a very versatile tool for scroll cutting at any stage of assembly.

The *cut-awl*, which is designed for light, detailed cutting, works best on profile and composition board. It also requires a padded bench or table for satisfactory results.

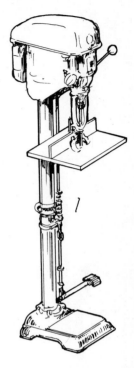

PARING TOOLS

(Figure 6–5a–k, page 164, l–o, right) Chisel or knifelike tools to smooth or shape wood are paring tools. A list of the most useful:

Hand Tools	*Power Tools*
(*a*) Drawknife	(*i*) Rotary planer (joiner)
(*b*) Block plane	(*j*) Disk and belt sander
(*c*) Chisel	(*k*) Router
(*d*) Smoothing plane	(*l*) Mortise machine
(*e*) Rasp	(*m*) Rotary shaper
(*f*) Rasp blade in holder	(*n*) Emery wheel
(*g*) Triangular metal file	(*o*) Lathe
(*h*) Flat metal file	

The simplest tool for freehand shaping of wood is the chisel. Although the hand chisel cannot compare in speed and accuracy to power tools, it can be used to do a limited amount of shaping and notching of wood. It is an excellent tool to clean up a power-cut dado, rabbet, mortise, or routed area. With skilled handling it can, if necessary, make any of these cuts itself. A set of chisels would include a variety of widths from ¼ inch to 1¼ inches.

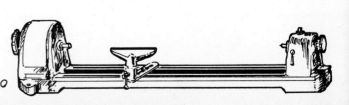

166   The drawknife is not a precision tool. It is useful to pare away waste, or roughly shape a surface before planing.

The smoothing plane can pare a surface to an accurate dimension. It is made to smooth with the grain of the wood while the small block plane is designed to work across the grain and to smooth or shape the end of a board.

The rasp is also used for cross-grain smoothing or shaping. Its sharp teeth tear the fibers so that unless a rough finish is desired the surface has to be smoothed with a fine rasp or sandpaper.

Power tools designed to do various shaping and smoothing operations are limited mostly to special cuts. The rotary planer or joiner, for example, can smooth a board, size a board by changing the depth of cut, bevel the edge by angling the fence, as well as cutting a rabbet on one side of the board.

Likewise the rotary shaper is designed especially to cut moldings. It can cut a variety of molding by changing or combining different blades.

The mortising machine, or mortising attachment for a drill press, with its square chisel, is limited to cutting the deep square hole of a mortise. It is a time-saving tool in a professional scenery shop where there is a lot of mortise and tenon joining.

Probably the most useful small power tool for shaping is the router. Besides routing to countersink hinges, it can cut tenons, dados, and rabbets. With special bits it can also do a limited amount of molding cutting.

Some of these shaping operations can be performed on the table and pullover saw. The circular table saw can be equipped with a dado head which is a set of special blades to cut a groove. Molding cutters can also be attached to the circular saw for simple molding cutting. The pullover saw can also be rigged to dado, shape, and rout. Any change over, of course, takes time and ties up the saw for other uses.

For finished smoothing, a power sander, both belt and disk, quickly and accurately smooths the end, edge, or face of a board. In this same category, the emery wheel is used to smooth and shape metal as well as sharpen hand tools.

BORING TOOLS (Figure 6–6*a-m* page 167).

Tools with a cutting edge that revolves about a central axis to cut a circular hole are boring tools. The tool is comprised of two basic parts: the bit, which is the cutting part of the tool, and the brace or some similar mechanism to rotate the bit.

There is, of course, great variation in the types of bit depending upon the size and depth of hole, kind of hole (clean bore, tapcr, ream), and the nature of the material (hardness, thickness). Likewise the power-providing part of the tool will vary with type of bit used and the speed of rotation necessary to do the work. The types of bit and means of rotation found in the average scenery shop are:

Bits	Rotating Tools
(*a*) Auger bit (square shank)	(*j*) Brace
(*b*) Twist drill (round shank)	(*k*) Hand drill
(*c*) Twist drill (square shank)	(*l*) Power hand drill
(*d*) Twist drill (¼-inch round shank)	(*m*) Drill press
(*e*) Power bit (¼-inch round shank)	
(*f*) Countersink, wood	
(*g*) Countersink, metal	
(*h*) Hole-cutter	
(*i*) Expansive bit	

The auger bit has a screw lead which, when rotated, pulls the cutting edges of the bit into contact with the wood. The auger bit does not need to rotate at a high speed. It is usually driven with the brace made to receive its square shank. The brace is a cranklike form designed to give the carpenter a mechanical advantage rather than to increase the speed of rotation. Augers are manufactured in size differences of $\frac{1}{16}$ inch. They are numbered by sixteenths; thus a ½-inch auger would be a No. 8 bit.

Twist drills have no screw lead and depend upon speed of rotation and pressure to advance into the material. The band drill is designed to increase the speed of rotation as well as provide some mechanical advantage. The high speed, portable, powered hand drill is excellent for this type of work.

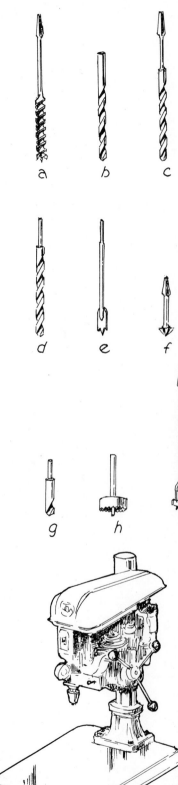

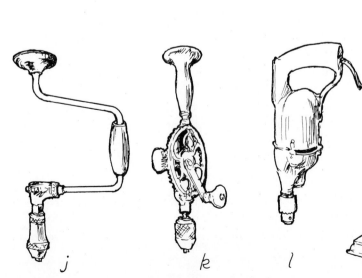

FIGURE 6–6.

168

The power bit is a wood-cutting bit made for high-speed rotation with a small round shank (¼-inch) for the small power drill.

Also in the auger-bit class are the gimlet and expansive bit. The gimlet is made to bore a small hole in an inaccessible place; and the expansive bit, which is adjustable, can bore a hole as large as 1¼ inches to 2½ inches in diameter.

The hole-cutter is made to cut oversized holes (1½ inches and up) at high speed. Although faster and cleaner than the expansive bit, it is limited in its depth of cut.

The drill press, which is a stationary power drill, has the added advantages of such controls as depth of bore and speed variation for precision work. The drill press with a mortising attachment makes a very useful tool in the scenery shop (Figure 6–6m).

WOOD-JOINING TOOLS (Figure 6–7a-x page 169)

The joining of wood is the last stage of carpentry. The tools that are used are designed to drive or set the joining hardware (nails, screws, or staples) in such manner as to hold the pieces of wood together. The hammer and hammerlike tools (staple gun) drive a nail or staple; the screwdriver sets a screw into wood; the wrench and pliers tighten a bolted joint; and the clamps hold a glued joint together until the glue has set. A list of the most frequently used tools follows:

(a)	Claw hammer	(m)	Staple hammer
(b)	Straight claw hammer	(n)	Scissors
(c)	Blacksmith's hand hammer	(o)	Tin shears
(d)	Ball peen hammer	(p)	Stillson wrench
(e)	Mallet	(q)	Bolt-cutter
(f)	Magnetic tack hammer	(r)	Nail-puller
(g)	Ratchet screwdriver	(s)	Pinch bar
(h)	Screwdriver	(t)	Grommet-setting die
(i)	Crescent wrench	(u)	Clinch plate
(j)	Pliers	(v)	C-clamp
(k)	Mat knife	(w)	Jorgensen hand screw clamp
(l)	Staple gun	(x)	Bar clamp

The bolt-cutter, tin shears, scissors, and mat knife are cutting tools that are used in the covering and assembly process of scenery construction.

PNEUMATIC TOOLS

A well-equipped scenery shop is not without the speed and efficiency of the pneumatic hammer or staple gun (Figure 6-8). As these tools require about 90 pounds per square inch of air pressure to operate, the

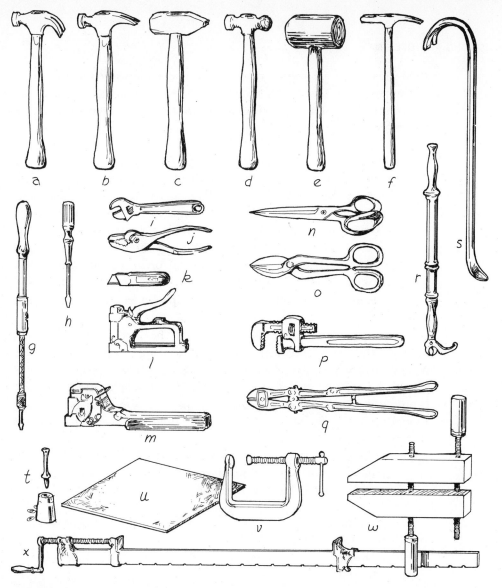

FIGURE 6–7.

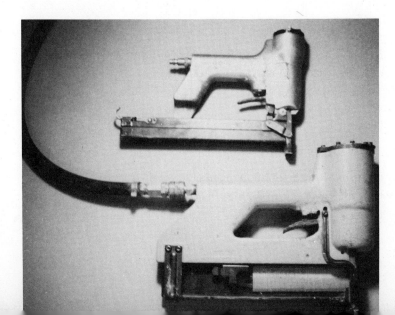

FIGURE 6-8. PNEUMATIC TOOLS.   Two useful pneumatic staplers suitable for attaching corner blocks and light-weight nailing.

170 shop must have a heavy-duty compressor or compressed-air service at convenient positions in the shop. Besides the air-hammer there is the pneumatic reversible drill with socket wrench and screwdriver attachments.

METAL-WORKING TOOLS (Figure 6–9a–g page 171)

The ever increasing use of structural steel, pipe, and tubing in scenery as either framing or decorative materials makes it advisable to include a few necessary metal-working tools in the well equipped scenery shop. Many of the basic hand tools for cutting and working metal have already been mentioned, including the hack saw and metal file as well as such power tools as the drill press for the drilling and countersinking of metal. Additional hand tools for the cutting and working of pipe not mentioned are the pipe-cutter, threader, bender, and vise stand.

The pipe-cutter, when rotated around the pipe, applies an even pressure to the cutting wheel, thereby insuring a square, clean cut. A pipe-threader set should include die heads to thread at least ¾-inch, 1-inch and 1½-inch pipe. Both the cutting and threading of pipe require a pipe vise. Rather than attaching a pipe vise to a fixed bench position, it is easier to use a portable vise stand which can be brought to the work on the stage or in the shop to minimize the handling of material. The vise stand shown in Figure 6–9d is also equipped with slots for limited pipe bending. For larger-scale bending of heavier pipe it is best to use a regular pipe-bending tool (Figure 6–9e).

Hand Tools	*Power Tools*
(a) Pipe-cutter	(f) Power hack saw
(b) Pipe-threader with ¾-inch, 1-inch, and 1½-inch die heads	(g) Power band saw
(c) Pipe vise	
(d) Portable vise stand	
(e) Pipe-bender	

The cutting of pipe or structural steel by hand can be time consuming and inaccurate. Two power tools, the power hacksaw and band saw, are designed to cut up to 2-inch stock pipe, structural steel, or cold-rolled steel bar at an adjustable angle cut of 45 to 90 degrees. Both tools are adaptable to mass producing or multiple cutting, with the band saw being the more accurate and of course the most expensive.

The occasional need to cut light-weight sheet metal or aluminum can be accomplished by using a metal-cutting blade in either the saber saw or regular band saw.

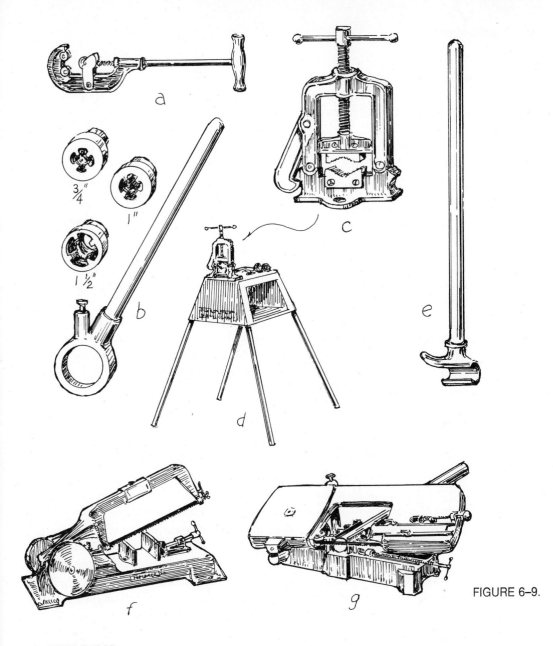

a

3/4"

1"

1 1/2"

b

c

d

e

f

g

FIGURE 6–9.

WELDING

The joining of metal structural or decorative members is obviously more complicated than the joining of wood. Structural steel may be joined by drilling and bolting; pipe may be joined by a coupling or union fitting, and so on. A faster method, which at the same time produces a rigid permanent joint, is welding.

Of the many welding processes there are two techniques that are adaptable to the theatre workshop. Although there is an increased use of metal in scenery for the theatre, the average workshop does not have the skill of a professional welder or the need of manufacturing techniques.

172   The two most useful welding processes adaptable to the construction and design of scenery are *gas-welding* and *arc-welding.*

GAS-WELDING EQUIPMENT

Oxy-Acetylene Welding (OAW) ignites an oxygen and acetylene mixture to produce one of the hottest flames known. Welding is possible with or without a filler metal. Gas-welding can perform a wide range of work. Besides joining or fusing the metals together it can be used for low-temperature welding or *brazing;* to cut metal with a cutting attachment; and to preheat metal for reshaping on the anvil. The chief disadvantage to gas-welding is heat warpage.

Unless handled very carefully, there is the possibility of warping the metal near the welded point. The choice of a welding rod which will melt at the same temperature as (or slightly lower than) the melting point of the steel will minimize the amount of distortion.

The relative harmlessness of the flame is another advantage of gas-welding when used in the scenery shop or on the stage. The only exception is when the cutting tip is being used. To cut metal with a torch, a tiny jet of oxygen is directed onto the white-hot metal, producing a rather spectacular shower of sparks. The operator should wear goggles and gloves, more for protection from flying sparks than from the intensity of the flame itself. Because there are no ultraviolet rays generated in the flame of gas-welding, it does not have to be isolated or shielded from other shop activity. Precautions should be taken, however, to guard the sparks from inflammable materials by using asbestos or sheetrock pads under and around the work.

The most cumbersome parts of a gas-welding outfit are the heavy tanks containing the two welding gases oxygen and acetylene. A tank truck is essential to make their handling easier. The methods of acquiring oxygen and acetylene vary with the suppliers. Some gas suppliers charge a fixed deposit on the tank which is refunded when the empty tank is returned, while others rent the container on a per diem basis. If a supplier insists on the tank-rental arrangement, it pays in the long run to purchase a set of empty tanks to exchange for each tank of gas and thereby eliminate the per diem rental charge which, though small, can mount up during idle times between productions.

A listing of the parts and attachments of a gas-welding outfit including the gas tanks is as follows (Figure 6–10a–p, page 173):

(*a*) Oxygen tank
(*b*) Acetylene tank
(*c*) Tank truck
(*d*) Gauges: oxygen regulator and acetylene regulator
(*e*) 25-foot twin $\frac{3}{16}$-inch hose with connectors

(f)   Welding butt

(g)   Cutting attachment

(h)   Welding nozzles, sizes 00, 1, 3 and 5

(i)   Cutting tip size 2

(j)   Tip cleaner set

(k)   Flint lighter

(l)   Welding gloves

(m) Goggles

(n)   Rods: ⅛-inch fluxcoated brazing rod (for thin-walled conduit)

        ⅛-inch mild steel rod (for structural steel)

(o)   Flux

(p)   Wrench

FIGURE 6–10.

174 ARC-WELDING EQUIPMENT

The heat of arc-welding comes, as the name implies, from the arc of a high-amperage short between the metal and the rod of electrode. The work has to be grounded to complete the circuit from the rod to the holder through the electrode cable to the transformer. *Shielded Metal Arc-Welding* (SMAW) is the most adaptable arc-welding technique for the theatre workshop. Upon striking the arc it is enveloped in a shield of inert gas as the coating of the rod burns. This shield of inert gas keeps the oxygen in the air out of the critical metallurgical change of the welding process.

Of the two welding methods, arc-welding requires more skill. It takes practice to develop a steady hand to strike an arc and draw a good bead. Arc-welding's chief advantage is in the speed of the welding operation. Because a welding temperature is reached almost instantaneously and in such a small area, the amount of heat warpage is negligible. This is important in the welding of a preassembled part when its fit is critical to the final shape of the completed structure.

A transformer of at least 25 to 230 amperes capacity with multiheat selection is an ideal welder for stage and scenery application. With the proper rod it will solder, weld bronze, steel, or cast iron and, with special attachments, heat metal for reshaping.

The most obvious disadvantage of arc-welding is the harmful intensity of the flash. Because of the presence of ultraviolet rays, it is very injurious to the eyes to look directly at the flash for a prolonged interval. Hence it becomes necessary to shield the eyes of the operator with ray-absorbing glass and a protective hood. As bare arms and hands are also subject to ray burns, gloves and protective long sleeves are an added precaution for the operator.

The flash can also affect the casual observer or fellow worker in the shop. If arc-welding cannot be isolated in a special area away from other shop activities, it is possible to shield the flash from others with a folding screen.

The parts of an arc-welding outfit are as follows (Figure 6–11 a–j, page 175):

(a) Transformer: 40–230 amperes
16–20 heats
Supply cable (20 feet for greater mobility)
(b) 18-foot electrode cable
(c) 18-foot ground cable
(d) Electrode rod holder
(e) Ground clamps
(f) Helmet, fiber glass with ray-absorbing viewing glass
(g) Gloves

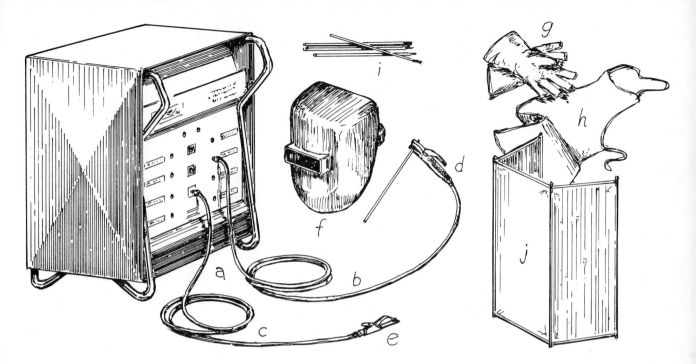

(*h*) Apron or smock

(*i*) Rods: ⅛-inch mild steel rods (structural steel and pipe)
       ⅛-inch hard surface rods (chrome carbon steel)

(*j*) Folding screen

FIGURE 6–11.

GAS-METAL ARC-WELDING

A third welding process which is rapidly becoming adaptable to theatre shop use is the gas-metal arc-welding method commonly referred to as *Metal Inert Gas* or MIG. MIG uses a wire-fed electrode through a gas hose and gun nozzle to the work. The arc is surrounded with an inert gas shield and is automatically fed with a wire electrode in the center of the nozzle. Welding is a simple one-handed operation easy to learn. The heat of the arc and gauge of the wire can be altered to weld various metals including aluminum. A special spot-welding fitting can be attached to the end of the nozzle for temporarily tacking or permanently joining adjacent surfaces. Some MIG units can also switch to stick-welding (regular arc-welding with rod) without the use of gas.

As welding equipment MIG is more expensive than arc or gas, but is easier to operate and provides a variety of uses. Its chief disadvantage is its weight and bulk. It is not very mobile for other than metal-shop use.

Tungsten Inert Gas or TIG is also a gas-metal arc-welding system. TIG uses a tungsten electrode in the gun nozzle rather than a wire feed. The tungsten electrode has the advantage of eroding more slowly than other refractory metals and can withstand higher currents. The electrode, however, does not act as a filler metal as in MIG and therefore requires the two-handed skill of the gas-welding method to operate.

Because an arc is involved in gas-metal arc-welding it is subject to all the safety precautions of arc-welding mentioned earlier. The components of MIG equipment are as follows (Figure 6-12).

(a) Power unit MIG—160 Amperes DC at 22 volts

(60% duty cycle)

STICK—160 amperes DC at 28 volts

(35% duty cycle)

Supply cable

(b) Gas cylinder—Mixture of Argon and CO_2 or Helium

(c) Gauges—tank pressure

work pressure

(d) Gas hose-cable

(e) Automatic wire-feeder

Built-in wire-feeder is a feature of this

particular unit (AIRCO, DIP/STICK 160)

(f) Gun and nozzle

(g) Ground cable

(h) Electrode cable for stick-welding

(i) Spot-welding attachment

(j) Helmet, fiberglass with ray-absorbing viewing window

(k) Gloves

(l) Apron or smock

(m) Rods for stick-welding

(n) Folding screen

(o) Angled grinder to smooth weld

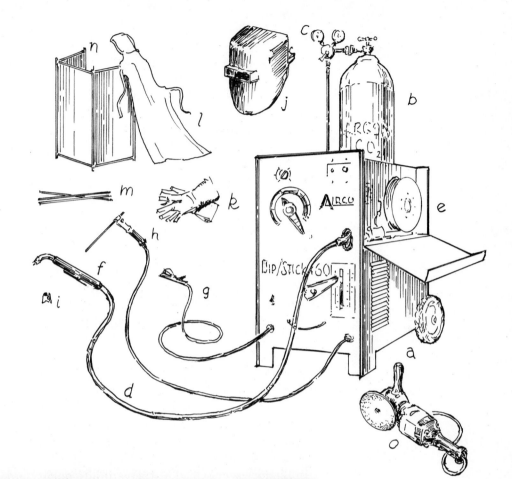

FIGURE 6–12.

178   MATERIALS

Although some materials will be mentioned relative to the construction of certain types of scenery, it may be wise to consider briefly all the materials that are used for making scenery. To compile a conclusive list is, of course, next to impossible, for designers and technicians are constantly bringing new materials into the theatre every day as well as discovering new uses for old materials.

Materials can be divided and classified into four groups of similar functions: (1) structural (lumber and metal), (2) cover stock (fabric and hard surfaces), (3) hardware (joining and stage hardware), (4) paints and related supplies.

STRUCTURAL MATERIALS

Lumber is the principal framing and structural material, supplemented and reinforced on occasion by structural steel, pipe, and aluminum. As supplies and prices change, aluminum may become the framing material and wood the supplementary or decorative material. Until this is an actuality, lumber remains the chief structural element.

Lumber.   To fill the needs of scenic construction, lumber must be lightweight, strong, straight, and inexpensive. The best combination of weight and strength is found in white pine. Although woods such as redwood and spruce are lighter, they do not have the strength and tend to splinter and split. The hardwoods are stronger, of course, but weigh and cost too much.

Lumber is classified at the yard into quality groups. The straightness of grain and freedom from knots determine the quality. Hence, clear white pine is of the highest quality. It is further classified as to its expected use. A board that is to become trim or a finished surface is of a higher quality than a structural member hidden from view.

The finishing lumber, or, "select" grades, are designated by the letters A, B, C, and D. Hence B-select or better is a high-grade pine. C-select is the usual quality of lumber used in professional scenery.

The common grades are numbered 1 to 5. They are not intended for a finished surface although many times 1- and 2-common are used as knotty-pine paneling. No. 2-common is the usual framing material for amateur scenery unless the theatre is in an area of the country where the better grades of pine are available at reasonable prices.

The stock sizes of lumber refer to the rough-cut size and not to the finished dimension after the wood has been dressed (planed or smooth on all sides). Thus 1 by 3 is really ¾-inch by 2½-inch. The longest stock length is 16 feet, although longer lengths can be obtained on special order.

Because lumber is cut in a variety of widths and thicknesses, it has a unit of measurement, the board-foot, common to all sizes. A board-foot is a 1-foot-square unit measuring 1 inch in thickness. A piece of lumber

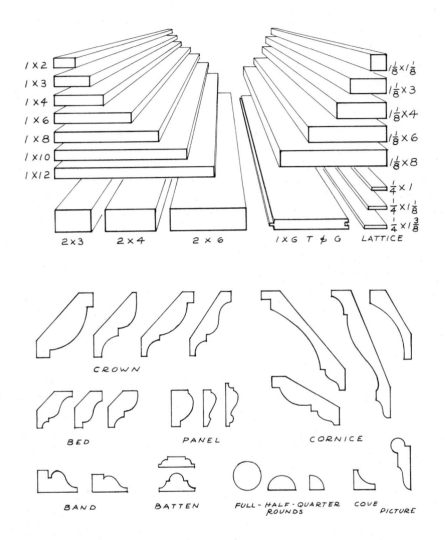

FIGURE 6–13. STOCK LUMBER SIZES AND MOLDING SHAPES.

of any size can be reduced from its linear dimensions into board-feet. A 16-foot length of 1 by 3, for example, contains 4 board-feet. All lumber prices are based on the board-foot measurement.

Special shapes like "rounds" are stocked in diameter from ¾-inch to 1½-inch and sometimes as large as 3 inches in diameter. Dowel is available in ⅛- to 1-inch diameter and 3-foot lengths made of maple and birch.

Other special shapes are stock moldings which are made in a great variety of sizes and contours. A few of the most frequently used moldings are illustrated in Figure 6–13 along with the stock lumber sizes.

METAL

Structural steel has many special uses in scenery construction. The sizes and shapes in relation to their uses are illustrated in Figure 6-14.

Uni-strut with its fittings is a method of knockdown framing in special channel-shaped steel that is adaptable to platforming and trussing in the theatre. It eliminates the necessity of welding and cutting, and is available in different forms.

Thin-Wall Conduit.   Thin-wall galvanized-steel conduit pipe has become a very popular structural and decorative material in the theatre. With walls too thin to thread and therefore easy to bend, it has many uses in scenery construction (Figure 6–14). It comes in three diameters, ½-inch, ¾-inch, 1¼-inch, in 10-foot lengths. It is lightweight, inexpensive, and easy to gas-weld with fluxcoated brazing rod.

Pipe.   Malleable iron pipe is used for battens to support hanging scenery; as a weight or bottom batten for a drop; for lighting booms; and as structural elements. Pipe-fitting and pipe-bending increase the number of uses pipe can perform in the theatre. Figure 6–15 shows the stock sizes and fittings, and some of the uses.

Sheet Metal and Screening.   Galvanized iron, aluminum, tin, and zinc are the most frequently used sheet metals. Light pans, shadow boxes and special effects are a few of the uses of sheet metal in scenery construction.

The metal screening such as hardware cloth (¼-inch mesh), galvanized screen ($\frac{1}{16}$-inch mesh) and chicken wire (1-inch mesh) are primarily used as structural materials. Occasionally, galvanized screening is used to simulate window glass.

COVER STOCK

The material used to cover the structural frame of scenery, thereby providing a surface for painting, is known as cover stock. The frame can be covered with a fabric or hard surface depending upon the use and handling of the particular piece of scenery. A translucent backing, for example, is framed and covered differently from a section of wall that must support the weight of an actor.

Covering Fabrics.   The usual covering fabrics for framed scenery are 8-ounce canvas duck and 5- to 6-ounce unbleached muslin. Muslin is more frequently used as a drop material than as cover stock for framed scenery. However, almost any fabric can become a covering

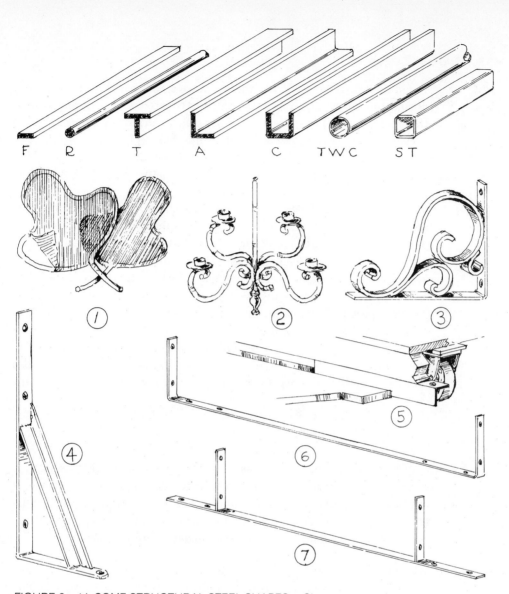

FIGURE 6—14. SOME STRUCTURAL STEEL SHAPES.   Shown are a few of the basic lightweight structural steel shapes and their uses in scenery construction: *(F)* Flat or strap iron. *(R)* Round or rod. *(T)* Tee. *(A)* Angle. *(C)* Channel. *(TWC)* Thin-wall conduit. *(ST)* Square tube. *Decorative Uses of Rod and Strap Iron:* (1) Stylized leaf forms. (2) Chandelier or candelabra shapes. (3) Decorative bracket. *A Few Familiar Uses of Steel in Scenery Construction:* (4) Special jack or over-sized footiron. (5) "Knife" guide in the track of a guided wagon. (6) Sill iron used under door opening in a flat. (7) Saddle-shaped sill iron.

material to serve as a special effect or as an unusual painting surface. Burlap, velour, scrim, terry cloth, and even string rugs have been used as covering fabrics. The thin, translucent materials are backed with canvas, of course, if the surface is supposed to be opaque.

Hard Surfaces. If the surface has to withstand active handling during the action of a play, the frame is covered with a harder surface than canvas. The most frequently used hard-surface material is ⅛-inch plywood board called EZ curve or profile board. It is lightweight, but still strong enough to supply a hard surface with a minimum of framing. Tek board, ⅛-inch laminated wood and paper, is a close substitute for profile board although not quite as strong.

Other hard-surface materials are: ⅛-inch and $\frac{3}{16}$-inch Upson board, an inexpensive but weaker substitute for profile board made of laminated paper; ¼-inch fir three ply, a very sturdy but heavy board (also used for keystone and corner blocks); ½-inch Homosote, a paper-pulp board with very little strength but thick enough to be carved or textured; and $\frac{3}{16}$-inch Masonite, a very heavy, hard surface of compressed wood pulp. The tempered Masonite is an extremely hard surface that is occasionally used as a floor covering. Double-faced corrugated cardboard is an inexpensive hard surface for limited profiling and covering providing the scenery is not subjected to excessive handling. Some shops also include ¾-inch and 1-inch five ply as cover stock, although its chief use is for platform tops.

Most of the cover-stock materials are available at the local lumber yard in stock 4-by-8-foot sheets. Occasionally, oversized sheets, such as 5 feet by 9 feet, 4 feet by 10 feet and 4 feet by 12 feet, are stocked.

Plastic Surfaces. Because the use of modern plastic as a scenery surface is usually related to a textured or relief-sculptured surface, it is reserved for discussion later under Textured and Sculptured Surfaces (page 211). Here the techniques of working plastics such as Styrofoam, urethane foam and thermoplastics are studied.

HARDWARE

In the scenery shop, hardware is divided into two categories: joining hardware and stage hardware. Joining hardware is an important part of normal scenery construction. It includes all the necessary nails, screws, and bolts for joining wood or metal. Stage hardware is a part of knock-down construction methods, stage assembly, and handling techniques peculiar to scenery.

FIGURE 6-15. VARIOUS USES OF IRON PIPE. *(a)* Top batten for drop, cyc, or stage drapery. *(b)* Bottom batten for a drop-in pipe sleeve. *(c)* Curved bottom batten using tielines. *(d)* Free-standing platform legs. *(e)* Special bracing. *(f)* Lighting booms and battens. *(g)* Bent pipe and welded railing. *(h)* Cut pipe and fitted railing. *Some of the Screw Fittings Used to Join Section of Pipe:* (1) Coupling. (2) Nipple. (3) Reducing coupling. (4) Tee. (5) Cross. (6) Union, ring end. (7) Union, screw end. (8) Cap. (9) 90-degree elbow. (10) 45-degree elbow. (11) Street ells. (12) Floor flange. (13) Adjustable elbow (railing fitting). (14) Pipe strap. (15) Batten inside sleeve splice. (16) Saddle tee, double strap. (17) Roto-lock. (18) Pipe hanger.

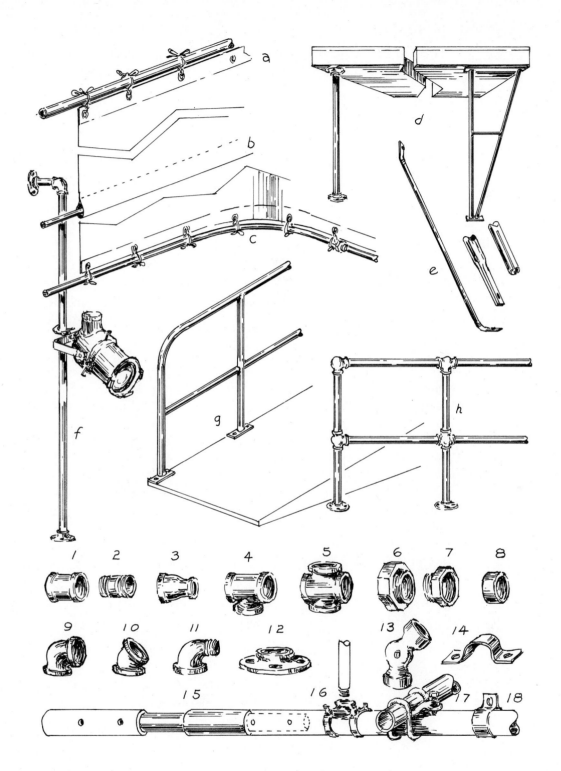

184 A list of joining hardware most frequently used in the construction of scenery would include:

Nails: Common—8d, 10d
Box—3d, 6d
Finish—4d, 6d, 8d
Clout—1¼-inch (or 3d box nail)

Screws: Flat-head bright steel:
No. 8—¾-inch, ⅞-inch, 1¼-inch
No. 10—2-inch, 3-inch

Tacks and Staples: Carpet—No. 6, No. 10
Gimp—½-inch
Staples—⅜-inch, ½-inch

Bolts: $\frac{3}{16}$-inch stove—2-inch, 3-inch
⅜-inch carriage—3-inch, 4-inch, 6-inch

Washers: ¼-inch ID (inside diameter)
$\frac{7}{16}$-inch ID

Supplementary to this list are many special items which might or might not be stocked, depending upon the personal whims of the shop carpenter and his construction techniques. Such items as lag screws and machine bolts are sometimes used under special conditions. Corrugated fasteners, wire brads and nails, screw eyes, eye bolts, and decorative-headed tacks are often needed.

Stage Hardware. The necessary portability of scenery leads to the use of many pieces of hardware made especially for the stage. Most of it is designed to brace, stiffen, and temporarily join units of scenery as well as provide rigging hardware for the flying of scenery (Figure 6–16). A list of essential stage hardware would be:

Stiffening: Batten hooks
Loose-pin hinge (back flap)

Bracing:
Footirons (straight, bent, and hinged)
Stage brace
Stage peg
Stage screw and plug
Brace cleat

Joining: Lash cleat and eye
Stop cleat

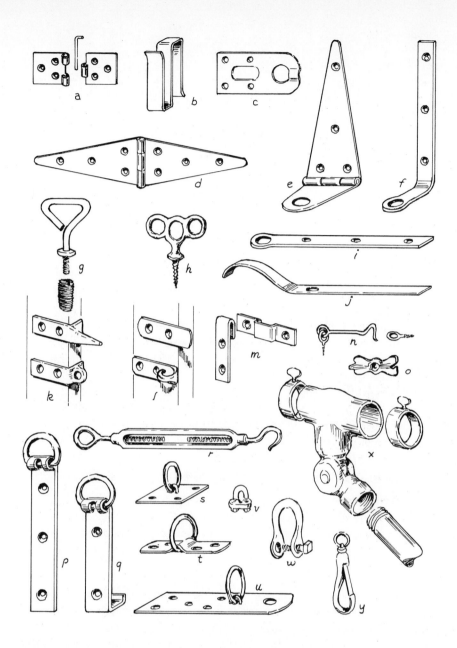

FIGURE 6–16. STAGE HARDWARE. *(a)* Loose-pin back-flap hinge. *(b)* Batten hook. *(c)* Brace cleat. *(d)* Strap hinge. *(e)* Hinged footiron. *(f)* Bent footiron. *(g)* Stage scew and plug. *(h)* Stage screw. *(i)* Straight footiron. *(j)* Floor stay. *(k)* Lash cleat and lash eye. *(l)* Stop cleat and lash hook. *(m)* Picture-frame hanger. *(n)* Hook and eye. *(o)* Turn button. *(p)* Hanger iron, straight. *(q)* Hanger iron, hooked. *(r)* Turnbuckle. *(s)* Square plate and ring. *(t)* Oblong plate and D-ring. *(u)* Ceiling plate. *(v)* Cable clamp. *(w)* Shakle bolt. *(x)* Cyc knuckle. *(y)* Swivel-eye snap hook.

Loose-pin hinge (strap, butt, and back flap)
Hook and eye

Rigging: Hanger irons (straight and hooked)
Ceiling plate
Wire clamps
Rope clamps
Shackle bolts
Turnbuckles

ROPE, CABLE, AND CHAINS

Pertaining to rigging and joining of scenery are some specific types of rope, chain, and cable. A listing of their specification and uses on the stage is as follows:

Rope used in the theatre is of two general types: cotton braid and stranded manila. The cotton braided rope is softer (easier to handle), more flexible, but of course not as strong as the stranded manila rope.

Rope (cotton braid):
No. 8 sash cord is used as lash line, lightweight rigging, and as an occasional draw line on a lightweight traveler.
No. 10 braided rope—draw line for heavy traveler track.
⅛-inch awning cord—lightweight curtain rigging and trick line to trigger a mechanical effect from an offstage position.

Manila rope:
¾-inch three-strand manilas—purchase line of counterweight system (see Chapter 7) and heavy rigging line.
½-inch, ⅜-inch manila—lightweight rigging, breasting, and bridling.

Wire rope or cable is used to hang scenery when the supporting wires will be in view. The wire rope is very strong for its small diameter and can inconspicuously support a fairly large unit of scenery. The types of wire rope used most frequently in the theatre are aircraft cable, tiller rope, and hoisting rope.

Aircraft cable:
$\frac{1}{32}$-, $\frac{1}{16}$-, ⅛-inch—nearly invisible at a distance, very strong for size, flexible but expensive.

Tiller Rope (6 by 42):
⅛-inch (smallest diameter)—strong, flexible, and less expensive.

Hoisting Rope (6 by 19):
¼-inch (smallest diameter)—extremely strong, less flexible, and not too expensive for its weight.

Chain, outside of instances of special rigging, is used primarily as weight for stage draperies.

Jack chain:

½-, ¾-inch (single or double)—curtain weight.

FIGURE 6–17. METAL SCENERY. *(a)* Sheet metal (16 to 18 gauge) over square tube structural framing, *(b)* rear view of welded frame. The Tyrone Guthrie Theatre production of *Oedipus the King* by Sophocles. Designer— Desmond Heeley. (Photo—Kewley)

FIGURE 6–18. STRUCTURAL STEEL AND PLEXIGLASS
SCENERY.   A setting for Shakespeare's *A Midsummer
Night's Dream* at the Guthrie Theatre using square tube
structural steel, plexiglass, and Mylar surfaces.
Designer—John Jenson.   (Photo—Kewley)

FIGURE 6–19. DECORATIVE USE OF THIN-WALL
CONDUIT. Forest scene from *As You Like It*.
Designer—John Kavelin. Carnegie-Mellon University.
(Photo—Nelson)

The 7 Construction of Scenery

The scene designer is interested in the construction of scenery not only to become familiar with building techniques but also to become aware of the uses of various materials and their limitations. The more he knows about present-day theatrical materials and techniques the better able he is to introduce new materials and original methods into his designs as well as develop a knowledgeable use of contemporary types of scenery.

TYPES OF SCENERY

Scenery construction may seem at first glance to be unduly flimsy and unnecessarily complicated. This is due, chiefly, to the unique demands placed upon scenery by the theatre. First, it must be portable and lightweight in structure so as to move easily on the stage and from theatre to theatre; second, scenery has to be able to assume large-scale proportions for either decorative or masking reasons, therefore large areas of scenery must be furnished with the minimum of structure and the maximum of portability; and last, because scenery is here today and gone tomorrow, its construction must be economical. To be economical does not necessarily apply to the buying of the cheapest materials. It is the balancing of costs against the weight and structural demands of a material. It also means the economical use of scenery. Higher material costs can be afforded if a scenic element has more than one use, or can be reused at a later date.

For the purpose of discussing construction techniques, the various types of scenery are divided into groups which are similar in construction and alike in function as well as related in handling methods. Scenery is broadly divided first into two general classifications, two-dimensional and three-dimensional scenery.

Two-dimensional scenery, under this broad division, is meant to include all flat scenery with reference to its basic shape rather than to the way it is used on the stage. Although units of flat scenery, for example, may be assembled together to make a three-dimensional form on the stage, the individual pieces are still classified as two-dimensional scenery.

Two-dimensional scenery is further subdivided into two groups, framed and unframed, or soft, scenery. Within these two groupings falls the bulk of the scenery that is used on the stage either in the form of stage draperies and drops or wings and flats.

Three-dimensional scenery obviously refers to the pieces that are built in three dimensions to be handled and used as solid forms. Some three-dimensional units, particularly platforms, knock down into smaller, nearly flat, pieces for ease of handling, but, because of their weight and use, they are still classified as three-dimensional scenery.

Three-dimensional scenery is also separated into two basic groups, weight-bearing solids, meaning the weight of the actor, and nonweight-bearing forms. Steps and platforms are examples of weight-bearing scenery as compared to such nonweight-bearing examples as tree trunks, logs, and the like.

SOFT-SCENERY CONSTRUCTION

Numbered under soft scenery are such large unframed pieces as stage draperies, the drop, and the cyclorama, or "cyc." They all have the same function, to provide a large area of scenery with a minimum of construction and a maximum of portability. Being soft, they are dependent upon hanging from a batten or pipe for support. As a result they can be easily folded or rolled for transportation or storage.

STAGE DRAPERIES

The large panels of stage draperies are made by sewing small widths of materials together with vertical seams. There are three sound reasons for using vertical seams. First, because the direction of the weave or decoration is with the length of the fabric, it hangs and looks better in a vertical position. Second, a vertical seam is less conspicuous as it is lost in the folds of the drapery. Third, there is less strain on a vertical than on a horizontal seam, which carries the cumulative weight of each width of material from the bottom seam to the top.

The seams are face to face to present a smooth front surface. The top is reinforced with a 3- to 4-inch webbing through which are set the grommet rings at 1-foot intervals for the tielines. The bottom has a generous hem containing a chain which functions as a weight for the curtain. Occasionally, the chain is encased in a separate sound-deadening pocket which is sewn on the backside of the drapery instead of being enclosed directly in the hem.

Drapery fabrics may be sewn on the top webbing, or may be gathered or pleated onto the webbing to give a fixed fullness to the curtain. Fixed fullness is an advantage for a front curtain or traveler curtain. However, it is not as flexible as a flat curtain panel, as the latter can be hung either flat or with varying degrees of fullness in a greater variety of uses (Figure 7–1).

Drapery Materials. Stage draperies can be made of a variety of fabrics depending upon the specific use they are to perform and the limitations of the budget. Are the draperies to be opaque, translucent, or transparent? Are they to be pictorial, decorative, or just masking? Are they to be stock draperies or a one-shot special effect? Answering such questions as these helps to decide the kind of material to choose in relationship to its cost and use.

Velour, although expensive, is the favored drapery material. Its pile weave has a rich texture under the stage lights that cannot be duplicated with cheaper substitutes. It hangs and drapes beautifully and is also easy to maintain, handle, and store. Among the more economical velour substitutes which bear mentioning are duvetyn and flannel.

Duvetyn is almost as opaque as velour but drapes poorly and lacks as rich a surface quality. Flannel drapes a little better than duvetyn, and it has almost the same opacity. Its woolly-nap surface is a fair texture under stage lights.

Stage draperies are made of other materials not with the intention of imitating velour but to create their own effect. Cotton rep and monk's cloth have enough texture to make an interesting inexpensive curtain when hung in fullness. Wide-ribbed corduroy is another drapery texture which, though semi-opaque, drapes and hangs well.

Sometimes draperies are expected to be translucent or on occasions, transparent. Dyed muslin is the least expensive translucent fabric. It

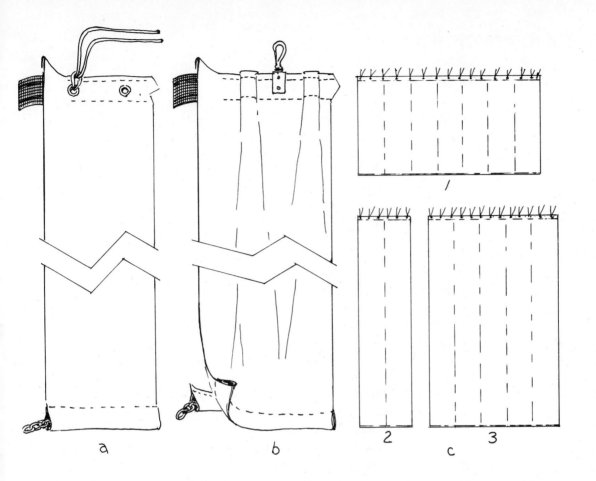

FIGURE 7–1. STAGE DRAPERIES. *(a)* Flat drapery construction. Webbing with grommets and tie-lines at top; hem enclosing chain weight at bottom. *(b)* Gathered drapery. Fullness gathered on top webbing; chain pocket attached above hem at the bottom. *(c)* Types of stage draperies: (1) border, (2) leg, (3) panel.

has a further advantage of coming in wider widths than such materials as satin or nylon crepe in the translucent class.

Gauze, the general term applied to all transparent materials, is available in a variety of fabrics such as cotton or nylon net, chiffon, and organdy, to name a few familiar commercial textiles. Although these fabrics are available at the local dry-goods store, their chief disadvantage is their narrow width which increases the number of seams in a curtain. The seams become visible when the transparent curtain is backlighted. There are gauzes, as well as muslins, that are woven on wide looms especially for theatre use. Bobbinet and shark's-tooth scrim, two transparent materials, are made in 30-foot widths. Bobbinet is a hexagonal net that is more sheer but weaker than shark's-tooth scrim, which has a rectangular or ladder pattern. The shark's-tooth, besides draping well, is dense enough to provide a dye-painting surface and still become transparent when back-lighted.

DROPS

Another large-area piece of scenery is the drop, taking its name from the fact that it hangs on a batten and is dropped in, as opposed to the older method of the shutter that slid on stage from opposite sides. The drop is made with horizontal face-to-face seams to create a smooth surface. The horizontal seams, when the drop is hanging, are under enough tension from the weight of the material and bottom batten to stretch into a smooth surface. A drop can be made to fold or roll depending upon whether it is to be translucent or opaque.

A translucent drop is dye-painted and can be equipped with tie-lines at the top and tielines or a pipe pocket at the bottom. The position of the seams of a translucent drop become important because if they are not carefully hidden in the design they produce a distracting shadow line. For this reason, translucent drops are sometimes made with vertical seams and with irregular spacing, or, if the budget permits, they are made seamless by using 30-foot-width muslin.

Since opaque scene paint is used on a regular opaque drop or a drop with opaque areas, it cannot be folded and therefore is rolled on the bottom batten. The opaque drop has a top and a bottom batten. Its construction and shape variations are shown in Figure 7–3.

Drops are commonly made of muslin because it is available in wide widths and is an excellent inexpensive translucent material. Drops are sometimes made of other materials, frequently for an unusual textural **quality, such as burlap, velour, and terrycloth.** And, of course, drops can be made of the gauze materials. Shark's-tooth and bobbinet are used more often than other sheer fabrics because they come in wider widths.

FIGURE 7–2. GAUZES. The three basic gauze materials: net, bobinette, and scrim are illustrated to show their difference in weave. *(a)* Net, square weave. A larger mesh (one inch) is knotted like a fish net. Loose, tabby-weave materials are sometimes called gauze. The fabric, which looks like surgical gauze, has very little strength. *(b)* Bobinette, hexagonal weave. Very transparent and strong, but stretches out of shape easily. *(c)* Shark's-tooth scrim, ladder weave. Strong, but not as sheer as bobinette. Best for dye painting.

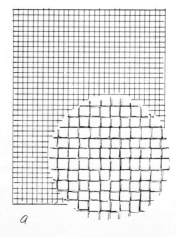

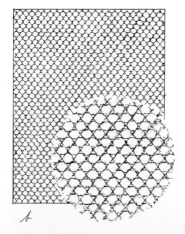

a *b* *c*

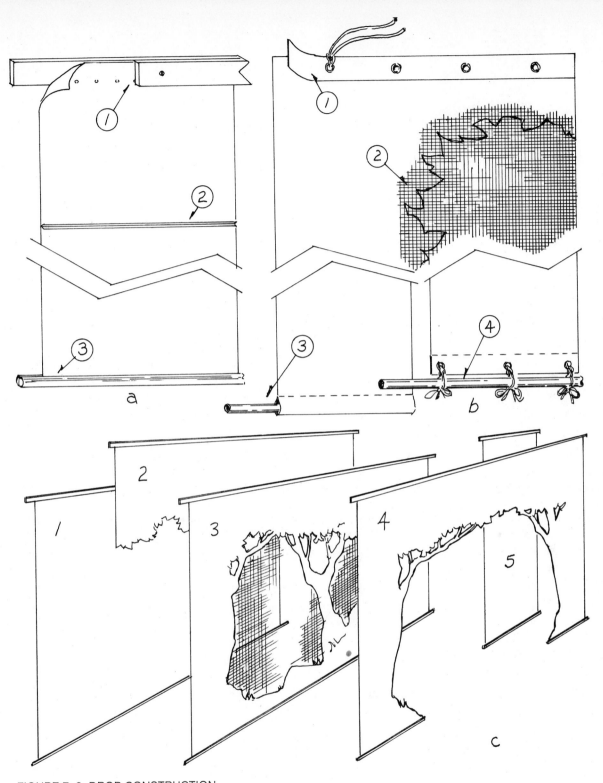

FIGURE 7–3. DROP CONSTRUCTION.
(a) Rear view of a roll drop. (1) Top batten, double 1 x 4.
(2) Face-to-face horizontal seam. (3) Bottom batten, doubles 2 inches
half round. *(b)* Rear view of a folding drop. (1) Top webbing with
grommets and tie-lines. (2) Netting glued over openings or cut edges
to support loose ends. (3) Drop bottom with pipe sleeve for the
removal of bottom batten. (4) Drop bottom made with grommets and
tie-lines. Below. *(c)* Types of drops: (1) Plain back drop. (2) Cut border.
(3) Cut drop, netted. (4) Leg drop. (5) Also referred to as leg drop or leg.

196   The cut-drop in Figure 7–3c is often backed with bobbinet or scrim more for a lighting effect than for strength. The cut edges of a drop or border are better supported with a special lightweight net which has a 1-inch-square mesh. When the net is dyed to match the background it becomes nearly invisible.

THE CYCLORAMA

The largest single piece of scenery in the theatre is the cyclorama or "cyc." As the name implies, it encircles or partially encloses the scene to form the background. The cyclorama's most familiar use is as a sky or void backing a setting or elements of scenery placed in the foreground. Because the flat center of the cyclorama is blended into the sides with a gentle arc it cannot be made on rigid battens like the drop. It is kept soft by using dyed material which is fastened by the tielines to a curved top-and-bottom batten of pipe.

A cyclorama is not always a sky or void. Occasionally it is painted with a decorative or pictorial scene to fit a specific show. Sometimes, stage draperies are hung in the same position to form a drapery cyclorama.

The sky cyclorama presents the greatest problem in its necessity to create a large, uninterrupted, smooth surface. Because the "cyc" material, dyed or dye-painted canvas, is hung flat without fullness from a curved batten, the direction of the seams becomes important. If the seams are horizontal the tension on the seams draws the surface smooth, but the resulting strain distorts the shape of the curve as the seams turn the corner.

Vertical seams round the corners better than the horizontal seams, but they do not present as smooth a finished surface. In both cases the seams are sure to show under a high level of illumination. This can be corrected by hanging a large flat panel of dyed (very light blue) shark's-tooth scrim directly in front of the canvas cyclorama using the same

FIGURE 7–4. THE CYCLORAMA.   (1) Cyc backing, white vertical-seamed canvas. (2) Cyc face, shark's-tooth scrim dyed pale blue. (3) Bottom pipe, made of various curved sections that can be joined to match the contour of the top. (4) Top batten, a combination of shallow and deep curves to provide a variety of contours. (5) Spot-sheaves, spotted on gridiron over the general shape of the top batten. (6) Mulling blocks, a change-of-direction pulley to direct the lifelines towards the headblock. (7) Headblocks. (8), (9), (10) Some of the cyc contours achieved by selecting various curve combinations in the top batten. (11) A drapery cyc hung from the same top batten.

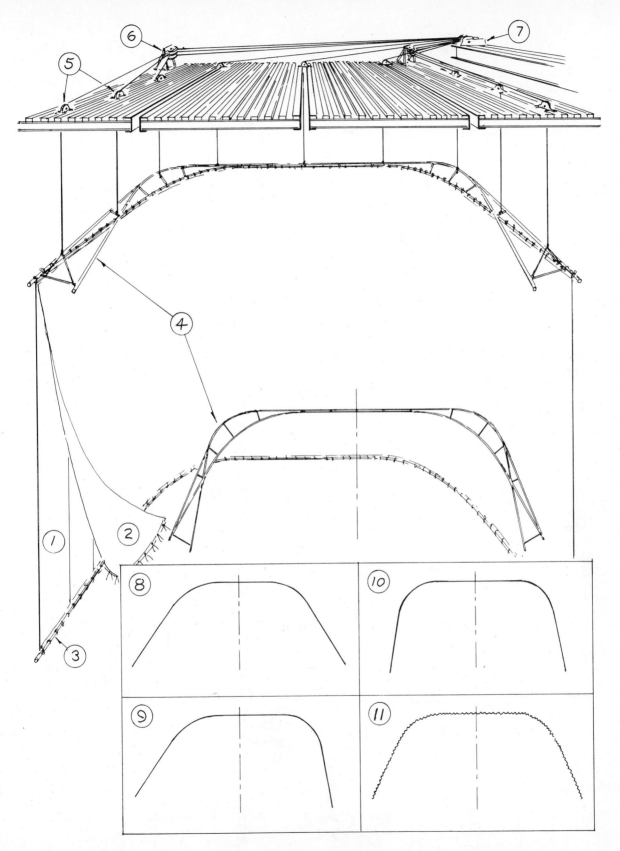

198 batten. Because it is a wide-width material the number of vertical seams can be reduced to two on the normal cyclorama. The scrim becomes the reflecting surface and the canvas acts as a backing (Figure 7–4).

FRAMED SCENERY

The structure of framed scenery is planned to support itself in a standing position. Although a framed piece may be aided by hanging support, or may be flown altogether, the basic framing principle remains the same. Framed scenery, as a construction technique, does not lend

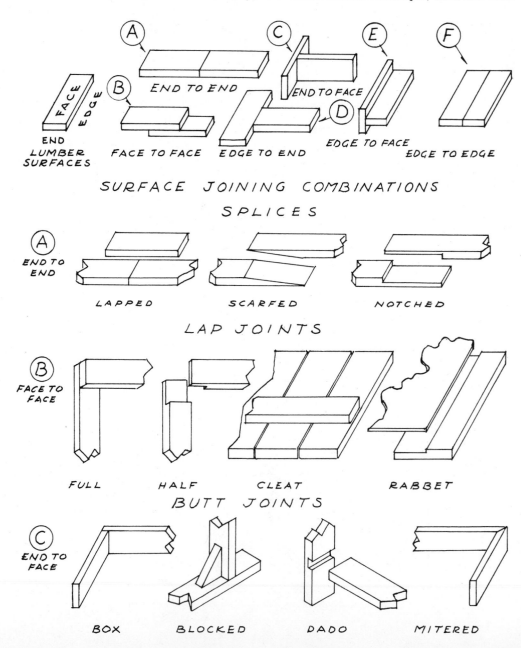

itself easily to the framing of a large area. It is possible to develop the framing for a large area, but to do this, it has to be hinged to fold into a smaller size or be dismantled into smaller parts to move in and out of the theatre. Most framing, then, deals with relatively small modules when compared to the large sizes of unframed scenery.

WOOD JOINTS

Scenery construction, although special in its framing techniques, employs the normal methods of joining wood. The various wood joints

FIGURE 7–5. Left and below. TYPICAL WOOD JOINTS USED IN SCENERY CONSTRUCTION.

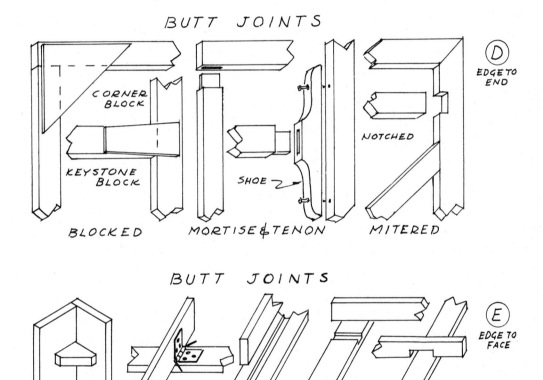

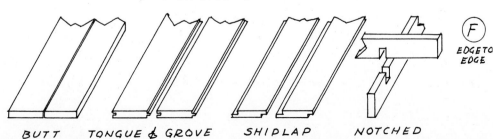

are derived from the many ways of combining lumber surfaces. The surfaces of lumber are described as its face (flat surface), edge, and end. The surface-joining combinations are classified as: end to end, face to face, end to face, edge to end, edge to face, and edge to edge.

The making of a joint has two steps: first, the cutting and fitting of the joint; second, the securing of the joint with hardware or glue. In scenery construction the joint is not always fixed but is many times temporarily secured or hinged. The fixed or permanent joint is used on standard-sized units of scenery, or smaller. The knockdown or temporary joints are used on oversized pieces that must be dismantled to get in and out of the theatre.

Figure 7–5 illustrates the numerous joints used in scenery construction classified in groups that combine the same surfaces. Fixed joints are secured with nails, clout nails (soft nails that clinch on the opposite side of the joint), screws, and glue. Knockdown or temporary joints are held with bolts, loose-pin hinges, keeper hooks, pegs, and turn buttons.

The framing of a simple flat illustrates the basic technique that is applied to any size or irregular shape (Figure 7–6). The area is enclosed with a lightweight frame of 1 by 3 white-pine lumber. The face of the lumber is kept flat in one plane causing edge-to-end butt joints at the corners. In this way, the wide surfaces of the framing boards are in position to support the canvas which is tacked to the inside edge of the outer frame and then pasted down. The end-to-edge joint is strengthened by one of two methods, or both. The joint can be mortised and tenoned with glue, or a simple butt joint reinforced with a ¼-inch three-ply plate or corner block. The mortise and tenon, although a stronger joint, takes longer to cut because it requires special power machinery or special attachments. It also reduces the amount of lumber that can be salvaged if the scenery undergoes remodeling. Unless the scenery is going to be subjected to excessive handling, the butt-joint keystone and corner-block method provides a simple, sturdy joint.

Toggle rails and diagonal braces are the internal members which function to strengthen and hold square the shape of the outside framing. If the flat has an opening, they also help to frame the opening. Any irregular shape involving profile edges or elaborate openings is framed in fundamentally the same manner (Figure 7–7).

THE FRAMED DROP

As mentioned earlier, it is possible to frame a large area of scenery. The framed drop and ceiling piece are examples of this technique. They use a droplike construction except that the battens are single instead

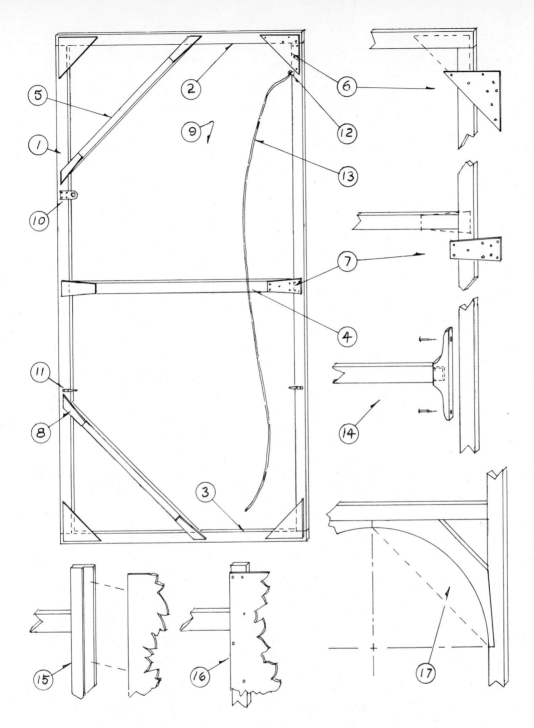

FIGURE 7–6. FRAMED SCENERY.   Basic framing techniques for the single unit of framed scenery, the flat. (1) Style, vertical member. (2) Top rail. (3) Bottom rail. (4) Toggle rail. (5) Brace. (6) Corner block. Note nailing pattern. (7) Keystone block. (8) Split-keystone block. (9) Canvas 8-ounce duck. (10) Brace cleat. (11) Lash cleat. (12) Lash-line eye. (13) Lash line. (14) Toggle rail and shoe. (15) Profile edge. Style rabbeted for profile board. (16) Profile edge. Cut profile board attached over style. (17) Method of setting curved sweep into flat. Note that the sweep butts to the toggle and is notched into the style. Sweep can be cut into any shaped curve.

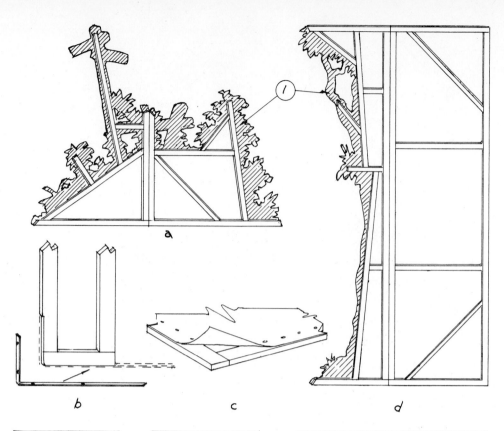

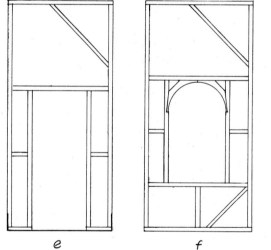

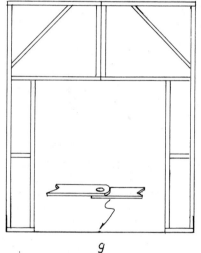

FIGURE 7–7. TYPES OF FRAMED SCENERY.   *(a)* The framing of a set-piece with profile edges of three ply (1). *(b)* Detail of sill iron used across the bottom of a door opening in a flat. *(c)* Detail of canvas-covering technique. Note that tacks or staples are set on the inside edge of the external frame work. The loose outside edge of canvas is then pasted to the flat surface of the frame. *(d)* Flat with profile edge. (1) Three ply. *(e)* Door flat. *(f)* Window flat. *(g)* Two-fold flat with double-door opening. Note hinged sill iron.

of double and therefore are made of heavier lumber stock (1 by 4 or 1⅛ by 4). The top and bottom battens are held apart by stretcher bars at about 6- to 8-foot intervals. They are bolted by means of ceiling plates to the battens. The loose ends of the drop are laced around the two end stretchers (Figure 7–8). A ceiling piece is made in the same manner, but will of course hang flat instead of vertically like the drop. Both the drop and ceiling fold and roll on their battens when the stretchers are removed.

DOORS

Doors and windows are those important details that are often neglected in the haste of preparing a set. A door, in a sense, is a moving piece of scenery that is used by the actor. In a split second, its malfunction can not only give away the scenic illusion but can also break the carefully built-up mood of a scene.

The building and hanging of a door is a skilled and time-consuming job. For these reasons, the average amateur group is better off to make or have made a set of good stock door casings that can be used in a variety of ways.

In the making of a door the normal scenery-framing techniques are often too lightweight. There was a time when the audience would accept a canvas door painted to look like oak planking but sounding and handling like a screen door. The modern audience, schooled by years of movie and television realism, is jarred by this obvious theatricality. There is a limit, however, to the weight of a door that can be supported in framed scenery which doesn't have the solidity of the stud framing or the masonry it is simulating. Hence it is necessary to reach a compromise in a construction technique that will keep the door portable and lightweight enough to shift while at the same time achieving a degree of solidity and sturdiness for the action.

A door unit is made up of three basic parts: (1) the actual door, sometimes called "shutter"; (2) the reveal, comprised of the jambs (vertical members), header (top), and sill (bottom); (3) the trim which forms the decorative frame around the door opening. The door is always hinged to the reveal. The trim, however, is constructed in one of two ways: it may be attached to the reveal, or it may be kept as a separate member and applied to the face of the flat. The first method, called a "cased door," is a complete unit. With the trim permanently attached to the reveal, the reveal of the cased door assembly slides through a prepared opening in the flat which is considerably larger than the size of the door itself (Figure 7–9a).

In the second method, referred to as a "scene door," the trim is not attached to the reveal which is built to the exact size of the flat open-

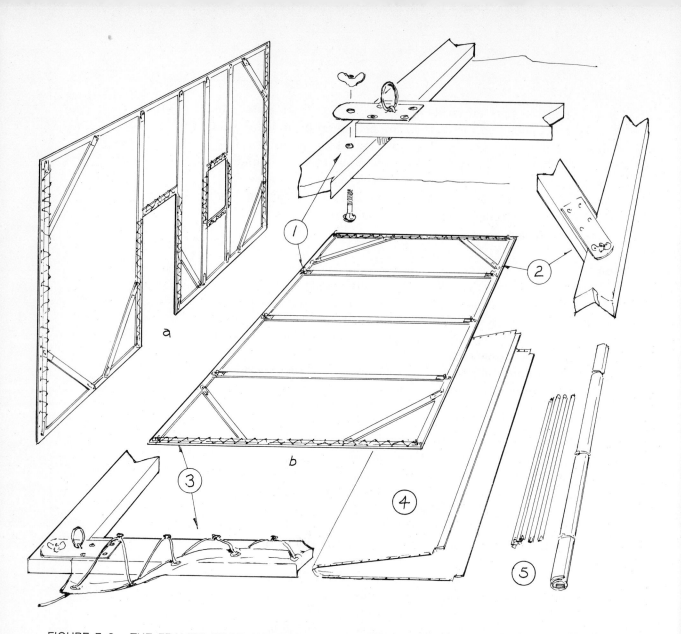

FIGURE 7–8. THE FRAMED DROP AND ROLL CEILING. Above. *(a)* Rear view of a framed drop. Notice how the canvas is laced around the ends and through the openings. The canvas is permanently attached to the top and bottom battens. The vertical stretchers and braces are removable. *(b)* Rear view of a roll ceiling which is very similar to the framed drop in construction. (1) Detail of ceiling plate on the end of the stretcher. The stretcher is bolted to the two battens. (2) Same technique used on the diagonal brace. (3) Detail of lacing. (4) To roll, stretchers are removed and battens are brought together, face to face. (5) Ceiling rolled on battens.

FIGURE 7–9. STOCK DOOR CONSTRUCTION. Opposite page *(a)* Cased-door unit: (1) Door reveal and trim built as one unit. (2) Flat with a standard door opening. (3) Detail of door construction. (4) Angled strap hinge on jamb to hold door unit in the opening. (5) Blocks to hold trim in place. (6) Cross section of door unit through the header. (7) Plan of the cased-door unit showing the hinging. (8) Butt hinge on door. *(b)* Scene-door unit: (1) Separate trim. (2) Flat with a standard door opening. (3) Door and reveal. (4) Corner blocks to hold reveal frame square. (5) Rim lock. Attached on back side of door. (6) Tubular latch. Sets into edge of door.

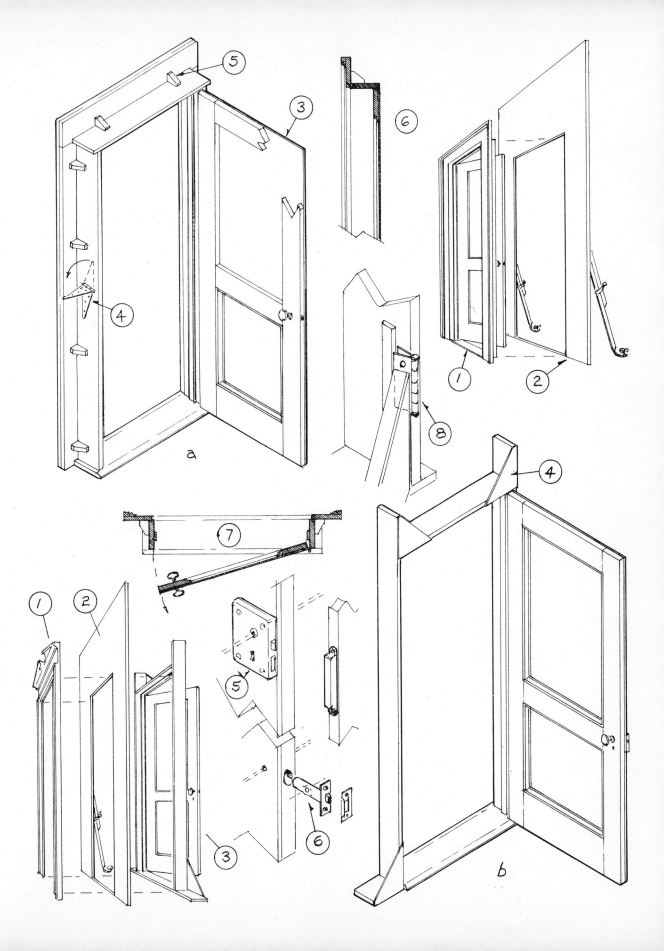

a

b

ing. The reveal, containing the shutter, "butt fits" to the opening from behind (Figure 7–9a). The scene door provides a great deal more flexibility in the ways the trim can be handled. It can, for example, be completely painted, or attached and set away from the opening to increase the apparent size of the doorway (Figure 7–10a).

The action of a door affects its construction. For example, a door that swings onstage requires double facing; a double-action door (kitchen door) takes special hinging as does a Dutch door; sliding doors involve tracking; and additional rigging becomes necessary for the trick door that, as if by magic, opens and closes by itself.

WINDOWS

Similar to the door, a window has a reveal and trim, but the window sash takes the place of the door. The arrangement of panes within the sash varies with the style of the window. Because the window sash is more open than a door, it is difficult to build. The pattern of the thin mullions often becomes too fragile for normal stage framing unless the window is far enough upstage to fake them in profile board. Delicate tracery is frequently reinforced by a backing of galvanized screening that passes for glass and strengthens the mullions at the same time. To simulate glass, panes are sometimes left clear or backed with netting. The net, although nearly invisible, has enough density to give the feeling of glass. It is more apparent by contrast if the window is opened during the action of the play.

Window action, like that of the door, involves sliding or swinging on hinges. A window may have the vertical sliding action of a double-hung window, or slide horizontally. It may have the vertical hinging of a casement window, or the horizontal hinging of the awning-type window.

It is a little more difficult to plan a set of stock windows than doors because of the greater variation in sash styles. Certain often-used conventionally styled windows can be standardized and put into stock. Also the casing (reveal and trim) may be kept in stock to be used with interchangeable or new sashes for each show (Figure 7–11).

TRIM

Decorative trim appears in a set in other places than around door and window openings. Some additional areas of trim, painted or practical, are baseboards, chair rails, wainscoting, cornices, and overmantel decoration. Trim that is attached in these areas must be removable so the flat scenery will fold easily.

The attached trim requires additional framing within the flat for

FIGURE 7–10. VARIATIONS IN DOOR TRIM AND PANELING.
(a) Various methods of handling the trim around the same-size
door opening, possible with a scene-door unit: (1) Wide-set trim.
(2) Close-set and high trim with transom. (3) Painted trim. *(b)* Door
paneling: The paneling of (2), (3), and (4) are all constructed within
the basic paneling of a stock door (1). (5) The flush side of a stock
door painted and cleated to look like a planked door.

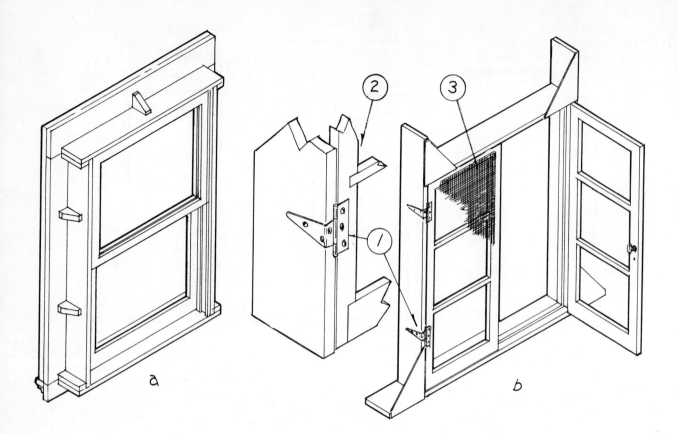

FIGURE 7–11. WINDOW CONSTRUCTION. *(a)* Double-hung window. Trim is attached to reveal in the same manner as the cased door. *(b)* Casement window. The reveal is constructed in the same way as the scene door with hinged sashes. (1) a bent T-strap hinge in place of the butt hinge. (2) *Notched* mullions. (3) Galvanized screening to strengthen the sash and simulate glass.

support. Chair rails and baseboards are easy to attach but the construction and hanging of a cornice is more complicated. Although trim details are slightly oversized for the stage the average cornice can be made up of stock moldings. To keep the framing lightweight, the molding is nailed to blocks set at about two-foot intervals and backed with 3-ply or longitudinal framing strips. The whole assembly is attached to the wall flats with bolts or turnbuttons (Figure 7–12).

THREE-DIMENSIONAL SCENERY

WEIGHT-BEARING STRUCTURES

Certain elements of scenery cannot be reduced to flat planes or, because they are so small, it is more practical to build them as a three-dimensional form. This is especially important if the form is to bear the weight of a sitting or standing actor. Weight-bearing structures are present in such architectural forms as steps, ramps, and raised levels; in the irregular forms of rocks; and in the free form of an abstract design. The raising of a large portion of the stage floor and the use of steps and ramps brings excitement to the design composition, variation to the staging, and headaches to the stage technician. In the absence of any mechanical means of raising sections of the stage floor, the problem becomes one of creating a second floor at a specific distance above

FIGURE 7–12. CORNICE CONSTRUCTION.   A cornice is a lightly framed three-dimensional element of trim designed to attach along the length of a wall. The perspective view shows the block-framing technique and a method of attaching the cornice to the scenery. (1) An elevation of the cornice showing the amount of overhang. (2) Stock crown molding. (3) Nailing block. (4) Three-ply face. (5) Linear support for blocks. (6) Bed molding, stock. (7) Carriage bolt. (8) 1 x 2 stiffener along the back of the blocks. (9) Added support at the top of the flats.

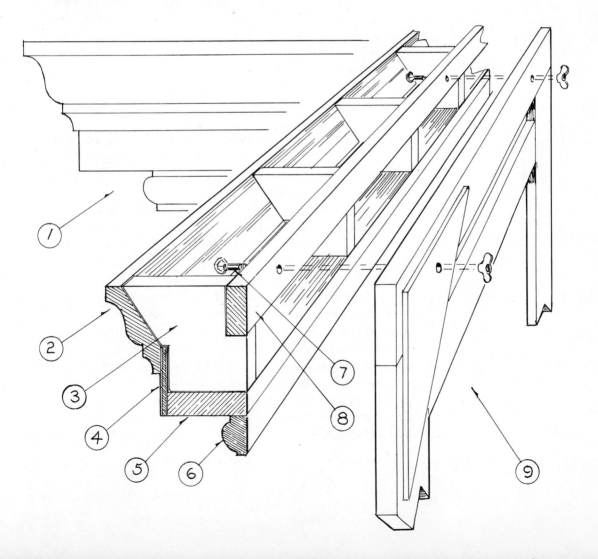

the stage floor. The level must be structurally sound enough to support actors and furniture with a minimum of deflection and, at the same time, be portable and economical. A large expanse of platforming is subdivided into smaller units for ease of handling. A single unit is made to knock down into even smaller parts.

The Parallel. The familiar way of providing a raised level for the stage is the parallel method. The parallel is a hinged trestle structure that opens to support a top and folds into a flat pack when not in use (Figure 7–13).

As a stock platforming method, the parallel has the advantage of being lightweight, easy to assemble and transport, and fairly sturdy. It also can be adapted to irregular shapes as well as to the conventional rectangle. Its chief disadvantage is a storage problem. To maintain any variation in levels, duplicate sets of parallels of different heights have to be kept in storage.

A convenient stock size for regular-shaped parallels depends upon first, general handling and storage conditions; second, the construction of the top; and last, the riser heights of stock steps which work with the platforms.

If the top is to be made of ¾-inch 5 ply, a 4-by-8-foot top is the most economical size. Planked tops, however, can be made smaller or larger without material waste if space permits the storage of larger parallels.

Stock parallel heights, obviously, should be at intervals related to riser heights of the steps, 6- or 7-inch intervals being normal. Parallel heights usually vary at double-riser intervals such as 12-, 24-, and 36-inch, or 14-, 28-, and 42-inch intervals.

There have been various attempts to standardize platforming construction with the aim first, to cut down the size of stored parts; second, to reduce the amount of internal framing (by using material other than wood) and at the same time to provide a sound structure. The post-and-rail and scaffolding methods (Figure 7–14) are ventures in this direction. Both succeed in reducing the storage space of spare parts and each provides a very sturdy platform with a minimum of framing. The techniques, although very practicable for regular shapes, do not lend themselves readily to irregular shapes. The limits placed upon design, however, are minor when compared to the stage-space and sightline limitations imposed by some theatre buildings.

Steel pipe and aluminum tubing have been used as platforming materials in two different methods. The first method involves the adaptation of construction scaffolding for stage uses. Each scaffold

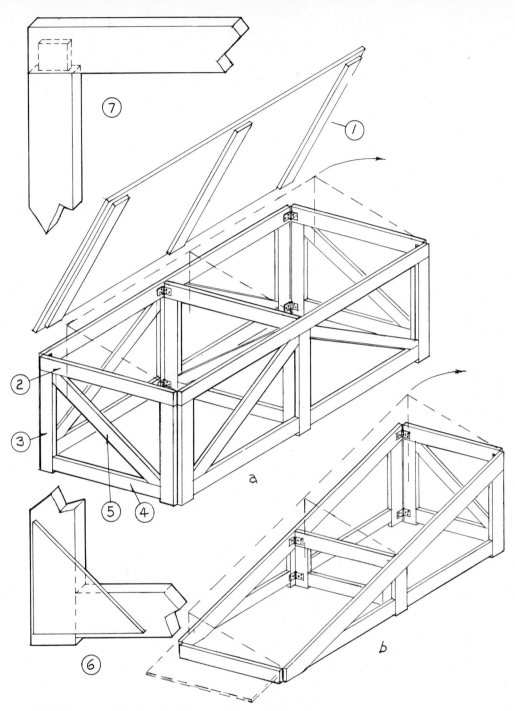

FIGURE 7–13. THE PARALLEL PLATFORM.   *(a)* Basic parallel construction with open-corner hinging. (1) Top ¾ inch 5-ply with cleats. Typical trestle framing includes (2) top rail bearing on (3) the post, tied by (4) the bottom rail, and strengthened by (5) the diagonal brace. The framing may be joined either by (6) corner blocks, or (7) by mortise and tenon joints. *(b)* The parallel technique used on a slanted platform or ramp.

unit is made out of aluminum tubing and at heights of 1 to 3 feet at 1-foot intervals. Figure 7–14c illustrates how the various heights of scaffolds interlock, or stack, one on top of the other. Each set has its own system of cross bracing.

A more recent use of pipe for platforming is in the parallel method (Figure 7–14d). The unique feature of the design is the making of the corner into its own hinge. The unit takes a 4-foot-square top which is overhung 1 inch to allow for a facing flat.

Other examples of steel in platform framing involves the use of manufactured shapes of structural steel. The shapes are designed to interlock and bolt together. Figure 7–15 illustrates the use of Unistrut channel, Telspar and Dexion slotted angle as platform. Dexion, with its slotted flat angles, offers ample surfaces for combining wood with steel in platform construction.

Regardless of whichever type of platforming is favored, the parallel method is, like the framing of a plane flat, an example of basic structural framing. With this basic knowledge the carpenter can modify or embellish the technique to fit his special needs.

Platform Construction. Any platforming technique can be resolved into its three structural members which are always present in some form or other; they are the top, rail, and post. The top, which is the actual bearing surface, is directly supported by the rails. Crossrails run parallel to the shortest dimension of the level. Their interval is linked to the material and thickness of the top. The average top, made of 1 by 6 tongue-and-groove planking or ¾-inch 5-ply board, should be supported at 30-inch intervals. The span, however, can be increased by use of cleats or stiffeners on the underside and thereby, in effect, increasing the thickness of the top material.

FIGURE 7–14. OTHER PLATFORMING TECHNIQUES. *(a)* Post-and-rail method which knocks down into individual 2 x 3 units. *(b)* Detail of post-and-rail corner bolting. *(c)* Scaffold method. (1) Tubular steel or aluminum scaffold unit. (2) Spacer to interlock units. (3) Foot. (4) Cross braces to space and stabilize scaffold units. (5) The stacking of one scaffold unit upon another to gain height. *(d)* Steel parallel method. A smaller moduled tubular steel and angle iron-framed parallel. (1) Top overhangs unit to allow for facing flat. (2) Spacer to interlock and stack units. (3) Corners become hinges. (4) Pin attached to top to lock it in place. (5) Internal pin of hinge corner made up of (6) and (7). (6) Opened-end trestle. (7) Closed-end trestle. (8) Foot. (9) Extended foot.

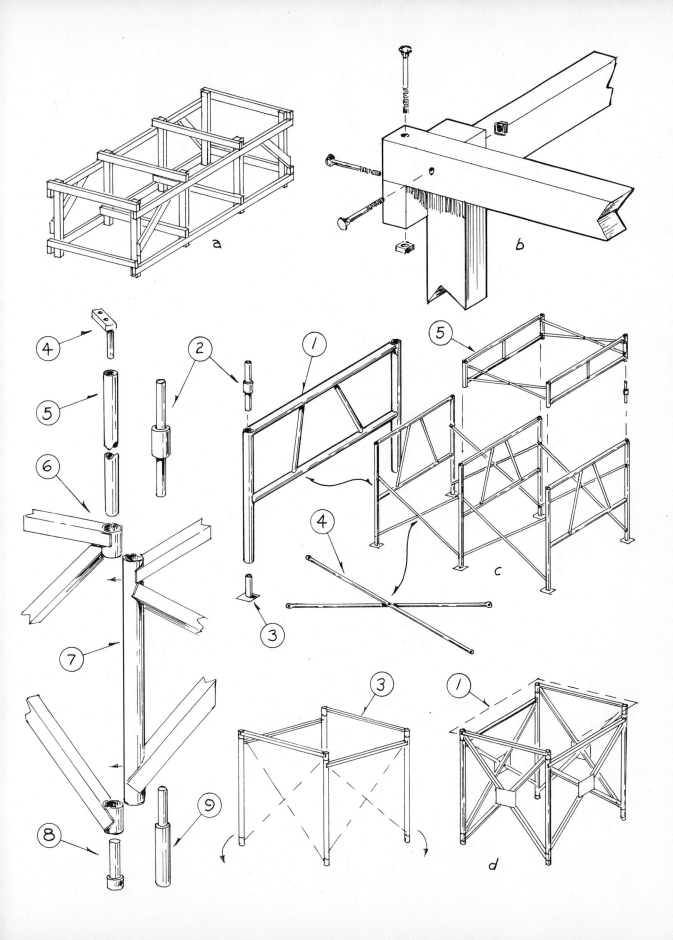

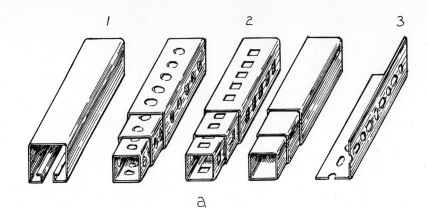

FIGURE 7–15. PLATFORMING TECHNIQUES USING PREFORMED STEEL.
(a) Commercial performed steei shapes. (1) Unistrut channel. (2) Three
types of *Telspar*, a telescoping square pipe shape manufactured by
Unistrut Corporation. (3) *Dexion,* a slotted angle iron also made in bar
and channel shapes. *(b)* A corner view of a platforming technique using
Unistrut channel as the basic corner post. Longer extensions of optional
lengths are attached with stock Unistrut fittings and cross bracing. *(c)*
Slotted angle framing with a basic post of slotted channel. Iron pipe is
used as the extension. *(d)* Slotted angle framing with a slotted channel or
Telspar basic post. The extension is Telspar. (Drawing after designs by
Philip Eck and Ned Bowman)

The rail is, in turn, supported by the post. The interval of posting is dependent upon the size of the rail. A 1 by 3 rail (on edge) should be posted at not more than three-foot intervals and at four-foot intervals for a 1 x 4 rail.

The framing of a single trestle or "gate" of a parallel employs the post-and-rail technique. In Figure 7–13a note that the top rail is borne by the two vertical members, or posts, which carry through to the

FIGURE 7–16. THE IRREGULAR-SHAPED PLATFORM. *(a)* the hinging and assembly of an irregular-shaped platform are solved individually. *(b)* To fold: (1) loose-pin-hinged internal trestle is detached after top (2) has been removed. (3) By unpinning the hinges of one corner, the parallel will fold into a flat pack. *(c)* The use of a "spanner" allows the removal of internal trestles in cases where it is necessary to keep the area under the top clear. (1) Spanner is of heavy enough stock, usually 2 x 4 or 2 x 6, to make strong span. (2) Detail of keeper-hook on end of spanner.

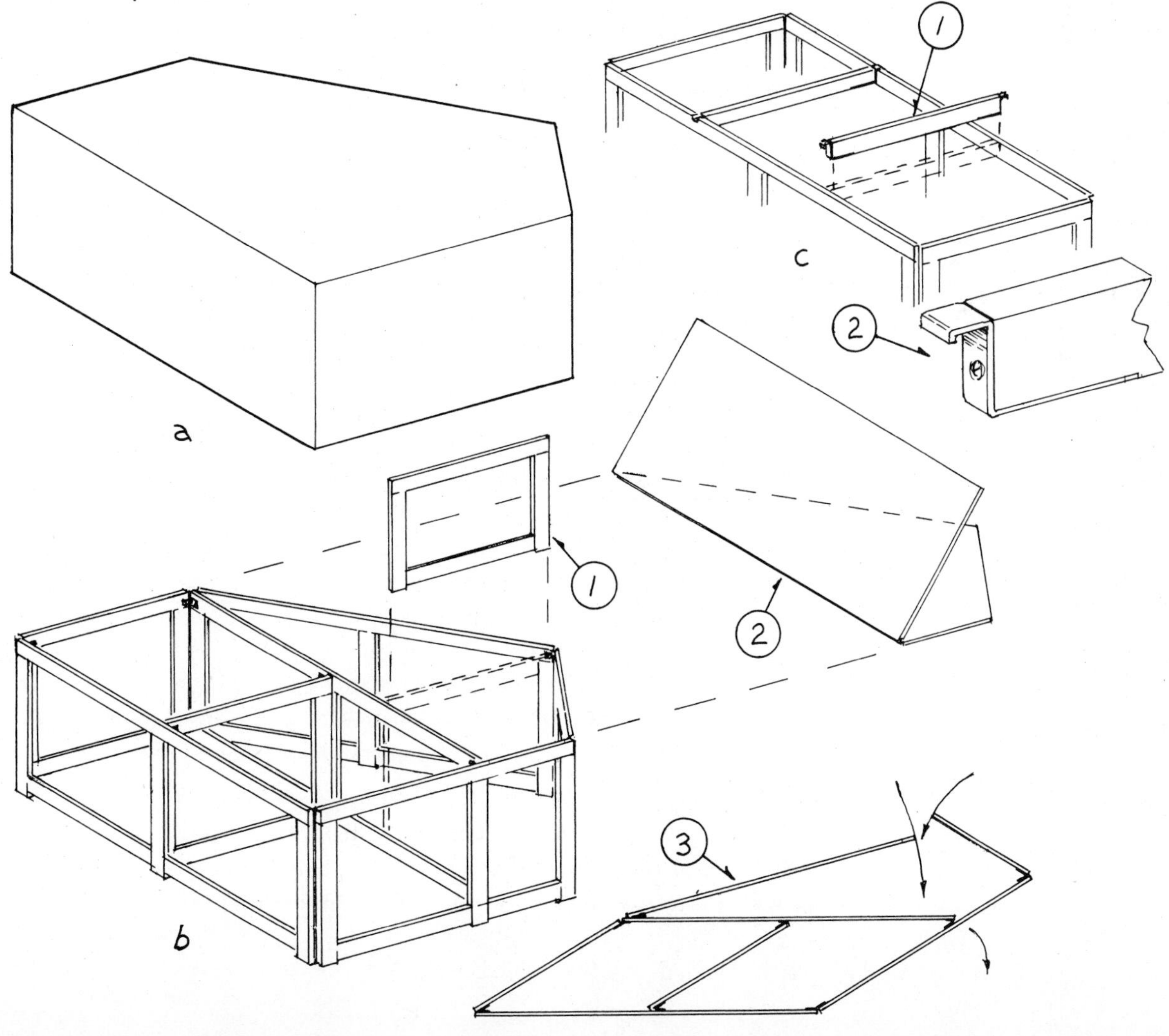

floor. The bottom rail is merely a tie-rail that completes the rectangle. The diagonals are necessary to hold the gate square and eliminate side sway or "rack" in the finished platform. The single gate, though light-weight, gathers strength when it is hinged to the other members of the parallel. The parallel to fold flat must hinge as shown.

Any irregular shape that can be reduced to flat planes may be constructed by the parallel method. The gates can be loose-pin-hinged together rather than folding, for many times the pattern of the supports is so irregular the parallel cannot fold flat (Figure 7–16).

Free Forms. The irregular surfaces that cannot be reduced to a series of flat planes have to be constructed as a three-dimensional unit. Rock pieces and abstract forms that have to bear weight are examples of this type of irregular surface.

The framing of an irregular surface is, of course, more or less extemporaneous and dependent upon some final sculptural touches by the designer to complete the form. For this reason the design drawings of a free-form should be accompanied with a scaled model. The form usually suggests the manner of construction, nevertheless there is a basic method that can be adapted to most irregular shapes.

The method of construction of a rock piece demonstrated in Figure 7–17 goes through the following steps: (1) The exact shape of the base of the rock is framed in the conventional flat-scenery technique. (2) Across the shortest dimension of the base is set a series of contour pieces that follow the contour of a section taken at that point (see Sections, Chapter 5). (3) The contour pieces are stiffened with cross-bracing and all bearing surfaces are reinforced. (4) Over the contour pieces is placed 1-inch chicken wire or ½-inch screen wire, which is pinched or stretched in the desired shape. (5) The final surface is applied to the screen wire. The kind of covering material depends upon the nature of the texture that is desired. The best results are usually obtained with burlap. It is applied by first dipping it into a mixture of strong glue size and base color. The burlap is then draped over and tacked to the framework, and allowed to harden. A form made in this manner is lightweight, inexpensive, and surprisingly sturdy.

A harder exterior surface is sometimes built up by using asbestos pulp applied on a ¼-inch wire-screening undersurface.

Ramps. The parallel as a platforming technique can also be adapted to a ramped surface (Figure 7–13b). The side trestles are built to the angle of the incline. Gates of varying heights connect the outside trestles and are hinged to fold like a regular parallel.

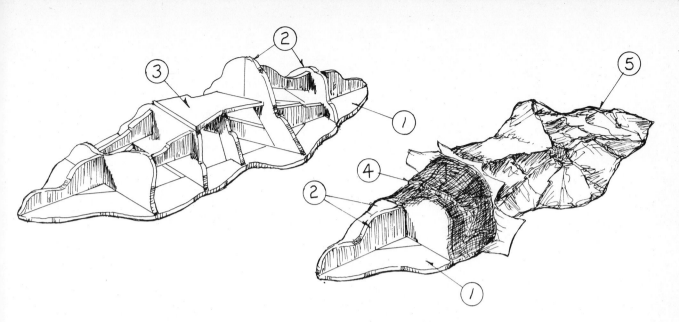

Steps.   Whereas the ramp is a gradual change of level, the step is more direct, dividing the change into a series of intermediate levels. A flight of steps is made up of risers and treads. The tread is the bearing surface and the riser is the interval of change in level. The rule of thumb guiding the size relationship of the tread to the riser is based upon the ease of movement up and down the steps. The sum of the

FIGURE 7–17. CONSTRUCTION OF ROCK FORMS.   Opposite page. (1) Shape of form on floor. Conventional framing. Above. (2) Contour pieces. (3) Cross bracing. (4) Wire screening. (5) Burlap.   Photo below: *(a)* Three dimensional shape before covering with burlap. *(b)* Same shape covered.

riser and tread in a continuous flight of steps is kept about eighteen inches. Hence a 6-inch riser would require a 12-inch tread; an 8-inch riser a 10-inch tread and so forth. Obviously the low-riser and wide-tread combination is more desirable for the onstage steps, permitting the actor to move easily and gracefully up and down.

A flight of steps can be built for the stage in one of two ways. One method is a modified platform trestle construction with each tread supported by a complicated post-and-rail framework (Figure 7–16a). This way the steps are a part of a bulky three-dimensional platform which is difficult to store and move.

Steps can be made to knock down into more easily handled parts by the use of the carriage method of construction (Figure 7–19b). The pattern of the riser and tread is cut from a wide board running parallel to a line drawn through the nosing of each step. The nosing is at the intersection of the top of the riser and the outside edge of the tread.

A carriage is cut from a wide enough board to retain at least three inch of uncut board along the bottom edge. The thickness of a carriage depends somewhat on its unsupported length. Frequently 1⅛-pine stock is used, chiefly for its lightness as well as strength. Sometimes 1-inch pine stock is substituted for lightweight construction while 2-inch stock is used for a heavier structure.

The choice of carriage stock is also affected by the nature of the riser material. Is the riser made of 1-inch pine or ¼-inch three ply, or is it left open? As the riser material becomes lighter, the carriage stock should increase in thickness.

A flight of steps would have, of course, two carriages. Additional carriages would depend upon the thickness of the tread and the width of the steps. For example, a tread ¾ inch thick would need a carriage every 30 inches of width.

The lower step of the carriage sits on the floor and the top step rests on a prepared cleat fastened on the front of a platform, thus eliminating the need of a post underneath. The steps, or carriage unit, can be lifted off the cleat to be handled and stored separately.

The facing of stairs (also levels) is a separate piece of scenery attached to the downstage edge of the step or platform. The facing of a stair is a more complicated unit because it includes the stair rail, balusters, stringer, and newel post (Figure 7–19e). The stringer, which

FIGURE 7–18. STEEL STAIRCASE.   Welded structural square-tube framing, I-beam carriage, and plexiglass treads. The unit was moved on air-bearing casters.   (Photo—Kewley)

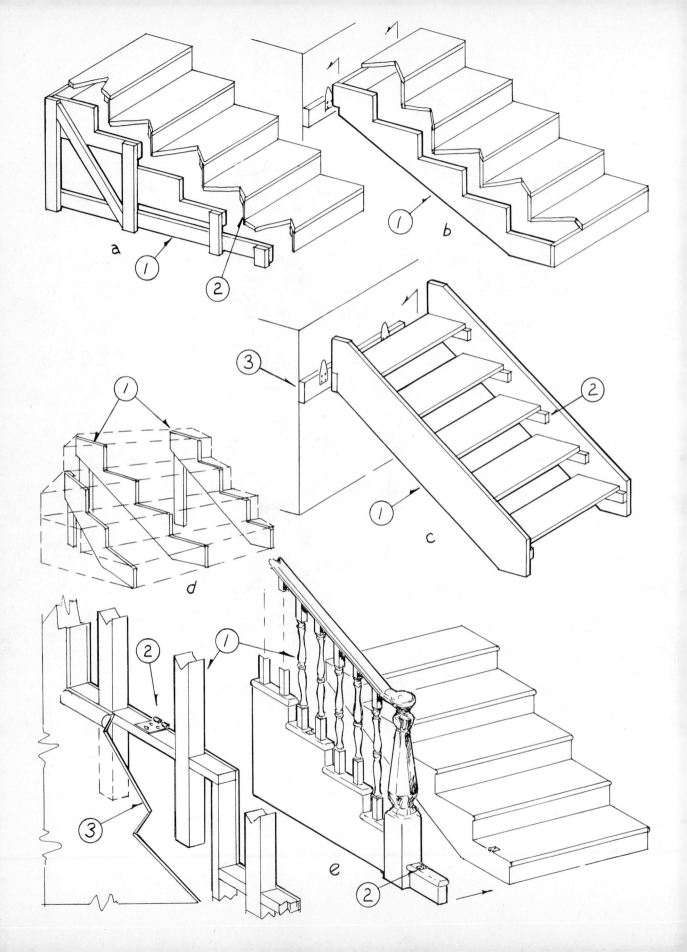

FIGURE 7–19. STAIR CONSTRUCTION TECHNIQUES. *(a)* Trestle method. (1) Trestle with the top edge framed to riser-tread pattern. (2) Three ply used as riser stock. *(b)* Cut-carriage method. (1) Carriage cut to riser tread pattern. Step unit leans on platform for support. *(c)* Closed-carriage method. (1) Closed carriage can only be used on the outside of stair unit. Hence this type of construction limits the width of the stairs. (2) Cleat to hold tread. Note that no riser is used. *(d)* Cut-carriage method used on an irregular-shaped flight of steps. (1) Carriages with same riser height but varying tread dimensions. *(e)* Stair facing, framed out of 1⅛ inch-baluster stock (1) which is pin-hinged to steps (2). If both faces are covered with 3 ply (3), the facing unit becomes reversible with minimum alterations.

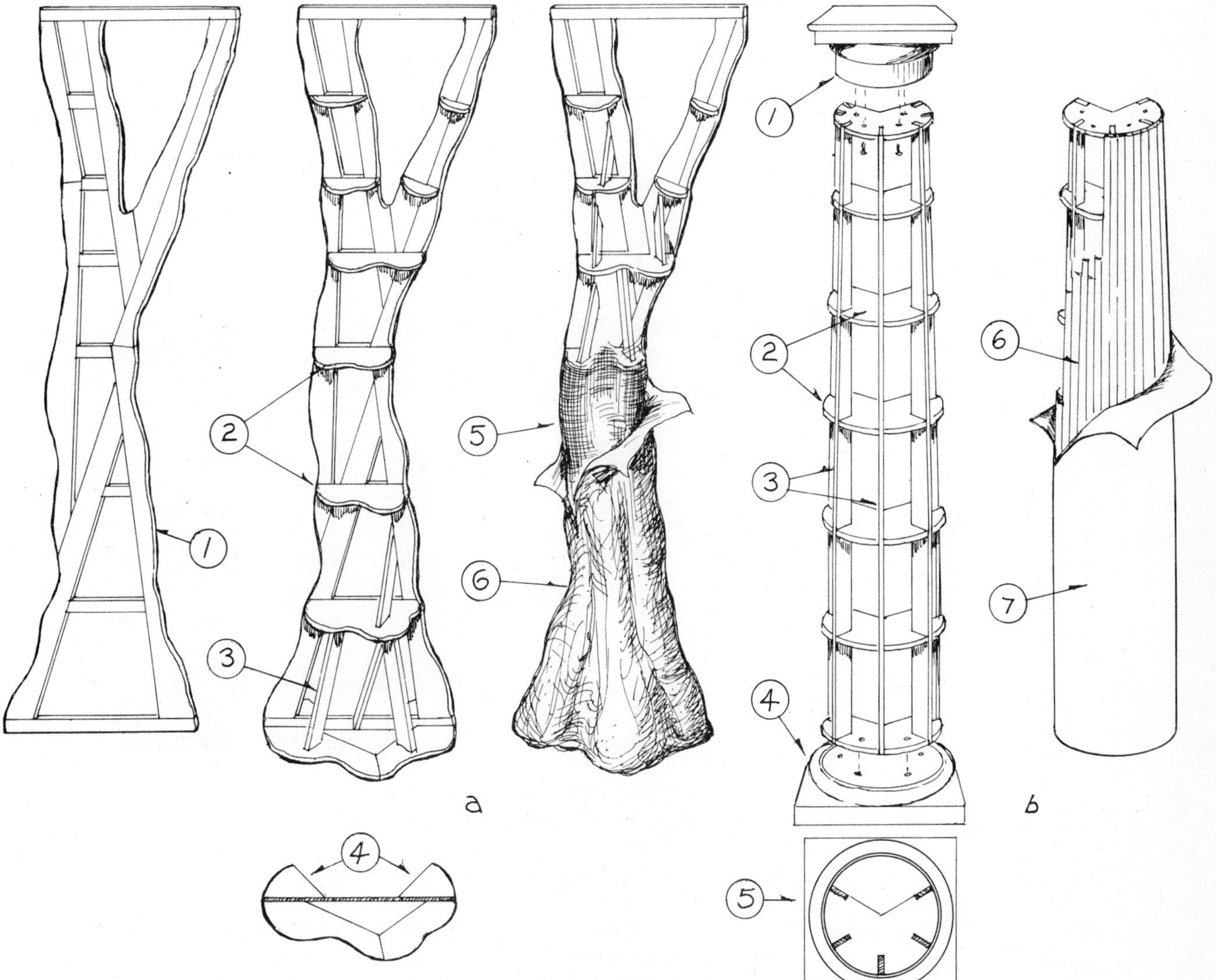

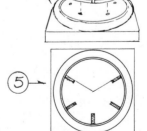

a

b

FIGURE 7–20. COLUMNS AND TREE TRUNKS. *(a)* Construction of a tree trunk. (1) Framing of basic silhouette. (2) Contour pieces set at intervals. (3) Cross bracing. (4) Pie-shaped contours to fill out base of tree where it meets the floor. (5) Wire-screening or chicken wire. (6) Burlap. *(b)* Stock column construction. (1) Removable cap. (2) Contour pieces. (3) Vertical stiffeners. (4) Removable base. (5) Top view showing stiffener spacing. (6) Lattice slats. (7) Canvas cover.

FIGURE 7–21. THREE-DIMENSIONAL SURFACE.   Shown are the steps in the construction of a highly textured surface such as a stone wall. (1) Hard undersurface, either ⅛ ply wood, upson board, or double-faced corrugated cardboard, shellacked to reduce warpage. (2) Surface is diagramed into areas representing the shape of each stone. Cutout appliques of corrugated board are helpful in reaching a desirable composition. (3) Each stone surface is built up with glue-soaked newspaper or rough-hewn Styrofoam. (4) Individual stone is covered with a square of cheese cloth to give it its final form. (5) After the covering has dried, the entire surface is covered with a thick coat of texture paint and then painted.

parallels the carriage, supports the bottom ends of the balusters. It can be an "open stringer," revealing the tread and risers, or it may be a "closed stringer," masking the ends of the steps with an uncut surface.

The railing completes the stair facing. It spaces the top ends of the balusters while being supported by them. The whole assembly of the stair-facing flat and steps must be kept to a practical size or it can become too large to handle.

NONWEIGHT-BEARING STRUCTURES

Columns, tree trunks, and any other objects that have to have dimension but do not bear weight form the last type of scenery. Since the structure need only be strong enough to hold its shape, the framing is lightweight in comparison to weight-bearing structures.

An irregular shape is built in three dimensions by the use of two structural elements: the basic silhouette of the object and numerous contour pieces. In a tree trunk, for example, the basic silhouette is the vertical outline of the trunk and branches. The contour pieces are spaced at intervals perpendicular to the silhouette frame. After sufficient bracing and stiffening, the form of the trunk is rounded into shape by attaching chicken wire or wire screening over the contour pieces (Figure 7–20). The chicken wire is covered with burlap or canvas for the finished surface.

In a rock, the basic silhouette is horizontal and the contour pieces are vertical which, as has been mentioned, can become structural if the rock has to bear weight.

Columns are a regular shape and lend themselves to a slightly different construction method. It is not necessary to use a silhouette piece. The circular or semicircular contour pieces can either be attached to a central core or be held at intervals by slats on the outer surface (Figure 7–20a).

The exterior surface of the column can be handled in two different ways. The surface can be made up of thin vertical slats (best for a column with a taper or entasis) that are covered with canvas after all of the slats have been rounded with a plane or rasp.

The column can also be covered with a flexible paperlike ⅛-inch EZ curve, or for a temporary column, heavy building paper can be used. When a light exterior covering is used, the amount of bracing between contour pieces has to be increased to stiffen the column.

TEXTURED AND SCULPTURED SURFACES

The designer has always been fascinated by a deeply textured surface. It reacts well under stage lights and gives the scenery a feeling of authenticity and stability. A deeply textured surface like the

FIGURE 7–22. CARVED AND
TURNED RIGID FOAM. Below.
left: Turned rigid urethane foam,
left, baluster with wooden core;
right, turned finial. Right: Relief
carving, Styrofoam, sealed with
flexible glue, finished with casein
paint.

FIGURE 7–22 (cont'd).
Opposite page: Sculptured
Styrofoam and mulched wood
imbedded in polyurethane foam
with welded iron cyclone fencing.
Oedipus Rex by Stravinsky-
Cocteau. Final ritual masks were
each nine to twelve feet high.
The set measured fifty-four feet
at the highest point.   Designer
—John Ezell.

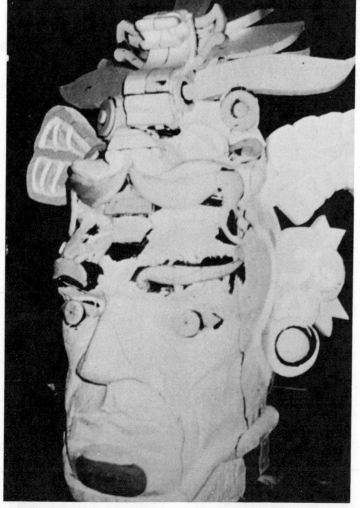

FIGURE 7–22 (cont'd).
Carved low-density Styrofoam.
Over-sized Aztec sculpture for a
Latin American version of
Shakespeare's *Julius Caesar*,
Guthrie Theatre. Left: Blocks of
Styrofoam glued together with
Dow mastic to form a solid
head. Above: Consoles sculpted
with hot wire and applied to the
hollow base that will support
the head. Both head and base
were sealed with flexible glue and
then covered with five coats of
fiberglass, resin, and matte.

stone wall in Figure 7–21 is usually accomplished by using the laborious technique of applied papier-maché. New plastic foams and forming techniques have made it easier to texture a surface or create sculptural relief and architectural details, as well as many three-dimensional forms.

RIGID FOAMS

The demand for greater perfection in the design and construction of decorative details on both properties and small elements of scenery, growing out of the intimacy of the thrust and arena theatres, has helped to uncover easier methods of simulating a sculpture form. The closeness to the audience, the increased amount of handling, and the change of design focus from scenic background to set properties are the basic influencing factors of the new theatre forms.

Styrofoam, the trade name of Dow Chemical's low-density rigid polystyrene foam (RPF), has been used successfully as a lightweight material that is easy to carve into three-dimensional details or textured surfaces. Blocks of Styrofoam can be glued together or to a scenery surface for convenient carving.

Regular Styrofoam is low density and therefore very porous. This limits detailed carving and reduces its strength. *Urethane* is a high-density, rigid foam (RUF) that, because of its high density, is easier to carve in detail or turn on a lathe. It also has greater strength than a low-density foam. Sections of RUF can be glued together around a wood core for even greater strength. Hyde glue works best if the special Dow Chemical adhesive, Dowmastic No. 11, is not available.

Sculpture surfaces can be primed with casein paint or flexible glue and then finished with scenery paint. For an extremely hard finish the surface can be coated with a mixture of fiberglass resin and hardener in about five to one proportions. Further uses and techniques can be seen in Chapter 11.

Both foams, of course, are very lightweight and many times have to be counterweighted or attached to heavier units of scenery to maintain the proper esthetics. Nothing is more disconcerting than to see a supposedly quarter-ton Greek statue bounce like a ping-pong ball if accidentally knocked over.

FOAM CASTING

If a sculptural element recurs several times on a set it is often better to prepare a mold and cast the detail to insure a matching likeness. The "Arothane system" is a method of casting foam into a negative mold. The system brings together two chemicals that produce a rigid foam of considerable strength and stability.

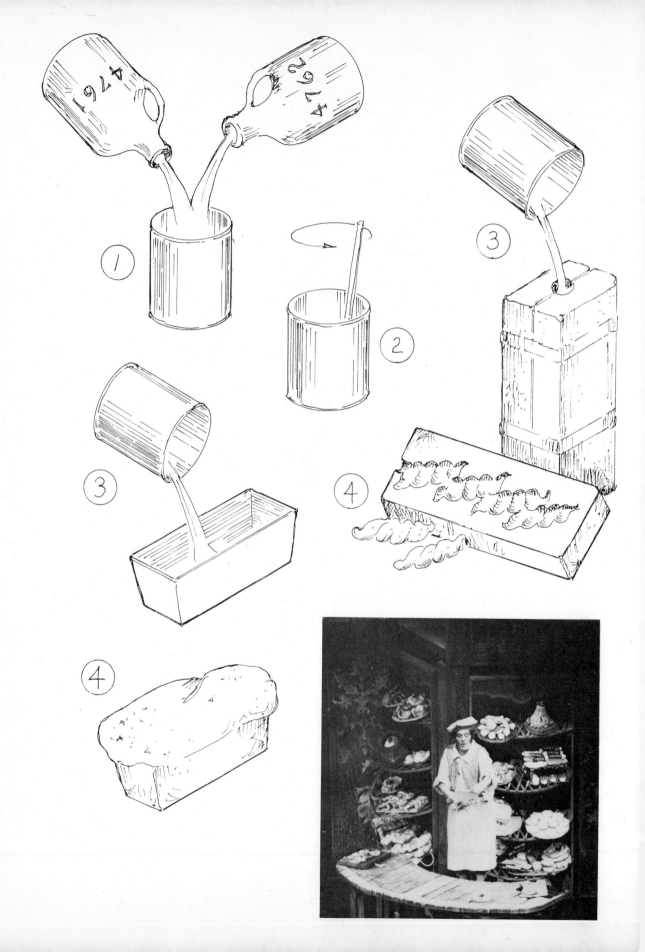

FIGURE 7–23. FOAM CASTING. Demonstrating one of the many forms plastic foam casting can take. Drawings show the steps taken to duplicate various forms of bakery goods. (1) Mixing Foamart plastic foam No. 4761 with foaming agent No. 4762 to produce a light-weight rigid foam. (2) Mixture is stirred vigorously for thirty seconds. (3) Mixture is poured in molds prepared with a parting agency such as wax or Foamart No. 7, mold release. (4) After the liquid foams and expands into the mold (about 20 minutes) the castings are removed from the mold. With the excess foam cut away, the form is ready for painting. Photo: bakery shop full of foam cast bakery goods. *Cyrano de Bergerac*, Guthrie Theatre. Designer—John Jenson. (Photo—Kewley)

The chemicals are described by their manufacturer, ADM Chemicals, as, first, Arothane 8760-A, a "quasi-prepolymer" used at one to one ratio by weight with Arothane 8764-B, a resin-catalyst material to produce a rigid polyurethane foam. A similar foam product called Foam Art is sold by Adhesive Products Corporation. It brings together two chemicals, 4761 and 4762 in equal proportions by weight to produce a urethane foam suitable for casting. The density of the foam can be varied by altering, to the manufacturer's instructions, the two chemicals in the mixture.

Both foam casting products are prepared in the same manner. The chemicals are mixed in a disposable container such as a No. 10 can, beaten with a high-speed mixer for about forty seconds, then poured into a hollow mold the surface of which has been sealed with shellac and coated with wax or paraffin which also functions as a parting agent.

As the chemical action is toxic, precautions should be taken to insure proper ventilation and protection of hands. Acetone is a solvent before the foam sets-up, and the skin should be washed with soap and water immediately after contact.

FOAM TEXTURE

Polyurethane foam when applied under pressure hardens into an interesting deep-textured surface. Two chemicals are brought together under pressure inside a spray gun and mixed in the air as they are shot onto a surface where the mixture foams into a bubbly texture in a matter of seconds. To control the chemical proportions that establish the density of the foam requires a high-compression tank; specific spray gun and nozzles (two hoses); and the necessary valves and gauges to vary the quantity of chemical from each tank. It is easier to use *Insta-Foam*, a trade name for aerosol urethane foam in a disposable kit form.

Insta-Foam, manufactured by Insta-Foam Products, Inc. is sold in a variety of mixtures for specific commercial uses and construction techniques. The Insta-Foam *Froth-Pak* in the Standard Foam mixture is ideal for the textured surface just described. The kit consists of two aerosol tanks of chemicals; two hoses to a mixing spray gun; and a variety of nozzles. The several nozzles not only give a selection of distribution (fan to round), but are also expendable. The nozzles clog with hardened foam very easily if work is stopped for any length of time, and have to be replaced. The chemical content of the two tanks is Polymeric Isocyanates in the first and Polyops with Amines and Fluorocarbons in the second.

The mixing process is toxic and should be performed only in a well-ventilated room. Prolonged breathing of the vapors or spray mist should be avoided. The empty tanks should be vented; the valves removed, with caution; and the chemicals drained. An unvented aerosol tank can be dangerous if handled unknowingly by someone else or if stored carelessly near heat (over 120° F). Safe storage for full tanks is 60° to 80° F.

Insta-Foam, although developed for the building trades, is adaptable for stage use. It will adhere firmly to any surface except polyethylene, a transparent filmlike plastic called Vis-Queen, which, incidentally, can be used as a parting agent or separator between units of scenery. The foam, after it has hardened, can be painted with dye or scene paint. For added texture, materials or objects can be imbedded and held by the foam. The hardened foam is quite durable. It compares in density and hardness to high-density rigid urethane foam. It will withstand normal handling on the stage but would have to be handled with care were it to go on tour.

FIGURE 7–24. FOAM TEXTURE. The Insta-Foam texturing process. Below, left: Froth-Pak tanks and surface ready for spraying; articles to be imbedded are in place on the scenery surface. Right: Mixing nozzles and foam spray in action. Opposite page, top left: Detail of texture. Top right: Finished unit ready for painting. Bottom: Foam texture and welded metal sculpture, *The Song of the Lusitanian Bogey* by Peter Weiss. Designer—Dennis McCarthy.

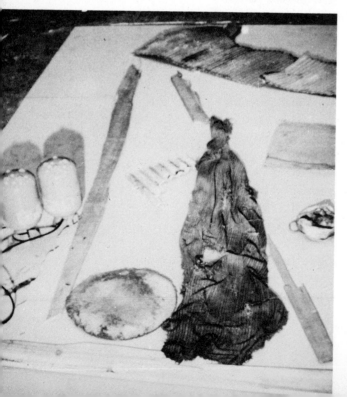

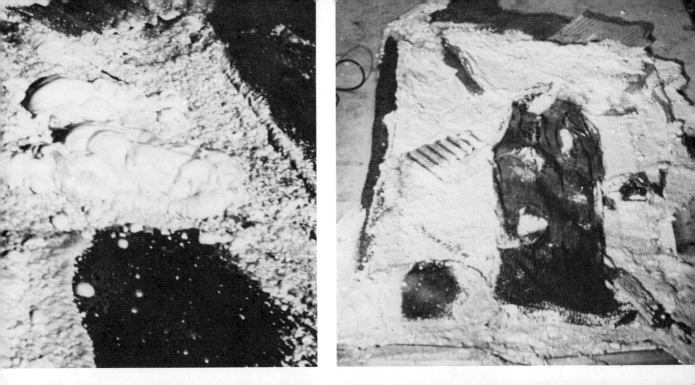

FIGURE 7–25. FOAM TEXTURED SCENERY.   Except for some
architectural fragments the entire set was covered with a foam
texture, with bits of mirror, straw, and other bits of rubbish embedded
in the surface. *The Devils* by Whiting.   (Photo—Nelson)

THERMOPLASTICS

Another method for the shaping of three-dimensional details, such as arabesques, props, masks, armorplate, or the duplication of real objects, is the vacuum forming of sheet plastic. Formerly a manufacturing technique that was out of reach of the average scenery shop, it is fast becoming an important construction method for those hard-to-execute details. Thanks to the detailed research by Nicholas L. Bryson on thermoplastic scenery (see Additional Reading on Technical Production) the trial and error approach has been taken out of the process.

The chemical structure of a thermoplastic is such that when heated it loses its rigid state and becomes ductile. While it is in this pliant condition it can be reshaped or stretched over a positive (or negative) mold, then allowed to cool and return to a hardened state. The fact that a true thermoplastic can be reheated and reshaped without a discernible change in its physical properties makes it economically feasible for theatre use.

Of the many thermoplastics available there are three that seem best suited for use in the theatre. This usage requires that they be opaque, translucent, or transparent; have a selection of color or take paint and dyes; be noncombustible; and be strong enough to withstand normal handling onstage and the mechanics of fastening (nailing, stapling, and so on). The three thermoplastics meeting these requirements are high-impact polystyrene, low-density polyethylene, and cellulose acetate. The working thickness need not be greater than .040″ (40 thousandths of an inch); it depends on how rigid or flexible the final form is meant to be.

High-Impact Polystyrene, as the name implies, has a high impact strength; great flexibility for intricate forming; a wide range of colors; and is obtainable in opaque or translucent sheets.

Low-Density Polyethylene is also tough and flexible. It is normally milky-white (no colors) and opaque, but turns translucent when heated and formed.

Cellulose Acetate is a well-known plastic with excellent forming characteristics. It is also very sturdy with the distinct difference of being completely transparent.

VACUUM FORMING

The heated thermoplastic sheet, in order to take an accurate impression copy of the mold, must be tightly drawn or sucked by a

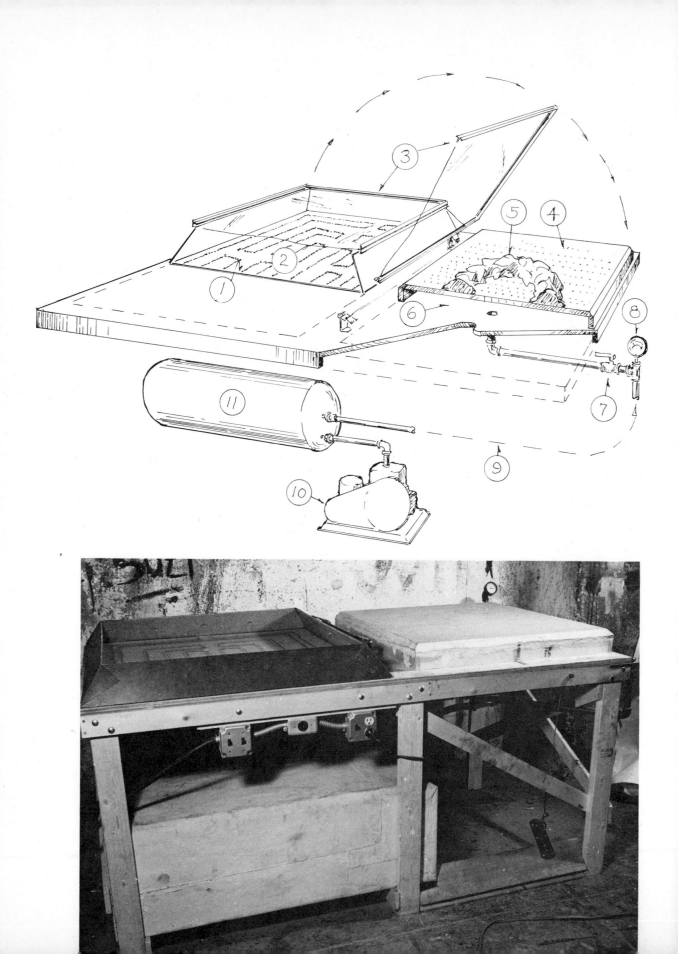

FIGURE 7–26. THERMOPLASTICS.   Above: The cut-away drawing of a vacuum-forming machine suitable for a scenery shop. (1) The oven has slanted metal sides with asbestos lining. The floor of the oven is covered with a pattern of coiled resistor wire forming a heating element. (2) Plastic sheet in angle-iron frame. (3) Frame is hinged to swing off of the oven and onto the mold and forming table when the plastic sheet is ductile. (4) Forming table. Floor is pierced with one-eighth-inch holes spaced at one-inch intervals to vent the vacuum chamber underneath. (5) Mold. (6) Vacuum chamber. (7) Bleed valve; can be rigged for pedal action. (8) Gauge reading inches of mercury. (9) Air hose or pipe to reservoir tank. (10) Vacuum pump. (11) Reservoir tank. Below: Photograph of a vacuum-forming machine suitable for piecework and original designing but not mass production. Note that the reservoir tank is made of wood. It is reinforced internally to resist pressure or sealed on the outside with canvas, flexible glue, polyethelene, mastic, and enamel paint. (Constructed, after designs by N. L. Bryson, by Les Zellan.)

vacuum around the form. The process is called vacuum forming. The basic steps of vacuum forming are: (1) Heat the plastic sheet uniformly to the temperature that renders it flexible (750–1000° F). (2) Transfer it quickly to a forming table where it is stretched over the mold and its edges clamped to the table in an airtight seal. (3) The air is removed through the forming table by a vacuum tank and pump, thereby sucking the heated plastic sheet over the mold. (4) Allow the plastic to cool and harden into its new shape. (5) Break seal and remove the plastic form for trimming, painting, and attaching to scenery, costume, or any other formed unit.

The use of a reservoir tank permits a rather rapid vacuuming action that is necessary or the plastic will cool and return to a rigid state. The pump then recovers the vacuum in the tank while the next sheet of plastic is being heated. Figure 7–26 illustrates the various components that make up a vacuum-forming machine.

Heat Gun.   There are some additional tools that are useful accessories to the thermoplastic-forming process. The heat gun, which is capable of delivering a blast of hot air (750–1000°F) from an enclosed heating element and turbo fan, is used at close range to soften portions of the plastic sheet that may not have taken to the mold accurately.

Welding Gun.   Similar to the heat gun, the hot-air welding gun produces a fine jet of hot air (400–700° F) which, when directed at a seam or thermoplastic welding rod, can weld plastic sheets or plastic forms together. Because the welding gun needs a jet flow of air it has to operate from an air compressor.

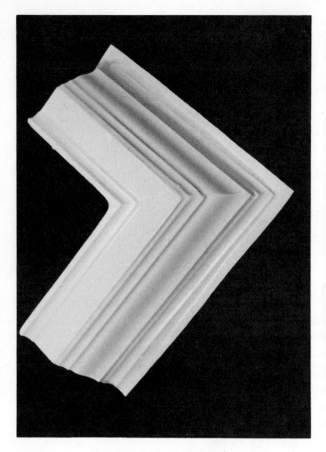

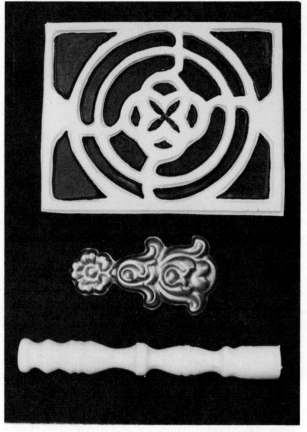

FIGURE 7–27. THERMOPLASTIC FORMS. A few of the many architectural and decorative details that can be vacuum formed for use oh the stage setting. Above, left: A cornice section. In this category, column capitals and bases, pilasters and panel molding can be included. Above, right: Open grill work, split baluster, and decorative details. Right: Low relief panel decoration. Additional thermoplastic forms can be seen in Figure 11–10.

FIGURE 7–28. FABRICATION OF RIGID FOAMS.   Two examples of forms created directly in the material by bringing together rigid foams, sealent rods (flexible polyethylene rods), hot glue, and fiberglass resin over a wooden armature. Above left: Bodies in House of Atreus. Right: Garden Sculpture. (Photo— Bakkum)

FIGURE 7–29. CAST PLASTICS.   Shown is the altar of *Oedipus the King* which was designed to look like an oversized, polished half of a geode. The top surface is made of layers of tinted Clear-cast, a clear polyester available at local craft shops, supported on a hollow frame of wooden ribs with a Celastic covering. The crusty edge is modeled fiberglass resin and Cav-o-sil, an inert powder that gives the mixture body for modeling. (Photo— Bakkum)

238

Hot-Wire Cutter.   Although not used in the thermoplastic process the hot-wire cutter is a handy tool for cutting and shaping rigid foam. Both the table hot-wire cutter and the hand cutter using the flexible wire loop (Figure 7–30) are useful to cut large blocks and to carve small forms. The wire loop is made of a high-resistance wire conductor (Chromel or Nichrome resistor wire). The wire's resistance generates enough heat to melt the rigid foam, thus enabling it to cut the block cleanly and quickly.

Other three-dimensional forming techniques such as fiber glass, Celastic, and the like are discussed in Chapter 11, since they relate to properties, furniture, and costume accessories.

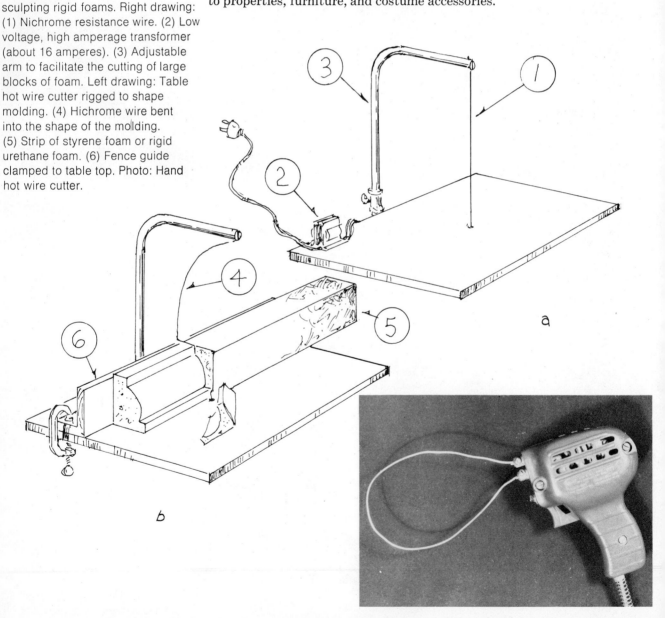

FIGURE 7–30. HOT WIRE CUTTERS. Table and hand hot wire cutters for sculpting rigid foams. Right drawing: (1) Nichrome resistance wire. (2) Low voltage, high amperage transformer (about 16 amperes). (3) Adjustable arm to facilitate the cutting of large blocks of foam. Left drawing: Table hot wire cutter rigged to shape molding. (4) Hichrome wire bent into the shape of the molding. (5) Strip of styrene foam or rigid urethane foam. (6) Fence guide clamped to table top. Photo: Hand hot wire cutter.

FIGURE 7–31. COMMERCIAL VACUUM FORMING OF STAGE PRODUCTS.   Shown are process pictures of the more sophisticated vacuum-forming equipment developed in the Tobins Lake Studios for the mass production of stage properties, armor, and architectural elements. Although this special equipment is capable of producing more than the average scenery shop, the studio's output is still far short of commercial manufacturing production. Top, left: View of forming table. Note overhead oven. Top, right: Plastic sheet in place over molds. Middle, left: After the "pull" with the oven raised. Middle, right: The making of a permanent mold to withstand the heat and pressure of numerous pulls. A fresh pull from the prototype is used as a negative mold. It is backed with sand for stability. Bottom left: The negative mold is filled with epoxy resin sometimes loaded with aluminum to save weight. The final mold is drilled with a pattern of small holes to improve the suction of the pull. Bottom right: Storage shelves of permanent molds.

8 Color in the Theatre

Although the final step in the execution of the design, the painting of scenery, is yet to be discussed, it is imperative to examine first the use of color in the theatre as it relates to painting, lighting, and the designing of scenery and costumes. This might be begun by asking the question, "What is color?"

"Color is *light*," says the physicist as he refers to the small visible portion of the electro-magnetic spectrum. "Color is *paint*," replies the artist, "light merely reveals it." "Color is in the *eye*," says the physiologist, "for no two people see color in the same way and some are color-blind." "Color is in the *mind*," the psychologist insists, to explain why some experience color with their eyes closed or in their dreams. All these attributes, of course, are present in any color experience. To these the artist in the theatre might add, as a part of its creative use, critical analysis and emotional response—the *philosophy* of color.

Although the designers in the theatre (scenery, costume, and lighting) desire knowledge of color to the same degree, they have slightly divergent interests in its use. The lighting designer, for example, is more involved with the physics of color while the scene and costume designers are interested in the painting and dyeing of color as well as the manipulation of colored materials. Whatever the final use of color may be, the individual designer has need of the same knowledge of color as his associates, for eventually all areas of design must come together onstage to form the total visual effect. The beginning designer in the theatre must be aware of the separate uses of color and seek a color explanation that satisfies both the use of color as light and as paint.

It can be seen that any explanation of color in the theatre must, therefore, involve either the separate study of color in light and color in pigment, or the integration of the two into an inclusive scheme. As it is almost impossible to discuss color without involving both light and pigment either by comparison or explanation, it seems logical to try integrating the two approaches to color into a sympathetic definition.

Basic Terminology. It is always difficult to talk or write about color, for words trigger individual images and do not convey accurate information. There are, however, a few terms that are so much a part of the description of a color that it is impractical to converse without knowing their meanings.

The three variants of color, *hue, value,* and *chroma,* are the most familiar terms used to describe a specific color. All will be discussed and illustrated in detail later, but briefly, one can describe a color by hue identification (red, yellow, and so on); value level, or the black to white relationship of a color; and the degree of chroma or freedom from neutralization by mixture with another hue.

Within the framework of these variants an elusive color can be described in simple semiscientific terms by referring to its hue, degree of chroma, and value level. In normal communication their use brings to mind a more consistent image of a specific color than would emotionally charged labels such as blushing pink or passionate purple.

COLOR IN LIGHT

A basic knowledge of color begins with its presence in light. Without light there would be no color. Everyone has seen in some form or other the breaking-up or refraction of sunlight into a spectrum of color. The refraction of sunlight through a bevel-edged window or in a rainbow are simple examples. The physicist with more precise laboratory prisms can produce an accurate spectrum with wavelength values for each hue. He can explain the existence of these hues, from infrared to ultra-violet, as a visible part of the electromagnetic spectrum. This is the beginning of *hue*, the first variant of color (Figure 8–1).

Hue. The position of a color in the spectrum determines its hue. The number of hues than can be separated or identified as principal hues in the spectrum is arbitrary. Six easily identified hues are red, orange, yellow, green, blue, and violet. The expanding of the number of discernible hues is dependent upon the ultimate use or application of the hues into a color theory or system of color notation. The use of color by the artist, for example, is linked to a medium such as paint or dye. Light, on the other hand, is colored by passing it through stained glass or colored plastic. Because of the purity of the color mediums in light, it is possible to establish *light* primary hues.

A primary is a spectrum hue that is basic and cannot be produced by the mixing (see Additive Mixing) of any other hues. Red, green, and blue are the light primary hues. The remaining hues or secondaries are produced by cross-mixing any pair of primaries.

It is important to mention at this point that the mixing of paint as a color medium is not as accurate as the mixing of colors in light. It involves a different physical process, hence the painter requires a finer separation of spectrum hues to creatively mix and use color (see Color in Paint).

Additive Mixing. Light secondary hues are formed by the mixing of a pair of primaries in the air. This can be illustrated by crossing the rays of a spotlight with a red color medium over the rays of a blue spotlight. The resulting color is the secondary hue red-violet, which was mixed in the air. The new color was produced by addition of hues from the color spectrum and therefore is referred to as additive mixing. The most spectacular example of additive mixing is the combination of the apparent hue opposites green and red. Their mixture produces a yellow hue, which is not too surprising when it is noted that the yellows and oranges fall between red and green in the color spectrum.

The additive mixing of a secondary and a primary or of all three primaries results in a synthetic white. It is obvious that the additive mixing of all hues results in white light, for that is what they were before being refracted into the color spectrum (Figure 8–2).

Value. The movement toward white by additive mixing illustrates the second variant of color, value. The light to dark relationship of a hue or mixed color is its value. The lighter values, nearer white, are known as *tints* and the darker values, approaching black, are referred to as *shades*. Both represent a variation from the true hue.

The use of value as a color variant or control is more the tool of the painter than of the lighting designer because of the necessarily greater range in pigment mixing. Subtle value differences are easier to accomplish in paint, particularly in the darker ranges.

The number of steps in a value scale is arbitrary. The limiting factor is usually the ability of the eye to distinguish the difference between adjacent steps. Seven steps between black and white seem to be a comfortable number (Figure 8–3).

Some hues come from the spectrum with a natural value difference. The light to dark difference of yellow and violet is the most extreme example. Other hues have less value difference and some, of course, are about equal. Hues that have little value difference contrast each other with another force. They are usually hue opposites. When certain hue opposites are placed side by side the color contrast is so high that it produces an apparent vibration in the eye. Because this phenomenon involves both the physics and optics of color it will be discussed later, after all the aspects of color have been examined.

Hue opposites, however, do perform another function. When mixed in equal parts they tend to neutralize each other. Hue opposites in light produce white, while their mixture in paint results in neutral tones. This change in the purity of a hue is the third variant of color, *chroma*.

Chroma. The instant the purity of a principal hue is modified, the change is referred to as a change of its chroma. The degree of pureness, or freedom from neutrality, like the value scale, can be measured in steps. The number of steps from pure hue to complete gray varies according to color theories. A very precise measuring and mixing method can produce a great number of steps. The artist, however, can see and work easily in quarter portions; thus, he moves from a fully saturated hue to one-quarter neutral through one half, then three-quarters to full neutrality. This serves merely as an explanation of chroma, and the artist is free to use more steps for a more subtle change if he so desires.

It is interesting to note in Figure 8–4, which shows the value and chroma changes produced by the mixing of orange and blue hues, that when the value of either orange or blue is raised or lowered its chroma is also changed as the tint or shade becomes more neutral. On the other hand, the quarter steps on the direct horizontal line to the value scale represent a chroma change without a value drop. This is accomplished on the orange side by the proportional mixing of blue (the hue opposite or complement of orange) after it has been raised to the matching value of orange. In other words, it is possible to

244   change the chroma of a hue without affecting its value, but it is impossible to change the value of a hue without modifying its chroma.

All neutralization can be accomplished, theoretically, by the use of black or white paint. It is possible under scientifically controlled conditions of paint manufacturing, but the scenic artist knows that certain opaque colors do not respond to mixing with black. The use of a complementary color to neutralize a hue gives the painter a chromatic neutral that has a little more life under the stage lights. The neutralization of a pigment hue or its modification by another color is due to the particular method of mixing colors in paint. When the painter mixes colors on the palette or in the bucket he is using *subtractive mixing*.

Subtractive Mixing.   It has been shown that when hues are mixed in the air the process is the additive blending of light colored by its transmission or reflection from two or more sources. The opposite technique is to mix colors by crossing or combining color mediums in front of a single source of light. Figure 8–5 illustrates the effect of combining two color mediums, blue-green and yellow, in front of a light source containing all the spectrum hues. The green color that is transmitted is the only hue not subtracted or filtered out of the light by the combined color mediums. It is not as visually apparent, but the same subtractive results are present when the artist mixes the two colors, blue-green and yellow, in paint.

It is characteristic of subtractive mixing in paint and light to move toward neutrality and darker shades. This is particularly evident when the hues are complementary colors. It is understandable that the closer the color mediums are to hue opposites the less light can be transmitted, until a block or point of negative transmission is reached. The mixing of complementary colors in paint results in a nearly black neutral for the same reason. Because the painter uses subtractive mixing most of the time, he has a slightly different attitude toward color than the lighting designer.

COLOR IN PAINT

Color in paint is, of course, dependent upon light to realize its physical properties. The color of a surface reaches the eye by the reflection of the light that is illuminating it. Just as a light color medium transmits a color by absorbing some spectrum hues and letting through others, so a colored surface absorbs and reflects only the colors of the paint (Figure 8–6). These are the physical properties of a paint surface that begins with its coloring agent, pigment.

Pigment.   The term *pigment* is an inclusive title for the coloring agent in paints, dyes and in nature. It can be best explained as the chemical properties of color that create hue. At first, pigments came from natural sources; the indigo and madder plants are familiar examples. Minerals and semiprecious stones were also pulverized and made into pigments. The crude chemistry of the past established many of the traditional names of colors still used today, such as madder lake and indigo blue.

Colors, other than those found directly in nature, were often made synthetically from known minerals and their compounds. In the mid-nineteenth century organic colors made their first appearance as organic dyes. Most of the present-day colors are a product of organic chemistry, which essentially deals with the carbon compounds. The names of organic colors often signify their chemical origin, such as chrome green, alizarin crimson and calcium red.

Modern chemistry has given the artist many new colors which have allowed him to increase his palette. Because of the subtractive result of most paint mixing the painter cannot begin with a palette of primary hues to develop a full range of colors. The intermediate colors of combined primaries are not pure and do not relate to the spectrum hues. Hence, the painter prefers to begin with a larger palette that might include all the principal hues of the spectrum. While a small palette made up of the six principal colors already mentioned is usable, the scenic artist favors a twelve-principal-color palette for reasons of flexibility and economy.

Twelve Principal Hues.   Beginning with the six original hues: red, orange, yellow, green, blue, and violet, six additional hues are formulated by introducing intermediate steps. The new hue takes its name from the two original hues on either side. The hue between yellow and orange, for example, would be *yellow-orange* and so on around the color wheel (Figure 8–7).

The new intermediate color is not thought of as a paint mixture of the two adjacent colors but as a full chroma hue from the spectrum. The result is a working palette of twelve full-intensity hues which will reduce the amount of neutralization from subtractive mixing that might have occurred with a smaller palette. Some scenic artists prefer a palette with even more than twelve hues. Also, under certain conditions such as the commercial or industrial use of color, the number of principal colors is expanded to twenty-four or more. In any event, the expansion is based on the twelve principal hues that become a basis of reference for individual use.

246   *The Color Wheel.*   Reference was made to the *color wheel* to help explain the formulation of the twelve principal colors. A question may be raised as to the value of arranging the hues in a circle when they appear in the spectrum in a line. Hues are located in the spectrum according to their wave length, moving progressively from the longest wave length, infra-red, to the shortest, ultra-violet. It is important to note that both of the fringe colors are red or have red content. If the eye begins with yellow in the near center of the spectrum and moves in progressive steps to the left or right, it is easy to conceive of completing a circle by bringing together the related hues, red and violet.

Besides showing a contiguous relationship, the circular arrangement of the twelve principal colors also emphasizes hue opposites. Complementary colors appear diagonally opposite each other in the circle. The hues in the color wheel shown in Figure 8–7 are pigment hues and are therefore related more specifically to the painter. Colors in light can be arranged in the same kind of color wheel. Because the wheel is developed from the light primaries, the values of the secondary and intermediate colors raise slightly as a result of additive mixing (Figure 8–8). By accepting a slight difference in chroma the complementary hues in light can be made to interrelate with the hue opposites of pigments.

The Light Color Wheel.   Lighting designers vary in their choice of color mediums to be used as primaries. The colors chosen are frequently dependent upon the immediate requirements. There is a great difference, for example, between primaries elected to light a sky cyclorama, a painted drop, or acting areas. With some latitude, light primaries can be described in terms of Roscolux color mediums (Rosco Laboratories, Inc.) as: (1) a red with some orange content (Roscolux No. 26, light red) designated as Ro (small orange); (2) a blue containing some red (Bv) difficult to match in a single medium (Roscolux No. 47, light rose purple, coupled with No. 65, day light blue). (3) The remaining primary, green, is obtainable by combining No. 89, moss green, and No. 12, straw. These primary hues are close enough to be thought of as red-orange (RO), blue-violet (BV), and yellow-green (YG), as they appear in the pigment color wheel. (Figure 8–8).

The light secondaries which are the result of the additive mixing of two primaries are the complementary colors located directly opposite each primary in the pigment color wheel. Yellow-orange (YO) is opposite light primary blue-violet (BV) and can be produced in light by doubling Roscolux No. 03, dark amber. Blue-green (BG) is across from primary (RO) and is near Roscolux No. 70, sea blue; and red-violet

(RV), the complement of primary (YG), is almost the same as Roscolux No. 48, rose purple. It will be noted that the light secondaries are lighter in value than their corresponding pigment hues because of the additive mixing that formulated them.

With some latitude light primaries can be described in terms of Roscolux color mediums (Rosco Laboratories, Inc.) as (1) a red with some orange content (Roscolux No. 26, light red) designated as Ro (small orange). (2) A blue containing some red (Rv) Roscolux No. 47, light rose purple plus No. 65, daylight blue, is very close to a primary blue. (3) The remaining primary, green, is obtainable by combining No. 89, moss green, and No. 12, straw. These primary hues are close enough to be thought of as red-orange (RO), blue-violet (BV), and yellow-green (YG) as they appear in the pigment color wheel (Figure 8-8).

The light secondaries are the result of the additive mixing of the primaries. They are complementary colors and are located directly opposite each primary in the pigment color wheel. Yellow-orange (YO) is opposite light-primary blue-violet (BV) and can be produced in light by doubling Roscolux No. 03, dark amber. Blue-green (BG), across from primary (RO), is near Roscolux No. 71, sea blue; and red-violet (RV), the complement of primary (YG), is almost the same as Roscolux No. 48, rose purple. It will be noted that the light secondaries are lighter in value than their corresponding pigment hues because of the additive mixing that formulated them.

THE COLOR EXPERIENCE

The source of color can be scientifically explained; the mixture of color can be diagramed; and all the variants of color can be schedduled into a system of notation. What the eye sees and the brain interprets, however, is an individual and personal color experience. The eye, functioning very much like a camera, receives light through its lens which focuses the image or impression onto the retina layer of the inner-eye. The innumerable nerve endings of the retina culminate in the optic nerve which carries the impression signal to the brain for interpretation. The impression is registered in terms of color and intensity (brightness), which is another way of saying hue and value. A few people can only distinguish value differences and not hue variances. Because the greatest hue difference falls in the middle of the value scale the color-blind individual cannot see the difference between reds and greens.

The physiological process of interpreting color is complete when the brain makes the final decision. Beside the intellectual action that determines color, the mind (often subjectively) undergoes an emotional response to color as a part of the total color experience.

The psychological effect of color on a theatre audience is difficult to measure as a group reaction. The designer depends upon measurable individual responses, hoping they will multiply. The emotional response to a color within an individual is primarily conditioned by a lifetime of influence exerted by nature's colors and natural lighting. The repulsion to strong colors that produce unnatural flesh tones or discolor foods are obvious examples. The expressive content of a color can stimulate, relax, or depress the feelings of the viewer. Reds quicken the heartbeat, greens are restful, and neutral hues can be depressing.

Tradition, such as the centuries of social and religious conventions buried deep in the mind, can also condition an emotional response to color. We also react to contemporary color symbols such as traffic lights and color coded road signs. Within the framework of tradition, training and conventions, the six basic spectrum hues can be described in terms of their emotional response, as follows:

Yellow   Radiant, light giving, golden, saintly; in light values near white, virginal.

Orange   Festive, earthy, peasant colors, neutral shades, nature in the fall.

Red   Active, passionate, full of inner warmth, fiery, strong, forceful.

Violet   Royal, piety, deeper shades, shadows, terror, chaos, a reddening color.

Blue   Passive, receding, deep, cool, purity, icy tints.

Green   Tranquility, compassion, nature in the spring and summer.

The psychological description of a hue is, at best, very general. The emotional response to a color can be countered or modified by adjacent colors, as well as the color of the background. The intercolor experience, which involves both the psychological response and the physiological limitation of the eye, can also be tricked by an optical illusion. This phenomenon of fooling both the eye and the mind is dependable enough to be considered an important part of the impact of color on a theatre audience.

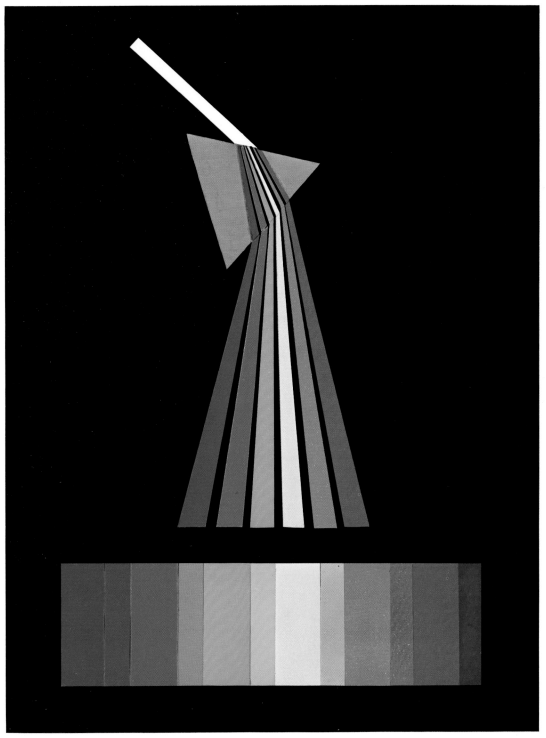

Figure 8–1. SPECTRUM HUES.
The breakdown of sunlight through prism refraction into first six and then twelve spectrum hues.

Figure 8–2(a).   ADDITIVE MIXING.

The additive mixing of the light primaries by the crossing of the spotlight rays. Note that the secondary hues formed by the mixing of two adjacent primaries are lighter in value, and that the mixing of three primaries results in white light.

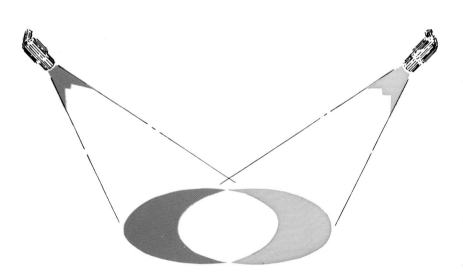

Figure 8–2(b).   APPLICATION OF ADDITIVE MIXING TO STAGE LIGHTING.

The simple mixing of complementary colors to produce white light in an acting area. The white light can be "warmed" or "cooled" by altering the intensity of one side or the other, or by moving the choice of color medium slightly off a true complementary scheme. *Left*—Daylight blue—Roscolene No. 851—spectrum hue, blue, raised in value. *Right*—No color amber—Roscolene No. 810—spectrum hue, orange, raised in value.

Figure 8–3.   HUE-VALUE RELATIONSHIP.
The twelve principal spectrum hues are
arranged next to the value scale in their natural
light-to-dark relationship. The middle value of
the seven steps between black and white
is referred to *medium* value while the three
steps above are known as, *lowlight, light*
and *highlight.* The lower value steps are
called *highdark, dark* and *lowdark.*

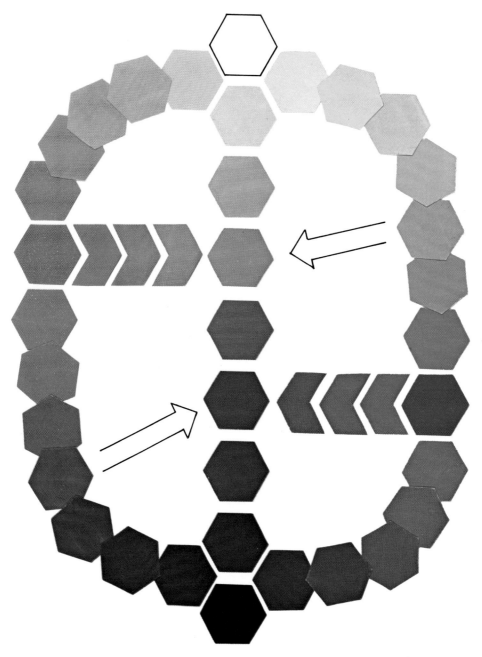

Figure 8–4. VALUE AND CHROMA. The complementary hues, blue and orange, are subjected to value and chroma changes first by alternately mixing each color with white and black in the outside ring to effect a value change. Chroma changes at a fixed value are accomplished horizontally by mixing the color with its complementary hue after it has been raised or lowered to the same value (arrow) *Note* that to change the value of a hue automatically alters its *chroma* without necessarily affecting value.

It is possible, of course, to alter chroma at each value step and completely fill the circle with a variety of tints and shades. This mixing procedure (although impossible to reproduce accurately), applied to any set of complementaries, is important to the stage designer as a method of creating new and unusual colors as well as matching existing shades.

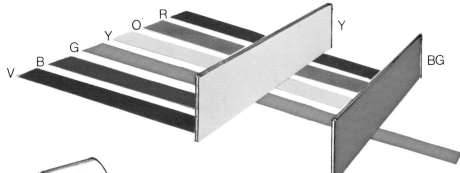

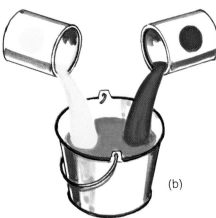

Figure 8–5.   SUBTRACTIVE MIXING.
(a) Six basic hues of the spectrum are shown passing
through two color mediums, first yellow and then
blue-green. All hues are absorbed or subtracted by the
two colors except green.
(b) *Subtractive mixing in paint.* The result is the same
when blue-green and yellow paint are mixed.

Figure 8–6.   COLOR REFLECTION.
The horizontal orange strip represents an orange-colored
surface. It appears orange under sunlight because only
the red, yellow, and orange hues of the spectrum have
been reflected. The other hues have been absorbed.

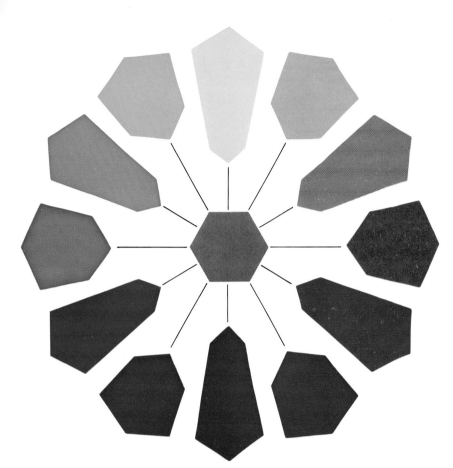

Figure 8–7.   PIGMENT COLOR WHEEL.

Twelve principal colors of the spectrum arranged in a circle. Diagonals are color opposites. Their subtractive mixing would produce a neutral shade similar to the gray lozenge in the center.

Figure 8–8.   LIGHT COLOR WHEEL.

The same twelve hues in a circle arrangement, but showing decided value changes resulting from the additive mixing of the light primaries. The largest lozenges are the light primaries, yellow-green, red-orange, and blue-violet. Two adjacent primaries mix to form an intermediate secondary which becomes the complement of the remaining primary located diagonally opposite. The secondary hues are progressively lighter in value as are the remaining intermediate hues. As the additive mixing of complements produces white light the center lozenge is white.

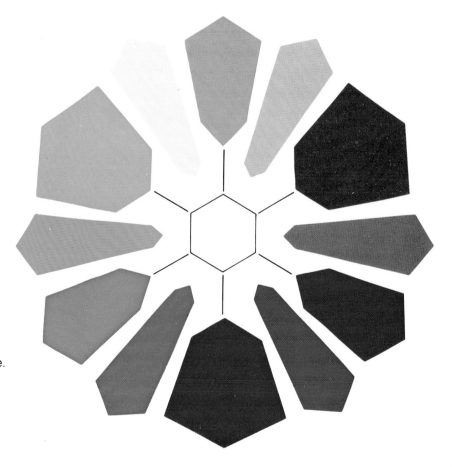

Figure 8–9.   THE COLOR OF CAST SHADOWS.
A cast shadow takes on a color that is complementary to the hue
of the light source. The color of the shadow becomes a more positive
tint when it is illuminated with a subtle secondary light source. In
the diagram the major light source is blue-green in color. The shadow
is a red-orange tint, the hue opposite of blue-green.

Figure 8–10. INTERACTION OF COLOR HUE REACTION INFLUENCING A NEUTRAL.
A small neutral figure is influenced by the color of the ground that surrounds it. The neutral in each of the six basic spectrum hues appears to be tinted with the complementary color of the background. The influence can be noted in each case when compared with the same gray tone to the right of each hue.

Figure 8–11. INTERACTION OF
COLOR CHROMA REACTIONS.
The chroma of the six basic
spectrum hues appears to take on
more brilliance as the background
is darkened.

Figure 8–12. INTERACTION OF
COLOR VALUE REACTION.
The value of the center of each
area of color is the same. It appears
to be lighter or darker is it is influenced by the surrounding color.

Figure 8–13.   MONOCHROME COLOR SCHEME.
A sketch for a velour dye-painted traveler curtain in shades and tints of one color, blue.

Figure 8-14.   COSTUME COLOR SCHEMES.
The control of color within a single costume. (a) A fifth-interval color scheme using blue-green, red-violet, and yellow-orange as principal hues with slight value changes to provide interesting variation. Emilia from *The Winter's Tale*. Designer—Frank Bevan. (b) A third-interval color scheme involving blue-green, yellow-green, yellow-orange, and red-orange. The Y-O has been raised in value and the blue-green lowered. Baron Ochs' chasseur from *Der Rosenkavalier*. Designer—Frank Bevan. (Courtesy of Beinecke Rare Book and Manuscript Library, Yale University)

Figure 8–16.   NEUTRAL COLOR SCHEME.
The high contrast of a red, white, and blue color scheme is modified into a close harmony composition by neutralizing the red and blue and by using a light gray instead of white.

Figure 8–17. COLOR PLOT TO COSTUME SKETCH.

From the simplified colors in a color chart of Moliere's *The Learned Women* the costumes of two characters have been developed in final individual color schemes. Designer — June DeCamp

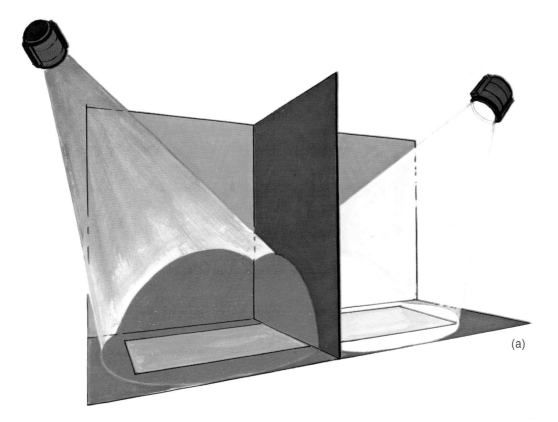

Figure 8–18. COLOR MODIFICATION.
(a) A demonstration of the subtractive mixing effect when a colored surface is modified by a colored light. (b) Color modification chart of the twelve principle colors under the influence of the light primaries.

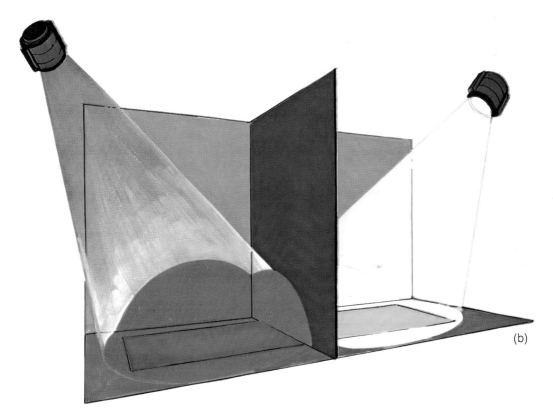

THE OPTICS OF COLOR

Some artists believe in balancing the colors in a painting, contending that color in nature is balanced and therefore points the way to achieving a natural effect on canvas. In the effort to not reproduce nature, the modern artist frequently unbalances the colors of his composition with spectacular results. The eye of the viewer, however, tries to balance the color impression. The strain of a prolonged view of a single colored form results in an *after-image* of the object upon its removal, but it appears to be colored in the exactly opposite hue, or complementary color.

A theatrical demonstration of the after-image phenomenon was present in the Russian Ballet's production of *Le Coq d'Or.* The first scene, a garden, is dominated by a brilliant red-orange tree. During twenty minutes of dancing the eye was saturated with an unbalanced color scheme; upon changing to the next scene the audience was plagued by a blue-green after-image of the first-scene tree floating ethereally about the stage. The impression was in the eye, of course; the tree was not onstage.

The phenomenon of after-image or the color-balancing tendency of the eye is present in other forms. The shadow cast from a colored light source, for example, appears to the observer to be in a complementary color. Figure 8–9 illustrates the pale red-orange shadow cast from a blue-green light which is not there in reality, but is an optical illusion or color impression within the eye. It should be mentioned that the shadow has to be faintly illuminated with a colorless light to accomplish the demonstration accurately.

Modern abstract art has taken optical color demonstrations out of the laboratory and turned them into exciting examples of so-called OP-ART. This and other phenomena of intercolor action, however, are not new. It was in 1886 first referred to as the *simultaneous contrast of color* by M. E. Chevreul, the grandfather of color theorists. In 1960, Joseph Albers referred to the same effects more correctly as the *interaction of color.*

The Interaction of Color.   How a color reacts to an adjacent hue or to its background is known as the interaction of color. Certain reactions are painfully obvious while others are extremely subtle. The degree of color interplay is a critical element in the use of color by all stage designers. Aside from the mixing and creating of colors itself, the designer's choice and arrangement of colors become the most forceful elements in stimulating an emotional or intellectual response in the audience.

The interaction of colors affects all the variants of color. The *value* of a color can seem to change by juxtaposition; a neutral can be influenced by a surrounding color and appear to take on a *hue*; and the *chroma* of a color can be sharpened or deadened by its background. Figures 8–10, 11, 12 are a few classic examples of obvious color interactions that have an influence on the designer's use of color or choice of a color scheme.

COLOR MANIPULATION

The Color Scheme. Like a production scheme or visual style convention, a color scheme is the control of color within a stage composition by the designer. The color scheme may be inherent in the play, an outgrowth of the visual style, or the necessary unifying force of a multiscene production or ensemble of costumes. Sometimes the color control is very striking with a strong design feeling, while at other times the control is subdued and only apparent to another designer. The presence of design in a composition is more obvious when it counters the balance of color in nature and thereby expresses a man-made control. Nature, however, has its own dramatically unbalanced moments such as a sunset or moonlighted landscape.

The first and most evident control is to use a single color. A *monochrome* scheme is based upon limiting a composition to one hue and maintaining contrast by the variation of chroma and value (Figure 8–13). A second harmonious color scheme is produced by *analogous* or closely related colors on the color wheel. Yellow-green, yellow, and yellow-orange, for example, would be a close-harmony analogous color scheme.

Color schemes can progress from the more harmonious consequence of closely-related colors to *third* and *fifth* interval selections. The extreme of hue contrast terminates with a *complementary* color scheme. The most vibrant combination of hue opposition is the bringing together of red-orange and blue-green (Figure 8-15).

An interesting color composition does not end with the selection of hues. There is infinite variety in the way color can be put together through the manipulation of chroma and value. The neutralization of very positive hues can often change their impact and meaning. The patriotic red, white, and blue color scheme in Figure 8–16 has a reduced emphasis when all the colors are forced into the neutrality scale.

The Color Plot. The control of color within a composition is only a portion of the color planning that occurs in designing for the theatre. As the designer develops the color scheme for each setting of a multiscene play he also has to consider the *whole* production.

Most designers use some form of a *color plot* to make preliminary studies of the entire production. Although it is a view of the show the audience will never see, it does serve as a color guide for his associates, the lighting and costume designers. Through the color plot the over-all development of color can be studied. The functionability of connecting colors and hue accents is clearly visible. The progressive unfolding of color change within a scene or throughout a production as well as moments of high contrast or subdued uniformity can be demonstrated in the color plot.

The color plot is perhaps more important to the costume designer. Not only can he study the over-all relationship of all costumes in the production, but he can also plot small scenes and families of color that may help to visually define sympathetic characters and rival groups or individuals. The focus or center of attention in a large group scene can be planned as well as the control of the over-all emotional impact or mood within the scene. The color plot also establishes the progression of colors from scene to scene and act to act.

Age and station in society can enter the color plot in the broad, symbolic statement of a single color note. The costume designer, however, frequently uses more than one color to note a single costume as a means of studying color accents and harmonies between characters. The costume color plot in Figure 8-17 illustrates in particolor swatches the color interaction and character relationship within Molière's *The Learned Women*.

Color Modification. It has been shown that color can be changed by mixing; influenced by interaction; and materialized by optical illusion. Surface color can also be modified by colored light. The constant use of colored light on a colored surface is unique to the theatre. The designers in the theatre not only have to consider the colors of a painted background, costumes, and other materials of a set, but also the colors of the lights that will reveal them. This is especially true if the lighting for the scene is unusual such as a romantic moonlight scene or the arbitrary flooding of the stage with red or green hues to provide an unnatural effect.

Fortunately, color modification is not quite as complicated as it seems. The effect of colored light on a colored surface is a result of subtractive mixing. In other words, if a red light is thrown on a mixing surface, the yellow is modified into orange tones (Figure 8–17).

The modification of a color in a costume or on scenery by colored light is a theatrical example of the joining of the two color media, pigment and light. The designers in the theatre are constantly aware of the cross influence of colored light and pigment. They are always prepared to compensate in either medium to create a natural effect, or to deliberately cause dramatic reversals of color.

Color modification charts can be prepared for the reference of all designers in the theatre by systematically matching the shade of the modified color chit on the white-light side of the dividing shield of a testing apparatus similar to the setup indicated in Figure 8–18. If each of the twelve principal colors is subjected to the influence of at least the light primaries, a rather informative set of color notes is collected. It will be noted that when alike hues are brought together, blue light on blue pigment, for example, the modified pigment hue is raised in value. This slight alteration of value is true of all alike color combinations. The degree of value change in a given situation depends upon the relative value of the background surrounding the color chit and the comparative intensity of the two light sources.

The chart will indicate the many possibilities under light primaries, however, unusual color combinations should be checked under the exact lighting conditions. Some designers prefer to use a miniature duplication of the planned stage lighting setup to check their color schemes and plan color effects. The consideration of the color of the stage lights is, of course, most important to the scene designer when he is preparing to paint the scenery.

The painting of scenery is a highly skilled and specialized portion of creating a setting. It is also a very interesting and fascinating part of scene design and technical production. Most of the methods and techniques of handling scene paint are familiar to one with visual-arts training. The main difference between painting scenery and easel painting is that of scale. Instead of painting at a small drawing-board size, the scenic artist paints at life size or larger.

Because scene painting is large in scale, the scenic artist uses a broad technique, sometimes so broad that what appears to be slaps and dashes up close does not take form until viewed at a distance. Learning to paint on a large scale and in a broad technique is an easy adjustment for the visual artist. The uninitiated, however, should first become accomplished in handling water colors in sketch form before attempting large-scale painting. Sketching and painting from still life or landscape not only improve the student designer's drawing and painting ability but also increase his perception of light and color in nature. These processes serve to point up the significance of color as an element of design.

253

254 PAINT AND COLOR

The design of a setting can succeed or fail in the strength of the painting. Hence, the designer should carefully plan how the scenery is to be painted. The most important part of the planning and actual painting is the use of color. A scene designer must be familiar not only with the mixing and use of pigments, but also with the use of colored lights.

The prominence and forcefulness of color as an element of design was mentioned in Chapter 3. The attributes of the color experience and the philosophy of the use of color in the theatre were discussed in Chapter 8. The scenic artist or scene designer, if he is painting his own scenery, employs the same philosophy, terminology, and mixing procedures in his use of color for scenery as would any other visual artist.

SCENE PAINTING PALETTE

The scenic artist's first act is to establish a working palette of scene paint that will relate to the twelve principal hues of the spectrum. The size of the palette will vary from at least twelve to many additional pigments depending on the individual artist's tastes and working methods; the quality of the pigments available as to pureness of hue and mixing behavior; and finally, the relative cost of individual colors balanced against their actual usefulness.

As the designer chooses his paint colors he is judging the color in comparison to the corresponding spectrum hue. If the paint sample does not match favorably in hue, value, and chroma, he may have to compensate by choosing colors on either side of the spectrum hue and stock two pigments instead of one. The pigment red is a good example. Because a true spectrum red is not obtainable, two reds are usually stocked, one that will mix with blue and the other with yellow.

There are two types of scene paint, the unmixed dry pigments and ready-mixed paints. The mixture in this case refers to the presence of all or part of the properties of paint as a medium, which will be discussed separately under mixing procedures. The choice of a palette in either type of paint is related to the mixing of colors or of one pigment with another.

Dry Pigment Palette. Dry pigments are ground for theatrical use and, therefore, the spectral hues at least are available only at supply houses specializing in scenic paints and supplies. Earth colors can be found in local paint shops, although many times they are of inferior quality for painting scenery.

In preparing a list of stock scenic colors it is natural to compare the quality of the pigment's hue to the twelve principal colors of the color wheel. A good scene-painting palette would include them as well as some special colors and the earth colors.

The following hues have been selected from Gothic Scenic Paints (Gothic Color Company, Inc.).

Yellow

Light Chrome Yellow   A straight yellow, close to a primary hue. It is important to have a yellow with a sharp cut-off (minimum green or orange content).

Yellow Orange

Medium Chrome Yellow   Excellent yellow-orange hue. Not necessary to stock with light chrome yellow. Some painters, however, prefer stocking two yellows, warm (slight red content), and cool (slight blue content).

Orange

French Orange Mineral   Excellent spectrum hue. Heavy, therefore a little expensive.

Red Orange

American Vermilion   Brilliant red orange.

Red

Turkey Red Lake   Good red, slight yellow content.

Alizarin Crimson   Excellent red, close to spectrum red but is not always available.

Red Violet

Magenta Lake   A brilliant bluish red, makes rich violets with blue. Expensive but goes a long way.

Violet and Blue Violet

Purple Lake   A rich, brilliant violet. Very expensive. Special, not necessary to stock with magenta lake at hand.

Blue

Cobalt Blue   A pure primary blue although a little high in value.

Ultramarine Blue   A rich blue with a touch of red content. Mixes well to make purples, but poorly for greens.

Blue Green

Italian Blue   A brilliant turquoise, although not a true blue green (high in value), it is a very useful color. Mixed with primrose yellow, it makes vibrant yellow greens and greens.

Prussian Blue   Dark, rich blue green. Difficult mixer, good for near-black tones.

Green

Emerald Green   Intense green, slight yellow content.
Medium Chrome Green   A straight green but a little low in value.

Yellow Green

Primrose Yellow   A cold yellow. Not necessary to stock with light chrome yellow, except as a special color.

Earth Colors

The earth colors are inexpensive neutral shades that can be used in place of the expensive method of neutralizing the more intense colors.

French Yellow Ochre   Rich ochre or neutral yellow shade, extends into good cream shades.
Raw Italian Sienna   Warmer and richer than ochre.
Burnt Italian Sienna   Terra cotta and brick color.
Raw Turkey   A cold brown, has greenish cast. Not too useful by itself. It is used to neutralize other colors.
Burnt Turkey Umber   Rich brown, good wood-graining color.
Van Dyke Brown   Very rich brown, but hard mixer. Excellent wood color.
Ivory Drop Black   A bone black (avoid using lampblack which is commonly mistaken for bone black. Lampblack is greasy and therefore a hard mixer).
Zinc White   A white pigment not whiting. Sometimes called Permanent White.

Danish Whiting   Pure whiting, doesn't settle out. Excellent filler.

Ready-Mixed Paints.   The color range of ready-mixed paints is not as extensive as that of dry pigments. Although their colors are brilliant there are not as many intermediate tones. The following paint colors are from Gothic Casein Fresco Paints. They are fairly representative of the range of colors found in all casein paints.

Yellow

Lemon Yellow   A good straight yellow close to spectrum hue.

Yellow-Orange

Golden Yellow   Not quite a full yellow-orange in hue. Closer to an orange-yellow.

Orange

Orange   Has more red than a spectrum orange.

Red-Orange

Bright Red   Excellent spectrum hue.

Red

Red   Good spectrum hue. Just a shade off in chroma.

Dark Red   A step lower in value than red and has a little blue content.

Red-Violet

Magenta   The hue is right but it is about three steps too high in value.

Violet and Blue-Violet

Purple   Excellent spectrum hue. When mixed with ultramarine blue it produces fine blue-violet.

Blue

Ultramarine Blue   A blue with a red content. Too deep in value to be a true spectrum blue.

	Blue-Green
Turquoise Blue	Excellent spectrum hue.
Cerulean Blue	A brilliant blue-green but high in value. Makes vibrant yellow-greens when mixed with lemon yellow.

| | *Green* |
| Emerald Green | Excellent spectrum hue. |

| | *Yellow-Green* |
| Cerulean Blue and Lemon Yellow | No prepared yellow-green available. |

	Earth colors
Yellow Ochre	Rich neutral yellow.
Raw Sienna	Neutral yellow. Warmer and richer than ochre.
Burnt Sienna	Darker and less red than traditional burnt sienna.
Raw Umber	Cold brown. More blue than green, the cast of traditional raw umber.
Burnt Umber	Good rich brown.
Black	Deep flat black. Covers and mixes well.
White	Opaque. Good tinting white.

MIXING PROCEDURES

THE COMPONENTS OF SCENE PAINT

The three basic components of scene paint are pigment (color), binder, and vehicle. The pigment and binder are suspended in a liquid medium which allows the paint to be brushed or sprayed onto a surface. The vehicle then evaporates and the binder holds the pigment to the surface.

The dry colors used for scene paint are the pigments which are suspended in a water vehicle with a water-soluble glue as a binder. A fourth ingredient is frequently added to scene paint as a filler. Whiting, which is an inexpensive chalk and not a pigment, is often added to the mixture to give the paint body and opacity. As whiting affects the intensity of the color it is not used in pure or full-intensity colors.

The mixing of scene paint begins with the preparation of the binder and vehicle or "size." The mixing proportions of a working size depend upon the kind of glue that is being used. Ordinary flake or ground glues are strong and usually have to be cut about 16 to 1 to make a size. Rubber and gelatine glues, although more flexible and easier to handle (dry slower) make into about a 10-to-1 size. Both types require advance preparation. They have to be soaked and cooked in a double boiler to soften them into a liquid state. Once the glue has been made into size, it stays in a liquid state. The size will deteriorate, however, if it is allowed to stand for too long a period. A small quantity of carbolic acid or formaldehyde added to the size acts as a preservative.

Because scene paint dries about two to three values lighter than it appears when wet, it is easier to mix the dry colors together first to acquire the desired tone. The size is then added to the premixed pigment, thereby saving repeated testings and sometimes the mixing of twice as much paint as is needed in the attempt to match an elusive shade. The size is added slowly, first making a pulp or paste. If the paste is vigorously stirred to make sure all the dry color is thoroughly moistened before thinning it to a painting consistency, there is no need to break up the unmixed lumps by hand. If the dry paint refuses to go into suspension (some colors such as Van Dyke brown and Prussian blue are poor mixers), a little alcohol added to the paste helps to wet the troublesome color.

READY-MIXED PAINTS

The question may be raised as to whether or not it wouldn't be wiser to use ready-mixed paints and thereby avoid all the bothersome procedure of mixing the dry scenic colors. Casein and latex based paints are two water-color paints that are sometimes used in the theatre. Casein (a milk derivative) is the binder in a casein-based paint which is available in prepared mixtures of dry or pulp form. The dry casein colors, however, have a very limited color choice and the pulp mixtures are expensive when compared to the cost per area of coverage of dry scenic colors. Iddings and Luminal Fresco Colors are the two brands of casein paints most frequently used in the theatre.

One important thing to remember in using casein paints is that when they "setup" or dry they are water repellent. This can play havoc with uncleaned brushes or buckets. It also means that scenery painted with casein paint cannot be washed down for repainting. Casein paint, however, covers very well, one coat usually being sufficient. The water-repellent quality of casein is, of course, an advantage for scenery that is to be used outdoors.

Latex-based paints are also adaptable to scenic painting. Vivid-Deep Color (Long Island Paint & Chemical Co.) produces a complete range of colors. Although most Vivid colors are in full chroma and concentrated they are liquid in consistency and therefore do not go as far as a pulp

260

mixture. As latex and casein paints are compatable the painter is free to select favored hues from each system as stock colors.

The most recent scene paint to become available is *Roscopaint,* a product of Rosco Laboratories, Inc. Roscopaint is not a ready-mixed paint but does combine the conveniences of ready-mixed and the flexibility of dry color mixing into a scene painting system. Rather than cans of paint the Roscopaint system is composed of three ingredients: the pigment, binder, and water added later by the painter. The pigments, which have a wide range of high chroma colors, are suspended in mineral oil ready for mixing with one of the two bases. Each base is highly concentrated and must be diluted with water. The neutral or clear base (a vinyl acrylic binder) does not affect the chroma of the color. It has a very favorable mixing ratio of one part pigment to eight parts of concentrated neutral base. One gallon of color mixture makes three gallons of finished paint. Further thinning does not change the color's chroma but does, of course, reduce its opacity.

The white base is used to opaque the pigment. Its mixing ratio is sixteen parts of white concentrate to one part pigment. The amount of water added will naturally affect its opacity. The white base with titanium white is used to produce tints.

Roscopaint dries into a nonreflective matte finish. A gloss or semi-gloss finish can be obtained, however, by mixing it with a concentrated gloss medium provided with the system.

The mixed colors do not spoil and with the slight mineral oil content in the pigments do not readily dry out. Because of the high concentration of its major elements, the system is more economical when measured gallon to gallon of ready-mixed paint.

The acrylic binder holds on all surfaces and even with the addition of unrelated ingredients will still bind. Whiting or sawdust, for example, can be added to create texture as well as the combination of metallic powder or dyes for other surface effects.

PAINTER'S ELEVATIONS

The designer must prepare for scene painting even if he is going to do his own painting. His painting ideas are expressed in the painter's elevations, which, unlike his sketch, remove all the atmosphere of stage lighting to show the true colors and exact form. The painter's elevation is a scaled drawing showing in detail the cartooning, or line drawing, a notation of actual color, and a clear indication of the painting technique. The scale of the drawing varies with the designer, some preferring to work at a small scale and others in a large scale. The larger the scale, however, the more accurately it can be interpreted. The painter's elevations for most settings can be done at ½-inch scale, with details shown at a larger scale.

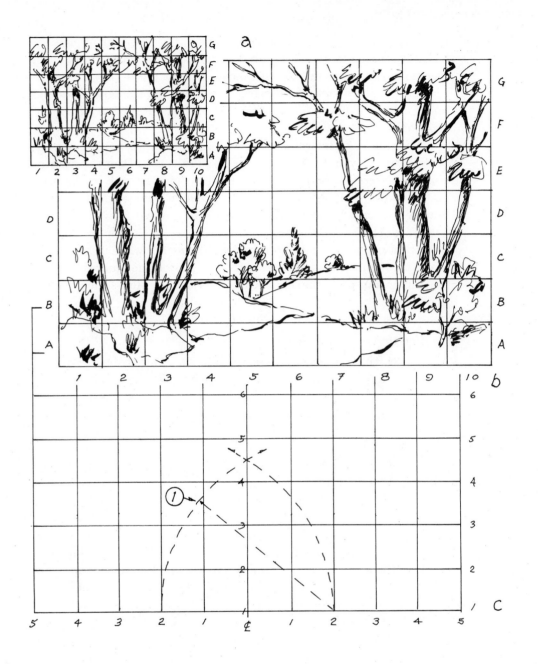

FIGURE 9-1. METHODS OF PROPORTIONAL ENLARGING. (a) The designer's elevation with a grid of two or three foot squares. Spaces are numbered from right to left and lettered from bottom to top. (b) Full-scale layout of the drawing with the same labeling method. (c) Full-scale grid with the lines numbered from the center line in opposite directions and from the bottom to top. The base line and center line are established first. (1) A perpendicular center line is constructed off the base line through the intersection of two arcs swung from centers equidistant to the center point.

If a designer is painting his own scenery, the preparing of painter's elevations becomes a time to think through the appropriate painting technique and procedure. At this point, if lights are to play an important part of the design, the designer can check the painter's elevations under colored lights to foresee the effect of the stage lights on the setting colors.

The painter, as he works from the painter's elevation, has a method of proportionally enlarging the drawing to full scale. Over the drawing he places a grid of horizontal and vertical lines, spaced, in the scale of the drawing, at 2-foot intervals. A similar grid, at full scale, is drawn on priming coat of the surface to be painted.

Ways of numbering or lettering the grid vary. In Europe, for example, the artists prefer to number the spaces (Figure 9-1) while in the United States the numbering of the lines is favored. Proceeding square by square, the painter transposes the small-scale elevation into a full-scale lay-out of the design.

PAINTING PROCEDURE

The three steps toward preparing a surface for decorative painting are the size, prime, and base coats of paint. Their individual use or omission varies in accordance with the complexity of the design, the nature of the surface, and the painting technique.

SIZE COATS

The first step toward preparing new canvas or muslin is the size coat which shrinks the canvas and glazes the surface without filling it. There are several uses and ways to mix size coats that bear mentioning. First, the starch size, which is used to prepare canvas or muslin for dye painting or very thin opaque paints. It can also serve as a surface for opaque paints, especially if the opaque coat is not completely covering the surface, but is applied so as to leave large areas of unpainted background. A starch size is made by adding a cup of cooked laundry starch to a 16-quart bucket of hot working size of about 20-to-1 proportion. A touch of dye or scenic color is added to make it more visible for brushing on the canvas. The resulting coat is a taut, slightly glazed surface that is excellent for dye painting.

Second, the alum size which is used over old painted canvas to stop the old coat of paint from picking up or bleeding through following coats of paint. Formaldehyde is sometimes used in place of alum with the same effect. A small quantity of powdered alum (½ cup to a 16-quart bucket) is mixed into working size of about a 10- or 16-to-1 proportion.

A third use of a size coat is as a glaze. A glaze is a thin, transparent coat that is more of a painting technique than a preparation step. It gives the surface a slight gloss without covering up the under-coat. A glaze mix is prepared by weakening or strengthening the working size, depending upon the degree of gloss that is desired. The stronger the size, the higher the gloss. The technique can vary from a filmy, transparent wash to a fairly glossy finish. A glaze technique is tricky and difficult for a beginner. It has to be applied quickly and lightly to avoid moving the painted detail underneath.

PRIME COAT

The second step in preparing new canvas is the prime coat, which has the function of filling the canvas. When painting on new canvas it is necessary to have it filled or the colors will "strike in" and lose brilliance. This is very noticeable when old canvas is used beside the new canvas on a flat.

A prime coat is made of working size and whiting with a touch of color to facilitate the application. It is kept thin so as not to overload the canvas. Because the prime coat fills the canvas it tends to be an opaque coat and therefore cannot be used over areas of the canvas that are to be translucent or dye painted. If there are no translucent areas on the flats, the size and prime coats are sometimes combined into one operation, shrinking and filling the canvas at the same time.

All cartooning or layout drawing is done in charcoal on the prime coat. After the drawing is completed, key points or portions of the cartoons are "inked" in a fine line of dye or indelible pencil. The rest of the charcoal is "flogged" or dusted off the surface in preparation for the base coat. The inked-in portions of the design will bleed through the base coat and serve as a guide for later detailed painting.

BASE COAT

The base coat is the under painting for the final decorative painting and texturing. The application and color of the base coat then depends upon what is to follow. For example, a base coat may be of one tone as a basis for a slick, modern paneled wall; it may be a scumbling of two or three tones in preparation for an antiqued, weather-beaten surface, or it may become a graded wash under a stenciled wallpaper design.

As a mixture, the base coat is kept thin so as not to overload the canvas. Because it is more intense in color than the prime coat, it will have less whiting and more pigment.

DETAIL AND DECORATIVE PAINTING

The final step of scene painting is the definition of form or the illusion of form through the various painting techniques of lining, texturing, and stenciling.

FIGURE 9-2. SCENERY PAINTING PROCEDURE.   Painter's elevations to finished scenery. Above: Painter's elevation of an oleo drop prepared by the designer. The drawing has been gridded with two-foot squares in preparation for enlarging. Opposite page, above: Proportional enlarging. The muslin has been sized and the drop has been gridded with charcoal and snap line to full-scale dimensions. The design is sketched in with charcoal so that mistakes and construction lines can easily be "flogged" or dusted off. Opposite page, below: Inking the cartoon. the charcoal drawing or cartoon of the design is fixed to the muslin with a thin dye outline. Page 266, above: Painting into the cartoon. Wash backgrounds and detail painting can proceed without fear of losing the cartoon, for the dye will bleed through the paint and be visible as guide lines. Page 266, below: Finished drop. An oleo drop for *Under the Gas Lights* by Augustin Daly. Designer—Glenn Gauer. (Photo—Nelson)

FIGURE 9–2(cont'd).

Lining. The technique of lining, with straight edge or free hand, **267**
is to represent in two dimensions the complicated surfaces of the moldings in a cornice, chair rail, panel, or door trim.

Careful lining, in addition to local color, is done with a minimum
of three tones: high light, shade, and shadow. Sometimes in showing a
large cast shadow two shadow tones are used consisting of a light and
dark shadow. The high light is cooler and, of course, lighter in value
than the local color, while the shade and shadow are in warmer and
darker tones.

The order of lining for a panel or cornice is determined after first
studying a cross section of the molding and the direction of the light
that would reveal the molding if it were real. The position of a window
or artificial-light sources are clues for fixing the general direction of
light for each wall in the set. If the paneling is for a stock set that
will be used in many positions, the light source is standardized as if
it were coming from above and left of the surface (Figure 9–3).

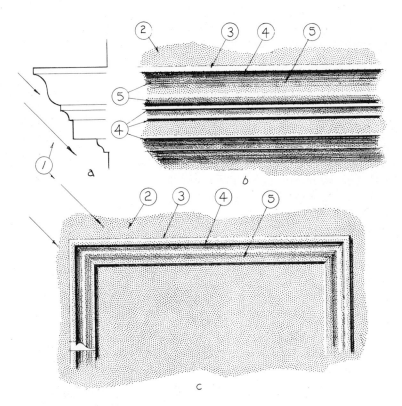

FIGURE 9-3. LINING TECHNIQUES. (a) Profile of cornice to be
painted. (1) Assumed direction of light. (b) Lining of cornice molding. (2)
Local color. (3) Highlight. (4) Shadow, darkest tone. (5) Shade. (c) Lining
of a raised panel molding.

Texturing. To avoid the starkness of a single tone and to bring more depth to a flat surface, the painter uses various texturing techniques. Because the stage lighting is from many sources compared to the limited sources found in nature, most of the natural shadows and reflected-light tonalities are eliminated. Much of this natural variation of tonality has to be painted into the set through the use of texturing techniques.

One of the simplest texturing techniques is to wet-blend or scumble three or more tones of a color on a surface. Using three brushes, one in each bucket, the three tones are brushed or blended together on the canvas while the paints are still wet. The result is an impression of one color with more depth and quality than is found in a single flat tone. This technique is usually handled on a broad scale with subtlety or obviousness depending upon the contrast or harmony of the tones.

A scumbling technique can also be done over a dry surface by blending the tones together with a dry-brushing or feathering. Dry-brushing, as the name implies, is done with the tip of a relatively dry brush so as to cover the under surface only partially and let it show through. Feathering refers to the direction of the brush stroke. The brush is drawn from the wet surface toward the dry so that the stroke ends in a featherlike pattern.

Other techniques that do basically the same texturing function at a smaller scale are sponging, stippling, spattering, combing, use of paint roller, and spraying. Each technique creates an individual feeling of texture as well as blending the tones into a vibrant surface (Figure 9-4).

All these techniques can be used to simulate the textural qualities of a specific material such as stone, plaster, wallpaper, and the like. Some materials, however, require texturing techniques that border on decorative painting, wood and wood graining being a prime example (Figure 9-5).

The painting of wood graining employs the same movement of color found in the other techniques. The grain pattern, of course, will vary with the type and use of the make-believe wood. Is it to be matched-grain walnut veneer on a late Empire break-front secretary, or knotty-pine vertical paneling? Any attempt at realistic representation of wood graining on the stage should be preceded by a careful study of the real wood's color and grain characteristic.

If the wood is a door or door trim and should appear as a varnished finish, the graining can be glazed. Glazing, however, not only reduces the contrast between colors, but also lowers their value. This must be taken into consideration in the preparation of the grain colors.

The glazing of grain that has a varnished finish can be accomplished in two different ways. The first method has been mentioned, which is to grain the surface first, then apply a glue, shellac, clear latex, or flat-varnish glaze. Of the three glazes, clear latex is the easiest to handle and gives

FIGURE 9-4. TEXTURING TECHNIQUES.   (1) Wet blending or scumble.
(2) Dry scumble. (3) Spattering. (4) Combing or dry brushing. (5) Rag
rolling. (6) Spraying. (7) Feather duster. (8) Paint roller. (9) Taped paint
roller to add a pattern to texture.

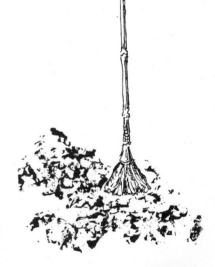

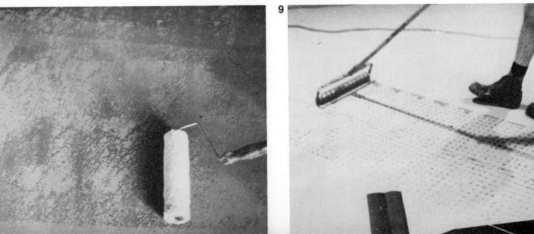

 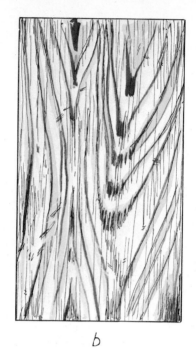 

a b c

FIGURE 9–5. WOOD-GRAIN AND MARBLE
TEXTURING. *(a)* Pine grain. *(b)* Oak grain.
(c) Marble.

the best results. The results, however, are hard to predict especially
if there is a change of surface materials, such as from wood to canvas
or vice versa.

A safer and easier approach is to put something with the paint
(dry color) that will give a gloss and eliminate the necessity of glazing
the surface at all. Scenic paint can be mixed directly with a flat varnish,
which serves as a binder as well as giving the paint a slight sheen.
Liquid wax mixed with scene paint produces the same effect and is
even easier to handle. Either method can be brought into a higher
luster by polishing with paste wax later. Glazed surfaces must be
handled with caution, however, for there is always the danger of creating a surface that is too reflective; it then becomes annoying to actors
and audience.

Stenciling. The chief use of the stenciling techniques is for a
painted wallpaper or similar condition in which a design motif is repeated in an interlocking over-all pattern. The cutting and printing of
a stenciled design is the fastest and most effective method of repeating
a small motif. After the means of interlocking the motif has been carefully figured out in relation to the size of the wall area, the motif is

traced upon a sheet of stencil paper. Stencil paper is a tough, oil-impregnated paper prepared especially for stencils. It is readily available in art shops or paint and wallpaper stores, or can be made by applying a half-and-half mixture of linseed oil and turpentine to a heavy wrapping paper.

A well-planned stencil has at least one full motif with portions of adjacent motifs to key the stencil into an interlocking scheme. The size of the motif and the amount needed for interlocking the design more or less determines the size of the stencil sheet. Care should be taken not to create too large a stencil that might become too awkward to handle. The motif is cut out of the paper with a sharp knife, razor blade, or Exacto knife, being sure to leave some tabs within the open parts to support the loose ends and strengthen the stencil as a whole. Two or more stencils can be cut at one time, for it is wise to have more than one stencil, especially if there is a large area to cover. They can be alternated in use so as to minimize the tendency of a stencil to become damp and misshapen from hard use.

After the stencil is cut, it is framed at the outside edges with 1 by 2 on edge to further strengthen it and at the same time provide a shield to the spray if the paint is being applied with a spray gun. The stencil is coated with clear shellac or any water-repellent plastic spray as an additional protection from the water-soaking effect of scene paint.

The stencil print can be made by three different methods: by spray gun, by brush, or by sponge. The spray gun is fast but sometimes messy. Stenciling with a brush is slower. The brush should be kept fairly dry and stroked toward the center of the openings to avoid dribbles. The use of a sponge or soft cloth to apply the paint works best on an open stencil, for the print is purposely textured and not clean cut (Figure 9–6).

Pouncing.   Pouncing is another method of transferring and repeating a design motif. It is generally used when the motif is either too large for a stencil, doesn't repeat enough times for one to bother cutting a stencil, or is repeated in reverse. Pouncing differs from stenciling in that only the outline or cartoon of the motif instead of a painted print is transferred as in the stencil.

The pounce pattern is made by first drawing the design on a piece of wrapping paper and then perforating the outline with a pounce wheel. The best type of pounce wheel (Figure10-6c)has a small swivel-mounted perforating wheel. It works better on a padded surface, such as a blanket or fold of canvas, than on a hard table top or floor.

After the design is perforated and the back-side rough edges are lightly sanded, the paper is laid on the canvas in the desired position. The pattern is rubbed with a pounce bag made of a thin material such

a

b

c

1

2

3

4

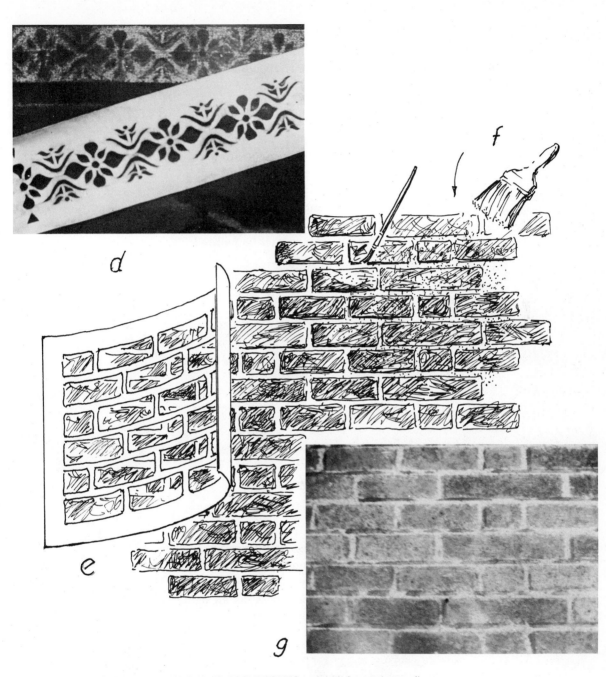

FIGURE 9-6. STENCILING TECHNIQUES. *(a)* Unframed stencil
for dry-brush application. *(b)* Framed stencil for spray-gun
application. Note how the stencil is keyed at the top and bottom.
As this stencil follows a vertical line it is not necessary to key it
horizontally. *(c)* Pouncing: (1) Pounce, or perforated design. (2)
Pounce wheel. (3) Pounce bag. (4) The pounced design
transferred onto the canvas. *(d)* Border stencil. *(e)* Brick stencil. *(f)*
Lining and spattering the stencil pattern. *(g)* Finished brick
pattern.

as cheesecloth filled with a dry color or charcoal dust. The outline is strengthened after the pouncing with charcoal, paint, or dye, depending upon the painting technique to follow.

TEXTURED SURFACES

Although their value on the stage is debatable, textured surfaces are sometimes desirable. Important points to consider before texturing a surface are: (1) a textured surface cannot be reclaimed for a different use without re-covering the piece of scenery; (2) deeply textured surfaces will not stand excessive handling or wear; (3) unless the texturing is in the position on the stage to get the proper lighting (preferably side lighting), it may as well be painted.

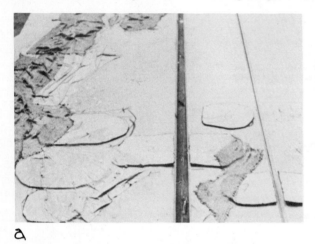

a

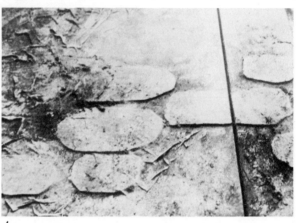

b

TEXTURE COMPOUNDS

Spackle.   The use of a prepared mixture of plaster and whiting called Spackle is the most familiar method of texturing. Because of the tendency of any texture coat to crack and flake off, Spackle is applied on a base of the same color unless, as an aging technique, some areas are

FIGURE 9-8. WALLPAPERING.   Occasionally the scenic artist is expected to hang wallpaper. The surface, if canvas, should be sized and based with casein or latex paint. If the wall surface is hard a size coat is sufficient. (a) Wallpaper strips of approximate length face down on pasting board. Wheat paste is used for regular wallpaper, or vinyl paste on vinyl wallpaper. (b) Paste-covered strip is folded one third as shown. (c) Exposed portion of pasted strip is smoothed onto wall being careful to match the pattern. Bubbles are smoothed-out with wallpaper brush. (d) Strip is unfolded and brushed flat. (e) Cutting wheel and roller. Edges are trimmed and, if paper is being applied to a hard surface, the edges are rolled. (f) Wallpapered unit of scenery. (g) Wallpapered panels.

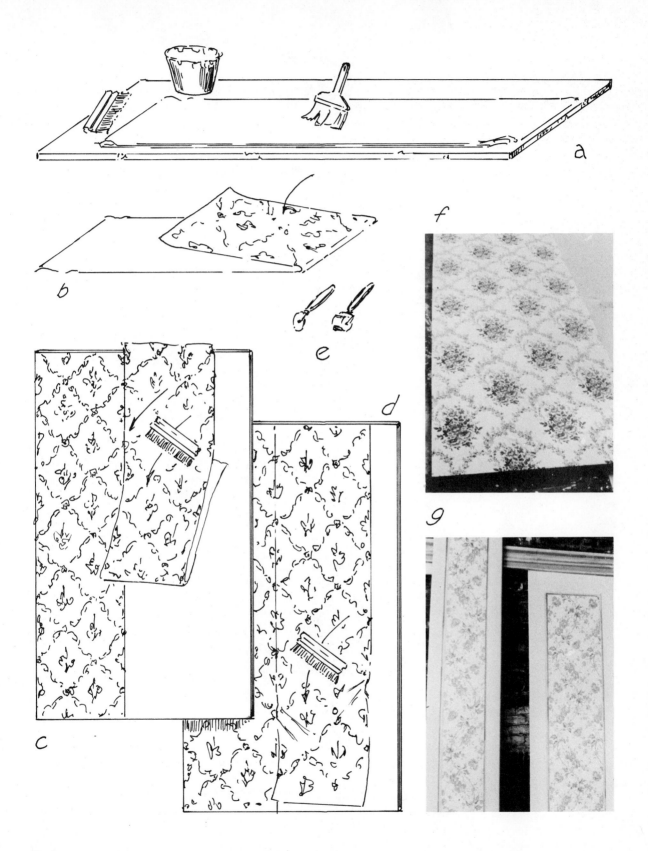

FIGURE 9-9. TEXTURED DETAILS.   Decorative details such as this
Rinceau pattern are often in slight relief. (1) A cut-out of the border
pattern is prepared in Upson board. Thick texture paint (J.C. Penney) is
applied with a cake decorator to the cut-out which is then glued to the
architrave position of the entablature. (2) After dry, all recessed surfaces
are stained dark and later brushed with metallic gold paint. (3) Final
assembly.

purposely knocked off to reveal an undercoat of a contrasting color. The Spackle, which can be obtained at local paint shops, is mixed in cold water, colored with dye, and applied in about ¼-inch layers. While it is damp it may be roughed, combed, or grained for more texture. Sawdust, cork, or wood chips may be added to the mixture for extra texture. After the Spackle coat dries (about 24 hours), it can be shellacked and detail painted.

Sawdust Coat. Sawdust or wood chips can be mixed directly with scenic paint and applied as a texture coat. The size should be stiffened a little to bind the sawdust firmly. A sawdust coat requires less preparation and dries more quickly than Spackle but does not have as deep a texture.

Water Putty. Durham's Water Putty, a commercial surface repair mixture in powder form, can be used as a texture coat. It works best on a hard surface (3-ply or wood) and can be combed or stippled into a deep texture. Although it dries off-white it can be colored either with dye during the mixing or with paint after it has dried. When hardened it is tougher than Spackle but still subject to chipping.

Joint Cement. A compound developed commercially to cement tape over dry-wall joints in house construction. It will hold a deep texture if a little white glue is added to the compound before application.

TEXTURE PAINTS

J. C. Penney Texture Paint. A prepared texture paint that is easy to apply. It holds a deep texture on a hard surface and is flexible enough to hold a medium texture on canvas.

Marble Coat. A texture paint made of marble dust that sets-up extremely hard. It takes a deep texture, can be colored when mixing, and when hardened it can be handled with the minimum of chipping. It is the hardest of the prepared texture coats.

SURFACE MATERIALS

Related to texturing a surface are the various materials that are used as a painting surface. Their varied uses are primarily for textural reasons. Each has its special handling and individual effect.

Irish linen has, of course, long since disappeared from the American theatre as the standard covering for framed scenery. Its durability and excellent texture have not quite been replaced by the scene canvas now in common use.

Canvas, which is 8-ounce cotton duck, has been discussed (see Size Coats) as a painting surface. It is the standard and most frequently used painting surface for all types of scenery. All other surfaces are limited in use to a special effect.

Muslin (unbleached) is the next most frequently used covering material. Although it lacks the texture and durability of canvas, its lightweight weave is useful for other purposes. As was mentioned, muslin is an excellent dye-painting surface for translucencies.

Scrim can be used as a painting surface outside of its general use as a dye-painted transparency. It can be used as a covering material if backed by canvas or some other opaque fabric.

Unbacked scrim can also be painted (dry brushed) with thin scenic colors. They are not as good as dyes, for they tend to stiffen the scrim which is a disadvantage if it has to fold or roll. To paint large areas of scrim it is best to use a spray gun to avoid stretching it out of shape.

Scrim mesh can be filled to create opaque areas with a mixture of latex and powdered chalk kept thin enough to spread, but thick enough to fill the mesh of the scrim.

Burlap is frequently used as a covering material chiefly for its texture. Burlap should be backed or fastened to a firm surface, for it is jute and may stretch or sag under a heavy coat of paint. Sometimes it helps to paint and dry it horizontally.

Burlap needs to be heavily sized to keep the color from "striking in." However, this may be a desirable effect if it is to be an old tapestry or wall hanging.

METHODS OF PAINTING

Scenery is painted in two different positions, horizontally and vertically. The various methods of painting are devised to facilitate either way of painting.

HORIZONTAL PAINTING

Painting on the floor is the oldest and simplest method requiring the least mechanical assistance. Long handles on the brushes, charcoal-holders, and straightedges help take the backache out of horizontal painting. The most essential requirement is lots of smooth floor space (preferably wood) and good overhead illumination (Figure 9–10).

Although some painting techniques are best employed horizontally, others are accomplished more easily in a vertical position.

STATIONARY FRAME AND BOOMERANG

It is easy to fasten scenery against a wall or on a stationary frame along a wall, but it is not so easy to reach all areas without using a ladder. A rolling platform or *boomerang,* as it is called, provides the painter with two or three painting levels (Figure 9–11).

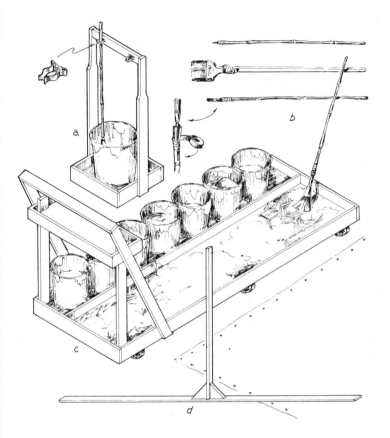

FIGURE 9–10. PAINTING ON THE FLOOR. Extensive floor painting is made easier with the use of proper tools and the right type of brushes. *(a)* Individual paint-bucket carrier. *(b)* Long handles for the brushes. *(c)* Paint cart with palette area for mixing paint. *(d)* Straight edge with handle.

MOVING FRAME

The moving paint frame which raises or lowers past the working level brings the greatest flexibility to vertical painting (Figure 9–11). The frame lowers into a well or to a second painting level. Some unusually high frames many times have two or three decks so that the painters can work at different levels at the same time.

TOOLS AND EQUIPMENT

The painter's most important tool is, of course, his brush. A good brush should have long bristles and a full shape (avoid hollow centers). Pure bristles are so expensive, especially in the larger sizes, that many painters have turned to nylon brushes. A nylon brush with sandblasted tips is about half the price of the pure-bristle brush of the same size. The difference in price offsets the slight disadvantage of nylon. Water color tends to run off the nylon, causing it to hold less paint than a pure-bristle brush.

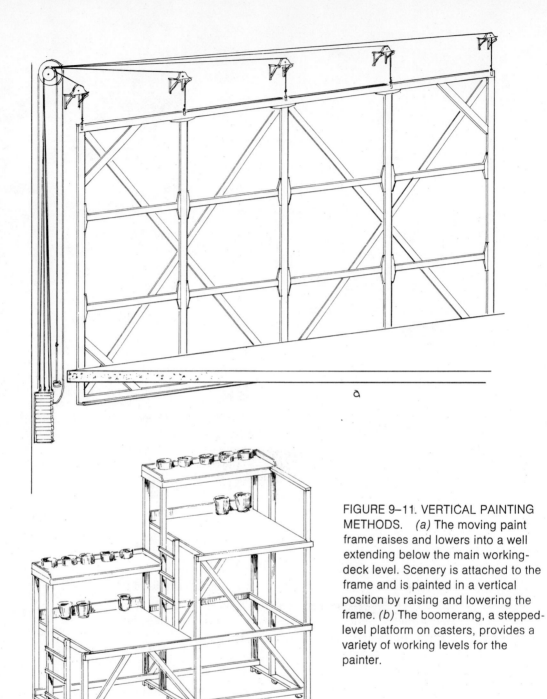

FIGURE 9–11. VERTICAL PAINTING METHODS. *(a)* The moving paint frame raises and lowers into a well extending below the main working-deck level. Scenery is attached to the frame and is painted in a vertical position by raising and lowering the frame. *(b)* The boomerang, a stepped-level platform on casters, provides a variety of working levels for the painter.

Because scene-painting brushes are used predominately in water colors, the bristles should be rubber set. Some brushes set in glue are suitable for oil paint, but will break down with continued use in water color.

TYPES OF BRUSHES

The types of brushes for scene painting are classified by the work they do, such as priming, base-coating or "lay-in," decorating, and lining (Figure 9–12).

The priming brush is the widest brush (6 to 8 inches). It holds a large quantity of paint which makes it good for spreading size and prime coats quickly and efficiently.

The lay-in brush is about 4 inches wide for the more careful painting of a base coat, blending, spattering, and similar techniques.

A decorating brush is from 1½ to 3 inches wide with a long handle. Sometimes called a foliage brush, it is used for most of the decorative painting, including the tree leaves. The foliage brush is a pure-bristle brush made especially for scene-painting and consequently is quite expensive. A sash tool, which is a long handled brush for painting window sashes, makes an inexpensive decorating brush.

Liners are also long-handled brushes varying in width from ¼ to 1 inch. Liners should have long pure bristles to perform well. A 1-inch sash tool can do limited lining, but there is no substitute for the smaller brushes.

PAINTING TOOLS

Besides brushes and paints, the painter uses other implements to prepare, lay out, and paint scenery. Other necessary painting tools are:
(1) Beveled straightedge (6 feet)
(2) Rule or steel tape
(3) Snap line (50 feet)
(4) Charcoal stick and holder
(5) Large compass (36 inches)
(6) Tank sprays
(7) Spray gun and compressor
(8) Pounce wheel
(9) Plumb bob
    Buckets (14 and 16 quarts)
    Small pots or cans (No. 10 cans)
(10) Bow snap line (6 to 8 feet)
(11) Burner and double boiler for glue
(12) Flogger
(13) Paint roller

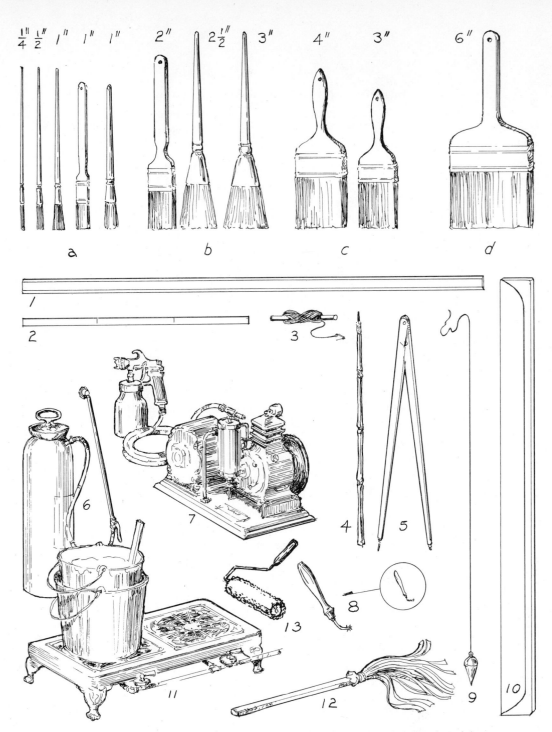

FIGURE 9-12. BRUSHES AND TOOLS. *Scene-painting brushes: (a)* Lining brushes, flat and oval. *(b)* Decorating brushes. *(c)* Lay-in brushes. *(d)* Priming brushes. *Painting tools and accessories:* (1) Beveled straight edge. (2) Yard stick. (3) Snap line. (4) Charcoal and holder. (5) Large compass. (6) Tank spray. (7) Spray gun and compressor. (8) Pounce wheel. (9) Plumb bob. (10) Bow snap line. (11) Burner and double boiler for glue. (12) Flogger. (13) Paint roller.

RELATED MATERIALS

ANILINE DYES

Aniline dyes are available in almost all the standard colors. They are used for inking in outlines, thin wash glazes, translucencies, and for dip-dyeing fabrics.

Dyeing or painting with dyes is a different process than painting with scene paints. Scene paint changes the color of a surface by covering it with a pigment which is held in place by a binder. Dyeing, on the other hand, is a chemical process. The dye color becomes a part of the material it is dyeing. It is important that the dye and material have an affinity for each other or a complete chemical action will not take place.

To dye cotton duck or muslin it is sometimes necessary to add a little acetic acid or vinegar to the dye solution. The acetic acid increases the affinity of the cotton for the dye causing the fabric to absorb more color from the dye bath. The addition of a little salt also helps to increase the amount of absorption. Salt counteracts the tendency of dye stuffs to go into solution, making it easier for the dye color to be absorbed by the material.

The presence of too much salt in the mixture, possibly from salted dyes or flameproofing compounds frequently mixed with the dye bath, can keep the dye from going into solution. It is important that all the crystals dissolve or streaks of concentrated color will appear on the surface of the canvas. If the dye is separating, the addition of some alcohol will insure a complete solution. Normally, the crystals go into solution in hot water without any trouble.

For extensive dye-painting, as in painting a translucent drop, the muslin is prepared with a starch size (see Size Coats). If the painting is being done on a fabric that cannot be starch-sized, such as velour or silk, a little starch can be added to the dye mixture to keep it from spreading on the fabric.

Dip-dyeing is used mostly on small pieces of fabric such as window drapes or tablecloths. Occasionally, large gauze pieces are dipped with excellent results.

The preparation of the dye for dip-dyeing is the same as for dye-painting except, of course, larger in quantity. It is important to be sure enough dye has been mixed, for to run out of dye mix in the middle of a dipping is disastrous. The color of the mix should be checked by dipping a sample of the fabric before preparing it for dipping.

In preparation for dip-dyeing, the fabric is first dipped in water. If it is new material, it should be washed to remove the size. After wringing, the still damp fabric is dipped into the dye mix. If it is a stage gauze, after squeezing or wringing out the excess dye, it should

284 be stretched to dry, or hung in place and stretched back into shape as it dries.

An important thing to remember is that dip-dyeing will take out any flameproofing that might have been in the material. It has to be reflameproofed later, or better still flameproofing mixed into the dye solution. The regular sal ammoniac and borax mixture (see Flame-proofing) can be cut to half strength by adding water and still give a satisfactory test. It is best, however, to run some test experiments under dipping conditions before taking a chance with a large piece.

FLAMEPROOFING

Canvas and muslin can be purchased already flameproofed but if the scenery has been washed for reuse the canvas will have to be flameproofed again. A mixture of one pound of sal ammoniac, one pound of borax, and three quarts of water is an inexpensive flameproof-ing formula. It is brushed or sprayed onto previously dampened material for the best results. Sheer materials, such as scrim or bobbinet, should be dipped to insure a successful test.

As the flameproofing mixture is highly corrosive to metals, brushes and spray cans should, after use, be washed thoroughly in cold water. A small amount of acetic acid in the water helps to counteract the corrosive action.

ADDITIONAL SUPPLIES

There are some additional supplies that supplement the dry colors, glue, and dyes which are directly associated with scene painting. Some have been mentioned in relation to a particular painting technique. These supplies and their uses are:

White shellac	For glazes, water-repellent finishes, binder, and hardener.
Alcohol	Solvent for shellac and speeds the dissolving of colors that are poor mixers.
Flat varnish	Glaze finish and paint binder.
Turpentine	Solvent for varnish and oil paints.
Liquid wax	Glaze finish and paint binder.
Metallic paints	Powder mixed with strong size or clear acrylic for metallic surfaces. All right for scenery, but not for props. Spray cans (Krylon) have harder finish, good for props, more expensive.
Glycerin	Added to paints for slow drying.
Formaldehyde	Preservative.

Alum	For alum-size preparation.
Sal ammoniac	Flameproofing chemical.
Borax	Formula—1 lb borax, 1 lb sal ammoniac to 3 qts of water.
Oil paints	Limited use in the theatre. When they are used they are the flat Japan color, or Coach colors.

10 The Handling of Scenery

When the designer is confronted with a multiscene play, he has to consider early in planning a method of handling the many settings. From the numerous ways of moving scenery he can develop a production scheme into his design concept. Consequently, the more he knows of the mechanics of the modern stage and theatrical techniques for moving scenery, the closer he can come to fully realizing his designs. This is especially true of theatre away from New York and its unlimited budgets, where the designer has to be clever not only to overcome limited funds but many times poorly equipped stages. Some hold the belief that too much technical knowledge inhibits a designer's imagination. To the contrary, it can help him solve his scenery-shifting problems with an ingenuity that often becomes inventively original.

METHODS OF HANDLING SCENERY

The four basic methods of handling scenery, in the order of their increasing complexity and additional construction are: first, the moving or running of scenery on the floor; second, the flying of scenery; third, the moving of scenery on casters, including such large units as wagons and revolving stages; fourth, the handling of scenery through the stage floor by elevators.

INFLUENCING FACTORS

How scenery is to be handled is influenced by four major factors: the play, the theatre and its stage, the design of the production, and the budget.

PLAY STRUCTURE

The form of the play or its plot structure are the primary influences on the handling of scenery. A play, for instance, may have many unrelated episodic scenes, a flash-back technique, several simultaneous scenes with continuous action, or the conventional three-act form. The structure of the play, besides determining the number of scenes or locale changes in their order of appearance or reappearance, also establishes the *kind* of change.

The most common interval for a change of scene is between acts. The act change, which can be as short as three minutes or as long as fifteen minutes, presents no great problem under optimum conditions, assuming the stage has adequate flying and offstage space. Even under limited stage conditions, an act change usually allows enough time to maneuver the scenery although it may require more ingenuity and manpower.

A change within the act, or scene change, can be as short as thirty seconds to as long as a minute and a half. If the time interval of a scene change is too long the play's continuity is seriously interrupted.

A scene change, by necessity a fast change, can be handled several different ways. It may be a hidden change, taking place behind a curtain, or without a curtain, but hidden by a blackout. It may be a *visible* change (avista) made in full view of the audience with a display of theatrical magic, or by actor-stagehands frankly moving elements of scenery as a part of the action.

In contrast to the other kinds of changes, the avista, or visible change, becomes more a part of the play, by calling attention to the movement of scenery. As a theatrical technique, it obviously fits only certain types of plays and production schemes.

THEATRE AND STAGE

The shape of the theatre and the size of the stage, of course, have an important influence on the movement of scenery. The amount of flying space and equipment, the extent of offstage and wing space, the size of the proscenium opening, and sightline conditions obviously help determine the way scenery can be handled.

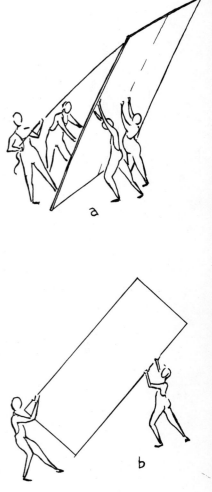

c

Some stages have more elaborate mechanical aids or stage machinery for shifting scenery such as built-in revolving stage, tracking and offstage space for full-stage wagons, or elevator stages. The existence of one or more of these mechanical aids in a theatre cannot help but influence scenery-handling techniques.

Other scenery-shifting considerations are those of a traveling production. Instead of one theatre and stage the designer has to consider the size and sightline conditions of many stages and auditoriums as well as the physical limitations and extreme portability expected of scenery for a road show.

Elaborate scenery-moving devices such as turntables and treadmills are sometimes duplicated so as to reduce the setup time in each theatre. Two crews are used. The first specializes in assembling the shifting aid which might be a turntable, for example. They work in advance of the second crew who are running the show. The second crew, when the run is finished, moves the show from theatre A to theatre B onto the pre-assembled turntable No. 2, leaving behind turntable No. 1. The first crew then returns to theatre A and moves turntable No. 1 in leap-frog fashion to theatre C, and so on.

DESIGN AND SCHEME OF PRODUCTION

The scene designer combines the influences of the play and the stage and adds a third control, the scheme of production. The designer's production scheme stems from the kind of scene or locale change inherent in the play, the physical limitations of the stage, and his visual concept of the play's setting (Chapter 4). A designer cannot design a large production without thinking through, at least in basic terms, a method or scheme for handling the changes.

BUDGET

The influence of budget on the handling of scenery is felt directly through the control of the scale of the set designs and general size of the productions. Although the operational budget has little direct effect on the form of the physical stage, it does influence its operation in providing funds for an adequate production staff. A large stage with a small technical staff, for example, would limit the amount of scenery that could be efficiently handled.

An operational budget also is tied in with the estimated length of run. A Broadway show with a prolonged run, for example, can reduce its operational costs by spending more money on costly mechanical aids to shift the scenery, thereby cutting down the number of stage-hands on the weekly payroll.

d

The operational budget of university or community theatre influences scenery handling in a slightly different way. The decision to use an extensive mechanical aid is based upon its reuse value for other productions so as to spread the cost throughout the season's operational budget.

BACKSTAGE ORGANIZATION

The layman who has seen a fast change from a backstage vantage point is often amazed by the teamwork and precision with which the large pieces of scenery, properties, lights, and actors seem to move. This is due, to some extent, to careful rehearsing, but largely it is the result of normal backstage organization and its division of responsibility. Under the coordinating management of the stage manager a production has two major divisions: acting and technical. The technical responsibilities are divided between the scenery, electrical, property, and costume departments.

e

STAGE MANAGER

Once the production is on the stage, the stage manager becomes its field commander. The responsibility of the performance is in his hands. He starts each performance, gives all cues, calls the actors, and posts all daily calls. He is charged with maintaining production standards set by the director and company discipline onstage.

STAGE CARPENTER

Although taking his cues from the stage manager, the master carpenter is in charge of the shifts, the rigging, and the general condition of the scenery. Responsible to him is the crew, which is made up of assistant carpenters, grips (stagehands), and flymen.

MASTER ELECTRICIAN

The responsibilities of the master electrician include the hanging and focusing of the lighting instruments, the maintenance of all electrical equipment, and operation of the switchboard for the lighting cues. Any movement of lighting equipment during a shift comes under the supervision of the stage carpenter but may be done by grips assigned to the electrical department.

MASTER PROPERTY MAN

The property man's duties include the care and maintenance of the set and hand props, rugs, ground cloth, mechanical sound effects, and any trick device handled by the actors too small to be classified as

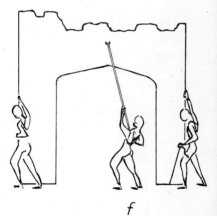

f

scenery. He supervises the handling of props during a shift with the help of grips assigned to the property department.

Sometimes electrified props cause what may seem to be double handling. A living room lamp, for example, is placed on the set by a member of the prop crew, but it is connected and lighted by the light crew. The offstage storage and visual appearance of the lamp is the responsibility of property men, while all electrical maintenance is done by the electrician. The division of responsibility is clearly and logically defined.

SOUND MAN

Although traditionally a member of the electrical department, the sound man is established in many theatre organizations as a separate department. The increasing use of high-fidelity recording for a major portion of the sound effects and incidental music warrants in many cases the creation of a sound department.

The sound man is responsible for the recording and editing of each show tape as well as the operation of sound equipment for sound cues. He supervises the placement and installation of speakers and microphones, maintains all sound equipment, the stage manager's inner-communication, and for a permanent producing group might organize and service a sound-recording library.

WARDROBE MISTRESS

The care and maintenance of all costumes is the responsibility of the wardrobe mistress, as well as the assistance of actors during a fast costume change. The backstage organization of community and university theatres often places the supervision of make-up in the costume department.

THE RUNNING OF SCENERY ON THE FLOOR

Running or "gripping" of scenery is the simplest handling method and requires the least additional construction. As the units are usually strong enough to support themselves, the only additional support that is needed is horizontal stiffening of two or more units; the vertical bracing of the piece in an upright position; and the quick and easy method of joining together the various parts of the set. Occasionally the extreme height of scenery combined with its traditional thinness makes it difficult to move, to anyone not experienced in handling scenery.

The designer frequently thinks through a method of handling a particular piece of scenery before deciding on the scale or fragileness of its design. Some of the many ways of handling single flats, twofolds,

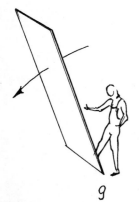

g

FIGURE 10-1. RUNNING SCENERY.   The running or "gripping" of scenery is the simplest handling method although, occasionally, the awkward shape or extreme size of a piece may require experience to handle it successfully. Page 287: (a) "Walking-up" a stiffened two-fold. (b) "Edging-up" a single flat. Page 288: (c) Running or "gripping" a single flat. (d) Making a lash. Page 289: (e) Running a two-fold. (f) Three men running a top-heavy piece. Above: (g) "Floating" down a single flat.

and partially assembled units of scenery on the floor are illustrated in Figure 10–1.

STIFFENING, BRACING, AND JOINING

Because scenery has to travel in units of relatively small, lightweight sizes to get in and out of theatres, it depends on joining or unfolding these smaller units into larger shapes. The new larger shape requires stiffening to be safely handled in a shift.

A stiffener is usually a horizontal stiffening member (1 by 3 or 1 by 4 on edge) that is loose-pin-hinged into place as the set is assembled. A vertical stiffener is often called a "brace," especially if it is in the form of a "jack," to brace the unit in an upright position. Bracing and stiffening can take a variety of forms depending upon the shape and size of the scenery they are reinforcing (Figure 10–2).

Joining appears in three different categories again related to the portable nature of scenery and the degree of permanence of the joint. Elements of scenery may be joined together by fixed or permanent joining, by assembly joining, or by temporary joining. The kind of joint and its location is often important to the design as the designer seeks ways to avoid a crack or open joint in a conspicuous area of the setting.

Fixed joining occurs as the scenery is being built (with use of nails, screws, and so on). A fixed hinged joint is made with tight-pin hinges so that large units composed of several small pieces may unfold into larger sizes. The smaller pieces remain fixed together and travel or move from shop to stage folded, to be unfolded and stiffened into their final shape in the theatre (Figure 10–3a,b,c,d).

On the other hand, large areas of scenery may be made in separate small pieces to be assembled in the theatre. Loose-pin hinges, bolts and wing nuts, and turn buttons are some of the most frequently used methods of assembly joining pieces of scenery together into a larger unit. After it is stiffened and braced, the larger unit can be handled in its assembled form until time to leave the theatre (Figure 10–3e,f,m).

The temporary joining of scenery occurs at the time of the striking and making of a set during an act or scene change. The lashed joint is the most common means of temporarily joining units of scenery. Loose-pin hinges, turn buttons, and hooks and eyes are some additional ways that scenery may be temporarily joined (Figure 10–3e,j,k).

A *lip* is often used to cover a flush temporary joint between two flats. The lip, which is made of a 4-inch strip of ¼-inch plywood with both edges beveled is secured to an edge on the face of one of the joining flats. It is attached under the canvas with about an inch overhang (Figure 10–3a).

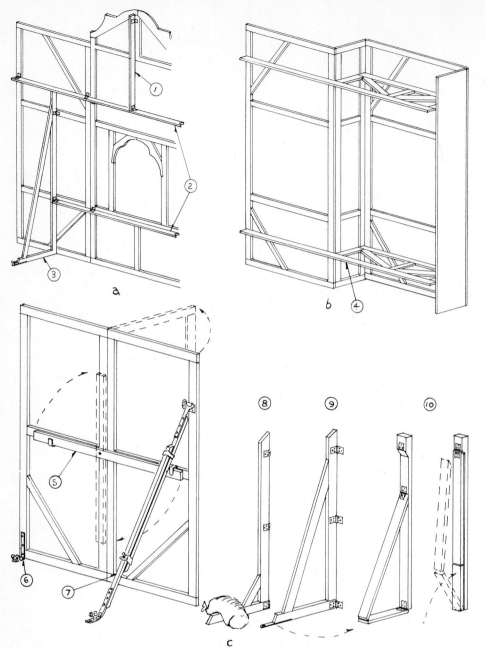

FIGURE 10–2. BRACING AND STIFFENING. *(a)* Stiffening a fla wall: (1) Vertical stiffener. (2) Horizontal stiffener. (3) Bracing o "jack." *(b)* Stiffening a jogged wall: (4) A framed stiffener which conforms to the shape of the wall *(c)* Other bracing and stiffening techniques: (5) A swivel keeper bar and keeper hooks. (6) Bent footiron and stage screw. (7) Adjustable stage brace. (8) L-jac and sandbag (no stage screw). (9) Hinged jack. (10) Folding jack

FLYING SCENERY

The designer is always interested in the size of the stage house and the type of flying system, if any, over the stage, for the extent of flown scenery he may design depends upon their presence or absence. A good stage house that is designed to handle scenery in the air will have an adequate flying system and generous amount of hanging space, which means a high and wide loft. The two common methods of flying scenery

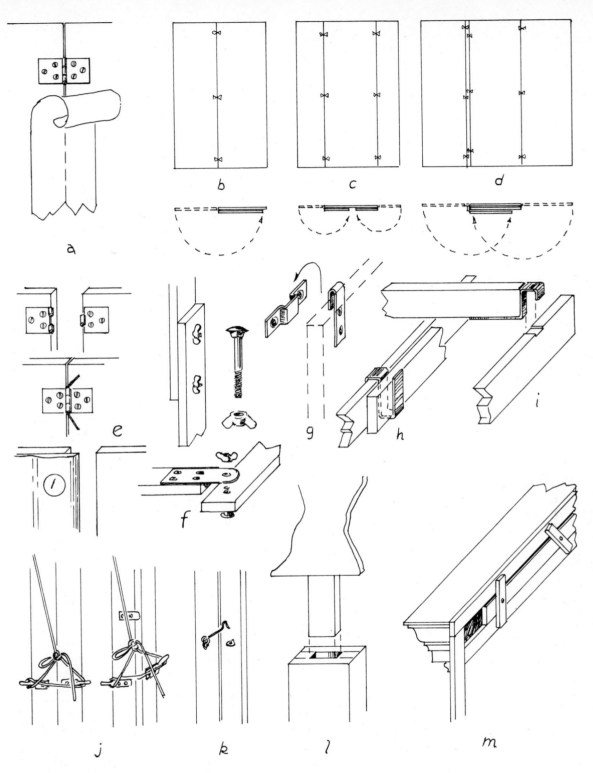

FIGURE 10–3. THE JOINING OF SCENERY. *Fixed joining: (a)* Tight-pin hinge and dutchman. *(b)* Two-fold, two flats tight pin-hinged together. *(c)* Three-fold, two jogs, and a flat hinged together. *(d)* Three-fold and "tumbler" to hinge three full-width flats together. *Assembly joining: (e)* Loose-pin hinge. (1) Front view of a lip as it is used to cover a flush joint. *(f)* Bolting. *(g)* Picture hanger. *(h)* S-batten hook. *(i)* Keeper hook on end of a spanner. *Temporary joining: (j)* Lashing, flush and around corner. Note stop cleat. *(k)* Hook and eye. *(l)* Tongue and socket. *(m)* Turn buttons.

are the pin-and-rail and counterweight systems. Both are based on the presence of a gridiron over the stage to support the sheaves or pulley blocks and the extended control of the line sets to one of the side walls. They differ in the complexity of the rigging, cost of installation, and the flexibility of use.

GRIDIRON

As the name implies, the gridiron is a grid or open floor of iron high over the stage. The average gridiron has at least three and sometimes four or five channels which run up and down stage and are spaced at approximately ten-foot intervals across stage. Across each channel opening, which is about six to eight inches wide, sit the sheaves that make up the line-sets. Each line, as it runs over the sheave, drops through the channel to the stage floor.

The space between the channels is floored with strips of 3-inch channel iron running parallel to the main channels. The channel-iron strips are set far enough apart to allow the spotting of additional sheaves for special spotlines (Figure 10–4c–1).

Recent gridiron designs employ the use of many more channels at about four-foot intervals. Swivel loft blocks are suspended above the gridiron floor from beams over each channel. The multichanneled gridiron is discussed in more detail later in this chapter and is illustrated in Figure 10–6.

LINE-SETS

A line-set refers to the grouping of three or more lines into a set to be handled as one line. The sheaves of a line-set are usually placed over each channel opening and are all at the same distance from the proscenium, thus forming a line parallel to the footlights.

FIGURE 10–4. FLYING SYSTEMS. *(a)* Pin-and-rail or "hemp" system: (1) Short line. (2) Center line. (3) Long line. (4) Tandem head block. (5) Double pinrail on fly door. (6) Sandbag counterweight. (7) Clew or "sunday" on a line-set. *(b)* Counterweight system: (1) Pipe batten, a fixed line set. (2) Hoisting cable for liftlines. (3) Head block, multigrooved. (4) Trim chains at top of arbor. (5) "T" track. (6) Purchase line. (7) Lock and safety line on lock rail which may be on a fly floor or the stage deck. (8) Idler pulley. *(c)* A demonstration of the flexibility of the pin-and-rail system: (1) Spot sheaves used to fly a drop at an askew angle. The spotlines use the same or adjacent head blocks. (2) The separation of a single line from a line-set to use in a spot-sheave.

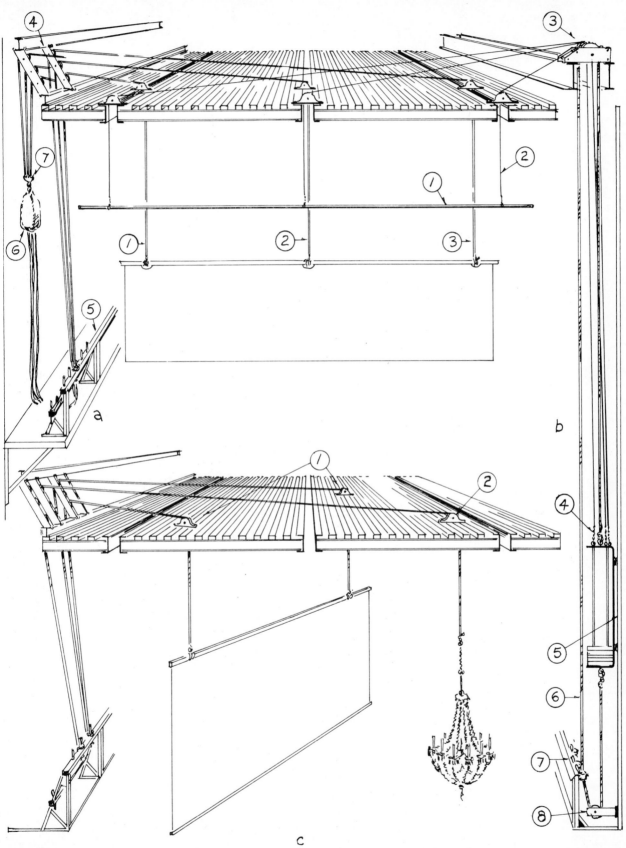

The number of lines in a line-set depends upon the number of channels in the individual gridiron. A stage with a wide proscenium opening might have as many as five lines in a set, while a small stage usually has only three lines to a set.

The lines are named by their length and position on the stage. The line nearest the control side (pinrail or lock rail) of the stage is the short line and the line to the far side of the stage is the long line. The line in between is, of course, the "center line." A four line-set would have two center lines, a "long center," a "short center," and so on.

PIN-AND-RAIL

The pin-and-rail system is the older though more flexible of the two flying systems. It is a less costly installation but does, however, require more skill and greater manpower to operate. The "hemp" system, as it is sometimes called, uses ¾-inch manila rope for liftlines. As illustrated in Figure 10–4a, the individual line in a line-set (1), (2), (3) comes up from the stage, passes through the loft block, travels horizontally to one pulley in the head block (4) located on the left or right stage wall. From the head block in which the pulleys are mounted in tandem, the lines are brought together as a set and tied off at the pinrail (5). The lower rail of the pinrail is usually the trim tie for the drop in its "in" or working position, and the top rail receives the tie for the "out" or stored position. A line-set can be "clewed" or bound together (7) and sandbagged (6) to counterweight a heavy piece for easy handling.

As can be seen, the pin-and-rail system has great flexibility in its ability to use, as desired, only part of a line-set, add a spotline to a line-set, or, in some instances, cross line-sets. The adding of a spotline employs a single rope and loft sheave occasionally placed in a remote position on the gridiron to fly a raked, or angled, piece of scenery (Figure 10–4c–1).

The chief disadvantage of a "hemp house" is the amount of manpower that is required to run a show, as well as the professional skill necessary to rig and safely counterweight heavy pieces of scenery. To the designer, this disadvantage is far outweighed by the greater design possibilities inherent in the flexibility of the pin-and-rail system.

THE COUNTERWEIGHT SYSTEM

Unlike the pin-and-rail system which can separate lines or add a single line to the line-sets, the counterweight system uses fixed line-sets. Although the counterweight system was born in an era of box settings and raked scenery as theatrical styles, it is, paradoxically, rigidly based upon wing and backdrop staging. It keeps the lines in sets, fixed to a pipe batten parallel to the footlights.

The system, as illustrated in Figure 10–4b, begins at the pipe batten (1) and the permanently attached wire-cable liftlines (2). Lifting the batten, the lines pass through the individual loft blocks at each channel, over a multigrooved, single-pulley headblock (3) and attach to the top of the counterweight arbor (4). The arbor is guided by a "T" track (5), or guy wire, and controlled by a separate purchase line. The purchase line (6) is also attached to the top of the counterweight arbor and passes through the large groove in the head block. It then turns toward the floor and after going through the lock (7) on the lock rail and around the idler pulley (8) fastens to the bottom of the arbor.

Pulling down on the outside purchase line lifts the arbor and lowers the scenery hanging on the batten. A corresponding amount of weight placed on the arbor balances the weight of the scenery. Although the counterweight system is easy to run with parallel scenery, it is less flexible due to the fixed line-sets. Most of the rigging time used to hang an angled or raked piece is spent in overcoming rather than using the system.

WINCH SYSTEMS

There have been attempts in the past to electrify a flying system, such as the use of a single electric-motor-driven winch to lift a battened line-set. In this system, all the lines in the set are wound upon a single drum which turns in only one direction to lift the batten. A mechanical clutching and braking device disengages the drum from the motor allowing the weight of the attached scenery to bring the batten back down to the stage floor. Its only advantage over the limitations of the fixed line-sets of the counterweight system is the saving of manpower by placing the remote-control operation under one person. The slow fixed speed and insensitivity of the system combined with the rather hazardous braking operation has caused the "electric batten," as it was called, to fall into disuse.

A new but short-lived method of flying scenery is the synchronous-winch system designed by George Izenour (Figure 10–5). It is based upon a radically different approach to the control and placement of the winches as well as a unique gridiron concept. Although the synchronous-winch system promised to give the theatre both the flexibility of the pin-and-rail and the weight-lifting capacity of the counterweight system, plus the added feature of a centralized electronic control, it failed in its initial obligation—synchronization. Repeated attempts to improve the design only proved that the system could never provide a dependable trim over a group of winches. While the synchronous winch

298

has fallen short of being the ultimate method for flying scenery, it has proven moderately successful in installations where it is combined with both the pin-and-rail and counterweight systems. It functions best when limited to scenery loads involving a scattered pattern of liftlines and conditions where accurate trim is not critical.

Perhaps the most important by-product of the synchronous-winch venture is the new look of the gridiron. The two features that have improved the gridiron for any flying system are, first, the increased number of channel openings positioned to extend from wall to wall of the stage, and second, the use of swivel loft blocks suspended at head height over each channel.

To have more channel openings at closer spacing (about four- to five-foot intervals) makes it easier to spot lines away from the playing area to positions offstage. The gridiron can now provide a spotline in any area of the stage without involving a major rigging problem to overcome rather than extend a flying system.

The overhead swivel loft block provides a cleaner gridiron floor which is normally filled with sheaves and fixed line sets. A single bolt or pin holds the swivel block in the overhead channel beam making it a simple operation to loosen and slide up- or downstage, or, move to another channel.

An additional feature contributing to an uncluttered gridiron floor is the mounting of all fixed line-sets under the gridiron floor in a lower set of channels at the conventional spacing of a counterweight system.

An equally important outgrowth which, perhaps, made the new gridiron possible is the use of ⅛-inch aircraft cable as liftlines in place of hoisting cable or hemp rope. The use of the smaller, more flexible steel cable and resulting smaller sheaves and working parts has become an accepted practice.

The newest flying system to be developed by Izenour and his associates at Yale is a motor driven spotline system. It is apparent in the pictorial drawing of the system (Figure 10–6) that the basic concept is to use an individual driver motor on a specially designed double-purchase counterweight line-set. The theory is that after the weight of the scenery on the individual arbor has been counterweighted the work

FIGURE 10–5. THE SYNCHRONOUS-WINCH SYSTEM (drawing opposite page). (1) Gridiron, channels running up and downstage. (2) Winches mounted on proscenium and back wall of stage (photograph of a winch with cover removed). (3) Liftlines, ⅛-inch aircraft cable. (4) Swivel loft block. (5) Cross section of channel beam holding loft block. (6) Truss batten to increase span and reduce the number of liftlines in a line-set. (7) A group of lines in operation. (8) The console. (9) Control group. (10) Driver group.

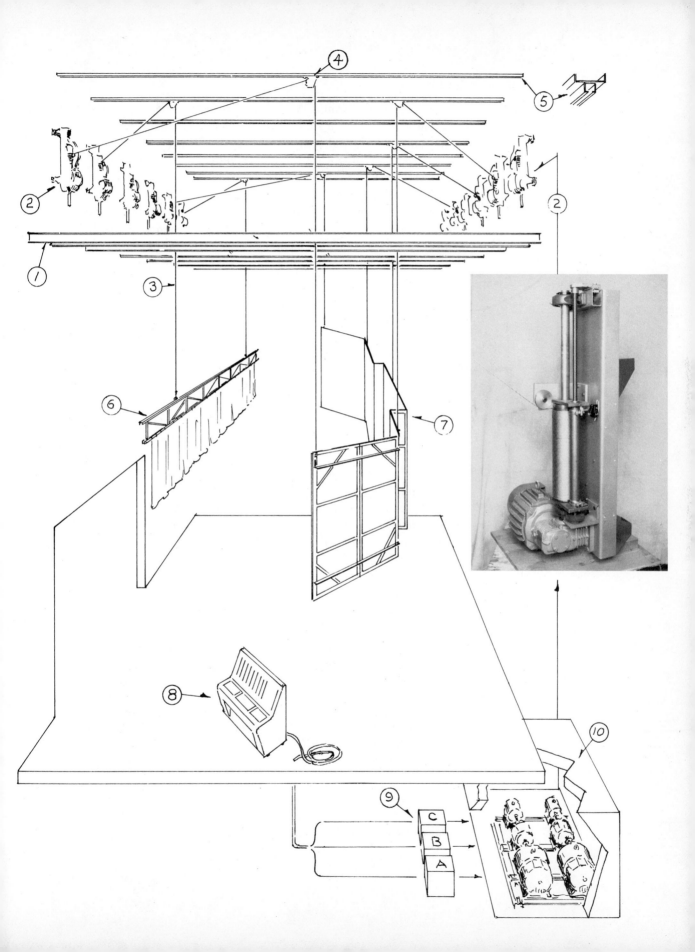

load on each motor would be more or less the same, which keeps the horsepower of the drive small and eliminates the need for synchronization, line to line, within the working set. The electronic read-out of the exact position of the arbor has been retained from the synchronous-winch system but the operational accuracy is greatly improved.

The driver which is a variable-speed three-quarter horsepower d-c electric motor is placed either under the stage floor or through the stage wall to minimize noise. It is attached through a quadrature reduction gear to the lower portion of the purchase line by a sprocket and roller chain drive and utilizes both dynamic and electromechanical braking.

The top of the arbor is not connected to the conventional fixed line-set arrangement but utilizes new spotline and trim adjustment features. The head block, although in tandem mounted position, is made up of individual caster-mounted swivel pulleys which increase the "fleet angle" or spread of the lines in the set. The swivel head block, while allowing a wide spread to the pattern of the loft blocks in the line-set, is dependent upon the adjustable length of each line in the set to be completely flexible. The length adjustment of an individual line is accomplished by taking up each line on a trimming winch at the trimming gallery position. This small hand winch is located at what would normally be the end or "dead tie" of a single liftline in a double-purchase system.

To base the motor-driven arbor on a double-purchase counterweight system, however, gives the flyman cause for concern because of its tremendous demand for counterweights. The nature of the rigging produces a mechanical disadvantage of two to one thereby creating a counterweight load twice the weight of the scenery it is lifting. The storing of counterweights, the endless job of loading and unloading an arbor are tasks that are not eliminated but are doubled when the double-purchase system is employed.

FIGURE 10–6. MOTOR-DRIVEN SPOT-LINE SYSTEM. *(a)* A pictorial drawing of the rigging for one line-set. (1) Driver motor, a ¾ horsepower, variable speed d-c motor. (2) Sprocket and roller chain drive. (3) Movable bull-winch to retrieve empty arbor for loading. (4) Arbor. (5) Grooved pulleys to return the four liftlines to (6) Grooved muling pulley, the normal dead-tie position on the regular double-purchase counterweight system. (7) Trimming winches to adjust the length of each liftline. (8) Swivel head blocks in tandem mount. (9) Swivel loft blocks. (10) Channel openings at about four-foot intervals. (11) Underslung channel supporting loft blocks for rigid line sets. (12) Head block for rigid line-set. (13) Pipe batten. *(b)* Schematic diagram of the motor driven spot line system.

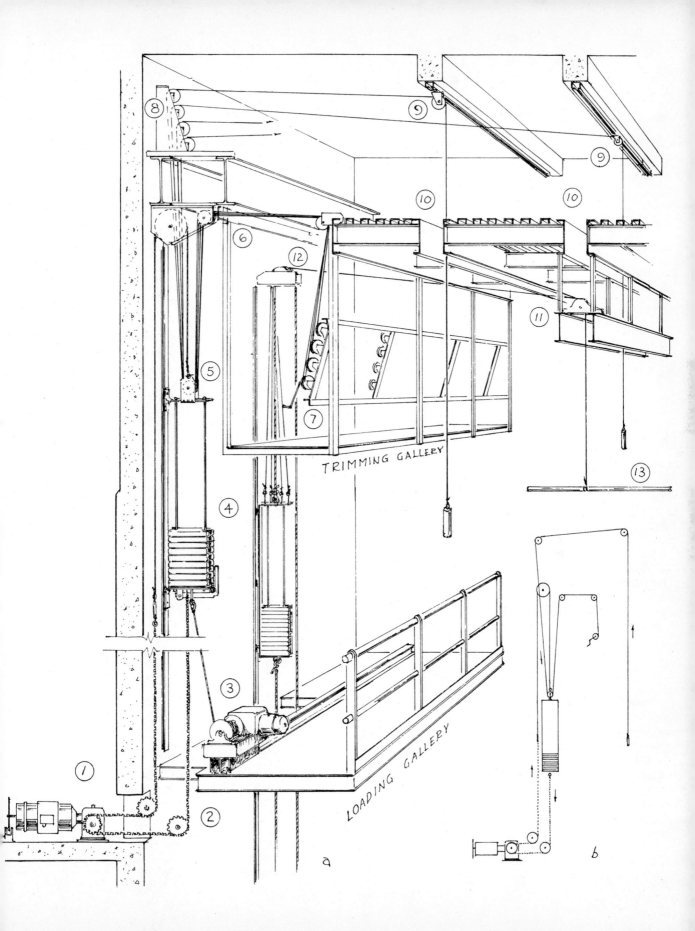

TRIMMING GALLERY

LOADING GALLERY

a

b

The advantages of the new motor-driven spotline system over the synchronous-winch are three-fold. First, the number of lines to each motor has been quadrupled; second, the synchronizing problem within a line-set has been eliminated and improved between line-sets; and last, by using the double-purchase rigging, the top speed has been doubled from 2 feet per second to 4 feet per second.

In its present concept the motor-driven spotline system is not intended to be the sole method of flying scenery in any given theatre. An installation including twelve to twenty-four motor-driven arbors interspersed with several counterweighted rigid line-sets, as well as the always flexible pin-and-rail line-sets, would be considered ideal.

RIGGING

Whether a stage is equipped with a pin-and-rail, counterweight, or synchronous-winch system, there are several flying and rigging techniques common to all systems. While many of the routine problems inherent in the older systems are eliminated in a winch system, certain specific problems pertaining to the movement of scenery in relationship to its hanging position and loft height will be forever present.

Stage rigging begins with the relatively simple process of hanging scenery and includes the more complicated maneuvers of breasting and tripping scenery elements. The handling of stage curtains (such as the traveler, tableau, and contour curtains) and the unframed drop are also a part of stage rigging.

FIGURE 10–7. THE HANGING OF SCENERY. *(a)* Hanging hardware: (1) Top hanger iron, straight. (2) Ceiling plate and ring. (3) Bottom hanger iron, hooked. *(b)* Trim adjustments: (1) Trimming hitch using hemp rope of sash cord. (2) A snatch line. The snap hook on the end of the liftline makes it possible to unhook a flown piece of scenery. (3) Turn-buckle on wire cable, another way to adjust the trim of a flown piece of scenery. *(c)* Various methods of hanging a drop: (1) Tie around top batten. (2) Tie through batten. (3) Drop holder. (4) Tie-lines to pipe batten. (5 and 6) Floor stays.

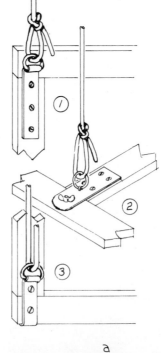

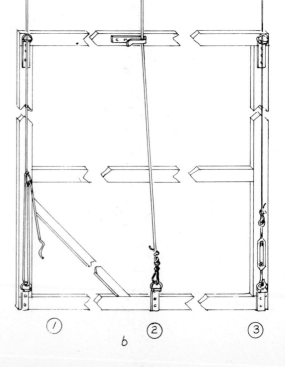

a

b

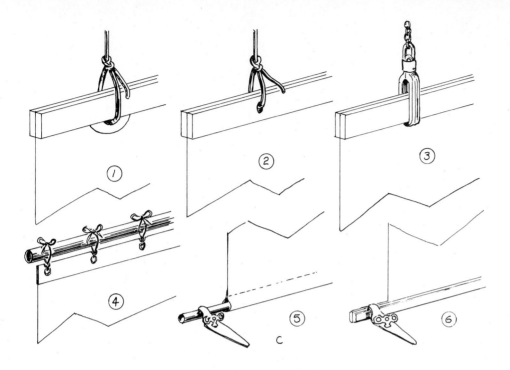

Hanging Scenery. An early step in rigging is the preparation of scenery to hang by providing hardware or some other means of attaching the liftlines. Hanger irons or D-rings, which are used on framed scenery, should be bolted to a vertical member of the framing for greater strength. On extremely tall or heavy pieces two rings are used, the one at the top serving as a guide for the liftline which is attached to the bottom. To lift the load from the bottom is not only a safer procedure, but it also provides a convenient position to trim each line (Figure 10–7a,b). The use of the turnbuckle or trimming hitch as illustrated is, of course, not necessary on the pin-and-rail system, for each line can be brought into trim from the flyfloor. The same is true of the winch system which can "inch" an individual line into exact trim.

Unframed pieces of scenery, such as drops and borders, are hung from their top battens and can be fastened to a pipe batten, or picked up by a set of lines in many ways (Figure 10-7c). The long thin batten requires numerous pick-up points, about every six feet (see Bridling), to keep it from sagging and thereby spoiling the trim of the drop.

Knots. Safe stage rigging requires the use of many familiar knots. The stage technician, and the designer who has to supervise his own rigging, should be skilled in the use of at least a few of the knots and hitches that appear in stage rigging. Some of the most frequently used knots are illustrated in Figure 10–8 along with notations of their uses for stage rigging. A more detailed and comprehensive manual of knots

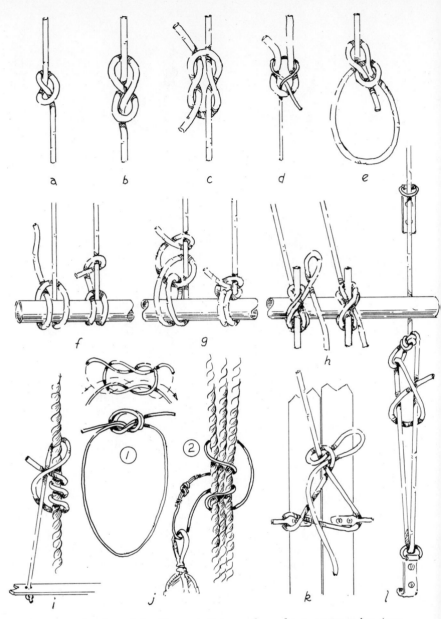

FIGURE 10–8. KNOTS USED IN STAGE RIGGING. *(a)* Half hitch or overhand knot. *(b)* Figure eight, used to put a knot in the end of a line to keep it from running through a pulley or eye. *(c)* Square knot, for joining ropes of the same size. *(d)* Sheetbend, for joining ropes of different sizes. *(e)* Bowline. A fixed loop used on end of litfline through ring. *(f)* Clove hitch on a batten, finished with a half hitch. It grips firmly under tension, but is easy to adjust or untie. *(g)* Fisherman's bend. Excellent for a tie onto a batten. Not as easy to adjust as the clove hitch. *(h)* Half hitch over a belaying pin. Used as tie-off on pinrail. *(i)* Stopper hitch, made with a smaller line in the middle of a larger rope. The safety line on the counterweight lock rail uses a stopper hitch on the purchase line. *(j)* Sunday: (1) A method of joining the ends of a small loop of wire cable without putting a sharp kink in the cable. (2) The loop is then used to clew a set of rope lines together so as to counterweight them with a sandbag. *(k)* Lashline tie-off. *(l)* Trimming hitch, to adjust the trim of a hanging piece of scenery.

and splices can be found in the catalogue of cordage companies (see Bibliography).

Breasting Scenery. Two pieces of scenery, regardless of which flying system is being used, cannot occupy the same space at the same time, although the designer may wish they could. Consequently, it sometimes becomes necessary to hang a unit away from its working position and rely on breasting lines to bring it to its proper location. A breasting line (sometimes called a checkline or restraining line) is usually dead-tied at one end to the gridiron or side-stage position and fastened to the scenery at the opposite end. When the piece is in its

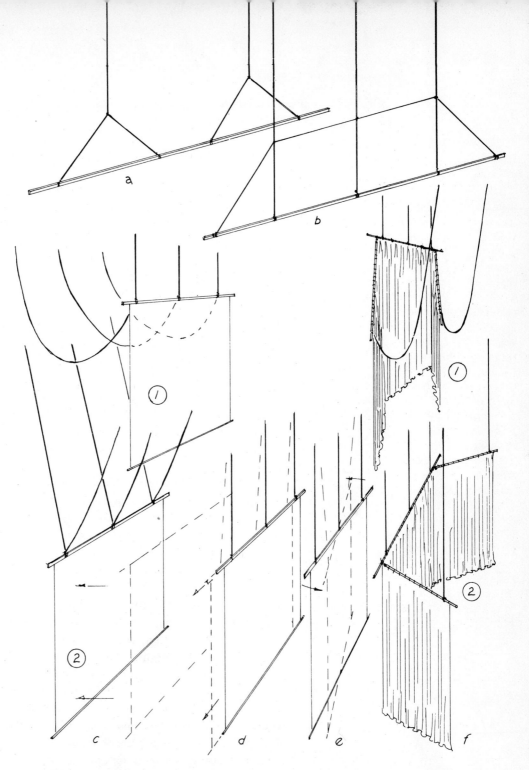

FIGURE 10–9. BRIDLING AND BREASTING TECHNIQUES. *(a)* A simple bridle. *(b)* A bridle of a set of lines to support the overhang of an extra-long batten. *(c)* Breasting a drop up- and downstage: (1) Stored position. (2) Working position. *(d)* Breasting across stage. *(e)* Twisting a batten into an angled position. *(f)* Breast lines on the side-tab arms of a drape cyc.: (1) Stored position, arms hanging down. (2) Working position, arms pulled by breast lines into spread position.

flown position the breasting line is slack, but as the piece comes into its working position the breasting line becomes taut and breasts the unit off dead-center hanging. (Several breasting maneuvers are illustrated in Figure 10–9c,d,e,f).

Bridling. The bridle is a simple rigging used to spread the load picked up on one line (Figure 10–9a,b). The number of lines in a set can be reduced, or the number of pick-up points increased by the bridling technique.

Tripping Scenery. Many rigging problems result from too low a loft or the complete absence of one. Tripping, which can only be used on soft or semi-soft scenery, is one way of flying scenery in a limited space (Figure 10–9d,e,f). By picking up the bottom of a drop as well as the top, it can be flown in half the height necessary to clear a full drop. The height can be further reduced by picking up the drop a third of the height off the floor and thereby tripping it in thirds.

An extreme variation of tripping a drop is to roll it on its bottom batten or drum at the bottom edge of the drop (Figure 10–10a,b,c). The old opera house "oleo" drop was rigged in this manner and it still is a good way of flying a drop on a stage with reduced flying space.

Levitation. The flying of objects or persons, as if in defiance of gravity, requires special rigging. A designer, to create a workable setting for flying actors or objects, should be familiar with the special rigging that is required for a flying effect. The right kind of background, the properly planned exits and entrances and atmospheric lighting can serve to mask or camouflage any exposed support wires and dramatize the illusion.

An object, to create the illusion of floating in space, must be supported on as fine a wire as possible so that the support will disappear from view at a distance. Lightweight objects, such as a bat or a bird, can be supported on fishing line (20-pound test) which becomes invisible at a very short distance. The size and strength of the support wire to fly an actor, however, is more critical.

The kind of wire used in the flying apparatus for an actor depends upon whether or not the wire has to go over a pulley. Wire rope, such as airplane strand, is extremely flexible and strong for its size—$\frac{1}{16}$-inch aircraft cable tests at 500 pounds and has a recommended safe load of 100 pounds; 20-gauge (.045 inches) piano wire has great tensile strength (500 pounds) for its size but is a single strand and cannot be run through a pulley. Any sharp bend or kink quickly weakens piano wire to the point of breaking.

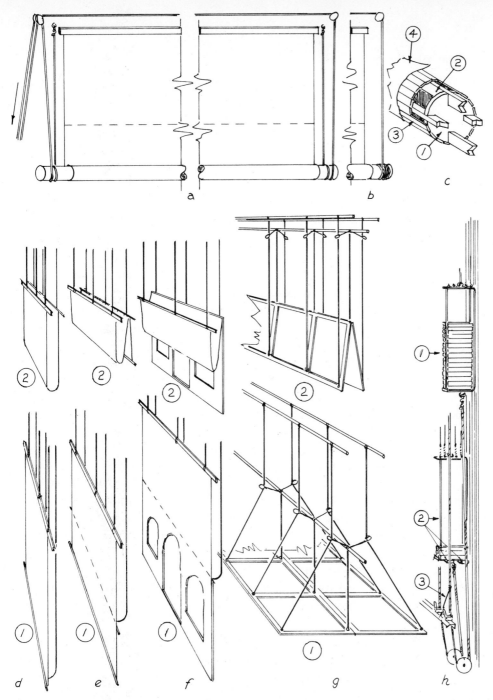

FIGURE 10–10. TRIPPING TECHNIQUES. *(a)* The "oleo" drop which rolls on the bottom batten or drum. Note: the rigging of the rope gives operator a mechanical advantage of two. Drop is made with horizontal seams to make roll flat. *(b)* An alternate rigging. Liftline has equal turns on the end of drum, in reverse direction of drop. When liftline is pulled, it unwinds as the drop winds onto the drum and thus rises. *(c)* Detail of drum construction: (1) Contour pieces. (2) Linear stiffeners. (3) Lattice slats. (4) Padding and final cover. *(d)* Tripping a drop; back set of lines is attached to bottom batten: (1) Working position. (2) Stored or tripped position. *(e)* Tripping in thirds. Upstage batten is attached at one-third height of the drop off the floor: (1) Working position. (2) Tripped position. *(f)* Tripping a drop which has the lower portion framed: (1) Working position. (2) Tripped position. *(g)* Book ceiling rigging: (1) Working position. (2) Booked position. *(h)* Carpet hoist, handling a variable load: (1) Free arbor (no batten attached) carrying counterweights. (2) Working arbor with batten that handles the variable load. (3) Free arbor is locked-off at top position allowing working arbor to run free of counterweight after load has been removed from batten (rigging is only usable on light loads of 100-150 pounds).

308

Flying Apparatus. A flying apparatus begins with a harness for the actor. It is made of strong webbing and is fitted about the legs and chest like a parachute harness. The ring, to which the wire is attached, is placed approximately in the middle of the back, a little above the actor's center of gravity. The harness, of course, is worn under the costume with only the ring protruding.

The Variable Load. Of the many rigging problems experienced with the conventional flying systems, the most annoying is the variable load or unbalanced condition resulting from the removal of part or all of the scenery load from a set of lines. The *deus ex machina,* descending with a live cargo of gods or goddesses and then ascending to the heavens empty, is an example of a variable load.

The carpet hoist is one way of compensating for the varying load if the weight variation is not too great (100–150 pounds). The counterbalancing weight to the variable load is not directly attached to the load-bearing batten but is handled on a separate purchase line. Figure 10-10h shows a carpet hoist rigging on a counterweight system. The counterbalancing weight is on the first arbor (1) which is a "free arbor" meaning that it is not attached to a batten or line-set.

The second arbor (2), which carries only enough weight to bring the arbor down, is attached to the batten handling the variable load. The extending hooks on the bottom of this arbor pass under and engage the first arbor to utilize its weights. It will be noted that when the first arbor is locked or tied off in an up position at the moment the variable load is being removed, the second arbor is free to disengage and return to a down position. The counterbalancing weight can be returned to the second arbor by reversing the procedure and unlocking the first arbor.

Any larger weight variation has to be handled by an electric floor winch, or a hand winch which provides a mechanical advantage to off-

FIGURE 10–11. LEVITATION. Types of rigging for flying objects or persons: (a) Pendulum and breast line: (1) Pendulum line, placed off center, has long arc when it is swinging free of breast line. (2) Breast line shortens arc and lifts object up and out of sight. (b) Pendulum and double breast line: (1) Pendulum line. (2) First breast line. (3) Second breast line. (c) Harness for actor. (d) Schematic diagram of Joseph Kerby's flying rig for Peter Pan: (1) Piano wire lead. (2) ⅛-inch wire cable feeds through swivel sheave at gridiron to a drum off stage. (3) Operating line turns large drum, thereby achieving a mechanical advantage and avoiding the use of counterweights. (e) Double-line counterweighted rigging provides a very flexible lateral movement although the actor has to remain attached to rig.

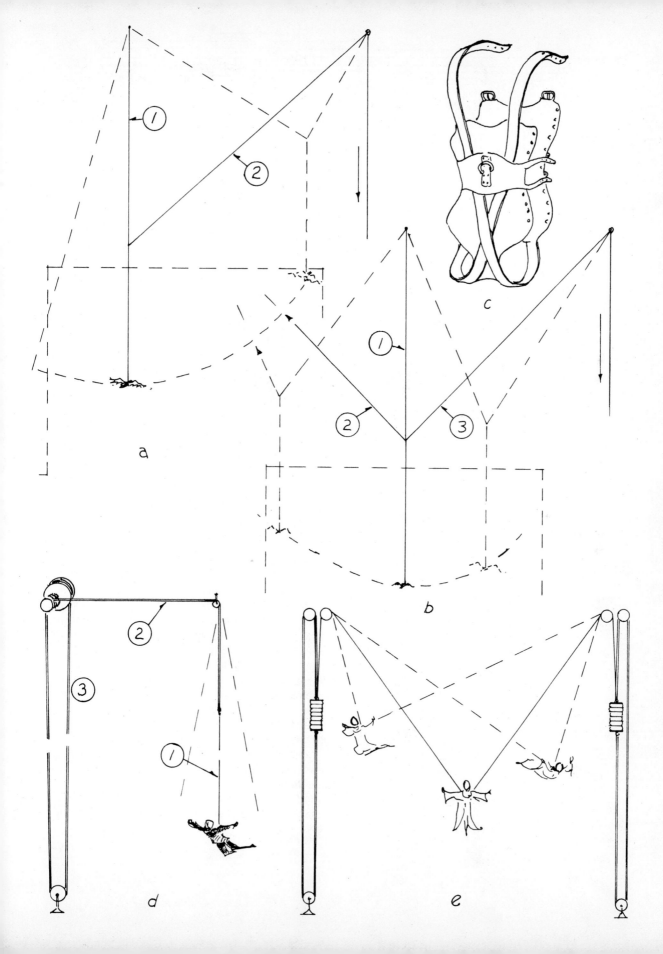

a

b

c

d

e

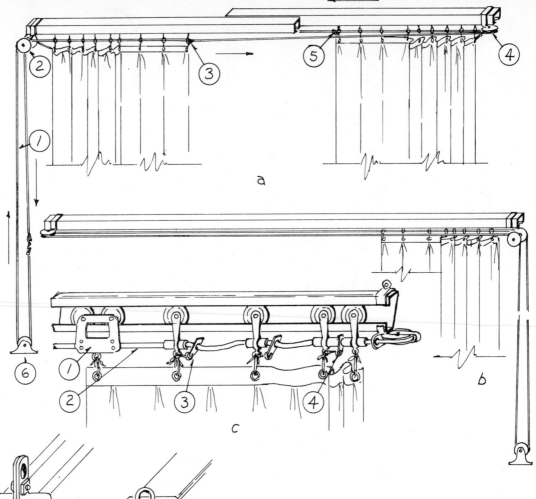

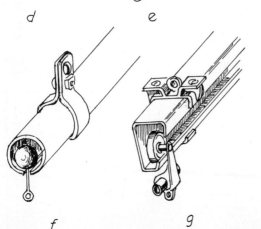

FIGURE 10–12. TRAVELER CURTAINS AND TRACKS.
(a) Rigging of a draw curtain or two-way traveler:
(1) Draw line. (2) Head block. (3) Lead carrier on
downstage curtain, fastened to drawline. (4) Change-of-
direction pulley. (5) Lead carrier on upstage curtain also
fastened to drawline. (6) Floor block. *(b)* One-way
traveler curtain. *(c)* Detail of rear-fold attachment. All
carriers move at once with drawline and curtain folds
offstage rather than bunching onstage. (1) Lead carrier.
(2) Drawline. (3) Rear-fold attachment grips drawline
until it is straightened up by bumping into the next
carrier. (4) Drawline now passes through the rear-fold
attachment. *Various Types of Traveler Tracks and
Carriers* (left): *(d)* Wooden track with ball carriers.
(e) Square steel track with double-wheel carrier.
(f) Round steel track with ball carriers. *(g)* Triangular
steel track with side opening and single-wheel carriers.
(Vallen, Inc.)

set the unbalanced load condition. The synchronous-winch system, of course, eliminates any variable load problem because it is based upon a direct lift and not a counterbalanced lift.

The type of rigging for levitation depends upon the movement of the actor both in the air and on the floor. For instance, the Rhine maidens in *Das Rheingold* keep flying in a lateral pattern, back and forth across the stage. On the other hand, Peter Pan, besides flying in all directions, also lands and walks about on the floor.

Most flying apparatus is based upon a pendulum action whether the pattern of movement is lateral or in all directions. The pendulum is usually placed off center for a lateral movement and center stage for a free-movement pattern. Figure 10–11 illustrates, schematically, the various pendulum riggings as well as other methods of flying actors, some of which require two wires and more complicated apparatus.

CURTAIN RIGGING

The actions or movements of a stage curtain, other than being raised and lowered on a batten, are classified into three groups. A curtain can be drawn horizontally from the sides, tripped diagonally into a tableau shape, or tripped vertically into the varied patterns of a contour curtain.

Traveler or Draw Curtain.   The conventional action of a traveler curtain is the drawing together of two curtain halves on two over-lapping sections of track. The track guides the carriers which are attached to the top edge of the curtain at about one-foot intervals. The draw line is fastened to the first or lead carrier which pushes or pulls the rest of the carriers to open or close the curtain. The many track and carrier designs as well as the rigging of the drawline are illustrated in Figure 10–12.

Sometimes a one-way traveler is needed, which means that the curtain instead of coming from opposite sides of the stage is drawn on stage from one side on a single long track (Figure 10-12b). Also illus-trated is a rear-fold device which causes all carriers to move at once rather than being pushed or pulled by the lead carrier (Figure 10-12c).

Tableau Curtain.   Like the traveler, the "tableau curtain" is made up of two curtain panels hung, with a center overlap, from a single batten. Each panel is lifted or tripped open by a diagonal draw-line attached to the central edge, about a third of its height off the floor, and running through rings on the back of the curtain to a pulley on the batten (Figure 10-13a). The tableau has a quicker action than a traveler, but doesn't lift completely out of sight unless the batten

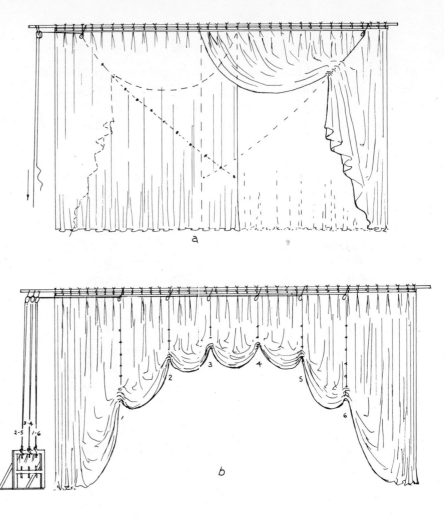

FIGURE 10–13. FRONT CURTAIN RIGGINGS. *(a)* Tableau curtain. *(b)* Contour curtain. (Opposite page: above) *(c)* Brail curtain. *(d)* Detail of the liftline rigging for a brail curtain. The same technique can be applied to the contour curtain and, when placed on the diagonal, to the tableau curtain. (1) Pierced wooden or fiber balls to keep rings from fouling. (2) D-ring sewn at regular intervals to (3) a vertical strip of webbing usually attached to the curtain seams. (4) ⅛ inch aircraft cable lift line. (5) Curtain weight to bring the curtain back to its down position.

is also raised at the final moment. Because of the picturesqueness of the tableau curtain drape it is frequently left in view as a decorative frame for the scene.

Contour Curtain.   The contour curtain is made in a single panel with great fullness, usually about 200 percent. The curtain, which is made of thin or soft material to drape well, is tripped by a series of vertical drawlines attached to the bottom edge of the curtain and running through rings on the back to pulleys attached to the batten. By varying the lift on certain lines the bottom edge of the curtain takes on many different contours (Figure 10–13b).

Brail Curtain.   The front curtain in a no-loft stage is sometimes rigged as a Brail curtain to achieve a faster and more desirable lifting action than the slower side motion of a traveler curtain. In this case the amount of lift on each drawline is equal, eliminating the need for the abnormal fullness of a regular contour curtain. To add a decora-

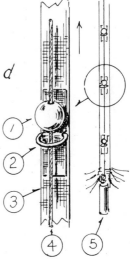

tive quality the curtain may have the horizontal fullness which is obtained by gathering material on the vertical seams thereby producing a series of soft swags (Figure 10–13c).

SCENERY ON CASTERS

The moving of a three-dimensional piece of scenery on the floor is made easier and faster if it is mounted on casters. The mounting of scenery on casters can vary from a single caster on the edge of a hinged wing to the large castered platform or wagon to move an entire set. In between are such techniques as castered tip and lift jacks, and outrigger wagons for rolling three-dimensional units of scenery.

CASTERS

The stage places special demands on the kind of caster it uses. A good stage caster should first of all run quietly, which requires a rubber wheel or a rubber-tired wheel. The rubber-tired wheel is a better long-time investment because the tires can be replaced as they wear.

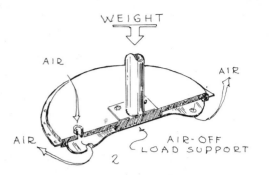

WEIGHT

AIR

AIR

AIR

AIR-OFF
LOAD SUPPORT

2

FIGURE 10–14. THE AIR BEARING CASTER. Top photos: Basic air bearing unit. Sketch: Cross section of the unit showing the flow of the compressed air into the flexible inner tube and out through the vent holes, thereby lifting the object on a film of air for a frictionless movement. Bottom photo: Theatrical use of the air-bearing caster for a production of *The Tempest* at the Tyrone Guthrie Theatre. The upstage supports function as a pivot. (Caster photos, courtesy of Rolair System, Inc., Santa Barbara, Calif.; Guthrie production photo—Bakkom)

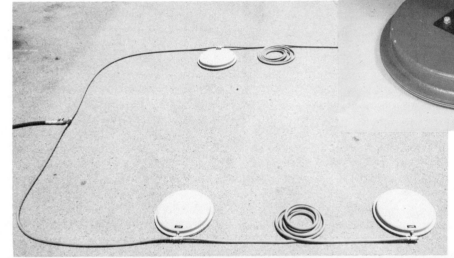

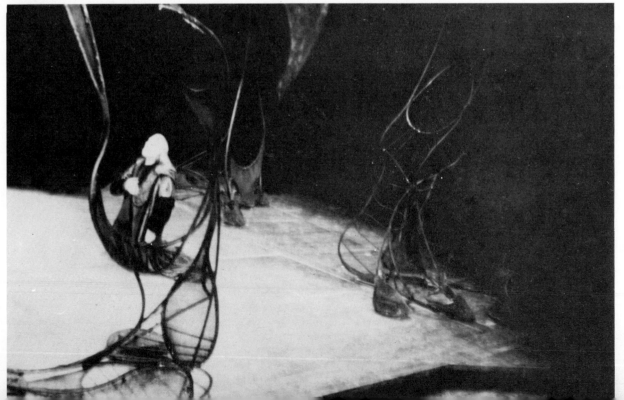

Secondly, the caster wheel should have as large a diameter as possible (3½ to 4 inches). A wagon on 4-inch-diameter caster wheels rolls with little effort and is not as easily stopped by small obstructions such as rugs, padding, ground cloth, or lighting cables.

Casters are of two general types: those made to move freely in any direction and those made to move in a fixed direction. The swivel caster has a free action that allows it to move in any direction, while the fixed caster is limited to one direction in a guided or tracked movement. Because both fixed and swivel-action casters are used on the stage, it is more economical to invest in swivel casters which, when necessary, can be blocked into a fixed position for a tracked movement (Figure 10-15). An alternate method is to purchase swivel casters and

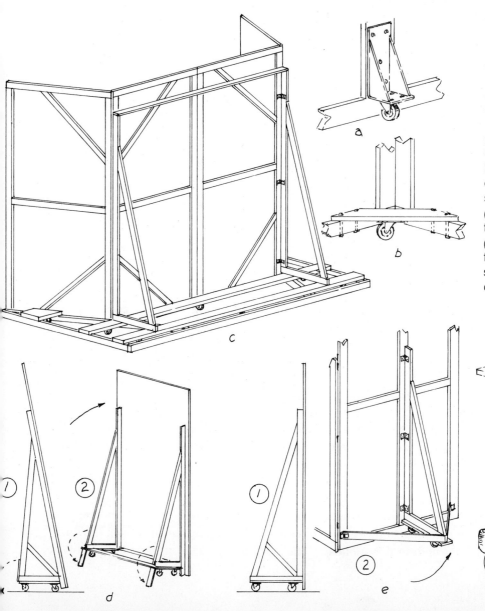

FIGURE 10–15. CASTERING TECHNIQUES. *(a)* Single caster mounted on rear of flat. *(b)* Single caster mounted in corner. *(c)* Outrigger wagon. *(d)* Tip jack: (1) Scenery tipped back to rest on casters. (2) Scenery upright, blocked-off caster in working position. *(e)* Castered jack: (1) Side view showing how scenery is held clear of floor. (2) Caster jack on a hinged or "wild" piece of scenery. *(f)* Flat-top swivel caster. *(g)* Flat-top fixed caster. *(h)* Stem-type swivel caster for furniture. *(i)* Small stem-type ball caster for furniture. *(j)* Large stem-type swivel caster. Mounts into bottom of scaffolding pipe.

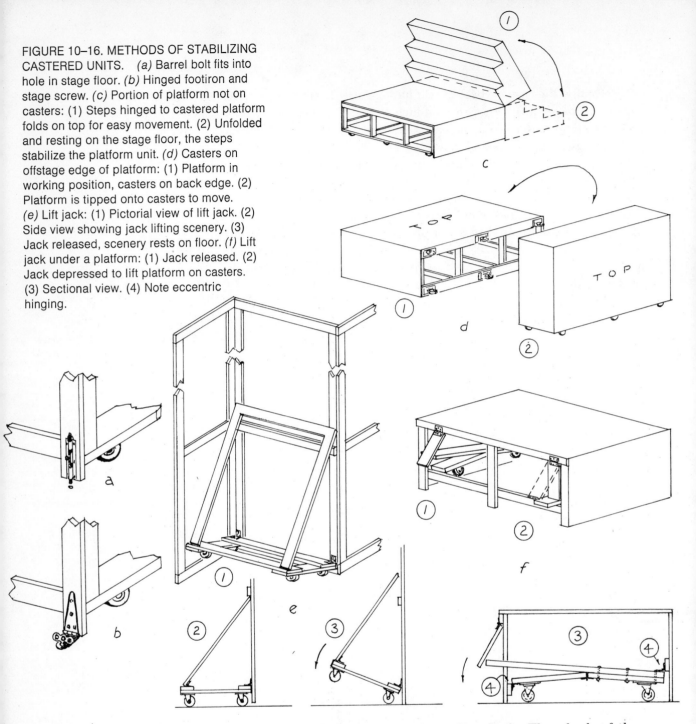

FIGURE 10–16. METHODS OF STABILIZING CASTERED UNITS. *(a)* Barrel bolt fits into hole in stage floor. *(b)* Hinged footiron and stage screw. *(c)* Portion of platform not on casters: (1) Steps hinged to castered platform folds on top for easy movement. (2) Unfolded and resting on the stage floor, the steps stabilize the platform unit. *(d)* Casters on offstage edge of platform: (1) Platform in working position, casters on back edge. (2) Platform is tipped onto casters to move. *(e)* Lift jack: (1) Pictorial view of lift jack. (2) Side view showing jack lifting scenery. (3) Jack released, scenery rests on floor. *(f)* Lift jack under a platform: (1) Jack released. (2) Jack depressed to lift platform on casters. (3) Sectional view. (4) Note eccentric hinging.

a matching set of fixed forks without the wheels. The wheels of the swivel casters may be removed and inserted into the forks for an easier to mount fixed caster.

TIP AND LIFT JACKS

The mounting of scenery on casters to make it move easily creates the paradoxical problem of anchoring, or keeping the unit from moving at an undesirable moment. The lift and tip jacks are methods of lift-

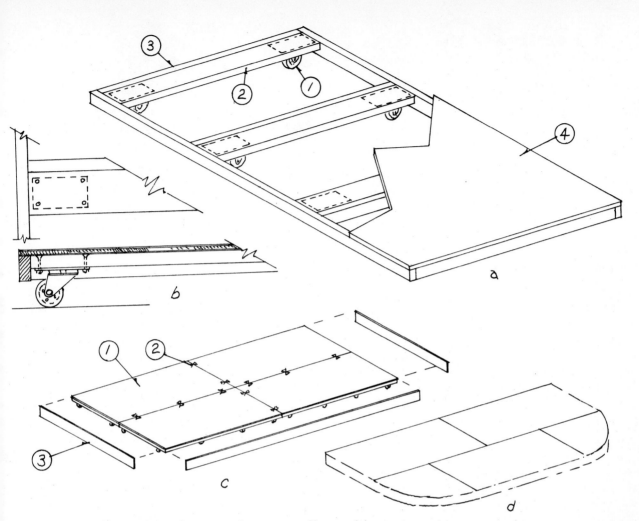

ing or tipping a piece of scenery from a standing position onto casters to move (Figures 10–15d, 16e,f). The scenery, however, sits firmly on the floor when it is in its working position.

Another way to anchor a castered platform or a bulky three-dimensional piece of scenery is to attach it to units that are sitting on the floor, or by tipping the piece onto casters mounted on its off-stage or upstage edge (Figure 10–16d).

OUTRIGGER WAGONS

An outrigger wagon is essentially a pattern of castered jacks or braces around the outside of a set or portion of a set. The scenery remains on casters. It is a skeleton wagon intended to brace and caster the scenery. The action of the scene is played not on a wagon but on the stage floor (Figure 10–15a).

WAGONS

The low-level platform (6 to 8 inches) on casters, or wagon, can carry a large portion of a setting including the set props. Large wagons often carry an entire setting which can swiftly and easily move into

FIGURE 10–17. THE WAGON UNIT. *(a)* Construction of a stock wagon: (1) 4-inch swivel casters. (2) 2 x 6 caster planks. (3) 2 x 3 frame. (4) 4 x 8 foot, ¾-inch 5-ply top. *(b)* Cross section. *(c)* Large wagon made up of stock units: (1) Stock unit. (2) Units pin-hinged together. (3) Facing boards. *(d)* A different shape made of three stock wagons and two special corner pieces.

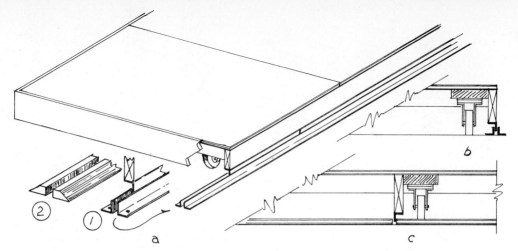

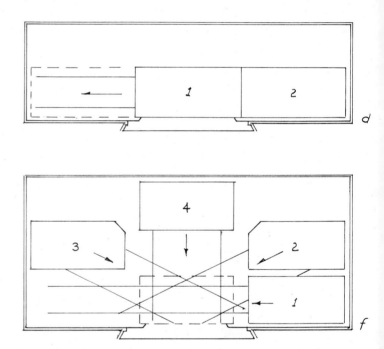

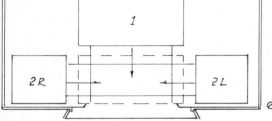

FIGURE 10–18. TRACKED WAGON MOVEMENT.
(a) Tracks on top of the stage floor. (1) Steel angle irons. (2) Beveled wood which though subject to wear is quieter than steel on steel. *(b)* Section detail. *(c)* Section showing track cut into the stage floor. In an elaborate tracked-wagon scheme such as those diagramed in d, e, and f, a temporary stage floor is installed with space beneath the track groove for cables to drive the wagon unit by hand winch from an offstage position. *Types of Tracked Wagon Movements:* *(d)* Transverse movement. *(e)* Split transverse wagons and a large single wagon moving up- and downstage. *(f)* Multimovements: transverse, diagonal, as well as up- and downstage.

place for a scene change. Although requiring ample floor space, the wagon is a flexible and efficient method of handling scenery.

WAGON CONSTRUCTION

Wagon construction is basically the same as platform construction. The caster in a sense becomes the post of the platform. If the casters are mounted on caster planks (2 by 6 feet or 1⅛ by 6 feet) the minimum span between supports can be increased. The caster plank, besides providing a sturdy mount for the caster, serves as a cleat for the top to increase the overstrength of the wagon. Normally, unless the wagon is to carry an extremely heavy load, such as a piano, the spacing of casters at 3-foot intervals is sufficient to remove any noticeable deflection.

Stock wagon units made in a convenient size (3-by-6-foot or 4-by-8-foot modules) for handling are pin-hinged together to make larger units (Figure10-17). Although stock wagons use more casters than are necessary for the total area, the flexibility of arrangements, handling and storage ease justify the module system.

WAGON MOVEMENTS

Aside from the free movement of a wagon carrying a full or partial set, there are several controlled or tracked movements that can become a scheme of production for handling scenery entirely on casters. The scheme may be based upon a pair of alternating wagons that allow the scenery and props to be changed on the offstage wagon while the alternate wagon is in the playing position. The transverse, jackknife, and split-wagon movements operate on this principle(Figures10–18, 10–19).

When there are many small sets in a production it is sometimes desirable to keep each set intact upon separate wagons. The stage then becomes packed with wagon sets and the shifting is accomplished by shuttling each wagon into position. The pattern of the movement varies with the size and shape of the sets and their order of appearance in the play.

THE REVOLVING STAGE

Another controlled movement of a castered unit is around a fixed center. A revolving stage that is not permanently built into the stage floor is similar to the wagon in structure. To remain portable, a turntable is made in small pie-shaped sections which are bolted or pin-hinged together (Figure10–20).The casters are mounted in a pattern to properly support each unit and are fixed in a position perpendicular to a radius line drawn through the point of attachment. If the casters are carefully mounted, the turntable will revolve about its pivot point with very little effort.

Another method of assembling a portable turntable is to reverse the normal position of the casters under the table and place them upside down on the stage floor (Figure 10–21b). The casters are placed in concentric circles as bearing points on a prepared rolling surface on the under side of the table. Each caster is shimmied to the same height to insure a level turntable floor. Although the assembly time is longer and the table is a little higher off the stage floor, the result is a smooth running, quite turntable. Figure 10–21c illustrates the assembly steps, as well as the cable-drive and motor method of powering a revolving stage.

Single Turntable. The revolving stage as a basic device can assume a variety of sizes and uses. The most familiar type is the large single turntable. Unless the stage is especially designed for a large turn-

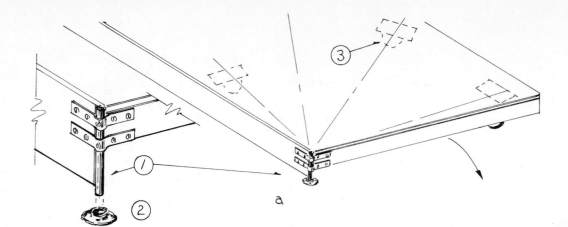

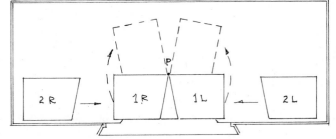

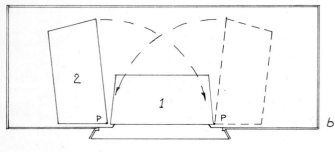

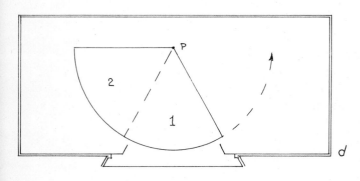

FIGURE 10–19. PIVOTED WAGON MOVEMENT.
(a) Pivot mounted on the corner of the wagon. (1) Pivot detail. (2) Socket fastened to the floor at the pivot point. Although the pivot and socket positions are often reversed in a turntable installation, it is best under the illustrated conditions to place the socket on the floor. A corner pivot, besides being an awkward mounting position, may also have to bear weight as the nearest caster is usually about four feet away. (3) Fixed caster set perpendicular to radius. *(b)* Jackknife wagons. *(c)* Type of jackknife in combination with split wagons. *(d)* Pivoting a segment of a circle, semi-revolving.

table, its diameter is limited by the depth of the stage. If the stage happens to be shallow in proportion to the proscenium opening, a single turntable will leave an awkward corner in the downstage right and left positions. Attempts to fill the area with a show portal, or hinged pieces on the turntable which unfold and mask the corner, more or less negate the basic function of the single revolving stage (Figure 10–23a).

Two Turntables. A shallow stage is adaptable to the use of two turntables, either touching in the center or held slightly apart. This method removes the awkward corners of the single turntable, but it

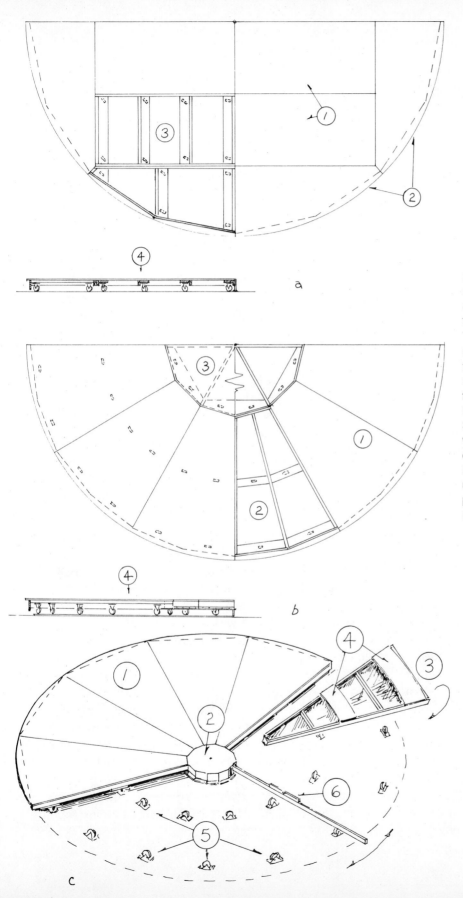

FIGURE 10–20a-b. THE REVOLVING STAGE.   A portable revolving stage or turntable can be built many ways. Shown here are two methods. *(a)* Turntable made up of stock wagon units with special-shaped wagons to form the curve of the outside edge: (1) Stock wagon. (2) Special wagon to complete circle. (3) Casters blocked perpendicular to radius. (4) Section. *(b)* Turntable made of wedge-shaped units around central core. Fewer casters are used creating less noise: (1) Basic wedge-shaped unit. (2) Top removed showing the position of casters. (3) Central core. (4) Section.

FIGURE 10–20c. TURNTABLE CONSTRUCTION, REVERSE CASTERING.   (1) Basic wedge-shaped unit. (2) Central core, ballbearing pivot. (3) Single unit viewed from underneath to show framing. (4) Bearing surface in path of casters, three-quarter-inch five-ply or particle board. (5) Casters mounted on the stage floor in patterns that are the same circumference as the caster-bearing surface on the underside of the turntable. (6) Spirit level and rotating bar to check the level of each caster mount to insure a steady, level rotation. Although the reverse caster turntable takes longer to assemble, it is quieter and easier to turn than the conventionally castered unit.

creates a design problem—that of joining all the sets in the center (Figure 10–23b).

Three Turntables.   Occasionally, a large turntable is combined with two small disks in the downstage right and left positions. The small disks either carry scenery related to the large set in the center or are small independent sets. The production scheme for *I Remember Mama* designed by George Jenkins used this technique(Figure10–23e).

The Ring and Turntable.   A great deal more variety of movement is achieved by using a ring and turntable combination. The ring and turntable are individually powered so that they can turn in the same direction at identical or different speeds, or they may revolve in opposite directions. The possible combinations of fixed units on the ring and turntable are almost endless. If the changes are made avista it becomes a delightful scheme of production. The settings for *Protective Custody* designed by Peter Larkin were handled in this manner (Figure 10–23f).

Two Rings and Two Turntables.   Although less adaptable to revolving fixed units than the single ring and turntable, two rings around two turntables are a very flexible method of changing elements of scenery and properties. This was demonstrated in the production of *Lady in the Dark,* designed by Harry Horner. With the help of flown pieces of scenery, the settings were able to blend from one scene to the next in full view of the audience (Figure 10–23c).

Semirevolves and Combinations.   The remaining variations of the revolving technique are the semirevolving stage and the combination of a turntable and a wagon.

The semirevolving stage is a portion of a ring or turntable tracked to swing in half an arc and then return to its original position (Figure 10–23g).The semirevolving stage may be large or small, used singly or in pairs, or, in some cases, combined with a turntable.

A combination of revolving and lateral movements can be accomplished by building a turntable into a full-stage transverse wagon (Figure 10–23d).This combination works best when a portion of one set is reused many times during the show. The lobby of *Grand Hotel,* for example, was saved in this manner. Most of the lobby setting remained on the left side of the wagon while a portion moved on the turntable. The smaller rooms and other scenes in the hotel occupied the remainder of the turntable and were moved in better sightlines by sliding the wagon to the left.

The scheme can be varied by setting the turntable into the center of the wagon and having elements of scenery on both sides instead of one side.

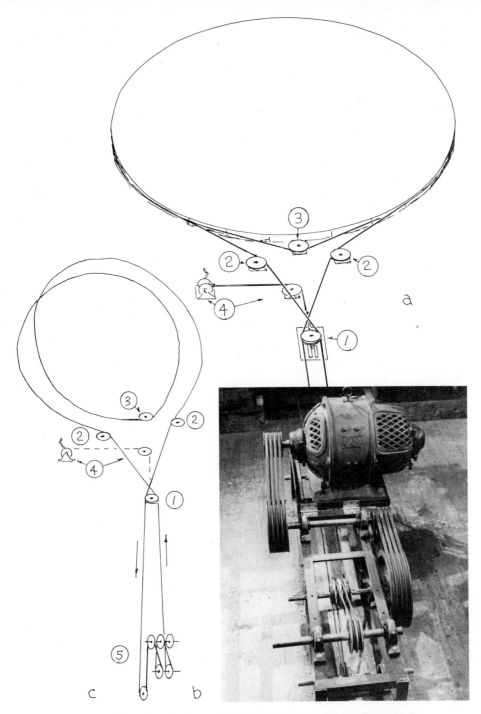

FIGURE 10–21. MOTORIZED CABLE DRIVE FOR A SINGLE TURNTABLE.
Sketch (a): (1) Tension idler. (2) Mulling pulley to change direction of the
cable. (3) Centering pulley. Keeps cable from creeping and binding as it
winds and unwinds on the edge of the turntable. (4) Winch to control the
tension on the cable. Photo (b): Motor and reduction pulley system. The
drive is a 2.5 horsepower, variable speed, reversible, 230-volt d-c motor.
Instead of a drum, a system of pulleys is used to keep the cable from
binding and still provide enough friction to move the turntable. Sketch
(c): A diagram of the threading of the cable which is one-quarter inch of
flexible steel long-spliced into a continuous loop.   (Photo—Tom Eaton)

324 FIGURE 10–22. METHODS OF POWERING A SINGLE TURNTABLE. *(a)* Cable and winch. (1) A spliced cable with one turn around the outside edge of the turntable is held taut by (2) a tension idler and powered by (3) a hand winch. *(b)* Motor driven turntable. A reversible and variable speed electric motor underneath a highly mounted turntable. (1) Motor. (2) Reduction gear box. (3) Spring loaded friction drive wheels, or bevel gears. (4) Drive ring for friction drive, or gear ring for bevel gear drive. (5) Raised, fiber-padded track for fixed casters. (6) Steel channel-beam frame work. (7) Roller-bearing pivot. It should be noted that both (a) and (b) turntables are usually surrounded by a raised temporary stage floor flush with the top of the turntable. *(c)* Drive wheel power unit. An example of a turntable on top of the stage floor with an eccentric pivot position making the use of the ring drive or cable drive impracticable. (1) Basic platform structure on fixed casters perpendicular to radius. (2) Pivot located off the center of the platform. (3) Wheel drive power unit hidden by (4) superstructure of the setting. (5) The path of rotation. (6) Components of the power unit: 5-horsepower, reversible d-c motor linked to (7) gear reduction box. (8) Drive wheel which turns the platform by friction drive off of the stage floor. It is connected to the gear box by a sprocket and roller-chain drive. (9) Ball-bearing socket fixed to the platform. (10) Turn indicator. A self-synchronizing motor (SELSYN) mounted on the wagon with its shaft fixed to the pivot and wired to a companion motor mounted offstage. An arrow attached to the shaft of the second "selsyn" becomes a pointer to indicate the exact position of the turntable. (11) Dial face of the turn indicator. (Original installation designed, and constructed by George B. Honcher and Pat Mitchell).

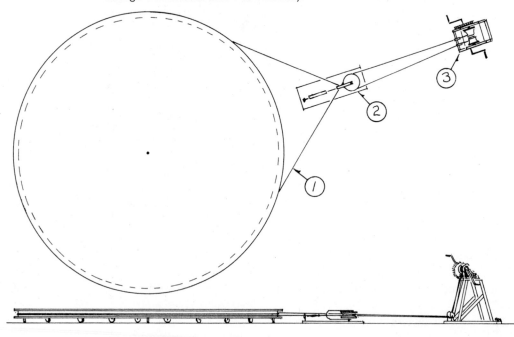

a

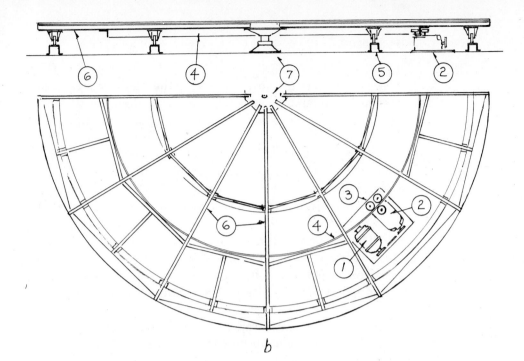

b

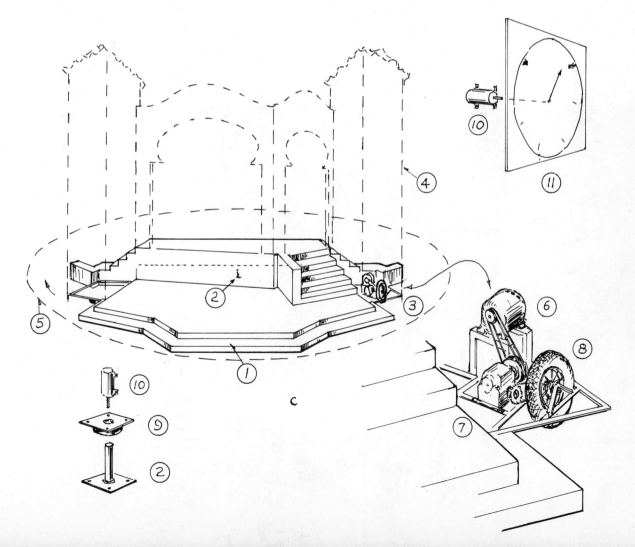

c

326   ELEVATOR STAGES

As a means of moving scenery, the elevator stage requires the maximum amount of stage machinery. Unless the theatre is in the position to make constant use of the equipment, or the elevators have a second function, such as a scenery and property lift to remote storage areas, the installation is extravagant. With few exceptions (The Metropolitan Opera, Radio City Music Hall, and similar presentation houses), the normal legitimate theatre in the United States has little use for the elevator stage as a method of changing scenery (Figure 10–23).

The financial organization and scale of production of numerous state theatres in Europe make the elaborate elevator stage a more feasible method of handling scenery than could be supported by the unsubsidized theatres of the United States.

SMALL ELEVATORS AND TRAPS

Aside from the doubtful chance of using a full-stage elevator, the designer may encounter a limited use of elevators in the raising of small elements of scenery through the stage floor.

Although the average stage may not have an elevator system, it usually has a portion of the floor area made in sections or "traps." The traps can be removed to give access through the stage floor into the trap room below. Entrances by stairs or ladder can be made from

FIGURE 10–23 (Left). ELEVATOR STAGE.   A backstage view of the elaborate elevator installation at the Metropolitan Opera House, New York.

FIGURE 10–24 (Right). TURNTABLE AND RING COMBINATIONS.   *(a)* Single large turntable. *(b)* Two small turntables. *(c)* Two small turntables with rings. *(d)* Single turntable in a transverse wagon. *(e)* Large turntable with two small disks. *(f)* Large turntable with ring. *(g)* Semi-revolving ring-segment and small turntable. *(h)* A pair of rings.

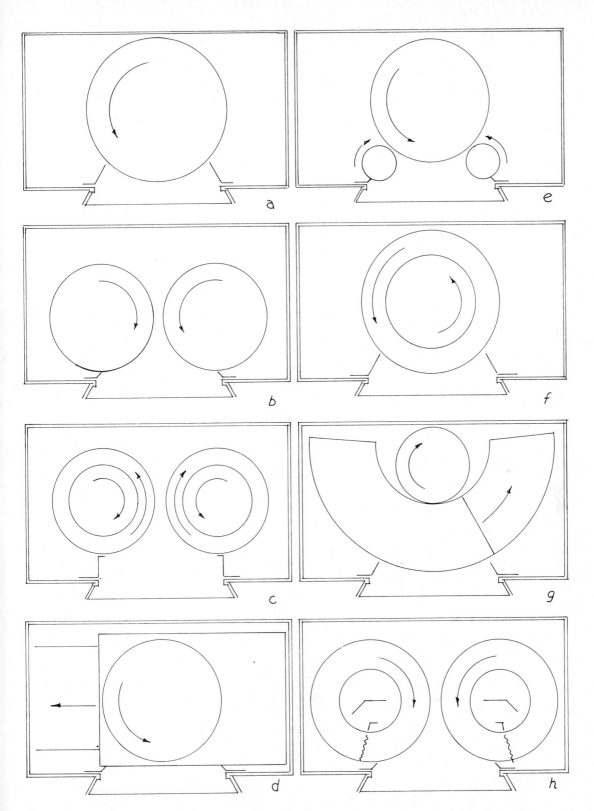

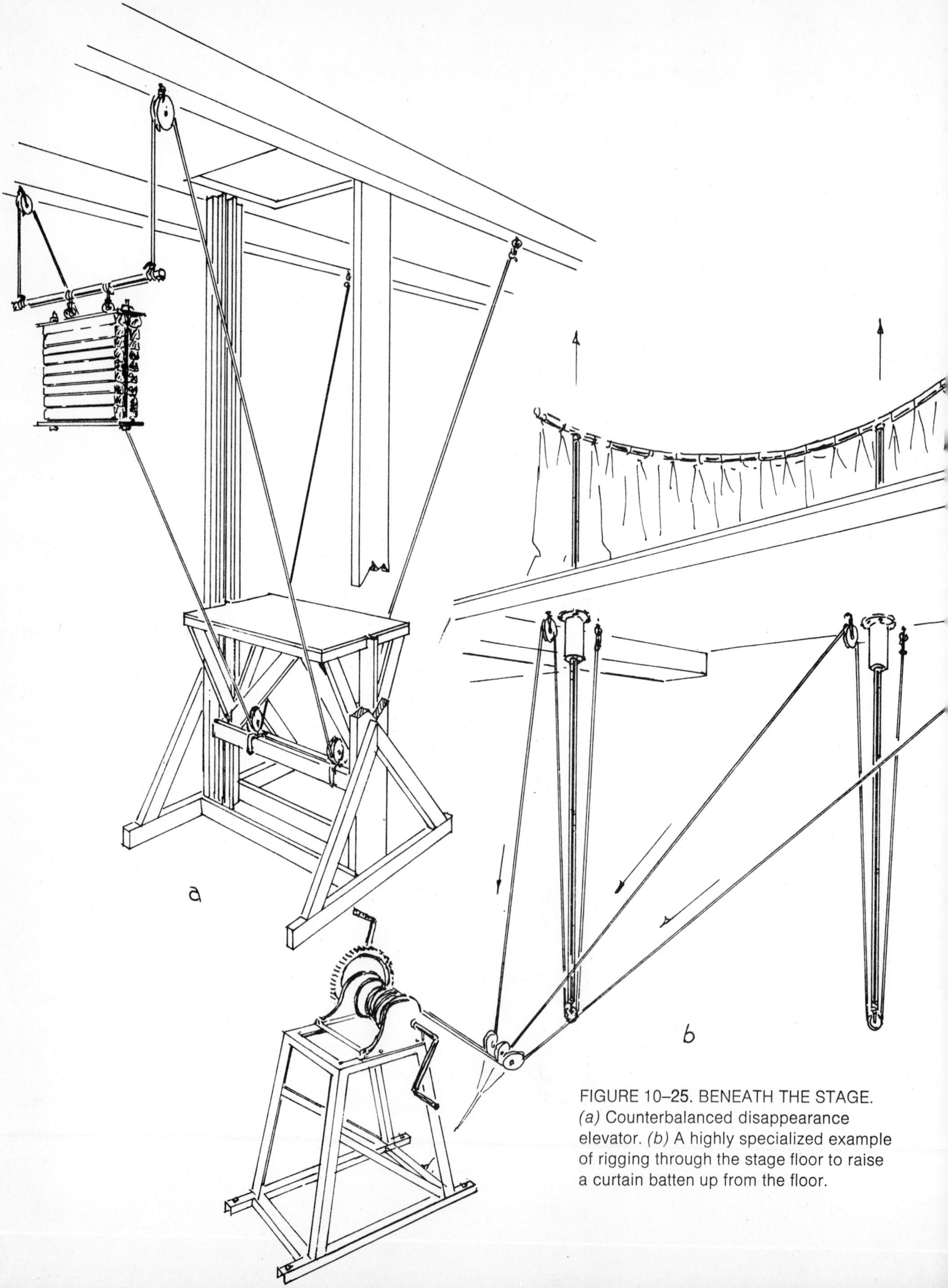

FIGURE 10–25. BENEATH THE STAGE.
(a) Counterbalanced disappearance
elevator. (b) A highly specialized example
of rigging through the stage floor to raise
a curtain batten up from the floor.

below through such an opening. Trap openings are made between transverse beams that run parallel to the footlights. As a result the designer has great freedom in planning the size and position of an opening running across stage. Openings running up- and downstage, however, are limited by the transverse beams.

The construction of a temporary lift which can be used for scenery or actors is shown in Figure 10–24a. Although the elevator platform can be as large as a single trap opening, the example illustrated is smaller. A larger elevator would require more guides and liftlines. Figure 10-24b. is an example of an elevatorlike mechanism under the stage floor designed to raise a small curved batten supporting a curtain. The technique is probably very similar to the methods used to raise a curtain out of the front pit of the Roman theatre.

THE ELEVATOR FLOOR

The elevators designed to move scenery should not be confused with the short-run elevators used to shape the stage floor in some of the more recent theatres. In this instance, sections of the stage floor,

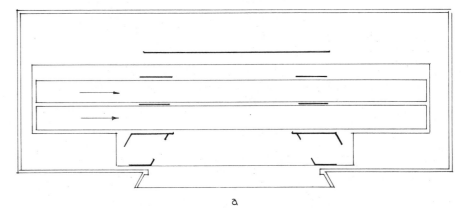

a

FIGURE 10–26. THE TREADMILL. *(a)* Plan of a pair of treadmills showing the amount of offstage space needed to use treadmills effectively. *(b)* Construction diagram of a treadmill with continuous action. *(c)* A simpler treadmill design, however, action is not continuous. The belt moves first to the left and then to the right as it winds or unwinds off the drums.

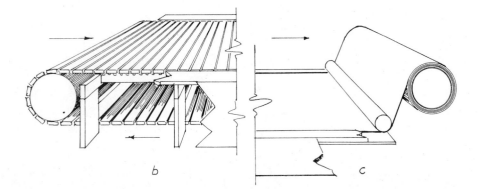

b   c

which can be raised or lowered by elevators to make levels or pits, are not a method of moving scenery. They can, however, be considered as a means of changing the appearance or form of the stage floor, which in a sense creates a new scene although they are not literally moving scenery.

THE TREADMILL

Like transverse wagons, the treadmill has a lateral movement. It is a conveyor-belt method of moving light scenery and properties to the right or left. It consists of an endless horizontal belt or flexible surface made of narrow wooden slats, held apart by two drums on opposite sides of the stage. Like a conveyor belt which is taut around the drums, the treadmill surface will move to the right or left when the drum is turned. As the belt has to return underneath itself, the space has to be kept clear of obstructions. This limits the width or height of the platform, for the wider the belt the higher the platform to allow for the framing of the span over the returning belt. The usual belt is about four feet wide which keeps the platform about a foot in height (Figure 10–25b).

A rather unique variation of the treadmill was developed by the Tobin Lake Studios, South Lyon, Michigan, which allows the belt (vinyl plastic) to rest on the floor. The belt is rolled onto motor-driven drums at opposite sides of the stage. The action is limited in one direction by the length of the belt which is not endless but rolls up on one drum or the other. Besides not requiring extensive platforming, this type of treadmill has the added advantage of being extremely simple to install (Figure 10–25c).

Stage Properties and Effects 11

Besides the large scenic background elements of the stage setting, the designer is responsible for the design and selection of stage properties and smaller bits of scenery more closely related to the actor. His responsibility for stage properties may vary from finding a marble-topped Louis XV console table to making an exotic sofa for a Turkish Cosy Corner; or from the borrowing of a Victorian tea set to the fashioning of tree leaves. Whether borrowed or constructed, each property is carefully coordinated into the design composition and adjusted to the production scheme, as well as being checked for size and ease of use by the actor.

Stage properties are in essence the design details of the over-all visual composition. Although the visual significance of properties applies more specifically to a realistic interior setting than to an exterior or abstract scene, their contribution cannot be overemphasized. Stage properties are, many times, the accent or artistic touch that makes or breaks the effectiveness of a stage setting.

Perhaps a more significant use of properties occurs on the thrust and arena stages, both of which are almost entirely dependent on

331

332

properties to set the scene visually. Because of the close audience-stage relationship in both cases, the finished detail and workmanship of all properties are subject to closer inspection than they are on the proscenium stage.

Another visual consideration of a stage property of equal importance to its compositional value is its rightness for the play. Again applying more to the selection of furniture, the designer has to continually ask such questions as: Is this chair in the right historical period and nationality? Is the sideboard the kind Mama would choose? And so on. The selection and designing of furniture and properties is done in close collaboration with the director so as to insure not only its rightness for the play but also to check its part in the staging of the action. Reference is made to the specific size and position of furniture in the setting in relation to other properties and the movement of the actors. Large furniture may hinder movement between the pieces, or a high-backed chair may block off a view of upstage action.

Real furniture is, of course, used in the modern theatre although it is often altered to become stageworthy. Scale and color are sometimes changed to improve its relationship to the stage composition. Because of these alterations even real furniture takes on a theatrical look. It becomes a stage property suggesting, sometimes faintly, sometimes openly, that it is no longer real. The name, property or "prop," is often synonymous with the unreal or the theatrical.

Properties of a setting should be planned and built simultaneously with the rest of the scenic elements. Their importance to the design and production scheme is sometimes overlooked in the planning period. The construction of built properties is often started too late, or too many decisions in the selection of furniture or decorative features are postponed until the final hectic rehearsals. This often occurs when the designer, overworked and pressed for time, places the responsibility of organizing the properties on the shoulders of a willing but not-too-able apprentice.

To make better use of his time, the designer, besides having a competent background in historical furniture styles and period decorations, should be thoroughly acquainted with the traditional uses of properties in the theatre. He must also be able to evaluate a property in terms of its importance to the action of the play and its sheer decorative qualities.

PROPERTIES VERSUS SCENERY

What defines a prop? When does a small piece of scenery become a property, or a large property become scenery?

Stage properties are traditionally defined as: (1) all objects carried or handled by the actor; (2) separate portions of the set on which the actor may stand or sit such as rocks, stumps, or logs; (3) decorative features not permanently built or painted on the scenery (pictures, draperies, and so on); (4) the ground cloth and rugs; and (5) all sound and visual effects that are not electrically powered.

In the average show, the categorical division of properties is based for the most part upon these traditional definitions of a property. An occasional exception or collaboration is made with the agreement of all concerned. Hence, a tree trunk may be scenery and the foliage a property; a pair of glasses discovered on the stage is a property while those brought on stage by the actors are costumes. Heavy properties often become scenery because of their size or necessity to be fastened to the scenery for movement.

Besides the distinction of properties from costumes and scenery there is the further classification of properties into groups related to their size and use. A property can be designated as either a hand, set, or dress property, or as a visual or sound-effect property.

HAND PROPERTY

The small objects handled by the actor on the stage are hand props. They include such items as teacups, books, fans, letters, and many more similar articles.

SET PROPERTIES

As the name implies, set properties are the larger elements more closely related to the scenery, but still used by the actor. This group includes furniture, stoves, sinks, rugs, ground cloth, and any domestic object used by the actor. Exterior set props consist of small rocks, stumps, bushes, foliage, real dirt (*Tobacco Road*), grass mats, and so on.

Set properties are in the care of the property man, who supervises the placing of the set prop on the stage and its removal to a stored position offstage.

DRESS PROPERTIES

More closely related to the setting are the dress properties. Their chief function is decorating the set. They comprise all the elements not specifically used by the actor which serve to fill in and complete or dress the set. Window curtains, pictures, wall hangings, flower groupings are a few typical dress properties.

Dress properties, as a class, are not necessarily superficial. They can become a strong decorative feature in a setting. Because they are not used by the actor they can often be faked so as to be handled more easily or in a different way than the normal set property. Bookcases,

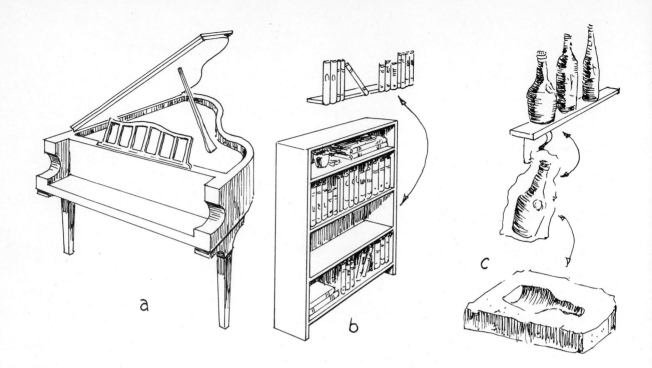

FIGURE 11–1. DRESS PROPERTIES. *(a)* Fake spinet piano. *(b)* Dummy books in book case. *(c)* Papier-mâché bar bottles.

for example, may have faked books and be attached to the scenery. A saloon back bar is often dressed with fake plastic or papier-mâché bottles to cut down the weight. A period piano or spinet, which is hard to find and harder to borrow, can be easily built and faked as a dress prop (Figure11–1). These are, of course, just a few of the many, many types of faked dress properties.

THE SELECTION OF SET AND DRESS PROPERTIES

The designer is responsible for the compositional unity, period continuity, and color relationships of the set and dress properties. Their first notation appears in the designer's sketch which may or may not be clear as to the indication of the real form. Once the general idea of the design has been accepted the designer can turn to a more careful study of period line and availability of each piece.

The final decision on each piece of furniture is made by the designer with the director's approval. To help reach this decision at an early stage in the planning, the designer uses individual sketches or illustrational clippings. The selection of set properties can be further facilitated by the use of a furniture plot and compositional elevations, as suggested in Chapter 5, which give exact references to the size of the individual piece in relation to its surroundings.

PERIOD STYLES AND ORNAMENTATION

Needless to say, a scene designer must be well grounded not only in furniture styles, but also in period interior decoration and architecture. The more familiar the designer is with the historical background of a period style, the better able he is to design and select, and sometimes make up, set and dress properties which bring a feeling of authenticity to the setting. This, of course, is more applicable to the naturalistic setting, but can be the springboard for abstraction.

Throughout the period of selecting or designing the properties and setting the designer draws heavily on a knowledge of period style. He cannot hope to recall at an instant the details of a certain period, but he should have a general sense of period style at the tip of his pencil. For detail and enrichment of the general form he depends on research. Research doesn't always mean leafing through reference books or old periodicals. It frequently involves study of the real thing in a museum or in actual surroundings. Again the designer resorts to sketches or photographs to collect this information. Although these are not presentation drawings they become important to the designer as personal reference material.

A designer soon learns to conserve energy and legwork on research by avoiding duplication. Generally much more material is gathered than is finally used. If all the research examples are filed and catalogued, they may come in handy at a later date on another show. The designer in this way soon finds himself in possession of an efficient reference library, to which should be added several inexpensive illustrated books, such as those listed in the bibliography, containing collections of furniture styles and ornamentation which also can serve as quick-and-easy reference. More extensive research, of course, may be needed to back any one style, depending upon the needs of the play.

DRAPERIES

Of all the dress properties used onstage, draperies are the decorative detail that brings character to an interior setting. Their elegance or cheapness, style or lack of style, or complete absence contributes immeasurably to the visual expression of the kind of place and people in the play.

From historical references, the designer can plan his draperies which, depending upon the period, may include window, door, fireplace mantel, picture, and mirror draperies. The designing of draperies is based upon a knowledge of the way the material drapes or hangs and the methods of cutting and assembling the material into the desired effect.

A New York designer needs only to prepare a carefully scaled or dimensioned drawing of the assembled drapery, specifying the material and the action, if any. Window curtains, for example, may have to be drawn for a tableau during the action of the play.

For university and community theatre production, the designer is expected to guide the execution of the draperies and therefore needs to know something about drapery patterns and assembly techniques.

The Window Drapery.   Although draperies may occur in many positions other than at the windows of a setting, the fundamental parts making up the decorative portion are the same. The basic parts of window drapery, which may or may not be used all at the same time, are: glass curtains, shade, overdrapery, and valance. The overdrapery and the valance are the frame, so to speak, while the glass curtains and shade diffuse the light, or cut off the view into the room from the outside. Each is made of a different type of material.

Drapery Materials.   The materials for window draperies are divided into three groups: the transparent or sheer fabrics for glass curtains and some types of draped shades; the translucent materials for the shade, unless it is opaque; and the opaque materials of the overdrapery and valance. The sheer materials may be chiffon, organdie, net, or theatrical gauze to name a few. Muslin, silk, and handkerchief linen are samples of translucent fabrics. Though the opaque materials for overdraperies are numerous, they usually are made of a fabric that will drape well such as velour, velveteen, corduroy, monk's cloth.

Types of Draperies.   As most of the decorative emphasis of a drapery is in the valance, it requires the greatest variety of draping techniques. A valance may be made up of plaits, swags, tails or wing pieces, or even festoons. The festoon, which is one continuous piece of material, is the basis for the more exaggerated shape found in the swag and tails. Although the swags and tails are cut separately they are frequently sewn together to look like a continuous piece of drapery. Examples of the types of draperies and their patterns are shown in Figure 11–2.

The side draperies, which are vertical members of the overdraperies, are usually a simple rectangular piece of material hung in fullness and drawn into a gentle or deep swag with a "tie-back" or decorative loop. Side draperies are sometimes shaped by cutting the bottoms on the diagonal similar to the festoon pattern (Figure 11–2e). Side draperies, although frequently draped symmetrically, can take on an eccentric draping depending upon the design and period style.

SHADES

A shade normally is not included in a stage window unless there is action in raising or lowering it. Roll shades are fairly easy to make and install. A dye-painted shade of muslin or handkerchief linen can be attached to a commercial spring-loaded roller, which has been cut to fit any special size of window.

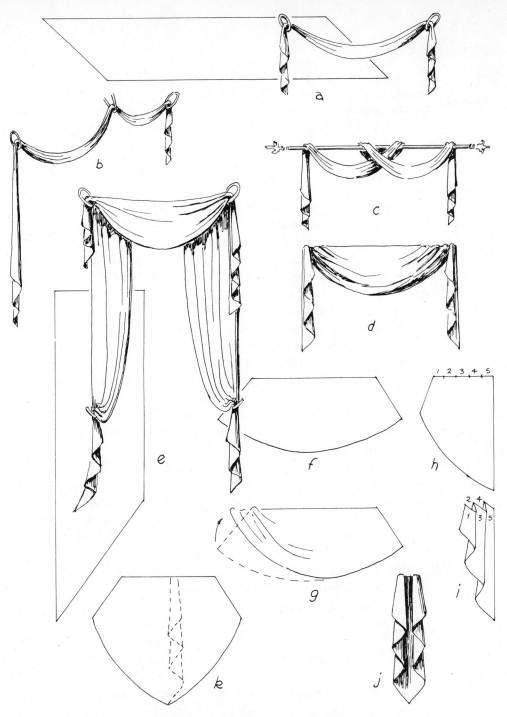

FIGURE 11–2. TYPES OF DRAPERIES AND VALANCES. *(a)* Festoon valance and pattern. *(b)* Eccentrically draped festoon valance. *(c)* Crossed festoons as valance. *(d)* Valance of swag and wing pieces. *(e)* Festoon valance and side draperies showing pattern for side drapery. *(f)* Pattern of a swag. *(g)* Draping a swag. *(h)* Pattern of a wing piece or tail. *(i)* Draping or folding a wing piece. *(j)* A double or central tail. *(k)* Pattern of a central tail.

A more special type of shade for a very grand window is the festoon-draped shade, sometimes called a French drape or Brail curtain. It is pulled up from the bottom by a series of vertical liftlines, which have been threaded through rings on the back of the curtain like the rigging of a contour curtain (Figure 11–3). The bottom of the festoon-draped shade is shaped so that its top position becomes part of the valance design. The shade may work in front of or behind the side draperies.

BORROWING OR RENTING PROPERTIES

Nonprofessional producing groups rely on renting and borrowing furniture or try to maintain in storage a collection of stock period furniture for continuous use. The storing of select period pieces is by far the most satisfactory method of securing properties for a repertory or stock company. Stock furniture can be varied with new upholstering and painted for reuse in many different productions.

A producing group which depends upon borrowing furniture and other articles must make an effort to maintain good will. Its members are part of the community, and if they want to continue to do business within the community, it pays to be businesslike when borrowing properties. Unfortunately, many a property room has been furnished with unreturned props, which is obviously not the way to build good will. A few simple rules for borrowing help to create a friendly, businesslike way of handling the loan.

1. Establish a method of recording each article borrowed, listing: name and address of owner; date borrowed and date to be returned; estimated value; description of article noting its condition (scratches, cracks, or parts missing); remuneration (cash, complimentary tickets, or program credit); and a signed receipt from the owner upon return of the article.

2. Centralize the responsibility. Handle all borrowing transactions through one person rather than selecting a different person to be responsible for each production.

3. Never borrow priceless heirlooms or irreplaceable antiques.

4. Take preferential care of borrowed properties on the stage, using dust covers and padding to prevent undue damage from movement of the scenery.

5. Return borrowed pieces promptly and on the date promised.

6. Secure a receipt and file it. If a record of the transaction is kept, it can become an excellent source for quickly locating and reborrowing for another production.

FLOOR COVERING

Floor covering serves two purposes, one esthetic and the other technical. First, any special floor covering helps to unify the stage composition by bringing colors and forms related to the setting into the

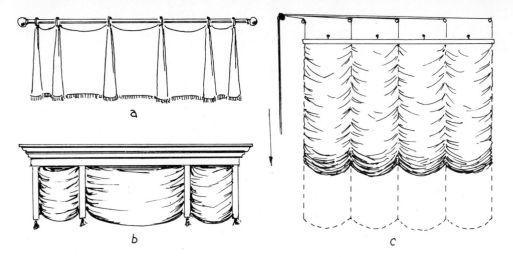

FIGURE 11–3. SHADES AND VALANCES. *(a)* Café-curtain valance. *(b)* Boxed-festoon drapery valance. *(c)* Festoon drapery shade.

floor. A painted ground cloth simulating wood planking, marble, or just a related hue help to anchor the setting to the floor. A setting on an unrelated or contrasting floor may appear to float in space. It loses stability and unity. This does not mean that every setting needs a special ground cloth, but rather that the designer, when using a stock ground cloth, consider its color so as to interrelate the setting to the floor covering. If the tone of the stock ground cloth is about a medium gray to low-light gray, it is not too difficult to relate the setting colors. Ideally, the presence of two stock ground cloths is more adaptable, especially if one is a warm neutral or brown tone and the other a gray shade.

Because regular scene paint will dust off when walked on, ground cloths are usually painted with dyes. The cloth can be folded for storage easily when it has been dye-painted. Occasionally ground cloths are painted with oil paints, or casein paints, to obtain a harder water-repellent surface for scenes where water is spilled on the floor in the course of the action. Oil or casein paints, however, tend to shorten the life and effective reuse of the cloth.

The technical reasons for using a ground cloth are, first, to pad or cover padding and thereby deaden the sound of the actors' movements. For deep, permanent padding, ozite or ordinary rug padding is used. It is expensive but it can be reused indefinitely. A double layer of deadening felt, an inexpensive paper-pulp product found at most lumber yards, is used under the ground cloth for thin, temporary padding.

Second, if the show is traveling, the spike marks locating the working position of the scenery and properties are carried on the ground cloth. Once the cloth is laid to the center line in each stage the marks are located correctly, ready for setup.

There are many examples of unusual floor covering that go beyond the conventional ground cloth such as real dirt in *Tobacco Road* and *Bury the Dead,* artificial snow in *Ethan Frome,* grass mats in *Three Sisters,* Masonite pavement in *Dead End.* Most ballet companies and dance groups prefer a vinyl floor covering which provides a better surface for dancing.

340

Ground-Cloth Construction.   Ground cloths are made of heavy canvas (12- to 14-ounce duck) to withstand the wear of action and scenery. The seams, which run parallel to the footlights, are double-stitched flat felt seams for strength. The edges and corners are reinforced with webbing to take the tacks that fasten it to the floor. A convenient size is usually two or three feet wider than the proscenium opening and two-thirds the depth of the stage.

The shape is usually rectangular; however, a more flexible shape is achieved by adding to the long edge a tongue of one width of canvas (about 36 inches) slightly narrower than the proscenium opening. For a play with action on the apron, the ground cloth can be laid with tongue downstage protruding through the proscenium opening to cover the apron. It can also be reversed with the tongue upstage and the straight edge downstage at the tormentor line in the more conventional position.

MAKING AND REMAKING FURNITURE

The making of cabinetmaker's styles of furniture is too difficult for the average scenery shop which is not equipped to finish or work hard woods. There are, however, several carpenter styles and rustic pieces of furniture that are more often easier to make than to find or borrow. Some of the unupholstered, carpenter-style pieces shown in Figure 11–4 can be made without too much trouble.

The alteration of furniture is often easier than making new furniture, especially if the alteration is cutting down rather than adding to the original structure. The practiced eye of the designer can see in the otherwise hideous neo-Grand Rapids masterpiece, after a little painting, reupholstering, and trimming away of excess parts, a Louis XIV side chair that would fool Molière. Armed with a background of period style the designer frequently can turn a second-hand furniture store into a treasure house of antiques (Figure 11–5a).

UPHOLSTERING

Invariably when the sundry set properties are brought together on the stage for the first time, some or all may have to be upholstered for either color or compositional reasons. Extensive reupholstering is not recommended on borrowed pieces, although it is possible to cover the existing surface with a new material by catching it lightly with a needle and thread. This should not be attempted on antiques which might have old and therefore weak upholstering. Bright colors or shiny materials on a borrowed piece can be dulled by covering them with a black net.

To reupholster furniture that belongs to the theatre, it is best to follow the same method of covering used originally. If the old covering

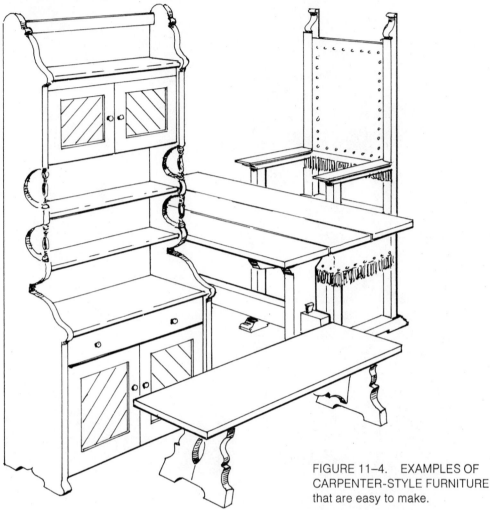

FIGURE 11–4.   EXAMPLES OF
CARPENTER-STYLE FURNITURE
that are easy to make.

is removed carefully, the pieces can serve as a pattern for cutting the new material. While the upholstering is off, repairs can be made to the springs and webbing that holds the springs, as well as refreshing or altering the padding (Figure 11–5b).

If the piece of furniture is going to be kept in stock, the padding can be covered first with muslin which serves as a base for any future changes in upholstering.

Expert upholstering hides or covers the tacking. This is accomplished in many ways. The material can be tacked on a hidden edge in back or underneath, tacked to a surface that is later hidden by a covered panel, or the exposed tacks can be covered with a decorative gimp braid or fringe. Sometimes the tacks are studded and are left exposed as a decorative feature in themselves (Figure 11–7).

FIGURE 11–5. REMAKING FURNITURE.
(a) Remodeling a sofa: (Above.) The original sofa before alterations. (Below.) Back removed, reupholstered, and freshly painted.

FABRICATING AND CASTING TECHNIQUES

In the designing and making of properties there is frequent need of decorative details or bold relief at an exaggerated scale beyond that of conventional furniture. These and other forms such as architectural details, costume armor plate, small properties and various free-forms are often made in the shop to obtain the exact shape and dimension

FIGURE 11–5, Continued.
(b) Reupholstering, Tufting:
(Above.) Tufting a sofa.
(Below.) Rear view of ties
used to form tufts (Photos–
Gene Diskey).

the designer is seeking. The forms may be fabricated or cast from the real object or from a prepared mold of a three-dimensional shape.

PAPIER-MÂCHÉ

The term "mâché work" has grown to include all techniques and materials used to mold or fake carved relief detail on furniture or scenery. The original papier-mâché technique used paper or paper pulp,

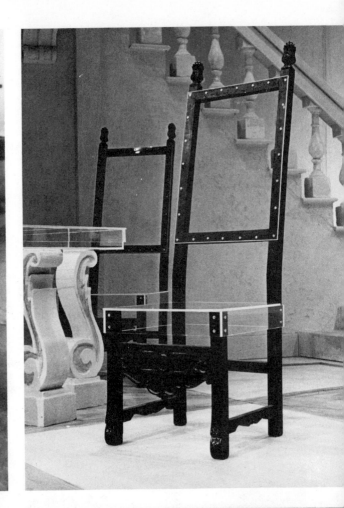

FIGURE 11–6. MAKING NEW FURNITURE.   Above, left: A hard-to-find tete-a-tete is constructed in the property shop. Frame and webbing ready for padding and upholstering. Below: Finished settee. Above, right: Plexiglass seat and back give a side chair a new look. On the far left, rigid urethane foam with wooden core carved into legs for a console table. In the right background, turned rigid foam baluster.

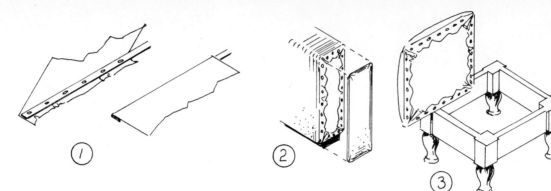

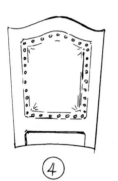

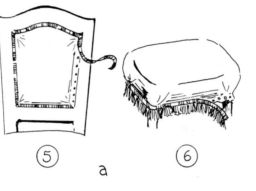

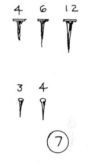

FIGURE 11–7. UPHOLSTERING TECHNIQUES. *(a)* Tacking: (1) Hidden tacking. (2) Tacking covered by a panel. (3) Tacking kept on an unexposed surface. (4) Decorative tacking. (5) Tacking covered with gimp braid. (6) Tacking covered with fringe. (7) Upholstering tacks, 4, 6, 12, and gimp tacks, 3, 4. *(b)* Fringes and braid: (1) and (2) Ball fringes. (3) and (4) Tassel fringes. (5) Bullion fringe. (6) Braid. (7) Gimp braid. (8) Ruffle. *(c)* Plaits: (1) Pinch plait. (2) Box plait. (3) Accordion plaits. (4) Gathering.

346 which was either modeled directly on the surface, or to duplicate a large number, was fashioned from a plaster mold.

When modeling directly with papier-mâché, a poriferous paper is used, such as tissue, paper toweling, or newsprint. The paper, after being torn into convenient strips and dampened in water, is dipped into binder consisting of wheat paste and strong glue size. The excessive binder is lightly squeezed out of the now near-pulp mass, and then is applied to the furniture surface to be modeled into the desired shape. If the relief is high, some preliminary modeling can be done with wire screening to which the mâché is applied as the final surface. The technique is very similar to that described in Chapter 5 for construction of large irregular shapes.

To duplicate identical forms, the same process can be applied to a greased positive or negative mold. In molding mâché there is a noticeable amount of shrinkage in the size of the final shape that has to be taken into consideration.

ASBESTOS PULP AND CELASTIC

Because papier-mâché-relief appliqué is rather fragile with excessive handling, a sturdier substitute is occasionally needed. Although more expensive, relief forms of asbestos pulp and Celastic are made more quickly and are stronger than papier-mâché. The process of molding and shaping asbestos pulp is slightly different. The pulp is moistened with size water to a consistency that can be modeled and applied to the furniture surface, or to a preshaped screen surface. Although taking longer to dry than papier-mâché, it dries with a very hard surface. The wet pulp also can be pressed into a negative mold to duplicate many shapes.

Celastic or Sculpt-o-fab is, of course, a different technique. It is a cheese-cloth impregnated with cellulose nitrate and a fire retardant. This rather stiff fabric, when softened in a special solvent, becomes pliable, and can be shaped or molded in a negative or positive mold. As the very volatile solvent evaporates, the cellulose nitrate hardens into the new shape. The Celastic form will separate easily from a mold that has been covered first with aluminum foil. There is very little shrinkage and the resulting shape is extremely sturdy (Figure 11–8).

FIBER GLASS

Fiber-glass fabricating is easily adapted to the making of three-dimensional details occurring on either scenery or properties. The technique, like the papier-mâché and Celastic procedures, shapes a fiber-glass cloth over a positive form or into a negative mold after first coating the mold with a releasing agent. The pieces of fiber-glass cloth are

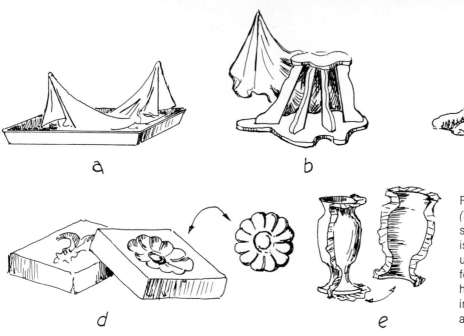

FIGURE 11–8. CELASTIC. *(a)* Fabric softened in special solvent. *(b)* Softened fabric is draped over prepared understructure. *(c)* Final form after Celastic has hardened. *(d)* Celastic used in negative mold. *(e)* Over a positive mold.

saturated and cemented together with a solution composed of a fabricating resin and a hardener. As the hardener is the catalytic agent of the mixture, the amount of it present controls the degree of hardness of the final form. The proportion of resin to hardener is usually about five to one, but, because the strength of these plastics may vary from dealer to dealer any mixture should be tested for its finished hardness before beginning extensive fabrication. Acetone, which is the solvent for the plastics, is used to clean brushes and hands.

There are many types and weights of fiber-glass cloth. Woven glass cloth is available in light, medium and heavy weights. The woven glass cloth is most suitable for making objects with opaque surfaces that are to be painted. The medium and heavyweight cloth, for example, works very well for making costume armor plate and helmets. The matted glass cloth is generally lightweight and quite translucent. It is adaptable for fabricating shapes like lamp globes or similar translucent forms.

An easy way to experiment with the technique is to purchase a fiber-glass boat repair kit and follow the directions in the manual. Although the kit may not supply a releasing agent it can be purchased separately.

Body Armor and Mask Making.   Some of the "mâché" techniques can be applied to the making of full or partial masks to be worn by the actor, or, in some cases, to appear as decorative details on scenery. Figure 11–9 illustrates the designing and making of masks in the three basic forming techniques, papier mâché, Celastic, and rubber latex. Fiber glass and thermal plastics (Chapter 7) lend themselves to the forming of body armor, such as breast plates and helmets (Figure 11–10).

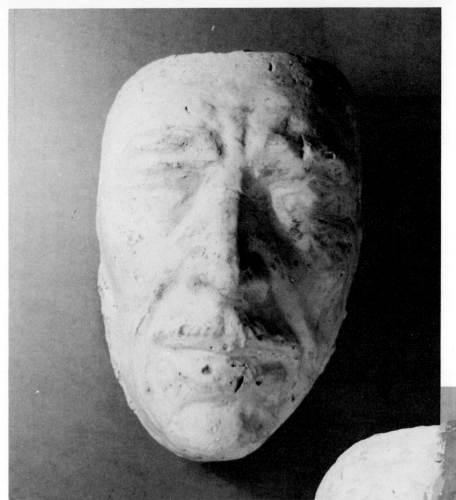

FIGURE 11–9 a. MASK-MAKING
TECHNIQUES.   A simple half
mask is used to demonstrate
the steps taken to design and fit
any mask to the actor's face. A
life mold cast from a surgical
gauze (plaster impregnated
gauze) impression of the actor's
face.

FIGURE 11–9 b. The new form
and dimension of the mask is
modeled directly on the mold in
plasticine clay. The completed
design form is cast in plaster to
create a negative mold of the
mask.

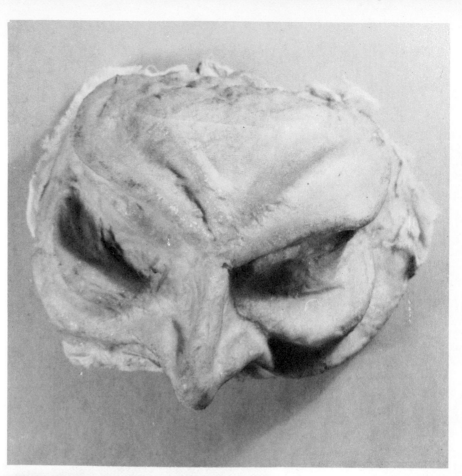

FIGURE 11–9 c. Raw latex mask cast from the negative mold. At this stage, any one of several processes can be used such as Celastic, Polysar, liquid rubber, or papier mâché.

FIGURE 11–9 d. The finished mask, painted and decorated.

FIGURE 11–9 e. An example of a full-face mask and its negative mold. Ritual or larger decorative masks can be reproduced in number by using the vacuum forming technique if water clay is used in place of plasticine to make the mold. Designer—Pat Moser.

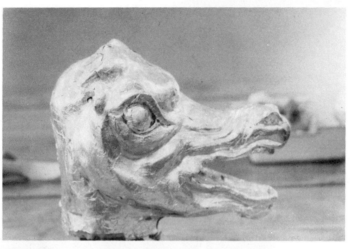

FIGURE 11–9 f . FANTASY MASK.
Positive mold technique using Celastic.
Top: Plasticine clay orginal. Second:
Foil covering the clay mold as a parting
agent. Third: Softened Celastic strips
applied to the mold. The hardened form
is then cut off the mold and sealed
together to complete the raw mask.
Bottom: Finished mask with a velour
covering and applied hair. Designer—
Louise Krozek.

FIGURE 11–10. PROPERTIES AND ARMOR.   A few of the innumerable vacuum-formed articles for theatre use from Tobin Lake Studios. Above: Prop telephone, architectural details, armor breastplate, and other articles are shown in various stages of assembly and surface finish. Below: Full armor and shields of vacuum-formed from vinyl plastic sheets. The swords in the display are made of tempered steel.

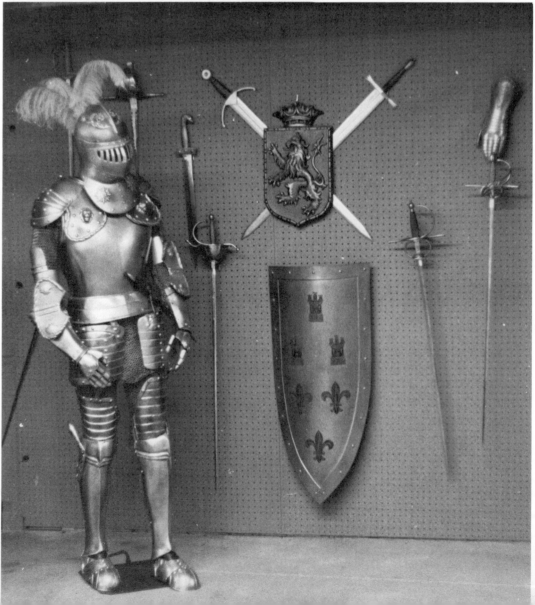

LAMINATED FELT

Another method for constructing small set or dress properties is the laminated-felt technique. It is a process that works best for hollow forms, such as vases, goblets, and body armor. It can also be used to make open filigree or oversized costume jewelry.

Working over a positive form covered with aluminum foil to insure its "parting," the shape is built up with laminated strips of felt coated with Elmers or Poly-vinyl glue. Decorative detail is appliquéd in the same manner. Once the shape is hardened it is painted with a glaze made up of shellac cut one half with thinner. The glaze is applied in successive coats to build up a hard surface. Aniline dye may be added to the glaze to serve as an undercolor or as an antique effect if it is the final coat.

If the surface is metallic to simulate silver, gold, or bronze the dry metallic powder is brushed into one of the glaze coats as high lights. A metallic surface developed in this manner has a very authentic look on the stage.

Felt can be kept flexible by using a flexible glue rather than Elmers glue. A flexible glue made by Swift and Company, Adhesive Division, is a transparent poly-vinyl which can, with dye staining, make felt look and feel like leather. The same flexible glue is also an excellent sealer for Styrofoam and Artfoam prior to painting.

EFFECT PROPERTIES

There was a time in theatre history when visual and sound effects were the major concern of the property department. Before the advent of high-fidelity recording many sound effects were created mechanically by the property man. Most of these machines are now gathering dust in the property room. An adequate sound system can bring any effect to the audience with a truer quality and a more sensitive control than the mechanical sound effect. There is one possible exception, which is the effect of offstage gun fire. The recordings of distant battle scenes are fairly convincing, but close rifle or revolver shots are better when a gun with blank cartridges is fired backstage.

More as historical record and less as modern practice, Figure 11-11 shows some of the mechanical sound effects that are a part of the property department. Directors, on occasion, have requested all the old mechanical sound effects for certain kinds of productions for their theatrical quality as opposed to the movielike realism of electronic sound.

Although some visual effects have become electrified, most of them have remained mechanical or partially so. Smoke, fire, and flash explosions are usually electrically controlled; however, smoke can be made nonelectrically if necessary (Figure 11–12).

FIGURE 11–11. MECHANICAL SOUND EFFECTS. *(a)* Wind machine. *(b)* Rain, shot in rotating drum. *(c)* Rain, shot in tray with wire-screen bottom. *(d)* Thunder sheet. *(e)* Rumble cart. *(f)* Falling rubble after an explosion. *(g)* Wood crash. *(h)* Gun shots. *(i)* Slap stick. *(j)* Horses' hoofs.

Some familiar visual effects that are mechanical are the snow cradle and rain pipes which are shown in Figure 11–13 along with other special effects that call upon the ingenuity of the stage technician and property man to rig and trigger on cue.

BREAKAWAYS

Many times pieces of furniture, dishes, or other objects have to break on stage. The chairs that collapse and the flag pole that falls down in *Cockadoodle Dandy,* the bullet fired through the windowpane in *Front Page,* or a railing that breaks during a fight scene are a few examples of properties or scenery breaking on cue and in a predetermined manner.

In Figure 11–14, a railing breakaway is prebroken and lightly glued together. Thin strips of orange crate are tacked to the back of the repair to give a convincing splintering sound as the railing breaks again. The pattern of the break is carefully planned so as to control the fall of the pieces in the same manner for each performance.

Breakaway Windowpanes and Mirrors. The breaking of real glass on the stage, although frequently done, is somewhat dangerous. Flying glass plus broken glass left on the floor can become a hazard. If the actor is too close to the breaking glass it is sometimes desirable to use other materials. One familiar substitute for glass used often in the motion picture industry is candy glass. Candy glass or hardened sugar and water is prepared like old-fashioned rock candy. After bringing a supersaturated solution of sugar and water to about 260 degrees Fahrenheit it is poured on a smooth surface into a thin sheet. The sheet hardens into a clear, transparent solid. Candy glass, however, has a low melting point and may soften under stage lights or excessive handling.

FIGURE 11–12. SMOKE EFFECTS. *(a)* Smoke bomb. *(b)* Dry ice and water. *(c)* Water mixed with titanium tetrachloride. *(d)* Heated sal ammoniac. *(e)* Heated mineral oil. *(f)* Squibb, means of electrically firing a flash or firecracker. *(g)* Flash box containing flash powder over low-amperage fuse wire for electrically firing flash and smoke.

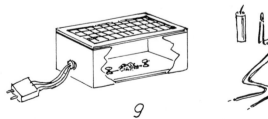

A clear-sheet breakaway can be made of powdered plastic. Santolite MHP, manufactured by Monsanto Chemical Company, can be easily melted and cast into transparent sheets, which upon hardening, break easily into dull-edged fragments. The best results are obtained by casting the sheets on a cellophane-covered, tempered Masonite surface. The MHP in sheet form also tends to soften easily but at a higher temperature than candy glass. Whenever possible it is wise to cast the plastic directly into the window or mirror frame to avoid excessive handling. A mirror is made by painting the back of a clear sheet with a metallic paint.

The fragments, as an added advantage, can be reclaimed and melted down again although the plastic begins to discolor after repeated remeltings.

Pottery Breakaways. Opaque shapes, such as teacups, dishes, or small objects of art are much easier to make into breakaways. Because they are not transparent, inexpensive pottery or china pieces may be

FIGURE 11–13. VISUAL EFFECTS. *(a)* Snow cradle. *(b)* Rain pipe. *(c)* Water reflection.

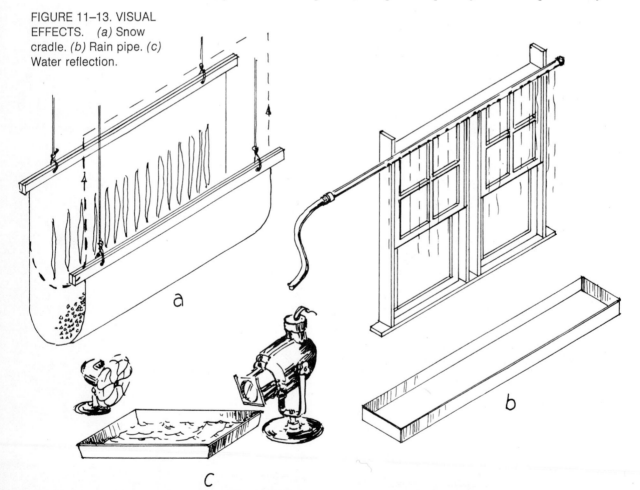

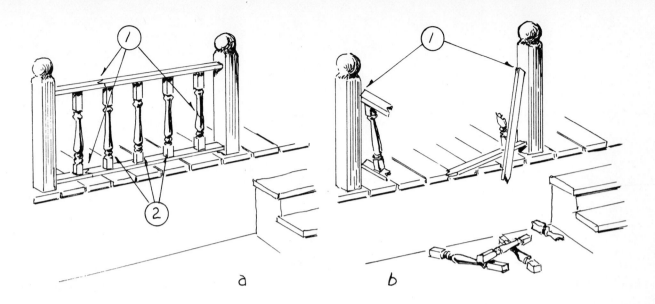

prebroken and lightly glued together again to insure their breaking onstage. As the second breaking usually shatters the piece beyond reclaiming, a breakaway should be prepared for each performance.

Special opaque breakaway shapes can be prepared by casting a mixture of plaster and Styrofoam into a mold of the shape. To keep the casting hollow for easy breaking requires a core mold which makes the whole casting process very complicated and time consuming.

If the authenticity, both in sound and looks, of the breakaway object is extremely important to the play a replica can be made in clay bisque. A clay slip or solution of powdered water clay and water is poured into a mold of the object and after allowing to set a few minutes is poured out. A thin shell of clay adheres to the mold making a hollow casting of the object. After drying thoroughly (48 hours) the raw-clay casting is fired in a ceramic kiln to bisque hardness. A great number can be prepared this way.

Electrically Triggered Breakaways. To cue a breakaway in a remote position it is frequently easier to use an electrical trigger rather than a manual operation. A chandelier shattered by gunfire; a picture falling off the wall; or the decapitation of the weathervane cock in *Annie Get Your Gun* are a few examples of remote breakaways.

A mouse-trap spring can be released by shorting-out the low amperage fuse wire that is rigged to hold the spring under tension. Melted fuse wire can also be used to break a support chain of a chandelier (Figure 11-15).

The magnetic power of the *solenoid* coil can be used to withdraw the support of a picture on the wall or as a trigger for any other breakaway. When a current is passed through the coil of the solenoid it becomes an electro-magnet which draws the spring-loaded center pin into the coil. Upon breaking the circuit the pin is released with considerable force. Either action can be used to trigger a breakaway.

FIGURE 11–14. BREAKAWAY RAILING. *(a)* Railing prepared for breaking: (1) Prebroken spots, lightly glued. (2) Loose spindles, lightly glued. *(b)* Railing after breaking: (1) prepared hinge points.

FIGURE 11–15. ELECTRICALLY TRIGGERED BREAKAWAYS. (*a*) The mousetrap is a simple mechanism that can be used to trigger a breakaway. (1) Fuse wire holding trap in "set" position. An electrical short melts fuse wire and the trap is sprung. This action can be used to break glass or *spring-load* a hinge as in (*c*). (*b*) Breakaway chandelier. (1) Fuse wire link which can be located anywhere on chain. The effect is helped if there is a little sand or dust in bowl to spill after the break. (*c*) Decapitating a weathervane cock. (1) Fuse wire holds spring-loaded hinge in upright position. Head folds behind body when fuse wire melts. 3 to 5 ampere fuse wire usually works best. If spring is too strong fuse wire can be doubled for strength. (*d*) Falling picture. (2) Solenoid coil mounted on rear of (3) picture batten. In *off* position the spring-loaded pin is extended through the batten to hold picture frame in place. When current is sent into the coil the pin withdraws and picture falls.

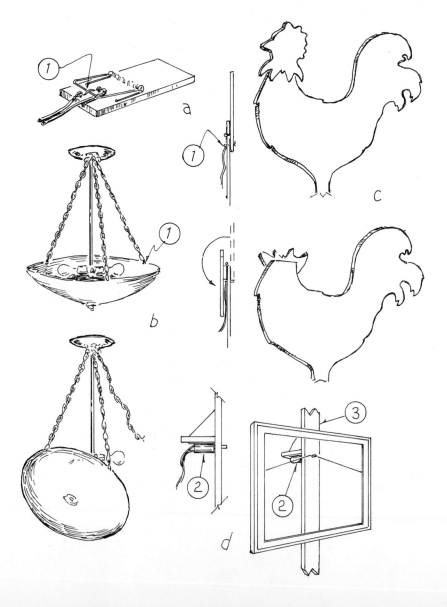

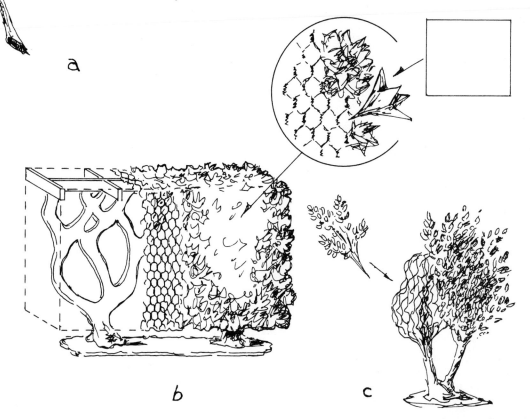

FOLIAGE

Artificial flowers and the foliage of hedges, bush pieces, and small trees are considered properties as well as live flowers, potted plants, and sprays of real leaves used to dress the setting. The expression "prop bush" besides meaning that the bush is not real, implies that it is shaped in three dimensions, as opposed to a flat, painted set piece.

Lifelike artificial flowers can be obtained easily from display houses, local variety stores, or at the home-decoration section of a department store. Although they are more expensive than real flowers, with proper care they can be used over again.

FIGURE 11–16. FOLIAGE.   (a) Artificial leaves wired or taped to real tree branches or section. (b) Trimmed boxwood hedge made of frame covered with inch-mesh chicken wire. Crepe-paper or fabric squares are pushed into openings (color is more convincing if two or three shades of green are used). (c) Untrimmed box or ilex bush; chicken wire shaped over basic frame and filled with sprays of artificial boxwood or ilex.

Stylized or caricatured blossoms have to be specially made. Their scale and design determine the material used. Exotic tropical flowers in a musical comedy, for example, have been made of velveteen or satin with leaves made of wire loops covered with sheer chiffon.

Banks of blossoms and box hedges can be made of shaped 1-inch mesh chicken wire with ruffle-edged colored crepe paper or silk pushed into the openings. A more realistic box hedge can be made of chicken wire holding sprays of artificial boxwood or ilex leaves (Figure 11-16). Large mesh chicken wire can be used to support clumps of leaves on a tree branch, or as a hanging border related to a tree trunk. The leaf material, which can be either paper or fabric, should have sufficient stiffness to hold a leaflike shape, or it will have to be stiffened with wire. Window-shade stock, which comes in several shades of green, makes a good leaf fabric to staple onto a branch or chicken-wire frame.

PART 3

Designing the Lighting

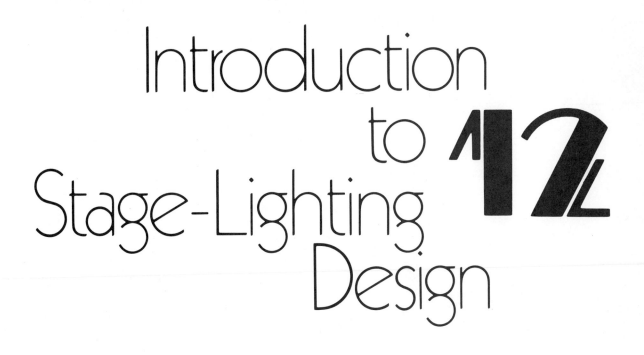

Introduction to Stage-Lighting Design

12

Scene design, unlike the other visual arts, is deeply dependent on the use of light as a part of the final composition—the dramatic picture. And stage lighting holds such importance in contributing to the total visual effect that no designer should neglect to familiarize himself with its techniques.

The design of lighting usually begins with the scene designer's sketch. Here he presents a suggestion of the light that will illuminate the scene. It may appear to be coming from such natural sources as the sun, the moon, or a fire—or from artificial sources as table lamps or ceiling fixtures. In contrast, the sources may be frankly arbitrary and depend on the position and color of the instruments used to build the composition. If the sketch is carefully done, the direction and color of the light will be apparent. To indicate any changes in brightness, color, or direction, the designer will have prepared several sketches to show such altered composition and mood.

Such sketches, however, are only a start in the planning of stage lighting. Although a sketch represents an artistic concept, it must be technically sound to be properly realized. The floor plan that accom-

363

364 panies the sketch gives the first clues as to the credibility of the designer's lighting ideas. Many a beautiful sketch has been based on a floor plan that revealed, on closer study, impossible lighting angles and insufficient space for the lighting instruments.

Ideally, a single person should design the entire production—scenery, costumes, and lighting—thus assuring a unified concept. But all too often a highly gifted designer will disclaim sufficient knowledge of the technical aspects of stage lighting, or is too busy to devote enough time to it. But whether the scene designer is one of the notable exceptions who light their own sets, or whether he depends on a specialist, often his assistant, to do it for him, he will certainly broaden his design concepts if he makes a study of stage lighting, and even more surely he will escape the pitfalls that await the uninformed.

STAGE LIGHTING

What is the magic of stage lighting? The demands on it are many. The costume designer, after considering period, silhouette, color, and character in choosing the fabric for a costume, also wonders how it will look *under the lights*. The scene designer, while selecting the colors of draperies and upholstery or deciding the scale of detail on the scenery, hopes they will show *under the lights*. The actor in the dressing room ponders if his makeup will look right *under the lights*.

Good lighting—and there is much that it not good—should tie together all the visual aspects of the stage. Ninety percent of the time stage lighting is cast in the supporting role of revealing scenery forms, enhancing costumes, and defining the acting areas. There are occasions, however, when stage lighting becomes more visually expressive. Scripts often call for startling effects such as an explosion, a fog, a flashing sign, lighting, or a hearth fire. Effects usually occur either to advance the plot or establish the mood for a scene.

Recent trends in stage design have given lighting such a conspicuous share of the total visual effect that it often is the basic element of scenery. The new scenic role of light can vary from the conventional use of a projected scenic background or shadow patterns (see Light as Scenery) to the more extreme abstract forms of psychedelic lighting.

Between these two extremes—the conventional illumination of scenery forms and the uninhibited use of light for light's sake—lies the world of the lighting designer.

The Lighting Designer. In contemporary theatre, the lighting designer is the newest member to join the design team of the average

FIGURE 12–1. THE SCENE DESIGNER'S SKETCH. The planning of stage lighting usually begins with the scene designer's sketch where the kind of illumination, its distribution, color, and general atmosphere are indicated. The sketch is for the opening scene of *Don Juan, or the Love of Geometry* by Max Frisch.

theatre production. Except for a few scene designers who enjoyed lighting their own scenery, the lighting of most Broadway productions in the not-too-distant past was neglected and became, by default, one of the innumerable duties of the stage manager or stage electrician. It was inevitable that lighting specialists would move into the neglected field and demonstrate with startling results what could be done if one person devoted his sole attention to the planning of lighting.

Although the lighting designer is an integral part of present-day stage designing he was not always so. The early lighting designer, for example, often felt the necessity to make an independent statement within the total visual effect and thus called attention to the lighting. This statement was usually expressed in color and frequently the costumes and scenery were sacrificed in the process.

Contemporary theatre training and awareness of total theatre on the part of the lighting designer has brought greater unity to the visual side of today's theatre. The lighting designer must have compassion for and understanding of the total design effort since he is the only design member who does not make an advance statement in visual terms of what he intends to do. The costume and scene designers submit a multitude of sketches, material samples, and models as visual examples of their intent. The lighting designer, on the other hand, submits a light plot and a verbal description, which

FIGURE 12–2. MOOD. The barn scene from *The Visit* by Friedrich Duerrenmatt is a good example of a mood-dominated setting. The low intensity, limited distribution, and dramatic patterns of light reveal the scenic forms with the proper atmosphere for the scene.

FIGURE 12–3. THEME.   Tennessee Williams   *A Streetcar Named Desire* is an example of a theme-dominated play. The lighting designer is asked to support the theme with a distribution of light that follows the action in all areas within the apartment (above) as well as revealing the outside through transparent walls (below). Set designer—Edward Pisoni. (Photo—Nelson)

means less to the other designers than his established integrity as an artist who will faithfully interpret their designs as well as the intent of the play.

STAGE LIGHTING AND THEATRICAL FORM

The development of the importance and scope of stage lighting is visibly linked to the evolution of theatrical form. The prolonged dominance of the *literary theatre* placed lighting as well as costumes and scenery in an interpretive role that followed the inspirations of the playwright. The literary theatre, leaning more toward literature than theatre, tends to be tied to the reality of the present or past. Narrative and dialogue are its most theatrical ingredients. Most of this textbook is devoted to the problems and skills connected with designing scenery and lighting for a dramatic production or play.

The *musical theatre*, from musical comedy to opera, is connected to literary theatre by a mere thread. The sung dialogue and dance

movement of musical theatre make it a completely different theatrical form. Concerned less with the logical development of a plot, it deals with the essences of human emotions, of people's hopes, fears, their tragedies. Music, an abstract form itself, lifts musical theatre into another dimension, thereby freeing lighting to fill a more expressive role.

The *audio-visual* form, as was mentioned in Chapter 1, places the emphasis on sound and sight rather than on the spoken word. Ballet, dance, and mime are prime examples of this theatrical form. Stress on the visual aspect makes lighting and the use of light projections extremely significant.

Avant-garde experimental combinations of theatrical forms and *mixed-media* create a new and imaginative theatrical form relying heavily on sensation and shock to stimulate an audience. The demand and opportunities provided by this kind of theatre for lighting expertise is very apparent.

FIGURE 12–4. STORY. The use of lighting to assist the staging of the story is apparent in a play like *Summer Tree* by Ron Cowen. The lighting reveals all or a portion of the formalized setting as the story moves back and forth in time. Set Designer—Richard Churchill. Lighting—Bertrand Cottine. (Photo—Nelson)

THE PHYSICAL FORM

The shape of modern theatre also has had an influence on the development of stage lighting. Beginning with the *proscenium theatre* and its traditional audience and stage arrangement, lighting, for the most part, is essentially *shadowbox* illumination catering to theatrical realism or the illusory theatre.

The *thrust stage*, with its audience on three sides, minimizes the use of scenery and makes illusion a greater responsibility of the lighting designer. This new-old form of theatricality (popular in the sixteenth century) relies chiefly on lighting, costumes, and properties for its visual composition.

Center staging surrounds the stage area with audience. The arena-theatre form increases the demands on stage lighting and virtually eliminates scenery.

Theatre of total environment (see Chapter 1), the most recent form, not only brings back scenery elements but also expands the use of lighting to even greater dimensions by surrounding or immersing the audience in the atmosphere or environment of the play. The circle has been completed by returning to a prosceniumlike form. The production, however, is not contained behind the frame, but is allowed to spill out and surround the audience.

Flexible staging should not be neglected for it is capable of achieving, on a small scale, any of the aforementioned audience–stage arrangements and even more. It is, by its sheer flexibility, a frankly impromptu form with its exposed lighting instruments and temporary seating arrangement.

It can be seen by now that, between the rapid expansion of imaginative theatrical forms and the numerous physical forms in the explosion of new theatres, the lighting designer is facing demands on his skills that are totally different in taste and technical capabilities of only a generation or so ago. The opportunities are challenging. The reader by now may be asking, "Where does the study of stage lighting begin?"

Setting aside the technical aspects of electricity, instrument and control design, and the nitty-gritty of plotting, scheduling, and hanging of equipment, the lighting designer is concerned first with the esthetics of light. To develop a sense of composition and taste in color so that he may extend theatrical judgment, a lighting designer must start by familiarizing himself with the qualities and limitations of his medium, light, itself.

THE QUALITIES OF LIGHT

Once light is created, whether it be from the sun or an artificial source, it has certain inherent qualities that become characteristic of the light medium. Just as paint has traits peculiar to its medium, so light conforms to a similar set of attributes. The physical characteristics of light itself as a design potential are discussed in Chapter 3 where *light* is presented as a very important element of design in context with the development of scene design as a visual art. The separate study of *light* in its application to stage lighting involves these same qualities: *intensity, distribution,* and *color.*

Intensity. The first and most obvious quality of light is its intensity or *brightness.* It can be the *actual* or *comparative* brightness of light itself. The actual brightness of the sun, for example, can be contrasted to the comparative brightness of automobile headlights at night. Spotlights in a darkened theatre offer the designer the same comparative brightness under more controlled conditions.

Distribution. Light rays follow an energy path which is known as distribution. The control of the distribution of light gives it *direction* and *texture* as a design feature. The various kinds of distribution begin with the general radiation of direct emanation through the more specific reshaping of the light rays by reflection or optics to the parallel rays of the laser beam. The sharp or soft-edged quality of the light beam coupled with its degree of brightness give texture to the light itself.

It is easy to see how the distribution of light can affect the ultimate design of a scenic form. The considered use of the direction and texture of light can introduce highlight, shade, and shadow into the composition. The angle or direction of the light that is illuminating the actor, for example, becomes very important in giving the actor a natural look as might occur under sunlight. Unnatural angles such as illumination from below distort the face with unusual shadows and misplaced highlights.

Color. The third property of light is its ability to transmit and reveal color. Color, besides being a forceful element of design in *all* phases of the visual side of the theatre, is the most effective and dramatic quality of light. Setting aside the physics of color and its origin in the electromagnetic spectrum (see Chapters 8 and 12) and turning to the design aspect of color in light, we find that its chief contribution is the transmitting of color or *colored light.* The modification of the local color of a scenic form by colored light is a design technique unique to the theatre. *Color modification* and the *additive mixing* of colored light are two rather basic concepts of *color* as a quality of light that has to be understood by *all* designers in the theatre. Both are discussed in detail later.

Composition.   The principles of composition are the same for the lighting designer as they are for the scene designer or any visual artist (see Chapter 3). Composition is the organizing of the visual elements of design into a unified form or arrangement of forms. The *meaning* attached to forms in a stage composition is, for the most part, a visual interpretation of the playwright's ideas. Lighting is the final unifying force of the stage composition.

Unlike a painting, a stage composition is not static but is an ever-changing arrangement of forms with a moving center of interest. Although light can have composition of its own (projected patterns, and so on) its chief function is to reveal stage forms in the proper relationship to other forms and the background. And here the complexity of compositional lighting begins.

Compositional lighting means: lighting one form and not lighting another; lighting two-dimensional forms to look three-dimensional; keeping shadows off the background; lighting three-dimensional forms to look three-dimensional (not as easy as it seems); and many other similar problems, the most important of which is the compositional lighting of the actor.

THE QUALITIES OF LIGHT AND THE ELEMENTS OF DESIGN

If lighting design and the lighting designer are going to assume the title of *designer* in the context of the other designers in the theatre (scenery and costumes) there must at least be an awareness of the elements of design that are part of the creative process of the scenery and costume designer. A complete knowledge and skill in all areas of design would approach the present-day definition of the scenographer—an ideal which only a few are able to attain. Nevertheless the goals and guidelines of scenography are significant to stage lighting if for no other reason than to be aware of the creative process of the visual artist with whom the lighting designer has to work.

The fundamentals of design as applied to scene design are discussed in detail in Chapter 3 where the basic *elements of design* are presented and their contribution to the stage composition is explained. The elemental factors that make up any visual *form* can be listed in the order of their importance to the creative process. They are: *line, dimension, movement, light, color,* and *texture.*

Line   as an element of design defines *form.* Its force is present in a composition in many ways. Line can enclose space as *outline* creating shape (two-dimensional form), or as *contour-line* suggesting three-dimensional form. Strong backlighting, for example, would emphasize the silhouette or *outline* of a form while directional side lighting reveals its contour.

Line can appear in a composition as *real line* in many different modes (straight, curved, spiral, and so on) or as *suggested line* simulated by the eye as it follows a sequence of related shapes.

Line as a path of action frequently assumes *direction*. A strong beam of light cannot help but establish direction. The linear shape of the beam coupled with a concentration of brightness creates a strong focus in the composition.

Dimension   is the size of *form*. As an element of design, it is not only concerned with the *size* of a shape or mass, but also with the relationship of the size of one shape to another—large to small, large to large, and so on. Hence the size of the interval has a definite effect on the apparent size or mass of a form and to its proportional relationship to other forms in the composition.

The control of the distribution of light on either the form or the interval influences the dimension of one or the other. Light can reverse the feeling of dimension by making a two-dimensional shape look three-dimensional and vice versa.

Movement   is the action of *form*. It is the kinetic energy of composition. Motion can exist in a stage design as *real movement,* and as the movement of the eye or *optical motion* within a static composition.

The *real movement* of lights; of the actor; and on occasion, animated elements of scenery, are all very much part of a theatrical production. Any visible change of intensity, distribution, or color is the movement of light. The movement of a follow-spot beam; the change of a color on the cyclorama; and the raising or lowering of lights on different areas of the stage are a few examples of real movement.

Optical motion is the movement of the eye over a composition. When a form or arrangement of forms is static optical motion is dependent upon the sequential arrangement of forms or elements of design. Suggested line is most frequently used to create optical motion as the directional attitude of real line or linear shapes. Strong directional light rays or the sequential arrangement of light sources are examples of the use of light as optical motion. The subtle gradation of one color and the vibration of two hue opposites are the extreme uses of color as optical motion.

Light reveals form.   The dominant presence of light in all areas of stage design makes it imperative that light be considered as a basic influence in the beginning of the creative process and not something to be studied later. The early awareness of light as a design element is as important to the scenery and costume designer as the appreciation of all

FIGURE 12-5. TEXTURED AND LOW-RELIEF SURFACES. Demonstrating the effects of angle and distribution of light on a highly textured surface or low-relief carving. Above: a low-relief sculptural form lighted with a single source from the front. Below: the same form lighted with two side-angle sources of different intensity or color.

the elements of design is to the lighting expert to whom this section of the book is devoted.

Color modifies form.   As an element of design it is a powerful stimulus within the composition. It can change the dimension of form; reverse the direction of line; alter the interval between forms; and generate optical motion. Color in the theatre comes from two basic sources: pigment or dye colors present on the surface of the form, or colored light that modifies the color of the form. For a more detailed discussion of color in the theatre and light see Chapters 8 and 12.

Texture   is the tactile aspect of *form*. It is the treatment of surfaces, which is of interest to the lighting designer. Surfaces may be highly polished, rough-hewn, or rusticated, to name a few that may reflect light or cast interesting shadows. Real texture is best revealed by directional side light (distribution) while painted or simulated texture appears more real under a wash of light without a strong sense of direction. Light itself can have texture, as has been mentioned earlier.

FIGURE 12-6. LIGHTING STYLES.   Besides the lighting styles created by the realistic quality of natural distribution and the abstract style of light coming from arbitrary directions there are some styles more closely related to production. (*a*) *Documentary* style of Brecht. Stark, colorless with exposed light sources in an effort to deny theatrical make-believe. *The Measures Taken*. Designer — Frederic Youens. (Photo — Nelson) (*b*) *Theatrical* in a historical style. Warm, colorful, and nostalgic, capturing the period light quality coming from candles of the chandeliers and footlights. *Love for Love*. Designer — Robert E. Jones. (*c*) *Theatrical* in the contemporary style. A theatrical use of contemporary lighting sources and the modern concept of lighting. *After the Fall*. Designer — Ladislav Vychodil — Bratislava. (*d*) *Symbolic* style. A hollow pyramid of light symbolizing the vision interludes of the play. *Owner of the Keys*. Designer — Josef Svoboda — Prague. (Photo reprinted from *The Scenography of Josef Svoboda* by permission of the Wesleyan University Press. Copyright © 1971 by Jarka Burian.)

a

b

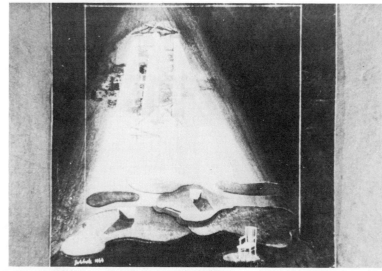

c

d

376 THE FUNCTION OF STAGE LIGHTING

It might be argued that the basic obligation of light on the stage is to give the actor or performer *meaning* in his surroundings and to provide him with an atmosphere in which he may logically interpret his role. At the same time, stage lighting, like scene designing, has to assist in creating an environment suitable for the action of the play that brings to the audience the full meaning and emotions of the playwright's concept.

Although the lighting designer does not begin until the setting has been designed, he is guided by the same fundamentals of dramatic form as the set designer. Through the use of light in all its aspects, intensity, color, distribution and movement, the lighting designer assists in creating the proper environment for the play by helping to place the action, establish the mood, reinforce the theme, and stage the story of the play or related theatrical form.

Placing the Action. In some plays the designer may find that mood and theme are so much a part of the story line that it is hard to separate their functional differences. On the other hand, the action of a play is usually easy to isolate. Action, the designer soon discovers, can vary from a static, wordy, psychological study to a fast-moving farce, or to the violent contact of a murder mystery. The physical action of a play or any theatrical performance is of prime importance to the lighting designer. He wants to know where the action has to

FIGURE 12–7. NATURAL DISTRIBUTION. Below: Natural lighting and surroundings make up the environment of *You Can't Take It with You.* Opposite page: Close-up of a scene from *The Miracle Worker.* The lighting is realistically motivated although the setting, with its cutaway walls is less conventional. The black and white photograph does not show the difference in colors of the exterior and interior acting area lights. The strong directional light of the exterior can be seen in contrast to the soft, diffused light of the interior. Set designer—Wayne Linder. Lighting designer—Steve Ross.

be clearly seen, half seen, or not seen at all. To follow the action, the designer frequently manipulates the intensity and distribution of light.

The placing of the action usually happens in the opening moments of the performance and can set the tone of the show. Whether it be a specific room in a house, a street in a village, a cabaret, or just action in limbo, it is still the place of the action that will, of course, set the proper environment for the rest of the scene. Making the action visible to the audience is the first and most obvious use of light. The placing of the action relies heavily on some degree of visibility to let the audience see what should be seen.

Visibility. We cannot define visibility as a fixed degree of brightness or an established angle of distribution. It is the amount of light needed for a moment of recognition deemed appropriate for that point in the action of the play. "To see what should be seen" may mean the revealing of only the silhouette of a three-dimensional form, the solidity of its mass, or the full detail of all surfaces with decoration and texture. Each degree of visibility cannot help but take on an atmosphere or mood that will affect the action.

Establishing the Mood. The over-all mood of a play or scene is the next important clue to the lighting designer. A strong color impression comes from mood, as well as a suggestion of the intensity

378 and distribution of light. The word "mood" tends to suggest dark and moody surroundings, but a bright comedy or nonsensical farce is also a type of mood.

Although an abstract or dramatic mood is more impressive and eye-catching than the realistic visibility of a conventional interior setting, it is far easier to accomplish with light. How many times have the dancing shadows of an actor sitting in front of the *single* source of a hearth fire won more aclaim for the lighting designer than the hours of careful lighting of a realistic interior.

Reinforcing the Theme. The key word here is "reinforcing." Because the visual expression of theme is dependent upon the scene designer's interpretation of the playwright's message, the lighting designer is concerned with the compositional revealing of the thematic forms of the setting. The theme-dominated play, *A Streetcar Named Desire*, for example, asks the lighting designer to reveal the fragmented setting first as a structure having solid walls, then as a transparent, see-through skeleton; finally, he is asked to illuminate the constantly moving center of attention from room to room, interior to exterior.

In the more extreme theme-oriented or documentary plays of Bertolt Brecht the theme is pointed up by removing the moodiness of stage lighting and playing the show under a clear, uncolored wash of light. Lighting, however, is used to reinforce the theme visually through the use of projections. These take the form of propaganda pictures or subtitles and are used in the place of scenic background.

Staging the Story. The story line of a play may be developed very simply as in a one-set, seven-character, domestic comedy or as in an extremely difficult, episodic marathon with a cast of hundreds. The narrative may require the cross-section of a house or the establishment of many unrelated locales in a single-setting arrangement. The movement from scene to scene or from area to area is planning in logistics for the scene designer, while for the lighting designer it is an exercise in control of precise distribution and delicate intensities of light. Movement or transitions within a scene, or from scene to scene by lighting become a connecting or unifying factor for the production.

There are many plays that are examples of the use of this type of staging and lighting. *Inherit the Wind, Desperate Hours* and *Summer Tree* are a few of a long list of plays that require special attention in both staging and lighting.

LIGHTING THE ACTOR

The actor, when he walks onstage, must be seen in proper relationship to his background. This relationship, of course, is different for each play or dramatic situation. In general, the designer turns to the manipulation of intensity, distribution, and color of the lights to solve his problem. Distribution is of primary importance because it involves the angle and direction of the light reaching the actor to reveal him, especially his face, in natural form.

The expression "in natural form" is the clue. It means the actor's face should be seen as it appears under natural lighting. Our eyes have been schooled by a lifetime of seeing one another under sunlight or interior lighting coming from above. We are so accustomed to seeing the features of the face disclosed by light from an overhead direction that to light it from below, for example, produces for us an unnatural-looking face.

Anyone who has done outdoor photography knows how to maneuver his subject into a position where the sun will reveal the subject's face most favorably. He also discovers that overly bright sunlight from a single direction will cast such deep shadows that that visibility of the face will be reduced. While in the diffused light of shade or an overcast sky the face appears in full visibility, though it is missing the dramatic accent of the brilliant sunlight.

Through the elaborate control of intensity and distribution that is possible in stage lighting it is easy to see that by choosing the proper position and direction of the light sources, the face of the actor can be lighted as it is in nature.

It has long been a practice of artists and architects to render their drawings as though light were falling on the subject from over the artist's shoulder at an angle of about 45 degrees. The lighting designer adopts the same concept. By using a specific lighting instrument, like a spotlight, the beam may be directed on the actor at a 45 degree angle above and at 45 degrees from the right and left. To give the face an accent of brightness or color difference on one side, the intensity or color of the right or left spotlight may be varied. The face is then disclosed by a wash or *fill-light* on one side and an accent or *key-light* on the opposite side. This slight difference in color and intensity not only improves the visibility of the face but also adds interests to the composition.

Back Lighting.   Cross lighting and modeling of the face have been discussed as beginning techniques for the lighting of the actor. A third angle can be employed to further define the actor by lighting

FIGURE 12–8. UNNATURAL
DISTRIBUTION.   Light coming
from below (apron) at an unnatural
angle. Above: It can be used as
an added dimension to the already
abstract form of the dance. Right:
An example of sharp cross lighting
in contrasting colors and
brightness. Design and photos—
Steve Ross.

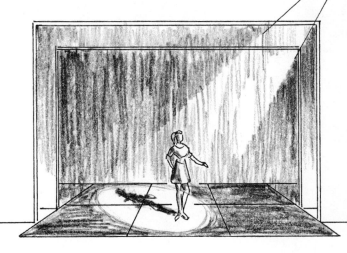

FIGURE 12–9. LIGHTING THE ACTOR.
THE FOLLOWING SERIES OF
PHOTOGRAPHS (through page 385)
ILLUSTRATES THE EFFECT OF THE
NUMEROUS ANGLES OF LIGHT ON THE
COMPOSITION OF THE FACE.

Above: Front light from the left,
forty-five-degree angle. Lack of
visibility on the dark side of the
face.

Below: Front light from the left and
right, forty-five-degree angle. The
right side of the face has a higher
intensity light suggesting the
direction of the motivating or ''key''
light.

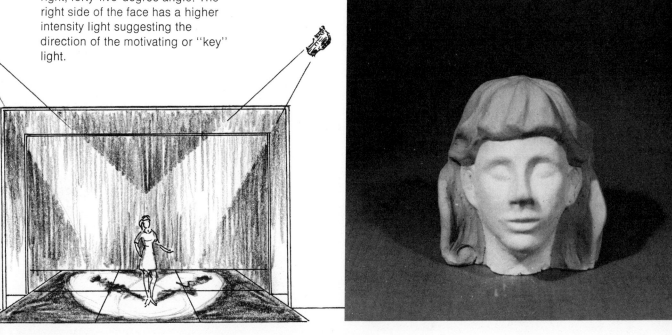

LIGHTING THE ACTOR (cont'd).
Side light from the right,
forty-five-degree angle.

LIGHTING THE ACTOR (cont'd).
Side light from the right,
thirty-degree angle.

LIGHTING THE ACTOR (cont'd).
Side light from the right and left,
thirty-degree angle. Note the
shadow in the center of the face.

LIGHTING THE ACTOR (cont'd).
Full front light. Note lack of
definition.

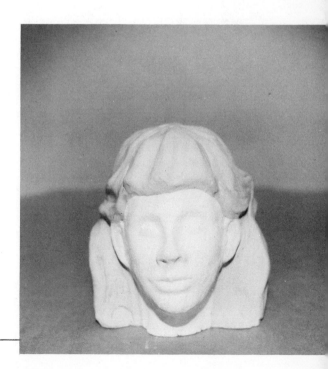

LIGHTING THE ACTOR (cont'd).
Backlight producing a halo or
''rim'' effect.

LIGHTING THE ACTOR (cont'd).
Three angles: right and left front
light and back light. The key light
is from the left from a forty-five-
degree angle, fill light from the
right front and rim light from the
overhead rear.

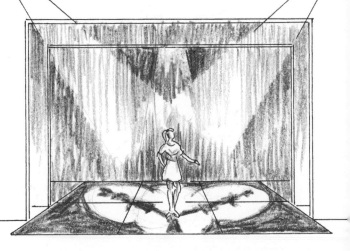

LIGHTING THE ACTOR (cont'd).
Downlight or ''pool,'' ninety-degree
angle.

LIGHTING THE ACTOR (cont'd).
Upward angle from the footlights
or apron. An unnatural, though
dramatic, angle.

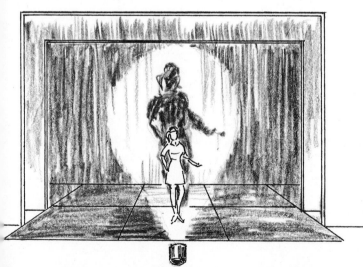

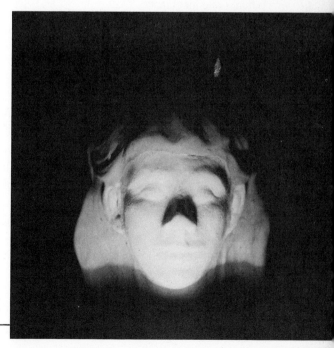

him from overhead and behind. Back lighting is a stratagem borrowed from movie and television lighting. Because of the need to separate the actor from his background, it is a necessary angle in television lighting. (The tendency of the camera is to flatten or shorten distances appearing on the reception screen.) The use of back lighting on the stage to separate the actor from his background also adds another dimension to the stage composition. It allows the lighting designer to put a brighter light on the background than he could otherwise, and it permits the scene designer to use colors without fear of failure to bring the actor's face into relief. Back lighting produces highlights on the head and shoulders of the actor that give a *halo* effect if the light is too intense. When it is kept in proper balance with the front lights the actor is etched clearly against the background. The designer, however, can use additional angles to further enhance the composition.

Side Lighting.   Side lights (or *glint lights*) are a compositional plus. They are not absolutely necessary, but if there is flexibility in color selection from scene to scene they do add a sparkle to colorful costumes. Side lighting, coming from the wings or tormentor positions, is best when directed parallel to the apron. As side lights hit the actor from the extreme right and left they need not be the same colors as the front lights. They can be used with more chromatic colors to accent costumes, or to add colored highlights to white or neutral costumes. The side lighting is frequently used for musical productions as a part of this more presentational style of theatre.

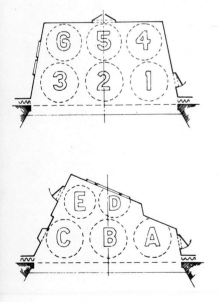

DIAGRAM 12–10. THE ACTING AREAS.   Top: A conventional box setting. Note the numbering of the areas from downstage left to upstage right. The total number of areas will vary with the shape and number of settings in the production. Bottom: An irregularly shaped interior setting. Some designers prefer to designate the areas with letters to avoid confusion with dimmer and instrument numbers.

LIGHTING THE ACTING AREA

The lighting of the actor from various positions and angles is, of course, easy when the subject is posed or remains in a fixed position on stage. The actor, however, must move. Therefore, to produce the same coverage as on a stationary figure, the lighting designer must constantly duplicate the focus of spotlights on many similar areas over the entire playing area.

By dividing the playing portion of the setting into convenient areas and then lighting each area with the same number of spotlights, the acting area is covered with a balanced illumination that reveals the actor in the degree of visibility that is most suitable for the immediate situation.

The area method of lighting the actor, which was first developed by Stanley McCandless in the 1930s, has proven to be a very efficient and systematic technique. As the style of scenery has changed and

lighting instrument design has improved, the method has been modified and expanded. The original concept of providing a smooth coverage with a minimum of instruments has given way to double and triple
hanging in the name of greater flexibility in color control and distribution. The resulting instrument count in some shows is of staggering
proportions. Though the area method was first developed for the
proscenium theatre it can be and has been applied to other theatre
forms such as thrust and arena (see Chapter 21).

The designer soon learns, as he begins to use the area system, that
areas have to have a generous overlap of lighting or the actor will
walk into dark spots as he leaves one area for another. He also finds
that he cannot always maintain the ideal angle of 45 degrees from
both sides of each area. The extreme right and left sides of the stage
are unavoidably covered by spotlights from an almost head-on angle.

The placement and choice of the number of areas is the lighting
designer's decision and, of course, varies with the size and shape of
the setting Diagram 12–11a).The action of the play or the staging of
the production also helps to determine the number of areas and the
distribution of the coverage. In a multiscene production some of the
areas can be planned for use in more than one set, providing the floor
plans are close to the same configuration.

AREA FLEXIBILITY

The demand for greater and greater flexibility stems from the
trend toward increased complexity of staging, more frequent repertory
organizations where several shows are kept in rotation, and high labor
costs that force the elimination of unnecessary handling or manual
operation of equipment. It is cheaper, for example, to hang a few
extra instruments than to pay a man to be present at each performance to change a color medium.

Double Hanging. To improve the limited flexibility of simple
cross lighting Diagram 12–11d)the designer can hang two more instruments, right and left, as additional lights for each area. This offers
him many alternatives. By duplicating the area color scheme on each
side he has several possibilities for color control. He can (1) change
the warm-cool accent from left to right; (2) change the area color by
independently mixing the colors from either the right or left; (3) flood
the stage with only one of the two area colors. If the setting is open
enough to permit it, the back lights can also be double-hung, providing even further flexibility.

388   *Triple Hanging.*   A third spotlight may be added to each position lighting an area Diagram 12–11e).The extra light can give further dimension to color control, increase the intensity of the area, and provide greater flexibility of distribution for the area. An area, for example, can have both *tight* and *wide coverage.* To achieve tight coverage, the two extra spots are focused onto a smaller portion of the stage so that the focus on the scene is more concentrated.

Blending the Acting Areas.   Sometimes the flexibility of control in area lighting is limited either by the number of circuits on the con-

DIAGRAM 12–11. LIGHTING THE ACTING AREAS. *(a)* The *area system* with a minimum of spotlights for each area. (1) Beam or ceiling position in front of the proscenium covering the downstage areas, 1, 2, and 3. (2) Teaser position. Spotlights on the first pipe batten upstage of teaser or proscenium opening are focused on the upstage areas, 4, 5, and 6. *(b)* A sectional view of the area system. (1) Beam spots. (2) Teaser spots. (3) Side lights and (4) back lights are additional angles that can be added into each area. (5) Extreme vertical sightline. *(c)* Front view showing the angle of side lighting for areas, 1, 2, and 3. *(d) Double hanging* on the left side. Only the downstage areas, 1, 2, and 3,are shown. The stage right beam spots are cool in color while the spots on the left are both warm and cool to allow a color selection in the acting areas. *(e) Triple hanging* on area 2, double hanging on areas 1 and 3. The center area has a *tight* and *open* focus as well as a selection of color and direction of *key* light in each area.

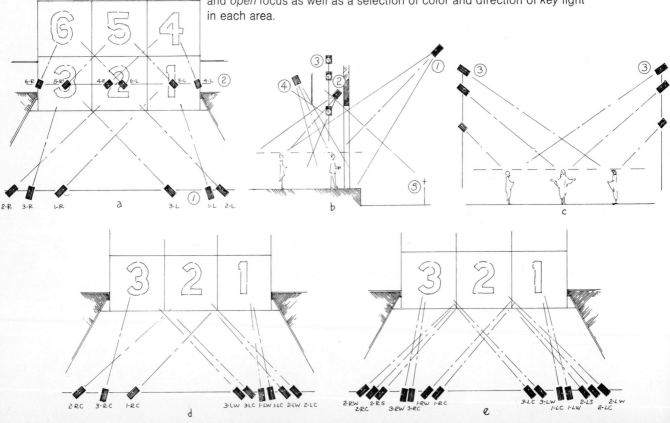

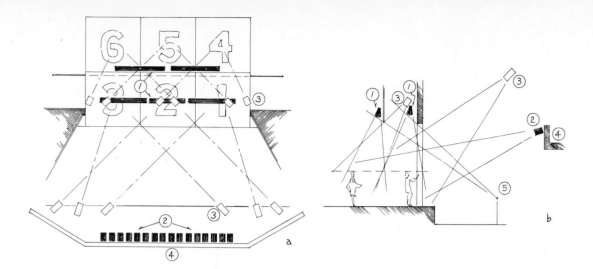

DIAGRAM 12–12. BLENDING THE ACTING AREAS.   Two methods of blending the acting areas when a minimum of acting areas spots are used. *(a)* Plan. (1) Three-color borderlight strips. (2) Balcony front spotlight group to provide a three-color wash of light on the stage. The method can be simplified, of course, to a two-color or single color set-up thereby reducing the number of spotlights by one-third or two-thirds. (3) Area spotlights. *(b)* Section. (1) Borderlight strips. (2) Balcony front wash spots. (3) Area spotlights. (4) Balcony. (5) Extreme vertical sightline.

trol board or by a lack of equipment. Under these conditions the designer may find it necessary to stretch the area coverage by filling irregularities between areas with a wash of light from flood instruments; in this way the areas are blended together. This soft wash of light which functions as a *fill-light* is best achieved from the backstage teaser position through the use of three-circuit compartment or reflector-lamp striplights. It provides a shadowless illumination with color selection and controlled distribution.

Fill-lights can also come from the front of the house (usually balcony front position). A battery of spotlights at flood focus and controlled by one circuit can provide a wash of light from a frontal direction.

LIGHTING THE BACKGROUND

The lighting of scenic elements in relation to the area lighting is an extension of compositional lighting and is more frequently a part of proscenium theatre than of the thrust or arena stages. The mood of the environment surrounding the action of the scene is often so fully expressed in the intensity, color, and distribution of the area lighting that, except for special occasions, the area lights themselves are the major portion of the illumination of the setting.

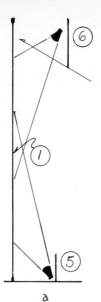

a

DIAGRAM 12–13. LIGHTING THE BACKGROUND. Various methods of lighting the backdrop and background arrangements. *(a)* Painted backdrop (1) lit from above and below. (5) Horizon or base striplights behind a groundrow. (6) Overhead strip behind a border. *(b)* Painted backdrop (1) lit only from above. *(c)* Translucent drop (3) is illuminated by backlight reflected off a reflecting drop (2) lit by base strips (7) and overhead strips (8). Frontlight comes from a second overhead strip (9). *(d)* A translucent drop upstage of a scrim. The drop has front and back lighting to change its quality or time of day. The scrim has front lighting to add depth and atmosphere. (10) Base strip. (11) Overhead strips for backlighting. (3) Translucent drop. (12) Base strip. (13) Overhead strip for front lighting. (4) Scrim. (14) Overhead strip for frontlighting scrim.

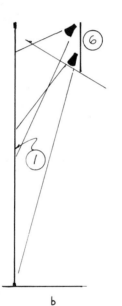

b

In a conventional interior setting, the area lighting will usually suffice to light the walls of the set, particularly when border-strips are contributing their blending wash. Background areas and backings, however, are a different matter. Many times the problem is small, as the backing behind a doorway, rarely seen for more than a moment at a time, and then not directly by most of the audience. Not very elaborate equipment is needed to give these backings enough illumination so that an actor, when leaving the stage, does not seem to be retiring into a dark closet.

Backings can assume greater proportions such as a section of exterior seen through a large window which might contain groundrows of distant hills or hedges and a section of sky. Rooftops or the exterior walls of an adjoining building may also be seen in a more detailed backing. Such backings usually demand greater attention to distribution and color control (to perhaps simulate different times of day) than the simple doorway backing.

For the most complicated backgrounds such as vast areas of sky, sometimes with a painted scenic vista, large backdrops or cycloramas are usually used. These require rows of high-wattage instruments, both from above and below, in order to give the proper amount of light, as well as even distribution and blending of color over the entire surface. Greater control of color is required if the mood of the background is expected to change with the time of day or the arbitrary change of washes of color. Changes in distribution can also occur, especially if the backdrop is partly translucent, allowing a cross-fading from front lighting to back lighting furnished by an additional bank of lights behind the drop.

Successful background lighting depends on the close cooperation of the lighting and scene designers. All too often the scene designer does not leave enough space between groundrows and the backdrop

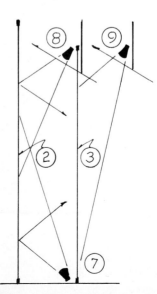

c

or between borders and the cyclorama to allow sufficient distance for proper distribution of the striplights. Backgrounds representing distant fields are sometimes so close to a window or door that it is impossible to keep the area lights from casting shadows on the background thereby destroying any illusion of distance.

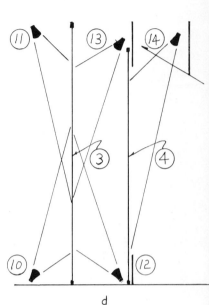

MOTIVATING AND MOTIVATED LIGHTS

In addition to the acting-area lights and background illumination there is a special group of lights that keynote the compositional aspect of stage lighting. The first category includes the *motivating* lights which are the visible sources on the stage that *seem* to be giving the light, or a portion of it, to the stage picture. Chandeliers, wall sconces, lanterns, and hearth fires are typical of this category. Usually, each must be naturalistic enough to appear to be furnishing a plausible amount of light to the scene, which means it must be slightly brighter than its supposed field of illumination. Its eye-catching brilliance gives it a strong emphasis in the over-all composition and must be handled with extreme caution and taste.

The second category is *motivated* illumination, which seems to be emanating from some real, but not always visible, source. The burst of sunlight through a window that was mentioned earlier is an example of a motivated light. A motivated light is usually very directional and therefore becomes a dramatic part of the composition. The position and direction of motivated lighting give the designer a clue to the direction of the key-light in the planning of the color and intensity of the acting area lights. If a strong, warm, motivated light is coming from stage left it would inspire the use of a warm, intense, area light on the left side of the actor's face. It is an accent over and above fill-light from the other directions and gives the lighting some meaning.

AREA SPECIALS

There is a variation to regular area lighting that should be considered. It takes form in the use of special instruments that specifically define or emphasize a part of the setting or draw attention to an actor at a given moment and in a certain position on the stage. This may include a *door special*, an extra spot carefully framed to catch an actor in the doorway; a *couch special*, extra punch on the couch or settee where an important scene take place; or a *pin-spot*, a narrow beam of light on an actor's face that is held a moment longer than the rest of the stage lights on a final dim-out. It can be seen that the area specials influence composition for they tend to pull the eye, by increased intensity, to the center of action.

SPECIAL VISIBILITY

In a sense *area specials* are also a part of special visibility which strives to emphasize an actor by increasing the brightness of the light on him over the general intensity of the stage lights. The basic difference is that area specials are designed for fixed objects or static situations while special visibility deals with the moving actor under more arbitrary or abstract conditions. The movement of light can be achieved in one of two ways. The actor can be covered by a series of carefully focused spotlights on his path of movement that rise and fade at the proper moment. The more classic technique is to use a *follow spot*. The movement of the actor is followed by a single, freely mounted, spotlight. The follow spot has long been in use in musical comedies, revues, and other presentational productions where realism is of minor importance. It usually appears as a sharply defined, brilliant circle of light outshining all the stage lights. In recent years the follow spot has come into more general use in straight drama, where it is, however, soft-edged and reduced in intensity so that it follows the action unobtrusively. If it is used properly the audience is not aware that an accent exists, but only feels its effect.

SPECIAL EFFECTS

Under the heading of special effects are listed all the uses of light that are not directly involved in lighting the actor or illuminating the background. This is often a dramatic use of light and hence makes more of an impression on the audience, thereby providing a moment of creative "fun" for the designer. Explosions, fires, ghosts, or psychedelic effects are all examples of the spectacular use of light that for a brief moment gives the stage lights and the lighting designer "stage center."

Light projections, the projected patterns of light or complete pictures whether moving or fixed, plays a dominant role in the category of special effects. The recent improvements in instruments and lighting techniques have led to greater and more successful use of projected scenery. The problems and possibilities in the use of projections are discussed in Chapter 18, *Light as Scenery*.

Elements of Electricity 13

ATOMIC THEORY

According to presently accepted theories, all matter consists of molecules, which are made up of atoms. Each atom is composed of a positively charged center called the nucleus around which are distributed a number of negatively charged bodies called electrons. The nucleus of an atom consists of protons and neutrons. Neutrons have no electric charge, but each proton has a positive charge exactly equal to the negative charge of an electron.

Every normal atom has as many electrons surrounding the nucleus as it has protons within the nucleus, and thus has an equal quantity of positive and negative charges. Thus hydrogen has one proton in its nucleus and one electron outside it; helium has two protons and two electrons; lithium has three of each, carbon has six, copper has twenty-nine, and so on up to uranium which has the most: ninety-two protons and ninety-two electrons. It is thought that the electrons are in constant motion, revolving around the nucleus in orbits much the same as the planets revolve around the sun. Figure 13–1 shows a few examples.

The hydrogen atom, the simplest of all, has its single electron revolving around its single positive proton, which acts as the nucleus of this atom. The negative charge and the positive charge being exactly equal, the atom is electrically neutral.

The helium atom has two electrons revolving about a nucleus which contains two protons and two neutrons. Again, this atom is neutral.

In the atom of lithium, the lightest of all metals, the three protons are balanced by two electrons in the inner orbit plus one in the outer orbit. Carbon also has two electrons in the inner orbit, plus four in the outer orbit, to balance the six protons. Copper requires four orbits to take care of its twenty-nine electrons.

It must be understood that actually the various orbits are not all in the same flat plane, like a plate, but rather they are at angles to each other, somewhat like a number of rubber bands stretched haphazardly about a baseball.

FIGURE 13–1. SCHEMATIC DIAGRAM OF THE STRUCTURE OF CERTAIN ATOMS.

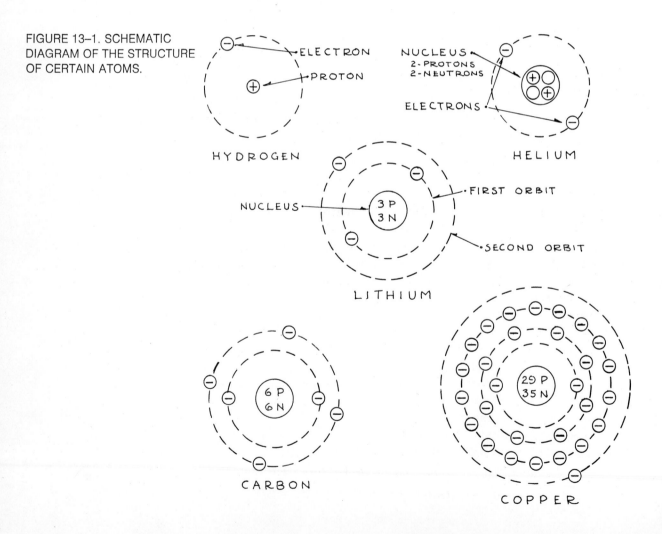

The lone electron in the fourth and outer orbit of copper may be easily dislodged, providing a free electron, the basis of current flow. The same is true of the outer electron in the lithium atom. In fact, all metals have electrons that can be readily dislodged.

CONDUCTORS AND INSULATORS

To allow electric current to move through circuits of any kind it is necessary to provide a path through which the electrons may move as easily as possible. Materials made up of atoms that release free electrons readily also permit the movement of electrons through them and are known as conductors. Actually there is no material that will not offer some resistance to such movement, but all metals are relatively good, and silver is the best of any substance known.

Obviously the use of silver for extensive wiring is not very practical, and some less costly material must be used. Copper is this material: its conductivity is almost as good as silver's, it is relatively inexpensive, and it is easy to work—to form into wires and other parts. Aluminum is coming more and more into use in some applications, and brass is valuable for large, permanent parts that need to be especially rugged. Other materials are also used for special purposes, but by and large when we think of electric wires, switch parts, and the like, we think of copper.

Some sort of insulation is necessary to prevent the electrons that are flowing in a conductor from short-circuiting—that is, escaping into other channels. This they will incline to do if the alternate path offers less resistance than the one that they were intended to travel. Obviously this would cause a lowering or even complete loss of available power. More important, this short may result in severe shock to anyone chancing to come in contact with the new and unprotected channel of flow. And because it may offer little resistance, it may allow a higher flow of current than the legitimate circuit was designed to carry, thereby causing damage to it.

Just as there is no material that is 100 percent conductive, so there is nothing that has 100 percent insulative properties, but there are many that can serve for various practical purposes. Glass and ceramics are excellent for small permanent parts such as sockets and switches, slate for larger switch and fuse panels, and asbestos where heat is involved. For wires and cables, rubber and fiber are used, while plastics are becoming increasingly common. The most useful insulator of all is dry air. If this were not so, every open socket or wall outlet would drain off current!

Permanent wiring, which should be laid by a licensed electrician only, may have a solid copper core through which the current flows, but the temporary wiring used on the stage always has a core made up of a number of small strands of wire. This is to provide proper flexibility in handling and laying. Standard stage cable consists of two or three such standard cores, each surrounded by a strong rubber insulation. For physical strength, tough fiber cords are laid alongside, and the whole surrounded by either a rubber or a fiber sheathing.

Stage cable comes in different sizes, or gages, each of which is designed to carry a specific maximum amperage. These limits should never be exceeded. The most useful sizes are:

Size (gage number):	18	16	14	12	10	8	6
Capacity (amperes):	3	6	15	20	25	35	50

Occasionally, for a very small load and a very short run, ordinary lamp cord (or zip cord), which has an 18-gage core, may be used, but this should be kept to a minimum and carefully guarded against abuse.

SOURCES OF ELECTRIC CURRENT

Just as you cannot get water to flow out of one end of a pipe unless there is water being poured into the other end, so free electrons will not move through a conductor unless there is a supply of free electrons being introduced into it. Such a supply of electrons is known as an electromotive force, or emf. It can be built up in a number of ways.

THE BATTERY

A very common device for supplying an emf is a battery, such as one consisting of a glass container filled with a dilute sulphuric acid solution, into which are placed a strip of copper and a strip of zinc. Now if a meter is connected between these two strips, it will show a small electric current passing from one to the other through this connection (Figure 13–2). This is caused by the acid attacking the zinc, which dissolves into the solution and releases two electrons from each of its atoms. These electrons are left on the zinc strip, and because the acid will not permit them to return to their atoms, they flow through the wire to the copper strip.

DIRECTION OF CURRENT FLOW

In the early days of electrical experimentation it was mistakenly thought that electricity moved in the opposite direction: from the copper to the zinc, or from plus to minus. This is known as "Franklinian current" or "conventional current." It is still used in marking voltage and current meters, in many books, and—this is especially important to remember—by nearly all practicing electricians. It is suggested that the student keep in mind that the actual electron flow

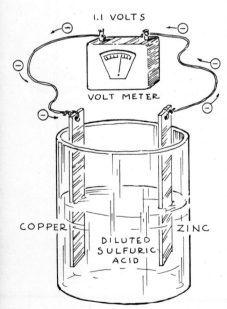

FIGURE 13–2. A SIMPLE CARBON-ZINC-ACID BATTERY.

is from minus to plus, but to be prepared to read texts or to talk with people who are not impressed by electron movement but use the conventional theory that the current flow goes from plus to minus.

Actually current may move through a conductor in either of two ways. Direct current, referred to as dc, flows in one direction only, while alternating current, or ac, reverses its direction one hundred twenty times each second. This is known as sixty-cycle current and is standard in most American installations, though many foreign countries use fifty cycles or even fewer.

OTHER SOURCES

An emf may be built up in a number of ways other than the battery. *Electrostatics* produces electricity by rubbing two dissimilar substances together. *Photoelectricity* is the action of sunlight on certain photosensitive materials. *Thermoelectricity* is the application of heat to the junction of two dissimilar metals that have been welded together. *Piezoelectricity* is the mechanical compression of certain crystals. And newer techniques are being developed. But the method of most importance to the stage electrician is that of "electromagnetism" in the form of a generator, powered by water, by steam or otherwise.

THE GENERATOR

The principle of the generator is the relative movement of a conductor within a magnetic field. The conductor may be moved while the field is stationary, or the field may be moved and the conductor remain stationary. The latter is usual in very large installations, but it is somewhat easier to comprehend the operation by considering a moving conductor in a stationary magnetic field.

Before we examine the production of an emf by a generator, we must establish the direction of the current induced by the movement of the conductor through the magnetic field. Fleming's right-hand rule may be applied. Hold the thumb, forefinger, and middle finger of the right hand at right angles to each other, the forefinger extended as if pointing, the thumb straight up at right angles to it, the middle finger half closed at right angles to the palm.

Now if the hand is adjusted so that the thumb points in the direction in which the conductor is moving and the forefinger points in the direction of the magnetic lines of force (from North to South pole of the magnet), the middle finger will point in the direction of the induced electromagnetic force (or current flow). But it must be remembered that the actual movement of the electrons is in the opposite direction from the conventional current flow.

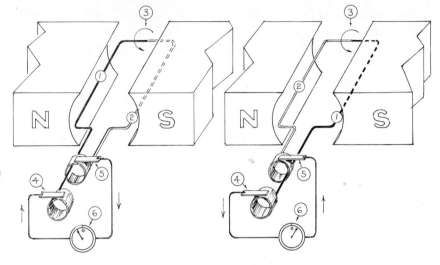

FIGURE 13–3. SIMPLE A-C GENERATOR (OR ALTERNATOR). (1) Side 1 of coil (2) Side 2 of coil (3) Direction of rotation of coil (4) Slip ring A (5) Slip ring B (6) Volt meter.

In Figure 13–3 the two diagrams show a highly simplified a-c generator, usually called an alternator. We see an armature in the shape of a single coil of wire being rotated through the magnetic field between the two poles of a magnet. The first diagram shows side *1* of this coil descending past the S pole, while the *2* side rises past the N pole. This induces an emf in the coil causing negative electrons to accumulate at slip ring *4* and flow off the slip ring through the brush and thence along the connecting wire and through a voltmeter to slip ring *5,* whence they re-enter the coil. In the second diagram the sides of the coil have reversed positions and directions, so now the electrons will accumulate at slip ring *5,* pass through the connecting wire and

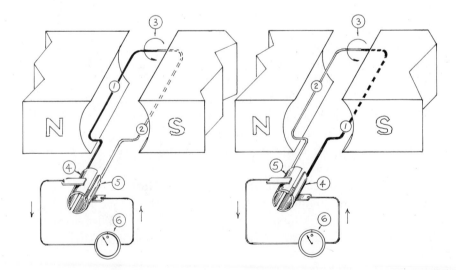

FIGURE 13–4. SIMPLE D-C GENERATOR. (1) Side 1 of coil (2) Side 2 of coil (3) Direction of rotation (4) Half commutator, side 4 (5) Half commutator, side 5 (6) Volt meter.

meter and reenter the coil at slip ring *4*. Each complete revolution of the coil is called a cycle, so for one half of each cycle the electrons move in one direction and for the other half in the opposite direction. Thus the current is said to be alternate.

In Figure 13–4 the two diagrams show a simplified d-c generator which is identical to the alternator except that in place of the two stationary slip rings a single ring, split into two equal sections and called a commutator, which revolves with the armature, is substituted. In the first diagram we see the induced emf causing the electrons to accumulate on the *4* portion of the commutator, to be passed through the wire and meter to the *5* portion, or, it might be stated, leaving the *1* side of the coil and re-entering at the *2* side.

But in the second diagram the electrons leave on the *2* side and re-enter on the *1* side of the coil, so they have all passed through the wire in the same direction and this movement is described as direct current.

In Figure 13–5 we see the construction of the sine curves that represent the variation of the induced emf for any portion of the complete cycle of the armature through the magnetic field. At the exact instant in time that the armature is passing the 0-degree point in its rotation it is moving parallel to the magnetic field, not through it, and hence is producing no emf at all.

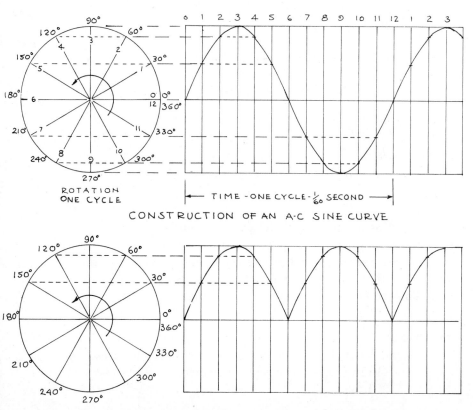

CONSTRUCTION OF AN A-C SINE CURVE

FIGURE 13–5. THE CONSTRUCTION OF A-C AND D-C SINE CURVES.

CONSTRUCTION OF A D-C SINE CURVE

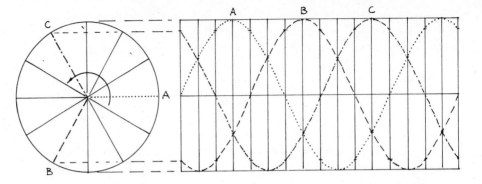

FIGURE 13–6. OVERLAPPING SINE CURVES PRODUCED BY AN A-C GENERATOR WITH THREE ARMATURES AT 120 DEGREES TO ONE ANOTHER.

As it reaches the 30-degree mark it is cutting into the magnetic field somewhat and hence is generating a small emf as depicted by extending a line from the 30-degree point to a somewhat later point in time than the 0-degree reading of 0. At the 60-degree position, an emf of greater magnitude is produced, and at 90 degrees the maximum emf. After this the emf drops back to 0 and then in an a-c generator it starts to build up in the opposite direction as depicted below the time line. But in the d-c generator the commutator rings prevent a reverse, or negative, emf, but rather add another direct, or positive, curve.

For the sake of economy it is practical to build not a single armature into a generator, but several of them. As these must be at angles to each other, it is obvious that their respective emfs will not reach any one point at the same instant, but rather they will produce sine curves as indicated in Figure 13–6. Here we see the very common arrangement of three armatures each producing its own curve. These are known as phases A, B, and C and will be discussed later.

ELECTRIC UNITS OF MEASUREMENT

There are four basic measurements that can be made in any electric circuit. Their definitions and relationships are below.

THE VOLT

The volt is the difference in electrical potential between two points in a circuit. Another way of putting it is to ask: how many more free electrons are there at point A than at point B, to which they will flow if a path is opened for them? This is also called electromotive force. The symbol is E, from the latter term.

THE AMPERE

The ampere is the rate of flow of current through a conductor: how many electrons pass a given point in one second of time? In working with mathematical calculations, the symbol for the ampere, I (for intensity of current flow) is used.

THE OHM

Every substance offers some resistance to the flow of current; some, as copper, offer very little while others, as rubber, offer a great deal. The ohm is the measurement of such resistance and its symbol is R.

THE WATT

The watt is the rate of doing work, whether it be turning an electric motor, or heating an electric iron, or causing a lamp to glow. Its symbol is P, for power.

OHM'S LAW

Ohm's law is the statement of the relationships among the potential that pushes the electrons, the resistance it encounters, and the current flow that will result. It states that the current will equal the potential divided by the resistance, or:

$$I = \frac{E}{R}$$

THE "PIE" FORMULA

The "pie" formula equation expresses the relationships among the potential, the current flow, and the rate of doing work. It states that this rate is equal to the product of the current and the potential or: P = IE. It should be noted that this equation has exactly the same meaning as the familiar "West Virginia law" or: W = VA, meaning watts equal volts times amperes.

COMBINATIONS OF THE EQUATIONS

Naturally these equations may be transposed or substituted one in the other to arrive at any arrangement suitable for solving any specific problem. Below are listed all the possible relationships of these four units:

$$I = \frac{E}{R} = \frac{P}{E} = \sqrt{\frac{P}{R}}$$

$$E = IR = \frac{P}{I} = \sqrt{PR}$$

$$R = \frac{E}{I} = \frac{E^2}{P} = \frac{P}{I^2}$$

$$P = IE = I^2R = \frac{E^2}{R}$$

402

DIRECT AND ALTERNATING CURRENT

Before the quite recent development of new techniques, direct current was not an efficient way to transport electricity for long distances. However, it was the only way known in the early days of electricity and for that reason was installed in the downtown areas of many cities, where it is still to be found, produced by comparatively small generating plants for neighborhood consumption. Elsewhere it has almost entirely been replaced by the more versatile ac.

Alternating current has the great advantage of being easily changed from low voltage to high and from high voltage to low by means of transformers. A transformer consists of an iron core, frequently doughnut shape, about which is coiled two wires, the primary and the secondary. When an alternating current is sent through the primary coil, it sets up a magnetic flux in the iron core, and in turn this flux induces a new current in the secondary coil. It must be understood that there is no electrical connection whatever between the two coils.

If the primary has few turns about the core and the secondary has more, the voltage induced in the secondary will be higher than that in the primary, but if the primary has more turns than the secondary, then the induced voltage will be lower. These are known as "step-up" and "step-down" transformers, respectively.

Figure 13–7 depicts a portion of a typical arrangement for a modest alternating-current service. At the left side we see the a-c generator station producing an emf of 1200 volts. This is fed to the substation where a transformer boosts it to 6000 volts, because the higher the voltage the less loss there will be in transit (some high-power transit lines carry as much as 500,000 volts!). As the current nears the neighborhood in which it will be consumed, it passes through another substation where the emf is reduced to 600 volts. This is sent out over the local wiring system until it reaches a house, where a small transformer on a pole by the highway reduces it still further to 120 volts for use in the home.

In this country the most common household service is 120 volts ac at 60 cycles. This accounts for almost two thirds of the installations, with most of the rest at 115 volts. The few remaining d-c services are 110 volts. Many foreign countries use quite different voltages, ranging from 105 to as much as 240, and these are usually at 50 cycles or even fewer.

FIGURE 13–7. SCHEMATIC OF A-C TRANSPORTATION FROM THE GENERATING STATION TO THE HOME.

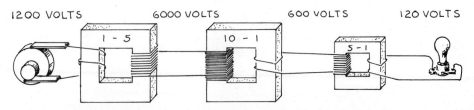

ELECTRIC SERVICES

It is essential that the stage electrician know by just what system of wiring the electricity is brought into the theatre or other area in which he may be working. This is especially true when a touring company moves into an unfamiliar building and must connect up its portable control board and other equipment. Let us glance briefly at the three forms of service in common use (Figure 13–8).

The first of these is the two-wire system, carrying either dc or ac, in which one line is said to be "hot" and the other "neutral." The potential between them usually is 120 volts, though it could be 115 or 110 volts depending on the voltage supplied in that particular locality, as explained above. Practically all portable lighting equipment will operate almost equally well on any of these voltages.

The second form of service is the three-wire system, which also may be either ac or dc. In this the two outside wires usually have a potential of 240 volts between them, but each has a potential of only 120 volts between it and the third wire, the common neutral. A familiar domestic application of this service is found in many homes where the electric lights are on two or more circuits of 120 volts each, while the electric range operates on 240 volts. Great care must be taken when working with such a system to avoid connecting any apparatus designed for 120 volts across the two hot lines. The 240 volts will blow the lamps at once, ruin other equipment promptly, and provide grave danger of fatal shock. The British, who use 240 volts for all their home lighting, must take precautions that would seem very irksome to us, who are used to our comparatively mild 120-volt service.

The third type of service, and one that is on the rapid increase due to its efficiency in distribution, is the a-c 120–208-volt, four-wire system, also known as the three-phase system. The generation of these three phases is illustrated in Figure 13–6. The emf produced by each phase is said to be at 120 degrees to the others. If the emf in relation to a common neutral conductor is 120 volts, then any two phases will be 208 volts from each other, this being the product of 240 volts times the sine value of angle 120 degrees, or .8660. Many motors are built to run on this 208 voltage, but this is of little concern to us, except that we must be sure never to connect standard-voltage equipment between two hot lines of a three-phase system.

SERIES AND PARALLEL CIRCUITS

Once the current has been received from the supplying mains in any location, regardless of how it reaches the building (by two-, three-, or four-wire systems), it is distributed in two-wire systems, similar to the one diagrammed in Figure 13–8. And the various elements that work

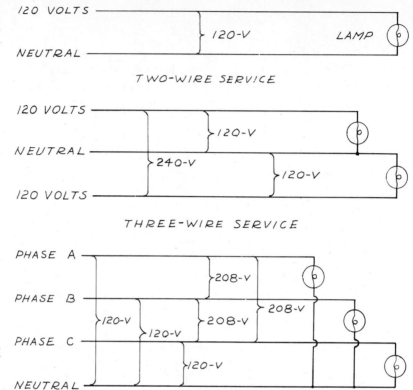

FIGURE 13-8. THE THREE KINDS OF ELECTRICAL DISTRIBUTION SERVICE.

in these circuits—lamps, switches, dimmers, fuses, and the like—may be connected in either of two ways.

One of these is the series circuit in which the flow of current passes through the various elements successively. In the top diagram of Figure 13–9 it will be seen that the current must pass through each of the four lamps, one after the other, before returning by the neutral wire. But in the center diagram the same four lamps are connected "in parallel," and it is apparent that a portion of the total current can flow simultaneously through each lamp.

Almost all practical lighting circuits are a combination of these two. The bottom diagram of Figure 13–9 shows a typical example. The switch and fuse are in series, and they are also in series with each of the lamps. But the four lamps are in parallel with one another. Let the switch be opened or the fuse blown and all the lamps will be extinguished. But one of the lamps may be removed and the remaining three will not be affected. In other words, the series portion is used to control the circuit as a whole, while the parallel portion is valuable as a distributor of the current.

In stage lighting we find that switches, fuses, and dimmers are put in series with the stage lights for the sake of control. The switch

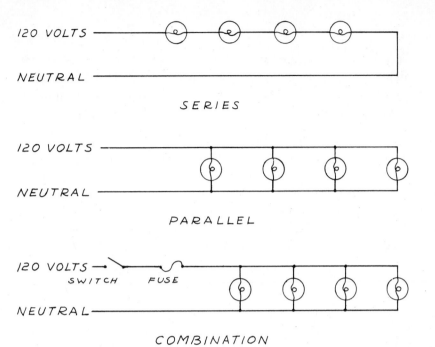

FIGURE 13–9. TYPES OF ELECTRIC CIRCUITS.

controls the lights by turning them off and on; the dimmer controls them by making them more or less bright; while the fuse, which does not actually control the lights themselves, does protect them as well as the switch, the dimmer, and the wiring against a short circuit or an overload that would result in a current flow too great for one or more of these elements.

But the lights themselves are always in parallel, as several spot-lights ganged on one dimmer, or the lamps in one color circuit of a striplight. In each case these are simultaneously under the control of the switch, the dimmer, and the fuse, but each is independent of the others. If they were connected in series, none could burn at full bright-ness, as will be demonstrated presently. One or more lamps in a paral-lel circuit may be removed, or, providing no overload is involved, one or more may be added in parallel, without affecting those already in the circuit.

THE MATHEMATICS OF SERIES CIRCUITS

Because the current flow must pass through all the resistances successively, the total resistance must equal the sum of the individual resistances:

$$R_T = R_1 + R_2 + R_3 + R_4$$

The current flow must be the same throughout the circuit (just as one car in a train must move at the same speed as any other car), and so:

$$I_T = I_1 = I_2 = I_3 = I_4$$

A portion of the emf will be consumed in forcing the current through the successive resistances (this is known as the "voltage drop across a resistance") and the entire emf will have been used up after the final resistance:

$$E_T = E_1 + E_2 + E_3 + E_4$$

It must be kept in mind that the current will distribute itself instantly in the proper proportions throughout the entire system, so it does not matter which element comes first in the circuit; a stable condition will be reached at once.

Let us assume that the four lamps shown in series in Figure 13–9 have resistances of 10, 20, 30, and 40 ohms respectively. Then:

$$R_T = 10 + 20 + 30 + 40 = 100 \text{ ohms}$$

The electric service furnishes 120 volts, so:

$$I_T = \frac{E_T}{R_T} \quad \frac{120}{100} = 1.2 \text{ amperes}$$

Thus 1.2 amperes in the current through each lamp and likewise the current through the entire circuit.

The voltage drop through each lamp can be calculated:

$$
\begin{aligned}
I \times R_1 = 1.2 \times 10 = E_1 = &\ 12 \text{ volts} \\
I \times R_2 = 1.2 \times 20 = E_2 = &\ 24 \quad '' \\
I \times R_3 = 1.2 \times 30 = E_3 = &\ 36 \quad '' \\
I \times R_4 = 1.2 \times 40 = E_4 = &\ \underline{48 \quad ''} \\
\text{Total voltage drop}\ &120 \text{ volts}
\end{aligned}
$$

But let us suppose that we have only three lamps in series and their resistances are 10, 20, and 30 ohms. Now:

$$
\begin{aligned}
R_T &= 10 + 20 + 30 = 60 \text{ ohms} \\
I_T &= \frac{120}{60} = 2 \text{ amperes} \\
E_1 &= 2 \times 10 = \ 20 \text{ volts} \\
E_2 &= 2 \times 20 = \ 40 \quad '' \\
E_3 &= 2 \times 30 = \ \underline{60 \quad ''} \\
\text{Total voltage drop}\ &120 \text{ volts}
\end{aligned}
$$

Note that the resistances offered by the lamps do not change, as these are factors of the dimensions of the filaments. But with less total resistance the current is higher and the voltage consumed by each lamp is greater.

As a practical matter, there is so little voltage consumed by each lamp in the first example that only the 30-ohm and 40-ohm lamps will be seen to be burning at all, and then very dimly. In the second example, the 20-ohm and 30-ohm lamps will give off but weak glows.

In this type of circuit, the current will flow through all the resistances simultaneously, pushed by the full 120 volts in each case. The total resistance will be less than any of the individual resistances, and the total current flow will be the sum of all the individual current flows.

A helpful analogy might be two parallel streets through a city, one wide (offering little resistance) and one narrow (offering considerable resistance). More cars will be able to pass through the broad street than through the narrow one, but the total resistance will be less than through either street alone, and the total number of cars will be greater than through either street.

The following formulas apply to parallel circuits:

$$\frac{1}{R_T} = \frac{1}{R_1} + \frac{1}{R_2} + \frac{1}{R_3} + \frac{1}{R_4}$$
$$I_T = I_1 + I_2 + I_3 + I_4$$
$$E_T = E_1 = E_2 = E_3 = E_4$$

Using the same 10-, 20-, 30-, and 40-ohm lamps as before, we find:

$$\frac{1}{R_T} = \frac{1}{10} + \frac{1}{20} + \frac{1}{30} + \frac{1}{40} = \frac{5}{24}$$
$$5R_T = 24 \qquad R_T = 4.8 \text{ ohms}$$
$$I_T = 12 + 6 + 4 + 3 = 25 \text{ amperes}$$
$$E_T = 120 = 120 = 120 = 120 = 120 \text{ volts}$$

Again let us remove the lamp with the 40 ohms resistance, and we will have:

$$\frac{1}{R_T} = \frac{1}{10} + \frac{1}{20} + \frac{1}{30} = \frac{11}{60}$$
$$11R_T = 60 \qquad R_T = 5.45+ \text{ ohms}$$

This is greater than in the previous example, because we have removed one of the paths through which the current formerly flowed.

$$I_T = 12 + 6 + 4 = 22 \text{ amperes}$$

This is a smaller flow than in the previous example for the same reason.

$$E_T \text{ remains 120 volts.}$$

An additional calculation of the utmost importance in parallel circuitry is to ascertain quickly the ampere flow in a circuit. This is usually necessary when several stage instruments are ganged together, or several striplights are fed through each other.

Suppose we have four spotlights ganged on one circuit, each one burning a 500-watt lamp. We may invert the $P = IE$ formula to read $I = \frac{P}{E}$. Then:

$$I = \frac{4 \times 500}{120} = 16.67 \text{ amperes}$$

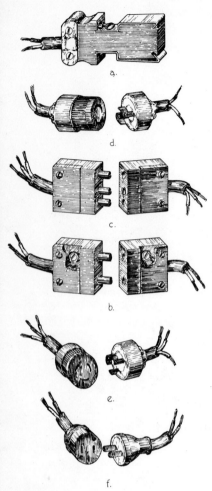

FIGURE 13–10. CONNECTORS. *(a)* Full stage plug. *(b)* Male and female pin-connectors. *(c)* Male and female three-wire pin-connectors. The extra wire is to provide a ground for the instrument should a short-circuit develop. *(d)* Female and male twist-lock connectors. *(e)* Female and male three-wire twist-lock connectors. *(f)* Female and male heavy duty parallel-blade plugs.

If our circuit is fused at 20 amperes we are safe. But if we wish to change the lamps to the more powerful 750-watt variety, then:

$$I = \frac{4 \times 750}{120} = 25 \text{ amperes}$$

This is too much for our 20-ampere fuses, so we must go back to the 500-watt lamps or put one or two of the spotlights on a different circuit.

CIRCUIT ACCESSORIES

CONNECTORS

Because lights on the stage are temporary, being moved after each production, and often between scenes of a play, it is not wise to make permanent connections of the cables to the various lighting instruments. Devices that can be easily connected and disconnected are needed. Ordinary household plugs, with parallel blades, are used on some small stages, but because they are easily disconnected in error, are usually very fragile, and have limited capacities, they are not advisable. A departure from this style that is coming into popular use is the twist lock, roughly similar in appearance to a heavy-duty parallel blade plug, but with a design that permits the male and female caps to be locked together quite easily, yet firmly (See Figure 13–10).

Probably used as much as any other devices are the pin connectors, heavy-duty fiber blocks with sturdy brass pins and sockets. They have the disadvantage of not always giving a firm electrical connection, and they can be easily pulled apart by mistake unless the two cables are tied together. As in the case with cables, all such connectors come in different sizes, each rated to carry specific maximum amperages. For the smaller stage it is wise to settle on a single-size connector, as well as a single type, to save confusion and wasted time —the 15-ampere pin connector or the 20-ampere twist lock being the usual choice.

The connectors described above can all be used to join an instrument to a cable, or two cables to each other, or a cable to a switchboard or cross-connect panel. There is also a device known as a stage plug which is used solely to connect a cable to a switchboard or a plugging box designed to accept it. The stage plug is a block of hard wood with a strip of brass down each of its edges that fits into a porcelain receptacle of rectangular shape. The standard plug is about 1 inch thick and is rated to carry 50 amperes. A half-plug is also made, about ½ inch thick and rated for 25 amperes. A pair of these will fit into the standard porcelain receptacle, thus forming an easy way to gang two instruments on the same switch or dimmer. In some localities, however, the half-plugs are not permitted.

SWITCHES

A switch is a device, put into a circuit, to interrupt and to restore the flow of current as desired, or, as it is usually stated, to open and close the circuit. There are many types of mechanical switches, from the familiar domestic wall type to great knife-blade arrangements that handle many hundreds of amperes. Like everything else electrical, the type and size to use depends on the duty it is expected to perform and the load it is intended to carry. A contactor is an electrically operated device whereby a small switch, located at some convenient place on-stage, controls a magnet which operates a large-capacity switch in a remote spot. This has the double advantage of keeping the dangerously high current at a distance from the operator and allowing the heavy-duty portion, which is very noisy, to be placed where it cannot distract the audience.

FUSES

No chain is stronger than its weakest link, and should an electric circuit suffer damage that permits a short circuit somewhere along the line, the ampere flow will increase to a point where *something* must burn out. The same thing will happen in the case of an overload—that is, if too many lamps are connected to the circuit. By using the "pie" formula we see that if six 500-watt lamps are connected to a 120-volt circuit, 25 amperes will flow through it. So if no. 14-gage wire, which has a capacity for only 15 amperes, is used, its limit will be greatly exceeded, and again something must burn out.

To protect against such occurrences, fuses of suitable capacities are inserted to form the weakest link in the electrical chain. Then, should the current flow grow dangerous, it will be the fuse that gives way, thus breaking the circuit and preventing more serious damage. The trouble is then located and corrected, and a new fuse is inserted with a minimum of trouble.

Figure 13–11 shows various forms of fuses in common use at the voltages usually encountered in stage-lighting circuitry. Everyone is familiar with the plug fuse which screws into a socket like a lamp. There is a special and very useful variation of the plug fuse known as nontamperable or "Type S", which has one thickness of threading for ratings up to 15 amperes and a different threading for those rated 16 to 30 amperes. The socket is designed to take either one threading or the other but not both. When wiring up a switchboard, for example, the electrician will install a socket that takes only the proper-

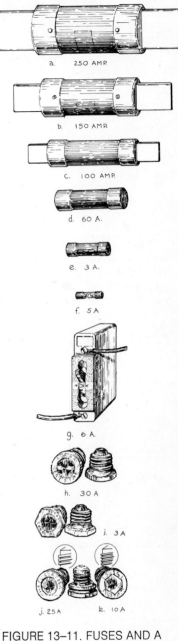

FIGURE 13–11. FUSES AND A CIRCUIT BREAKER. *a, b,* and *c* are knife-blade cartridge fuses, capacities as indicated. *d, e,* and *f* are ferrule-tipped cartridge fuses. *g* is a typical circuit breaker. *h* and *i* are standard plug fuses. *j* and *k* are type-*S* plug fuses (note the difference in the threads as shown in the inserts).

capacity fuse, depending on the other elements in that circuit. Thus no one can change to a higher-capacity fuse, and the circuit is always protected.

Both the standard plug fuse and the type S have an easy identification for capacities up to 15 amperes: either the head is hexagonal instead of round, or the window in the head is hexagonal.

A different shaped fuse is the cartridge, which is available in contact types, sizes, and ratings as listed below.

Contacts	Lengths	Capacities
Ferrule	2 inches	up to 30 amperes
	3 inches	31 to 60 amperes
Knifeblade	5⅞ inches	61 to 100 amperes
	7⅛ inches	101 to 200 amperes
	8⅝ inches	201 to 400 amperes
	10⅜ inches	401 to 600 amperes

FIGURE 13–12. SCHEMATIC DRAWINGS OF THREE TYPES OF CIRCUIT BREAKERS.

THERMAL

THERMAL — MAGNETIC

FULLY MAGNETIC

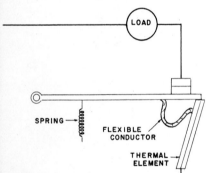
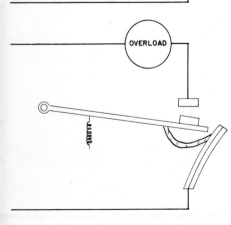
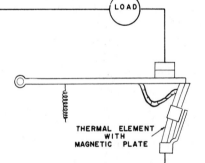
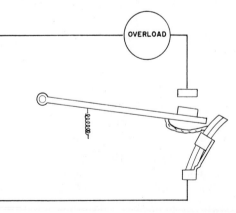
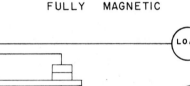
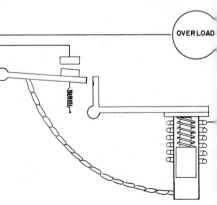

If fuses continue to blow whenever replaced, it is a sign that there is either an overload or a short circuit, and immediate steps should be taken to eliminate the hazard. Overfusing, or bypassing a fuse, is a dangerous and foolish practice.

CIRCUIT BREAKERS

Today, in many installations, the fuse is being replaced by the circuit breaker. This, briefly, is a form of switch that is automatically opened when the current flow becomes higher than it should. For most installations the circuit breaker is a great convenience: it saves the trouble of keeping a supply of fuses on hand, it cannot be carelessly replaced by one of the wrong capacity, and, if of the magnetic variety, it can also serve as a switch for the circuit.

Figure 13–12 shows schematics of three types of circuit breaker. The first two depend on the overcurrent heating a strip of two metals with different coefficients of expansion under heat. The metal that expands the most forces them both to bend and thus releases the spring-loaded arm and so break the circuit. The third one uses a solenoid, or electric magnet, which will pull the catch down, releasing the arm. All three may be reset by means of an exterior switch lever which is not shown.

Color in
14 Light

The relationship of color in light to all the uses of color in the theatre is discussed and illustrated in Chapter 8, *Color in the Theatre*. The beginning of color in the refraction of light, the chemistry of color in paint, and a system of color notation bringing the two media together are exemplified there in detail, as well as an over-all philosophy regarding the use of color in all the areas of design, costume, scenery, and lighting.

At this point, however, it is necessary to be more specific. Color in light, like color in paint, has to be studied in greater detail in order to fully understand the differences and similarities of the two media. In both cases, the reader is referred to Chapter 8 for illustrations in color as further examples of the importance of color in the theatre.

THE ELECTROMAGNETIC SPECTRUM

Light is caused by certain waves of radiant energy. The electromagnetic spectrum (see Figure 14–1) contains waves as long as 3100 miles, those of electric current produced by standard sixty-cycle generators. It contains waves as short as one ten-thousandth of an angstrom unit (and 254,000,000 angstrom units make up only one inch!). These very short waves are cosmic rays which come to the earth from outer space. The waves which produce to our eyes the sensation we recognize as light range from 3800 to 7600 angstroms. Radiant energy in waves between these two limits make up the visible spectrum.

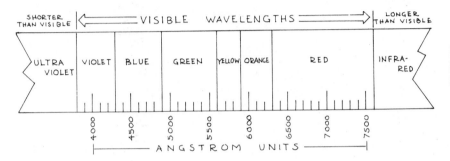

FIGURE 14–1. THE ELECTROMAGNETIC SPECTRUM.

The shortest of such waves, 3800 to 4300 angstroms, produce what we call violet light. Next longer waves make blue light, followed by green, yellow, orange, and finally (between 6300 and 7600 angstroms) red light. All these together make white light.

Waves somewhat shorter than 3800 angstroms are called ultra-violet (*ultra* being Latin for "beyond"). Their effects are not visible to the human eye, but they have many uses, such as killing germs and creating photochemical, photoelectric, and fluorescent effects. Also they give to some a beautiful summer tan and, to the less fortunate, painful sunburn. The waves longer than 7600 angstroms, also invisible, and called infrared (or "below red"), are useful for heat therapy and commercial drying processes.

It is recommended that the designer read carefully the material on color in pigment, found in **Chapter 9,** before proceeding with this discussion of color in light.

PRIMARY COLORS IN LIGHT

As stated, all the waves in the visible spectrum together form white light. But it is not necessary to use every single wave length for this result. White light can be produced quite effectively by mixing, in the proper proportions, red, blue, and green light. Red, blue, and green are, therefore, considered the primary colors in light, for no mixtures of other colors will produce these at full purity, but these three together, in varying proportions, can produce any color that can be conceived. This differs from the pigment colors in which red, blue, and yellow are the primaries, and it is sometimes difficult for painters

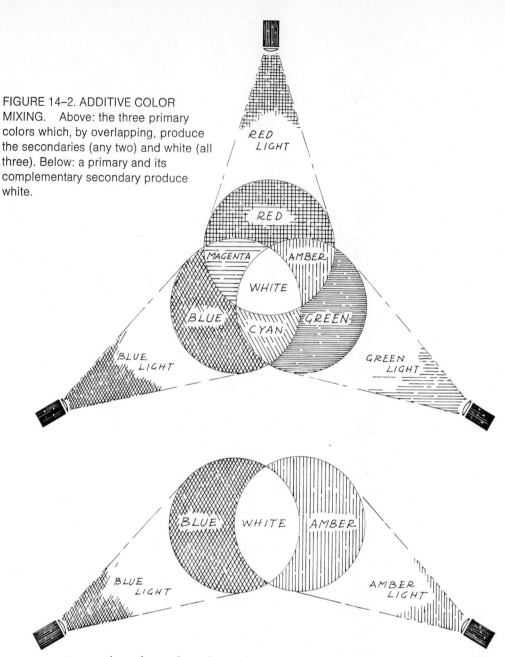

FIGURE 14–2. ADDITIVE COLOR MIXING. Above: the three primary colors which, by overlapping, produce the secondaries (any two) and white (all three). Below: a primary and its complementary secondary produce white.

to convince themselves that in light green takes the place of the familiar yellow as a primary.

COLOR MIXING

Now if we mix red and blue light together, we get a color that we call magenta; if green and blue are mixed the result is a blue-green that is referred to as cyan-blue or cyan; while red and green mixed will form a yellow light that is usually called amber. These are the secondary colors in light, and just as red, blue, and green can be mixed to form white light, so can magenta, amber, and cyan produce white (Figure 14–2). This should be obvious, for the secondaries are nothing but combinations of the primaries. In fact, by mixing the secondaries in varying proportions, we can achieve almost any color of the spectrum except those very close to the purest primaries themselves.

Likewise if we mix any secondary with the primary that has not gone into its making—say amber and blue—we again get white, for the amber already contains the red and green waves.

When we have used the word "mix" above, we have been employing it in the sense that the various beams of colored light were being focused, one on the other, against a common neutral surface and the resulting effect is what we see on this surface. This is additive mixing and is one of the two ways of producing and changing color in light and light effects.

COLOR FILTERING

There is a second way of altering the color of light, sometimes known as subtractive mixing, but more accurately called color filtering. It is best explained by examples. Suppose we have a beam of white light falling on a neutral surface. That surface will reflect to us white. Now, if we place a sheet of pure red glass or red gelatin in the path of this beam, the red sheet will absorb all the blue and green waves of the white light and allow only the red waves to pass through to the neutral surface which will now appear red. Or, if we put a sheet of pure blue in the beam, the red and green waves will be removed, the blue waves will pass through, and the neutral surface will appear blue.

But if we put both the red and the blue sheets before the beam, no light whatever will come through, for the red sheet will filter out the blue waves, the blue sheet will absorb the red waves, and both will remove the green waves—leaving nothing to strike the neutral surface! (Figure 14–3).

FIGURE 14–3. COLOR FILTERING. Above: white light, when filtered through two secondaries, produces a tint of their common primary. Below: light, when filtered by two primaries, is completely absorbed so that no light whatever emerges.

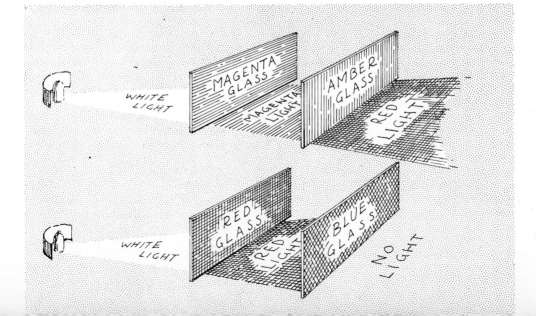

416   If we put a piece of magenta glass and a piece of amber glass in the same beam, the magenta will filter out the green in the amber while the amber will stop the blue in the magenta. Result: red, which is common to each. Notice that this red is produced by the negative approach of filtering out the other colors, not the positive approach of adding or mixing colors to achieve it, so our statement that a primary cannot be produced by mixing other colors still holds.

USES OF MIXING AND FILTERING

Both color mixing and color filtering are extremely important in stage lighting. Our lighting instruments give out beams of approximately white light and the only practical way to color these beams is to intercept them with a sheet of colored transparent material: color filtering. Then when we have produced our colors—say red and green—in this way, we may direct the two beams on a single surface producing an amber effect.

Usually mixing and filtering are used for more subtle effects than adding two primaries to produce a secondary. For example, let us see what we can accomplish by the use of a green-blue color filter and a lavender one. We might use these colors from opposite sides of the stage to give the effect of a cold wintry moonlight from one side and the glow of a small bed of coals from the other. The over-all effect will be quite chilly, despite the slight warmth of the lavender. Where the two mix in equal proportions on a surface, the net result will be a somewhat palid, cold blue.

Now let us try the same colors in a filtering process. Suppose we want a blue that has just the faintest tinge of green in it. Our green-blue filter is too much on the green side for our requirements, but by putting the lavender in the same color frame, we find that a great percentage of the green is killed, but just enough comes through to give us the exact tint we were looking for.

Although an understanding of the filtering and mixing processes is most easily achieved through the study of the primary and secondary colors, it must be clearly understood that the same principles apply to all colors, tints, and shades. But, because most of these are rather complex mixtures, the exact results of their mixing or filtering usually cannot be predicted with precision.

However, it is most necessary to consider these other less strong colors, for they are of vast importance on the stage. Were we to attempt to light our acting areas with strong colors, except possibly for brief and unreal effects, the actors would appear far too distorted and unnatural for an audience to accept. And if we bathe our stage scenery with too rich a tone, the eyes of the spectators will soon tire of it. Far more often only tints and hints of color are used, or two or more of the stronger shades may be used to blend with each other and thus approach a more tolerable white light. The human eye tends to neutralize all colors it sees, so a startlingly vivid effect at the opening of the curtain will soon lose its impression on the spectator, but meanwhile his eyes are being strained and his nerves exhausted.

As has been mentioned earlier, modern productions frequently call for violent effects, unnatural colors, and the like—often for shock alone. Obviously what has been said in the previous paragraph will not apply in such circumstances.

WARM AND COOL COLORS

In general, most people recognize red as typifying anger and war, amber as warmth and comfort, blue as restraint and coolness, green as restfulness. These and similar identifications should always be foremost in the designer's mind when selecting his stage colors. But for us there is no advantage in going deeply into the psychology of color, about which there are many (and often contradictory) theories.

There is one psychological aspect, however, that cannot well be ignored: the matter of the relative warmth and coolness of colors. Few people would deny that a bright red-orange suggests warmth; most would agree that a brittle blue-white gives an impression of cold. Whether these sensations arise from association with flames and ice respectively we cannot tell with any assurance.

Given samples of twenty different tints and shades, rarely will two people list them in exactly the same order from most warm to most cool. But in general we can say that the reds, oranges, and ambers are considered in the warm group, while the blues, violets, and greens fall within the cool range. Some mixtures of hues from the opposing groups seem on the border line, and the particular effect they give at any moment is in contrast to whatever other color is seen in relation to them.

As a matter of fact, the precise feeling given by most tints is purely a matter of contrast. A pale blue that seems positively icy in contrast to a strong amber will appear quite warm when placed next to a stronger shade of blue. Pink and lavender are frequently used on the stage as free-wheeling tints whose effects we can reverse merely by changing the hues used in association with them.

Many people overlook the most versatile and least expensive color of all—clear light! Opposite a cool color, such as the palest of blues or greens, uncolored light will appear quite warm. But when it is opposite a pink or pale amber, white light will definitely be on the cool side in contrast. Nor is it necessary to use a clear gelatin or plastic medium; it is sufficient just to leave the color frame empty.

COLORED LIGHT AND THE ACTOR

In a later chapter, we will suggest actual colors to be used in different types of productions, but it may be advisable here to give a little thought to the general effects desired in the various portions of the stage picture. For the acting areas, for example, it is well to stay clear of startling and unnatural shades that will adversely affect the faces and costumes of the actors. Unless the production style is abstract or unworldly the light designer should not use colors so saturated as to distort the natural flesh color of the actor's face.

Like their faces, the actors' costumes should not be adversely affected by the stage lighting. This is sometimes more difficult to handle. Often the acting areas are lighted with tints of pinks and ambers, flattering enough to the human face, but deadly to green materials. Because the scene may definitely call for such colors in the light, the light designer should warn the costumer sufficiently ahead of time to prevent later distress and tears.

Beware of Green! It should be noted that green light has limited use on the acting areas of the stage. Green on the human face is extremely unbecoming, muddying the natural healthy colors of cheeks and lips, deadening blonde and reddish hair, and exaggerating to the point of grotesqueness the slightest blemish in the complexion. This is pathetically true of the blue-green light filtered through the gelatin commonly advertised as "moonlight blue." It is difficult to conceive of anything more alien to romance.

This does not mean that green should never be used. It is an extremely useful color, especially for the enrichment of costumes and scenery. But it should be handled with considerable care, unless, of course, a distorted effect is actually desired.

COLORED LIGHT AND THE SCENERY

Just as the actor is entitled to his own face, the scene designer has presumably painted his settings the way he wants them to appear. And it is the utmost impertinence for a lighting designer to attempt to improve on his artistry. Enhance it, yes, but strictly in accordance with the scene designer's wishes. Ideally, of course, the scene designer should light his own settings, and many of the finest do just that. But, if he does not do so, he and the lighting designer should work in the closest collaboration. The result will usually be that nearby scenery, as the walls of an interior setting, will, like the acting areas, receive tints of light only. Strong colors, as we have made clear, will tire the audience and will alter the appearance of the painting. Furthermore, being so close to the acting areas, it is almost impossible to separate light on such scenery from other portions of the stage.

It is on the deep backgrounds that the light designer can cut loose. These are usually skies or distant scenery, and much stronger colors can be used here to depict the different times of day, conditions of the weather, or purely arbitrary effects. Setting up the instruments, selecting his colors, and juggling the intensity of his lights for a rip-roaring sunset should go far to relieve the tensions of the otherwise frustrated light designer.

In connection with backdrops and cycloramas the question frequently arises: is it better to try to select a single color medium that will give the exact hue desired, or is a blending of several colors to achieve the desired tint preferable? Of course, if there is to be a change in color effect during the scene, then more than one color must be provided to enable a smooth blend from one to another. Likewise more delicate and precise shadings can be achieved if several different colors are blended into one. However, on a stage with limited equipment, especially for intensity control, it may be far easier, if not essential, to pick a single tint and let it go at that.

COLOR MEDIA

We have spoken of color media without stating just what these may be. There are three kinds in general use today.

Gelatin. The most common, and certainly the cheapest, gelatin comes in the form of very thin sheets that are relatively inexpensive and in a vast range of colors. It has to be cut with care to prevent tearing, it dries out and becomes brittle with age, and it loses all form when dampened, drooping like a wet dishrag in folds that adhere to each other and can never be separated. Some of its shades, particularly the blues and pinks, fade quite easily and must be replaced in the instruments frequently—sometimes after a single performance, if used with one of the largest instruments burning at high intensity.

Plastic Media. Fairly new media are the plastics, which also come in sheet form, but are sturdier than gelatin. These stand up better under rough usage. They are completely unaffected by water and are therefore essential for outdoor productions or theatres in particularly damp localities, such as near the ocean or a large lake. Plastics come in almost as many shades as gelatin, but are considerably more expensive. Despite some claims to the contrary, their resistance to intense heat and to fading is not much greater than that of gelatin.

A new piece of plastic may, when placed in the heat of a light beam, give off considerable steam for a period. This effect, which appears to be smoke, can be quite distracting, if not alarming, to the audience. It is wise, therefore, to test new plastic well before curtain

420

time and, if it smokes, leave the instrument switched on to dry it out before the show starts. Further, the surface of some makes of plastic has a tendency after exposure to heat to break out in a multitude of striations that have much the same effect as a frost gelatin in diffusing the light beam.

To allow the heat of an instrument to escape when plastic is used as its color medium, it is a good idea to perforate it with numerous small holes. These will not affect the performance of the plastic in any way, except to prolong its life, nor will the holes appear in the beam pattern. An ice pick, nail, or awl may be used for this purpose, but the neatest and easiest method is to run a pounce wheel several times over the full sheet before cutting it to size.

It is possible to paint on plastic, using either transparent or opaque paints. This is a very great convenience when preparing slides for Linnebach projectors or the like. Because plastic has some rigidity, it need not be framed when cut for use in the smaller instruments.

One annoyance for anyone ordering either plastic or gelatin is the matter of identification of colors. The names given certain hues have little accuracy of description. Generally a number code is used, but no two companies use the same system. A collection of sample books, experience, and an accurate memory are all needed by the light designer when he orders color media.

Mylar Media. Deep-dyed clear mylar, another plastic of course, seems to resist the heat and color fading tendency of the tungsten-halogen lamp better than other plastics.

Colored Glass. The most expensive medium of all is glass. While gelatin and plastic may be cut to any size or shape desired, glass must be ordered for exactly the purpose required. It comes in few colors, is heavy and bulky to store, and though it never fades, is rarely affected by heat, and stands up well under ordinary usage, it can be smashed. It has one great advantage in addition to its heat-resisting qualities in that it can have molded into it markings and prismatic lines that

that what?? Diffuse light?

Glass filters, specially prepared for use in striplights, are called roundels and can be obtained with the following features:

Plain For color filtering only.
Stippled For color and also to diffuse the beam.
Spread For color and also to spread the beam laterally, so that the various colors will blend more readily.

Stripped   Very thin glass in narrow strips to color the light
            from extremely hot-beamed instruments.

COMPARISON OF COLOR MEDIA

The choice of colors to use in the lighting of a stage production, as has been mentioned, is based on: colors in the setting and costumes; mood of the scene; style of the production, and the taste, knowledge, and judgment of the lighting designer to fulfill these requirements and still make an interpretive statement of his own. There are many manufacturers of color media from which to choose. It is futile to attempt a published list comparing their colors because of the ever-changing market. Most manufacturers advise a review of their color list every three years because unpopular colors are frequently dropped and new tints added, thereby creating a new list.

The prominent manufacturers can be mentioned and their colors and qualities commented upon, but the designer should compare color lists and note the range and purity of each product before making a color choice.

Roscolyne,   a product of Rosco Laboratories, is a plastic color medium listing 62 tints. It is a little less expensive than *Roscolux* which comes in 102 colors. The latter plastic is *body colored* as opposed to *surface coating* and is the color to withstand fading under the intense heat of the modern quartz light.

Gelatran,   manufactured by Berkey Colortran, is a *deep-dyed* clear mylar capable of resisting high temperatures. Because Berkey Colortran manufactures chiefly for television and photographic studios they pay more attention to the wavelength and color temperature of colors than is normally needed for stage lighting. This, of course does not detract from their use on the stage but might add to the over-all cost. Gelatran lists a selection of 60 colors with wavelength charts.

Cinemoid and Cinbex   are two British imports distributed in the United States by Century Lighting, Inc. Both are heavy plastic designed for greater durability and heat resistance. Cinemoid comes in 48 colors and Cinebex in 46. The number coding sometimes becomes confusing for colors have been added in this country and some of the numbers have been changed.

Brigham   gelatin, also carried by Century Lighting, Inc., is one of the older mediums. It comes in 75 different colors, including Special Chocolate, Chocolate, and Gray.

FIGURE 14–4. COMPARISON OF THREE COLOR MEDIA.

COLOR	ROSCOLUX	BRIGHAM	CINEMOID
			Pale Rose
			Gold Tint
			Pale Gold
RED	Bastard Amber	Light Scarlet	
	Dark Bastard Amber		Pale Salmon
			Light Rose
			Light Salmon
		Special Light Red	
RED	Orange Amber		
	Light Red	Light Red	
		Medium Scarlet	
		Pink Red	
	Fire Red		
		Fire Red	Primary Red
			Ruby
	Medium Red		
	Pure Red	Pure Red	
PINK	No Color Pink	Light Flesh Pink	
	Flesh Pink	Flesh Pink	
	Medium Pink	Medium Pink	
	Medium Pink DuBarry		
		Pink	
	Deep Pink	Rose Pink	
	Rose Pink	Dark Rose Pink	
			Bright Rose
	Deep Pink	Deep Pink	
		DuBarry Pink	
MAGENTA			Middle Rose
		Light Magenta	Dark Pink
	Light Magenta		
	Medium Magenta	Medium Magenta	
			Magenta
			Deep Rose
	Dark Magenta	Dark Magenta	
		Rose	
VIOLET	Dark Lavender	Rose Purple	
	Rose Purple	Dark Rose Purple	Mauve
	Dark Purple		
	Violet	Violet	
			Pale Violet
			Pale Lavender
	Special Lavender	Special Lavender	
	Medium Lavender	Medium Lavender	
		Dark Lavender	
	Light Purple	Light Purple	
	Medium Purple		

VIOLET	Royal Purple	Purple Royal Purple Medium Purple Dark Purple	
			Purple
			Steel Blue
	Daylight Blue	Daylight Blue	
			Pale Blue
		Light Sky Blue	
	Azure Blue		Light Blue
	No Color Blue	Light Blue	
		Light Navy Blue	
	Special Steel Blue		
		Special Steel Blue Light Blue Special	
BLUE			Bright Blue
	Light Blue		
		Medium Sky Blue Medium Blue Special	
			Medium Blue
	Medium Blue Med. Non-Fade Blue Medium Blue	Medium Blue	
			Dark Blue
		Medium Navy Blue Dark Sky Blue	
	Urban Blue Dark Blue Dark Urban Blue Dark Non-Fade Blue	Non-Fade Blue Dark Blue Dark Navy Blue	
BLUE			Deep Blue
		Urban Blue	
	Light Green Blue Sky Blue	Light Green Blue	
		Moonlight Blue Nile Blue	
	Green Blue		
		Light Blue Green Medium Blue Green	
BLUE GREEN			Peacock Blue Blue Green
	Blue Green Medium Blue Green	Blue Green Dark Blue Green	
			Pale Green
	Yellow Green		
			Pea Green Moss Green Light Green
GREEN	Light Green	Light Green Medium Green	
			Dark Green

GREEN	Medium Green		
	Medium Green		Primary Green
		Dark Green	
			Pale Yellow
YELLOW	Medium Lemon	Light Lemon	
		Medium Lemon	Yellow
	Dark Lemon	Dark Lemon	
	No Color Straw	Very Light Straw	
	Light Straw	Light Straw	
	Straw		
			Straw
		Medium Straw	Canary
			Light Amber
	No Color Amber	Dark Straw	
	Pale Amber		
	Light Amber	Light Amber	Medium Amber
	Medium Amber	Medium Amber	
			Deep Salmon
AMBER			Deep Amber
	Golden Amber		
		Amber	Orange
			Golden Amber
	Amber	Dark Amber	Deep Orange
	Dark Amber		
	Orange	Orange	
GRAY	Special Chocolate	Special Chocolate	
	Chocolate	Chocolate	
	Neutral Gray		
		Gray	
			Clear
DIFFUSING			Light Frost Special
	Frost	Frost	Heavy Frost

Light Sources 15

THE INCANDESCENT LAMP

The most common source of light used on the stage today is the incandescent filament lamp, a gas-filled glass bulb containing a tungsten filament which emits light when a current is impressed through it by the prescribed voltage, 120 being the most common in this country. The three important parts (Figure 15–1) of an incandescent lamp are the bulb (the glass envelope that encloses the inert gas), the base (to hold the lamp in position and to make electrical contacts), and the filament (to pass the current, yet offer enough resistance to effect the transfer of electrical energy into light energy).

LAMP FILAMENTS (Figure 15–2)

The filament is the most important part of the incandescent lamp. It is the tungsten wire which emits the light. To keep it compact, it is usually coiled. Its arrangement within the bulb is of great importance. Among the filament forms used in stage-lighting equipment are the barrel (C–5) and the corona (C–7). These are designed to throw out their light equally in all directions. On the other hand, the monoplane (C–13)

425

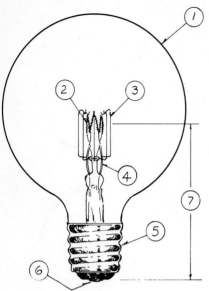

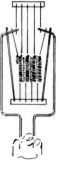

1. *GAS-FILLED G-SHAPED BULB*

2. *BARREL FILAMENT*

3. *FILAMENT SUPPORTS*

4. *LEAD-IN WIRE*

5. *SCREW BASE*

6. *BOTTOM CONTACT BUTTON*

7. *L.C.L. (LIGHT CENTER LENGTH)*

FIGURE 15–1. A TYPICAL INCANDESCENT LAMP.

and the biplane (C–13D) emit most of their light in two opposite directions only, thereby permitting a larger proportion to be picked up and made useful by a reflector or a lens.

The LCL (or light-center length) of a lamp is the distance from the center of the filament to some definite place in the base. With a screw-base lamp, the measurement is to the contact button at the end of the base (Figure 15–1). With a prefocus base it is to the fins, and with the bipost to the shoulder of the pins. It is particularly important to know the LCL when a lamp is to be used in conjunction with a reflector or a lens, for the center of the filament must be exactly aligned with the centers of such optical devices.

One characteristic of the incandescent filament which can be important in stage lighting and is extremely critical in color television is that when a lamp is taken down on dimmer the color of the light emitted becomes quite reddish. This can definitely change the appearance of colored materials, such as costumes and scenery, and even the faces of the actors.

LAMP BULBS

Lamp bulbs vary greatly in three ways: their size, their shape, and the finish or color of their glass. Obviously a small, compact bulb is preferable, but two factors cause the higher-wattage lamps to have bulbs of larger sizes: the dimensions of the larger filaments demand a more roomy envelope and a larger surface is necessary to dissipate the greater heat emitted by them. Bulb sizes are expressed in numbers representing eighths of an inch: thus a bulb of five-inch diameter would be called a 40.

FIGURE 15–2. FILAMENTS FREQUENTLY USED IN STAGE LIGHTING INSTRUMENTS. The upper row shows a side view, the bottom row an end view of each. (a) The barrel. (b) The corona. (c) The monoplane. (d) The biplane.

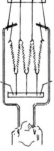

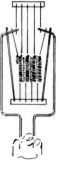

a

b

c

d

The shape of the bulb is designated by a letter. The A (for arbitrary) and PS (for pear-shape with straight sides) are common forms seen in the general line of household lamps (Figure 15-3). Many lamps used in stage-lighting instruments are globe-shaped (G) to permit the even dissipation of heat, or tubular (T) to allow the filament to be brought closer to some optical feature. There are a number of other shapes, some of which are purely decorative. The line of reflector lamps will be discussed separately.

Bulb Finishes and Color.   Usually lamps used on the stage are made of clear glass, which is essential for any source used in an instrument with reflector or lens. But the smaller wattage A and PS lamps are more readily obtained with an inner frost finish that is intended to diffuse the light. If desired, these sizes can also be ordered in the clear-glass style, but this is seldom necessary as they are rarely used in stage lighting instruments of any precision. There are many kinds of finishes available, some purely decorative and others for some special application. The side-silvered showcase lamp that can be tucked away behind very little cover is often handy on the stage for throwing a little light in difficult corners.

Colored-glass lamps are obtainable in the smaller wattages only and are not very useful on the stage except in the smallest installations. There is one exception: the pale-blue "daylight" lamps which give off a color not much different from that seen outdoors on a slightly overcast day, or the light that comes through a north window. These can be used effectively to illuminate small backings or, in combination with other tones, larger areas, or to imitate general daylight (not sunbeams) pushing through a window. Daylight lamps are in sizes to 1500 watts.

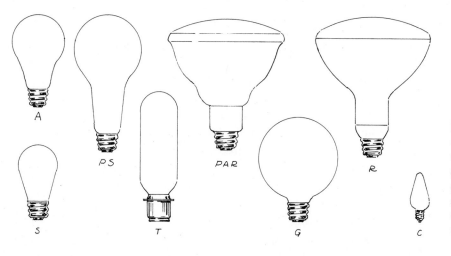

FIGURE 15-3. TYPICAL BULB SHAPES. *(A)* Arbitrary designation. *(S)* Straight side *(PS)* Pear shape, straight neck. *(T)* Tubular. *(PAR)* Parabolic aluminized reflector. *(G)* Globular. *(R)* Reflector. *(C)* Cone shape.

SCREW

PREFOCUS

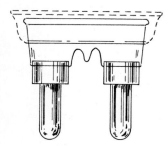

BIPOST

BAYONET

FIGURE 15–4. COMMON BASE SHAPES.

LAMP BASES

The base of a lamp is generally made of copper, though aluminum is now being used for many of the smaller wattages. The base may be any of several sizes, but the medium size (as the common household lamps) with a 1-inch diameter and the mogul with a 1½-inch diameter are the ones most commonly used in the theatre. While compactness is obviously desired, these sizes are required for two reasons: the larger bulbs need the stability of the greater physical support, and the heavier currents demand larger electrical contacts.

The bases may also vary in type, with the common screw base (which comes in all sizes) being the simplest (Figure 15–4). Frequently this type is sufficient, but in certain cases it is necessary to provide some sort of locking device in the base so that the lamp and particularly its filament may be held in a precise relationship with some optical feature of the instrument in which it is designed to burn. Two such devices are used in the medium and mogul sizes. There is the bipost base which consists of two pins that push down into carefully aligned holes in the socket, and the prefocus base with side fins of different sizes that lock into the socket by a quarter turn. In the smaller sizes the bayonet, a variation of the prefocus base, is used. There are also a number of other forms, such as the screw base with a spring button at the end, the end prong, side prong, bipin, disk, and others too numerous to mention. In most cases these demand a special socket or contact; usually their mode of operation is apparent on inspection.

THE R AND PAR LAMPS

A feature in lamp design that is constantly gaining in importance is the "instrument-contained-in-the-lamp," marketed under the two lines of R (reflector) and PAR (parabolic aluminized reflector) lamps. Because all the light emitted by the filament is reflected out of these lamps in a useful direction and because this reflector is sealed into the bulb itself, these lamps are extremely efficient.

PAR lamps are made of molded, heat-resistant glass and can be used outdoors without danger of their cracking if snow or rain strike them while they are hot. They are a good deal heavier and sturdier than the R's, which are of blown glass, light in weight, and fragile. Most R lamps should not be used outdoors without some sort of hood to protect them from the elements. In deciding which of the two to buy, there are considerations other than suitability for outdoor use. A PAR may cost almost twice as much as an R of the same wattage, but it gives out a much more powerful beam, which makes it worth the extra expense in many applications.

LIGHT DISTRIBUTION FROM R AND PAR LAMPS

In the 75-watt and 150-watt lamps of both series, and the 300-watt and 500-watt R lamps, two types of lights are available for each—spots and floods. In general the R flood gives the smoothest pattern of light, followed by the R spot and PAR flood, while the PAR spot throws a very irregular beam pattern, which may not be important when several beams overlap, as those from a striplight. The 300-watt and 500-watt PAR's come in three styles, the wide flood, the medium flood, and the narrow spot. While the other PAR's and R's have conventional screw-type bases, the 200-watt, 300-watt, and 500-watt PAR's have either the side- or end-prong base and are held firmly in place in instruments fitted with clamps which grasp the edge of the heavy glass bulb. All R and PAR lamps have diffusing marks of one sort or another on their faces, which should not be confused with true lenses.

Because of the great breadth of beam typical of these lamps, they can be very useful in striplights, where it is necessary to blend the light from different-color circuits smoothly and at short range. Since the reflectors are sealed into the bulbs, there is no worry over dirt or corrosion affecting their surfaces. Further, providing the same type and size of base is involved, it is a simple matter to change from type to type, depending on the precise effect desired, such as using PAR spots for a long, very intense throw and R floods for a short throw where smoothness is more important than brightness. Single lamps may also be useful as small floodlights.

Attempts have been made to use PAR and R spots as substitutes for conventional spotlights. For a small stage and a short throw they have enough punch, but it is impossible to control the very same side spill that makes them useful in striplights or as floods. A variety of hoods are advertised as answers to this problem, but the fact remains that there will be no real control over the unruly beam unless the lamp is placed in a hood at least 2 feet long, a very inefficient expedient as so little of the illumination will then be used. However, the smaller hoods can be handy for mounting the lamps, focusing them, and holding color media in place.

COLOR IN THE R AND PAR LAMPS

Both R and PAR lamps have recently added a line of colored bulbs. So far these are offered only in the 100-watt size for the PAR's and the 150-watt size for the R's. They seem to have distributional characteristics midway between their respective spot and flood models. Red, yellow, blue, green, pink, and blue-white are available, but it must be noted that even the full colors do not have the purity that is obtained from gelatin. These colored lamps are particularly effective in striplights and other blending arrangements, and the blue-whites have the same uses as the daylight-blue lamps described earlier.

It seems that future developments in these two lines of lamps may offer greater possibilities for the stage. At the present time, however, the R's and PAR's have limited uses in good dramatic lighting though they can be extremely valuable on the low-budget stage if used with an appreciation of their limitations.

LAMP LIFE

The "rated-average life" of any type of lamp may be found listed in the catalogs. For the common household varieties, this is usually 750 burning hours, but for many stage-lighting lamps it is only 200 hours. This expected life is determined by many factors. It would be possible to build a lamp that never burns out, but such a lamp would give very little light for the current consumed. On the other hand, photoflash lamps are simply those in which the sudden burst of intensity is more important than continued life.

A few of the G lamps come in two styles, designated, quite inaccurately, "spot" and "flood." The difference is that the spot has a life of 200 hours but gives out much more light than the flood which is expected to burn for 800 hours. Their uses are identical, and which one to select depends on the comparative importance to the buyer of life versus output.

"Rated-average life" is determined by the manufacturer, who takes a number of lamps at random and leaves them burning under normal conditions until either (1) they burn out completely or (2) their light output drops to 80 percent of what they were originally. Among the great number of specimens tested at one time, a few will burn out or lose output quite rapidly; more will last longer, and some will continue to be good long after the others have failed. But the majority will last for approximately the same number of hours and this is known as the rated-average life for this particular type and wattage of lamp.

Rated-average life is presumed to apply under usual operating conditions. But a lamp's life may be shortened in a number of ways. It will give out more quickly if burned while enclosed in an excessively hot place such as one from which its own heat cannot escape. Rough handling may break some interior part, even though the outer appearance is not changed. If connected to a higher voltage than it was designed for, a lamp will burn out rapidly, even abruptly. And in the case of many lamps used in stage instruments, burning in the wrong position results in rapid failure. The correct burning position, if important, will always be marked on the end of the bulb and should be consulted if any doubt exists.

T lamps are particularly susceptible to failure due to being burned in the wrong position. A T lamp designed to be used in an ellipsoidal spotlight should be burned base up, or nearly so, for the filament is close to the end of the bulb which would be melted by the heat if it accumulated there. On the other hand, a T lamp intended to be used in a Fresnel spotlight should be burned base down or no more than 90 degrees from the perpendicular, for the filament is close to the base and if the heat should concentrate there it would crack the cement seal between bulb and base.

Such lamps have been designed to be used in specific instruments and their burning position is that which they would occupy when the instrument is used in a normal manner. In each case there is ample space for the heat to dissipate above the filament (Figure 15–5).

If a lamp that has been designed to be used on 120-volt service is fed with only 110 volts, the lamp will last almost four times as long as it would on 120 volts, but there will be only about 74 percent as much light and the cost will be 17 percent higher.

On the other hand, if this same lamp is fed 130 volts, there will be 31 percent more light at a cost of only 86 percent, but the lamp will last only a third as long as it should.

This relationship of voltage, light, cost, and life must be kept in mind, especially when bargains in "lamps that will burn twice as long" or the like are offered. It also explains why stage lamps often last a far longer period than anticipated: they have been burned at low dimmer readings!

TUNGSTEN-HALOGEN LAMPS

Invented during the 1950s and known during its early years as quartz-iodine, the tungsten-halogen lamp has recently sprung into prominence in all branches of illumination including stage lighting.

The light from this lamp originates in an incandescent filament, hence the word "tungsten" is its approved name. It was pointed out earlier in this chapter that as an ordinary filament lamp becomes older, it loses some of its light output. This is partly because the tungsten evaporates from the hot filament and deposits itself on the glass bulb, thereby darkening it. Naturally as the filament continues to lose tungsten, a point will be reached when not enough remains to carry the current and the lamp burns out. For many lamps used in stage lighting the rated-average life is as low as 200 hours!

In the tugsten-halogen lamp, known as a T-H lamp, a halogen gas, usually iodine, but possibly one of the other elements of this group, is introduced into the bulb. As a particle of tungsten evaporates from the filament and moves toward the glass, it makes contact with the halogen and combines with it. The new compound is attracted back to the

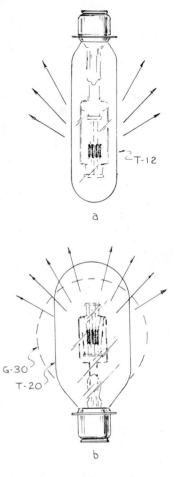

FIGURE 15–5. DISSIPATION OF HEAT FROM INCANDESCENT LAMPS. *(a)* A lamp designed to be burned base up. *(b)* Lamps designed to be burned base down.

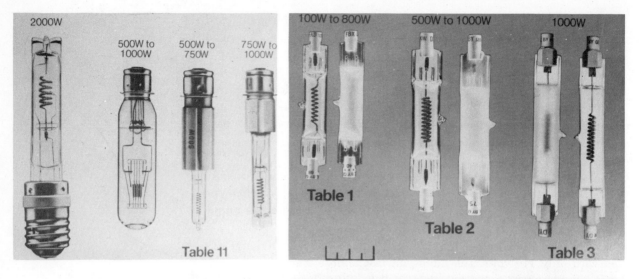

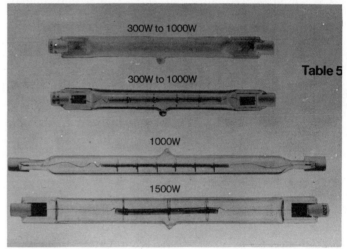

FIGURE 15–6. TUNGSTEN-HALOGEN LAMPS.   A few of the many types. *(a)* General Electric's "Quartzline." Single-ended lamps, compact filaments, screw and prefocus bases. *(b)* Double-ended, compact filament quartzline lamps. *(c)* Double-ended, linear-filament quartzline lamps.

filament, where the tungsten is redeposited while the halogen floats free to continue its good work. Because the combining of the two elements will take place only in very high heat, the bulb must be very small and for this reason is usually made of heat-resistant quartz glass. Hence the old name, quartz-iodine, which was frequently accurate, but not always. The newer name, tungsten-halogen, has the advantage of making it clear that a tungsten filament and one of the several halogen gases are involved.

With the filament constantly replenished, it lasts a great deal longer and continues to emit light of the same color regardless of its age. The color of the light from this form of lamp has less red in it, and therefore is closer to white, than that emitted by the older filament lamps. Because there is no blackening of the lamp as it grows older it is hard to predict failure without logging burning time of each instrument to avoid losing a lamp during a production.

The efficiency of the T-H lamp is not quite as high as claimed but it does give about 10 percent more light per watt than the comparable incandescent lamp. The T-H lamp, being smaller, burns *hotter* than a conventional lamp but, of course, the amount of heat per watt is equal if not a little less.

The very small bulb—some bulbs are little longer than a cigarette, and scarcely thicker—and the compact filament make it possible to place the source at the exact focal point of a reflector or a lens. Some manufacturers of stage-lighting equipment have redesigned their instruments to take the tungsten-halogen lamp as it is, a small, thin tube. Others have arranged with the lamp-makers to encapsulate the tungsten-halogens inside the same large bulbs that were formerly used, thereby making it possible to use the same instrument for either old or new types of lamps.

High Intensity—Low Voltage Lamps.   High intensity lamps operating on low voltage such as those designed for the automobile (sealed beam) or aircraft landing lights are adaptable to stage use. Their extreme brightness and controlled distribution make them more useful as a design statement than as illumination (Chapter 18).

The General Electric Quartzline FCS 24-volt lamp is used in the theatre. It is miniature in size, one and one quarter inches high, and about 250 watts. Originally designed for the photographic studio, it makes an excellent source for a Linnebach projector (page 474). All low voltage lamps, of course, require a transformer for operation in the theatre.

PURCHASING LAMPS

When ordering lamps it is advisable to use the manufacturer's code number, found in his catalog, to be certain of receiving the exact type of lamp needed for your equipment. If there is any doubt, list all possible factors in making out your order: base size and shape, bulb size and shape, filament form and LCL, bulb color or finish, and so forth. The importance of being specific can be seen in the fact that the General Electric Large-Lamp Price Bulletin lists no fewer than thirty-seven 100-watt lamps, twenty-six of which have the medium screw base, and nineteen 500-watt lamps.

One fact, in addition to the code number, that must always be specified in ordering lamps is that of the voltage. The term "standard voltage" is sufficient in most circumstances, but if a locale has service above 125 volts or under 115 volts, it must be specified.

Many of the lamps used in stage-lighting instruments are not readily available outside the largest centers, and it therefore becomes

434 necessary to foresee one's probable needs well in advance and to keep on hand an inventory against the future. Lamp manufacturers put up their products in standard packages, such as 120 to the carton for the common 100-watt A lamp, 24 for the 500T12 which is extensively used in ellipsoidal reflector spots, and so forth. It is recommended that orders be placed for these packaged amounts or multiples thereof. The lamps will be better protected in transportation and can be stored quite conveniently in the same cartons.

Your lamp company's catalog is a valuable source of information of all sorts. If your local dealer cannot supply you with one, write to the company's nearest sales office, or to its headquarters. They are usually happy to supply enough copies for an entire class studying lighting.

THE CARBON-ARC LIGHT

One source of light that is not an incandescent lamp yet has a long history in stage use is the carbon arc. In this device a current is passed through two touching carbon pencils which are then drawn slightly apart forcing the electrons to leap (or arc) the gap. This bombardment of electrons burns into the receiving carbon a crater which emits an extremely intense light of slightly bluish tinge. Mounted in a hood, with a condensing lens, devices for shaping the beam, and a method of focusing the beam in different directions, the carbon arc becomes extremely useful as a follow spot for emphasizing portions of the stage or members of the cast. The carbon-arc spotlight will be discussed in detail in Chapter 17.

Short-Arc Lamps. Two tungsten electrodes in a strong glass enclosure of gas under high pressure produce an intense light source when the current arcs between the electrodes. The result is a brilliant, white, point source. Because the arc is shielded from the oxygen in the air the tungsten electrodes do not burn up as do the carbons in the arc light.

Of the two short-arc lamps available the *xenon lamp* is the oldest. The xenon lamp which is filled with high pressure xenon gas burns with a brilliant, cool, white light. Its high efficiency and long life help to compensate for its high cost. Because of its efficiency and long life it is standard installation in motion picture projectors and long-range follow spots. The lamp, however, has to be handled with care and proper safety precautions. The high pressure of the gas in the lamp increases the danger of explosion.

The more recent *HMI lamp* is constructed like the xenon lamp but with the gas under a much lower pressure. It, too, is a good film projector lamp although the light is so cool that it needs a warm filter to correctly project the colors of the film or slide (Figure 15-7).

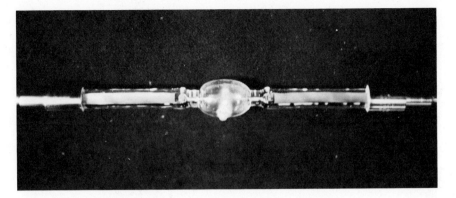

FIGURE 15–7. SHORT-ARC LAMPS.   The HMI lamp, 2500 watts.

GASEOUS DISCHARGE LAMPS

Although the xenon and HMI lamps can also be considered gaseous discharge lamps, the more familiar form is the *fluorescent tube* which never did achieve its promises of becoming a new light source in the theatre. Current passing through a pressurized mercury vapor causes a gaseous discharge, predominantly in the ultraviolet zone, which is absorbed by the phosphorous coating on the inside walls of the tube. The coating reemits the energy, becoming the light source itself.

As the fluorescent tube is a line-of-light and not a point source, its uses in the theatre are limited to producing a wash of light on a cyclorama or back drop. The shape of the lamp makes it difficult to achieve smooth color blending. The fluorescent hoods, however, can be installed with *black light fluorescent tubes* to flood the stage with ultraviolet light for a black light effect.

A *black light effect* is the illuminating of a surface treated with fluorescent paint or dye with ultraviolet light (UV). The fluorescent surface becomes, in effect, the light source as it reemits the energy of the ultraviolet light.

The *mercury vapor lamp* with a UV filter is another effective instrument to produce black light. Both the black light fluorescent tube and the mercury vapor lamp require a ballast and warm-up time and cannot be dimmed.

It should also be mentioned that the arc light follow spot can be equipped with a UV filter and be used for a black light effect.

Reflection, Refraction, and Absorption

When a beam of light passing through air encounters anything in its path, three things can happen. The light may be absorbed (as by a sheet of black material), it may be refracted (as through a lens), or it may be reflected (as by any opaque substance it strikes). Actually, none of these things will happen completely: a mirror or a lens will absorb a small portion of the light, the blackest of materials will still reflect some of it, a piece of colored glass will absorb certain light rays and allow others to pass through. By understanding the laws by which these phenomena operate, we can better understand how stage-lighting instruments work and why light behaves as it does when it strikes the stage and actors.

REFLECTION OF LIGHT

The law of regular reflection explains what happens to a light beam when it strikes a smooth, shiny surface, such as a mirror. It is reflected at an angle equal to the angle at which it struck, but in the opposite direction (Figure 16–1). A moment's contemplation of a mirror will make this clear. Of course, if the beam strikes the surface head on, it will reflect directly back over the same path.

436

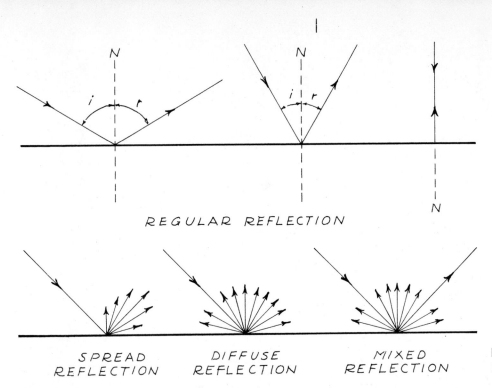

REGULAR REFLECTION

SPREAD REFLECTION   DIFFUSE REFLECTION   MIXED REFLECTION

FIGURE 16–1. TYPES OF REFLECTION.

If the beam strikes not a mirror but a surface with slight irregularities, as etched aluminum or foil paper that has been crumpled and smoothed out again, the same law applies, but due to the fact that there are now innumerable little surfaces, rather than a single, perfectly flat one, the reflected rays will tend to spread out somewhat, but will not diverge too greatly from a basic direction. This is known as spread reflection.

A piece of blotting paper, or soft, cotton cloth, will produce a diffuse reflection, due to the vast number and varied angles of the surface. In this case, there will be no single direction to the reflected light. Rather the whole surface will appear much the same from whatever angle it is viewed.

Last, we have mixed reflection, a combination of regular and diffuse. A piece of crockery with a high glaze will produce this: the rough surface of the ceramic will create diffusion, while the shiny glaze will act like a mirrored surface to give regular reflection. Furthermore, the diffused light will show the color of the material itself, while the regularly reflected light (or high light) will have the color of the source.

THE SPHERICAL REFLECTOR

Now, if polished metal is made into a reflector in the form of a part of a sphere, and a source of light is placed at the center of the curvature of this form, each ray of light that strikes the reflecting surface will do so squarely. Therefore, it will be returned through the source and will augment the light emanating from the source in the opposite direction (Figure 16–2).

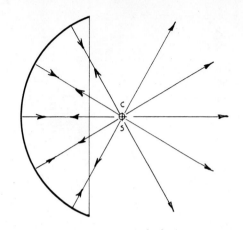

SOURCE (S) AT
THE CENTER (C)

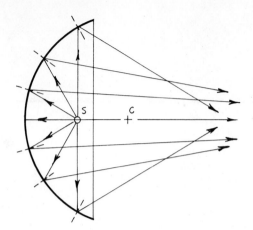

SOURCE INSIDE
THE CENTER

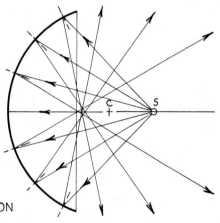

SOURCE OUTSIDE
THE CENTER

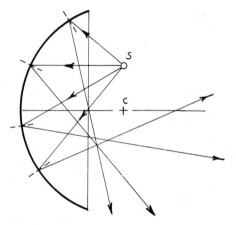

SOURCE AT ONESIDE
OF THE CENTER

FIGURE 16–2. REFLECTION
FROM A SPHERICAL
REFLECTOR UNDER
DIFFERENT CONDITIONS.

Naturally, it would be necessary for the source, say the filament of a lamp, to be located precisely in relation to the reflector, or its rays would not strike the reflector straight on but at various angles and would be reflected equally in various directions in accordance with the law of regular reflection.

THE PARABOLIC REFLECTOR

Some stage-lighting instruments make use of reflectors with shapes other than the spherical. The nature of a parabolic reflector is such that if a light source is placed at its focal center, all rays that strike the reflective surface will emerge parallel one to another (Figure 16–3). This will naturally give a great concentration of light in a tight beam, rather than the spread effusion from a spherical reflector.

THE ELLIPSOIDAL REFLECTOR

A third form of reflector that has great use is the ellipsoidal. By mathematical definition an ellipsoid has two conjugate focal points. When a reflector is constructed in the form of half of an ellipsoid and a source is placed at the focal point at that end, all rays of light that strike the reflector will be diverted through the second focal point (Figure 16–3). The result is that an enormous percentage of the light from the source is directed in a manner that makes it easily usable, as we shall examine in Chapter 17 under the section on spotlights.

REFRACTION OF LIGHT

Refraction is a phenomenon that has been observed by anyone who has ever looked into a pool of water and noticed how a straight stick will seem to bend sharply as it passes beneath the surface. The law of refraction states that when a ray of light passes into a denser medium (as from the air into the water) it is bent toward a perpendicular drawn to the surface at the point of entry, and when it emerges into the less dense medium again, it is bent away from the perpendicular drawn at that point.

THE PLANO-CONVEX LENS

Now if the two surfaces of a sheet of glass are parallel, the path of an emerging ray will be parallel to its entering path, but slightly offset (Figure 16–4). But if the two surfaces are not parallel, then the emerging ray will take a different course depending on the angle at which it strikes each surface. This is the principle of all lenses, of which

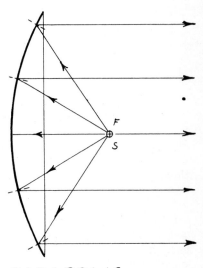

PARABOLIC REFLECTOR

SOURCE (S) AT THE FOCAL POINT (F)

FIGURE 16–3. REFLECTION (above) FROM A PARABOLIC AND (below) FROM AN ELLIPSOIDAL REFLECTOR.

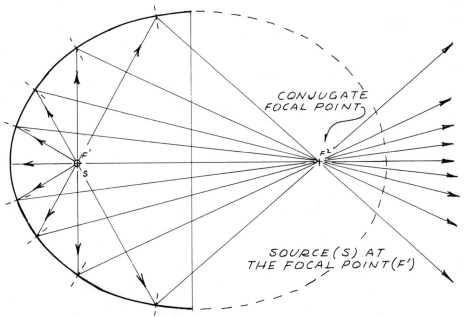

ELLIPSOIDAL REFLECTOR

440   there are many forms, but the plano-convex lens, with one flat side and one curved surface (or modifications of this) is the only one of importance to us. It is the simplest and least expensive lens for concentrating the spreading rays into a compact beam of great brightness.

It has been observed that many students are confused as to the actual paths the rays take relative to the perpendiculars drawn at their points of emergence from a plano-convex lens. This is correctly illustrated in the upper right-hand diagram of Figure 16–4. Should these rays emerge on the other sides of their respective perpendiculars,

FIGURE 16–4.
REFRACTION OF LIGHT.
Upper left: refraction of rays of light on passing through a sheet of glass. Upper right: refraction of rays of light on passing through a plano-convex lens. Below: refraction of light passing through a plano-convex lens under different conditions.

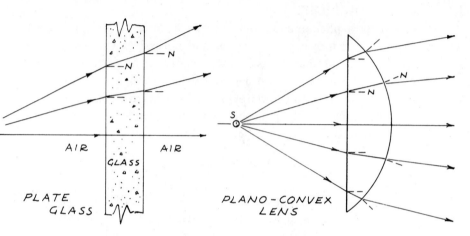

REFRACTION

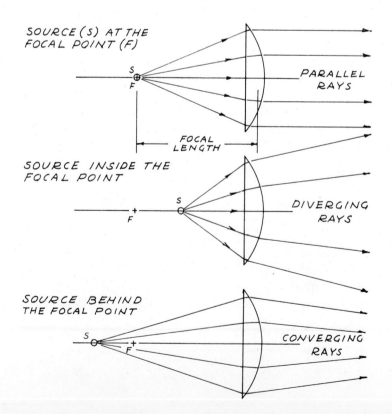

the resulting beam would be wider spread than it is when emerging from the lamp and before striking the lens. If this were the case, common sense would lead one to inquire, "Then why bother with a lens at all if it is going to spread the rays instead of concentrating them into a powerful beam of light?"

Every lens has a focal point. This should not be confused with the center of curvature of the surface. If a source of light is placed at the focal point of a lens, all the rays of light that emerge from the lens will be parallel one to another. Conversely, if parallel light rays (as from the sun) strike a lens, they will converge at the focal point. Lenses are identified by two numbers, the first of which states the diameter while the second gives the focal length: the distance from the focal point to a plane approximately two-thirds of the greatest thickness of the lens, measured from its plane face. Thus, a 6-by-8-inch lens would have a diameter of 6 inches and a focal length of 8 inches. The greater the curve of the convex face, the greater the refracting power of a lens. Therefore, a thick lens will have a shorter focal length than a thin one.

FINDING THE FOCAL LENGTH

As it is usually desirable to know what the focal length of a given lens happens to be, and as this information is rarely marked on it, a quick method of ascertaining this fact is good to keep in mind. If the sun is shining, the lens may be carried outdoors and held, plano side down, so that the sun's rays are concentrated on the ground. Then a ruler will measure the distance from the ground to the focal plane. For lenses used in stage-lighting equipment the focal lengths are in even inches.

Often the sun is not available, in which case some indoor light must be used, but as far away as possible. The resulting measurement will be, in this case, somewhat longer than the true focal length, because the rays were not parallel but diverging, when they struck the curved surface. But this excess will be less than an inch; so by simply eliminating the fraction, we can calculate the exact focal length quite accurately. For example, if the measurement is 11½ inches, we know the focal length is 11 inches; if we measure 9¼ inches, we know the focal length is 9 inches.

Importance of Focal Lengths. If a source of light be placed between the focal point and the lens, the emerging rays will diverge; if the source be placed further from the lens than the focal point, the rays will converge and eventually cross one another (Figure 16–4).

Because the light source may be placed closer to the lens when the focal length is short, it is obvious that such a lens will be able to gather

442

and make use of a larger percentage of the emanating light and is therefore more efficient than a lens with a long focal length. But there is a drawback in that the thicker glass of the short focal-length lens will absorb more of the light and therefore crack more easily from the greater heat that results. In some lighting instruments this can be corrected by using two lenses of long focal length to form a lens train of total shorter focal length.

FRESNEL AND STEP LENSES

Because this is not always practical, two solutions have been developed, both using the technique of cutting away part of the thick glass, yet retaining the basic relationships between the curved and the plane surfaces. The first of these is the Fresnel (pronounced Fr'nel) lens, in which the plano face is retained, but the curved face is cut back in steps. More recent is the step lens, in which the convex side retains its shape, while the plano face is cut back (Figure 16–5).

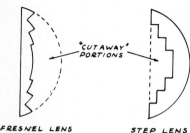

FRESNEL LENS   STEP LENS

FIGURE 16–5. SIMPLIFIED DIAGRAMS SHOWING HOW FRESNEL AND STEP LENSES ARE DERIVED FROM THE PLANO-CONVEX LENS.

ABSORPTION

Absorption takes place to some degree whenever light strikes any object, no matter how mirrorlike or crystal clear it may seem. But absorption is more particularly important to us in connection with solid objects.

WHITE LIGHT

If a beam of ordinary white light strikes a white surface, most of it will be turned back by reflection, but 10 percent or more will be absorbed, regardless of how purely white the surface appears. If the same light is directed at a black object, it may reflect 5 percent or so, but the greater part of the light is absorbed. In each case, of course, the reflected light will be white light, for nothing will have occurred to make any change in the color. In each case the reflecting surface will appear as it is: the white one white, the black one black, for nothing has happened to change their colors.

On the other hand, if this white light were to strike a pure-red surface, over 80 percent of the light would be absorbed but the balance would be reflected as red light. That is how we identify the surface as red. The only way we can tell the color of any object is by the color of the light that is reflected from it to our eyes.

COLORED LIGHT

Now suppose we direct a pure-blue light at this red surface, we will see it as black, for the red will reflect only red waves and no red waves were directed on it. This is similar, of course, to what we learned about white light and colored gelatins. Because pigments used to paint walls and dye cloth are seldom completely pure, we cannot count on a perfect demonstration of this phenomenon on every occasion, but the principle holds good and should be constantly kept in mind.

On the other hand, if we shine a red light on a neutral surface, whether white, gray, or black, we will find that the object will appear red, for that is the only light available for reflection. Further, if a red light is directed on two surfaces, one the same red and the other white, both these surfaces will seem to be almost exactly the same color to the viewer. This is a most important phenomenon to be kept in mind by the designer, lest, by use of strong tints, he may make large portions of the scenery or costumes appear just the same as something that had been intended to be a strong accent.

PROBLEMS OF ABSORPTION VERSUS REFLECTION

Other factors than pure colors enter into the picture of absorption versus reflection, the texture of the surface being of the utmost importance. Hard, shiny surfaces have a tendency to reflect light better than soft, woolly ones, even though both are apparently the same color. Such hard surfaces also may produce highlights when viewed from certain angles. These may be difficult to control on stage. For this reason metals, glass, and the like are usually confined to small adornments on costumes, or are soaped or otherwise dulled to prevent their disconcerting flashes and images. Mirrors or large mirrorlike surfaces are occasionally used on the stage as a design feature. Their highly reflective quality is accepted as a part of the design with some of the audience being treated to a perfect reflected image while others see only a pitch black surface.

Before we leave the subject of absorption, other warnings must be issued. White, or extremely pale colors, will always reflect a large portion of the light and are, therefore, inclined to be very obvious on stage. A white costume, beloved of all actresses, will draw attention away from more important action no matter how the stage is arranged. The best-lighted actors will appear as silhouettes before a very bright backdrop, and this effect can trouble the audience greatly. While on the other hand, no matter how black the scenery, of whatever material used, it will reflect a certain amount of light, even that which has been already once reflected from the stage floor! The "living darkness of the theatre" is one of its most difficult concepts to attain if, indeed, it can be achieved at all, except with charcoal on the scene designer's sketch pad.

17 Stage-Lighting Instruments

The term "stage-lighting instrument" is used to designate any device employed on the stage to hold a lamp in correct position, to direct and often to shape its output of light, and to hold color media in the resulting beam. Electric current is fed to all conventional instruments through short wire leads with asbestos insulation to protect them from the intense heat generated by the large-wattage lamps. There may be two or three leads. If three, the third one is to serve as a ground wire to draw off in safety any current that might have leaked into the metal hood from a short circuit within the instrument. The leads terminate in some sort of a connector, as described in Chapter 13.

To avoid confusion, discussion of instruments using the tungsten-halogen (quartz-iodine) lamps is saved for a special section at the end of this chapter. Up to that point only instruments employing the older types of incandescent filament lamps are discussed.

Because stage workers have a habit of referring to whole classes of instruments by the trade names of certain manufacturers or other slang terminology, there seems to be a bewildering complexity of such instruments. Actually, there are just a few basic types.

444

SPOTLIGHTS

On the modern stage the spotlight is far and away the most important instrument of all. Fundamentally, the spotlight is a metal hood containing a high-powered source of light which is made more effective by use of a lens and usually a reflector as well. The resulting beam of high-intensity light can be shaped by various means to forms that may be useful in the stage picture.

THE PLANO-CONVEX SPOTLIGHT

The first incandescent spotlight, and for many years the only kind, is what is known today as the plano-convex spot. In a simple hood a G-shaped lamp is mounted on a sliding carriage attached to which there is also a small spherical reflector that rides behind the lamp and is always in correct relationship to it (Figure 17–1). As was explained in **Chapter 16**, such a reflector sends all rays that strike it back through the original source, thus augmenting the forward emanation to a considerable degree.

In front of the lamp and carefully aligned with its filament is placed a plano-convex lens which refracts all the rays that strike it and bends them into a comparatively narrow beam. When the lamp is close to the lens in flood position the percentage of the total light that strikes the lens is quite high, but because this spreads into a wide angle after leaving the lens there is no great intensity to the beam at any distance from the instrument. When the lamp is moved back toward the focal point of the lens, the angle of acceptance of the lens is less and the beam much narrower. So, although a smaller percentage of the light is utilized, the beam then has greater intensity for all the light is concentrated in the narrower shaft. The inside of

FIGURE 17–1. THE PLANO-CONVEX SPOTLIGHT. (1) Asbestos-covered lead wires. (2) Pin connector. (3) Vertical adjustment knob. (4) Spherical reflector. (5) G-shape lamp. (6) Yoke. (7) Pipe clamp. (8) Ventilation holes. (9) Lamp in flood focus position. (10) Spring ring to hold lens in position. (11) Color-frame holder. (12) Plano-convex lens. (13) Focus-adjustment knob. (14) Movable lamp socket.

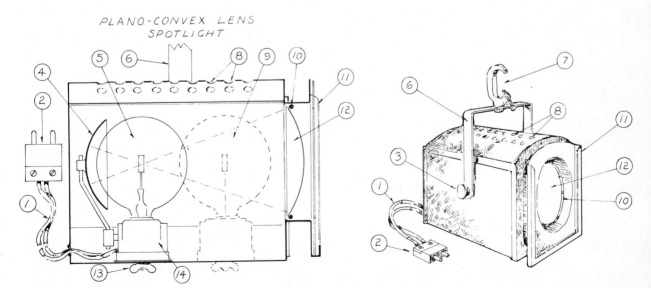

PLANO-CONVEX LENS SPOTLIGHT

446   the hood is painted a flat black to absorb all rays of light that do not strike the lens directly.

Spotlight Accessories.   The lens of a plano-convex, indeed of any, spotlight, is held in place by a strong metal spring-ring. Above and below the lens opening in the hood there are small troughs to hold color media frames. Every spotlight has some means of mounting it, usually a yoke held in place on side studs by large nuts or set wheels. Ventilation must be supplied—above to allow hot air to escape and below to let cool air in. The ventilation holes or slots are fitted with baffles to prevent light spill. And except on the smallest models, an access door permits the electrician to inspect the hood's interior and change the lamp without otherwise disturbing instrument or focus.

Beam Characteristics of the Plano-convex Spot.   When focused on a flat surface, the plano-convex spotlight's beam pattern is circular with a sharp, distinct edge. But the field is quite irregular in intensity, while aberrations in the form of rainbow effects are seen at the edges. When the lamp is moved back to the exact focal length of the lens, a precise image of the filament appears. The basic circular pattern can be easily changed by the insertion of mats (small metal or foil forms) into the color frame. This permits an exact shaping of the beam, often necessary to keep unwanted light off portions of the stage, to hold the light pattern to a precise location, and the like. Or an iris can be used to alter the size of the beam pattern without changing its circular shape.

Although the plano-convex spotlight does not have the importance it once held, it is still a useful instrument on many occasions, and it is far less expensive than the ellipsoidal-reflector spotlight, the other instrument that throws a sharply defined beam, although much less powerful.

Sizes of the Plano-convex Spot.   The P-C, as the plano-convex spot is frequently called, can be obtained in three sizes, the smallest and least powerful of which has a 5-inch lens and burns G-shaped lamps of 250 and 400 watts. It is useful for short throws, as on a very small stage and can be hidden in nooks where other instruments would prove too large. This little spotlight is usually referred to as a "baby."

Larger "brothers" are those with 6-inch and 8-inch plano-convex lenses. The various manufacturers furnish different lines of these, but in general it may be said that the 8-inch type burns 2000-watt lamps while the 6-inch models range from 500 to 1500 watts, all of the G type. These cannot be recommended for the well-equipped stage ahead of the far more efficient Fresnels and ellipsoidal-reflector spotlights. But when nothing else is available, they can be used very effectively if the intensity demands are not too great.

THE FRESNEL SPOTLIGHT

Because its short focal length allows it to gather such a large percentage of the light from a source, the Fresnel lens has been incorporated into the spotlight line. Essentially the only difference between the hoods of the plano-convex and the Fresnel spots is that the latter is considerably shorter, as the short focal length of the Fresnel lens makes a long movement of the lamp unnecessary.

The Fresnel spot throws a beam of much greater intensity than does the plano-convex for the same current consumed. Moreover, the beam pattern of the Fresnel is far smoother and without a sharp edge. In fact, it is hard to find its limits at all, so gently does it drop off, thereby permitting easy blending of two or more beams without a noticeable break.

This same softness of beam edge makes matting the Fresnel not as sure and certain as with the plano-convex. But satisfactory jobs can be achieved with this softer edge that is often preferable as it keeps the drop-off from being too obvious.

Fresnel Sizes. Fresnel spotlights come in a number of sizes, the smallest of which has a 3-inch lens and burns a 150-watt G-shaped lamp. Like the baby P-C, this little instrument though not possessing much punch is very handy for tucking into small corners. A streamlined version of the 3-inch Fresnel is sold in most camera-equipment shops for use in photographers' studios.

An extremely useful instrument on any stage is the 6-inch Fresnel, burning 500- and 750-watt T-shaped lamps. This spotlight is a true workhorse, being invaluable for the upstage acting areas where its soft-edged beam fades away on the scenery without leaving obvious and distracting lines and patterns. It throws a good punch with the typically smooth beam pattern. And for the larger stage the 8-inch Fresnel can be almost as valuable and with its 1000- and 1500-watt G lamps has a powerful beam that can be put to many uses.

The Fresnel type of spotlight is also sold with lenses from 10 to 20 inches in diameter. These have little importance for the conventional stage, being primarily designed for television and motion-picture studios. They might have significance for outdoor productions, where exceptionally long throws are often the rule. Another feature that has been introduced for television purposes is the Fresnel lens that throws an oval beam. This can be very useful on the stage as well, to spread the light laterally, making cross-stage blending easier.

Today the Fresnel is second only to the ellipsoidal-reflector spotlight in popularity and importance.

FIGURE 17–2. The FRESNEL SPOTLIGHT. Above: A modern example that uses the tungsten-halogen lamp. Below: Section. (1) Three-wire twist-lock connector. (2) Asbestos covered lead wires. (3) Spherical reflector. (4) Ventilation holes. (5) Yoke. (6) T-shaped lamp, base down. (tungsten-halogen or incandescent) (7) Fresnel lens. (8) Color-frame holder. (9) Hinged lens front for interior access. (10) Lead-screw drive for movable lamp socket and reflector. (11) Movable lamp socket. (Photo—Kliegl Bros.)

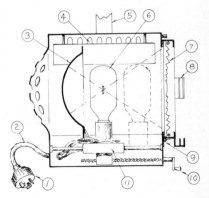

448

THE ELLIPSOIDAL SPOTLIGHT

This is, unquestionably, the most important, the most useful, and the most common stage lighting instrument in use today. In Chapter 16 we saw that if a source of light be placed at one of the focal points of a reflector built in the shape of half an ellipsoid, all the light rays that strike this reflector are diverted through the conjugate focal point. By placing a lens just in front of this secondary focal point a spotlight of great efficiency and power can be constructed. Such an instrument, properly called an ellipsoidal-reflector spotlight, is more often known by one or another of its various trade names.

Because the primary focal point is extremely close to the reflector, it is necessary to employ only T-shaped lamps in order to get the filament placed precisely (Figure 17–3). Inasmuch as this type of instrument is almost invariably used with its nose tilted down about 45 degrees from the horizontal, lamps that are to be burned "base-up only" are used and the socket that holds them is uppermost when the spotlight is in its usual burning position.

In front of the conjugate focal point, where the rays of light are starting to spread again, a lens is mounted to refract these rays into a comparatively narrow beam. In certain ellipsoidal spotlights, where a particularly short focal-length lens is needed, it is usual to employ two thinner lenses to get the effect of the one thick one. Today Fresnel and step lenses are taking the place of the plano-convex type pretty completely in these instruments for the double purpose of providing the short focal length and because these are less subject to breakage under the extreme heat concentrated on them.

These two types of lens cause the beam pattern to be much smoother and to have a fairly soft edge, which makes blending very much easier. Unfortunately with their use there is a tendency for the

FIGURE 17–3a. THE ELLIPSOIDAL-REFLECTOR SPOTLIGHT. (1) Pin connector. (2) Monoplane (or biplane) filament, with its center at the focal point, "f." (3) Ellipsoidal-shaped reflector. (4) Bottom shutter, which shapes the top of beam. (5) Color-frame holder. (6) Prefocus base socket. (7) T-shaped lamp, to burn base up. (8) Top shutter, which shapes the bottom of the beam. (9) The "gate," with typical reflected rays crossing at the conjugate focal point, "f¹." (10) Two plano-convex lenses. (11) Spring ring, to hold lens. (12) Alternate position of lens system.

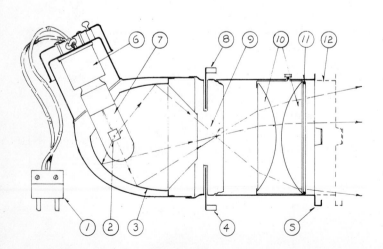

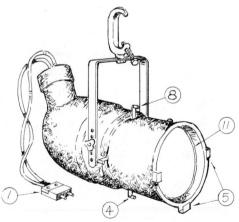

ELLIPSOIDAL REFLECTOR SPOTLIGHT

instrument to flare, that is, to send some of its rays outside the desired beam pattern. Such misdirected light is very difficult to mask off the proscenium walls, the ceiling, and even the audience!

Shaping the Beam of the Ellipsoidal-Reflector Spot. Just before the conjugate focal point, where the various rays are still converging, is a baffle known as the "gate." This cuts off stray rays of light that are not useful in forming a well-controlled beam, and it is an image of the opening in this gate which appears as a round and reasonably smooth pattern when the ellipsoidal spotlight is focused on a plain surface. Various other features to shape the beam may be placed at the gate, a common and useful device being four shutters which, by proper manipulation, can change the beam pattern into almost any simple shape. An iris is sometimes inserted here, allowing the circular form of the beam to be made smaller or larger at will, though this is of more pertinence when the instrument is to be used as a follow spot.

Or special shapes may be cut from sheet metal and placed at the gate. The common term for one of these is a "gobo."

Other Beam Characteristics. The ellipsoidal-reflector spotlight throws an extremely powerful beam of light which cannot be shaped by external means such as placing mats in the color frame, but this is no problem because the internal shutters achieve the same results. Because the lamp, reflector, and lens are in static relationship, there is no flood and spot focus, as with the plano-convex and Fresnel spotlights. But the lenses may be moved a few inches, back and forth, thus allowing the beam pattern to be thrown out of focus and so softening to some extent the hard, sharp edge of the field.

FIGURE 17–3 b. ELLIPSOIDAL REFLECTOR SPOTLIGHT. Hood engineered for an axially mounted tungsten-halogen lamp. (1) 3-wire pin-connector. (2) Monoplane (or biplane) filament. (3) Ellipsoidal-shaped reflector. (4) Bottom shutter, shapes top of beam. (5) Color frame holder. (6) Prefocus medium base socket axially mounted. (7) T-H lamp. (8) The "gate" with typical reflected rays crossing at the conjugate focal point f′. (9) Top shutter, shapes bottom of beam. (10) Two plano-convex lenses. (11) Alternate position of lens system.

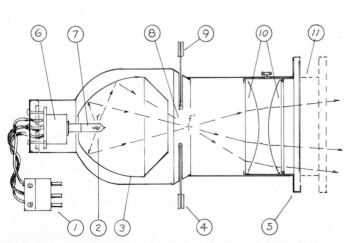

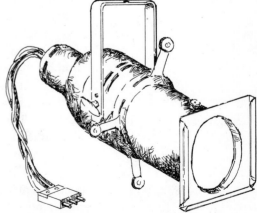

ELLIPSOIDAL REFLECTOR SPOTLIGHT

Because of the delicate relationship between filament and reflector, it is easy for the instrument to get out of adjustment, particularly if an inexperienced electrician tampers with the adjusting devices on the socket cap. Often, especially in those instruments that use the prefocus lamp, the base has not been properly seated in the socket. At other times it is necessary to focus the spotlight on a plain surface and manipulate the adjusting devices until a firm, circular field is found again. Or the instrument may be dimmed down until the filament barely glows, the lenses removed, and an inspection of the alignment of the filament and the reflector made from the front.

Ellipsoidal-Reflector Spotlight Sizes. The ellipsoidal-reflector spotlight comes in several sizes, from one with a 4½-inch lens that burns 250- and 500-watt lamps and throws a wide beam, suitable for small stages and auxiliary use on large stages, up to a 12-inch model that uses a 3000-watt lamp for a very narrow and extremely powerful beam intended primarily for follow-spotting from a distance. There are a number of models in the 6- and 8-inch sizes, some using 500- and 750-watt lamps and others those of 1000, 2000, or 3000 watts. The differences in design are too complex for analysis here, and are continually undergoing changes. But the buyer should study the latest catalogs carefully before placing his order and demand specific answers from the manufacturers as to the exact performance in the way of beam spread, foot-candle readings at various distances, and the like.

New Silhouettes. The successful development of the tungsten-halogen lamp has triggered new instrument design particularly in the ellipsoidal-reflector spotlight. The near point source, reduced size, and greater intensity of the lamp has increased the efficiency of the reflector and changed the hood design. The most notable design changes in this country are seen in Berkey Colortran's *Ellipsoid* and in the *Parellipsphere* manufactured by Electro Controls, Inc.

Besides an improved hood design the Ellipsoid provides a variable focal length adjustment of the front lens system which increases the number of uses of an individual instrument. The Parellipsphere also has a convenient mechanism to change focal length (almost a zoom lens) as well as a new reflector design. As the name implies, it involves three surfaces. The basic shape of the reflector is ellipsoidal with a parabolic apex at the lamp position and an off-axis spherical reflector in front facing the lamp to redirect outside rays back into the ellipsoidal portion of the reflector (Fig. 17-5). The increased efficiency and greater flexibility of both instruments make them useful though expensive ellipsoidal-reflector spotlights.

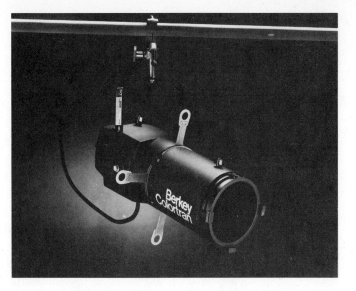

FIGURE 17–4. THE ELLIPSOID. An axially mounted T-H lamp, ellipsoidal reflector, spotlight. (Photo courtesy of Berkey Colortran, Inc., Division of Berkey Photo, Inc.)

FIGURE 17–5. THE PARELLIPSPHERE. Although basically an ellipsoidal-reflector spotlight, the Parellipsphere has a more sophisticated reflector design and greater flexibility in the lens system. (Photo courtesy Electro Controls, Inc.) (1) 3-wire twist-lock connector. (2) Parellipse part of reflector. Apex of reflector is parabolic in action. (3) Kickback reflector with slight spherical configuration. (4) Bottom shutter. (5) Baffles. (6) Nonsymmetric biconvex lens. (7) Planoconvex lens. (8) Color frame holder. (9) Prefocus medium base socket axially mounted. (10) T-H lamp. (11) Top shutter. (12) Lens adjustment knob to change focal length of objective system. (13) Knob to change beam spread.

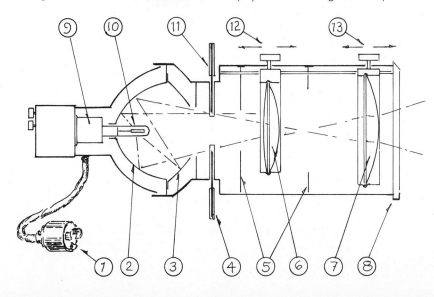

FIGURE 17–6. THE BEAM PRO-JECTOR. (1) G-shaped lamp. (2) Parabolic reflector. (3) Concentrated filament. (4) Lamp socket, adjustable. (5) Pin connector and lead wires. (6) Spherical reflector. (7) Color-frame holders. Photo of 11-inch Kliegsun Beam Projector, 500-1000 watts. Also available in 15 inch, 1000-1500 watts. (Photo — Kliegl Bros.)

THE BEAM PROJECTOR

Despite its narrow and extremely intense output, the beam projector is not a true spotlight. It has no lens, and, more important, its beam pattern cannot be greatly altered from the small and very bright circle that is its characteristic. True, the lamp can be moved slightly in relation to the reflector, which results in a somewhat larger pattern, but one which has a "hole" or dark spot in its center. In no case is the beam projector's pattern very smooth, and masking will not alter the shape in any way, but rather dims it in an erratic fashion.

This instrument makes use of a parabolic reflector which sends all the rays that strike it forward and parallel one to the other. In order to eliminate diverging rays of light that would not contribute to the tight beam pattern, but would prove undesirable and distracting, a spherical reflector is often placed in front of the lamp to redirect such rays as may strike it back to the parabolic reflector, from which they may augment the other parallel rays (Figure 17–6). In some styles of beam projector baffles or louvers serve to intercept and absorb such diverging rays. Basically the beam projector is a searchlight adapted to the theatre. Its stage uses are largely confined to strong shafts of light of great intensity but confined to small areas, as sunlight through a window. For musical comedy and the like, great banks of beam projectors may be employed, but for the modest stage this instrument has more limited uses.

The beam projector comes in various sizes, from 10 to 30 inches in diameter. The 10-inch style may take a 250- to a 750-watt T lamp, while the larger types use 1000- to 2000-watt lamps, in some models G's and in others T-shaped. Anything larger than 16 inches would scarcely be required for even a fairly sizable stage. Because of the tre-

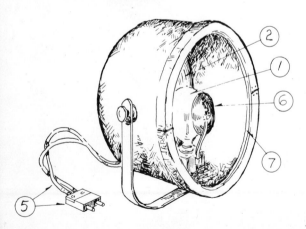

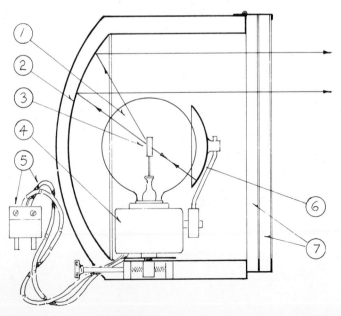

BEAM PROJECTOR

mendous punch of the light, the beam projector is very hard on gelatins or plastic color media, burning the color out of some shades within minutes after replacement.

THE FLOODLIGHT

A floodlight is, as its name suggests, a device for throwing a broad wash of light over a wide area. For many years the so-called Olivette was the standard instrument for such a purpose. Large and unwieldy, burning a 1000-watt G-lamp, the Olivette reflects a smooth wash of light from its boxlike hood and white-painted interior.

Floodlights are now a little more sophisticated, and a lot easier to manipulate. Most of them employ the ellipsoidal-reflector principle, but with a matte finish that distributes the light smoothly, without a sharp edge to the beam. A single such instrument can be valuable for lighting a fair-sized window backing, while a bank of them may be used to illuminate a drop or cyclorama.

Most of these floodlights are about 15 or 16 inches in diameter and burn general-service PS lamps of up to 2000 watts in some types. There is also a small 10-inch model that uses 250 and 400 G-lamps, or, occasionally, gives good service with a 100-watt A-lamp when only a very low illumination is required.

THE STRIPLIGHT

One form of stage-lighting instrument that predates the invention of the incandescent lamp is the striplight, which produces the effect of a line of light by means of a number of sources—formerly candles or gas, but now electric—adjacent to each other. In its crudest form, the striplight is often found as footlights—the only light source on a small, ill-equipped stage—a row of bare bulbs, sometimes as far apart as 12 inches, extending the entire width of the proscenium opening.

While permanently installed footlights of better design may be useful on some stages, the more general approach today is to have striplights prepared in lengths of between 3 and 9 feet. These sections may then be placed about the stage, including the usual footlight position on the apron's edge, or hung from overhead, as needed by the requirements of the particular play and its design concept. This system allows far greater flexibility in the use of equipment than does permanently installed striplights at many locations.

Certain basic principles in striplight design must be understood. The lamps should be wired in several color circuits, three being the most common, though four have much to recommend them. Then, by using different colors in each circuit and properly controlling their respective intensities, practically any color or tint of light may be attained. Obviously, the lamps should be closely spaced, so that their various

FIGURE 17–7. FLOODLIGHTS. (a) Soft Lite, 2000 watts, double-ended, linear filament T-H lamp. Also available, 4000 watts. (Photo — Kliegl Bros.) (b) Ellipsoidal Reflector Floodlight. Often called ERF's or "scoops." 300–500 watts, T-H lamp. (Photo — Kliegl Bros.)

454

beams will blend together more readily. Nothing is more ridiculous than the actor standing so near a badly designed footlight strip that his right foot is a rich magenta and his left a bright green.

TYPES OF STRIPLIGHTS

In the past various types of striplights were marketed and still are, unfortunately. The open trough is an abomination, as there is no possibility of using color media over the individual lamps. Only by employing the quite inefficient and unsatisfactory dipped-color lamps can any control over color be achieved.

An improvement over the open trough is the striplight in which each lamp has its own reflector, and various devices are provided for holding gelatin in front of it. The highly polished reflectors throw uneven light patterns, the matte finishes accumulate dirt. For the more powerful throws of light, larger lamps are necessary, and hence larger and more unwieldy instruments.

R and PAR Lamps in Striplights.   The advent of the R and PAR lines of lamps has made all this obsolete. For small and most medium stages, only one style of striplight is needed: that with the lamps on 6-inch centers, as all the reflector lamps that are necessary for use have diameters of no more than 5 inches. Color frames that will accept both gelatin and glass should be employed. Because the R and PAR lamps have built-in reflectors, these strips do not need any of their own—a saving in money and nuisance. The strips should be wired in three- or four-color circuits, depending on the preference of the producers; probably three is sufficient in the great majority of cases. And the small, low-budget stage can do very nicely with the colored R's and PAR's as described in **Chapter 15.**

The 150-watt R and PAR lamps prove adequate for many stages, though occasionally the 300-watt R spots may be needed for extra punch, as in lighting a large cyclorama. The 150-watt PAR spots are almost as effective, however, but throw too narrow a beam for anything but a sheet of light focused up or down a flat surface. For a very broad, smooth field of medium intensity the flood types of either R or PAR lamps are the most useful. Recently the commercial theatre has been employing striplights specially designed to take the 200-watt PAR-46, the 300-watt PAR-56 or the 500-watt PAR-64 lamps. These have no application, of course, for the small stage, and their value on a medium-sized one is questionable. But the group that plays on a very large stage, with vast cyclorama or sky drops, might find them a good investment, if properly designed for their specific needs.

COLOR WITH STRIPLIGHTS

Because of the extreme heat generated by R and PAR lamps, there is a great tendency for gelatin and plastic color media to burn out very rapidly. These media are satisfactory in front of the 150-watt lamps in a strip that is focused downward. But for larger wattages or for any striplight focused upward, glass must be used. Roundels of the 55-degree-spread variety are particularly valuable even though they cost a little more than other types. They have small prismlike ridges on the inner sides, and these serve to spread the light if the roundels are placed correctly, with the ridges running perpendicular to the long axis of the instrument. Certainly the primary colors should be stocked, as well as amber and blue-green. Such an inventory should prove sufficient for all but the most elaborate productions.

STRIPLIGHT LENGTHS AND COLOR CIRCUITS

There is an often misunderstood aspect in selecting striplights in short transportable lengths as advocated above. The actual measurements of these lengths depend on two factors: the size of the lamps and the number of color circuits desired.

If the strip is to use the 150-watt R's or PAR's, which are 5 and 4¾ inches in diameter, respectively, they should be spaced so that the centers of adjacent lamps are 6 inches apart. Disregarding the mounting studs at the ends, which add a few more inches to the long hoods, we can calculate as follows.

If there are to be six lamps, this will make the over-all length 36 inches (five spaces of 6 inches each, plus two end spaces of 3 inches each). If three-color circuits are wanted, they can be provided by having two lamps in each color, say, red-blue-green-red-blue-green. But if four-color circuits are needed, they cannot be supplied unless one is satisfied with something like red-blue-green-amber-red-blue, giving twice as many red and blue lamps as green and amber. This would give a very poor color balance from a single strip, and lead to a great deal of confusion when several strips are used end to end. Instead, a striplight 48 inches long should be used for four-color circuits with the lamps on 6-inch centers.

If 300-watt R lamps are required, their greater heat output makes it necessary to place them on 8-inch centers. Therefore the shortest useful strip would be 48 inches long, with two lamps of each color in a three-circuit strip, or 64 inches long for one with four circuits.

A chart correlating the number of lamps per color circuit and length of the striplight is on page 456.

FIGURE 17–8. THE 3½-INCH ELLIPSOIDAL REFLECTOR SPOTLIGHT.
This compact little instrument, with slight variations, can provide an enormous range of beam-widths and intensities, depending on which of several available lenses is used. It burns a tungsten-halogen lamp (whose tiny size makes the whole thing possible) of 300, 400, or 650 watts. It is excellent for short-throw lighting. (Photo—Kliegl Bros.)

RECOMMENDED STRIPLIGHT LENGTHS
FOR NUMBER OF LAMPS PER COLOR CIRCUIT

LENGTH OF STRIP	ON 6-INCH CENTERS		ON 8-INCH CENTERS	
	3 CIRCUITS	4 CIRCUITS	3 CIRCUITS	4 CIRCUITS
2 ft. 8 in.				1
3 ft. 0 in.	2			
4 ft. 0 in.		2	2	
4 ft. 6 in.	3			
5 ft. 4 in.				2
6 ft. 0 in.	4	3	3	
7 ft. 6 in.	5			
8 ft. 0 in.		4	4	3
9 ft. 0 in.	6			

Striplights longer or shorter than these are not recommended except for special and specific purposes. Additional suggestions about the placing of striplights in relation to a cyclorama or back drop will be found in Chapter 19.

TUNGSTEN-HALOGEN INSTRUMENTS

All the various types of stage-lighting instruments—ellipsoidal-reflector spots, Fresnel lens spots, floodlights, beam projectors, striplights—are available today with the new style lamps, and at least one large company has completely abandoned its former lines which used the conventional filament lamps. There are many reasons for this rapid acceptance of the tungsten-halogen source.

Longer life and undiminished light output for almost their entire lives are obvious advantages over lamps that dimmed and reddened perceptibly as time passed. At the same time, T-H lamps respond to any dimming system precisely as do the older types, so the same control apparatus may be used for both without adjustment.

The little lamps are mechanically stronger and less prone to suffer damage from careless handling. It is immaterial in what position they are burned. And, of course, their size helps solve the storage problem. Actually, because of the longer life, large inventories are no longer essential.

When these small lamps are used without an encapsulating bulb, their filaments may be placed with accuracy at the precise focal points of lenses and reflectors, giving a far better-controlled beam than with the larger, conventional lamps (see Figure 17–7). The size also makes possible the use of smaller reflectors, thus bringing new and more compact instruments into the market. This is typified by the 3½-inch ellipsoidal-reflector spotlight, shown in Figure 17–8, an instrument less than 18 inches long and 6 inches in diameter, which has a very wide

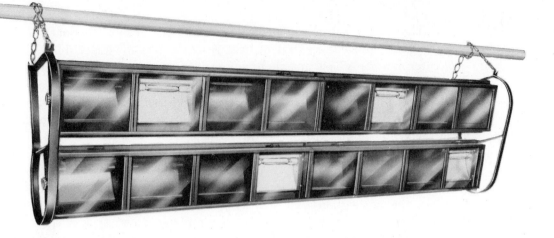

range of beam spreads and intensities to choose from. Another very natural application is in striplights, as seen in Figure 17–9

Tungsten-halogen lamps encapsulated in conventional bulbs, as the T-12, T-14, and T-20 sizes, may be used in instruments designed originally for the regular filament lamps without any change whatever. This is the path followed by some of the manufacturers of equipment for the stage for some types of instruments. And the PAR and R lines have come out with several new lamps in which the T-H bulb is encased in the old shapes and sizes. The PAR-38, PAR-56, and PAR-64, formerly limited to top wattages of 150, 300, and 500 respectively, are now available at 250, 500, and 1000 watts. All three have a life expectancy of 4000 hours! Similar improvements are noted in the R line of lamps. The new R-60 is offered at 1000 and 1500 watts with a tentative estimate of a life of 3000 hours. All these offer great expectations in the field of striplights, especially for backdrops and cycloramas.

Some question has been raised as to the danger of skin burn from exposure to a T-H lamp. Any tungsten filament emits a small amount of the ultraviolet wavelengths which cause suntan and sunburn. The glass used to make the bulbs of the conventional filament lamps absorbs most of these, but quartz glass has the property of passing a substantial amount of them. With the encapsulated T-H lamp there is no problem, for the outer bulb absorbs the ultraviolet waves. And the extremely "white" lamps used for color television are made with special bulbs to do the same. But it is true that in certain conditions a redness of the skin will be observed after an exposure of some time before an unprotected tungsten-halogen light. In stage terms, if a fair, untanned actor stands for something more than four hours about twenty feet from an ellipsoidal spotlight with a quartz glass lens and burning a 1000-watt T-H lamp, his face will show a perceptible reddening. If there were two such spotlights, the time of exposure would be halved.

FIGURE 17–9. STRIPLIGHTS. The rig that holds these two striplights permits either to be focused independently of the other, so each may wash a different portion of a backdrop. Note the four color-circuits. The lamps are 300 or 500-watt tungsten-halogen. (Photo— Kliegl Bros.)

458

Though the above example is an extreme one, it must be remembered that the same amount of light is used on many stages from a greater number of instruments hung considerably further away. Nonetheless it would seem that any danger involved is minimal. The use of any sort of glass color filter, or of a lens made of something other than quartz, will eliminate the ultraviolet. Probably gelatin or plastic color in the yellow-orange-red range will do the same.

THE ARC LIGHT

In Chapter 15 we mentioned the carbon arc as a source of light. When the two carbons and their associated apparatus are placed in a hood with a lens, it becomes essentially a plano-convex type of spotlight except for the source. The beam will have a sharp edge and, just as in the incandescent spotlight, the closer the source is to the lens, the more widespread the beam and the less intense the light. Then when the source is moved further back, the output narrows but becomes more brilliant.

It is not possible to control the intensity of the arc by conventional dimmers which alter the electric supply, for when the voltage drops, the arc simply goes out abruptly. But the *effect* of dimming can be achieved by moving the carbons toward the flood focus position, with the corresponding dropoff of intensity, and at the same time closing down the iris with which all good arc lights are equipped, so that the ultimate beam remains the same size. A skillful operator can do this so effectively that an observer cannot tell that mechanical means are employed, but it takes a great deal of practice and a piece of mechanism in fine condition.

Because these low-intensity carbon arcs operate on dc only, it is important that the instrument be properly connected to the supply service. Occasionally what is known as "reversed polarity" occurs—that is, the current is passing through the carbons in the wrong direction. This is easily recognized by the loud sputtering and the flickering imperfect beam—and is easily corrected by pulling out the plug, giving it a half-turn, and replacing it in its service outlet!

With any carbon arc a ballast (or fixed resistance) of proper capacity must be used to prevent an unrestricted flow of current when the carbons touch. An operator must always be in attendance, as the carbons burn away quite rapidly and must be fed back into proper relationship with each other. The d-c arc light is inclined to be noisy, which can be very disturbing to any of the audience seated nearby.

HIGH-INTENSITY ARCS

Once the only forms of carbon-arc spotlights available operated solely on direct current and drew a very high amperage. But for some

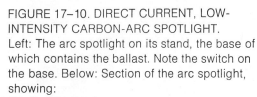

FIGURE 17–10. DIRECT CURRENT, LOW-INTENSITY CARBON-ARC SPOTLIGHT.
Left: The arc spotlight on its stand, the base of which contains the ballast. Note the switch on the base. Below: Section of the arc spotlight, showing:

(1) Positive carbon
(2) Negative carbon
(3) Crater
(4) Carbon clips
(5) Carbon feed screw
(6) Carbon feed handle
(7) Spot-to-flood focus handle
(8) Slot to permit spot-to-flood movement
(9) Lens
(10) Color-frame holder
(11) Insulation
(12) Feed wires
(13) Ballast
(14) Switch

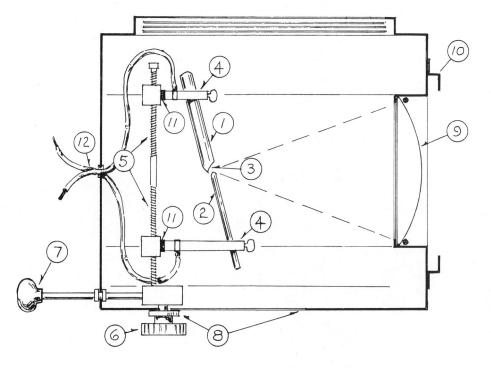

years now effective arcs that use alternating current, and little of that, have been on the market. These instruments are far more complete and include many accessories that the older types never had. They are expensive, but in any theatre where the throw must be over

FIGURE 17–11. HIGH-INTENSITY CARBON ARC SPOTLIGHT. The following features should be noted, starting at the left: (*a*) In the second from the rear compartment the two carbons, horizontal and point-to-point, backed by a reflector to direct any light from the negative carbon or from the arcing gases toward the front. (*b*) The gate, with an iris. (*c*) The lens system which can be adjusted to focus sharply at any distance. (*d*) The color boom, a rack of several different colors which can be selected as needed. All these items — carbon adjustment, iris control, lens focus, and color choice — can be handled by the operator without having to leave his position at the rear of his spotlight. (Photo — Century-Strand.)

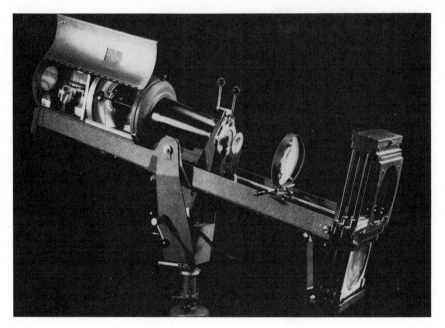

FIGURE 17–12. HIGH-INTENSITY FOLLOW SPOTS. (*a*) "Trouper" follow spotlight. High-intensity arc spotlight. Strong Electric Corporation. (*b*) Capitol "Quartz follow," 1000 watts follow spotlight. (Photo — Capitol Lighting). (*c*) Colorspot. A unique 1000-watt *lensless* follow spot. The lamp is mounted forward in the hood, aimed at a high-efficiency precision optical-projection mirror. (Photo — Berkey Colortran, Inc., Division of Berkey Photo, Inc.)

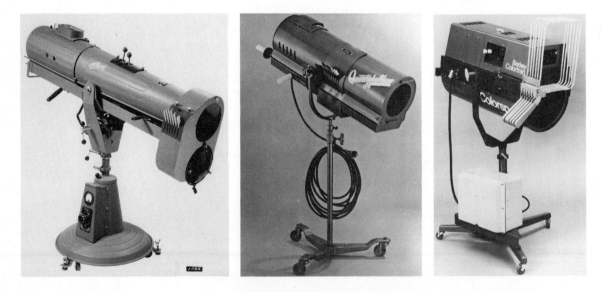

75 feet, they are essential. In smaller houses with shorter throws the new 3000- and 5000-watt incandescent follow spots will do the job just as well and with far less trouble, while a new, low-voltage lamp follow spot has recently appeared on the market and promises fine results.

ULTRAVIOLET EFFECTS

One field in which it is impossible to surpass the carbon arc is in the use of ultraviolet effects. Because the output from this instrument is rich in these very short waves, a black-light filter that removes practically all the visible waves will still permit the ultraviolet ones to pass through in good quantity. Objects painted with a medium susceptible to such waves will glow under this stimulus and, if all other light is removed from the stage, weird and unworldly effects can be achieved.

FIRE EFFECTS

Open fires are rarely convincing on the stage. Yet play after play calls for them. If it is possible to design the setting so that the hearth is located in a side wall, reasonably good results can be attained by simply letting a flickering light move over the far corner of the fireplace. Even this must be kept at low intensity so as not to take attention from the actors.

All too often the demands of the script force the designer to put his fire in full view of the audience. Sometimes no flames are actually demanded, and then a mere glow, through crumpled gelatin (orange and red), broken glass splashed with translucent orange paint, or the like, will suffice. If it is essential to show flames, then a glow on some form of rising smoke, or on thin streamers of chiffon, blown upward by a small fan, are often used. In every case, however, the designer is placed on the horns of this dilemma: whether to make the fire effects so realistic as to grab the attention of the audience—possibly to alarm them—or so phony as to arouse their ridicule. It must be stated emphatically that on the whole the less fire effect you can get away with, the more fortunate you and your production will be.

FLAMES

These remarks apply equally to other open-flame devices such as torches, candles, and oil-burning lanterns. Torches are a particular difficulty. Perhaps a flashlight hidden in the handle and focused on streamers of very light silk is as good a solution as any, but it is not very convincing, even when the torch is stationary and the silk can be blown upward by a hidden fan. Perhaps a smoke device can be incorporated and the flashlight trained on its fumes.

462   Oil-burning lanterns should never be used on the stage. To begin with, their use is strictly against all fire rules and insurance regulations. A real hazard is presented by their use, for in case of accident the stage becomes flooded with blazing oil. Fortunately oil lanterns conventionally have glass chimneys which can be realistically smoke-stained to hide a small lamp bulb placed inside.

If the lantern is never moved during the action, it can be connected to the regular stage wiring and dimmed up and down from the control board. Of course, actors, when pretending to adjust the wick, or touch a match to it, or whatever, must always be careful to mask this fakery by placing their bodies between the lantern and the audience until the process of dimming has been completed. Nothing brings more gleeful snorts from an audience than a lantern that continues to burn despite a strong puff from the actor, and then fades away as he draws his breath for a second try. If a lantern is to be carried about the stage a battery must be hidden within it and a switch provided for the actor to use as he pretends to touch a match or blow out the flame.

CANDLES

Unlike oil lanterns, candles which usually extinguish themselves when dropped, are permissible on most stages if properly handled. In some locations they must be encased in transparent mica shields. It is advisable to clear this matter with your local authorities if any doubt exists. In no case should candles be placed near draperies or other easily flammable materials, including human hair and frilly costumes.

But despite the permissibility of candles, they are not advised if they can be avoided, as their bright spots of light and particularly their flickering at the smallest breath of air can be most distracting for the audience. Very effective faking of candles can be done by means of a small battery or pencil flashlight hidden in a white paper tube. A tiny lamp on the top, with a twist of colored gelatin about it gives a steady and quite convincing glow.

LIGHTING FIXTURES

Chandeliers, wall sconces, table lamps, and similar household lighting fixtures offer no vast problems ordinarily except for the wattage of the lamps actually used in them. Such fixtures should never be counted on to produce all the light that seems to emanate from them. Frequently they are in quite the wrong locations to light the faces of the actors playing near them, so additional illumination must be provided by spotlights especially mounted for the purpose, or the acting area lights may be varied to give the effects desired.

This is particularly true when the fixtures have bulbs visible to the audience, for these, if at all bright, will throw a most annoying (even blinding) glare. Such bare bulbs must always be of extremely low wattage, and even then may have to be dimmed still further. Obviously little light will emanate from such fixtures, so the extra instruments become doubly important.

But if the bulbs are shielded by shades, then the glare is hidden and extra large-wattage lamps may be used to give a more realistic effect on an already bright stage. Such shades must be quite opaque, of course, or brown paper linings can be put inside them. Oftentimes an additional baffle of paper must be placed over the bulb to prevent an unsightly hot spot on the walls and ceiling of the setting. Basically then, it may be said that such household fixtures as chandeliers and sconces are more properly design features rather than functional lighting instruments on the well-appointed stage.

An interesting discussion on how the duties of handling and caring for such appliances are assigned in the commercial theatre is found in Chapter 10.

MOON AND STARS

Someday a playwright will call for a realistic sun on the stage! Until then we can have quite enough trouble with the moon and stars so often necessary. If the background is in the form of a cloth drop or cyclorama, quite a realistic moon can be devised by cutting the desired shape—fully round or crescent—into a large sheet of thin material such as cardboard or plywood, which is then pressed firmly against the back of the drop and a small spotlight is focused on the cutout from the rear. If the background is not a cloth, then a projection from an effect machine in front must be used, or an ellipsoidal-reflector spotlight with a gobo.

Stars can be quite effective, but are tricky to handle. The tiniest bulbs obtainable look like great blobs of light against a darkened sky. It is advisable to tape these over; a mere pin-prick will pass enough light. If a dark-blue gauze or scrim is hung a few feet in front of the sky drop, it will help cut down any overbrightness and also will hide the wiring to the star bulbs. When the cyclorama is a permanent one of plaster or wood, tiny holes are often drilled through it and clips provided on the back to hold the little lamps in place. Usually for such effects it is advisable to get strings of low-voltage lamps that can be bought at any hobby shop together with an appropriate transformer. Even Christmas tree strings can be used.

Stars can be projected from the front but, unless they are done by the gobo technique, they are rarely convincing as even the best slide equipment reproduces them as large and somewhat indistinct smudges of light. But for unrealistic, stylized effects, both stars and moon can be projected by a Linnebach with good results.

LIGHTNING

Lightning is a device in many plays. Fortunately it is usually not necessary to show forks springing from the sky, but only the sudden, rapid, and irregular bursts of high illumination as seen through windows or coming from the wings. By striking and breaking the contacts rapidly, a carbon arc can be used to give excellent results for this purpose. In fact a so-called arc striker that makes this even easier to handle is available commercially.

Another method is to switch rapidly on and off a number of small sources. It is better to use a striplight with many white and daylight-blue lamps of low wattage than a single large source which would respond more slowly to the irregular, staccato timing of typical lightning. A special switch may be devised to make the closing and the opening of the circuit easier to control, or the connectors themselves may be used to good advantage. Photoflash bulbs have also been used for offstage lightning.

If the lightning flash itself must be seen against the sky, a projection must be used. Because of the slow response of the high-wattage lamp, it is well to have the instrument already turned on and an operator stationed at it to reveal and conceal the beam of light by means of a cap or other masking device. And several different slides should be provided, rather than show the same shaped flash again and again. Scratches on black-painted slides can be drawn quite realistically for these.

EXPLOSIONS AND FLASHES

To produce these offstage, in the wings, the same general techniques can be applied as were suggested for lightning flashes, with the addition of mechanically produced noises when these are required. But for the same effects on the stage, in view of the audience, a flash pot is required.

A good flash pot consists of a metal pan with a tight-fitting wire screen over it. The bottom is covered by a piece of asbestos board, to which two electric terminals are fastened (small brass screws will do very nicely) but they must be carefully insulated from the box itself or a short circuit will develop. The two terminals may be about one inch apart. They are connected respectively to the two wires of a circuit that also contains a switch. Between the two terminals a single, very thin strand of copper wire is strung, wound firmly around each screw and lying flat on the asbestos board. A small quantity of flash powder is poured over this wire, covering all portions of it. When the switch is closed, the thin wire will burn out, igniting the powder. After each use the wire and powder must be replaced.

A variation of the flash box is a fuse of very low amperage set in an appropriate fuse clip or socket. The fuse is cut open—in the case of a plug fuse by prying out the isinglass window—with a cartridge fuse by cutting away part of the paper cover. Care is taken not to damage the fuse link. The resulting cavity is then filled with the flash powder. As with the flash box, the opened fuse and the powder must be renewed after each use.

Flash powder, when set off in this way, gives a good burst of light, but little smoke. If smoke is desired, some sal ammoniac powder may be mixed with the flash powder. In any case, the flash device must be well protected with a screen and should never be fired close to flammable materials or to persons. And an extra fuse, of higher amperage, should be placed in the circuit for additional protection.

And a most important warning: *very little powder should be used at one time—and it should never be tamped down,* but poured loosely into place.

FOG AND SMOKE EFFECTS

Many devices are used to produce smoke on the stage, but none is completely satisfactory. Perhaps the best known is sal ammoniac powder which after a few moments in a hot plate or in a heating cone will give off a good volume of white smoke. In ordinary quantities this is neither too odorous nor dangerous to breathe, but if allowed to become too dense, it can be very unpleasant. Cinnamon powder may be added to sweeten the smell for the actors. Sal ammoniac powder has disadvantages. It cannot be started suddenly, nor can it be stopped on cue. It is extremely corrosive on the producing elements.

Titanium tetrachloride combines with the moisture present in the air to give off a thin smoke that rises well. By adding a little water to it, or dropping a pinch of the powder into water, an instant response is produced that can be very effective, though the fumes are dangerous if breathed in quantity.

Dry ice can be dropped into water for a small quantity of smoke, but this tends to fall instead of rise. Dry ice may be quite effective in a fog machine (a metal drum with a heating element to keep the water from freezing when the solid carbon dioxide is lowered into it). If the drum is provided with a cover, quite a flow of fog can be produced suddenly and directed around the stage by means of a hose.

Smoke bombs are very smelly, impossible to control, and leave a greasy coating on the scenery and costumes. Steam is clean, but requires special piping and produces a loud hissing that makes it impractical for quiet scenes.

One device for generating smoke seems to be superior to any of the others mentioned. It consists of a container which is filled with a special

FIGURE 17–13. FOG MACHINE.   Solid carbon dioxide or dry ice changes state from a solid to a gas (vapor) without becoming a liquid. The rapidity of the change is increased when dry ice is submerged in hot water. The result is an almost instantaneous cloud of dense fog. Top left: Assembled fog machine. Top right: Top removed showing dry ice basket on end of the plunger. Middle right: View into the tank revealing electric heating element to heat water. Bottom left: Loading basket with crushed dry ice. Bottom right: The plunging of the dry ice in hot water produces a blanket of fog. (Pictures courtesy of Richard Thompson)

FIGURE 17–14. PORTABLE FOG MACHINE.   Small, lightweight tank vaporizes "fog juice" with electric heat. Fog is dense, white and dissipates quickly. Basket can be attached to front of machine with dry ice to slow down dissipation. Machine develops enough pressure to fill the stage very quickly. It can also be forced through PVC tube to remote parts of the stage. (Distributor — Mutual Hardware.)

liquid in which a heating coil is submerged. A handle for easy carrying is provided, and a plunger to pump the smoke about the stage at the desired rate and intensity. This mist tends to rise, but a cage is provided that may be filled with dry ice and fastened over the nozzle of the container. When this is done, the fumes hug the floor. Plastic hose hidden about the stage has proved an easy way to make this mist appear wherever wanted. A second fluid may be used to help disperse the smoke, and several essences are available to scent it pleasantly. Their value is strictly a matter of individual taste. Actually the fumes are not dreadfully unpleasant.

CONTROLLING SMOKE

Anyone using smoke of any nature on the stage is frequently faced with the problem of preventing it from flowing or blowing to where it is not wanted. Heavy smoke that tends to hug the stage floor may easily spill over the footlights into the auditorium—a touch that is seldom appreciated by the audience.

The lighter-than-air smoke that rises is subject to the slightest breeze or draft. A ventilator at the top of the stage house may draw it swiftly upward; a cross-draft may set up eddies and swirls; while an exhaust fan that evacuates stale air from the auditorium can bring the smoke billowing into the house.

Light as Scenery

18

Much has been said and written about the use of light in a supportive role to reveal the actor and illuminate the scene. Light, however, can become the basic element of a production. In recent years the use of light as scenery has reached an extreme height in popularity. Many reasons can be pointed out: (1) the increased use of theatre forms other than the proscenium stage, such as the thrust and arena stages where light is more obviously a major part of the total visual effect; (2) the impact of modern film techniques on live theatre as a stimulus for the use of film and multimedia experiments; (3) the sheerly sensational aspects of the psychedelic combination of light and sound both in and out of the theatre. The consolidation of all these influences is leading, in no uncertain terms, to a new attitude toward the use of light as a design element in all but the most conventional stage setting.

This new concept of lighting does not mean conventional illumination will disappear. Nor does it mean that scenery and the scene designer will cease to exist. It should also be apparent that flashy lighting does not fit every play or production; that the role of the

468

lighting designer is routinely supportive more often than it is freely innovative.

Light begins to be a scenic element the moment an open source is present on the stage. Such motivating lights as realistic chandeliers and sconces generally bring elegance and high-style to the scene. On the other hand, gaudy carousel lights or burlesque runway lights are frankly decorative and theatrical in their impact. Although motivating lights can make a strong visual contribution to the total design they are a supporting element and not the basic scheme of production.

PROJECTED SCENERY

The most familiar and accepted application of light as scenery is through the use of projections. Projections and projected scenery (usually backgrounds) are not new to the theatre. They are as old as the "magic lantern," which entered the theatre before the incandescent lamp, in the 1860s. The early experiments with the projection of moving images, first as crude animations and then later as motion pictures, are well known events in theatre history. The resurgence of projections in modern theatre is the result not only of improved equipment design but of a change in attitude toward their use.

Paint versus Light. It is most important to realize that a projection is *light* and not *paint* and that there is a world of difference between the two media. Because *color* in light is more brilliant than in paint, and has a limited value scale by comparison, its use in a projection is more dramatic and eye-catching. For these reasons, when projections are used as background to substitute for painted scenery, the actor has to fight for attention. This is not to say that projections do not work as background, for they can either at controlled levels of intensity or in a highly dramatic situation. The director and his designers soon learn that the most successful use of a projection is not as a substitute realistic background, but as a medium of its own, where it expresses itself best in abstract or thematic terms and almost becomes an additional actor.

Both paint and light, as an individual medium of expression, have their advantages and disadvantages which will be examined later. At this juncture it is important to realize that one is not the substitute for the other. This is one of the places where everyone concerned, the director and the scene and lighting designers, must be in full agreement and completely knowledgeable, or misconceptions will develop that will affect the end result.

FIGURE 18–1. LIGHT AS SCENERY. (*a*) The exposed light sources are a part of the visual composition. *Stop the World, I Want to Get Off,* by Leslie Bricusse and Anthony Newley. Set Designer — James Hooks; Lighting Designer — Steve Ross. (*b*) A curtain of light. The shape of visible light rays turns light into substance and becomes the design form. An early use of high-intensity low-voltage light sources by Josef Svoboda, the Czechoslovak scenographer. Light rays are caught in a special aerosol spray of minute electrostatically charged oil-emulsion droplets capable of staying suspended in the air for a prolonged time. The hyperdense air catches the light and takes on a form of eerie solidity. A light column is the central portion of the design by Svoboda for *Tristan und Isolde.* (*c*) Curtain or walls of light for *Sicilian Vespers.* (Photos reprinted from *The Scenography of Josef Svoboda* by permission of the Wesleyan University Press. Copyright © 1971 by Jarka Burian.) (*d*) Projected scenery (page 472). A simple, direct use of projected images as a design form in a show curtain for *Anastasia* by Guy Bolton, a dye-painted translucent muslin curtain with projected photographs from the balcony front. Designer — John Ezell. (*e*) Projections on scenic forms (pages 472–473). A strong visual expression and change of atmosphere is effected by the rear projection of patterns onto translucent scenic forms. *A Day in the Death of Joe Egg* by Peter Nichols. Set Designer — Edward Gallagher; Lighting Designer — Steve Ross. (Photo — Schonlau.)

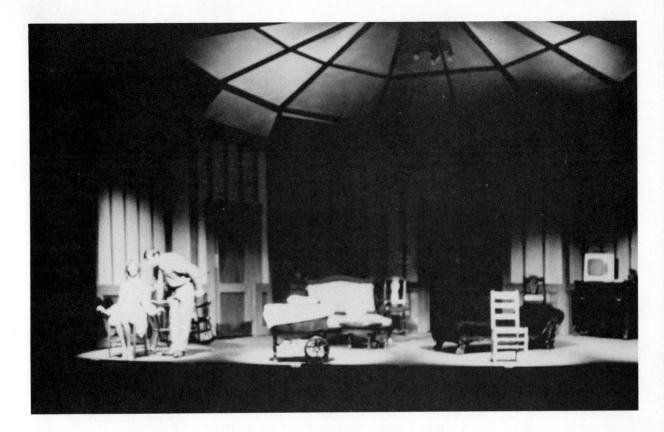

Projection Techniques.   Reduced to its simplest elements, the projection process consists of a *light source*, the object or *slide*, the projected object or *image*, and the projection surface most commonly known as the *screen* although it is possible to project the image onto almost any type of surface.

The image is projected by two different methods: *lens projection* or *shadow projection*. Though both images are *shadows* in essence, the term shadow projection is used to define all projections obtained without a lens.

The projection apparatus may be placed in front (downstage) of an opaque screen for a *front-projection*, or at the rear (upstage) of a translucent screen for a *rear-projection*. For a front-projection the source is normally hidden from view of the audience. It must also be placed so that it has to have a clear throw onto the screen. In a rear-projection arrangement the problem of hiding the source is solved, but, of course, backstage space still has to be kept clear of the throw to the screen (Figure 18–2).

Of the two methods of projection shadow projection is the easiest to achieve. Because the process depends upon direct emanation from the light source, without lens, the image is not as sharp or intense as a comparable lens projection.

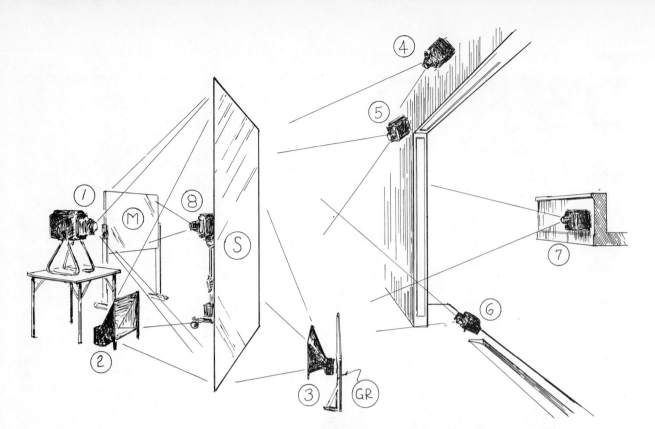

FIGURE 18-2. SCREEN AND PROJECTOR POSITIONS. The screen (S) is in the center of the stage. Rear projections. (1) Lens projector on platform to align with the center of the screen. (2) Linnebach projector on floor. Front projections. (3) Linnebach on floor masked by a groundrow. (4) Center teaser position. (5) High tormentor position. (6) Side apron position. (7) Balcony front. Rear projection under limited space conditions. (8) Lens projector angled upstage into a first surface mirror (M), which redirects the image onto the screen.

FIGURE 18–3. (*a*) The Linnebach Projector. (1) Slide holder. (2) Concentrated-filament T-shaped lamp. (*b*) Low-voltage, high-intensity Linnebach. A small, specially built shadow projector using a small source for a sharp projection. (1) Section view showing the position and adjustment of light socket. (2) General Electric Quartzline lamp, FCS 24 volts. The lamp, though miniature, is about 250 watts. It was designed for use in photographic studios. Adapted for use on the stage, it requires a variable transformer to reduce voltage.

The Linnebach Projector. The basic instrument for straight-line, shadow projection is the familiar device known as the *Linnebach Projector* (Figure 18–3a). It is a large, plain hood with a source of light—sometimes an arc but more often, today, a high-wattage incandescent lamp—at the center of a system of diverging sides. The outer edge of the hood has a slot for holding the slide.

The slide of the Linnebach projector or any variation of shadow projector can be a simple cardboard cut-out or painted glass. If the slide is kept parallel to the screen there is *no* distortion of the image on the screen. It is not always possible to place the instrument and the slide in this ideal relationship, hence the designer must be able to cope with *distortion*. Once the position of the instrument has been determined he can correct the distortion of the image by building in a counter distortion in the slide. Distortion on one plane is, of course, easier to correct than on two planes. Figure 18–4 diagrams the methods of correcting simple and complex distortions.

The Cinebach Projector.   Another variation of the Linnebach is the Cinebach projector, a homemade device that has proved extremely satisfactory for lighting the curved plaster cyclorama of a small stage. In its simplest form it is two D-shaped plywood panels, each about twenty inches wide, fastened about twenty-four inches apart to a plywood back piece. A sheet of acetate or of plastic color medium, clear or tinted, is tacked around the edges. On the bottom panel is a socket with a large-wattage lamp. Ventilation holes are drilled through both bottom and top panels, and frequently light baffles are built to shield these (see Figure 18–5).

Any sort of design may be painted on the plastic, just as on a conventional Linnebach slide. Because of the curved surface, this device is especially effective for lighting a curved surface and can be valuable even if no more than a plain blue wash is required for a sky. If the Cinebach (which gets its name from the use of Cinemoid as a slide material) is to be placed at the bottom of the curved cyclorama, the top panel may be built smaller than the bottom one to permit the light to spread upward more smoothly.

The Lens Projector.   The second and more complex type of instrument for projecting an image is the lens projector. The light source in a lens projector is concentrated on the slide surface by a condensing lens system. The illuminated slide is then transmitted into an image as it passes through the objective-lens system. The size of the image on the screen is determined by the beam-spread capacity of the objective-lens system. There are adjustments within the system of lens or lens train as it is called to bring the image of the slide into sharp focus. The determination of the size of the image and the focal length of the objective system is based upon the size of the slide and the distance the projector is from the screen (Figure 18–7). Figure 18–6 is an illustration of the lens projector "work horse" of the theatre, the *effect head*. It is an assemblage on the front of a plano-convex lens spotlight and consists of a condensing lens, slide holder, and

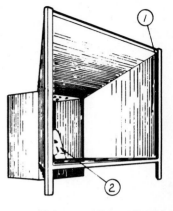

LINNEBACH   PROJECTOR

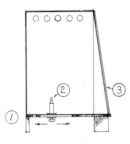

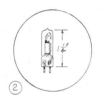

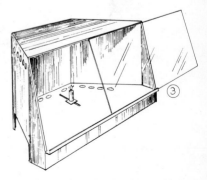

476 objective-lens system. The effect head is so named because it turns an ordinary working spotlight into a lighting instrument that produces effects beyond the spotlight's normal powers of illumination.

Moving Effects. There is an additional piece of apparatus that can be applied to the effect head assembly. A drumlike device with a motor drive known as an *effect machine* can be mounted on the spotlight at the slide position. It provides moving effects such as water ripples, flames, snowflakes, and the like. These are expensive and the results are rather too obvious for the tastes of today's audience.

FIGURE 18–4. CORRECTION OF DISTORTION. The Linnebach projector is tilted backward to project the image high on the screen. The plane of the slide is no longer parallel to the screen, resulting in a distortion of all vertical lines in the image. The diagram shows the method of countering the distortion with a corrected slide. (1) Keystoning or distortion of the rectangle. (2) Reference line established in slide view parallel to the plane of the slide. It is then located in the top view and vertical line plotted. (3) Corrected grid is constructed perpendicular to the plane of the slide and the verticals are plotted with information from the top view. The corrected slide is drawn into the new grid.

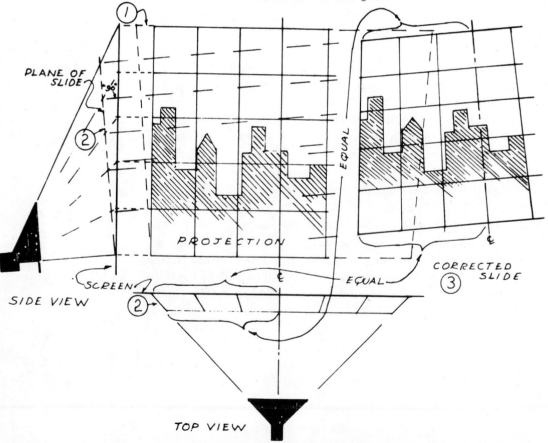

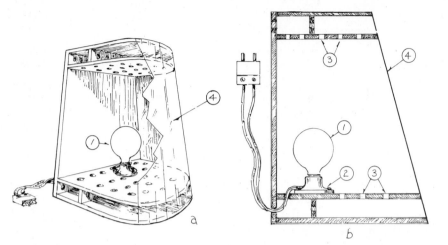

Gobos. One form of lens projection that does not require any special apparatus other than a common ellipsoidal-reflector spotlight was referred to in the previous chapter. This is the gobo, also known as a cookie, a circular sheet of highly heat-resistant material from which some shape, pattern, or design has been cut. When placed at the gate of an ellipsoidal spot, this pattern is projected by the lens (or lenses) onto any appropriate surface.

Commercial equipment houses sell gobos in a variety of designs; some are fairly realistic, but most are simply pleasant patterns. These are frequently used in television, where the background is rarely in sharp focus, to give interest to an otherwise plain drop or wall.

Patterns may be home designed and cut from heavy aluminum foil or the bottom of a cheap tin pie plate. Two especially useful effects are clouds, cut from foil, which may be wrinkled slightly to give out-of-focus soft edges, and stars, made by pricking tiny holes through a piece

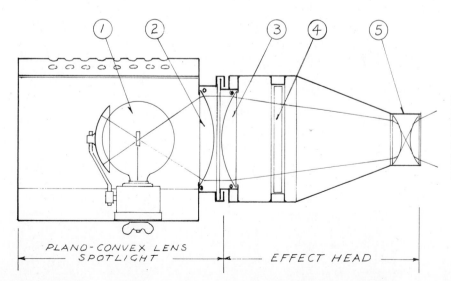

PLANO-CONVEX LENS
SPOTLIGHT

EFFECT HEAD

FIGURE 18–6. THE LENS
PROJECTOR. (1) G-shaped
lamp. (2) Plano-convex lens.
(3) Additional concentrating
lens (or "Dutchman"). (4) Slide.
(5) Objective-lens system.

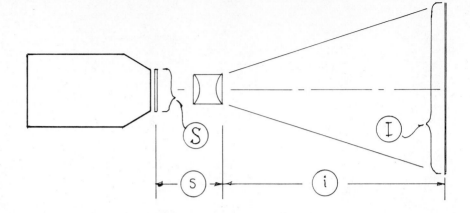

FIGURE 18–7. OBJECTIVE LENS TRAIN. (S) Slide dimension. (s) Distance between slide and objective lens system. (I) Image dimension. (i) Distance between image and objective lens system.

of tin, kept carefully flat to make all edges sharp. Both are projected in a white light against a blue drop or cyc.

Regrettably, neither color nor fine detail can be used at the present, as the only transparent material that will withstand the terrific heat at the gate of an ellipsoidal spot is a very expensive clear ceramic requiring special paints and a carefully controlled fixing process not available to the public.

MATHEMATICS OF PROJECTION

To eliminate the trial-and-error methods of selecting and placing the objective systems, the use of certain formulas should be understood. The first of these gives the size of the image at any distance. It is: $S/I = s/i$ when S = the size of the slide, I = the size of the image, s = the distance between the slide and the objective system, and i = the distance from the objective system to the image (Figure 18–7). It must be remembered that all these distances must be expressed in the same units, usually inches. If the horizontal dimension of the slide is used, the horizontal dimension of the image will be obtained, while if the vertical measurement of the image is needed, one must use the vertical measurement of the slide.

For example, let us assume that our slide is 3 inches wide, and we need an image of 15 feet across when our projector is to be placed 20 feet away from the screen. How far must the slide be from the lens? Using the formula we find that

$$\frac{3}{180} = \frac{s}{240}$$

(Note that all figures are expressed in inches). Therefore $s = 4$ inches, and the lens must be placed 4 inches from the slide.

THE OBJECTIVE-LENS TRAIN

The second formula gives us the focal length of the lens required to give the proper effect. It is:

$$\frac{1}{s} + \frac{1}{i} = \frac{1}{f}$$

when s and i have the same meanings as above and f = the focal length of the objective-lens train in inches. Continuing with the same problem as before, i is stated as 20 feet (or 240 inches) and we have found s to be 4 inches. Therefore:

$$\frac{1}{4} + \frac{1}{240} = \frac{1}{f} \text{ or } \frac{1}{f} = \frac{60 + 1}{240}.$$

Transposing, we find that $f = \dfrac{240}{61}$ or 3.934 inches, which is approximately 4 inches.

Now 4 inches is quite a short focal length for a lens, so we must try to achieve it by means of two lenses with longer focal lengths. Let us assume that we have two such, one of 6-inch focal length, the other of 8 inches. How can these be placed to make up a lens train of only 4-inch focal length?

Our third formula is as follows:

$$f = \frac{f_1 \times f_2}{f_1 + f_2 - d}.$$

As before, f is the focal length of the whole train, f_1 and f_2 are the focal lengths of the two lenses (which one is actually first and which is second has no significance), and d is the distance between these two. Now we can set up our formula as follows:

$$4 = \frac{6 \times 8}{6 + 8 - d} = \frac{48}{14 - d} \text{ or: } 1 = \frac{12}{14 - d} \text{ or: } 14 - d = 12.$$

Therefore, $d = 2$ inches, and the two lenses must be placed in their holder 2 inches apart.

Once these formulas are thoroughly understood, they can be utilized to solve any problem involving the assembly of an effect head. The objective-lens system for standard lens-projection equipment can be ordered from tables that compute the proper focal length for any given image size and distance from the screen arrangement.

LENS PROJECTION EQUIPMENT

Today's theatre is using a variety of very sophisticated lens-projector equipment. There is a wide selection in slide sizes at 35mm, $3'' \times 4''$, $5'' \times 5''$, $5'' \times 7''$, up to the continental size, $9'' \times 9''$; also provided are capacities from 500W quartz, 5KW tungsten, to the extremely brilliant xenon lamp. All instruments are equipped with automatic slide changing mechanisms (Figure 18–8).

The Overhead Projector.   The most unusual instrument in the lens-projector category is the overhead projector. Its rather large slide deck (about $12'' \times 12''$) is a translucent, horizontal surface with the light source underneath. The slide image, after passing through a vertically mounted objective-lens systems, is redirected by a 45-degree first-surface mirror onto the screen (Figure 18–9).

a

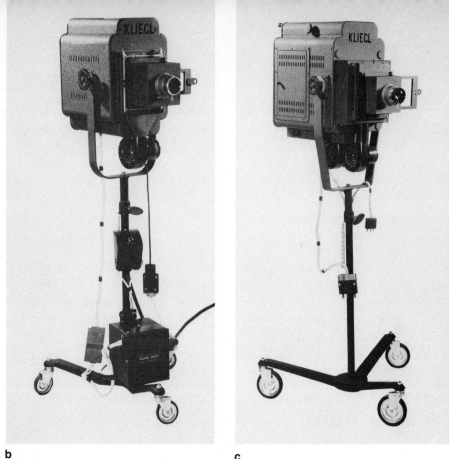

b

c

d

FIGURE 18–8. SLIDE PROJECTION EQUIPMENT. A few of the many slide and film projectors available for projected scenery. Separated into slide sizes and automatic slide-changing capabilities, they are: (*a*) Hi-Lite (Buhl Optical) 35mm carrousel changer, 1200 watts (incandescent or quartz). A dependable changer, small, good in remote positions. The same projector, a modified Kodak Carrousel, can be adapted to a Zenon package for a more brilliant source but less flexible dimming capabilities. (*b*) 2100-watt 3½-by-4″ slide projector. High-intensity, low-voltage light source (60 volts) Kliegl Bros. (*c*) 5000-watt 5-by-5″ slide projector. Excellent for rear projections: Kliegl Bros. (*d*) 5000-watt 7-by-7″ slide projector. Its one-for-one optics (one-foot coverage at a one-foot distance) makes it good for wide-coverage rear projections. The 7-by-7″ slide size is large enough to be hand painted if desired as well as adaptable to a conventional 5-by-7″ film size in Ektachrome color transparencies. (*e*) A 16mm 500-watt Baur film projector with an ECU-RP (Extreme Close Up Rear Projection) lens and a built-in mirror

e

f

g

h

system; lens — Buhl Optical. (f)
Film loop projector (moving projection) with speed control;
Kliegl Bros. Film Machine (moving projection). (g) Motor-driven
film loop mounts on 1000-watt
spotlight hood. Can be turned to
operate vertically or horizontally.
(h) View of film loop rollers.
Manufactured by Ryudensha
Co., Inc., Japan.

The advantages of the overhead projector, which was originally designed to animate or illustrate the classroom lecture, are twofold. (1) The large area of the slide permits handpainted slides, allowing the photographic process to be omitted, thereby saving time and money. (2) The horizontal position of the slide deck provides the opportunity to bring movement to the image. On-the-spot animation is possible by such actions as moving transparent film across the slide deck, agitating with an air jet a shallow transparent dish of colored dyes in oil or water, blowing smoke across the deck. The movement of smoke across the deck can appear on the screen as a descending fog, rising smoke from a fire, the engulfing black cloud of an approaching storm.

The overhead projector is not quite as efficient as a regular lens-projector, but because of its wide-angle objective system it can work close to the screen. It functions best with short throw, small-image projections.

As can be seen, the overhead projector requires an operator and therefore cannot be used in a remote position. It is ideal for rear-projections, although it has been used for front-projections from an extreme offstage side position.

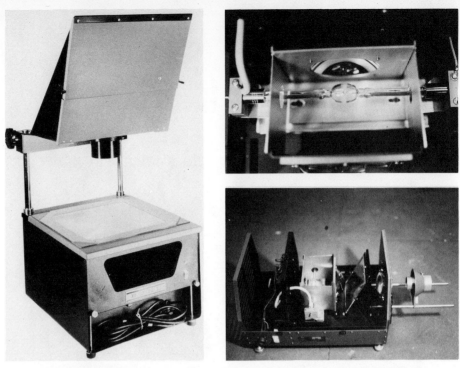

FIGURE 18–9. OVERHEAD PROJECTOR. Wide-angle overhead projector with a 10-by-10" transparent slide deck. The objective lens system can be operated vertically, as shown, or swung into a horizontal position. The hinged shutters at the top protect the mirror, which is at a 45-degree angle to the slide surface. (Buhl Optical)

FIGURE 18–10. SHORT-ARC LAMP SLIDE PROJECTOR. The Metro-lite ME 100 produces a sharp, high-intensity image. Right above, HMI 2500-watt lamp. Below, projector with top removed showing position of lamp, color filter, slide holder, condensing lens and objective system. George Snell Associates.

The Opaque Projector. There is another lens-projector that has not been mentioned, the opaque projector. The slide, which is *opaque*, is reflected by mirrors into the objective-lens system and projected onto the screen. As the slide is not transparent the image is not as bright. Because of the inefficiency of the instrument it is not very practical for stage use. Its chief use in the theatre is to facilitate the cartooning and painting of scenery. If a drawing bearing a grid of scaled squares is projected to match over a corresponding full-scale grid of a scenic element or drop, it can serve as a quick guide for drawing an enlargement of the original painting.

The Television Projector. The television projector is, at the moment, a very complex and highly specialized piece of equipment that is capable of projecting a live televised image. It has been used as a dramatic extension of action on stage or of a scene occurring just offstage. Intimate business or emotions expressed by live actors can be supported by simultaneously enlarged television projection elsewhere on the stage.

THE SCREEN

Aside from the increased efficiency of projection equipment, the innovative exploitation of the screen or projection surface is perhaps the greatest contribution to the imaginative use of light as scenery. Projected scenery has graduated in a very short time from the large single screen background, to multiscreen compositions, and to an infinite variety of sizes, shapes, and three-dimensional forms.

Under conditions where time and money are no obstacle the possibilities of the highly dramatic and imaginative use of projection is unlimited. The leader and prime innovator in the development of

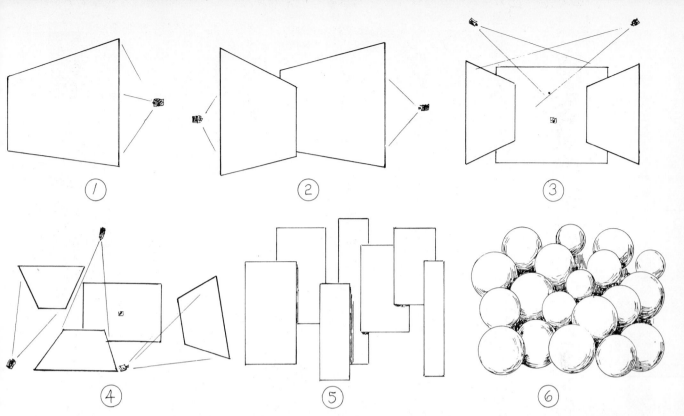

light as scenery is without a doubt the Czechoslovakian scenographer, Josef Svoboda. His inventive and artistic genius has unlocked traditional scenery and lighting practices and opened the doors to a less restricted attitude toward scene design and lighting.

Figure 18–11 illustrates a few of the many screen arrangements and projector positions. They range from a single rear-projection screen, a mixture of both rear- and front-projection screens, multishapes and sizes to three-dimensional front-projection surfaces.

FRONT PROJECTION VERSUS REAR PROJECTION

The single screen, rear-projection technique has been used as background for dramatic productions for some time. The original location of the projector and screen was governed by the need of having an operator, as well as the reluctance to stop thinking of the screen as a painted drop. An RP screen is translucent enough to diffuse the bright spot of the projector's source, yet transparent enough to transmit the image. A professionally made RP screen is constructed with the greatest density in the center to offset the hotspot of the projector source. Because of the general high density of an RP screen a lot of light is stopped and consequently a rear projection requires a higher intensity to equal a similar projection from the front.

FIGURE 18–11. PROJECTION SCREEN ARRANGEMENTS. Left: Rear projections. (1) Single screen. (2) Double RP screen arrangement. (3) Two front-projection screens right and left, with RP screen in center. (4) Multiscreen arrangement. (5) Three-dimensional surface made up of flat planes designed for a single projection. (6) A projection surface of balloons or Styrofoam spheres. Below: (1) Sculptural surface planned for many angles of projection. (2) Slanted surfaces. The downstage screen is scrim, providing the possibility of front, rear, and see-through projections.

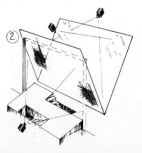

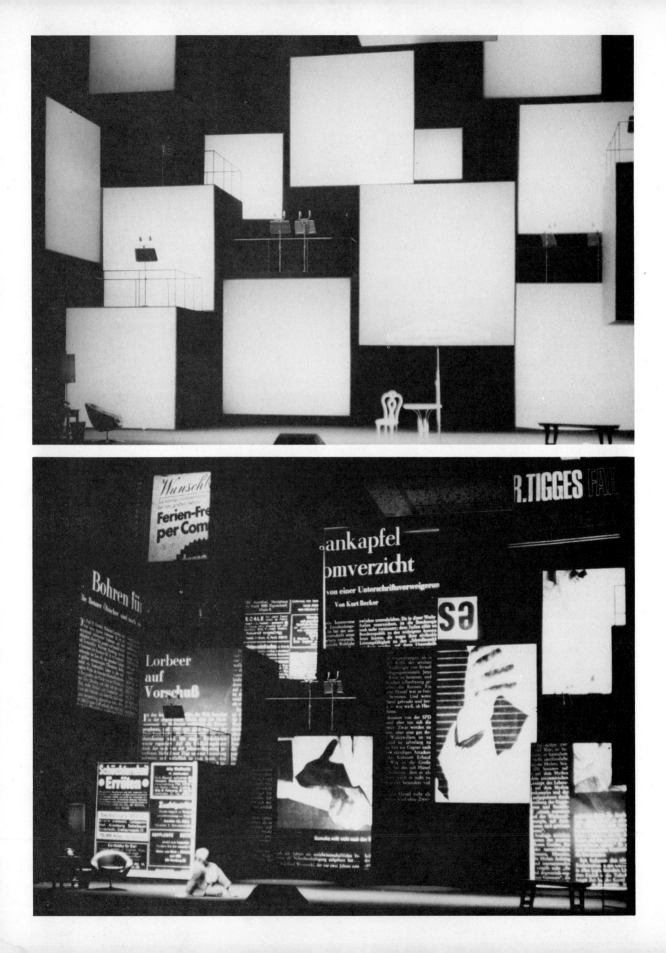

Another feature that may relate to the traditional frontal position of the RP screen is the rather noticeable fall-off of intensity as the spectator moves to an extreme right or left position. Beyond an angle of about 45 degrees the screen appears to go blank. This is especially apparent if two projectors are being matched on a single screen. They never seem to balance in intensity except in the center of the house. A front projection to the same screen position maintains its intensity through a much flatter angle of vision. The image, however, is distorted or foreshortened when viewed from an extreme angle, as would be expected.

Front projections have become more popular and practical for two reasons: the first, which has been mentioned frequently, is the change in attitude from thinking of projections as a substitute for painted scenery; and second, the great improvement in the efficiency and reliability of remote-control projection equipment.

On equal-intensity, distance, and size-of-image bases the front projection is brighter than a corresponding rear projection. To put it another way, it takes less wattage to project the same image from the front than from the rear.

Front projection does have the disadvantage of having to throw from a more extreme angle than does a rear projection because of the necessity of hiding the instrument from the view of the audience. The frequently remote position of front-projection equipment often requires the use of automatic changing devices unless a bridge or platform can be rigged for an operator.

The extreme angle of a front projection also causes distortion problems. They are not insurmountable but do necessitate extra drawing for the scene designer. If the side is to be a photographed transparency the designer has to make two designs. The first is the projection as it is to appear free of distortion, and the second shows the built-in counter distortion that is to be photographed and processed into a color transparency for the slide. If the slide is not too small or too detailed it can be painted directly on the slide-glass using the same counter- distortion control. The correction process for one-plane distortion is diagramed in Figure 18–13. The corrected grid on the slide should, however, always be checked under actual conditions before painting or photographing any quantity of slides.

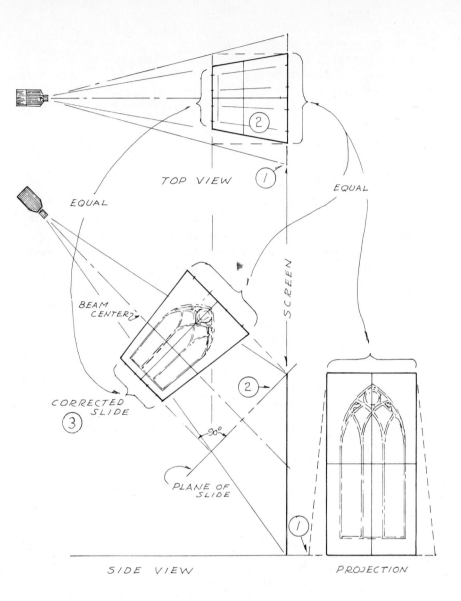

FIGURE 18–13. DISTORTION CORRECTION FOR A LENS PROJECTION. The projection position is perpendicular to the screen in top view but angled in the side view, resulting in a keystone distortion (1) of the image. Reference line (2) is constructed parallel to the plane of the slide. The counterdistortion is plotted in the top view of the slide plane (2). The corrected slide (3) is drawn perpendicular to the reference plane with information from the top view.

To demonstrate distortion-correction solutions for projections involving two-plane distortion a small, mixed-media production of Elmer Rice's *The Adding Machine* is shown in Figure 18–14. Depicted are the steps taken to make the slides for a pair of sharply angled front-projection machines. The expressionistic style of the play accepted the strong visual statement of the projections as an extension of the actor. Larger productions, more screens, or different angles of projections would follow the same approach for distortion solutions.

It should be mentioned that not all distortions need to be corrected. There are times when the distortions of an angled projection are accepted as part of the design, especially if the slide is abstract or nonobjective in style.

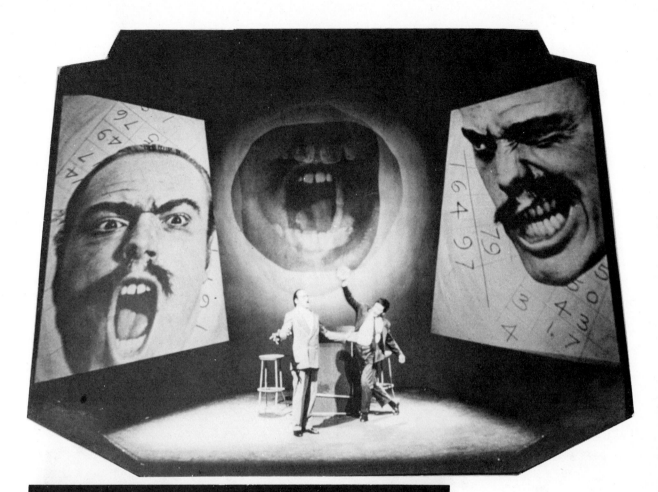

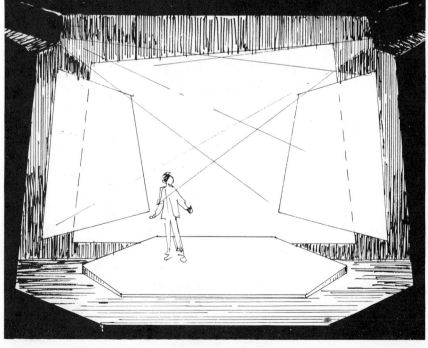

FIGURE 18–14. PROJECTED SCENERY. To illustrate the planning and execution of projected scenery, an all-projection production of Elmer Rice's expressionistic play *The Adding Machine* is illustrated in detail on this and the three following pages. Above: The pulsating images on the screen heighten the action in the scene. Below: Sketch of the screen arrangement. Three screens were used, two small downstage front-projection screens backed by a large rear-projection screen.

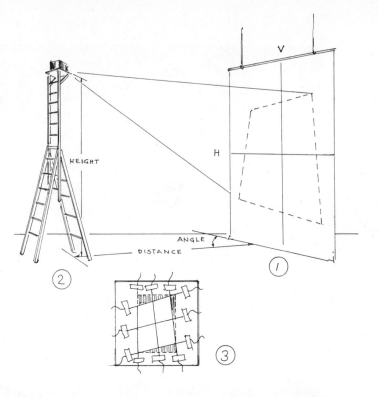

FIGURE 18–14. (cont.). Right: Sketch showing the method used to figure the counter-distortion of the front-projection slides caused by the steep angle of projection. (1) A temporary screen was hung at the site of the finished screen. The shape of the planned screen was drawn on the temporary surface with established horizontal (H) and vertical (V) center lines. (2) The right projector position at the

top of the ladder duplicated the distance, height, and angle of the final mounting position in the upper stage right of the portal. (3) Taped threads on a clear 35mm slide were moved by trial and error until the projection of the threads matched the outline and cross lines on the screen. The projector was tilted slightly to bring one projected edge of the slide into alignment with the upstage edge of the screen.

FIGURE 18–15. A special projector was developed for the multimedia product of *The Adding Machine*. A conventional Kodak Carrousel projector was rebuilt to take a 1200-watt projector lamp. The projector shown became the prototype for the Hi-Lite Projector manufactured by Buhl Optical (see Figure 18–8). The original model was developed by Douglas Pope with the cooperation of Buhl Optical.

PROJECTIONS AND THE ACTOR

The lighting of the actor in relation to a projected background is very tricky and varies with the direction of the projection, front or rear. A rear projection, for example, suffers from reflected light on the front of the screen which tends to wash out the intensity of colors and design in the image. Care must be taken to choose angles to light the actor that will not reflect off the floor onto the screen (Figure 18–16).

Besides the control of distribution, bounce light can be minimized in other ways: (1) The reflective quality of the floor can be deadened

FIGURE 18–16. PROJECTIONS AND THE ACTOR.   The effective use of large-scale projections as a background requires special lighting techniques. To avoid undue spill of reflected light onto the screen, the acting-area lights are kept at a steep angle along with the obvious use of back and cross lighting to throw the actors' shadows away from the screen. Left: Diagram of a rear-projection setup. (1) RP machine. (2) RP screen. (3) Black scrim drop hung in front of screen to absorb reflected light from the front. (4) Groundrow or screen frame to kill light reflected from the floor. (5) Unlit area, called *neutral zone,* about three or four feet in front of screen. (6) Back light on actor to help define him against a projected background. Note high hat or funnel on the front of the spotlight to prevent a flare of light onto the screen. (7) Sharply angled upstage-area spotlights to keep light and shadows off screen. (8) Front-area ceiling spotlight. The normal angle is usually good. (9) Center teaser position for front projection. Right: Front-projection setup. The lighting of the actor remains the same. The black scrim is removed to allow projections from the teaser position. Note the angle of front projection. It is planned to miss actors at the edge of the neutral zone.

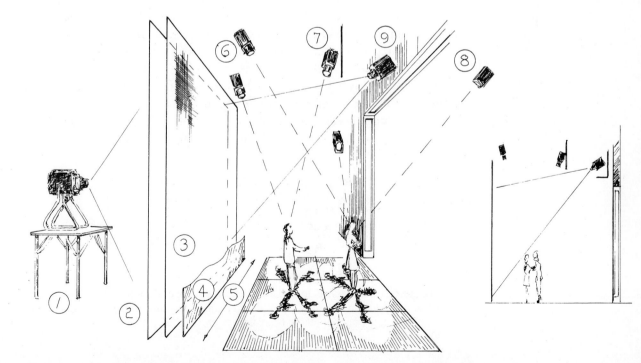

492

with a cover of black or dark gray felt or carpeting. (2) Reflected light can be kept off the screen by hanging a seamless black scrim about a foot in front. It serves to absorb the reflected light, but does not affect the quality of the image.

The reflected light problem can also be helped by the design and position of the screen or the image on the screen. If, for example, the screen or the image on the screen begins about four feet or more above the floor it is less likely to suffer from bounce light. This elevation coupled with the directing technique of keeping actors away from the screen by maintaining a so-called *neutral zone* of about four feet makes it easier to light the actor and not lose the intensity of the projection.

Back lighting and side lighting are especially helpful in separating the actor from a projected background. Otherwise, it is difficult to compositionally balance the intensity of the background and the area lights without one or the other becoming dull.

A front projection is less affected by bounce light. Nevertheless, the same precautions should be taken to avoid unnecessary spill from area lights onto the screen. Maintaining a neutral zone also helps because the projection throw is usually over the actor's head and his distance from the screen will reduce the chance of his shadow falling onto the projection.

The use of front projections allows greater creativity in the design of the screen. It can be three-dimensional; pierced, to permit action behind or through the screen; and, in a more practical vein, the screen position can be further upstage, thereby giving more space to the actor and providing an occasional scenic element.

Front projections can also frankly involve the actor as a projection surface or use the shadow that he casts as a part of the image. The imaginative mixture of light, projections, and performers is so successfully executed by Alwin T. Nikolais and his dancers that their performances become a stimulating experience in the theatrical form of sight and sound, as well as epitomizing light as scenery.

FIGURE 18–17. PROJECTIONS AND THE ACTOR.   (Facing page, top) A dancer or mime working with a large-scale projection. Note the strong focus of light that helps separate the central performers from the projection. *Tent,* a production of the Nikolais Dance Theatre. (Photo — Byron Manley.)

FIGURE 18–18. PROJECTIONS ON THE ACTOR.   The abstract form of the dance adapts easily to the unconventional use of projections on the actor or performer, thereby heightening theatricality and visual impact. *Scenario,* a production of the Nikolais Dance Theater. (Photo — Oleaga.)

Intensity 19 Control

Control of the intensity of stage-lighting instruments—commonly referred to as "dimming"—has two aspects. The more obvious one is the changing of lights in view of the audience, such as for a shift of emphasis or to mark a difference in time or simply to darken the stage at the end of a scene. The second—and equally important—aspect is the setting of the instruments at various intensities to achieve a precise effect in the complete stage picture, such as subduing the cooler colors to give an impression of a sunny warmth or adding more blue on the backdrop to paint a sky a richer hue, or bringing up the lights on one portion of the stage to center attention on action taking place there. It is understood, of course, that dimming includes making lights brighter as well as darkening them.

ARCHAIC FORMS OF DIMMING

The history of dimming is a long one. On seventeenth-century stages cans on cords were lowered over the candles to vary the light; and in the eighteenth century candles in the wings were frequently mounted on vertical boards that could be revolved to turn the light

494

away from the stage or back toward it. In the nineteenth century the gas table—a complex of pipes and valves—adjusted the flow of gas to the various jets about the stage and provided quite a complete control over intensities.

With the advent of the incandescent lamp, crude forms of dimming control were introduced almost from the start. These all utilized the principle of placing in series with the lamp some sort of resistance that could be varied at will. The carbonpile and salt-water dimmers were among these. But the most popular of all and one that lingers on even today is the resistance-wire dimmer, often called a rheostat. That this method of control is still in common use in the commercial theatre is more a comment on Broadway production methods than any indication that this archaic device retains any real merit. The fact that the resistance dimmer operates on both dc and ac is no valid excuse in the majority of modern situations. But because the resistance dimmer is still in some theatres the only form of intensity control available, it is necessary for us to give it attention.

PRINCIPLES OF THE RESISTANCE DIMMER

We discussed in Chapter 13 Ohm's law, expressed by the formula $I = E/R$. Therefore, the greater the value given R, the less value will I have. Or, we might state it: by increasing the resistance in a circuit, we decrease the current flow. Thus, if there is also an incandescent lamp in the same circuit, it will be deprived of current as the resistance is increased, and the brightness of the lamp will vary as the current is varied.

In order to dim an incandescent lamp evenly from full up to full out, a resistance of approximately five times the resistance of the lamp itself must be introduced into the circuit in series with it. The dimmer therefore provides a length of wire long enough to furnish a resistance five times as great as that of the lamp it is designed to control. By moving a shoe over taps spaced along this wire the amount of current available to feed the lamp is varied from the full supply of the house down to an amount insufficient to cause the filament to glow. The electrical energy that has been consumed by the wire is dissipated as heat.

TYPES OF RESISTANCE DIMMERS

The resistance dimmer is found in two standard forms. The less complex of these contains two coils of resistance wire placed parallel to each other and a short distance apart. The circuit enters at the top end of one coil and leaves at the top end of the other. A con-

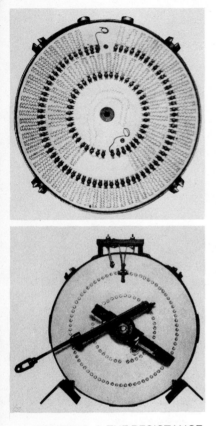

FIGURE 19–1. THE RESISTANCE DIMMER. (a) shows the plate of a two-wire, rotary resistance dimmer before the second coat of vitreous enamel has been applied over the concentric patterns of wire. (b) is the same plate with the vitreous enamel covering the resistance wires. The arm coming in from the left is operated by the handle on the face of the dimmer board. Here it is geared to the rotary sweep which makes contact at both ends with the protruding studs. (Photo—Ward Leonard)

ducting shoe slides up and down between the two coils making contact with each. When this shoe is at the top it bridges the gap in the circuit without introducing any resistance whatever. But when it has been moved to the bottom the full lengths of both coils have become part of the circuit. This so-called slider dimmer is quite simple in its operation but is so difficult to maneuver smoothly that the light tends to jump when its intensity is being changed. Further, it is impossible for one operator to manipulate more than two of these contraptions simultaneously.

The other form of resistance dimmer has its wire in the shape of a multi-pointed star, or as two stars, one within the other. The wire is fastened to a circular vitreous plate and is sometimes baked into it with only taps showing at the surface. The shoe is on the end of a pivoted sweep (when two coils are involved there is a shoe at each end of the sweep) and the sweep is moved by means of a projecting handle. Various refinements can be supplied with this type of rotary dimmer, such as a cutoff switch at the low end, provision for interlocking all the handles in a bank of them, and the like.

DISADVANTAGES OF THE RESISTANCE DIMMER

Because the resistance dimmer consumes full current as soon as it is switched on—whether the lamp burns full up or otherwise—it is extremely wasteful of electric power. And the heat generated by the coils can be quite overwhelming unless adequate ventilation is provided, a rare condition on most stages. But these are less important from the artistic point of view than the problem of fixed capacity. As we have stated, the length of wire in each dimmer is determined by the exact wattage of the lamp it is expected to control. If a lamp of a smaller wattage is used instead, the dimmer will not put it out completely, and what dimming it does accomplish will be at a different rate from those lamps of proper size on adjacent dimmers. This must be corrected by the expedient of connecting, in parallel with the stage light, a second lamp or "ghost load" hidden offstage and of sufficient wattage to make the total load on the dimmer approximate what it was designed to control.

DUAL-CAPACITY RESISTANCE DIMMERS

In an effort to offset the necessity of excessive ghost-loading, there has been developed a dual-capacity resistance dimmer, which really deserves a more accurate name since it effectively dims out lamps of any capacity between certain minimum and maximum wattages. In the commercial theatre these limits are usually 1500 to 3000 watts. The principle is that the resistance wire of the dimmer is long enough to offer sufficient resistance to dim out a 1500-watt lamp, which is twice the length needed to take out one of 3000 watts.

At first glance this might seem to be reversal of what one should expect, but by combining the two formulas given in **Chapter 13,** we see that:

$$\text{if } I = \frac{E}{R} \text{ and } P = I \times E$$
$$\text{then } R = \frac{E^2}{P}$$

Now we will assume that the electric service to the theatre is 110 volts dc, this being the most usual along Broadway where this type of dimmer is principally used.

Therefore:

$$R = \frac{110 \times 110}{P}$$

So the resistance offered by a 1500-watt lamp is 8.07 ohms, while that offered by a 3000-watt lamp is 4.03 ohms. Therefore if a wire is long enough to offer 5 times 8.07 ohms to take out a 1500-watt lamp, half the length will offer 5 times 4.03 ohms and will take out a 3000-watt load.

But at best, the resistance dimmer is an inefficient, uncomfortable, and not very flexible device.

THE AUTOTRANSFORMER DIMMER

Many complaints about resistance control are answered by the autotransformer dimmer. This device consists of an induction coil wound around an iron core (to increase its efficiency). The single coil serves as both primary and secondary induction circuits. As alternating current passes through the full length of the coil, it produces a magnetic flux through the iron core, and in turn this flux induces a reverse electromotive force which tends to counteract the voltage applied at the opposite end. The result is that the voltage varies within the coil from point to point, being a full 120 volts at one end and 0 volts at the other.

By means of a sliding contact shoe moving over the bared turns of the coil, the exact voltage required is drawn off. Because this tapped-off voltage does not depend on the relationship between the coil and the lamp, it will be the same regardless of what load is placed on it. Thus any lamp from the smallest to the highest allowable can be dimmed smoothly and effectively between full out and full up.

Because the only current drawn is that actually used by the load, the autotransformer is not wasteful of power nor does it create any

FIGURE 19–2. AUTOTRANS-FORMER DIMMERS. (*a*) A 1000-watt capacity rotary autotransformer dimmer. At the top is the handle which revolves the contact within the coil below. Note the provision for two-, three-, or four-wire service and two- or three-wire output. (*b*) A large capacity dimmer built in this shape to save space in a switchboard and to provide handle control and interlock possibility. (Photo —Superior Electric)

498

appreciable amount of heat. It is a heavy device however, and it will operate only on ac—though this should be a problem today in only a few locations. Autotransformers are built in two styles. One of these has a knob control and therefore is not suitable for stage use, as the most skillful operator can handle but two at the same time and it is doubtful if even then he can bring them smoothly and correctly to exact readings. The more useful kind is somewhat akin to the rotary resistance dimmer in that it can be mounted with others in a bank and has a protruding handle that makes manipulation simple, and this handle can be interlocked with those of its neighbors.

SWITCHBOARDS FOR RESISTANCE AND AUTOTRANSFORMER DIMMER CONTROL

Because the smallest stage should have provision to control individually no fewer than twenty different stage circuits—and for any quality of production far more are needed—it is pointless to think of dimmers except in relation to complete controlboards. In general design there is little difference between a switchboard utilizing resistance dimmers and one with autotransformers.

Any such board should logically be arranged so that banks of dimmer handles can be manipulated with ease by a minimum number of operators. All elements that pertain to any one circuit—dimmer handles, switches, pilot lights, fuses or circuit breakers, and if possible the stage-load plugs—should be placed in a logical association with one another. Mastering handles, master switches, and the like should be in one central location. All elements should be clearly identified. Running lights (lights by which the operators can see to manipulate the board) must be provided. Ideally, these should have a choice of brightnesses: high for usual operating conditions and a dim glow for use during stage blackouts. Clips to hold cue sheets, scripts, and notes in plain and easy view are a necessity often overlooked. And, most important, the board should be placed so that a clear, unobstructed view of the stage is provided at all times. Obviously, it should have all proper safety devices and precautions, physical as well as electrical.

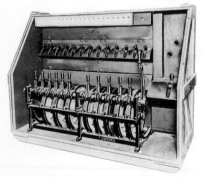

FIGURE 19–3. A RESISTANCE BOARD.   Here is an example of an early switchboard, built into a box for travel. At the right end of the row of dimmer handles is the long interlock handle and beyond it the master switch, above which can be seen holes for a three-wire service. An idle hour may be whiled pleasantly away conjecturing just how one reconciles what seem to be eight dimmer plates, eleven dimmer handles, thirteen circuit switches, and twenty-one receptacles for stage-cable plugs. Perhaps a glance at the fuse panel behind the hinged flaps would be enlightening. (Photo— Century -Strand.

FIGURE 19–4. A COMBINATION AUTOTRANSFORMER BOARD AND CROSS-CONNECT PANEL. At the left of this modern board are the master switch (white handle) and fourteen dimmer handles, with pilot lights behind them. At the right end of the dimmer handles is the master interlock handle. On the vertical face are the off-on switches for the fourteen dimmable circuits and circuit breakers for these and for the three non-dim circuits. Also houselight controls, emergency lights, etc., and the board master switch with lock. At the right end is a small cross-connect panel with forty plugs for stage circuits and seventeen groups of jacks for the dimmer circuits, plus non-dim circuits A, B, and C. Note the multiple jacks which allow four stage circuits to be ganged on a single dimmer. (Photo—Century-Strand.

STAGE CIRCUITS

One aspect that is frequently overlooked in controlboard consideration is just how many stage circuits are to be connected through it. The days when each dimmer was inflexibly wired to a certain instrument are happily gone. Present thinking demands that about the stage there be located at appropriate spots and in appropriate numbers outlets to any one of which any instrument in stock may be connected. Much as the wall outlet in a kitchen may serve at different times the percolator, the toaster, the electric iron, the fan, and even the hair curler, so an outlet in the stage floor may at different times be used for a backing flood, a fireplace effect, a special side-lighting spotlight, or one color circuit in a striplight.

CROSS-CONNECTING SYSTEMS

Now in order to make possible the connection of any stage outlet to any dimmer or indeed to place several stage loads under the control of a single dimmer of suitable capacity, flexible systems, variously referred to as interconnecting, cross-connecting, or patching, have been devised. These operate in any number of ways: by rotary switches, by push-button tables, by crossing grids of busses with contacts provided by movable clips. Each one has its own advantages and many refinements, and which should be employed in any particular case must be a matter of a study of the specific situation, the number of dimmer circuits and of load circuits, the probable amount of use, and particularly the experience and *competence* of the probable users.

Possibly the simplest and most common form of cross-connecting panel today is the type that has all the stage load circuits terminating in plugs at the end of retractable cables (Figure 19–5). The dimmer circuits end in jacks mounted in the panel. Any plug may be pushed into any jack; therefore any instrument may be under the control of any dimmer. Usually there are several jacks for each dimmer circuit, thus providing a simple way to gang several instruments on the same control if desired. It must always be remembered that the "plug" goes into the "jack." Confusion of these two terms is all too common.

MECHANICAL MASTERING

Because simultaneous intensity control is frequently required over several if not all stage circuits, various provisions may be incorporated into a properly designed controlboard to make this possible. The simplest and most obvious of these is interlocking. A number of dimmers mounted side by side may have their handles locked to a shaft that runs the length of the dimmer bank. This is usually done by twisting the end of the handle and thus releasing a spring-loaded plunger which drops into a spline, or groove, cut into the shaft. By means of a long master handle (for leverage), the shaft is turned and all dimmers locked to it will simultaneously turn to the same reading. When a handle is twisted in the opposite direction, the plunger is withdrawn from the spline and the dimmer may be worked independently of the others (Figures 19–3 and 19–4).

The drawback is obvious. If we want one dimmer to stop at a reading different from the others, it will take some fast and dexterous work on the part of the operator to disengage the proper handle at the proper place. If several dimmers must be dropped off at different readings during a fairly rapid dim, the whole process becomes impossible. Further, those that are dropped off correctly will have reached their desired readings while the other lights are part way to theirs.

Of course, the same thing happens in reverse when dimmers are set at different readings and the attempt is made to use the interlocking mechanism to take them to "out" simultaneously. Those dimmers that are set at the higher readings will start down first, and their lights will be part way out before dimmers set at lower readings are picked up by the revolving shaft. Interlocking, while better than no master control whatever, is an awkward, inartistic makeshift.

ELECTRICAL MASTERING

In order to get truly proportional dimming, a master dimmer of large capacity may be employed to control a number of smaller ones and their respective loads. Obviously such a master must have a capacity equal to the total capacities of the lesser dimmers combined, a limiting factor indeed. And of course, if these are resistance dimmers, all including the master must be loaded to full capacities for proper performance.

Obviously, the large-capacity dimmer is tied up to the single task of being a master, even at times when it would be more useful as an independent dimmer with its own stage load. To meet this situation various systems of wiring and switching have been devised to permit the large dimmer to serve either as a master or otherwise as the particular situation warrants.

It should be pointed out that a large-capacity autotransformer dimmer may be used to master several resistance dimmers, or a big resistance dimmer may control a group of autotransformer dimmers.

In many small theatres a transfer switch is associated with a large-capacity dimmer, such as a master, to enable it to be used to control the houselights. With the switch thrown one way, the dimmer can take out the house. Then the switch is thrown the other way, and the same dimmer brings up some of the stage lights. At the end of the act the process is reversed.

AUTOTRANSFORMER PACKAGE BOARDS

A "package board" is a compact unit containing several dimmers—a sort of miniature switchboard that may be transported without too great difficulty. For many years, only the autotransformer dimmer was used in such a unit, but today electronic packages are available and will be discussed later in this chapter.

A typical autotransformer package board offers several control circuits, often with provisions for mastering and interlocking. Switches, fuses, or circuit breakers, and some type of flexible plugging are incorporated. The whole is advertised as being readily movable, but it takes four husky lads to handle the larger sizes.

FIGURE 19–5. AUTOTRANSFORMER PACKAGE BOARDS. (a) At right is a package containing six 1300-watt autotransformer dimmers and one of 6000-watt capacity. By means of the white switches one or more of the small dimmers may be put under control of the large one, thus providing proportional dimming for up to a total of 6000 watts. Or the large dimmer may operate independently with its own big load and each small dimmer with its lesser one. Note the different color for each handle for easy identification, and the circuit breaker adjacent to each. (b) Below is a package with six 2500-watt autotransformer dimmers and an interlock handle to which several or all the others may be connected. Proportional dimming is not provided. This model is available with three, four, five, or six dimmers. The interlock handle is optional, but even without it several handles may still be locked to the shaft and the handle of any one of them used as the master. In both models the plugging is on the rear face. (Photo—Superior Electric)

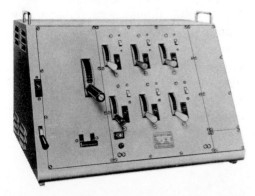

One of these devices is hardly adequate for even the smallest of stages and a minimum of artistic effort; two might be considered a minimum. But when more than two are employed, one might better invest his money in a conventional and permanent board.

One situation in which the package board does have merit is that found in many schools where plays are performed in a number of different locations. And in some places the drama group is requested, and expected, to provide lights for a dozen extraneous occasions: the dance in the gymnasium, the swimming extravaganza, the concert under the stars. Here a package board may be very useful, and when not on its social travels, it can earn its keep as a small auxiliary to the regular stage control system.

ELECTRONIC CONTROL

But the ultimate in intensity control will not be found in such devices, ingenious as some of them may be. Far more advanced apparatus is on the market today and installed in many places, here and abroad. These various forms of control fall under the general heading of electronic, but there are several ways in which the problem has been attacked. The names applied to different makes and types, some scientific, some proprietary, are very confusing, yet all electronic dimming systems have certain elements in common, as illustrated in the block diagram of Figure 19–6.

This diagram illustrates the flow of electric current through the entirety of any electronic dimming system. Starting at the top we see the entrance of 120-volt a-c service into the system. Its path immediately splits and to the left we see the 120 volts boosted to a higher figure. This is not necessary in certain systems and hence is shown in broken lines. Whether boosted or not, the current continues through a panel of circuit breakers that are inserted here to protect the system against any sudden overvoltage surge in the line supply. After passing through this protection, the current goes on to the dimming devices of whatever type they may be.

Returning to the split in the path of the entrance current, we see to the right the flow into a step-down transformer, for the heart of all electronic systems is low-voltage control. This transformer may reduce the emf to as low as eleven volts, though something in the twenties is far more common in most systems. The resulting low voltage now enters the control system proper through a master (or in some systems several masters and submasters) and then flows to the individual controllers which are, in a way, miniaturized dimmers. The complex of masters and controllers is usually called the manual. After being modified still further by these tiny devices, the low-voltage cur-

FIGURE 19–6. BLOCK DIAGRAM SCHEMATIC OF ANY ELECTRONIC INTENSITY CONTROL SYSTEM.

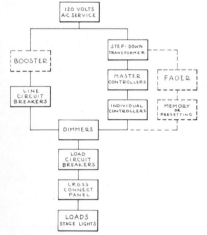

rent goes to the dimmers where it modifies in turn the higher voltages that have come down the left branch of our diagram.

The voltage that leaves each dimmer, whether reduced or not, is that which is wanted for the lamp. The current flows through the load breakers, placed here to protect the system against overloads or short circuits, and through the cross-connect panel where it is directed to whatever lamp has been selected, which will burn at the intensity set for it by the controllers. It may be noted that a few installations omit the cross connect panel and have dimmer and load permanently connected, with a resultant loss in flexibility.

On the extreme right is shown the memory system, in broken lines, because some systems do not have this important adjunct. This is where additional readings, for future scenes, are stored to be called on at the proper cue. Some systems eliminate the individual controllers and make all changes within the memory system, giving this a dual purpose. Others provide switching that can cut the control back and forth between the controllers and the memory as desired.

THE AIMS OF ELECTRONIC CONTROL

Before taking a look at the various types of apparatus, let us consider briefly what are the advantages of electronic control over the older systems. It must be emphasized that the object of electronic devices is not mere gadgetry, and certainly not complexity for the glorification of the technician. Rather the purpose is to free the artist from the tyranny of the crude mechanisms with which he has formerly worked. Under the older methods a simple shift of emphasis in the stage lights required the designer to instruct (either directly or through a boss electrician) several operators, who probably could not even see the results, in what he expected them to do, and coach them repeatedly and carefully in the timing he wanted them to follow. Then, if he saw exactly what he desired executed correctly once out of five times, he could consider himself fortunate.

With the low-voltage miniaturized control systems provided by electronics it becomes easy to master all the stage lighting, or any portion of it. Likewise it becomes practical to set up readings for future changes, which can be brought into effect on cue as wanted and at whatever rate of speed is desired. The nature of the dimming devices themselves is such that they are multicapacity: that is, each dimmer will successfully control any lamp load from the top capacity of the dimmer down to the smallest load desired (this does not apply to a few of the very largest-capacity dimmers, but these would certainly be put to other uses in a practical situation without the need of a ghost load. And because the current is low in both amperes and volts,

504   and the controls are miniature, the control panel is compact and may
be located anywhere in the theatre that is practical, rather than being
pushed into a corner backstage. This allows the operator to follow the
action on stage with ease and to make his changes with accuracy.

TYPES OF ELECTRONIC CONTROL

As shown in the block diagram, all electronic systems have basic
elements in common. In fact, the same set of controllers, masters, and
memories can be used, with slight modification, to control any of the
dimmers used in the various systems. In at least one system in actual
use, identical controllers are used with forty-six thyratron-tube dimmers and eight silicon controlled-rectifier dimmers.

The Saturable-Core Reactor.   Though not strictly a fully electronic device, the saturable-core reactor was the first attempt along
these lines. It consists of a transformer built on a core shaped like
the figure eight. The primary and secondary coils are wound around
the opposite ends of the eight, and a low-voltage d-c control current
coil around the common central bar. By varying the control voltage,
the current flow in the secondary is affected, thereby furnishing the
lamps with greater or lesser voltage.

There are a number of disadvantages connected with the saturable-
core reactor which have prevented it from receiving as wide acceptance
as might have been expected. First, the load current and the control
current are related, so that the reactor can operate effectively only
in a comparatively small range close to its rated load. Secondly, the
reactor itself is a ponderous piece of apparatus, and it dims ponder-
ously, with a noticeable time lag between the giving of a control com-
mand and the resulting change of the light. However, reactors were
installed in a number of large houses during the 1920s and are still
giving satisfactory service.

The Thyratron-Tube.   The first truly electronic system was put
into operation by George Izenour in 1947 at Yale University. The
dimming device is a pair of thyratron tubes which are controlled by
varying their grid voltages from the control panel. This results in a
rapid switching on and off of the supply voltage which modifies the
familiar a-c sine-wave form, thus feeding more or less voltage to the
lamps.

The tubes are multicapacity, dimming any loads up to their top
rating; the reaction time is instantaneous and only the current that
is actually consumed by the load is drawn.

But thyratron tubes also have their disadvantages. They require
a certain warm-up time before loads may be placed on them. They
give off a good deal of heat that must be disposed of—as a matter

of comfort if they are placed on the stage itself—to prevent their early failure if they are enclosed in a small area. The tubes have a tendency to "drift"—that is, to get out of adjustment—and therefore demand frequent and careful attention. And they do need replacement now and again, making maintenance a time-consuming and costly affair.

THE MAGNETIC AMPLIFIER

During the 1950s it seemed that the magnetic amplifier might be the answer to the electronic dimming problem. A refinement of the saturable-core reactor, it is multicapacity, has a fast reaction time, needs no warm-up, gives off little heat, and has an unlimited, maintenance-free life. Its only disadvantages seem to be its bulk, its weight, and its cost.

The Silicon Controlled Rectifier. The silicon controlled rectifier is the present leader in the electronic sweepstakes. Usually referred to as the SCR dimmer, its name means "a silicon rectifier under control" and not "a rectifier controlled by silicon." A kind of large-capacity transistor, this device presents all the advantages of the magnetic amplifier, but it is quite small and light in weight and is a good deal less expensive. It is a bit delicate, however, both to overcurrents and to high ambient heat, but special fusing and fans seem to take care of these drawbacks. Another problem is that its rapid switching action often sets up a distinct and annoying hum in the lamp filaments, requiring the addition of a special filter to correct it.

At the present time, however, the SCR seems to be leading the field by a goodly margin, though what the future may present cannot be predicted.

CONTROLBOARD THEORY AND DESIGN

There are two schools of thought regarding the design of controlboards (usually called "consoles") for electronic dimming. One advocates a system of presetting every change to be made in the lighting during the running of the show, while the other prefers to handle most of the changes by means of groups of dimmers under several masters and submasters.

Presetting. Presetting provides, in addition to the direct, manual control of each dimmer from the console, an alternate-memory control. When but one duplication of controls is provided, it is usually identical to the manual control and located in the same panel (see Figure 19–7). Whichever set of controllers is energized at a given moment also acts as the manual control, while the readings on the other set of controllers are being adjusted as a preset that will shortly be used.

FIGURE 19–7. A TWO-SCENE-PRESET CONSOLE. The transparent disks with the white handles are the controllers for the thirty dimmers, one apiece for each preset. Below them is a row of off–on switches for each circuit. At the right end of the white plate may be seen the fader handle. The six switches to their left are for the non-dim circuits. At the extreme left is the master dimmer for house-lights and a lock for the board. (Photo—George Izenour)

FIGURE 19–8. A TEN-SCENE-PRESET CONSOLE. To the left is the preset panel with ten rows of 45 controllers each, for the 45 dimmers. The upper portion of the console desk contains the 45 manual units, each with its reading-indicator at the top, below which is the controller handle, and beneath this the transfer switch which allows the circuit to be placed under either manual or preset control. At the left end of the desk are the selector buttons for the ten presets, plus black-out. There are two rows, one for the "up" and one for the "down" position of the fader, which is adjacent. When the fader is "down" (as in the picture) the preset "selected" in the bottom row is energized. As the fader moves toward "up," the preset "selected" in the upper row fades into prominence, cross-fading the former selection, until the handle reaches its top limit, when the "down" preset has been eliminated a new preset may be selected on the bottom row. At the right end of the desk is the master dimmer handle, which dims all circuits on manual control proportionately down or up. (Photo—George Izenour)

When there are several duplicate controls, usually five or ten, they are placed in a panel adjacent to the console and an assistant sets the readings on them. In running the show with, let us say, ten presets already set up, the operator need only fade back and forth from one preset to another at the speed dictated by the cues and the action. If a set of readings is not required again once it has been used, it may be erased and a new preset recorded in its place. Thus as many as sixty or more complex readings may be utilized in desired sequence for a single performance. This is certainly a simple enough procedure and one not likely to cause confusion in the mind of the operator.

Figure 18–8 shows a multipreset board and its console.

But it must be understood that there are certain problems presented by the presetting approach. A completely new preset is required for the change of light from even a single instrument. True, it is sometimes possible to make such a minor change in the preset panel itself, but this is frequently awkward and, in some models, impossible.

Further, all fades between presets must be linear; that is, if it is desirable to dim spotlight A from 10 (full up) to 0 (full out), while spotlight B is moving from 0 to 10, when A reads 8, B will read 2— when A is at 5, so is B, and when A reaches 3, B will be at 7. But this is not always desirable. Suppose the intention is to bring B to a reading of 7 before A has started to dim (a nonlinear cross-fade); this is not possible without setting up an additional preset. If many instruments are involved, and changes follow swiftly one after another, the whole thing becomes hopeless.

CARD SYSTEMS. To make the settings of presets easier and less subject to human error, various card systems have been devised. There are a number of forms that the cards may take, but in all cases the principle is the same: On each card are recorded the readings for a single preset; the cards are then fed into the console, making the only chance for error that of feeding the cards in wrong sequence. The cards are useable again and again (if not damaged in handling) until the final performance, and even then they may be stored away for a possible revival of the play. The exact nature of the cards and how the readings are marked on them differ for each system, and even recording the readings on tape and other methods have been subject to experimentation. Figure 19–9 shows one example of a card preset-system console.

Group Mastering. The second method of designing a control-board does not depend exclusively on separate preset panels, but divides the manual board into various groups and subgroups, each with its own master control. This system is known as group mastering. The groups may be used as presets independent of each other, operated

FIGURE 19–9. A CARD-PRESET CONSOLE. This console controls twelve dimmers by a manual system and also by almost limitless presetting achieved by dropping the cards into the slots as rapidly as required. Note the master dimmers for each preset and the fader between them. The type of card shown here is one of several varieties on the market. (Photo—Superior Electric)

508 together, or used to pile on new readings on top of the old ones, as well as other combinations.

Unfortunately, the operation of such a console can become extremely complex if a great many changes are needed in rapid succession. There are just too many things for an operator to keep track of in a swiftly moving play. But for fewer cues and with a tempo that permits careful checking and preparation for the next change, this type of system has much to offer.

A very distinct advantage of the group system is that the console may be run effectively with little rehearsal, a great boon for multi-purpose auditoriums, while the preset system demands considerable preparation time to record the readings.

Combination Systems. It must be noted that even the staunchest advocates of the preset have recently been incorporating a certain degree of grouping into their systems, while the group enthusiasts often include presetting as an adjunct to theirs. Actually, a large proportion of all consoles installed today are custom designed to the purchaser's special requirements. Anyone proposing to buy an electronic dimming system should consult the manufacturers to ascertain how they can incorporate *his* particular needs into the system that *he* wishes to buy.

Electronic Package Boards. As has been mentioned, the package board using the autotransformer dimmer has been available for some time, but now several manufacturers are offering packages containing the SCR, which, with its light weight, makes an ideal dimmer for something designed to be readily transportable.

In some models the single package contains both dimmers and their controllers, but in most types the electronic package board actually consists of several packages. One will contain the controller units, usually six, and a master, and will be connected by a special cable to a second package in which the dimmers themselves are housed. The dimmer package, which has outlets to which the stage loads are connected, may be left backstage, its small size permitting it to be tucked away in a convenient corner. The controller package is carried to wherever it is needed—in the auditorium during rehearsal, for example. If more circuits are required, a second package of dimmers and a second of controllers with their connecting cable may be added, and a third or more, as desired.

One model provides for five sets of preset controllers and a fader in the controller package. Another gives the option of buying a second controller package and a master fader package, so that a two-scene preset system may be set up and units may be added, until as many as thirty-six dimmers, each with duplicate controllers, are under the single master fader.

FIGURE 19–10. ELECTRONIC PACKAGE BOARDS RISAT.
(*a*) This package is essentially a miniature console controlling six
1800-watt semi-conductor dimmers in a separate package (not
shown). At the top is a row of six controllers which permit direct
manual control over the dimmers. Below these are the respective
switches to throw control to the manual, to "off," or to the preset
controllers below. There are five rows of the latter, thus five presets.
Note to the left of each preset row the selector switch which directs
the preset to fade "up" or "down" with the movements of the fader
handle, which is on the extreme left. Additional control packages
with their respective dimmer packages may be linked to each
other in such a manner that one fader acts for all. This is possible
up to six control packages, or thirty-six dimmers. Below right (*b*)
These two pictures show a different approach. On the left is the
dimmer package with six fused, removable 2.4 km S.C.R. units,
two receptacles for each, plus a circuit breaker each. On the right
is a controller unit with six controllers and a master. Two such units,
plus a master fader package of the same size (not shown) will
provide cross fading as in a two-preset console. A single master
can handle six pairs of controller units and six dimmer units, a total
of thirty-six circuits (Photos — (*a*) Superior Electric. (*b*) Theatre
Techniques.) (*c*) Kliegpac 9. Portable dimming system with
interchangeable 2.4 kw and 6 kw dimmerpacs, 9 dimmers per
pack, 9 and 18 channel 2-scene preset control consoles.
(Photo — Kliegl Bros.)

a

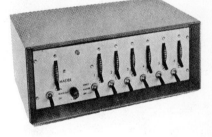

b

c

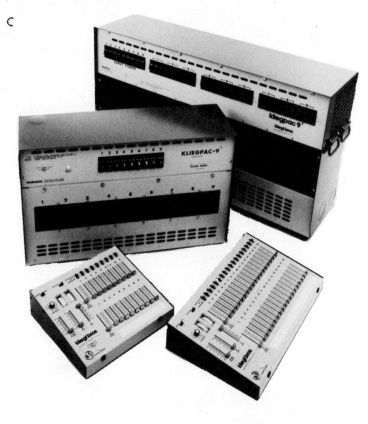

Perhaps, most of all, the operator requires a sensitivity and sense of timing akin to that of an actor's. He is, in a very real sense, himself an actor. He does not snap lights on, but dims in gently, with feeling, perhaps at a varying pace to suit best the action on the stage. If the actors are fast in their pace one night, he must adjust to the new tempo. If a cue is delayed, he must hold his hand. Many highly competent electricians can not adjust to this sensitivity. They may understand, but the delicacy of feeling isn't there: their lights are always a trifle off cue, a bit jerky on the fade-up, a little slow on the dim, a trifle rushed on the cross-fade sequence. Only experience will reveal who is the best conductor of this orchestra of lights.

FIGURE 19-11.   Q-FILE MEMORY SYSTEM. The first successful preset memory system designed and manufactured by Thorn Electrical Industries, Ltd. Originally developed for television lighting control, it has now revolutionized theatre lighting control. The console (top, opposite page) has fingertip control of a keyboard of close to 400 lighting-control circuits with a Servo Fader to control levels of one or a group of dimmers prior to memory storage; four faders grouped in inverted pairs with time-controlled cross-facing capabilities; a keyboard for the selection of nearly 200 memory positions; a status display panel to tell the operator at a glance (1) the control channels that are energized in the stage mode and (2) the channels being held in the next preset mode, and a peg matrix or patch panel. Extra features include an auxiliary control panel (lower right corner), a portable remote-control panel, and a library device in which an entire show can be stored on standard tape cassettes for recall at a later date. The console shown, installed at the University of Cincinnati's Conservatory of Music, has 80 control channels and 100 memories. Below, left: An isolated view of the library device and cassette. A close-up view (this page) of a typical Q-File control board. Q-Level Console (bottom right). The latest concept in memory system control, Q-Level, is a compact, low-cost version of the Q-File memory system. The Q-Level has fewer memory channels (50 to 100) and a smaller number of control circuits (40 to 160). A potentiometer for each control circuit takes the place of the punch keyboard for the selection of control channels. Each pot, however, contains two matching level-indicator lamps (LEDs) to match or monitor recorded levels in the memory circuits. The system also has an electronically-timed fade control and three master faders. The panel shown has 40 control channels and 100 memories. (Photos Kliegl Bros.)

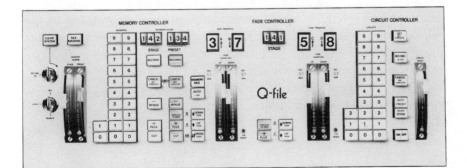

512   LOCATION FOR CONTROL CONSOLES

As we have pointed out, the low amperage and low voltage used by the control system permit the operator and the apparatus that he handles directly to be placed at any distance from the stage and in any location that seems appropriate. A projection booth at the rear of the balcony has been utilized in some houses, and while this is not a bad location from which to run a show, it is a poor place for the designer to light it because of the bad angle of vision to the stage, the impossibility of seeing the background scenery, and the distraction of light patterns on the stage floor. An orchestra pit is better, though too close for the designer to view the stage picture as a whole.

Of the practical places, the rear of the main floor of the auditorium is unquestionably the best. It is a good place from which to run the show, the view of the stage is satisfactory, and the operator and light designer are, during rehearsals, in easy and direct communication with director, scene designer, and others. In any event, it is inexcusable to place the control panels backstage, although the cross-connecting system should be there; the actual dimming apparatus—be it SCR's, tubes, magnetic amplifiers, or whatever—can be tucked away in the basement or other convenient location. This applies equally to a permanent installation consisting of console and preset panels and to the controller units of a package board.

THE OPERATOR

It would not be wise to leave the subject of electronic dimming without speaking of the person who will operate the controls. This is a very different task from that presented to an electrician standing backstage and manipulating several large handles, heavy with friction, under the direct supervision of a stage manager or a chief electrician.

A console operator is usually on his own in a booth out in the house. He may take telephoned cues from the stage manager, but frequently he operates by sight and sound cues from the stage itself. His apparatus is delicate and complex—not at all like a bank of simple and rugged resistance dimmers. If he makes an error with any of the master controls, or selects the wrong preset, it may result in every light on the stage assuming the wrong reading. Here is an actual example of this: The curtain rose on a scene taking place at midnight, but instead a bright summer afternoon with sunlight pouring in the window was revealed to the confused audience and the startled actors! In such a case no one can help the operator. He must have confidence, a cool head, and enough understanding of the apparatus before him and what it controls, to crawl out of his predicament with the least distraction to actors and audience.

It was inevitable that the combination of the SCR dimmer, low-voltage control circuits, and miniaturized parts would lead to computerized control of lighting. The ability of the computer to store information enables it to hold preset or *cue* information in whatever quantities a production situation might desire. A computer can be programed with the digital information of a cue and be randomly recalled with push-button speed. The only limit to the capacity is the size or number of computers in the memory bank.

MEMORY SYSTEMS.

Q-File (storage of cues) was one of the first memory systems on the market. Developed by Thorne Electric of Great Britain and Kliegl Brothers in this country, first for television and then for the theatre, it is referred to as a *random access memory control*.

It is possible at the Q-File control panel to set the intensity of the lights for a scene, assign a cue number, record the information in the memory bank, recall the cue in random order to a ready or *preset* position and, by use of the fader, cross-fade the working cue *out* and the preset cue *on* in one simple move. There are pile-on, cancel, and manual operations as well as a preview panel display of the entire cue setup, and a tape cassette attachment for recording and storing the entire production to be recalled at a later date (Figure 19-11).

Autocue. A little more sophisticated use of the computer is provided by *Autocue,* a *visible memory light control system,* manufactured by Skirpan Lighting Control Corporation. The system combines computer and video technologies. The Autocue control panel has a standard television monitor with an alpha-numeric display of all significant cue data. During the setup the operator uses a *light pen* on the monitor screen to set dimmer readings within the scene to be recorded, stored, and randomly recalled later. There are also pile-on, cancel, manual, and preset operations as well as a fader and lap dissolve. A teletype attachment gives a printed computer read-out for analysis or library storage. The entire production can also be stored on a digital cassette recorder. The simplicity of the operation to set and store cues reduces the chances of operator error.

Autocue has the added feature of including nondimming circuits into the memory system thereby allowing the storage of nonlighting cues. Other media, such as sound and slide changers, can be added to the system at additional expense (Figure 19-12).

FIGURE 19–12. AUTOCUE. A
visible memory light-control system. (*a*) The console and computer rack. Although shown together the console can be operated remotely. (*b*) Detail of display screen and lightpen, a dis-
tinguishing feature of the Autocue system.

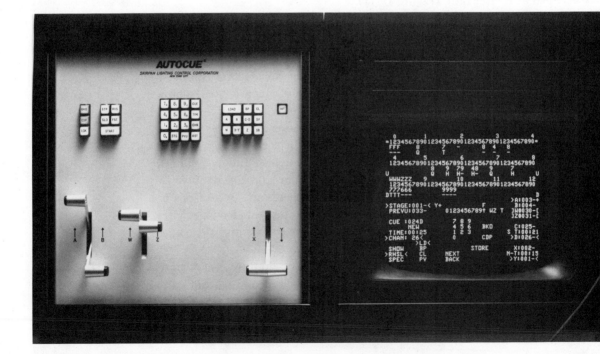

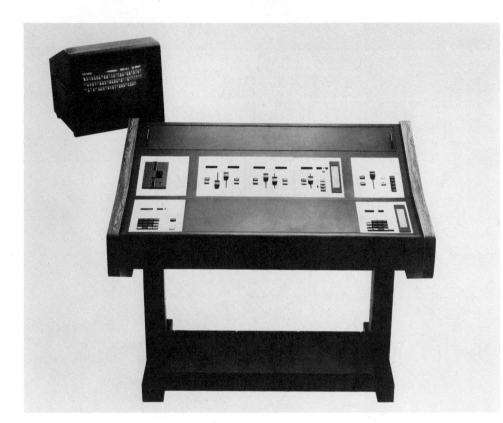

FIGURE 19–13. PERFORMANCE MEMORY CONTROL CONSOLE.
The latest memory control system designed and manufactured by Kliegl
Bros. The console has separate keypad access for channel selection
and memory storage; faders for playback include manual masters, cross
fader and automatic time fader. Optional features include second time
fader, video display unit, disc storage, hard copy printer, portable remote, group masters, pattern generator, and proportional patching. This
system is completely modularized so that elements can be rearranged,
added or deleted as the system grows.

20 Lighting Design for Typical Proscenium Productions

So far we have investigated the various tools of the light-designer's trade: instruments, color media, and control methods. Now let us see how these are employed in actually designing the lighting for a play. Because there are many forms of production these days, we will consider four typical but quite different sorts of presentation: a realistic interior, a realistic exterior, a wing-and-border setting, and a space stage. Each of these has its own special problems.

It must be noted that these four examples are deliberately designed to show the minimum number of instruments necessary to achieve acceptable lighting in each case. It would be hoped that in actual practice a much larger inventory would be available and would be used.

First, we must decide in what manner of theatre the four types of play will be produced. Let us assume that the theatre is of medium size. The stage will have a 30-foot proscenium opening. There will be ample provisions for hanging scenery and instruments above the stage. About twenty feet from an actor playing at the proscenium line will be a beam for mounting front spotlights.

DESIGNING ON PAPER

517

The importance of planning on paper the lighting design for any production cannot be exaggerated. It unifies the designer's ideas, enables him to foresee and eliminate many problems of both artistic and physical nature, and, when all the details are put down on paper, others are able to execute his wishes with assurance and precision.

A good layout shows the scenery in place on the stage and all the instruments in their proper locations, all drawn to scale to eliminate self-deception. Figure 20-2 shows the conventional symbols for instruments as used in most layouts. Instruments are numbered in a logical manner, and on an accompanying schedule they should be identified as to type, position, and purpose. Other details, such as lamp, color, and the like should also be specified. For some involved settings, it may be advisable to show a cross-section of the stage as well as the plan. Corrections and additions should be marked on the layout and schedule as the work progresses.

FIGURE 20–1. LIGHTING POSITIONS IN THE PROSCENIUM THEATRE. (1) Ceiling beams. (2) Box booms or house-slot position. (3) Balcony front. (4) Apron or footlight. (5) Teaser. (6) Tormentor boom. (7) Midstage backlight position. (8) Wing ladder. (9) Backdrop or cyclorama lights. (10) Cyclorama base or horizon lights. (11) Translucent drop backlight. (12) Follow spot.

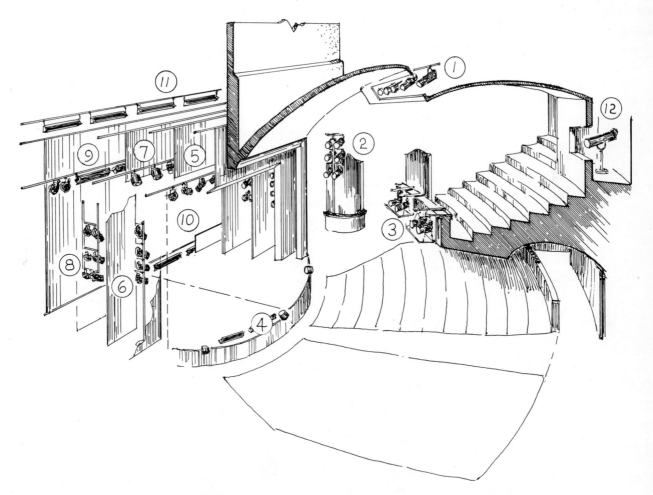

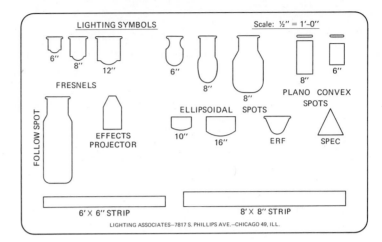

Symbols list (left column):

- ●— 8″ ELLIPS'L-REFL'R SPOTLIGHT
- ●— 6″ ELLIPS'L-REFL'R SPOTLIGHT
- ●— 4½″ ELLIPS'L-REFL'R SPOTLIGHT
- ■— 8″ FRESNEL-LENS SPOTLIGHT
- ●— 6″ FRESNEL-LENS SPOTLIGHT
- ▲— SPECIAL
- ■— 16″-BEAM PROJECTOR
- ◀— 10″-BEAM PROJECTOR
- ◀— 14″ ELLIPS'L-REFL'R FLOOD
- ◀— 10″ ELLIPS'L-REFL'R FLOOD
- ▬— 6′-0″ STRIPLIGHT
- ▬— 4′-6″ STRIPLIGHT

FIGURE 20-2. LIGHTING INSTRUMENT SYMBOLS. Conventional symbols for lighting instruments as used in the lighting layouts that follow. Silhouettes of contemporary instruments from a Lighting Symbols Template by Lighting Associates, Chicago. Below: Sketch of a realistic interior setting.

If the scale of the layout is large, say ½ inch equals 1 foot, it is possible and usually desirable to eliminate the separate schedule and include all the details on the layout itself.

THE REALISTIC INTERIOR

A realistic interior usually calls for some variation of the conventional box setting with a ceiling cloth overhead. The primary interest is within the walls of this set, while the backgrounds seen through windows and doors are of less importance. The lighting is sometimes completely motivated by apparent sources; in practically all cases it is realistically plausible.

In Figure 20-3 is shown such a setting. On the stage-left wall is a door, leading to some other room or passage. In the up-left corner a flight of stairs comes down into the room from off left. In the center of the upstage wall is an archway opening into a corridor with an entrance at the stage-left end.

No.	INSTRUMENT	LOCATION	PURPOSE	LAMP	COLOR	REMARKS
1	6" ELLIPS'L-REF'R SPOTLIGHT	BEAM – L	AREA 2 L	500 T 12	26	
2	" " " "	" "	" 1 L	"	26	FRAME OFF RETURN
3	" " " "	" "	" 3 L	"	26	
4	" " " "	BEAM – R	" 1 R	"	62	
5	" " " "	" "	" 3 R	"	62	FRAME OFF RETURN
6	" " " "	" "	" 2 R	"	62	
7	6" FRESNEL-LENS SPOTLIGHT	1ST PIPE – L	AREA 4 L	500 T 20	26	MAT TOP
8	" " " "	" – C	" 5 L	"	26	" "
9	6" ELLIPS'L-REF'R SPOTLIGHT	1ST PIPE – C	STAIR SPECIAL	500 T 12	62	FRAME TO STAIR
10	" " " "	" "	ARCH SPECIAL	"	62	FRAME TO ARCH
11	6" FRESNEL-LENS SPOTLIGHT	1ST PIPE – R	AREA 5 R	500 T 20	62	MAT TOP
12	" " " "	" "	" 4 R	"	62	" "
13	6" ELLIPS'L-REF'R SPOTLIGHT	STAND – L	STAIR BACKLIGHT	500 T 12	57	
14	10" FLOOD LIGHT	SCENERY – L	DOOR BACKING	250 G 30	57	HIGH ON SCENERY
15	" " "	FIRE PLACE	FIRE GLOW	100 A 21	61	GANG WITH #24
16	16" BEAM PROJECTOR	R – STAGE WALL	SUNLIGHT	1000 G 40	–	HIGH AS POSSIBLE
17	6" x 6'-0" STRIPLIGHTS	⎫			RED	⎫ 3-COLOR CIRCUITS
18	" "	⎬ APRON	FOOTLIGHTS	75 R30 FL.	BLUE	⎬ ROUNDELS
19	" "	⎭			GREEN	⎭ FEED THROUGH
20	" "	⎫ 1ST PIPE	X – RAYS	150 R 40	RED BL.WHITE	
21	" "	⎬		COLORED	AMBER	
22	6" x 4'-6" "	FLOOR – R	SKY BACKING	"	RED, BLUE, AMBER	
23	6" x 6'-0" "	BEHIND ARCH	HALL	"	RED, BLUE WHITE, AMBER	
24	SPECIAL	FIREPLACE	FIRE EFFECT	2- 60 A21	VARIED	GANG WITH #15
25	DESK LAMP	UL CORNER	LAMP	150 A 23	–	SHIELD TOP & SIDE
26	WALL SCONCE	L OF ARCH	WALL FIXTURE	15 FC/V		⎫ GANG – CANDELABRA
27	" "	R OF ARCH	" "	"	–	⎭ SOCKET ADAPTERS

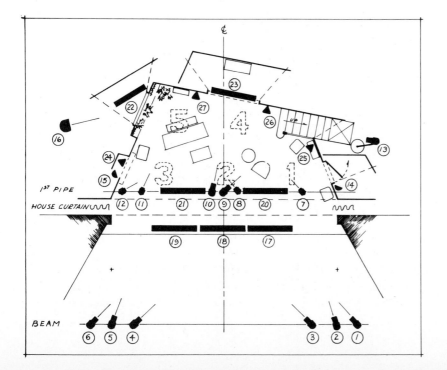

FIGURE 20–3. THE REALISTIC INTERIOR.   This and the following lighting layouts are simplified to demonstrate the basic instrumentation for some typical proscenium-type productions. They are illustrations and should not be considered professional lighting layouts. For professional planning techniques see Chapter 22. Above: Instrument schedule. Left: Layout of lighting instruments. Opposite page: Sketch of the setting.

The stage-right wall contains a window and a fireplace. Through the window is seen a backing with painted sky and a scene of distant hills.

Two scenes are involved. In Act I bright sunlight streams in through the window. In Act II it is dark night outside and a fire is burning on the hearth.

DOWNSTAGE AREAS

In dividing the stage into acting areas, we find that though the conventional three will be needed across the front section, only two will be required for the upstage band. To cover areas *1, 2, 3,* the downstage group, we mount 6-inch ellipsoidal-reflector spotlights in our front position. We select the ellipsoidal-reflector type over the plano-convex spotlight because of its far greater efficiency and punch of light, and over the Fresnel spot because the latter, though quite powerful, has such side spill that we would have light all over the proscenium wall to the great distraction of the audience. For a longer throw than the one we have assumed for this theatre, we would naturally use the 8-inch ellipsoidal-reflector spot with its narrow, more powerful beam. For a much shorter throw we could use the smaller, wider-beamed type.

In choosing the mounting positions for these instruments we attempt to achieve the ideal 45-degree angle, but note that we must mount the Area *1L* instrument somewhat in from the end of the beam in order to reach the extreme downstage-left corner of the stage without being cut off by the proscenium. In like manner, Area *3R* must come somewhat nearer the center.

Therefore, we have sacrificed to some extent the ideal angle in these cases, but this is a necessary compromise. The remaining four instruments can be placed just about where we prefer them. All six instruments are carefully framed so as not to spill distracting light on the face of the stage apron, on the overhead teaser, and, in the case of numbers *2* and *5,* on the proscenium.

UPSTAGE AREAS

To cover the upstage areas, numbers *4* and *5,* we will select 6-inch Fresnel spotlights and mount them on the first pipe. Fresnels are picked for this location because the soft edge of their beams makes blending between the areas much easier, and no sharp, distracting beam patterns will appear on the walls of the set. Numbers *7, 8,* and *12* can be focused at close to the 45-degree angle for their respective areas, but number *11,* focused on Area *5R,* must move in a little in order to keep spill light off the stage-right wall.

All five areas must be consistent in regard to colors. Because in both acts warm light (sunbeams and fireglow) seems to come from the right of the stage, we can use a warm gelatin in instruments *4, 5, 6, 11, 12*. The opposite side of the room would need a cool color for comparison in instruments *1, 2, 3, 7,* and *8*. Brigham Gelatin No. 62 (light scarlet) and No. 26 (light sky blue) make an excellent combination for such a situation without appearing too strong in either shade.

THE STAIRWAY

Of course, the stairway must not be overlooked. But rather than consider it another area, it is preferable to handle it as a special problem, due to its different levels. To catch it properly, yet to avoid spilling light where it is neither needed nor desired, we can use an ellipsoidal-reflector spotlight from the first pipe, framing its beam to the stairs themselves, and only high enough to cover the actor moving up and down. This would be instrument *9*, and because its beam is substantially at the same angle as the other stage-right instruments, its color should agree with these: a No. 62. To light the stairway from the other side, and particularly to catch the face of an ascending actor (always a fine effect) another ellipsoidal-spotlight (*13*) can be mounted on a high stand (or from an overhead line) at the head of the stairs, about eight feet offstage. The beam from this instrument may be presumed to come from a hall light at the head of the stairs, and a No. 57 (light amber) gelatin could be used here for realism.

THE ARCHWAY

An acting area of utmost importance is that immediately beyond the archway. Here the most vital entrances are made, and the actor must be well lighted as he prepares to come into the room. In fact, the director may even play brief, but important scenes in just this location. To cover this instrument *10* may be mounted in the center of the first pipe and framed carefully to the opening of the archway. As no particular angle is involved here, any plausible color may be chosen, such as the warm and flattering No. 62.

FLOODLIGHTS

Having listed the spotlights, we should next see what floodlights are desired. Two of the small, 10-inch variety are useful. Instrument 14 is placed behind the downstage-left door to throw illumination on the backing so this will not appear as a dark hole whenever the door is opened. This flood is placed at least ten feet high on the scenery to throw its light downward as from a ceiling or wall bracket. A 250-watt G-30 lamp will give ample illumination, and a No. 57 gelatin will provide a color that resembles the warm light usually associated with such household fixtures.

522 Instrument 15 has a very different use: it is placed in the fireplace to throw a warm glow over all who approach it. It need not be,
in fact should not be, too brilliant (and hence distracting) so a 100-
watt A-21 is all that is necessary, with a No. 61 gelatin (orange), a
more realistic color for fireglow than the traditional red.

SUNBEAMS

A large spotlight might be used for the strong beams of sunlight
entering the window, but a beam projector is better still, because of
the powerful punch of its parallel rays. No. 16 should be mounted
well offstage, if possible even farther than our layout indicates. A
producing group with ample equipment might even use two or more
instruments for this purpose. The height above the floor would depend
on the hour of day as expressed by the script; a great height for near
midday, a low, flat, angle for dawn or late afternoon. Likewise the
color to be used would depend upon the time. It is traditional to think
of sunlight as having a strong amber hue, but actually this is the case
only in the late afternoon. For such a scene a No. 58 (medium amber)
could be used. But noonday sun is much closer to white, and for such
an effect it is best to use no color medium at all.

FOOTLIGHTS

To give a unifying tone of color to the setting, footlights have
been installed: three 6-foot lengths, each burning twelve lamps, wired
in 3-color circuits. No strong burst of light is desired for this purpose,
so that the 75-watt R-30 floods will be ample behind red-, blue-, and
green-glass roundels. Of course, care is taken to place the glass so that
the colors run alternately through all three lengths, and to connect
the strips so that each circuit contains a single color only.

The best method for designating striplights connected in this manner is to give each length its own instrument number, and use the
name of the color to designate each circuit for the run of the strips.
Thus these footlights have been shown in our layout and schedule as
instrument numbers *17, 18,* and *19,* the circuits as red, blue, and green.

X-RAYS

Borderlights have also been hung: two 6-foot strips on the first
pipe, spaced slightly apart to allow certain spotlights to be mounted
between them. A little more punch is needed for these "x-rays," so
we have used 150-watt R-40 colored lamps in instruments 20 and 21,
with the circuits being designated as red, blue-white, and amber. Of
course, the regular 150-watt R lamps with appropriate gelatins would
be perfectly satisfactory. Considering that these lights are to blend

and tone an interior, we need not bother with any greens, nor very strong blues, while the cheerful warmth of the amber will be useful in both our sunlit and firelit scenes.

BACKING STRIPS

Instrument *22* is a 4½-foot striplight placed on the floor before the sky backing and focused on it. Considerable variation in color is desired here, so the 150-watt R-40 lamps would be in red, blue, and amber. The amber and blue mix to make a light blue daylight sky, while a rich night sky can be obtained by adding a little red to a blue on low reading. It should be noted that if people in the rear of the auditorium can see this striplight through the low window, or if there are balcony spectators who would surely see it, the better technique is to hang the instrument overhead and focus it down on the backing.

A 6-foot strip, *23,* is hung behind the header over the archway to light the passage and its back wall. Again the 150-watt R's can be used, but these may well be amber, blue-white, and red lamps as a more useful combination for this interior corridor.

Note that different length strips are employed for these two backings, because the area that can be seen by the audience varies: about nine feet in one case, and fifteen in the other. Such an analysis is always essential and is plotted carefully on the layout from the worst seat on each side of the auditorium through the extreme limits of the openings to the backgrounds.

SPECIALS

With the regular instruments cared for, we can turn to the specials. Instrument *24* is a fire effect: two 60-watt lamps hidden behind two or three logs. Their light will be seen through pieces of colored glass, or crumpled gelatins, to give the effect of glowing coals. Though this will be seen by only a small segment of the audience, it is a worthwhile device to give the fireplace a touch of realism and warmth.

In the corner between the wall and the stairs is another special, *25,* a conventional desk lamp with cord running offstage to connect with the regular stage cable. Because its shade has been made more dense by use of a brown-paper lining, a 150-watt lamp may be used to throw a strong downward light.

Finally on the upstage wall are two sconces or wall brackets, *26* and *27,* one on either side of the arch. These have unshaded lamps; therefore ones of small wattage must be used to prevent glare uncomfortable to an audience. The 15FC/V lamp, a flame-shaped decorative style, is employed. Because these have candelabra-sized bases, adapters

No.	INSTRUMENT	LOCATION	PURPOSE	LAMP	COLOR	REMARKS
1	8" ELLIPS'L SPOTLIGHT	CEILING-L	AREA 2L	750 T12	02	
2	8" " "	"	" 1L	" "	02	
3	8" " "	"	" 3L	" "	02	
4	8" " "	"	" 4L	" "	02	
5	8" " "	"	SPECIAL	" "	02	SOFA
6	8" " "	CEILING-R	AREA 1R	" "	60	
7	8" " "	"	SPECIAL	" "	60	SOFA
8	8" " "	"	AREA 2R	" "	60	
9	8" " "	"	" 4R	" "	60	
10	8" " "	"	" 3R	" "	60	
11	6" ELLIPS'L SPOTLIGHT	1ST PIPE	AREA 9L	500 T12	02	
12	6" FRESNEL SPOTLIGHT	"	" 5L	500 T20	02	
13	6" " "	"	" 6L	" "	02	
14	6" ELLIPS'L SPOTLIGHT	"	SPECIAL	500 T12	02	STAIR & LANDING
15	6" FRESNEL SPOTLIGHT	"	AREA 9L	500·T20	02	
16	6" " "	"	" 7L	" "	02	
17	6" " "	"	" 5L	" "	02	
18	6" ELLIPS'L SPOTLIGHT	"	SPECIAL	500 T12	02	UPPER LANDING
19	6" FRESNEL SPOTLIGHT	"	"	" "	02	WINDOW SEAT
20	3½" ELLIPS'L SPOTLIGHT	"	"	300W TH·L	60	FRAME ON TROPHY
21	6" FRESNEL SPOTLIGHT	"	AREA 6R	500 T20	02	
22	6" ELLIPS'L SPOTLIGHT	"	SPECIAL	500 T12	02	AREA 9-FRAME TO ARCH
23	6" FRESNEL SPOTLIGHT	"	"	500 T20	02	WINDOW SEAT
24	6" " "	"	AREA 7R	" "	60	
25	6" " "	"	" 9R	" "	60	
26	8" FRESNEL SPOTLIGHT	2ND PIPE	7·L BACK LT.	1000 G40	02	MAT OFF SCENERY TOP
27	6" " "	"	STAIR - LEFT	500 T20	02	" " " "
28	8" " "	"	2L BACK LT.	1000 G40	02	
29	8" " "	"	1R " "	1000 G40	CLEAR	
30	6" " "	"	AREA 8L	500 T20	02	
31	8" " "	"	3L BACK LT.	1000 G40	02	
32	6" " "	"	STAIR RIGHT	500 T20	60	
33	6" " "	"	AREA 8R	" "	60	
34	8" " "	"	2R BACK LT.	1000 G40	CLEAR	
35	8" " "	"	4L " "	" "	02	
36	3½" ELLIPS'L SPOTLIGHT	"	SPECIAL	300W TH·L	CLEAR	FRAME ON TROPHY
37	8" FRESNEL SPOTLIGHT	"	3R BACK LT.	1000 G40	"	
38	8" " "	"	4R " "	1000 G40	CLEAR	
39	6" " "	14' BOOM #1	KITCHEN LT.	500 T20	"	
40	6" " "	16' " #2	HALL + UPPER	" "	02	
41	6" " "	" "	LANDING	" "	02	
42	8" " "	SPOTLINE PIPE #2	STREET LTS.	1000 G40	62	
43	8" " "	"	" "	" "	62	
44	8" " "	"	" "	" "	62	
45	SPECIAL	SPOTLINE PIPE #1	PORCH LIGHT	100 W	CLEAR	
46	"	"	" "	"	"	D.S. FIXTURE IN VIEW
47	14" ELLIPS'L R. FLOOD	"	WINDOW WASH	500 PS	02	
48	9" " " "	HALL	WALL WASH	250 G30	02	
49	SPECIAL	HALL	CEILING FIXTURE	3/40W	CLEAR	
50	"	S.R. WALL	WALL FIXTURE	2/40W	"	
51	"	STAIR	" "	2/40W	"	

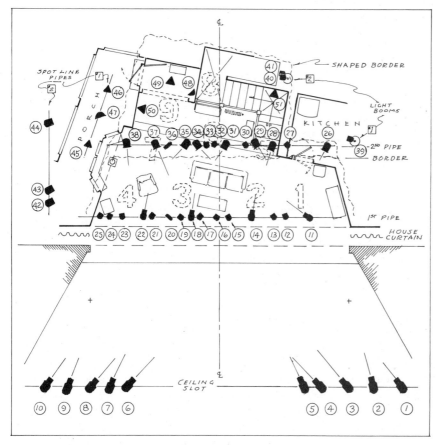

FIGURE 20–4. THE REALISTIC INTERIOR WITHOUT CEILING.
Present-day staging frequently omits the ceiling of an interior setting
to facilitate the lighting. Although the technique does allow "back-
lighting," at the same time it forces the upstage light-pipes higher into
the air if they are to mask, thereby increasing the size and wattage of
the instruments. Shown are the sketch of the setting, a layout of lighting instruments, and the instrument schedule.

must be placed in the regular sockets of the sconces, unless these are already of the proper, small size.

CONTROL

Modest as this layout is, it would still require no fewer than thirty dimmers to control the lights properly. There are twenty-seven listed instruments, but the two sconces can be ganged, as can the fire glow and fire effect. On the other hand, the striplights each have three color circuits, each demanding its own control. The largest loads would be 1200 watts for each circuit of the borderlights, 1000 watts for the beam projector, 900 watts for each color circuit of the footlights, and 600 watts for each color of the arch backing striplight. For the rest, 500-watt dimmers will suffice.

If the control board could not furnish the necessary circuits, some ganging would have to be done. Great ingenuity is often displayed in doing this, but a truly artistic use of lights and color values could not be maintained with much less than thirty dimmers.

REALISTIC EXTERIORS

The realistic exterior setting is one of the most difficult to light effectively, due to the many maskings needed to prevent the audience from seeing into the wings or up into the hanging space. These maskings—flat surfaces painted to resemble natural objects—are never very convincing and tend to catch stray, unwanted beams of light.

An exterior setting almost always includes a large sky area or a painted scene in the background that needs special attention. Apparent motivation is necessary for all the lighting.

AN EXTERIOR SETTING

Figure 20-5 shows a typical exterior setting including many of the features frequently encountered. On stage left three sets of woodwings, painted as tree clusters, serve to mask the wings on that side of the stage. On the right there is a cottage which masks that side. In connection with the downstage woodwings, leaf borders cross the stage to mask overhead. Across the back of the playing areas is a ground row, three feet high in its lowest portion and representing hills in the middle distance.

The backdrop consists of a translucency, the lower portion of which is painted with opaque media to represent rolling hills and woods; above this the translucency is painted with dye colors to permit the light to pass through from the rear for greater luminosity and depth.

There are two scenes involved. In Scene 1 the brilliant sunshine pours in from stage left. In Scene 2 moonlight floods the set from the same direction.

AREA SPOTS

The front lights are placed substantially as they were for the realistic interior, but because the sunlight and moonlight make two different effects necessary, the stage-left instruments are double-hung; that is, there are two instruments focused on each area from this side. One set works in the first scene, the other set in the second. Or they might be used together at different intensities.

The three upstage areas are handled the same way, but because the first leaf border will hang so low, the usual first pipe location cannot be used. Instead this pipe is moved behind the leaf border. Great care must still be taken to prevent stray beams from touching corners of the second cloth border. In fact, the most careful planning cannot predict this with exactness, and much remounting and refocusing will probably be needed on the actual set.

DOUBLE-HUNG SPOTLIGHTS

The stage-left instruments that will work when the sun is shining are called the left-warms and they have No. 57 (light amber) gelatins to give the effect of warmth on that side of the stage. Opposite them, in the stage-right spotlights, we use No. 17 (special lavender), a medium gelatin that will appear quite cool opposite the warm No. 57. But in Scene Two, when the moon is apparently lighting the left side, the left cools contain No. 29 (special steel blue) which is so very cool that the special lavender actually seems warm in contrast. This use of a medium or neutral gelatin on one side of the stage to work alternately against a warm and a cool on the other is a device that is often of extreme value when instruments or control circuits are not too abundant.

Many people would use, instead of lavender, no color at all. While it is true that the so-called white light from an ungelled spotlight is actually a trifle on the warm side of the spectrum, when used opposite a definitely warm color, such as amber, it will appear quite cool. Of course, opposite a cool color, it will seem even warmer than before. And the fact that you are using no color medium means that you will be getting that much more light. If you do not need a color, just omit the medium entirely; it is unnecessary to put a clear gelatin in front of the instrument, and to use a frost will result in changing the character of the beam into a broad, fuzzy-edged wash.

No.	INSTRUMENT	LOCATION	PURPOSE	LAMP	COLOR	REMARKS
1	6" Ellips'l-Ref'r Spotlight	BEAM-L	AREA 2L-WARM	500T12	57	SOFT EDGE
2	" " " "	" "	" 2L-COOL	"	29	" "
3	" " " "	" "	" 1L-WARM	"	57	FRAME OFF TORM.
4	" " " "	" "	" 1L-COOL	"	29	" "
5	" " " "	" "	" 3L-WARM	"	57	
6	" " " "	" "	" 3L-COOL	"	29	
7	" " " "	BEAM-R	" 1R	"	17	
8	" " " "	" "	" 3R	"	17	FRAME OFF TORM.
9	" " " "	" "	" 2R	"	17	SOFT EDGE
10	6" Fresnel-Lens Spotlight	1ST PIPE-L	" 4L WARM	500T20	57	
11	" " " "	" "	" 4L COOL	"	29	
12	" " " "	" "	" 5L WARM	"	57	
13	" " " "	" "	" 5L COOL	"	29	
14	" " " "	" "	" 6L WARM	"	57	
15	" " " "	" "	" 6L COOL	"	29	
16	" " " "	1ST PIPE-R	" 4R	"	17	
17	" " " "	" "	" 5R	"	17	
18	" " " "	" "	" 6R	"	17	
19	" " " "	2ND PIPE-L	" 7L WARM	"	57	
20	" " " "	" "	" 7L COOL	"	29	
21	" " " "	2ND PIPE-R	" 7R	"	17	
22	" " " "	3RD PIPE-R	" 7 SPECIAL	"	17	MAT OFF DROP
23	8" Fresnel-Lens Spotlight	1ST PIPE-L	MOONLIGHT	1000G40	26	FOCUS ON AREA 2,3
24	" " " "	" "	"	"	26	" " " 1,2
25	" " " "	2ND PIPE-L	"	"	26	" " " 5
26	" " " "	3RD PIPE-L	"	"	26	" " " 7
27	10" FLOOD	SCENERY-R	DOOR BACKING	250G30	58	MOUNT HIGH ON SCENERY
28	16" BEAM PROJECTOR	1ST PIPE-L	SUN LIGHT	1500G40	54	FOCUS ON AREA 2,3
29	" " "	" "	"	"	54	" " " 1,2
30	" " "	2ND PIPE-L	"	"	54	" " " 5
31	" " "	3RD PIPE-L	"	"	54	" " " 7
32	6"X6'-0" STRIPLIGHTS					FOCUS ON PAINTED
33	" "				AMBER	PORTION
34	" "	ON FLOOR BEHIND GROUNDROW	TRANSLUCENCY	300R40	BLUE	ROUNDELS
35	" "		FRONT LIGHT	FLOOD	BL-GREEN	
36	" "					
37	6"X4'-6" STRIPLIGHTS	4TH PIPE	TRANSLUCENCY	150 PAR38	36	
38	6"X6'-0" "	BEHIND	BACKLIGHT	SPOT	67	3-COLOR CIRCUIT
39	" "	TRANSLUCENCY			40	FEED THROUGH
40	" "	VERY HIGH				FOCUS ON
41	" "					TRANSLUCENT
42	6"X4'-6" STRIPLIGHTS					PORTION

FIGURE 20–5. A REALISTIC EXTERIOR SETTING. Opposite page: Instrument schedule. Above: Sketch of setting. Below: Layout of lighting instruments.

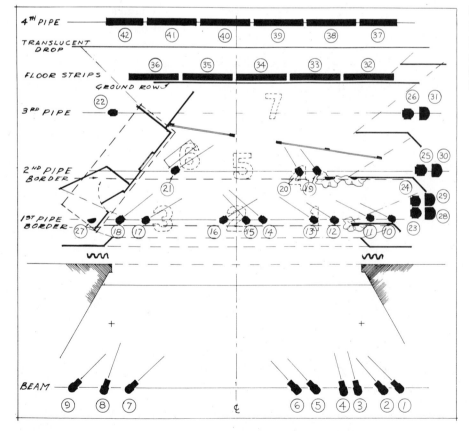

Because the space just beyond the fence would be frequently used, especially for entrances, we are considering it a seventh area, with instruments (numbers *19, 20,* and *21*) mounted behind the second border. To make sure that an actor leaving or entering at stage right is completely covered, we place an additional spotlight (*22*) off right. The sunlight and moonlight coming in from stage left (as explained below) will take care of that side of the stage.

SUNLIGHT AND MOONLIGHT

For a completely realistic effect, a great many powerful instruments would probably be needed for the sunlight and moonlight. But to keep our example within proper bounds, we will use only four for each. Because the moonlight need not be as bright, we have used 8-inch Fresnels, which give a much smoother and broader beam. Numbers *23* and *24* would be placed behind the first woodwing with their focuses overlapping across the stage. The remaining Fresnels, *25* and *26,* would be mounted one each behind the other two wings. No. 26 gelatin (light sky blue) would give quite a realistic appearance as moonbeams.

The powerful beam projectors with 1500-watt lamps will be necessary for sunlight, to cut through the general light on the stage. These have been mounted in the same manner as the Fresnels ("moons") and a No. 54 (straw) gelatin used with them to give them a bit more warmth than the natural light from these instruments. This light will still appear whiter than the stage-left area lights with their No. 57.

It is not unusual on the stage with limited equipment to employ the same instrument for suns and moons, changing the color media between scenes, of course.

TRANSLUCENT BACKDROP

And finally we come to the background with a distant view painted opaquely at the bottom. This portion of course, must be lighted from the front and therefore five 6-foot lengths of striplights are placed on the floor, not too close, so that their various beams may have room to blend smoothly over the surface. They should be as close to the ground row as possible, so as to be hidden from the audience (this is especially important if there is a balcony). As the light to be thrown on this portion is limited to the realistic daylight and nighttime colors, we may use amber, blue-green, and blue roundels over the 300-watt R-floods. Glass is essential here, for gelatin would quickly burn out over these powerful lamps.

The upper portion of the backdrop is a true translucency, and therefore its light should come from behind. Four 6-foot lengths and two shorter lengths of strips with 150-watt PAR-spots are flown well above the highest visible part of the translucency and are focused down it to give it a sheet of light. A plain, white cloth might also be hung behind these, to reflect additional light through the drop. This is a particularly effective device to furnish extra punch. As these strips are focused downwards, gelatin may be used safely. Quite a variation of color is needed for this sky, so the three circuits may well have No. 36 (nonfade-blue), No. 67 (fire red), and No. 40 (light blue-green). By mixing the first and last, a daylight sky can be achieved; the 67 and 40 can give a sunset amber, while a touch of 67 added to the strong blue will provide a rich night sky. Many variations of these are possible.

It will noticed that neither footlights nor x-ray strips are employed with this setting. Footlights would throw unwanted shadows—of the cottage, the trees, the fence, the ground row—on the background, unless they were kept at such a low reading that they would serve no useful purpose. Likewise, strips in the usual x-ray (or first border) position would light up the overhead cloth borders, representing leaves and branches, but actually designed solely for the utilitarian task of masking the overhead stage machinery. Such maskings are best left unlighted—and the audience, therefore, undistracted.

CONTROL

In a setting of this nature it is amazing how rapidly the dimmer requirements mount up. Certainly the twenty-two area spotlights each deserve individual control. The four moons could be ganged but would then require a dimmer of 4000 watts capacity. Similarly the suns could be controlled together, but would need a 6000-watt dimmer or two of 3000 watts each.

The translucency front strips make up as three 20-lamp color circuits of 6000 watts apiece. There are 22 lamps per color circuit in the rear strips, at 3300 watts each.

If the largest dimmers are 2000 watts (many places do not approach this) then the moons will require two, the suns four, translucency fronts nine, and rear six—a total of twenty-one dimmers!

On many boards this would necessitate ganging area spotlights, always a great pity, with the resulting loss of artistic control. Of course it may be necessary to fall back on awkward replugging between scenes, using the same dimmers for the moons in the second scene as were used for the suns in the first, and the left area cools in place of the warms on the same group of controls.

532   WING-AND-BORDER SETTINGS

The wing-and-border setting presents problems very different from the realistic exterior and interior types. Here realism and plausibility are usually of little concern. Rather, the large expanses of flat scenery demand flat lighting, and against these brilliant backgrounds the actors must be picked out by powerful lighting directed on them. The use of follow spots for this purpose is universal.

SETTING FOR A MUSICAL

Figure 20-6 shows a wing-and-border set for a typical musical. Because a traveler show curtain with appropriate design is hung immediately behind the house curtain, the house tormentors and teaser have been removed and their functions assumed by a show portal hung just upstage of the show curtain. The zone across the stage just above the portal is usually referred to as "In One." Its upstage boundary is marked by a second traveler, a second portal, and a drop beyond. In turn, some feet upstage of this group is yet another consisting of a second drop, a third portal, and then two more drops. Finally, beyond all is a sky-blue backing.

The several drops will not all be solid cloth; some will be cut out in part so that the audience sees through to other scenic elements beyond. The various drops will work with the curtains and portals in different combinations as the show progresses, while set pieces, furniture items, and the like will be moved on and off stage for different scenes. Often special lighting is needed for such pieces.

In the sketch are shown the three portals, drop No. 2, representing a cutout of trees, and drop No. 4, a distant view.

LIGHTING THE IN-ONE ZONE

In order to provide the punch of light on the actors required by this type of presentation, we have double-hung all the area lighting spotlights. This means that in the beams there are twelve 6-inch ellipsoidal spotlights, two to a side on each of the three "In One" areas. Care must be taken to focus these spots far enough downstage on the apron to cover the probable movement of the players. In this style of production it is not uncommon for the actors to be brought clear down to the very edge of the stage, and they must be covered there just as much as when they are confined by the imaginary "fourth wall."

With four instruments on each area, considerable variation in the colors is possible. Rather than simply use the same tints on the opposite side of the stage, we prefer to put the flattering No. 3 (flesh pink) as the warm color on the left and No. 62 on the right. For most productions of this type, a generally romantic feeling is desired, so the cools should not be extreme. No. 26 is a deep enough blue to be used on the left, while the rather neutral No. 17 (Special Lavender) on the right will appear quite cool in comparison to the warm colors used with it.

FOLLOW SPOTS

Frequently, it is desirable to have special instruments in the beams to illuminate the decorative show curtain. But to keep this layout on the modest side, we have forgone these and will let the footlights do the job. But a pair of 8-inch narrow-beam ellipsoidal spotlights, burning 750-watt lamps and equipped with irises are used as follow spots. We assume that operators may be stationed in the theatre's beam. In plants where this is not possible, some other location must be found. Musicals without spotlights to accent the leading players on the brightly lighted stage lack a great deal of the theatrical glamor that goes with this sort of presentation. Most of the time these follow spots will be most effective with no color medium at all. If any is used, a No. 2 (light flesh-pink) is appropriate. Of course, for occasional and particular purposes other and stronger colors may be used, including a very dense blue filter especially made for ultraviolet effects. With an operator in constant attendance, color changes are easily accomplished.

THE IN-TWO ZONE

Moving to the "In-Two" zone, that between the second and third portals, we light the three upstage areas by means of twelve 6-inch Fresnel spots hanging from the first pipe. Their colors match the downstage area spotlights, as usual. These instruments must be carefully focused to pass under the second portal without touching the edges with a distracting glare. Many times a third set of spotlights is employed for the "In-Three" zone, but because ours is not deep and we are trying to be economical with instruments, we shall hope that the extra light is not needed this far upstage.

SIDE LIGHTING

Side lighting—lighting from the wings—has become a convention with the wing-and-border setting. It has three important aspects: its low angle from the side adds to the plasticity of the actor's appearance; it can add extra color effects; and it helps to tie together the zones across which it is focused. In each of our six side entrances we have provided two 6-inch ellipsoidal spotlights, mounted on stands. The upper instrument is focused across the stage to catch both the center and the far acting areas, and, because of this long throw, it

No.	INSTRUMENT	LOCATION	PURPOSE	LAMP	COLOR	REMARKS
1	6" ELLIPS'L-REF'R SPOTLIGHT	BEAM - L	AREA 2L WARM	500T12	3	
2	" " " "	" "	" 2L COOL	"	26	
3	" " " "	" "	" 1L WARM	"	3	FRAME TO PORTAL
4	" " " "	" "	" 1L COOL	"	26	" " "
5	" " " "	" "	" 3L WARM	"	3	
6	" " " "	" "	" 3L COOL	"	26	
7	8 ELLIPS'L-REF'R SPOTLIGHT	BEAM - C	FOLLWSPOT	750T12	CLEAR	
8	" " " "	" "	"	"	"	
9	6" ELLIP'S'L-REF'R SPOTLIGHT	BEAM - R	AREA 1R WARM	500T12	62	
10	" " " "	" "	" 1R COOL	"	17	
11	" " " "	" "	" 3R WARM	"	62	FRAME OFF PORTAL
12	" " " "	" "	" 3R COOL	"	17	" " "
13	" " " "	" "	" 2R WARM	"	62	
14	" " " "	" "	" 2R COOL	"	17	
15	" " " "	1ST STAND - L	CROSSLIGHT	750T12	29	FOCUS ON AREA 2,3
16	" " " "	" "	"	500T12	29	" " " 1,2
17	6" FRESNEL-LENS SPOTLIGHT	1ST PIPE - L	AREA 5L WARM	500T20	3	
18	" " " "	" "	5L COOL	"	26	
19	" " " "	" "	4L WARM	"	3	
20	" " " "	" "	4L COOL	"	26	
21	" " " "	" "	6L WARM	"	3	
22	" " " "	" "	6L COOL	"	26	
23	" " " "	1ST PIPE - R	4R WARM	"	62	
24	" " " "	" "	4R COOL	"	17	
25	" " " "	" "	6R WARM	"	62	
26	" " " "	" "	6R COOL	"	17	
27	" " " "	" "	5R WARM	"	62	
28	" " " "	" "	5R COOL	"	17	
29	6" ELLIPS'L-REF'R SPOTLIGHT	1ST STAND - R	CROSSLIGHT	750T12	57	FOCUS ON AREA 1,2
30	" " " "	" R	"	500T12	57	" " " 2,3
31	" " " "	2ND STAND - L	"	750T12	29	" " " 5,6
32	" " " "	" - L	"	500T12	29	" " " 4,5
33	" " " "	" - R	"	750T12	57	" " " 4,5
34	" " " "	" - R	"	500T12	57	" " " 5,6
35	" " " "	3RD STAND - L	"	750T12	29	FOCUS FAR
36	" " " "	" - L	"	500T12	29	" NEAR
37	" " " "	" - R	"	750T12	57	" FAR
38	" " " "	" - R	"	500T12	57	" NEAR
39	16" BEAM PROJECTOR	2ND PIPE - L	DOWNLIGHT	1000G40	2 & 62	FOCUS DOWNSTAGE
40	" " "	" - L	"	"	2 & 62	" "
41	" " "	" - R	"	"	2 & 62	" "
42	" " "	" - R	"	"	2 & 62	" "
43	6"×6'-0" STRIPLIGHTS				R	
44	" "	APRON	FOOTLIGHTS	150R40	G (ROUNDEL)	3-COLOR CIRCUIT
45	" "			FLOOD	B	FEED THROUGH
46	" "				"	
47	" "	1ST PIPE	1ST BORDER	150R40	58	
48	" "			SPOT	40	
49	" "				"	
50	" "	3RD PIPE	2ND BORDER	150R40	58	
51	" "			SPOT	40	
52	" "					
53	" "	4TH PIPE	BACK DROP	300R40	"	
54	" "			SPOT	32	
55	" "				57	

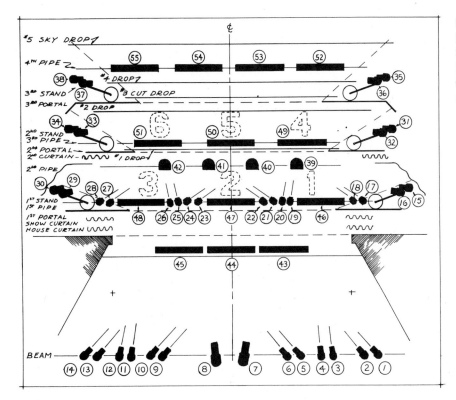

FIGURE 20–6. A WING-AND-BORDER SETTING. Above: Sketch of setting. Below: Layout of lighting instruments. Opposite page: Instrument schedule.

burns a 750-watt lamp. The lower one, mounted at least ten feet above stage level, ties in the near and the center areas and uses the 500-watt lamp. Because we are not using strong colors for our regular area spotlights, in these sidelighting instruments we choose No. 29 (Special Steel Blue) from the left and No. 57 (Light Amber) from the right.

DOWN LIGHTS

Another feature that is becoming almost a must for musicals are the downlights which we have placed over the "In-One" zone. These are hung quite high and just downstage of the traveler curtain and the second portal so that they tend to back-light the actors standing at the front of the zone. A combination of No. 2 and No. 62 gelatins in these 16-inch beam projectors with their 1000-watt G-lamps will throw a flattering high light on the head and shoulders of the actors and set them out from the scenery. A second set of down lights over the "In-Two" zone might not be amiss, but our list of instruments is already startlingly long.

FOOTLIGHTS

Striplights have been used extensively to tie in the various portions of the stage, to give tonal washes over scenery and actors, and generally, to provide quite a bit of the illumination. The footlights consist of the regular three 6-foot lengths, in this case burning 150-watt R-40 lamps behind glass roundels in the primary colors. The unusually high wattage here is to provide a strong wash of light for the show curtain. In general, musicals and revues demand rather strong footlights to supplement the regular front lighting especially for chorus-line sequences, to throw illumination under large hats, to wash the company with special colors, and the like.

BORDER LIGHTS

For the first and second borders, three 6-foot lengths each are used. Those of the first pipe must be placed well apart to leave room for area spotlights to be mounted between the lengths; on the third pipe less space is needed. But in both cases somewhat wider extension into the wings is necessary in order to wash properly the scenery hanging upstage of each set of strips. The 150-watt R-40 floods are used with colors approaching the secondaries: No. 11 (medium magenta), No. 58 (medium amber), and No. 40 (light blue-green), a combination that should allow almost any tint desired to flood the stage.

THE BACKDROP

And for the background, the cloth or other surface painted to represent the sky, there have been hung four lengths of strips, as far downstage from the surface as other flown elements permit, so that as smooth a wash as possible can be achieved. Here it is necessary to go to the 300-watt R-40 spots, as a good punch will be needed. A good dark night sky can be achieved by use of a No. 38 (dark navy-blue) and if this is a bit too deep it can be lightened a little by mixing in No. 27 (light blue). For a bright daylight sky we add No. 57 (light amber).

CONTROL

There are twenty-four area spotlights, all of which will be working at the same time in several scenes, so no replugging is possible in this production. While it would be pleasant to have an individual dimmer assigned to each cross-lighting instrument, we can get along by ganging the pair at each location, holding the dimmer requirements to six. Likewise the down lights may well be ganged: on a 4000-watt dimmer, if one is available—if not, in pairs on two 2000-watt dimmers.

The footlights and first and second border will each require three 1800-watt circuits—nine all together. But the backdrop calls for three circuits of 4800 watts apiece. On boards with only small capacity controls, these loads must be split up in some manner, depending on what is available.

Obviously individual control over the two follow spots is absolutely essential. The total and minimum demands for this layout, therefore, would be forty-three dimmers that can handle up to 2000 watts each, and three of far greater capacity. And this is a very modest plot for a musical play.

SPACE STAGES

Increasingly popular today is the type of presentation that is often referred to as space staging. In this form of production realism is completely lacking in the scenery, which is generally a dark background, an arrangement of platforms, and a form or two of suggestive but not very accurate shape. No specific locales are intended, or the locales may change as the play progresses. For example, a presentation of *Macbeth* might be given with the same scenery serving at various times for "A Heath," "Macbeth's Castle," "Birnam Wood," and so forth.

The lighting is usually done in limited areas at a time—a single actor pin-pointed by a spotlight, or a compact group covered by a slightly larger pool of light. Entrances are made from the dark. Often groups of actors stand in half darkness. Every instrument becomes, in effect, a "special." A grave problem is to keep the spill light off the background, to hold the beams to tight focuses, to eliminate, insofar as may be done, reflections from the floor. To this end the instru-

538 ments are usually mounted quite high and as nearly vertical as possible, and focused with care and precision.

A TYPICAL SPACE SETTING

Figure 20-7 shows a typical space-stage arrangement. Surrounding the stage is a cyclorama and wings of a soft, black material to absorb as much light as possible. Center stage is an irregular platform with steps from three sides, all painted a flat black. An arch that might be accepted as a number of things from a church window to a bower, and painted a dark shade of brown, stands on the platform. There is a trap to the left of it in the floor.

LIGHTING THE SPACE STAGE

In the beams four 6-inch ellipsoidal spotlights are used for the stage-level areas at quite sharp angles to avoid as far as possible letting their beams strike the cyclorama. One 8-inch spotlight to be used as a follow spot is also mounted there, while a 6-inch spot is placed

No.	INSTRUMENT	LOCATION	PURPOSE	LAMP	COLOR	REMARKS
1	6" ELLIPS'L-REF'R SPOTLIGHT	BEAM-L	DR SPECIAL	500 T12	29	
2	8" " " "	" "	FOLLOW SPOT	750 T12	54	
3	6" " " "	" "	R-CENTER SP.	500 T12	NONE	
4	" " " "	BEAM-R	DL SP. #1	"	57	
5	" " " "	" "	" " #2	"	26	
6	6" FRESNEL-LENS SPOTLIGHT	1ST PIPE-L	L-STEPS	500 T20	3/62	KEEP OFF CYC.
7	6" ELLIPS'L-REF'R SPOTLIGHT	" " "	UC SPECIAL	500 T12	NONE	
8	" " " "	" " "	"HORROR SP."	"	41	FRAME TO TRAP
9	" " " "	1ST PIPE-C	ARCH SP. #1	"	58	
10	6" FRESNEL-LENS SPOTLIGHT	" " "	R-STEPS	500 T20	17	
11	6" ELLIPS'L-REF'R SPOTLIGHT	1ST PIPE-R	ARCH SP. #2	500 T12	30	FRAME TO ARCH
12	" " " "	PLATFORM-DR	FOLLOW SPOT	"	26/29	
13	6" FRESNEL-LENS SPOTLIGHT	2ND PIPE-R	UR STEPS	500 T20	18	
14	6" ELLIPS'L-REF'R SPOTLIGHT	" " "	DS STEPS #1	500 T12	26	
15	" " " "	" " "	" " #2	"	57	
16	16" BEAM PROJECTOR	3RD PIPE UL	ARCH BACKLIGHT	1000 G40	54	FOCUS THRU ARCH
17	LINNEBACH PROJECTOR	BEHIND PLATFORM-L	PROJECTION ON CYC	1500 G40	SLIDE	HIDDEN OPERATOR - ADDITIONAL SLIDES
18	14" ELLIPS'L-REF'R FLOOD	BEHIND PLATFORM-R	FIRE GLOW ON CYC	500 PS	60	
19	" " " "	"	"	"	67	} GANG TOGETHER
20	" " " "	"	"	"	63	
21	6" x 4'-6" STRIPLIGHTS	1ST PIPE-L	X-RAYS	150 PS	29 58	3-COLOR CIRCUIT FEED THROUGH
22	" "	" " -R	"	OR R40-FL.	41	
23	SLIDE PROJECTOR	2ND PIPE-L	PROJECTION ON CYC	1000 G40	SLIDE	8" PLANO-CONVEX SPOT WITH EFFECT HEAD

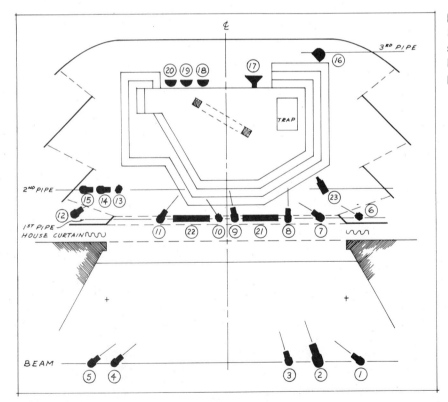

FIGURE 20–7. A SPACE-STAGE SETTING. Above: Sketch of setting. Below: Layout of lighting instruments. Opposite page: Instrument schedule.

high on a special platform in the right wing. Other 6-inch instruments, including a few Fresnels with hoods to control side spill are used from the first pipe to light the platform and step areas. Two cover the arch opening, a very important acting position; another is carefully focused on the trap. A large beam projector is also employed as back lighting through the arch from the upstage side.

Despite the blackness of the cyclorama, it can be used for special projections to good advantage. A Linnebach will throw general pictures as backings to the archway, while sharper images can come from the effect machine hung from the second pipe. A general glow is produced by three floodlights placed behind the up-right corner of the platform. Two spotlights are hung from the second pipe to wash the downstage portion of the steps. And two striplights are intended to give a very general low-intensity tone to the whole stage for scenes involving large groups.

CONTROL

This is a very modest layout; no doubt an actual script would suggest many more instruments than those to which we have optimistically limited ourselves. Frequently in such a production the demands for color changes force the hanging of identical instruments, side by side, and covering the same portions of the stage.

But those instruments we have used must, beyond question, have individual control. This should not be too difficult, as only twenty-two dimmers are required, and none need have a capacity greater than 1500 watts.

In plays of this nature the effects are largely achieved through the most delicate dimming and cross-fading. The biggest problem of control, therefore, is the timing on the control panel. If this is located, as is sadly the usual case, somewhere in the wings, the operators must be driven and drilled until they can accomplish their blindfold task adequately. But if the controlboard is properly located where the stage may be easily viewed, then the operator can perform his work with taste and understanding and become, in effect, an additional and very important actor.

FIGURE 20–8. THE TENSION WIRE GRID. A woven grid of aircraft cable under tension. Designed as a ceiling grid, it is weight-bearing and gives complete access to overhead lighting positions. (a) View of a grid installation over the auditorium of a proscenium theatre. (Photo —Eiseman.) (b) Detail of grid and lighting position. Developed by George Izenour. Manufactured by J. R. Clancy.

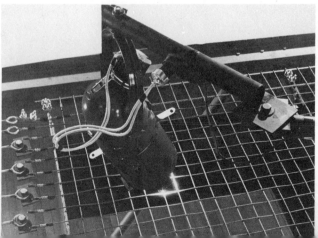

Designing the Lighting for Other Forms of Production 21

ARENA PRODUCTION

So far we have discussed only the types of production presented on a conventional stage with practically all action separated from the audience by "the fourth wall." But there are other forms rapidly gaining in popularity in which the division between audience area and acting area is less clearly marked. These vary from a regular stage with action coming out into the auditorium on side stages, ramps, and steps to the complete arena form in which the audience surrounds the playing area on all four sides. Obviously the techniques that are useful for lighting in-the-round stages must differ from those used for performances done on a proscenium stage.

The designer need not be bothered with lighting the scenery in a truly in-the-round production, for there is little scenery, and what there is is adequately lighted by the same beams that strike nearby actors. But this same lack of scenery deprives the designer of valuable mounting positions for his instruments, and, more important, denies him a background. He must light the actors from all sides, just as they must play to all sides.

541

ACCURACY OF FOCUS

With the spectators crowded closely—often too closely—about the playing areas, instruments that have hard-to-control beams are of little value. Floodlights are impossible. Striplights may be used discreetly and with side maskings to give an over-all tonality of rather low intensity. Fresnel spots must be focused with particular accuracy and in addition a funnel must be added to control the beam spill.

FUNCTIONS OF ARENA LIGHTING

Visibility remains, of course, the primary function in arena-production lighting, and this means that the actors must be effectively lighted for all members of the surrounding audience. Composition takes the form of holding the spectators' attention to the acting areas and thus demands that the lighting must have definition and form of great precision. Some plays suggest that certain sections of the stage always be related to certain locations, which adds another duty to composition: that of holding these areas to closely prescribed limits. Mood must be accomplished by means of general intensity and in color toning, but both within very limited ranges.

MOUNTING POSITIONS

Because there is such great variation among the different arena stages and the buildings surrounding them, it is difficult to suggest a typical lighting arrangement. An arena stage in the center of a large gymnasium floor, for example, would probably offer all sorts of lofty and convenient mounting places for overhead lighting instruments, while a formal hall with a plastered ceiling of no great height presents the utmost difficulty, ranging close to the impossible. However, let us assume a reasonable amount of overhead flexibility in our discussion of this form of presentation.

ARENA LIGHTING AREAS

It is convenient to divide the arena stage into a number of acting areas, each of which can be effectively covered by the beam of a spotlight mounted along the 45-degree angle. Just what type of spotlight this would be would depend on the mounting locations and their distances. If a good, long throw is possible, the narrow-beam ellipsoidal spotlight with a 500-watt lamp would be fine; for much shorter throws, say of 15 to 20 feet, the 6-inch plano-convex spotlight, using 500-watt or 1000-watt lamps or the wide-beam ellipsoidal can be very useful.

On the proscenium stage it is basic that each area be covered by two spotlights, ideally each 45 degrees on the actor, but in an arena with the actor seen from all sides, more instruments are a necessity.

There are two popular approaches to the solution. One is that three instruments per area be used, evenly spaced about the area and thus at 120 degrees from one another. The second approach is to use four spots on each area, putting them 90 degrees from each other.

COLOR IN THE ARENA

With either, the system of one warm and one cool color on each area is no longer applicable. With the three-spotlight plan the third instrument is assigned a neutral color, such as special lavender which, we have seen, appears cool opposite a warm gelatin and warm opposite a cool one. Light flesh pink is also a possibility for scenes that are basically warm and romantic. Or no color at all can be quite effective, and would permit lower-wattage lamps in such instruments as have no gelatin to cut down the output.

With the four-instrument system two variations suggest themselves. In the first, a warm and a cool are used on opposite sides, while the two intermediate instruments have a neutral medium. The alternate system is to use two warms, opposite each other, and two cools, also opposite each other. Probably the latter is the more satisfactory.

A word of warning about the choice of colors in arena productions is advisable: because the directionality of the spotlights on each side of each area is so definite, colors show up much stronger on the actors than in a proscenium production where there is far more mixing of different beams. Or perhaps the very closeness of the audience makes this seem true. At any event, the stronger colors are rarely advisable.

BLENDING

The use of blending strips to give a tonality to the scene, much as first border strips are used on a proscenium stage, may be quite effective if properly handled. Two or three of the 6-foot lengths might be hung down the center line of the arena, or two strips may be placed along opposite sides and focused across the stage. In a permanent arena setup, it might be easier yet to mount sockets on an overhead rig surrounding the stage and focused toward it, wire these in three circuits, and use the colored R-lamps. Striplights, so used, must be provided with blinders (side maskings) that will prevent their beams from falling on the audience, particularly that portion of it seated on the opposite side of the stage.

UNMASKED INSTRUMENTS

It is useless in a temporary arena setup to attempt to hide the instruments from the audience. They can, of course, be hung and maintained in a neat manner, with wiring carefully tied off and the

FIGURE 21–1. ARENA STAGE LIGHTING POSITIONS. Above: A perspective view of an arena stage showing a pipe grid over the audience and acting area. (1) The nearest frontal position behind the valance. (2) Extreme position on the outer edge of the grid. (3) Central position over the acting area for down lighting and back lighting. (4) Special position in the aisle for an occasional effect.

The acting areas are numbered from one to five. The number of areas is, of course, optional and would vary with the requirements of the production.

Below: A cross section through the arena showing the various angles of distribution. (1) Pipe grid. (2) Outside position. (3) Valance. (4) Inner position behind valance. (5) Central position. (6) Special position in aisle.

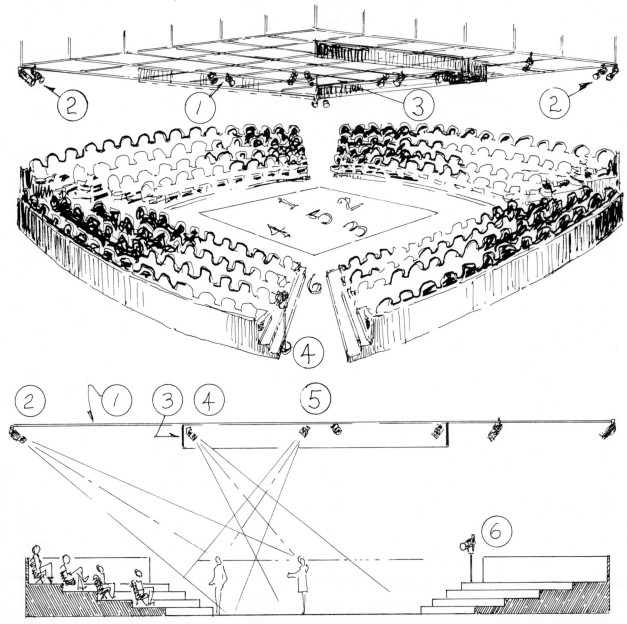

No.	INSTRUMENT	PURPOSE	LAMP	COLOR	REMARKS
1	6" Ellips'l-Ref'l Spotlight	Area 1	500 T12	802	
2	" " "	" 2	"	802	
3	8" Fresnel Spotlight	Moonlight Special	1000 G40	857	Focus Center
4	6" Ellips'l-Ref'l Spotlight	Area 2	500 T12	854	
5	" " "	" 3	"	854	
6	" " "	Divan Special	750 T12	826	Frame to Divan
7	" " "	Area 3	500 T12	805	
8	" " "	" 4	"	805	
9	" " "	" 4	"	842	
10	" " "	" 1	"	842	
11	6" Plano-Convex Spotlight	" 4	1000 G40	802	Mat Top
12	6" Fresnel Spotlight	" 5	500 T20	802	Funnel
13	6" Plano-Convex Spotlight	" 3	1000 G40	802	Mat Top
14	" " "	" 1	"	854	" "
15	6" Fresnel Spotlight	" 5	500 T20	854	Funnel
16	6" Plano-Convex Spotlight	" 4	1000 G40	854	Mat Top
17	" " "	" 2	"	805	" "
18	6" Fresnel Spotlight	" 5	500 T20	805	Funnel
19	4½" Ellips'l-Ref'l Spotlight	Center Accent	500 T12	Clear	Focus Center
20	6" Plano-Convex Spotlight	Area 1	1000 G40	805	Mat Top
21	" " "	" 3	"	842	" "
22	" " "	Divan Special #2	"	881	Mat to Divan
23	6" Fresnel Spotlight	Area 5	500 T20	842	Funnel
24	6" Plano-Convex Spotlight	" 2	1000 G40	842	Mat Top
25	Fixture	Table Lamp #1	40 A	-	Gang with #26
26	"	" " #2	40 A	-	" " #25

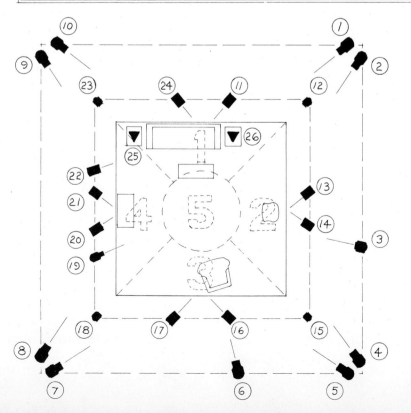

FIGURE 21–2. AN ARENA-
PRODUCTION SETTING.
Left: Layout of lighting
instruments. Above: Instrument
schedule.

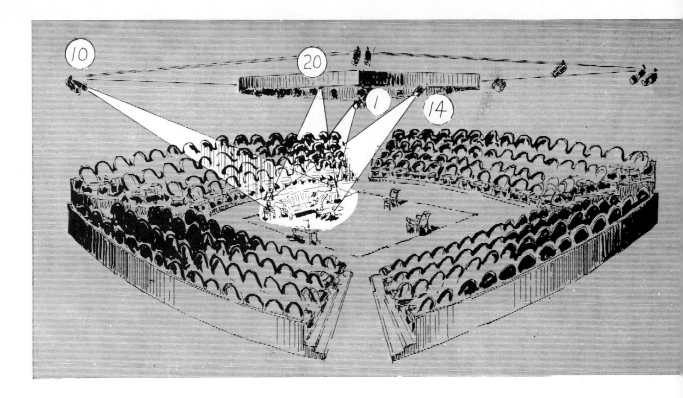

FIGURE 21–3. ARENA STAGE LIGHTING LAYOUT. Above: Illustrating the coverage on one of the five acting areas. Note the four different angles. Note Area 1 in floor plan showing lighting layout, p. 545.

like. But a frank acceptance of the fact that the instruments are there for all to view is better than a lot of makeshift, dust-catching, and fire-prone draperies.

However, if a stage house is designed especially for arena production, a false ceiling should be provided with openings through which the beams of light may be focused from instruments hung well above and out of sight. Catwalks must be installed, so the electrician can reach all instruments with ease for maintenance, for focusing, and for color changes. Provisions should also be made for closing off any unused openings.

BLINDING THE SPECTATORS

But the most difficult problem in any form of arena production is the matter of keeping the beams of the area spotlights out of the eyes of the spectators seated on the opposite side of the stage. As long as light persists in traveling in a straight line, and as long as directors wish to play their actors at the very edge of the arena stage, just so long will a compromise be necessary between a well-lighted actor and a half-blinded spectator. If the first row of the audience can be raised higher than the stage level, or be set back from it, or both, the problem is greatly eased. But in any event, this is one of the greatest problems confronting the light designer in arena production.

DESIGNING THE LIGHTING FOR AN ARENA PRODUCTION 547

Figure 21–1 shows a sketch of one variation of arena staging with properties in place on the stage floor. There are two boxes in which lighting instruments may be hung overhead. A layout and an instrument schedule for a suitable lighting design are also shown.

The designer has divided the stage into five subsidiary areas, which have been numbered clockwise from one through four, with area five in the center. Dotted lines on the layout mark the approximate limits of these areas, though it is, of course, understood that actually they will overlap one another and their lights will blend smoothly. The instruments have been numbered systematically, from the top, clockwise around the stage, in the outer box first and then the inner.

From each corner of the outer box a pair of 6-inch ellipsoidal-reflector spotlights are focused on the two closest areas, giving each of these two beams of light at approximately right angles to one another. From the inner box two plano-convex spotlights are focused on each of the same areas. The plano-convex type of instrument is used here because the upper portion of its beam can be effectively matted to prevent light from glaring into the eyes of spectators seated on the opposite side of the stage.

Area 5, in the center, is hit from the four corners of the inner box by 6-inch Fresnel spotlights. Here the danger of spill light annoying the audience is less marked than with the outer areas, but funnels are used on the instruments just the same. The typical soft-edged Fresnel-beam pattern is useful to blend this center light with the illumination on the adjacent areas.

The color system in Roscolene plastic is that of opposite warms and cools. The warm light, working diagonally out of the upper-right corner of the layout, is from a Roscolene No. 802 (special scarlet) gelatin. The identical color might have been employed also from the lower left, but the designer preferred to use a slightly different tint, Roscolene No. 805 (light straw). In like manner, the cools are not identical: from the lower right is a No. 854 (steel blue), while opposite it is a No. 842 (special lavender). This is not an especially cool color, but it has been chosen here because we are assuming that this is a warm, pleasant type of play. Had it been a cold, stark drama, we might have selected a combination of No. 851 and No. 854 for the cools, while the versatile No. 842 might have been one of the warms, with perhaps no color at all in the opposite instruments.

A few specials have been provided. On the right side there is an 8-inch Fresnel with a No. 857 (medium blue) gelatin to give the effect of moonbeams for a brief scene. Instrument 6, an ellipsoidal with a large-wattage lamp, is focused carefully on the divan with a romantic

No. 826 (medium-pink) for a tender moment. Toward the upper-left corner is another divan special with No. 881 (chocolate) for a different scene. Also on the left, a wide-beamed ellipsoidal-reflector spotlight without color serves as an accent on the central area for some special action there. And the two table lamps at either end of the divan are practical fixtures, ganged on the same dimmer, but capable of being turned on and off at their individual switches.

THE THRUST STAGE

THE EXTENDED APRON

In Chapter 2 there is an analysis of two forms of presentation that recently have become extremely popular: the extended apron and the thrust stage. The former is really a variation of regular proscenium production as far as lighting is concerned. Some additional spotlights in the beams, on the balcony front, in side slots in the auditorium walls, and on booms in side boxes can all be used on the extended stage. If it is not too deep, it may be back-lighted from behind the proscenium, except, of course, when the curtain is closed. The use of striplights and floods is impractical. The only real problem presented is that of keeping the beam patterns from being too prominent on the walls of the auditorium and off the audience itself.

AN APPROACH TO THRUST-STAGE LIGHTING

Any theatre designed for a thrust stage should include provision for good mounting positions for the lighting instruments. The simplest manner of doing this is a grid of pipes or other mounting structure over the entire stage and extending over the audience as well in all directions as far distant from the edge of the stage as the height of the grid above the stage floor. There should be a great number of electrical outlets provided on this grid, unless it is the intention to string cables from backstage to the specific instruments. If the grid is not too high, it can be reached by ladders from below. But if it is over fourteen feet above the floor, a network of catwalks, so numerous that an electrician can safely reach every inch of the grid from them, should be provided above the pipes.

Boxes or valances to hide the instruments are often provided, but the fact that it is necessary to be able to hang spotlights on any portion of the grid, especially over the stage itself, prevents these from being wholly effective. It is therefore extremely important that instruments be mounted and cabled neatly and securely so as to be neither a distraction nor a danger. Those spectators in the side seats particularly will find that the lenses of instruments focused in their general

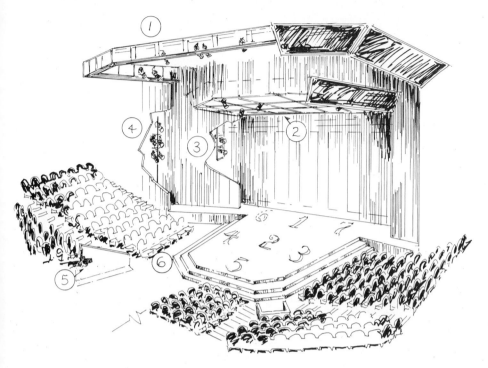

FIGURE 21–4. THRUST STAGE LIGHTING POSITIONS. A perspective view of a thrust stage showing its various lighting positions. The stage has been arbitrarily divided into acting areas which would vary with each production. (1) outer valance position. (2) Second valance and gridiron over stage. (3) Wing ladder, side lighting. (4) Tormentor boom. (5) Vomitory rail. (6) Gutter.

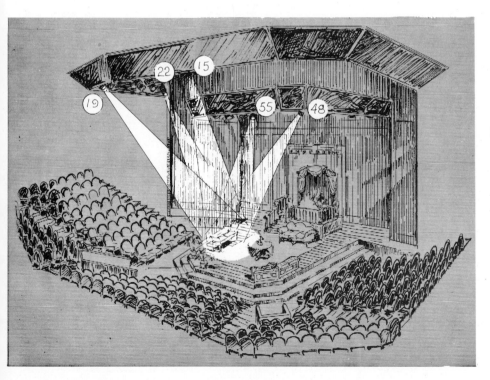

FIGURE 21–5. THRUST STAGE LIGHTING LAYOUT. (a) Illustrating the isolated coverage of a single acting area, Area 4. Note the five different angles. The following pages: (b) Instrument schedule. (c) Floor plan showing lighting layout. Note Area 4.

No	INSTRUMENT	LOCATION	PURPOSE	LAMP	COLOR	REMARKS
1	8" ELLIPS'L REF'R SPOTLIGHT	LEFT BOOM	AREA 1	750 T12	40	L. BOOM .TOP
2	6" " " "	" "	WASH - WARM	500 T12	34	" MIDDLE SOFT EDGE
3	6" " " "	" "	" - COOL	500 T12	19	" BOTTOM " "
4	6" " " "	2ND. VALANCE-L	AREA 3	750 T12	41	
5	8" " " "	" " "	" 2	"	41	
6	6" " " "	" " "	" 5	"	41	
7	6" " " "	" " "	" 3	"	40	
8	6" " " "	" " "	WINDOW SEAT	500 T12	40	
9	8" " " "	" " "	AREA 2	750 T12	17	
10	6" " " "	" " "	LEFT TUNNEL	500 T12	16	FRAME TO TUNNEL
11	6" " " "	" " "	AREA 5	750 T12	17	
12	8" " " "	2ND VALANCE-C	" 3	"	17	FRAME OFF AUDIENCE
13	8" FRESNEL-LENS SPOTLIGHT	" " "	WASH - COOL	1500 G40	19	BARN DOOR-OFF "
14	8" " " "	" " "	" - WARM	"	34	" " " "
15	8" ELLIPS'L REF'R SPOTLIGHT	" " "	AREA 4	750 T12	52	FRAME OFF "
16	6" " " "	2ND VALANCE-R	" 5	"	52	
17	6" " " "	" " "	RIGHT TUNNEL	500 T12	15	FRAME TO TUNNEL
18	8" " " "	" " "	AREA 2	750 T12	52	
19	6" " " "	" " "	" 4	"	51	
20	6" " " "	" " "	" 5	"	53/53	
21	8" " " "	" " "	" 2	"	53/53	
22	6" " " "	" " "	" 4	"	53/53	
23	8" " " "	RIGHT BOOM	" 1	"	51	R. BOOM - TOP
24	6" " " "	" "	WASH - WARM	500 T12	34	" MIDDLE-SOFT EDGE
25	6" " " "	" "	" - COOL	"	19	" BOTTOM - " "
26	8" " " "	LEFT LADDER	U.R. CORNER	750 T12	41	L. LADDER·TOP·FRAME SIDES
27	6" " " "	" "	AREA 1	"	41	" BOTTOM " US
28	6" " " "	" "	U.L. CORNER	500 T12	41	" " " " "
29	6" FRESNEL-LENS SPOTLIGHT	1ST VALANCE-L	" "	500 T20	17	
30	6" " " "	" " "	WASH - COOL	"	19	BARN DOOR-OFF AUDIENCE
31	6" " " "	" " "	" - WARM	"	34	" " " " "
32	6" ELLIPS'L REF'R SPOTLIGHT	" " "	AREA 1	"	17	
33	6" " " "	" " "	SOFA	"	17	
34	6" " " "	1ST VALANCE R.	"	"	52	
35	6" FRESNEL-LENS SPOTLIGHT	" " "	BENCH	500 T20	52	
36	6" ELLIPS'L REF'R "	" " "	AREA 1	500 T12	52	FRAME BOTTOM
37	6" FRESNEL-LENS "	" " "	WASH - WARM	500 T20	34	BARN DOOR OFF AUDIENCE
38	6" " " "	" " "	" - COOL	"	19	" " " "
39	6" " " "	" " "	U.R CORNER	"	52	
40	8" ELLIPS'L REF'R SPOTLIGHT	RIGHT LADDER	U.L. "	750 T12	53/53	R. LADDER ·TOP FRAME SIDE
41	6" " " "	" "	AREA 1	"	53/53	" BOTTOM " US
42	6" " " "	" "	U.R. CORNER	"	53/53	" " " " US
43	6" " " "	GRID. OVER STAGE	BENCH	500 T12	17	SOFT E. FRAME OFF AUDIENCE
44	6" FRESNEL-LENS "	" "	AREA 3	500 T20	CLEAR	BARNDOOR " "
45	6" ELLIPS'L REF'R "	" "	LEFT TUNNEL	500 T12	2	FRAME TO TUNNEL
46	6" FRESNEL-LENS "	" "	AREA 5	500 T20	CLEAR	BARN DOOR OFF AUDIENCE
47	6" ELLIPS'L REF'R "	" "	RIGHT TUNNEL	500 T12	2	FRAME TO TUNNEL
48	6" FRESNEL-LENS "	" "	AREA 4	500 T20	CLEAR	BARN DOOR OFF AUDIENCE
49	6" ELLIPS'L REF'R "	" "	STEPS	500 T12	52	SOFT E. FRAME TO STEPS
50	6" FRESNEL-LENS "	" "	AREA 2 DS	500 T20	CLEAR	
51	6" ELLIPS'L REF'R "	" "	ARCHWAY	750 T12	2	FRAME TO ARCHWAY
52	6" FRESNEL-LENS "	" "	AREA 2 US	500 T20	CLEAR	
53	6" ELLIPS'L REF'R "	" "	AREA 3	500 T12	"	FRAME L AND TOP
54	6" FRESNEL LENS "	" "	SOFA	500 T20	"	
55	6" ELLIPS'L REF'R "	" "	AREA 4	500 T12	"	FRAME R AND TOP
56	6" " " "	" "	LEFT RAMP	"	3	" OFF R. WALL
57	6" " " "	" "	RIGHT "	"	3	" " L. "
58	6" " " "	" "	UL ENTRANCE	"	3	" " R. "
59	6" " " "	" "	UR "	"	3	" " L. "
60	6" FRESNEL-LENS "	" "	UL CORNER	500 T20	CLEAR	
61	6" ELLIPS'L REF'R "	" "	AREA 1	500 T12	"	SOFT EDGE
62	6" FRESNEL-LENS "	" "	UR CORNER	500 T20	"	
63	6" " "	" "	HALL WAY - L	"	4	
64	6" " "	" "	" R	"	4	
65	6" " "	" "	WINDOW SEAT	"	CLEAR	BARN DOOR OFF AUDIENCE

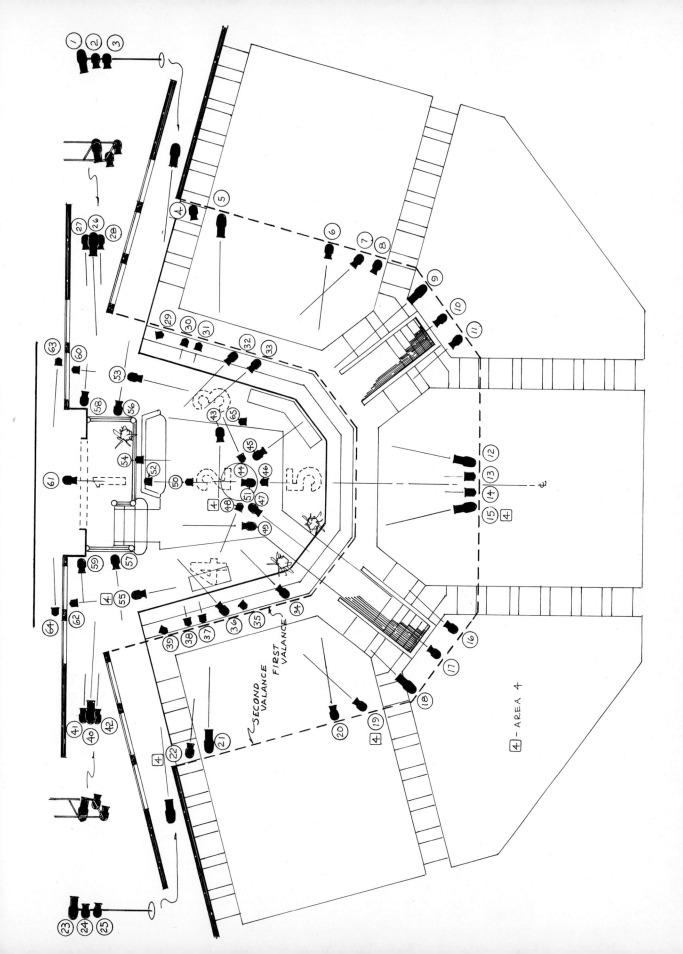

FIRST VALANCE

SECOND VALANCE

4 - AREA 4

552 direction will be in full view. But as long as they are not aimed directly at the audience, this should not prove too great a distraction, once it has been accepted. Great care must often be taken to mask or frame off the upper part of the beams from such instruments to be sure they do not glare directly into the eyes of those seated facing them. Ellipsoidal-reflector spotlights can use their internal framing shutters to good advantage; Fresnels should be provided with either funnels or barndoors, the latter being particularly recommended.

Often the arrangement of set pieces and properties will dictate how a thrust stage is best divided into acting areas, and each of these will require several instruments focused on it from several directions, for every actor is seen from three sides at the same time. Top or back lighting is also essential, to set the actor off from the background. Blending and toning are best accomplished by use of soft-beamed spotlights to throw color washes over large portions of the stage.

As with arena staging, strong colors are not indicated on the thrust stage, though we can become a little bolder, due to the one closed side. Spots to hit the stage at the familiar 45-degree angle from the front might use very pale tints, while other instruments on the same area can take stronger shades of the same basic colors, with those coming in directly from the sides using quite deep tones. The down or back lighting is usually not far from white light.

DESIGNING THE LIGHTING

Figure 21–5 shows a sketch of a typical thrust stage with properties and a few scenic pieces set for a play. On adjacent pages are a layout for lighting this production and a schedule of the instruments to be used.

The stage divides itself into five natural areas: the upper platform and archway being 1; the central section as outlined by the carpet, 2; and the margin of the platform surrounding the carpet, 3, 4, and 5. The designer has sought to put seven instruments on each area, but the difficulty of focusing to cover an area properly without hitting the audience at the same time has limited this in some instances. The further to the side the instruments are mounted, the deeper the colors they use. For this layout Cinemoid plastic is employed.

Taking area 1 as an example, we find that it is covered from the front by two 6-inch ellipsoidal-reflector spotlights, 32 and 36, mounted in the inner box. Two 8-inch ellipsoidals, 1 and 23, strike it from the booms placed in the ramp entrances on either side of the stage. Two more 6-inchers, 27 and 41, are on the ladders hung in the upstage entrances. One 6-inch ellipsoidal works as a back light from above the upstage archway. The colors, working from front to rear on the left side are Cinemoid 17 (steel blue), 40 (pale blue), and 41 (bright blue). On the right side they are 52 (pale gold), 51 (gold tint), and a double 53 (pale salmon). The back light is clear. The other areas use these same colors for instruments working from the same angles as do those on area 1.

A pair of 8-inch Fresnel spotlights strike the entire set from dead ahead to give it a tonal wash that may be varied by dimming the warm and cool instruments to different readings. Two pairs of 6-inch Fresnels, on either side of the inner box, and two pairs of 6-inch ellipsoidals in the ramp entrances work with the others. For the cool wash a Cinemoid 19 (dark blue) is used, for the warm wash a 34 (golden amber).

A great many specials have been hung. The extreme up-left and up-right corners, which might almost be considered areas in themselves, are each covered by three spots from front and sides, plus a back light. The tunnel entrances through the audience section, the entrances along the ramps left and right, and those at the extreme back, as well as the archway in the center of the backwall, are all lighted. The bench, the window seat, the sofa, and the steps leading up to Area 1 have appropriate coverage. Additional specials might be suggested, particularly as we see the development of the director's staging. He might, for example, place actors on the steps leading down from the platform, in which case, of course, suitable lighting would have to be provided.

The ellipsoidal-reflector spotlights have been used a great deal in this layout, because of the good control we have over their beam shapes, thus preventing light from spilling into the audience. When possible they are soft-edged by shifting the lenses to throw the gate out of focus, so as to cut down on sharp patterns and abrupt changes of intensity on the stage and actors. For the same reason Fresnel spotlights are used when their spill light will not be critical, and even then barndoors are suggested on many instruments.

DANCE

The following discussion on lighting for the dance is based in great part on the theories and techniques of Thomas Skelton, a leading practitioner in this field.

At first glance dance, which is almost always performed in a wing-and-border setting on a proscenium stage, would seem to require the same sort of lighting as do other forms of production. But there is one most important difference: when we attend a play we are vitally interested in the face of the actor to tell us his character, his thoughts, and his emotions. This is not true in dance, particularly ballet, in which it is the positions and movements of the dancer's body that tell us what the actor's face reveals. A knowledgeable lover of ballet will scarcely notice a dancer's face at all and will surely not concentrate on it. He is solely concerned with movement. Good dance lighting will reveal and emphasize movement.

To do this, the axis of the principal light should be along the axis of the movement. Thus a ballerina spinning in a pirouette should have the light hitting straight down on her or straight up from below. The latter, which has been used for trick effects in eccentric dance routines, would not be appropriate for serious ballet, so although light from directly overhead tends to make the human body appear shortened, it is still the best way to accent the rapid turning of the dance.

Or the same dancer faces the audience and raises her arm gracefully from her side to an angle of 45 degrees above her shoulder. This movement is best accented by a light striking her armpit along the center line of the angle through which her arm was raised. A spotlight about thirteen feet away at stage level would fulfill the requirements, and would be hidden from the view of the audience if the dancer is that close to the wings. If she is further away, the ideal angle is no longer possible, but this same location remains the best available position.

Of course it would be quite impractical to attempt to cover every single movement of a dance. It would require a prodigious number of spotlights and an extremely complicated list of cues and light changes. But provision can be made for a very few of the most significant

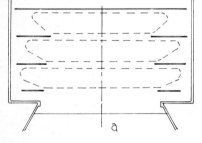

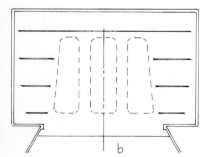

FIGURE 21–6. LIGHTING AREAS FOR DANCE.   These coincide with the principal movements of the dancers on the stage.
(a) *Cross-stage.* Dancers emerge from and disappear into the wings, dance across the stage, and work in lines that parallel the footlights. (b) *Up-and-down stage.* Dancers move toward the footlights and away again. In ballet the chorus frequently poses along the sides while the principals take center stage. (c) *Diagonal movement.* A most important aspect of modern dance. Dancers emerge from upstage wings and exit downstage on the opposite side, or vice versa. (d) *Center stage.* An obvious location for important dancing. The principal, or principals, or a small group, frequently work here in a circular pattern.
(e) *Special Spots.* These may be any place on the stage (a few possible ones are indicated) in which a tight movement by the leading dancer is performed.

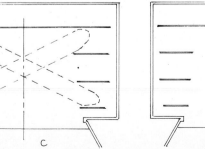

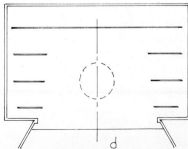

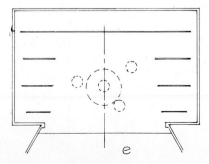

moments and for more general lighting that will best suit the major movements of the work. It is imperative that the light designer attend as many rehearsals as possible and take careful notes before sitting down to his drawing board. Fortunately, dances do fall into certain basic patterns of movement which can usually be covered successfully by one or more of the areas suggested in Figure 21–6.

LOCATION OF INSTRUMENTS

Among the more usual mounting positions for instruments, almost invariably spotlights, the following suggest themselves.

Low-Front. For the low-front position, light comes from the footlights. Such light is not flattering because this angle of lighting is not found in nature and rarely elsewhere. However, the footlights at a low reading are essential to wash out the shadows of the dancers' costumes caused by higher-placed instruments. This is the only location where spotlights are not used.

Medium-Front. For the medium-front position, the lights might be mounted on a low balcony rail. Though light from this angle tends to wash out body form, a little of it is desirable for the sake of visibility.

High-Front. The lights would be mounted on a second balcony or a beam position for the high-front position. Again, this does little for the body and accentuates the shadows of the dancers' costumes on their legs, so it should be avoided.

Low-Side. For the low-side position, light would come from the floor of the wings. Though this is an unnatural angle, it is flattering to women dancers, for it tends to lift the body.

Medium-Side. For the medium-side position, lights are mounted about eight or ten feet above the floor in the wings. This may be regarded as *the* basic dance-lighting angle. It throws a wash across the stage with little important shadowing. It may be desirable to mount another spotlight a few feet higher to carry across to the far side of the stage. In this case both long- and short-throw spots are focused so that the centers of their beams are parallel. Medium-side should not be confused with *high-side,* which is described below.

High-Side. Light in the high-side position comes from fifteen to twenty feet high in the wings. This tends to push the dancers down and makes them seem squat, and should be avoided if possible.

Straight-Back. In the straight-back position, light comes from above but also from behind the dancer. This is a very fine position, for it highlights the body in space, separating it from the background, and it does not cause one dancer to throw a shadow on the next one.

Diagonal-Back. As in the straight-back position, light comes from above and behind the dancer, but comes from an angle to the

a

FIGURE 21–7. LIGHTING LAY-
OUT FOR BALLET.   The scale
and style of both modern and
traditional ballet provide unique
lighting opportunities. Realistic
illumination is of less importance
than atmosphere and color.
Even classic ballet is a theatrical
extension of life into a highly
stylized performance technique.
(a) Sketch of the second act of
the traditional ballet *Giselle,* a
wooded bower sheltering the
grave of Giselle. (b) Lighting
layout. Note that only the down-
one area has been divided into
conventional lighting areas. The
balance of the plot is more dependent on side, down, and
back lighting for effect. Shin-
kickers (floor-level sidelights)
emphasize the dancer's legs.
The color of the scene is basic
moonlight blue that warms a little as dawn approaches at the
end of the ballet. (c) Schedule.
(Layout courtesy of Patricia
Simmons, Lighting Designer,
Pittsburgh Ballet Theatre)

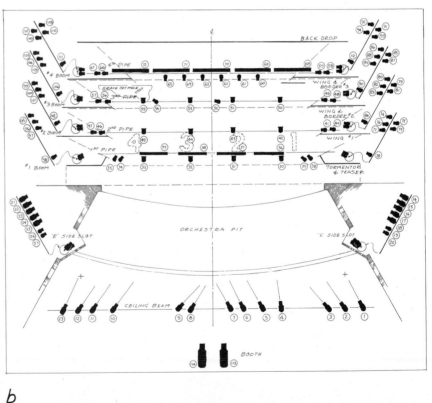

b

No.	INSTRUMENT	LOCATION	PURPOSE	LAMP	COLOR	REMARKS
1	8x12 ELLIPS'L SPOT	BEAM	AREA 1 DL	1000W QUARTZ	65	
2	"	"	" 2 DLC	"	65	
3	"	"	" 3 DRC	"	65	
4	"	"	SPECIAL	"	CLEAR	QUEEN WILLIE AREA
5	"	"	AREA 3 DR	"	65	
6	"	"	" 4 DR	"	65	
7	"	"	" 4 DRC	"	65	
8	"	"	" 1 DL	"	65	
9	"	"	" 1 DLC	"	65	
10	"	"	" 2 DLC	"	65	
11	"	"	" 2 DL	"	65	
12	"	"	" 3 DR	"	66	
13	"	"	" 4 DR	"	65	
14	8x10 ELLIPS'L SPOT	'L' SLOT	CROSS LT. DS	"	68	CUT OFF BACK DROP
15	"	"	"	"	68	
16	"	"	"	"	68	
17	"	"	"	"	68	
18	"	"	"	"	68	
19	6x14 ELLIPS'L SPOT	"	WASH DS	750 W Q	79	
20	"	"	"	"	79	CUTOFF ORCH PIT & DROP
21	8x10 ELLIPS'L SPOT	'R' SLOT	CROSS LT. DS	1000W Q	68	CUT OFF BACK DROP
22	"	"	"	"	68	
23	"	"	"	"	68	
24	"	"	"	"	68	
25	"	"	"	"	68	
26	6x14 ELLIPS'L SPOT	"	WASH DS	750 W Q	79	CUT OFF ORCH PIT & DROP
27	"	"	"	"	79	
28	6x12 ELLIPS'L SPOT	1ST PIPE	PIPE END	750W	65	CUT OFF WINGS
29	"	"	"	"	65	
30	8" FRESNEL	"	DOWN LIGHT	1000W	79	MID-SPOT FOCUS
31	"	"	"	"	79	
32	"	"	"	"	79	
33	"	"	"	"	79	
34	6x12 ELLIPS'L SPOT	"	PIPE END	750W	65	CUT OFF #2 WING
35	"	"	"	"	65	
36	6"x6" STEP LIGHT	"	BORDER WASH	150W R40	65	4-COLOR FEED THRU
37	"	"	"	"	79	
38	"	"	"	"	79	
39	"	"	"	"	64	
40	6x12 ELLIPS'L SPOT	2ND PIPE	PIPE END	750W	20	CUT OFF #2 WING
41	"	"	"	"	65	
42	8" FRESNEL	"	DOWN LIGHT	1000W	65	MID-SPOT FOCUS
43	"	"	"	"	79	
44	"	"	"	"	79	
45	"	"	"	"	79	
46	6x12 ELLIPS'L SPOT	"	PIPE END	750W	65	CUT OFF #2 WING
47	"	"	"	"	65	
48	"	3RD PIPE	"	"	65	CUT OFF #3 WING
49	"	"	"	"	65	
50	8" FRESNEL	"	DOWN LIGHT	1000W	79	MID-SPOT FOCUS
51	"	"	"	"	79	
52	6x9 ELLIPS'L SPOT	"	SPECIAL	750W	62	SOFT FOCUS - S'RAVE
53	8" FRESNEL	"	DOWN LIGHT	1000W	79	MID-SPOT FOCUS
54	6x9 ELLIPS'L SPOT	"	SPECIAL	750W	62	SOFT FOCUS - S'RAVE
55	8" FRESNEL	"	DOWN LIGHT	1000W	79	MID-SPOT FOCUS
56	6x12 ELLIPS'L SPOT	"	PIPE END	750W	65	CUT OFF #3 WING
57						

No.	INSTRUMENT	LOCATION	PURPOSE	LAMP	COLOR	REMARKS
58	6x12 ELLIPS'L SPOT	4TH PIPE	PIPE END	750W	65	CUT OFF #4 WING
59	"	"	"	"	65	" " #4 WING
60	6x12 ELLIPS'L SPOT	"	BACKLIGHT	750 W	64	HARD FOCUS
61	"	"	"	"	51	"
62	"	"	"	"	64	"
63	"	"	"	"	51	"
64	"	"	"	"	64	"
65	"	"	"	"	51	"
66	6x12 ELLIPS'L SPOT	"	PIPE END	"	64	"
67	"	"	"	"	51	
68	8'x7'6" STRIP LIGHT	"	BACK DROP WASH	150W QUARTZ	79	4-COLOR FEED THRU
69	"	"	"	"	64	
70	"	"	"	"	20	
71	"	"	"	"	91	
72						
73	6x12 ELLIPS'L SPOT	#1 BOOM-L	CROSSLIGHT	750 W	37	SHARP FOCUS - IN '1'
74	"	"	"	"	68	
75	"	"	"	"	37	
76	"	"	"	"	68	
77	6x9	"	"	"	68	
78	6x12 ELLIPS'L SPOT	#2 BOOM-L	"	"	64	CUT OFF HEAD
79	"	"	"	"	37	SHARP FOCUS IN '2'
80	"	"	"	"	68	
81	"	"	"	"	37	
82	"	"	"	"	68	
83	6x9	"	"	"	68	
84	6x12 ELLIPS'L SPOT	#3 BOOM-L	SHIN KICKER	"	68	SHARP FOCUS - OFF HEAD
85	6x12 ELLIPS'L SPOT	"	CROSSLIGHT	"	18	
86	"	"	"	"	68	
87	"	"	"	"	68	
88	6x9	"	"	"	37	
89	6x9	"	"	"	68	
90	"	"	SHIN KICKER	"	64	
91	6x12 ELLIPS'L SPOT	#4 BOOM-L	CROSSLIGHT	"	18	SHARP FOCUS IN '1'
92	6x12	"	"	"	68	
93	6x9	"	"	"	37	
94	6x9	"	"	"	68	
95	6x12 ELLIPS'L SPOT	#1 BOOM-R	CROSSLIGHT	750 W	68	SHARP FOCUS IN '1'
96	"	"	"	"	68	
97	6x9	"	"	"	64	
98	6x9	"	SHIN KICKER	"	68	SHARP FOCUS OFF HEAD
99	6x12 ELLIPS'L SPOT	#2 BOOM-R	CROSSLIGHT	"	68	IN '2'
100	"	"	"	"	68	
101	6x9	"	"	"	37	
102	6x9	"	"	"	68	
103	6x12 ELLIPS'L SPOT	#3 BOOM-R	SHIN KICKER	"	64	SHARP FOCUS OFF HEAD
104	"	"	CROSSLIGHT	"	68	IN '3'
105	6x9	"	"	"	68	
106	6x9	"	SHIN KICKER	"	64	SHARP FOCUS OFFHEAD
107	6x12 ELLIPS'L SPOT	#4 BOOM-R	CROSSLIGHT	"	68	IN '4'
108	"	"	"	"	68	
109	6x9	"	"	"	68	
110	6x9	"	"	"	68	
111	"	"	SHIN KICKER	"	64	SHARP FOCUS OFF HEAD
112	"	#4 BOOM-L	"	"	64	
113	'STRONG' XENON	BOOTH	FOLLOW SPOT			
114						

558

side as well. Frequently more desirable than straight-back because more of the dancer's body is lighted.

Down-Light. In the down-light position, lights are mounted directly overhead, which tends to push the body down. They are useful only for specific moments.

Follow-Spots. The follow-spot may come from the house or from some onstage location. This must be unobtrusive and should be used with a superior operator who can keep it so. Of course, in musical comedy dancing and the like, the blatant follow spots are all part of the show.

COLOR

For ballet, strong colors are not desirable, but a basic tint most certainly is. Pale lavender is frequently used, but for some ballets tradition may prescribe some other tint. Whatever color is selected becomes the neutral for the particular ballet. The other shades work in relation to it, and when blended together on the stage, approximate the neutral. Thus if lavender is the neutral, a violet next to it will appear quite warm, and a light blue will appear cool, while the violet and blue together will be close to lavender.

An excellent effect is often obtained by use of advancing and receding colors, which add apparent depth to the stage. The use of slightly cooler tints on the upstage dancers will make them appear further away than they would seem otherwise. Likewise, warmer shades on the downstage dancers will bring them even further forward.

OUTDOOR PRODUCTIONS

Theatrical Lighting Practice by Rubin and Watson gives an excellent description of lighting practices for outdoor productions on the grand scale, in auditoriums seating 3000 spectators or more. But we are concerned here with more modest presentations. Many schools, for example, give annual productions in a courtyard with a school building as background, others have a more-or-less permanent outdoors auditorium with planted hedges to create a proscenium wall, side wings, and a backdrop. Often there is no permanent area but an outdoor stage is improvised almost any place about the grounds.

Open-air theatrical productions would appear to have one advantage over those held indoors in that a truly all-enveloping darkness would seem to be an actuality. But even assuming that the outdoor stage is not located close to lighted areas and the performances do not start before night has fully closed in, there is rarely such a thing as complete blackness, even in rural sections. Moonlight, even starlight must be reckoned with. Blackouts are not long effective. And as conditions will vary from night to night, it is impossible to set definite dimmer levels.

ELECTRIC SERVICE

There are a number of problems facing the producers of open-air theatres, two of which deal with the supply of electric current. A permanently established outdoor layout will have made adequate arrangements to secure the proper service to the theatre, just as one would for a new theatre of any sort. But all too often a temporary outdoor presentation is attempted, and it is found at the last moment that adequate service is not available, without considerable expense, for running long cables or the hiring of a portable—and noisy— generator.

PERILS OF WEATHER

Second, there is the matter of weather. Cable and instrument connections, switches, dimmers, and other current-carrying parts that are perfectly satisfactory indoors are a hazard when exposed to rain, or even a heavy dew. Special equipment is needed for some parts, special housing for others. Equipment that has been rain-soaked and apparently dried out successfully may later reveal hidden and permanent damage. This is no field for the amateur electrician to risk his life and that of his fellows.

Artistically the weather may affect the best planned outdoor lighting by ruining gelatin color media. Gelatin when exposed to dampness loses its form completely and is entirely beyond control. This can occur as the result of condensation even indoors if close to the seashore or a large lake. Outdoors it is an impossible situation. Color media of glass or of plastic become essential.

FRONT LIGHTING

Front lighting is often a problem in an outdoor theatre. In order to attain anything close to the desired angles, it is usually necessary to erect poles beyond the seating area so as not to obstruct sight lines. Frequently this makes the throw to the stage an extremely long one, and the largest ellipsoidal-reflector spots, or even beam projectors, must be used.

These front lights may have to serve the entire stage, unless one is so fortunate as to have properly masked positions on the sides. Occasionally shrubs or trees are so located. Some permanent outdoor theatres have dense hedges that serve as proscenium wall and wood-wings and these are admirable to hide side-lighting spotlights. If natural features are lacking, it may be necessary to build towers near the stage with masking for the spotlights thereon.

Naturally no overhead lighting can be provided, so all thought of first and second pipes, border strips, and so on, may be discarded. Footlights, particularly if hidden by a low hedge, or similar natural device, can be effective in giving a general, low toning to the actors,

560

and any realistic scenery. Rarely in outdoor productions is there a large expanse of background corresponding to a backdrop or cyclorama. In fact, in many such presentations the background consists of trees or a hedge. In such cases no special lighting is desirable, and is even less so when the stage is backed by a view over a lake or of distant hills.

TELEVISION AND MOVIES

One tremendous advantage possessed by the television and movie lighting designers is that it is not necessary to mask instruments. Because the camera sees only what it wishes to, and its shots are carefully planned ahead of time, the lighting man need merely to keep his instruments and their associated equipment out of the picture. True, this is not always the easiest matter, but it is distinctly a help, particularly in the case of "tight" shots or close-ups when spotlights may be brought to within a foot or two of the actors.

BASIC TECHNIQUES

With this nicety of positioning possible, a great deal of precision can be brought to lighting a small scene, say a single commentator at his desk. Techniques vary, but a common one is to throw a general fill or base light on the actor from the front and then to set him apart from his background by means of low-hung spotlights coming in from behind to highlight his head and shoulders. To replace the plasticity lost by the flat fill lighting and to suggest a motivating source, a key light is used from one side at high intensity, while a modeling light of less brightness comes in at a different angle. Spotlights are used almost exclusively for these purposes.

GROUP SCENES

While these procedures are excellent for the lone actor, they need modification where there are two or three performers in a group. One head may throw a shadow on a neighboring face unless the instruments are placed with extreme care and foresight. An effect that flatters one of the actors may be uncomplimentary to his fellow who is facing in a different direction.

On the other hand, if there is a good deal of cutting back and forth from one camera to another when both are focused on the same scene but from different angles, it often happens that the key light, the motivating light, and the back light exchange duties for the various shots.

FULL-STAGE SCENES

When a scene becomes larger than a tight group of two or three actors, the lighting more nearly approaches the kind used in a conventional proscenium theatre. And when a full-stage picture, such as a dance sequence, is shown the similarity is quite marked. Although a discreet camera view allows greater liberties in placing of instruments, there are problems created by the medium that are not encountered on the legitimate stage, such as the danger of cameras, microphones, and personnel throwing shadows into view.

BACKGROUNDS

Usually a general wash of light over such scenic pieces is all that is necessary, though on occasions the addition of accents and modeling becomes desirable. Many times backgrounds are done by means of projections on a neutral screen or drop. Whatever technique is employed the great danger is that the intensity of the light on the background, or an overaccenting of some portion of it, may draw attention away from the actors in the foreground of the camera picture.

COLOR TELEVISION

The same general techniques apply equally to monochromatic and to color television, with two important exceptions. Color television requires a much higher intensity of light on every portion of the same picture. And with color it is vital that all the instruments used have the same color temperature: that is, if any two instruments are focused on the same neutral surface the color of their beam patterns must be identical with neither one more reddish nor a little to the blue side of the other. Special lamps are manufactured to insure this perfection.

If the color balance is not correct, two objects of identical color will appear quite different if they are lighted by different instruments.

INSTRUMENTS

The spotlight most frequently employed in the television field is the Fresnel type, from the smallest 3-inch size burning the 150-watt lamp up to the 10-inch models with 1000-watt lamps. Almost universal is the employment of "barndoors," shutters designed to cut the shape of the beam from round to a flatter pattern. This is necessary to eliminate the shadow of the microphones hung low above the actors' heads, while at the same time getting the full horizontal spread of the beam. A recent development has been an oval Fresnel lens that accomplishes the same purpose. Ellipsoidal-reflector spotlights, once used solely to project "gobo" patterns on a background, are now employed more and more for the tasks listed above. Follow spots— either the largest ellipsoidal-reflector type or arcs—are used in most large studios.

While striplights are rarely employed, floodlights are common. R lamps in clip-on holders, the ellipsoidal flood called a "scoop" with lamps up to 2000 watts, a boxlike flood with 750-watt lamp referred to as a "broad," and "pans" containing several fluorescent tubes are the common varieties. It is a rare studio that does not possess several of each type.

To keep the floor areas as clear as possible, most instruments are hung from overhead, though a few floods are kept on handy, castered floor stands, while the clip-ons, as the name suggests, are completely flexible.

INTENSITY CONTROL

Control over intensity levels is of far less importance in television than on the regular stage. Intensities are adjusted more by the size and location of instruments, or the use of noncolor filters. Scenes do not run long enough to need fades to suggest the passage of time, so the switching of circuits off or on suffices. And the camera itself, and its associated controls, can quite effectively handle many adjustments that on the stage require the most precise dimmer readings and changes.

In color television the control of intensity by dimming is absolutely out. As the voltage is reduced an incandescent filament not only dims but turns definitely toward the red end of the spectrum. As this would completely alter the all-important color temperature of the lamp, it can not be tolerated. Any dimming effect must be by mechanical means.

SUMMARY

Regardless of the technical differences that lie between proscenium-stage lighting and lighting for thrust stages, arenas, outdoor stages, and the eye of the camera, the same basic principles still hold true. The designer still uses the four tools of light: intensity, color, form, and movement. He still applies these, in varying degrees, to arrive at the desirable visibility, plausibility, composition, and mood for the play or the scene. And these, in turn, still contribute to the ultimate concern of the designer: to assist the actor to interpret his part in a suitable environment.

Lighting in the Commercial Theatre

22

Today, throughout this country, we see an amazing rebirth of the professional theatre, too long confined to New York and a few of the other large centers. Now it is a rare city that does not have its repertory or stock theatre, run by professional producers and directors and employing professional actors and designers. More and more college graduates, and even college students, are working in these theatres, on full- or part-time bases. This chapter is intended to give such people a picture of the differences between the lighting practices and limitations of the amateur (college and community) theatres and those of the commercial theatre.

The concern of this chapter is Broadway lighting practices, not that it is expected that any large percentage of those who use this book will soon be heading for New York, but because Broadway, for better or worse, is the ultimate in commercial usages and restrictions. Many of these pertain as well to resident professional theatres in other parts of the country, with considerable and unpredictable variations among localities. For example, what is common practice in A-town may be ignored in B-ville, while C-burg may employ it under

563

564   certain conditions. But by understanding the worst, so to speak, the person new to the commercial theatre can be better prepared for whatever the local situation holds in store.

EQUIPMENT IN A BROADWAY THEATRE

It is a surprise to most people to learn that no commercial theatre on what is commonly referred to as Broadway has any lighting equipment of its own beyond the few items here listed: There will be a dimmer for the houselights; there will be a company switch furnishing considerable power, frequently dc, to which a show's switchboards may be connected; there will be current at appropriate locations for the use of follow spots; and, a fairly recent addition, there will be wiring in conduit to the front of the balcony and to the box booms, vertical pipes erected on either side of the auditorium in the upper boxes closest to the stage. Occasionally there will be conduit to a second balcony, if one exists.

This means that everything else must come in with the show: all the instruments and their accessories, the switchboards and plugging boxes, cable sufficient to connect all instruments to the switchboards, booms for offstage instruments, asbestos cloth to protect flying scenery from lights hung above the stage, work lights, all special rigging devices, everything!

And, it may be added, when a show moves out of the theatre, taking with it all the above, a new show may move right in, bringing with it an almost identical list of equipment!

THE BROADWAY LIGHT DESIGNER

Before he is permitted to light a show on Broadway, the light designer must become a member of United Scenic Artists, Local 829 of The Brotherhood of Painters, Decorators and Paperhangers of America. To be admitted to this organization, whether as a full member entitled to design scenery and costumes as well as lights or as a Lighting Associate who is restricted to this one field, the applicant must pass a difficult examination given once a year in New York.

The light designer is hired, often at the suggestion of the director or the scene designer, by the producer of the play. Under the rules of United Scenic Artists he must receive a minimum fee of $1700 for a straight play and $2000 for a musical, though established designers ask for and get a great deal more than these figures. It is not uncommon for a well-known designer to receive, in addition to his straight fee, a royalty based on a percentage of the gross receipts, which, when the production is successful, can add up to a pretty sum.

For many years it was the practice for the same person to design the scenery, costumes, and lighting for a play. But today, with some very important exceptions, it is more common for a lighting specialist to be hired for this design element alone. It must be noted that many of the most successful lighting designers in the American theatre are women.

HIRING EQUIPMENT AND ELECTRICIANS

Because all expenses related to the play must be approved by the producer or his business manager, the light designer must work within the figures that they have in mind. All the equipment is rented, the usual contract calling for a down payment of 10 percent of its price for the first three-week period, a lower charge for the next three weeks, and a reduced rental for the balance of the run of the play. Sometimes a producer figures that he is about to open a sure hit that will run for a long time and will take advantage of an option that will permit him to buy the equipment if he decides that this will be cheaper than paying for a long rental. Some producers make a practice of asking for competitive bids from the few companies that are engaged in the rental of lighting equipment for the stage; others always work with the same company; some will accept the recomendations of the light designer to deal with a certain firm.

Equal in importance to the equipment costs are the wages paid to the electricians who set up and run the show. In New York these men must be members of Local No. 1 of The International Alliance of Theatrical Stage Employees, commonly called the IA. Some electricians are far better than others, and a good chief electrician can help the designer immeasurably. For this reason a designer well established on Broadway will probably have in mind someone who works well with him and will recommend that the producer hire this person. But the beginner must ask around to locate the best man available.

The chief electrician estimates how many men will be required to run the show, based on the number of instruments and switchboards used and the number and complexity of the cues. If the show has electrical sound effects, the sound man is also under the jurisdiction of the chief electrician.

PLANNING THE LIGHTING

After reading and rereading the script of the play, the light designer consults the playwright, the director, the scene and costume designers, and others. Sometimes a producer will hold meetings at which the light designer can exchange views with these co-workers, but on other occasions he must seek them out on his own. It is important that he study the color renderings of the scenic designer and visit the shop where the scenery is being built to note the painting. He will wish to see samples of the fabrics to be used in the costumes. He will consider the make-up to be worn by the actors. Most important, he will discuss with the director the visual effects that are desired for each scene of the play, and the nature of all changes and cues that affect the lighting. At all times he must remember that he is part of a team, each member of which is striving to make the production a success, and all of whom have opinions that merit respect and consideration.

Of course, right from the start he has been attending rehearsals to see how the director is interpreting the script and the style of the final presentation, so that his lighting may assist this, not clash with it. And toward the end of the rehearsal period he will want to assure himself of the movements and positions of the actors, the timing of the cues, and any variations in the approach that the director is taking.

The light designer will visit the New York theatre in which the play is to open and inspect it as to mounting positions and their distances from the stage, any possible difficulties in placing instruments exactly where desired, and all physical aspects that could affect the lighting of the play.

As soon as he can, and possibly before he has had a chance to attend to everything mentioned above, he will want to get his ideas down on paper. Most practitioners in New York draw their layouts to the scale of one-half inch equals one foot. This is large enough to permit much information, which otherwise would have to be included on a separate schedule, to be marked right on the layout, adjacent to the piece of equipment to which each item pertains.

CHECKING THE EQUIPMENT ORDERED

Two weeks before the rented lighting equipment is to move out of the contractor's shop, the chief electrician and his first assistant go there and carefully inspect and test everything ordered, rejecting all items that are not in satisfactory condition. They also mark the switchboards, frame the color media, label the bundles of cable, prepare any special effects, and otherwise organize matters as far as possible.

The light designer also visits the shop and checks over the colors to be sure he will have no surprises when he gets to the theatre. He will also check with the electrician to make sure that wall brackets and chandeliers are properly wired, and with the scene shop to be certain that the scenery on which lighting fixtures are to hang has been adequately braced. He will check the electrification of turntables and

FIGURE 22-1. THE EQUIPMENT LIST.   A portion of the equipment list for
the Broadway production of *Cyrano de Bergerac,* prepared by Gilbert
Hemsley, Jr., the Lighting Designer. The change of stage from thrust to
proscenium is not the only difference between the two productions of
Cyrano. The Guthrie Theater stage is fully equipped with lighting instruments,
outlets, and permanent control console; a New York theatre is not. Hence
all equipment to be rented or purchased is specified in detail by the lighting
designer. Instruments, cable, mounting fixtures, connectors, and traveling
switchboards are specified in the equipment list. Nothing is left to chance
or assumption.

CYRANO   Equipment List

A Richard Gregson – Apjac Production

Lighting – Gilbert V. Hemsley, Jr. 608-836-1197

Electrician – Joe Monaco   914-949-6587

Company Manager – Victor Samrock 212-751-1290

Load out to Toronto Feb. 15 or 16, 1973

Load in to Toronto   Feb. 18, followed by a possible
stand at the Colonial in Boston, and the Palace
in New York.

Balcony Rail   (This will be split between 2 Balconys in Toronto)

    24   750w 8 x 12 Lekos CC and CF

    16   750w 8 x 12 Lekos T and S, CC and CF

    12   750w 8 x 16 Lekos CC and CF

    6   500w 6 x 6 (Step Lens Wide Angle) CC and CF

    4 L.S. Units (Will come from Minn.)

    20   Twofers

    2   Threefers

            Rehearsal Worklites

            Cables and Jumpers   (CK with Royal Alex, Colonial, and Palace)

Box Boom Left

    24   750w 6 x 12 Lekos (Would prefer 6 x 16"s) CF

            Palace 12 Long Side Arms 2 T Joints Each (Same for Colonial ??)

            Royal Alex Possible C Clamps Ck with House

    12   Twofers

            Cables and Jumpers, ck with house

Box Boom Right

24   750w 6 x 12 Lekos (Would prefer 6 x 16"s) CF

12   Twofers

      Cables and Side Arms   See Box Boom Left

#1 Boom Stage Left

8   750w 6 x 16 Lekos CF

6   750w 6 x 12 Lekos CF

6   750w 6 x 9 Lekos CF

20   Side Arms

1   30' Boom (Welded with Ring top and Small Base)

10   Twofers

1   Bundle 4 Cables (Board #2)

1   Bundle 7 Cables (Board #1) (1 extra)

#2 Boom Stage Left

2   8 x 8-3 Circuit Striplight Sections with matching short hanging irons,

      with 300w PAR-56 Spot Lamps Color Frames and Blinders

      (Hang Blinders upstage)

1   30' Boom (Welded with Ring Top and Small Base)

1   Bundle 7 Cables (1 extra) (Board #4)

1st Electric (Downstage Bridge)

24   750w 6 x 12 Lekos T and S, CF and CC

8   Twofers

17   Cables (1 extra Board #5)

1   48' Pipe

4   Half Bumpers

Left Diagonal Pipe

1   8 x 8-3 Circuit Striplight 500w PAR-64 Hi Spot

1   8 x 4   "

      with matching Hanging Irons and CF and Blinders

      (Hang Blinders onstage)

7   Cables (1 extra) (Board #4)

1   16' Pipe

5th Electric (Upstage Bridge)

24	750w 6 x 16 Lekos (1st Priority) CC and CF
12	Twofers
13	Cables (1 extra) (Board #5)
1	48' Pipe

6th Electric (Upstage Bridge)

8	750w 6 x 16 Lekos (1st Priority) CC and CF
8	750w 6 x 16 Lekos (1st Priority) T and S, CC and CF
4	Twofers
13	Cables (1 extra) (Board #5)
6	Cables (extra for Specials) (Board #4)
1	48' Pipe

7th Electric (Upstage Bridge)

3	8 x 8-3 Circuit Striplights 500w PAR-64 Hi Spot Lamps with
	Matching Hanging Irons and Double Blinders CF

1st Pipe (Left Bridge)

12	750w 6 x 12 Lekos CC and CF
6	750w 6 x 12 Lekos T and S, CC and CF
9	Long Twofers
7	Cables (1 extra) (Board #3)
3	Cables (Board #4)
1	28' Pipe

3rd Pipe (Right Bridge)

3	750w 6 x 12 Lekos T and S, CC and CF
16	750w 6 x 12 Lekos CC and CF
5	Twofers
11	Cables (1 extra) (Board #3)
4	Cables (Board #4)
4	Cables (Extra for Specials) (Board #4)

Floor Stage Left

8	750w 6 x 12 Lekos CF
8	6' Adjustable Floor Stands
12	Cables (6 upstage, 6 downstage) (Board #6)

570

6	750w 6" Fresnels CC and CF
6	1500w 8" Fresnels (with painted risers if possible)
6	750w 6 x 9 Lekos T and S, CC and CF
18	750w 6 x 12 Lekos T and S, CC and CF (6 of these could be 6 x 16's)
2	8 x 8 Sections 3 Circuit Striplights with 300 PAR-56 Spot Lamps
	Hanging Irons and CF
2	21' Booms with 50lb Bases
24	Sidearms
4	Long Bundles of 4 Cables Each
	Lots of extra Gel Frames (Show is in a state of Flux)
4	24' Sections of Sky Climber Bridges. Undersides and Edges to be painted Black
	Perishables See Monaco
1	8 Way Cue Light System for Bob Currie
3	Mole Richardson Fog Machines Long Control Cables
	Extra Jumpers, Cables and Twofers See Monaco Also Pipe Stiffeners

Switchboards

#1	14 Plate 1500/3000 Resistance	
#2	14 Plate 6000w Auto Transformer	
3	6 Plate 3600 Autotransformer Boards. These are to be rewired so that 1 6 K Plate can Master 2 3600w Plates. The neutral must be split for each of the pairs, including the neutral to the pilot lite. These should be tested with a load before they leave the shop.	
2	6 Plate 1000w Auto Transformer Boards. These will have 1 Master only	
10	8 Plate 750w Preset Boards. (1 of these will work off 1 3K Master and the Hot Picket on the #1 Board---The remaining 9 will work off single masters. Plugging Boxes per Monaco.	

Special Note

Part of this list are 20 L.S. Units already on rent that will come to the Royal Alex from the Guthrie

Follow Spots

2	Super Troupers (It is possible that there are two at the Royal Alex)

FIGURE 22–2. PROFESSIONAL LIGHTING LAYOUTS.   The basic setting for
Cyrano de Bergerac as it was produced at the Guthrie Theatre. Designer—
John Jenson. Page 572: The lighting layout for *Cyrano* at the Guthrie Theatre.
Lighting Designer—Gilbert Hemsley, Jr. An examination of the layout will reveal
that the ceiling coves 1 to 6 form an inner ring of acting area lighting positions,
while ceiling coves 6 to 11 form an outer ring. The balcony rail provides a position
with a flatter angle for specials. The pipe bar over the vomitories or tunnels, right
and left, are additional front-light positions. Also note the tormentor ladders and the
downstage side-light booms, as well as the overhead back-lighting position in the
backstage area. The center cove over the thrust portion of the stage accounts for
the strange cluster of spotlights in the center of the stage. Because the Guthrie
Theatre production of *Cyrano* had to fit into a repertory schedule, 90 percent of the
layout is fixed to be reused in other productions with a minimum of additional
specials or color changes.

Page 573: A lighting layout for the Broadway production of *Cyrano de Bergerac*
by Gilbert Hemsley, Jr. Unlike most layouts there is no floor plan of the setting.
Because there are several arrangements of scenery it is difficult to show a
composite of floor plans without causing confusion. In such cases the lighting
designer frequently prepares his layout on transparent paper or pastic which he
places over each floor plan in turn. In any event the layout is not a representational
diagram but is a schematic working drawing for the lighting designer and his crew.

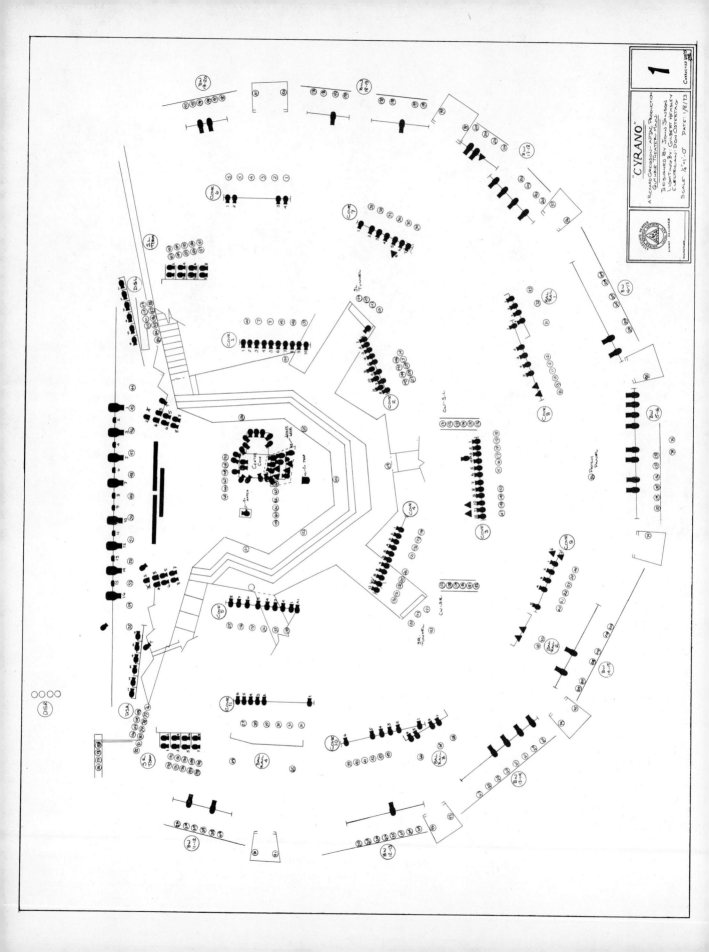

"CYRANO"

A RICHARD GREGSON - APJAC PRODUCTION
GUTHRIE THEATER - MINN.

DESIGNED BY: JOHN JENSON
LIGHTING BY: GILBERT HEMSLEY
ELECTRICIAN: DON OSTERTAG

SCALE: ¼" = 1'-0"   DATE: 1/8/73

UNITED SCENIC ARTISTS
LIGHT DESIGNER
SIGNATURE

CORRECTED 10/73

1

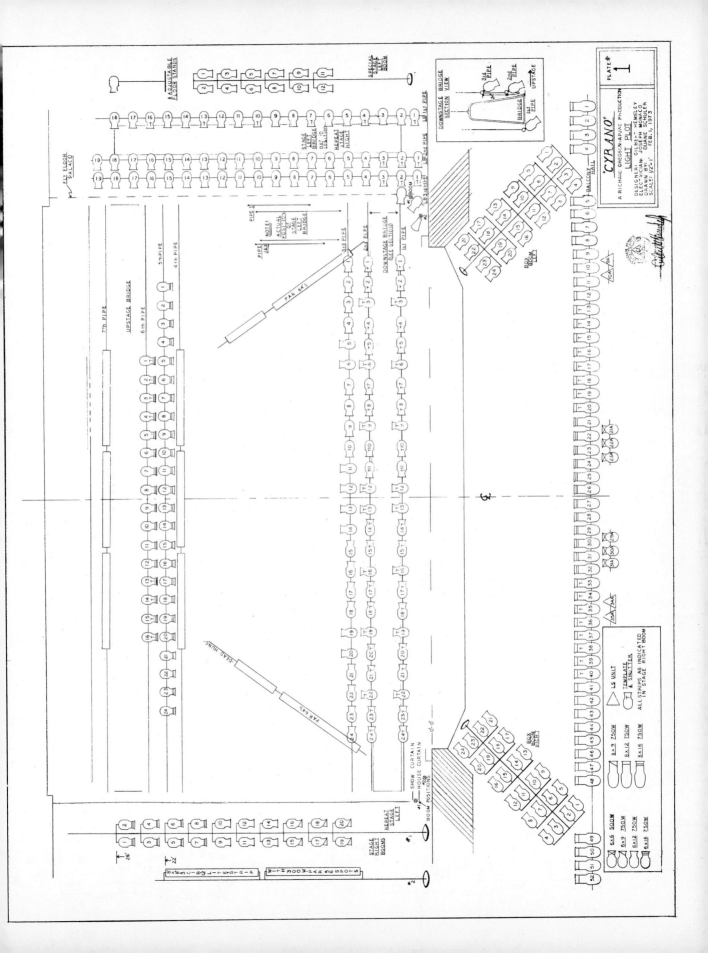

574 FIGURE 22–3. GENERAL HOOK-UP. Portions of the hook-up for the Broadway production of *Cyrano de Bergerac*. This organizes the nearly three hundred instruments of the layout into a scheme of control by designating the hook-up of each instrument to a dimmer in one of the system's six switchboards, ten auxiliary preset boards, or five auto transformer boards used for group mastering. The schedule also indicates the hanging position and type of instrument, its focus and color.

CYRANO
BOARD #1

SWITCH	POSITION	TYPE	FOCUS	COLOR
1	Box Boom L 9·10·11·12	4·750w 6×12	L AREA 1	½ C.B.
2	Box Boom R 1·2·3·4	4·750w 6×12	R AREA 1	½ C.B.
3	Box Boom L 5·6·7·8	4·750w 6×12	L AREA 2	½ C.B.
4	Box Boom R 5·6·7·8	4·750w 6×12	R AREA 2	½ C.B
5	Box Boom L 1·2·3·4	4·750w 6×12	L AREA 3	½ C.B
6	Box Boom R 9·10·11·12	4·750w 6×12	R AREA 3	½ C.B.
7	#1 Boom L 16-18 / #1 Boom R 4-6	2·750w 6×9 / 2·750w 6×16	AREA 1	½ C.B.
8	#1 Boom L 10-12 / #1 Boom R 10-12	2·750w 6×12 / 2·750w 6×12	AREA 2	½ C.B
9	#1 Boom L 4-6 / #1 Boom R 16-18	2·750w 6×16 / 2·750w 6×9	AREA 3	½ C.B.
10	#1 Boom L 15-17 / #1 Boom R 3-5	2·750w 6×9 / 2·750w 6×16	AREA 4	½ C.B.
11	#1 Boom L 9-11 / #1 Boom R 9-11	2·750w 6×12 / 2·750w 6×12	AREA 5	½ C.B.
12	#1 Boom L 3-5 / #1 Boom R 15-17	2·750w 6×16 / 2·750w 6×9	AREA 6	½ C.B.
13^M 131 132 133 134	BAL. RAIL 21 22 31 32	4·750w 8×16	SPECIALS	½ C.B.
14	BAL. RAIL 21A 22A 23A 29A 30A 31A	6·500w 6×6	FRONT CURTAIN WASH	911

1 OF 20

CYRANO BOARD #2

SWITCH	POSITION		TYPE	FOCUS	COLOR
15	BAL. RAIL	1 - 2 - 3 - 4 49 - 50 - 51 - 52	8·750w 8×12	FRONT DARK BLUE WASH	958
16	3RD PIPE	7 - 8 - 9 - 10 15 - 16 - 17 - 18	8·750w 6×12	TOP DARK BLUE	958 P-60
17	BAL. RAIL	9 - 10 - 11 - 12 41 - 42 - 43 - 44	8·750w 8×12	FRONT BLUE WASH	955
18 M 181 182	Box BOOM L Box BOOM R	17 - 18 - 19 - 20 17 - 18 - 19 - 20	4·750w 6×12 4·750w 6×12	Box BLUE L Box BLUE R	955 955
19	#1 BOOM L	1 - 2 - 7 - 8 13 - 14 19 - 20	4·750w 6×16 2·750w 6×12 2·750w 6×9	BOOM BLUE L	955
20	#1 BOOM R	1 - 2 - 7 - 8 13 - 14 19 - 20	4·750w 6×16 2·750w 6×12 2·750w 6×9	BOOM BLUE R	955
21	3RD PIPE	1 - 2 - 3 - 4 21 - 22 - 23 - 24	8·750w 6×12	TOP BLUE	955
22	BAL. RAIL	5 - 6 - 7 - 8 45 - 46 - 47 - 48	8·750w 8×12	FRONT STRAW WASH	805
23 M 231 232	Box BOOM L Box BOOM R	13 - 14 - 15 - 16 13 - 14 - 15 - 16	4·750w 6×12 4·750w 6×12	Box STRAW L Box STRAW R	805 805
24	BAL. RAIL	13 - 14 - 15 - 16 37 - 38 - 39 - 40	8·750w 8×12 w/TEMPLATE	FRONT HONEY WASH	911
25 M251 252	Box BOOM L Box BOOM R	21 - 22 - 23 - 24 21 - 22 - 23 - 24	4·750w 6×12 4·750w 6×12	Box HONEY L Box HONEY R	911
26	BAL. RAIL	17 - 18 - 19 - 20 33 - 34 - 35 - 36	4·750w 8×12 4·750w 8×12 w/TEMPLATE	FRONT CANDLELITE	918 915
27 M 271 to 278	BAL. RAIL	23 - 24 - 25 - 26 27 - 28 - 29 - 30	8·750w 6×16	FRONT SPECIALS	½ C.B.
28 M 281 to 288	3RD PIPE	5 - 6 - 11 - 12 13 - 14 - 19 - 20	8·750w 6×12	3RD PIPE SPECIALS	

CYRANO BOARD #3

SWITCH	POSITION		TYPE	FOCUS	COLOR
29	L BRIDGE	#2 PIPE 9 - 10 - 11 #3 PIPE 9 - 10 - 11	6·750w 6×12	L BRIDGE STRAW	805
30	R BRIDGE	#2 PIPE 9 - 10 - 11 #3 PIPE 9 - 10 - 11	6·750w 6×12	R BRIDGE STRAW	805
31	L BRIDGE	#2 PIPE 17 - 18 - 19 #3 PIPE 17 - 18 - 19	6·750w 6×12	L BRIDGE HONEY	911

32	R BRIDGE #2 PIPE 17-18-19 / #3 PIPE 17-18-19	6-750w 6x12	R BRIDGE HONEY	911
33	L BRIDGE #1 PIPE 3-6-9 12-15-18	6-750w 6x12	S.L. GALLERY HONEY BACKLITE	911
34	R BRIDGE #1 PIPE 3-6-9 12-15-18	6-750w 6x12	S.R. GALLERY HONEY BACKLITE	911
35	L BRIDGE #2 PIPE 1-2-3 / #3 PIPE 1-2-3	6-750w 6x12 w/ Template	S.L. BRIDGE GOBOS	½ C.B.
36	R BRIDGE #2 PIPE 1-2-3 / #3 PIPE 1-2-3	6-750w 6x12 w/ Template	S.R. BRIDGE GOBOS	½ C.B.
37	L BRIDGE #1 PIPE 1-4-7 10-13-16	6-750w 6x12 w/ Template	S.L. GALLERY GOBO BACKLITE	½ C.B.
38	R BRIDGE #1 PIPE 1-4-7 10-13-16	6-750w 6x12 w/ Template	S.R. GALLERY GOBO BACKLITE	½ C.B.
39 M 391 to 398	L BRIDGE #2 PIPE 4-8-12-16 / #3 PIPE 4-8-12-16	8-750w 6x12	L BRIDGE SPECIALS	
40 M 401 to 408	R BRIDGE #2 PIPE 4-8-12-16 / #3 PIPE 4-8-12-16	8-750w 6x12	R BRIDGE SPECIALS	

CYRANO
BOARD #4

SWITCH	POSITION	TYPE	FOCUS	COLOR
43 M 431 / 432	#2 BOOM L VERTICAL STRIPS / #2 BOOM R VERTICAL STRIPS	2-8x8 STRIP / 2-8x8 STRIP w/300w PAR 56 SPOT	S.R. GALLERY / S.L. GALLERY HONEY	911 / 911
44 M 441 / 442	#2 BOOM L VERTICAL STRIPS / #2 BOOM R VERTICAL STRIPS	SAME SET AS 43	S.R. GALLERY / S.L. GALLERY RED	918 / 918
45 M 451 / 452	L DIAGONAL STRIPS / R DIAGONAL STRIPS	1-8x8 ; 1-8x4 / 1-8x8 ; 1-8x4 w/300w PAR 56 SPOT	INSIDE S.L. GALLERY / INSIDE S.R. GALLERY DARK HONEY	912 / 912
46 M 461 / 462	L DIAGONAL STRIP / R DIAGONAL STRIP	SAME SET AS 45	INSIDE S.L. GALLERY / INSIDE S.R. GALLERY DARK AMBER	915 / 915
47 M 471 / 472	#2 BOOM L VERTICAL STRIPS / #2 BOOM R VERTICAL STRIPS	SAME SET AS 43	S.R. GALLERY / S.L. GALLERY BLUE	955/P-6 / 955/P-6
48 M 481 / 482	L DIAGONAL STRIPS / R DIAGONAL STRIPS	SAME SET AS 45	INSIDE S.L. GALLERY / INSIDE S.R. GALLERY DARK BLUE	958/P-8 / 958/P-6
49	L BRIDGE #2 PIPE 13,14,15 / #3 PIPE 13-14-15	6-750w 6x12	L BRIDGE DARK BLUE	958/P-8
50	R BRIDGE #2 PIPE 13-14-15 / #3 PIPE 13-14-15	6-750w 6x12	R BRIDGE DARK BLUE	958/P-6
51	L BRIDGE #2 PIPE 5-6-7 / #3 PIPE 5-6-7	6-750w 6x12	L BRIDGE BLUE	955
52	R BRIDGE #2 PIPE 5-6-7 / #3 PIPE 5-6-7	6-750w 6x12	R BRIDGE BLUE	955

SWITCH	POSITION		TYPE	FOCUS	COLOR
53	L BRIDGE #1 PIPE	2-5-8 11-14-17	6-750w 6×12	L GALLERY BLUE BACKLITE	955
54	R BRIDGE #1 PIPE	2-5-8 11-14-17	6-750w 6×12	R GALLERY BLUE BACKLITE	955
55 M 551 to 556	LS SPECIALS				
56 M 561 to 566	LS SPECIALS				

CYRANO   BOARD #5

SWITCH	POSITION		TYPE	FOCUS	COLOR
57	1 ST PIPE 4-5-20-21 2 ND PIPE 4-5-20-21		8-750w 6×12	TOP HONEY	911
58	1 ST PIPE 7-8-17-18 2 ND PIPE 7-8-17-18		8-750w 6×12	TOP AMBER	915
59	1 ST PIPE 10-11-14-15 2 ND PIPE 10-11-14-15		8-750w 6×12	TOP RED	918
60	1 ST PIPE 1-2-23-24 2 ND PIPE 1-2-23-24		8-750w 6×12	TOP STRAW	805
61	5 TH PIPE	1-3-5 7-9-11	6-750w 6×16	L BACK HONEY	911
62	5 TH PIPE	14-16-18 20-22-24	6-750w 6×16	R BACK HONEY	911
63	5 TH PIPE	2-4-6 8-10-12	6-750w 6×16	L BACK BLUE	955
64	5 TH PIPE	13-15-17 19-21-23	6-750w 6×16	R BACK BLUE	955
65	6 TH PIPE	1-2-3-4 13-14-15-16	8-750w 6×16 w/ TEMPLATE	BACK NEUTRAL	
66 M 661 to 668	6 TH PIPE	5-6-7-8 9-10-11-12	8-750w 6×16	BACKLITE SPECIALS	
67 M 671 to 678	1 ST PIPE	3-6-9-12 13-16-19-22	8-750w 6×12 w/ TEMPLATE	1ST PIPE SPECIALS	
68 M 681 to 688	2 ND PIPE	3-6-9-12 13-16-19-22	8-750w 6×12 w/ TEMPLATE	2ND PIPE SPECIALS	
69					

CYRANO
BOARD #6

SWITCH	POSITION	TYPE	FOCUS	COLOR
71	4TH PIPE STRIPLIGHTS	3-8X8 STRIPS	WALL FRONT AMBER	912
72	7TH PIPE STRIPLIGHTS	3-8X8 STRIPS	WALL BACK HONEY	911
73	4TH PIPE STRIPLIGHTS	SAME SET AS 71	WALL FRONT RED	918
74	7TH PIPE STRIPLIGHTS	SAME SET AS 72	WALL BACK DARK AMBER	915
75	4TH PIPE STRIPLIGHTS	SAME SET AS 71	WALL FRONT DARK BLUE	958
76	7TH PIPE STRIPLIGHTS	SAME SET AS 72	WALL BACK BLUE	955
77	BASEMENT 1-2-3 4-5-6	6-750w 6x12	BAKERY OVENS	918
78	SPECIAL BOOM S.L. 1-2-3 4-5-6	6-750w 6x12	TOP GATES OF PARIS	955
79	SPECIAL BOOM S.L. 7-8-9 10-11-12	6-750w 6x12	BOTTOM GATES OF PARIS	955
81 M 811 to 818	L FloOR STANDS 1-2-3-4 5-6-7-8	8-750w 6x12	AS NEEDED	
82 M 821 to 82.8	R FloOR STANDS 1-2-3-4 5-6-7-8	8-750w 6x12	AS NEEDED	

CYRANO
BOARD #7   8 PLATE   750w PRESET

SWITCH	POSITION		TYPE	FOCUS	COLOR
13 MASTER				FRONT SPECIALS	
131	BAL. RAIL	21	1-750w 8x16		½ C.B.
132		22	1-750w 8x16		½ C.B.
133		23	1-750w 8x16		½ C.B
134		24	1-750w 8x16		½ C.B.

CYRANO

BOARD # 8   6 PLATE   3600w AUTOTRANSFORMER

SWITCH	POSITION	TYPE	FOCUS	COLOR
18 MASTER				
181	Box Boom L 17-18-19-20	4-750w 6x12	Box Blue L	955
182	Box Boom R 17-18-19-20	4-750w 6x12	Box Blue R	955
23 MASTER				
231	Box Boom L 13-14-15-16	4-750w 6x12	Box L Straw	805
232	Box Boom R 13-14-15-16	4-750w 6x12	Box Straw R	805
25 MASTER				
251	Box Boom L 21-22-23 24	4-750w 6x12	Box Honey L	911
252	Box Boom R 21-22-23-24	4-750w 6x12	Box Honey R	911

CYRANO

BOARD #10   8 PLATE   750w PRESET

SWITCH	POSITION	TYPE	FOCUS	COLOR
28 MASTER			3 RD PIPE SPECIALS	
281	3 RD PIPE # 5	1-750w 6x12		
282	6			
283	11			
284	12			
285	13			
286	14			

CYRANO

BOARD #11   8 PLATE   750 W   PRESET

SWITCH	POSITION	TYPE	FOCUS	COLOR
39 MASTER		L BRIDGE	SPECIALS	
391	L BRIDGE #2 PIPE #4	1-750W 6x12		
392	L BRIDGE #2 PIPE #8			
393	L BRIDGE #2 PIPE #12			
394	L BRIDGE #2 PIPE #16			
395	L BRIDGE #3 PIPE #4			
396	L BRIDGE #3 PIPE #8			
397	L BRIDGE #3 PIPE #12			
398	L BRIDGE #3 PIPE #16			

CYRANO

BOARD #12   8 PLATE   750W   PRESET

SWITCH	POSITION	TYPE	FOCUS	COLOR
40 MASTER		R BRIDGE	SPECIALS	
401	R. BRIDGE #2 PIPE #4	1- 750W 6x12		
402	#8			
403	#12			
404	#16			
405	#3 PIPE #4			
406	#8			

CYRANO

BOARD # 13   6 PLATE   3600W AUTOTRANSFOAMER

SWITCH	POSITION	TYPE	FOCUS	COLOR
43 MASTER				
431	#2 BOOM L VERTICAL STRIPS	2-8×8 STRIPS w/300W PAR 56 SPOT	S.R. GALLERY HONEY	911
432	#2 BOOM R VERTICAL STRIPS	2-8×8 STRIPS w/300W PAR 56 SPOT	S.L. GALLERY HONEY	911
44 MASTER				
441	#2 BOOM L "	SAME SET AS 431	S.R. GALLERY RED	918
442	#2 BOOM R "	SAME SET AS 432	S.L. GALLERY RED	918
45 MASTER				
451	L DIAGONAL STRIPS	1-8×8 ; 1-8×4 w/300W PAR 56 SPOTS	INSIDE S.L. GALLERY DARK HONEY	912
452	R DIAGONAL STRIPS	1-8×8 ; 1-8×4 w/300W PAR 56 SPOTS	INSIDE S.R. GALLERY DARK HONEY	912

CYRANO

BOARD #14   6 PLATE   3600W AUTOTRANSFORMER

SWITCH	POSITION	TYPE	FOCUS	COLOR
46 MASTER				
461	L DIAGONAL STRIPS	SAME SET AS 451	INSIDE S.L. GALLERY DARK AMBER	915
462	R DIAGONAL STRIP	SAME SET AS 452	INSIDE S.R. GALLERY DARK AMBER	915
47 MASTER				
471	#2 BOOM L VERTICAL STRIPS	SAME SET AS 431	S.R. GALLERY BLUE	955/P·6
472	#2 BOOM R VERTICAL STRIPS	SAME SET AS 432	S.L. GALLERY BLUE	955/P·6

48 MASTER				
481	L DIAGONAL STRIPS	SAME SET AS 451	INSIDE S.L. GALLERY DARK BLUE	958/ P-60
482	R DIAGONAL STRIPS	SAME SET AS 452	INSIDE S.R. GALLERY DARK BLUE	958/ P-60

CYRANO

BOARDS # 15 + 16   2 - 6 PLATE   1000 w AUTOTRANSFORMER

SWITCH	POSITION	TYPE	FOCUS	COLOR
55 MASTER		L.S. UNITS	SPECIALS	
551	BAL. RAIL 9A - 10A	2 - L.S. UNITS		
552	BAL. RAIL 34A - 35A			
56 MASTER		L.S. UNITS	SPECIALS	

CYRANO

BOARD #17   8 PLATE   750 w PRESET

SWITCH	POSITION	TYPE	FOCUS	COLOR
66 MASTER	6TH PIPE		BACKLITE SPECIALS	
661	6TH PIPE # 5	1 - 750 w 6×16		
662	6	"		
663	7	"		
664	8	"		
665	9	"		
666	10	"		
667	11	"		
668	12	"		

CYRANO
BOARD #18 8 PLATE 750w PRESET

SWITCH	POSITION	TYPE	FOCUS	COLOR
67 MASTER	1st PIPE		SPECIALS	
671	1st PIPE #3	1-750w 6x12		
672	6	"		
673	9	"		
674	12	"		
675	13	"		
676	16	"		

CYRANO
BOARD #19 8 PLATE 750w PRESET

SWITCH	POSITION	TYPE	FOCUS	COLOR
68 MASTER	2ND PIPE		SPECIALS	
681	2ND PIPE #3	1-750w 6x12		
682	6	"		
683	9	"		
684	12	"		
685	13	"		
686	16	"		
687	19	"		
688	22			

CYRANO

BOARD #20   8 PLATE   750w PRESET

SWITCH	POSITION	TYPE	FOCUS	COLOR
81 MASTER	S.L. FLOOR		L FLOOR SPECIALS	
811	S.L. Floor Stand # 1	1-750w 6x12		
812	2	"		
813	3	"		
814	"			

CYRANO

BOARD #21   8 PLATE   750w PRESET

SWITCH	POSITION	TYPE	FOCUS	COLOR
82 MASTER	S.R. FLOOR		Floor Specials R	
821	S.R. FlOOR STAND # 1	1-750w 6x12		
822	2	"		
823	3	"		
824	4	"		
825	5	"		
826	6	"		
827	7	"		
828	8	"		

other electrical devices and scenic effects, make sure that lens systems for projections are correct, and the like, leaving nothing to chance but taking pains to assure himself that whatever will be delivered to the theatre is exactly what he requires.

SWITCHBOARDS

In the matter of control boards and wiring the commercial theatre is very different from the usual college or community situation. Most Broadway houses, as well as many in other cities, are furnished with d-c power only, thus making it impossible to use auto-transformer or electronic-dimming equipment. Also, at the present time, resistance dimmers are less expensive than other types. Recently there has been some success in introducing autotransformer and electronic devices, and persuading theatre owners to convert to a-c. This practice may soon be widespread but at the present moment it can be safely stated that the resistance dimmer is the only type in general use in the commercial theatre.

Switchboards using resistance dimmers are of three styles, each with a certain definite number and capacity of dimmers. The two largest types are called "piano boards" because the metal-lined boxes into which they are built resemble the crates in which upright pianos are shipped. These are also known as road boxes because they are designed to travel.

PIANO BOARDS

In each box, in addition to the dimmers, there is a bull switch, or master switch, that can energize or kill the entire board and is imperative for sudden blackouts as well as for general control. There is also a master interlock handle by means of which all the dimmers that are locked to the common shaft may be brought up or down simultaneously. There is a master fuse for the entire board, and fuses for the individual dimmers.

In the commercial theatre all instruments are joined by means of pin connectors to cables that reach to the switchboard area and end in a stage plug. These stage plugs are thrust into porcelain pockets on the dimmerboard. There are frequently two such pockets connected to each dimmer, so that two instruments may be connected to it. A two-way switch associated with each dimmer permits the electrician to choose whichever of the two loads he wishes, or, by putting the switch in its center, neutral position, to disconnect both loads.

There are two standard types of piano board available. One contains twelve dimmer plates, each with a capacity of 5000–6000 watts, which are usually used to control rows of striplights or banks of floodlights. Many shows do not require dimmers of this capacity.

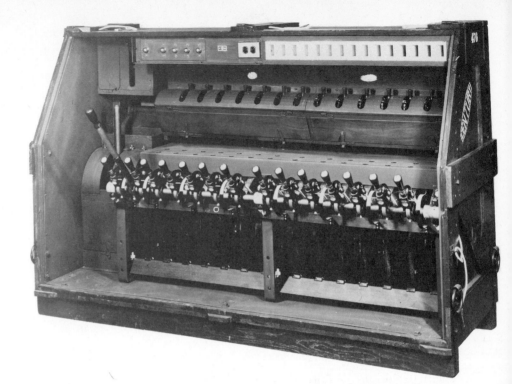

FIGURE 22–4. A ROAD BOX OR "PIANO BOARD." This is the standard 14-plate, 1500-to-3000-watt-capacity resistance board that is the basic control unit for practically all Broadway productions. The fourteen circular dimmer plates may be seen dimly at the bottom of the box, with the handles for each in the row just above. At the end of this row is the master interlock handle and just behind this the master or "bull" switch that kills the entire board. The hinged compartments above the dimmer handles are for the fuses, and above these are the switches for each circuit. Along the upper right is a row of fifteen stage-plug receptacles, fourteen for the dimmer circuits and one for a non-dim circuit, the switch for which is almost invisible in the top left corner. Note the heavy construction to withstand the rigors of touring, the skids for moving, the lift handles, and the box's metal lining, which is grounded for safety. The 12-plate, 6000-watt board is similar. (Photo—Century Lighting)

The other, and far more common, board has fourteen dimmers with a capacity of 1500–3000 watts each. These are used to control individual instruments, or gangs of instruments, or one group of smaller dimmers in an auxiliary board as described below.

PRESET BOARDS

Auxiliary or preset boards are comparatively small and are usually placed on top of the roadboxes for convenience. A standard preset board has either twelve 500-watt or eight 750-watt dimmers which generally are used to control a single spotlight each, though several small-wattage lamps occasionally are ganged together to be fed by a single dimmer. In turn, each group of four dimmers of a preset board is fed by one of the 1500–3000-watt dimmers of a 14-plate piano board and hence are mastered by it. Thus each instrument connected through a preset board may be set for a different reading, and all may be brought to these readings simultaneously and proportionately by bringing up the handle of the mastering dimmer. Each dimmer of a preset board has an associated switch so that instruments not required for a certain scene may be turned off.

GANGING INSTRUMENTS

Because it is often desirable for instruments in different parts of the stage to be put under the control of a single dimmer, plugging boxes are used. Such a box has a number of porcelain sockets to receive stage plugs, and these pockets all feed into a single cable which may be plugged to a dimmer in any of the boards in use. Standard plugging boxes come with two, four, or six sockets, each of which has its own fuse.

Like the preset boards, the plugging boxes are usually placed on top of the piano boards, forming, in effect, a sort of distribution panel, easily reached if it is necessary to replug any of the dimmers during the performance.

But if the instruments to be controlled by the same dimmer are hung close to each other on the stage, "twofers" are usually employed. These are two female pin connectors each with its own short asbestos-covered cable which feeds into a single male connector. Otherwise, "tap-off" blocks or other ganging devices may be used.

Because all the dimmers are of the resistance type, it is necessary that each be loaded close to capacity, as has been explained in Chapter 19. This will have been taken into account in preparing the shop order, and extra instruments have been provided to act as ghost loads, carefully placed offstage in such a manner as to keep their light from spilling onto the stage during dark scenes and blackouts.

OPERATING THE BOARDS

The usual practice for operating the boards is to place them in two rows, facing each other, so that one man can stand between them and operate two boards at the same time. Often one of the electricians will assist another when his cues are complex, but if everyone is too busy to help, extra hands must be hired. It is not uncommon for a producer, when told how many men will be required to run the switchboards, to insist that he can not afford that many, and the designer must then modify his layout and control.

It is customary to try to put all the front-of-the-house instruments (balcony and box booms) and the first pipe lights on the first board, but this will not be possible for a heavy show, such as a musical.

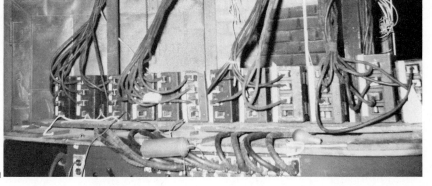

a

b

c

FIGURE 22–5. SWITCHBOARDS IN ACTION. (*a*) A row of plugging boxes, each with four outlets, arranged along the top of a piano board. (*b*) Two piano boards plugged for a show. Top center is a ten-plate auxiliary or "preset" board. Plugging boxes are on the left. Note the identifications of the loads on the various dimmers chalked above each. (*c*) A typical board arrangement for a fairly modest show. Note the cue book to the left, and to the right the speaker for the stage manager's cues. (Photos—author)

The upstage lights go on the next board or boards, and finally the cyclorama or, more usually, the backdrop, lights on the last board.

It may be remarked here that very often the switchboards are so located backstage that the electricians operating them can not see the stage at all. But whether they can or not, they always receive their cues from the stage manager or his assistant, and never by direct observation of the action on the stage.

SETTING UP THE LIGHTING
MOVE IN AND SET UP

On "move-in" day all the rented equipment is delivered to the theatre in which the show is to open. Because there is a vast amount of work to be done, and done fast, the chief electrician will have called for such additional men as he needs to get the instruments mounted and cabled. Under his direction, and following the designer's layout, this work proceeds while at the same time the scenery is being erected on the stage. Usually, to avoid conflict with the carpenters, the front-of-the-house lights are the first to be put in place, with the onstage equipment following. Great cooperation is necessary at this time between the two departments, and it is now that a competent electrician can prove his value to a production.

FOCUSING AND SETTING CUES

By the time the lights are in reasonably good shape—hung and connected to the switchboards—the light designer, who has been observing the work and double-checking the position of the instruments, takes over. He usually starts with the front-of-the-house spotlights, sometimes while the upstage equipment is still being hung. He will not have the exclusive use of the stage, but must carry on the work of focusing despite all manner of confusion on the stage as the other departments go about completing their business, and possibly even before all the scenery is in place.

If a regular technical run-through is scheduled, this is the time the designer may rough in the dimmer readings and cues. But all too often these delicate operations must be done under the most frustrating conditions, sometimes even with the houselights and stage work lights ablaze! And it is important that all be finished quickly, so that the regular crew will not run into overtime and the extra hands hired for the set-up may be let go. There can be no second guessing about the latter, for if it becomes necessary to send someone up a tall ladder at a later time, a ladder crew of four men must be hired for the minimum of half a day just to adjust one poorly placed instrument.

During rehearsals the lighting people continue their work, adjusting dimmer readings, sharpening cues, and taking copious notes for refocusing, rehanging, matting, masking, changing color media, and the like. The designer frequently has an assistant to do the paper work and to keep in touch with the stage manager, and perhaps with any followspot men, by means of a telephone or a public address system.

In this manner adjustments are made right up to the moment when the curtain rises before an audience, and once the play has started the designer will continue to make his notes during this and subsequent performances. All changes are passed on to the chief electrician as the man who henceforth is in charge of running the lighting. All cues are also given to the stage manager, since his department is responsible for warning the men on the boards of each cue as it approaches and giving the "dead cue" at the precise fraction of a second.

It must be emphasized that the light designer never goes backstage during either rehearsal or performance, regardless of any temptation to do so. Instead he delivers his notes after the final curtain and discusses with the electricians how any complex cues or unexpected changes in procedure may best be handled.

According to union regulations, under no condition whatever may the light designer or his assistant handle any lighting equipment, but must request one of the electricians to do it for him. This applies to even such innocent actions as handing a wrench to its owner, or steadying a ladder on which an electrician is working.

AFTER THE PRODUCTION HAS OPENED

It has long been a custom to open Broadway shows out of town, usually with a short run in one of the cities along the Atlantic seaboard such as New Haven, Boston, Philadelphia, Washington, and then move it on to some of the others, polishing the play as it goes, before the official opening on Broadway. When these tryout runs are scheduled, the first of such openings pretty much follows the procedures that have been described above. Occasionally the light designer will stay with the show through all its wanderings to New York. More often he will leave it at its first stop, possibly dropping in on it in another city, or, most likely, not seeing it again until New York is reached. Meanwhile the chief electrician and the stage manager are responsible for the lighting.

Recently it has become popular not to venture a play out of New York at all, but to run a series of preview performances right in the theatre in which it is scheduled to open officially. It is understood by the audience who have bought their tickets to such previews at a special low rate, that the play is not yet in its final form but is undergoing continual revisions. Such revisions include the lighting, of course, thus giving the designer ample time to experiment and make changes, bringing his concepts to perfection at comparative leisure.

But no matter how the play opens, it is advisable for the designer to drop in every once in a while during its run. Often he will find that things have started to slip a little from what he had originally set, and he must tighten them up again.

GOING ON THE ROAD

If, after its Broadway run, a show takes to the road—or a national company is formed to troup about the country—it is necessary for the designer to work out a simplified plot. This is desirable for the double reason that there should be less equipment to carry and fewer instruments to set up in the great rush that precedes the opening performance in every city visited. This is, of course, especially important if the show is to play in schools, municipal auditoriums, or any places other than conventional theatres.

Various techniques have been developed to make setting up and focusing as easy as possible. For one example, the original production may have used a great battery of beam projectors for back-lighting the actors. For the road there may be substituted large striplights burning high-wattage PAR lamps, which can be hung and focused in a fraction of the time required to mount a score of individual instruments.

Today when a show goes on the road its scenery, properties, costumes, and lighting equipment are always moved by truck. As a result, as frequently as possible, the lighting instruments are left right on their pipes and the whole unit is placed aboard the vehicle, where it is hung safely and securely until the next city is reached. More and more, instead of pipes, so-called tracks are used, to which instruments are hung and in which the cabling for them is enclosed. The use of either pipe or track permits many short cuts in the remounting of instruments in the next theatre.

One such labor-saving practice is, before striking the lighting in New York, to lower a pipe loaded with spotlights to a specific distance above the stage floor. The lights are turned on and the outline of their beam patterns are carefully marked on the floor cloth, which will travel with the show. At the next theatre the pipe is hung at the identical height as before and the beam patterns are fitted to the marks on the floor cloth. Then when the pipe is raised to its proper trim, the individual instruments will be automatically in their correct focus.

In like manner instruments mounted on booms are firmly fastened to these vertical pipes, so that they are all brought to focus by simply revolving the pipe to its proper position.

THE FINAL WORD

While a number of these commercial usages may be familiar practice in some noncommercial theatres, certainly as many are not, nor should they have any occasion to be. As stated at the beginning of this chapter, it is hardly expected that many of its readers will be moving on to Broadway. Rather, what can be predicted is that more and more of them will become involved in the wide-spreading field of regional resident professional theatre of repertory and stock companies, where some degree of commercial practice must of necessity prevail. It is well for these to have some idea of what may be encountered in the many and vastly differing groups of this nature.

But more important than commercial usage is the quite different matter of professional standards. No one should consider for a moment going into any level of commercial theatre unless he plans to devote all his energies and abilities to the routines and the problems that present themselves. It is no place for the casual enthusiast or the dilettante, nor for the easily discouraged, the supersensitive, or the noncooperative.

Though many of the customs on Broadway are wasteful, even stupid, the New York practitioners ply their trade, whether designer or electrician, with a high regard for perfection and a diligence to excel on every show they work. The best of them, and this might well read "the most of them," are eager to cooperate with their fellow workers of the theatre at all levels, and will go to amazing lengths in cases of emergency to keep the play flowing smoothly. Their generosity in sharing their knowledge with interested outsiders, especially students, is heartwarming. Their competence, dependability, and high professional standards can be an inspiration to all who love the theatre.

Glossary

ARC LIGHT: A spotlight that has for its source an electric current arcing between two carbon rods. The term is often misapplied to mean any brilliant light.

ASBESTOS: Fire-retardant curtain located at the proscenium opening.

AVISTA: Change of scene or movement of scenery in full view of the audience.

BACK CLOTH: English theatre expression for back drop.

BACKSTAGE: Much the same as OFFSTAGE but used generally in reference to stage workers and stage machinery rather than to actors.

BAG LINE: Pick-up or bull line on a sandbag to lift the weight of the bag while trimming or clewing a line-set.

BARN DOORS: A device consisting of two or four hinged metal flaps which is placed in front of a spotlight to reduce the beam spread in one or more directions.

BATTEN: (1) Pipe batten. Horizontal pipe hung from a line-set of a flying system. (2) Wooden batten. Top and bottom of roll drop.

BLACK-OUT: The instantaneous killing of all stage lights.

BLEEDING: Brightly colored undercoat of paint showing a second coat.

BLOOM: Specular reflection from mirror or highly polished surface.

BOARDS: Slang for stage.

BOOK: To set a two-fold of scenery in an open-book position.

BOOM or BOOMERANG: A vertical pipe for mounting spotlights.

BOUNCE: Reflected diffuse light off the floor or walls.

BREAK: To fold or unfold scenery.

BREAKAWAY: Scenery or properties rigged to break on cue.

BREAST LINE: Fixed line to wall or gridiron that drags or breasts a piece of hanging scenery into an excentric position. Also called a DRAG LINE.

BRIDLE: Means of dividing the load of each liftline by spreading the pick-up points along the batten.

BRUSH-OUT: Slow black-out or quick fade.

BULL LINE: Heavy, four-stranded hemp rope used on a winch to lift uncounterweighted scenery.

BUMPER: (1) Low platform downstage

of portal against which castered wagons bump. (2) Metal hoop fastened to a batten carrying lighting instruments to protect these from flying scenery and the scenery from hot instruments.

BUMP-UP: Sudden movement of lights to a higher intensity.

CLEWING: Several lines are held together by knots or clew so as to handle as a single line.

COMPANY SWITCH: A distribution panel with hook-up terminals to supply the power for a traveling company's switchboard. Usually three-wire 220 volts, 600 amps on a side.

CROSS FADE: To fade or dim from one lighting set-up to another without going through a dim-out.

CUE: A visual or audible signal from the stage manager to execute a predetermined movement of lights or scenery.

CYC: Short for cyclorama.

CYC KNUCKLE: Hardware for attaching side arms of a cyc batten to a regular pipe batten.

DARK HOUSE: No performance or inactive theatre.

DECK: Stage floor.

DIM: To change the intensity of a light, either brighter or less bright.

DIMMER: Apparatus for altering the flow of electric current to cause a light to be more or less bright.

DISAPPEARANCE TRAP: Special counterweighted elevator trap used as a quick exit or disappearance by an actor.

DOLLY: A type of wagon.

DONKEY: Electric winch.

DOUSER: Mechanical means of putting out a light.

DOWNSTAGE: The area nearest the footlights and curtain.

DRAW LINE: Operating line of a traveler curtain rigging.

DUTCHMAN: (1) Condensing lens in a lens projector. (2) Scab or mending

cleat. (3) Cloth strip covering a hinged joint.

EDGE-UP: Framed scenery maneuver. To raise a flat upright on its edge.

END FOR END: To reverse the position of an object.

ERF: Stage jargon for ellipsoidal reflector floodlights.

EYEBALL STRIPS: Striplights made of swivel-mounted PAR spotlight reflector lamps for selective focusing.

FEEL-UP: To take slack out of lift lines prior to setting the trim.

FEV: Short for French Enamel Varnish.

FILL LIGHT: Wash or soft light that fills in the light on the face from the direction opposite the key light.

FLAG: Small piece of cloth inserted into the lay of the purchase line as a trim mark.

FLAT: In the commercial theatre FLAT refers to the stiffening of two or more hinged wings into a flat plane or wall.

FLIPPER: Jog hinged to a single wing.

FLOAT-DOWN: Kitelike action when a flat is allowed to fall or float to the floor.

FLOOD: Widespread focus on a spotlight. Also, short for floodlight.

FLOODLIGHT: A lighting instrument that produces a broad spread of light. Often misapplied to other lighting apparatus.

FOCUS: (1) The direction in which a lighting instrument is aimed. (2) Adjustment of the size or shape of its beam.

FOLLOW CUE: A cue that is timed to follow an original cue so quickly it does not warrant a separate cue number.

FOOTCANDLE: The measurement of illumination. It is the amount of light from one candle that will fall on a surface one foot from the candle.

FRESNEL (correctly pronounced Fr'nel): A lens recognized by its concentric rings. The spotlight designed to use this lens.

FRONT LIGHTING: Illumination on the stage from instruments placed in the auditorium.

FUNNEL: Also known as a "top hat." A short metal cylinder that is placed in front of a spotlight to reduce the spread of its beam.

GOBO: A metal cut-out used with a spotlight to obtain a patterned beam.

GRAND DRAPE: Decorative first border in old proscenium-type theatres.

GREEK-IT: Fake lettering that has no meaning; doubletalk.

GRIP: Stage hand.

GRIPPING: Running scenery on the floor by stage hands or grips.

HALATION: Undesirable spreading of light from a spotlight. A halo of light around the beam.

HEAD BLOCK: Multigrooved pulley or multipulley sheave in a line-set.

HEAD SPOT: Very narrow beam from a spotlight focused on the actor's head. Also called pin spot.

HOUSE CURTAIN: Main curtain of a proscenium theatre designed to tie in with the house decorations. Also called act curtain.

IN-ONE: Foremost downstage acting position, traditionally in front of oleo.

IRIS: Mechanical means of closing the aperture of a spotlight.

JACK: Framed brace to hold scenery upright.

JACK KNIFE: Pivoting wagon movement like the action of blades in a jack knife.

JOG: Narrow-width wing.

JUICE: Commercial jargon for electricity.

JUMPER: Cable connecting two or more lighting instruments.

KEY LIGHT: Accent or highlight on actor's face. Usually from the direction of the motivating light for the scene.

KEYSTONING: Refers to the distortion of a projected image when the projector is oblique to the screen.

KLIEGLIGHT: A type of spotlight sold by Kliegl Bros. KLIEG is often used as a synonym for any bright light.

KNIFE: Steel guide for a tracked wagon.

LADDER: Hanging ladderlike frame for mounting spotlights.

LAMP: (1) Correctly, the name of what is often called a light bulb. (2) In the commercial theatre the term for any lighting instrument, particularly a spotlight.

LEAD: Cable from power supply.

LEFT STAGE: To the actor's left as he faces the audience.

LEKOLITE: A type of spotlight sold by Century-Strand. LEKO is often used as a generic term for any ellipsoidal reflector spotlight.

LIGHT-LEAK: Unwanted spill from an instrument or through scenery.

LINE-SET: A group of from three to five lines using the same head block to lift a pipe batten or unit of scenery.

LIP: A beveled three-ply strip attached so as to overhang the edge of a framed unit of scenery and thereby conceal the open crack of a joint with an adjacent unit.

LOAD: Lamp or instrument.

LOFT BLOCK: Individual pulley on the gridiron of a line-set.

MAKE-UP: To put together a setting.

MASK: To conceal from the audience, usually by scenic pieces or neutral hangings, any portion of the backstage area or equipment.

MAT: Shutter or matting material over the face of a spotlight to change the shape of the beam.

MULING BLOCK: Pulley to change the horizontal direction of a moving line.

OFFSTAGE: Out of sight of the audience. Away from the center of the stage.

OHM'S LAW: This states the relationship of current, electric potential, and resistance in a circut. It may be expressed by the equation: $I = \dfrac{E}{R}$.

OLEO: Traditionally the in-one back drop. A decoratively painted ad-drop from vaudeville days.

OLIVETTE: Old stand floodlight.

ON AND OFF: Referring to scenery sitting parallel to the footlights.

ONSTAGE: In sight of the audience. Toward the center of the stage.

P and OP: Promp and Opposite Promp. An English and old American method indicating the left and right side of the stage. Promp was the side of the prompter or stage manager.

PAR: Short for parabolic reflector lamp.

PEEK: To expose the backstage or see past masking.

PICTURE: The general composition of the setting as seen from the average and not extreme sightline seat.

PIG-TAIL: Short length of lead cable.

PIN-SPOT: *see* HEAD SPOT.

PRACTICAL: Can be used by the actor, as a window sash that can actually be raised, or a light that can be switched on and off by him.

PRE-SET: (1) A pre-arranged lighting set-up held in readiness for later use. (2) Pre-position scenery that will be revealed later in the scene.

PROP: Short for "property." Also refers to anything not real or practical.

PURCHASE LINE: Flyman's operating line in a counterweight system.

QUARTZ-IODINE: An early name for what is now known as the tungsten-halogen lamp.

RAKED: Scenery or stage floor angled to the footlights.

RETURN: Element of scenery that returns the downstage edge of the setting offstage to the right or left.

RIGHT STAGE: To the actor's right as he faces the audience.

RPF: Short for Rigid Plastic Foam. Styrofoam.

RUF: Short for Rigid (Poly)Urethane Foam.

SANDBAG: Counterweight for pin-and-rail flying system.

SHARP FOCUS: Narrow-beam focus of a spotlight.

SHOE: (1) Special construction on the end of the toggle rail, the internal framing member of a flat. (2) Framed platform to encase the legs of furniture for protection on tour.

SHOW PORTAL: Framed teaser and tormentor designed especially for the show.

SLASH: A diagonal beam of side lighting on a stage drapery or window curtain creating an arbitrary pattern of light.

SNATCH BLOCK: Pulley block with removable side to permit its insertion into rigging or tackle system without having to rethread all the line.

SNATCHING: To hook and unhook a flown piece of scenery during the shift.

SPIKE: Mark on floor to locate the working position of scenery or properties.

SPOT LINE: A fixed line spotted on the gridiron directly over its working position.

SPOTLIGHT: A lighting instrument with a lens that throws an intense light on a defined area. The term is often misapplied to other lighting instruments.

SPOT SHEAVE: The special placement of a loft sheave on the gridiron for an additional or single running line.

STAB: Low trim or tie-off on the bottom rail of the pin-and-rail flying system.

STAGE LEFT and STAGE RIGHT: *see* LEFT STAGE and RIGHT STAGE.

STAGE PEG AND PLUG: Bolt-threaded peg which fits into an inside threaded plug.

STAGE SCREW: Screw-threaded peg.

STRIKE: To take down a setting. To remove properties or lights.

SUNDAY: Knot used to clew or hold several lines together.

SURROUND or SHROUD: Carry-off platforms that surround a turntable.

SWITCHBOARD: Fixed or movable panel with switches, dimmers, etc., to control the stage lights.

TAILS: Lines dropped from a batten to hang scenery several feet below the batten.

TEASER: Top or horizontal member of the adjustable frame downstage of the setting.

TOP HAT: *see* FUNNEL.

TORMENTOR: Side or vertical members of the adjustable frame downstage of the setting.

TRAPS: System of openings through the stage floor.

TRICK LINE: Small line used to trigger a breakaway or trick device.

TRIM: Mark designating the height of a line-set. HIGH TRIM: Height of a flown piece when in *out* position. LOW TRIM: Height of flown piece when in an *in* (or working) position.

TRIPPING: Raising a piece of soft scenery from the bottom as well as from the top.

TUNGSTEN-HALOGEN: An improved form of the incandescent filament lamp which contains a small quantity of a halogen gas in the bulb.

UP AND DOWN: Referring to scenery sitting perpendicular to the footlights.

UPSTAGE: On the stage but away from the audience.

WAGON: Low platform on casters.

WILD: Hinged portion of a setting that is free to move.

WING: In the commercial theatre the term *single wing* refers to the basic unit of framed scenery, commonly called a *flat* in the noncommercial theatre.

WINGS: Area offstage right and left, stemming from the era of wings and backdrops.

X-RAYS: Old expression designating the first row of border lights.

Additional Reading
on
Scene Design

The following books are recommended as additional reading to increase the
reader's understanding of the philosophy and historical background of
scene design as part of the art of theatre.

THE DESIGN CONCEPT

Appia, Adolphe, *Adolphe Appia—A Gospel for Modern Stages. Theatre Arts Monthly,* August, 1932.
Entire issue devoted to Appia's influence on present-day scene and lighting design.

Bay, Howard, *Stage Design.* New York: Drama Book Specialists, 1974.

Brown, John Mason, *The Modern Theatre in Revolt.* New York: W. W. Norton and Co., Inc., 1929.

Burian, Jarka, *The Scenography of Josef Svoboda.* Middletown, Conn.: Wesleyan University Press, 1971.

Cheney, Sheldon, *Stage Decoration.* New York: The John Day Company, Inc., 1928.

Clay, James H., and Krempel, Daniel, *The Theatrical Image,* New York: McGraw-Hill Book Company, Inc., 1967.

Craig, Edward Gordon, *On the Art of the Theatre.* New York: Theatre Arts Books, 1956.

Fuerst, Walter R., and Hume, Samuel J., *Twentieth Century Stage Decoration,* New York: Dover Publications, Inc. Vol. 1, text; Vol. 2, ill., 1965.

Gassner, John, *Directions in Modern Theatre and Drama.* New York: Holt, Rinehart and Winston, Inc., 1965.

Gorelik, Mordecai, *New Theatres for Old.* New York: Samuel French, 1940.

Jones, Robert E., *The Dramatic Imagination.* New York: Duell, Sloan & Pearce, Inc., 1941.

Kernodle, George R., *From Art to Theatre.* Chicago: University of Chicago Press, 1944.

Laver, James, *Drama, Its Costume and Decor.* New York: The Viking Press, Inc., 1951.

Mielziner, Jo, *Designing for the Thea-*

tre. New York: Atheneum, 1965.

Nicoll, Allardyce, *The Development of the Theatre,* 5th ed. New York: Harcourt Brace Jovanovich, Inc., 1957.

Oenslager, Donald M., *The Theatre of Donald Oenslager.* Middletown, Conn.: Wesleyan University Press, 1978.

Oenslager, Donald M., *Scenery, Then and Now.* New York: Russell & Russell, 1966.

Pierson, William H. J. F., and Davidson, Martha (editors), *Arts of the United States* (Stage Design section). New York: McGraw-Hill Book Company, Inc., 1960.
A collection of color slides assembled by the University of Georgia under a grant by the Carnegie Corporation of New York. Contains an excellent essay by Donald Oenslager on U.S. scene design. Slides by SANDAK INC. New York.

Simonson, Lee, *The Art of Scenic Design.* New York: Harper & Row, Publishers, 1950.

Simonson, Lee, *The Stage Is Set.* New York: Harcourt Brace Jovanovich, Inc., 1932.

DESIGN APPLICATION

The following are recommended to broaden knowledge of the practicable application of design principles to modern theatre practices and related theatrical forms.

Albright, Halstead and Mitchell, *The Principles of Theatre Art.* Boston: Houghton Mifflin Company, 1955.

Boyle, Welden F., *Central and Flexible Staging.* Berkeley: University of California Press, 1956.

Bretz, Rudy, *Techniques of Television Production.* 2nd ed. New York: McGraw-Hill Book Company, Inc., 1962.

Carrick, Edward, *Designing for Moving Pictures.* London and New York: The Studio Publication, 1941.

Dean, Alexander, and Carra, Lawrence, *Fundamentals of Play Directing,* 3d ed. New York: Holt, Rinehart & Winston, Inc., 1974.

Koenig, John, *Scenery for Cinema.* Record of Exhibition, Baltimore Museum of Art. Baltimore, 1942.

Lambourne, Norah, *Staging the Play.* New York: The Viking Press, Inc., 1956.

Levin, Richard, *Television by Design.* London: The Bodley Head Ltd., 1961.

Southern, Richard, *Proscenium and Sightlines.* New York: Theatre Arts Books, 1964.

Traube, Shepard, *So You Want to Go Into the Theatre.* Boston: Little, Brown & Company, 1936.

Wade, Robert J., *Designing for TV.* New York: Farrar, Straus and Giroux, Inc., 1952.

DRAWING AND PAINTING

The following books are recommended to the student scene designer to help develop his skill as a visual artist and draftsman.

Albers, Josef, *The Interaction of Color.* New Haven: Yale University Press, 1963.

Clark, Arthur Bridgman, *Perspective.* Stanford, Calif.: Stanford University Press, 1944.

Chevreul, M. E., *The Principles of Harmony and Contrast of Colors.* New York: Reinhold Pub. Corp., reprinted 1967.

Container Corporation, *Color Harmony Manual, Ostwald Theory of Color.* Chicago: Container Corporation of America, 1948.

Evans, Ralph M., *An Introduction to Color.* New York: John Wiley & Sons, Inc., 1948.

Field, Wooster Bard, *Architectural Drawing.* New York: McGraw-Hill Book Company, Inc., 1922.

600

French, Thomas E., *A Manual of Engineering Drawing*. New York: McGraw-Hill Book Company, 1941.

Graves, Maitland, *The Art of Color and Design*. New York: McGraw-Hill Company, Inc., 1951.

Guptill, Arthur L., *Drawing in Pen and Ink*. New York: Reinhold Publishing Corp., 1961.

Guptill, Arthur L., *Sketching and Rendering*. New York: Pencil Points, 1929.

International Printing Ink Corp., *Three Monographs on Color*. New York: International Printing Ink Corp., 1935.

Itten, Johannes, *The Elements of Color*. New York: Van Nostrand Reinhold, 1970.

Jacobson, Egbert, *Basic Color, An Interpretation of the Ostwald Color System*. Chicago: Paul Theobald, 1948.

Kepes, Gyorgy, *The Nature and the Art of Motion*. London: Studio Vista, 1965.

Luekiesh, M., *Color and Its Application*. Princeton, N.J.: D. Van Nostrand Co., 1921.

Munsell, A. H., *A Color Notation*. Baltimore, Md.: Munsell Color Co., Inc., 1941.

Munsell Color Co., *Munsell Book of Color*. Baltimore, Md.: Munsell Color Co., 1942.

Ostwald, Wilhelm, *Colour Science*. Winsor and Wenton Limited, 38 Rathbone Place, London W. 1, England.

Parker, Oren, *Scenographic Techniques*. Pittsburgh: Carnegie-Mellon University Bookstore, rev. and enlarged, 1964.

Patten, Lawton, and Rogness, Milton, *Architectural Drawing*, rev. ed. Dubuque, Iowa: William C. Brown Co., 1961.

Pope, Arthur, *The Language of Drawing and Painting*. Cambridge, Mass.: Harvard University Press, 1949.

Scott, Robert, *Design Fundamentals*. New York: McGraw-Hill Book Company, Inc., 1951.

FURNITURE AND DECORATIONS

The following are recommended as general reference material for designing furniture and decorating interiors.

Aronson, Joseph, *The Encyclopedia of Furniture*, 3rd ed. New York: Crown Publishers, 1968.

Gottshall, Franklin H., *How to Design Period Furniture*. Milwaukee, Wis.: Bruce Publishing Co., 1951.

Grant, Ian (editor), *Great Interiors*. London: The Hamlyn Publishing Group, Ltd., 1971.

Hardy, Kay, *Beauty Treatments for the Home*. New York: Funk & Wagnalls Co., 1945.

Hayward, Helena (editor), *World Furniture*. London: Hamlyn, 1971.

Hunter, George Leland, *Decorative Furniture*. Grand Rapids, Mich.: Dean Hicks Co., *Good Furniture Magazine*, 1923.

Joel, David, *The Adventure of British Furniture, 1851–1951*. London: Theodore Brun, Pub., 1953.

Jones, Bernard E., *Furniture Making*. Philadelphia: David McKay, Publisher.

Jones, Owen, *The Grammar of Ornament*. London: Bernard Quaritch, 1910.

Otto, Celia J., *American Furniture of the Nineteenth Century*. New York: The Viking Press, Inc., 1965.

Potter, Margaret and Alexander, *Houses*. London: John Murray, 1948.

Potter, Margaret and Alexander, *Interiors*. London: John Murray, 1957.

Praz, Mario, *An Illustrated History of Furnishing*. New York: George Braziller, 1964.

Richter, G. M., *The Furniture of the Greeks, Etruscans and Romans*. London: The Phaidon Press, 1966.

Speltz, Alexander, *Styles of Ornament.* New York: Grosset & Dunlap, Inc., 1936.

Strange, T. Arthur, *A Guide to Collectors: English Furniture and Decoration.* London: McCorquodale & Co., 1903.

Strange, T. Arthur, *Historical Guide to French Interiors.* London: McCorquodale & Co., 1903.

Wilson, Jose, and Leaman, Arthur, *Decorating Defined.* New York: Simon and Schuster, 1970. A dictionary of decoration and design.

Additional Reading on Technical Production

The following books are recommended as additional reading to give the reader a greater insight into scenery construction techniques and general shop practices.

SCENERY CONSTRUCTION

Bowman, Ned, *Handbook of Technical Practice for the Performing Arts.* Winkinsbury, Pa.: Scenographic Media, 1972.

Bryson, Nicholas L., *Thermoplastic Scenery for the Theatre.* New York: Drama Bookshop Specialist, 1970.

Burris-Meyer, Harold, and Cole, Edward C., *Scenery for the Theatre,* rev. ed. Boston: Little, Brown & Co., 1972.

The Complete Woodworker. New York: David McKay Co., Inc., n.d.

Cornberg, Sol, and Gebauer, Emanuel L., *A Stage Crew Handbook.* rev. ed. New York: Harper & Row, Publishers, 1957.

Daniels, George, *How to Use Hand and Power Tools.* New York: Popular Science Publishing Co., Inc., 1965.

Dykes Lumber Company, *Moulding Catalog,* No. 49, Dykes Lumber Co., 137 West 24th Street, New York, N.Y., 10011.

Fitzkee, Dariel, *Professional Scenery Construction.* San Francisco: Banner, 1931.

Haines, Ray E., *Carpentry and Woodworking,* Princeton, N.J.: D. Van Nostrand Co., Inc., 1945.

Lacey, John L., *Handy Man's Carpentry Guide.* New York: Arco Publishing Co., Inc., 1955.

Parker, H., and Kidder, F. E., *Architect's and Builder's Handbook.* New York: John Wiley & Sons, Inc., 1931.

Ramsey, Charles G., and Sleeper, Harold R., *Architectural Graphic Standards,* 5th ed. New York: John Wiley & Sons, Inc., 1956.

U.S. Forest Products Laboratory, *Wood Handbook.* Washington, D.C.: Government Printing Office.

THE HANDLING OF SCENERY

The following provide a more specialized knowledge of the various methods of moving scenery, backstage organization, and rigging techniques.

Barber, Philip W., *The Stage Technician's Handbook.* New Haven, Conn.: Whitlock's Book Store, Inc., 1928.

Burris-Meyer, Harold, and Mallory, Vincent, *Sound in the Theatre.* Mineola, N.Y.: Radio Magazine, Inc., 1950.

Gassner, John, *Producing the Play,* with *New Scene Technicians' Handbook* by Philip Barber. New York: Holt, Rinehart and Winston, Inc., 1953.

Gillette, A. S., *Stage Scenery.* New York: Harper & Row, Publishers, 1960.

Halstead, William P., *Stage Management for the Amateur Theatre.* New York: Appleton-Century-Crofts, Inc., 1937.

How to Put Rope to Work, Plymouth Cordage Company, North Plymouth, Mass.

Irving, J., *Knots, Ties and Splices.* New York: E. P. Dutton & Co., Inc., 1934.

Kranich, Friedrich, *Buhnintechinik der Gegenwart,* Vol. I. Berlin: Verlag Von R. Oldenbourg, 1929.

Rose, A., *Stage Effects* (George Routledge and Sons, Ltd.). New York: E. P. Dutton & Co., Inc., 1920.

Southern, Richard, *Changeable Scenery.* London: Faber & Faber, Ltd., 1952.

Southern, Richard, *Stage Setting.* London: Faber & Faber, Ltd., 1937.

SCENE PAINTING

The following are recommended to expand skill in scene-painting techniques.

Appleton Publishing Co., *Theatrical Scene Painting.* Omaha, Neb.: Appleton Publishing Co., 1916.

Ashworth, Bradford, *Notes on Scene Painting,* edited by Donald Oenslager. New Haven, Conn.: Whitlock's, 1952.

Atkinson, Frank H., *Scene Painting and Bulletin Art.* Chicago: Frederick J. Drake and Co., 1916.

Brown, Van Dyke, *Secrets of Scene Painting and Stage Effects.* New York: E. P. Dutton & Co., Inc., 1913.

Pecktal, Lynn, *Designing and Painting for the Theatre.* New York: Holt, Rinehart and Winston, 1975.

Polunin, Vladimir, *The Continental Method of Scene Painting.* London: C. W. Beaumont, 1927.

GENERAL

The following books are recommended as supplementary reading in the generalized area of scene design, technical production, and stage lighting.

Adix, Vern, *Theatre Scenecraft.* Cloverlot, Anchorage, Ky.: Children's Theatre Press, 1956.

Bellman, Willard F., *Scenography and Stage Technology: An Introduction.* New York: Thomas Y. Crowell Co., 1977.

Friederich, Williard J., and Fraser, John H., *Scenery Design for the Amateur Stage.* New York: The Macmillan Company, 1950.

Helvenston, Harold, *Scenery, a Manual of Scene Design.* Stanford, Calif.: Stanford University Press, 1931.

Selden, Samuel, and Rezzuto, Tom, *Essentials of Stage Scenery.* New York: Appleton-Century-Crofts, 1972.

Smith, André, *The Scenewright.* New York: The Macmillan Company, 1926.

Additional Reading on Stage Lighting

The following books are recommended as supplementary reading, either to broaden the reader's view of the field or to assist him in understanding knotty problems. They would form an invaluable nucleus for the private library of anyone genuinely interested in the field.

The "General" list contains books of broad approach to the whole stage-lighting picture, and offers material of value in several facets of theatre lighting. The titles under the heading "Supplementary" contain matter related to specific aspects, and also include a few periodicals that frequently carry articles of interest to the lighting designer for the stage.

GENERAL

Bentham, Frederick, *Stage Lighting.* London: Pitman & Sons, Ltd., 1950. Covers the field well, but the American reader is warned that British terminology is sometimes confusing.

Fuchs, Theodore, *Stage Lighting.* Boston: Little, Brown & Co., 1929. Many portions are somewhat outdated today, but there is much pure gold still to be found in it.

Gassner, John, *Producing the Play,* rev. ed. New York: Holt, Rinehart & Winston, Inc., 1953. Contains a capsule survey of the field by one of Broadway's most successful lighting practitioners.

Kook, Edward F., *Images in Light for the Living Theatre.* New York: privately printed, 1963.

McCandless, Stanley, *A Method of Lighting the Stage,* 4th ed. New York: Theatre Arts Books, 1958. Though it does not go into the more technical aspects, this is probably the most influential book ever published on the subject.

McCandless, Stanley, *A Syllabus of Stage Lighting,* 11th ed. A reference book and dictionary of all stage-lighting terms.

Pilbrow, Richard, *Stage Lighting.* New York: Van Nostrand Reinhold, 1970.

Rosenthal, Jean, and Wertenbaker, Lael, *The Magic of Light.* Boston:

Little, Brown & Co., 1972.

Sellman, H. D., *Essentials of Stage Lighting*. New York: Appleton-Century-Crofts, 1972.

Williams, Rollo G., *The Technique of Stage Lighting*. London: Pitman & Sons, Ltd., 1952. Especially good on color. British terminology may confuse.

SUPPLEMENTARY

Bowman, Wayne, *Modern Theatre Lighting*. New York: Harper & Row, Publishers, 1957. Some good comments on practical electricity.

Century Strand Company, New York. Their equipment catalogues are a mine of information regarding instruments.

General Electric Company, Cleveland, *Fundamentals of Light and Lighting*, 1956. Excellent material on color, sources, and the behavior of light.

General Electric Company, Cleveland, *Large Lamp Bulletin*. Almost a textbook on sources. Excellent illustrations.

General Electric Company, Cleveland, *Lamb Bulletin*, 1956. Another fine and complete publication on lamps.

Illuminating Engineering Society, New York, *IES Lighting Handbook*, 4th ed., 1966. Pertinent information on color, instruments, equipment, and usage.

Kliegl Bros., New York. Equipment catalogues of all stage instruments.

Navy Training Courses, *Basic Electricity* (NavPers 10086-A). Washington, D.C.: U.S. Government Printing Office, 1960. Clear and simple presentation of the fundamentals of electricity. The best available text.

Rubin, Joel E., and Watson, Leland H., *Theatrical Lighting Practice*. New York: Theatre Arts Books, 1954. A survey of the usual lighting practices of all types and levels of dramatic production.

Tabs. This little magazine is brought out four times a year by Strand Electric and Engineering Co., Ltd., of London. It is available in this country from Strand Electric Co., 3201 North Highway 100, Minneapolis, Minn., 55422.

Theatre Design and Technology, the official journal of the U.S. Institute for Theatre Technology, is published four times a year. Circulation Manager, USITT, 245 West 52nd Street, New York, N.Y., 10019.

Theatre Crafts is published six times a year by Rodale Press Inc. Subscription Office, 33 East Miner Street, Emmaus, Penna., 18049.

Index

608

TE DUE